**Keep this book. You will
need it and use it throughout
your career.**

About the American Hotel & Lodging Association (AH&LA)

Founded in 1910, AH&LA is the trade association representing the lodging industry in the United States. AH&LA is a federation of state lodging associations throughout the United States with 11,000 lodging properties worldwide as members. The association offers its members assistance with governmental affairs representation, communications, marketing, hospitality operations, training and education, technology issues, and more. For information, call 202-289-3100.

LODGING, the management magazine of AH&LA, is a "living textbook" for hospitality students that provides timely features, industry news, and vital lodging information.

About the Educational Institute of AH&LA (EI)

An affiliate of AH&LA, the Educational Institute is the world's largest source of quality training and educational materials for the lodging industry. EI develops textbooks and courses that are used in more than 1,200 colleges and universities worldwide, and also offers courses to individuals through its Distance Learning program. Hotels worldwide rely on EI for training resources that focus on every aspect of lodging operations. Industry-tested videos, CD-ROMs, seminars, and skills guides prepare employees at every skill level. EI also offers professional certification for the industry's top performers. For information about EI's products and services, call 800-349-0299 or 407-999-8100.

About the American Hotel & Lodging Educational Foundation (AH&LEF)

An affiliate of AH&LA, the American Hotel & Lodging Educational Foundation provides financial support that enhances the stability, prosperity, and growth of the lodging industry through educational and research programs. AH&LEF has awarded hundreds of thousands of dollars in scholarship funds for students pursuing higher education in hospitality management. AH&LEF has also funded research projects on topics important to the industry, including occupational safety and health, turnover and diversity, and best practices in the U.S. lodging industry. For information, call 202-289-3180.

MANAGING
HOSPITALITY
HUMAN RESOURCES

D‸‸ D‸

Educational Institute Books

MANAGING HOSPITALITY HUMAN RESOURCES

Fourth Edition

Robert H. Woods

EDUCATIONAL INSTITUTE
American Hotel & Lodging Association

Disclaimer

This publication is designed to provide accurate and authoritative information in regard to the subject matter covered. It is sold with the understanding that the publisher is not engaged in rendering legal, accounting, or other professional service. If legal advice or other expert assistance is required, the services of a competent professional person should be sought.

— *From the Declaration of Principles jointly adopted by the American Bar Association and a Committee of Publishers and Associations*

The author, Robert H. Woods, is solely responsible for the contents of this publication. All views expressed herein are solely those of the authors and do not necessarily reflect the views of the Educational Institute of the American Hotel & Lodging Association (the Institute) or the American Hotel & Lodging Association (AH&LA).

Nothing contained in this publication shall constitute a standard, an endorsement, or a recommendation of the Institute or AH&LA. The Institute and AH&LA disclaim any liability with respect to the use of any information, procedure, or product, or reliance thereon by any member of the hospitality industry.

©2006
By the EDUCATIONAL INSTITUTE of the
AMERICAN HOTEL & LODGING ASSOCIATION
2113 N. High Street
Lansing, Michigan 48906-4221

The Educational Institute of the American
Hotel & Lodging Association is a nonprofit
educational foundation.

Printed in the United States of America
1 2 3 4 5 6 7 8 9 10 10 09 08 07 06

ISBN 978-0-86612-287-0

Editor: Priscilla J. Wood

Contents

Preface

T HERE WAS A TIME in the history of the hospitality industry when managing human resources was relatively simple. Back then, we could pick and choose the employees we wanted for our lodging, timeshare, or food service operations. More than likely, the employees we chose would stay with us for many years. Those were simpler times. Hospitality managers could operate their businesses in almost any way they desired.

Times have changed. In the past few decades, several factors have combined to transform the way we must manage. Because of this, today's hospitality managers must be attuned to the many internal and external influences that dictate how we do business.

Last summer, George Glazer (Vice President of Publications at the Educational Institute) and I were talking about an idea I had for this new edition of the book. That idea was to involve my graduate human resources class in helping to co-author chapters in the new edition. Graduate students write papers in classes, anyway. I thought writing a paper that had some meaning other than an academic exercise would be a better idea. With George's support, this is the project that we undertook. I can honestly say that revising a textbook in this way, with multiple authors, is more difficult than doing it myself. However, this method of involving future educators is much more rewarding, for both them and me.

Managing Hospitality Human Resources is divided into four major parts. Part I examines employment laws, planning, and staffing. This section includes a comprehensive overview of the various laws affecting the management of hospitality human resources. Readers will find a thorough description of the Americans with Disabilities Act, the Family and Medical Leave Act, and guidelines of laws enacted in recent years, in addition to practical guidelines for complying with these laws and discussions about recent court cases pertaining to the laws. Issues such as job analysis and design, selection, and human resources planning and recruiting are also thoroughly covered.

Part II details useful information on human resources development activities such as orientation, socialization, training, and evaluating employee performance. Readers will discover concrete recommendations for these important functions and become acquainted with various approaches to motivating and evaluating employee performance.

Part III focuses on compensation and labor issues. These chapters examine alternative methods of planning, developing, and implementing compensation and benefits programs, as well as the legal ramifications of compensation and benefits legislation. Labor relations and collective bargaining are explored in two chapters. These two chapters on labor relations include information on approaches used by unions to organize as well as methods used by management to combat organization.

Part IV considers safety, discipline, and ethical concerns of the hospitality workplace. Readers will find in-depth coverage of health and safety issues, employee assistance programs, turnover, employee discipline, and organizational exits. Our final chapter examines some of the complex ethical and social responsibility questions facing the modern hospitality manager.

Each chapter includes discussion questions, key terms with definitions, a list of suggested Internet sites, and either a case study, a mini case study, or other teaching tools as useful devices for reinforcing and applying the concepts in the text.

This project would not have become a book at all without the help of many people. The professional staff of the Educational Institute of the American Hotel & Lodging Association were instrumental in developing what appears on these pages. The book would be considerably less worthwhile without the tremendous help of these wonderful people. A special thanks is due to my editor at the Institute, Priscilla Wood, who spent so many hours over the last months bringing this project to fruition. I would also like to thank George Glazer for having the faith to renew this project and to take the leap of faith required to invite students to help co-author revisions to some chapters. Thanks, too, to all the wonderful educators and industry managers and executives who have helped to make this book a success over the past seven years. Finally, I want to thank my wife Jen and my three daughters, Kate, Jessica, and Colleen. Each has been patient and supportive of me throughout this project.

Robert H. Woods, Ph.D., CHRE
Las Vegas, Nevada

About the Author

Robert H. Woods, Ph.D., CHRE, ISHC, is a Professor in the William F. Harrah College of Hotel Administratoin at the University of Nevada, Las Vegas. He is a specialist in human resources and management issues and regularly consults with hospitality organizations and clubs on management, strategic management, service management, human resource, timeshare management, and corporate culture issues. He is co-author of the textbook *Leadership and Management in the Hospitality Industry* and of *The Job Description Handbook*. He has written more than 150 refereed articles. Woods has also written chapters for various books, including *Ethics in Hospitality Management* and *Contemporary Club Management*. Woods received his Master's degree and Ph.D. from the Hotel School at Cornell University and is a former Chair of the Hotel Managment Department at UNLV. Before returning to academia, he owned and operated a successful chain of restaurants and a hospitality consulting firm.

Part I

Employment Laws, Planning, and Staffing

Chapter 1 Outline

Competencies

1. Describe the EEOC and distinguish between EEO laws and affirmative action. (pp. 4–12)

2. Describe the evolution of EEO legislation from the 1960s through today. (pp. 12–25)

3. List major areas of EEO abuse and litigation, and identify critical EEO issues regarding women and older workers. (pp. 25–37)

4. Define *disability*, and describe the Americans with Disabilities Act (ADA) and its implications for human resource managers at hospitality operations. (pp. 37–43)

Employment Laws and Applications

BEFORE THE 1960S, DISCRIMINATION in the workplace was widespread in the United States. In fact, only government employees and union members had any type of protection at all. This does not mean, of course, that all employers abused their employees; it does mean, however, that employers could do so with impunity.

Because there was almost no regulation of human resource policies, widespread employment discrimination was often the rule, especially for some groups. For instance, women were relegated to positions traditionally viewed as "women's work" and were barred from many employment opportunities. The same was true for minorities.

These rampant inequities eventually led to social unrest. Finally, sweeping legislation was passed during President Lyndon Johnson's administration that radically affected the American work force. The **Civil Rights Act of 1964**, which prohibits discrimination on the basis of race, color, religion, sex, or national origin, became the cornerstone of change. **Title VII** of this act ensures fair employment standards. This single act is generally credited for initiating the equal employment opportunity (EEO) environment that exists in the United States today. Understanding and following the various EEO laws and regulations support a strong human resources focus, which helps an organization succeed.

Defining Discrimination

Human resources management is the practice of *legal* discrimination. There is a difference between legal and illegal discrimination. From a technical standpoint, selection, training, and appraisals are all discriminatory practices, since they all involve choosing one individual over another based on discernible differences. However, discrimination that follows the guidelines, laws, and regulations of the **Equal Employment Opportunity Commission (EEOC)** is legal. Practices that do not follow the law are illegal. They may also be very costly.

In 2003, the median jury award for employment practices liability claims in the United States was $250,000.[1] In recent years, we have seen significant increases in multimillion-dollar judgments against businesses in product liability and discrimination cases.[2] In *Zubulake* v. *UBS*, a female employee sued for sex bias and was awarded $9.1 million in actual damages and $20.1 million in punitive damages. The employee's salary was $650,000 per year.[3] The average out-of-court settlement of harassment and discrimination lawsuits is $300,000.[4] Valentino

Las Vegas, an Italian fine-dining restaurant, operated in The Venetian Resort • Hotel • Casino by Los Angeles-based Valentino Restaurant Group, reportedly agreed to a $600,000 settlement of a sexual harassment lawsuit involving at least five female employees.[5]

Equal Employment Opportunity Commission

The EEOC is the federal commission created by the Civil Rights Act of 1964 to establish and monitor employment standards in the United States. This independent agency interprets and enforces Title VII. The EEOC is made up of five members appointed by the president of the United States for a term of five years each.

The EEOC plays three principal roles. First, it oversees the administration of existing EEO laws and regulations, referring charges of violation to state or local equal employment opportunity agencies. Someone filing a complaint in Michigan, for instance, would have his or her case referred to the Michigan Civil Rights Department.

Exhibit 1 is an example of a charge filed with the EEOC. When an employee files a charge, the employer receives a copy of the paperwork. Regardless of whether the charge is filed with the EEOC or a state enforcement agency, the charge can still be heard in state or federal court. Even if the EEOC or state agency finds that the employer has not discriminated, the person filing the charge can still sue the employer.

The second responsibility of the EEOC is to issue guidelines for Title VII compliance. These guidelines are interpretations of the statute written by Congress. While not technically laws, EEOC regulations have been given the force of law by the courts, and have been viewed by the Supreme Court as important to the effective administration of EEOC operations.

The third role of the EEOC is to gather information. Each organization in the United States with 100 or more employees must annually file an EEO-1 report to a regional EEOC office. This report outlines the number of women and minorities employed in nine different job categories within the company. The EEOC analyzes these reports to statistically determine patterns of compliance and discrimination in the United States. If patterns of discrimination are found, the EEOC has the added responsibility of filing class action lawsuits to counteract such events. Exhibit 2 shows an EEO-1 form that employers use to report employee information.

In September 2004, the EEOC delivered on an old promise to provide better consumer access to its services through establishment of a centralized national call center. While only a two-year pilot project, the call center is designed to handle many of the millions of calls the agency handles annually. After the first year, the agency reported that 61 percent of the calls were requests for information. The remaining 39 percent were complaints that could lead to potential charges. The outsourced operation is located in Lawrence, Kansas, and is staffed to answer calls from 8 AM to 8 PM.[6]

Departments of Labor and Homeland Security

The U.S. Department of Labor (DOL) also plays a significant role in the interpretation of labor laws. For instance, the DOL Wage and Hour Division issues opinion

Exhibit 1   Sample Documents Used in a Discrimination Charge

	PERSON FILING CHARGE
EQUAL EMPLOYMENT OPPORTUNITY COMMISSION	Debella, Scarlette

THIS PERSON (check one)
☐ CLAIMS TO BE AGGRIEVED
☐ IS FILING ON BEHALF OF ANOTHER

```
┌                          ┐
  Mr. John Doe
  OWNER
  THE LION'S DEN
  101 PLAY LANE
  SNAFU, USA, 30000

└                          ┘
```

DATE OF ALLEGED VIOLATION	
Earliest	*Most Recent*
10/31/96	10/31/96

PLACE OF ALLEGED VIOLATION
SNAFU, USA,

CHARGE NUMBER
180871234

NOTICE OF CHARGE OF DISCRIMINATION
(See EEOC "Rules and Regulations" before completing this Form)

You are hereby notified that a charge of employment discrimination has been been filed against your organization under:

☒ **TITLE VII OF THE CIVIL RIGHTS ACT OF 1964**

☐ **THE AGE DISCRIMINATION IN EMPLOYMENT ACT OF 1967**

☐ **THE AMERICANS WITH DISABILITIES ACT**

☐ **THE EQUAL PAY ACT (29 U.S.C, SECT. 206(d))**

The boxes checked below apply to your organization:

1. ☐ No action is required on your part at this time.

2. ☐ Please submit by _____ a statement of your position with respect to the allegation(s) contained in this charge, with copies of any supporting documentation. This material will be made a part of the file and will be considered at the time that we investigate this charge. Your prompt response to this request will make it easier to conduct and conclude our investigation of this charge.

3. ☐ Please respond fully by _____ to the attached request for information which pertains to the allegations contained in this charge. Such information will be made a part of the file and will be considered by the Commission during the course of its investigation of the charge.

For further inquiry on this matter, please use the charge number shown above. Your position statement, your response to our request for information, or any inquiry you may have should be directed to:

Equal Employment Opportunity Comm
477 Michigan, Room 1540
Detroit, MI   48226

Earl Benson, Enforcement Manager
(Commission Representative)
123-4566
(Telephone Number)

☒ Enclosure: Copy of Charge

BASIS OF DISCRIMINATION

☐ RACE ☐ COLOR ☒ SEX ☐ RELIGION ☐ NAT. ORIGIN ☒ RETALIATION ☐ AGE ☐ DISABILITY ☐ OTHER

CIRCUMSTANCES OF ALLEGED VIOLATION

See enclosed Form 5, Charge of Discrimination.

DATE	TYPED NAME/TITLE OF AUTHORIZED EEOC OFFICIAL	SIGNATURE
01/24/97	A. William Schukar, Director	

RESPONDENT'S COPY

(continued)

Exhibit 1   *(continued)*

<table>
<tr><td colspan="2">CHARGE OF DISCRIMINATION
This form is affected by the Privacy Act of 1974; see Privacy Act Statement on reverse before completing this form.</td><td>ENTER CHARGE NUMBER
☐ FEPA
☒☒ EEOC 180-87-1234</td></tr>
</table>

_____ and EEOC
(State or local Agency, if any)

NAME (Indicate Mrs., Ms., or Miss.) Scarlette DeBella	HOME TELEPHONE NO. (Include Area Code) 100/555-1111
STREET ADDRESS CITY, STATE AND ZIP CODE 315 Brunson Drive Snafu, USA 30001	COUNTY Snafu

NAMED IS THE EMPLOYER, LABOR ORGANIZATION, EMPLOYMENT AGENCY, APPRENTICESHIP COMMITTEE, STATE OR LOCAL GOVERNMENT AGENCY WHO DISCRIMINATED AGAINST ME (If more than one list below.)

NAME The Lion's Den	NO. OF EMPLOYEES/MEMBERS approx. 20	TELEPHONE NUMBER (Include Area Code) 100/555-2222
STREET ADDRESS 101 Play Lane		CITY, STATE AND ZIP CODE Snafu, USA 30000
NAME		TELEPHONE NUMBER (Include Area Code)
STREET ADDRESS		CITY, STATE AND ZIP CODE

CAUSE OF DISCRIMINATION BASED ON (Check appropriate box(es)) ☐ RACE ☐ COLOR ☒☒ SEX ☐ RELIGION ☐ NATIONAL ORIGIN ☐ AGE ☒☒ RETALIATION ☐ OTHER (Specify)	DATE MOST RECENT OR CONTINUING DISCRIMINATION TOOK PLACE (Month, day, year) 10/31/96

THE PARTICULARS ARE (If additional space is needed, attached extra sheet(s)):

I was employed as a cocktail waitress at the Lion's Den. From September 1996 until my discharge, I was required to work in a sexually degrading environment and was subjected to unwelcome sexual advances from customers. On October 31, 1996, I was fired in retaliation for complaining about the sexual harassment aspects of my job. Other female cocktail waitresses were also adversely affected by the sexually degrading environment and unwelcome sexual advances from customers.

☐ I also want this charge filed with the EEOC. I will advise the agencies if I change my address or telephone number and I will cooperate fully with them in the processing of my charge in accordance with their procedures.	NOTARY - (When necessary to meet State and Local Requirements) I swear or affirm that I have read the above charge and that it is true to the best of my knowledge, information and belief.
I declare under penalty of perjury that the foregoing is true and correct. Date 11/7/96 *Scarlette DeBella* Charging Party (Signature)	SIGNATURE OF COMPLAINANT SUBSCRIBED AND SWORN TO BEFORE ME THIS DATE (Day, month, and year)

NOTICE REGARDING REPRESENTATION

OF RESPONDENTS

BY ATTORNEYS

It is not necessary that you be represented by an attorney while we handle the charge filed against your organization.

If you are represented by an attorney, however, we ask that you tell the Commission the attorney's name, address and telephone number, and that you ask your attorney to write to the Commission confirming that he or she does represent your organization.

The Commission has found that it is more efficient, in dealing with an organization, to work through just one representative of the organization. Therefore, if you have an attorney, the Commission will make all its contacts with your management officials through him or her, unless the Commission makes some other arrangement with you and your attorney.

Source: Equal Employment Opportunity Commission, Detroit, Michigan.

Exhibit 2 EEO-1 Report

Standard Form 100
(Rev. 3/97)

O.M.B. No. 3046-0007
EXPIRES 10/31/99
100-214

Joint Reporting Committee

- **Equal Employment Opportunity Commission**
- **Office of Federal Contract Compliance Programs (Labor)**

EQUAL EMPLOYMENT OPPORTUNITY

EMPLOYER INFORMATION REPORT EEO—1

Section A—TYPE OF REPORT
Refer to instructions for number and types of reports to be filed.

1. Indicate by marking in the appropriate box the type of reporting unit for which this copy of the form is submitted (MARK ONLY ONE BOX).

   (1) ☐ Single-establishment Employer Report

   Multi-establishment Employer:
   (2) ☐ Consolidated Report (Required)
   (3) ☐ Headquarters Unit Report (Required)
   (4) ☐ Individual Establishment Report (submit one for each establishment with 50 or more employees)
   (5) ☐ Special Report

2. Total number of reports being filed by this Company (Answer on Consolidated Report only) _____

Section B—COMPANY IDENTIFICATION (*To be answered by all employers*)

OFFICE USE ONLY

1. Parent Company
   a. Name of parent company (owns or controls establishment in item 2) omit if same as label

   a.

   Address (Number and street)

   b.

City or town	State	ZIP code

   c.

2. Establishment for which this report is filed. (Omit if same as label)
   a. Name of establishment

   d.

Address (Number and street)	City or Town	County	State	ZIP code

   e.

   b. Employer Identification No. (IRS 9-DIGIT TAX NUMBER)

   f.

   c. Was an EEO-1 report filed for this establishment last year? ☐ Yes ☐ No

Section C—EMPLOYERS WHO ARE REQUIRED TO FILE (*To be answered by all employers*)

☐ Yes ☐ No 1. Does the entire company have at least 100 employees in the payroll period for which you are reporting?

☐ Yes ☐ No 2. Is your company affiliated through common ownership and/or centralized management with other entities in an enterprise with a total employment of 100 or more?

☐ Yes ☐ No 3. Does the company or any of its establishments (a) have 50 or more employees <u>AND</u> (b) is not exempt as provided by 41 CFR 60-1.5, <u>AND</u> either (1) is a prime government contractor or first-tier subcontractor, and has a contract, subcontract, or purchase order amounting to $50,000 or more, or (2) serves as a depository of Government funds in any amount or is a financial institution which is an issuing and paying agent for U.S. Savings Bonds and Savings Notes?

If the response to question C-3 is yes, please enter your Dun and Bradstreet identification number (if you have one): ☐☐☐☐☐☐☐☐☐

NOTE: If the answer is yes to questions 1, 2, or 3, complete the entire form, otherwise skip to Section G.

(continued)

Exhibit 2 *(continued)*

SF 100 Page 2

Section D—EMPLOYMENT DATA

Employment at this establishment—Report all permanent full-time and part-time employees including apprentices and on-the-job trainees unless specifically excluded as set forth in the instructions. Enter the appropriate figures on all lines and in all columns. Blank spaces will be considered as zeros.

JOB CATEGORIES		OVERALL TOTALS (SUM OF COL. B THRU K)	MALE					FEMALE				
			WHITE (NOT OF HISPANIC ORIGIN)	BLACK (NOT OF HISPANIC ORIGIN)	HISPANIC	ASIAN OR PACIFIC ISLANDER	AMERICAN INDIAN OR ALASKAN NATIVE	WHITE (NOT OF HISPANIC ORIGIN)	BLACK (NOT OF HISPANIC ORIGIN)	HISPANIC	ASIAN OR PACIFIC ISLANDER	AMERICAN INDIAN OR ALASKAN NATIVE
		A	B	C	D	E	F	G	H	I	J	K
Officials and Managers	1											
Professionals	2											
Technicians	3											
Sales Workers	4											
Office and Clerical	5											
Craft Workers (Skilled)	6											
Operatives (Semi-Skilled)	7											
Laborers (Unskilled)	8											
Service Workers	9											
TOTAL	10											
Total employment reported in previous EEO-1 report	11											

NOTE: Omit questions 1 and 2 on the Consolidated Report.

1. Date(s) of payroll period used: 2. Does this establishment employ apprentices?
    1 ☐ Yes   2 ☐ No

Section E—ESTABLISHMENT INFORMATION *(Omit on the Consolidated Report)*

1. What is the major activity of this establishment? (Be specific, i.e., manufacturing steel castings, retail grocer, wholesale plumbing supplies, title insurance, etc. Include the specific type of product or type of service provided, as well as the principal business or industrial activity.)

OFFICE USE ONLY

g.

Section F—REMARKS

Use this item to give any identification data appearing on last report which differs from that given above, explain major changes in composition of reporting units and other pertinent information.

Section G—CERTIFICATION *(See Instructions G)*

Check one
1 ☐ All reports are accurate and were prepared in accordance with the instructions (check on consolidated only)
2 ☐ This report is accurate and was prepared in accordance with the instructions.

Name of Certifying Official	Title	Signature	Date
Name of person to contact regarding this report (Type or print)	Address (Number and Street)		
Title	City and State	ZIP Code Telephone Number (Including Area Code)	Extension

All reports and information obtained from individual reports will be kept confidential as required by Section 709(e) of Title VII. WILLFULLY FALSE STATEMENTS ON THIS REPORT ARE PUNISHABLE BY LAW, U.S. CODE, TITLE 18, SECTION 1001.

Source: Equal Employment Opportunity Commission, Washington, D.C.

letters interpreting the Fair Labor Standards Act (FLSA). The letters address a broad spectrum of issues under the FLSA, including the recent fair-pay regulations. On December 16, 2004, the DOL issued new regulations governing child labor. Under these regulations, 14- and 15-year-olds are allowed to perform kitchen work and other work involved in preparing and serving food and beverages, including operating machines and other devices used in performing such work.

In other regulatory developments, the Department of Homeland Security has expanded its Basic Pilot Employment Verification Program nationwide. The program is a new, voluntary Web-based system through which employers can verify the immigration status and employment eligibility of new hires.[7]

Equal Employment Opportunity and Affirmative Action

EEO and **affirmative action** are not the same. EEO refers to the laws and regulations that protect the rights of an identified group or class. Affirmative action represents an obligation employers have to hire members of protected groups to overcome past discriminatory practices. All employers are required to abide by EEO laws and regulations. However, only employers holding federal (and sometimes state) contracts are required to have affirmative action programs. An example of affirmative action would be a program designed to recruit, hire, or promote qualified members of a protected group, such as women, minorities, Vietnam-era veterans, or people with disabilities.

Affirmative action programs are acceptable only when they consider applicants on an individual basis and do not set rigid quotas that prevent people who are not in protected groups from competing equally. This key point stems from the famous *Bakke* v. *the Regents of the University of California* case decided by the Supreme Court in 1978. In that case, the medical school at the University of California at Davis set aside 16 of its 100 places for incoming students for minorities only. As a result, Bakke—a white male—could compete for only 84 spaces in the incoming class, while minorities could compete for the entire 100. Since this policy represented a formal, quota-based system in which one group was favored over another, it was ruled **reverse discrimination** and was overturned.

The Myths of Affirmative Action

Affirmative action was debated more intensely in the 1990s than at any other time during its history. In some states, the debate led to ballot measures designed to overturn many aspects of affirmative action. In California, for instance, a referendum to end affirmative action in state and local government was passed by a 54 percent vote in the 1996 elections.

Those who favor affirmative action and those who oppose it both offer strong arguments. Those who oppose affirmative action allege that it uses reverse discrimination to solve the problem of discrimination. While affirmative action does *not* require an employer to hire unqualified applicants, it can lead an employer to hire applicants in protected groups who are less qualified than some nonprotected applicants, who in turn often resent being passed over. This argument suggests that using affirmative action to reward one group over another fosters resentment and can perpetuate prejudice. In addition, those who oppose affirmative action argue that employees hired under affirmative action policies always bear the stigma of not being the most qualified, but simply the best pick from a limited minority group. Finally, the government encourages affirmative action through tax breaks, rebates, and contracts. To follow through on these incentives, the government must establish quotas, which leads employers to use reverse discrimination to qualify for incentives.

Those who support affirmative action also offer strong arguments. These arguments are summarized succinctly by social psychologist Stephen Plous, who presents and then refutes ten common arguments—or myths, as he calls them—against affirmative action.[8]

Myth #1: The only way to create a color-blind society is to adopt color-blind policies. Although this assertion sounds logical, color-blind policies often put racial minorities at a disadvantage. For instance, all else being equal, color-blind seniority systems tend to protect white workers against job layoffs because senior employees are usually white.

Myth #2: Affirmative action has not succeeded in increasing female and minority representation. Several studies have documented important gains in racial and sex equality as a direct result of affirmative action. For example, according to a report from the U.S. Department of Labor, affirmative action has helped five million minority members and six million white and minority women move up in the work force.

Myth #3: Affirmative action may have been necessary 40 years ago, but the playing field is fairly level today. Despite the progress that has been made, the playing field is far from level. More than 40 years after the Civil Rights Act prohibited gender bias in the workplace, women are still earning almost 25 percent less than comparably employed men. That means that, over a lifetime, each working woman will earn $700,000 to $2 million less than a man holding the same position.[9] For every dollar a man made in 2003, women made 75.5 cents, according to the U.S. Census Bureau. That was down from the record 76.6 cents that women earned for every dollar men earned in 2002. The median income for men working fulltime in 2003 was $40,668, not significantly different from the prior year, while the median income for women working fulltime was $30,724, down 0.6 percent from 2002.[10] And African Americans continue to have twice the unemployment rate of whites, half the median family income, and half the proportion who attend four years or more of college.

Myth #4: The public doesn't support affirmative action anymore. This myth is based largely on public opinion polls that offer an all-or-none choice between affirmative action as it currently exists and no affirmative action whatsoever. When intermediate choices are added, surveys show that most people want to maintain some form of affirmative action. Most members of the public oppose extreme forms of affirmative action that violate notions of procedural justice; they do not oppose affirmative action itself.

Myth #5: A large percentage of white workers will lose out if affirmative action is continued. Government statistics do not support this myth. According to the U.S. Commerce Department, there are fewer than two million unemployed African American civilians and more than 100 million employed white civilians. Thus, even if every unemployed African American worker displaced a white worker, less than two percent of the white work force would be affected.

Myth #6: If European and Asian immigrants can rapidly advance economically, African Americans should be able to do the same. This comparison ignores the unique history of discrimination against African Americans in America. As historian Roger Wilkins pointed out in 1995, African Americans had (then) had a 375-year history on this continent—245 involving slavery, 100 involving legalized discrimination, and only 30 involving anything else.[11] Europeans and Asians, on the other hand, have immigrated to North America often as doctors, lawyers, professors, entrepreneurs, and so forth. To expect African Americans to show the same upward mobility is to deny the historical and social reality that African Americans face.

Myth #7: You can't cure discrimination with discrimination. The problem with this myth is that it uses *discrimination* to describe two very different things. Job discrimination is grounded in prejudice and exclusion, whereas affirmative action is an effort to overcome prejudicial treatment through inclusion. The most effective way to cure society of exclusionary practices is to make special efforts at inclusion, which is exactly what affirmative action does.

Myth #8: Affirmative action tends to undermine the self-esteem of women and racial minorities. Although affirmative action may have this effect in some cases, interview studies and public opinion surveys suggest that such reactions are rare. In many cases, affirmative action may actually raise the self-esteem of women and minorities by providing them with employment and opportunities for advancement. There is also evidence that affirmative action policies increase job satisfaction and organizational commitment among those who benefit from the policy.

Myth #9: Affirmative action is nothing more than an attempt at social engineering by liberal Democrats. Affirmative action programs have spanned the presidential administrations of five Republicans and three Democrats. President Johnson, a Democrat, signed the originating document of affirmative action in 1965. The intent of Johnson's Executive Order 11246 was to strengthen affirmative action by increasing the number of minorities employed by federal contractors. The policy was significantly expanded in 1969 by Republican President Nixon. Republican President George Bush enthusiastically signed the Civil Rights Act of 1991, which formally endorsed the principle of affirmative action. Thus, despite the current split along party lines, affirmative action has traditionally enjoyed the support of Republicans as well as Democrats.

Myth #10: Support for affirmative action means support for preferential selection procedures that favor unqualified candidates over qualified candidates. Actually, most supporters of affirmative action oppose this type of preferential selection. Affirmative action selection procedures can be ordered along the following continuum:

- Selection among equally qualified candidates. The mildest form of affirmative action selection occurs when a female or minority candidate is chosen from a pool of equally qualified applicants. The public typically does not see this type of affirmative action as discriminatory.

- Selection among comparable candidates. A somewhat stronger form occurs when female or minority candidates are roughly comparable to other candidates.

- Selection among unequal candidates. A still stronger form of affirmative action occurs when qualified female or minority candidates are chosen over candidates whose records are better by a substantial amount.

- Selection among qualified and unqualified candidates. The strongest form of affirmative action occurs when unqualified female or minority members are chosen over other candidates who are qualified.

Although these selection procedures sometimes blend into one another (due in part to the difficulty of comparing unlike records), a few general observations can be made. First, of the four different procedures, the selection of women and minority members among equal or roughly comparable candidates has the greatest public support. Second, the selection of women and minority members among unequal candidates—used routinely in college admissions—has deeply divided the nation. And finally, the hiring and promotion of unqualified candidates is usually condemned (and rarely occurs because affirmative action does not require employees to hire unqualified applicants). By distinguishing among these four different selection procedures, it becomes clear that opposition to stronger forms of affirmative action need not imply opposition to milder forms.

Evolution of EEO Legislation

The evolution of EEO laws follows a pattern. The first set of EEO laws emphasized personnel policies. The second set targeted unequal treatment, while the third targeted perpetuation of the effects of past discrimination. The fourth and, to date, final stage of laws and regulations emphasize the **adverse impact** on protected groups. *Adverse impact* relates to those laws designed to reverse the effect of past employment practices.

The major EEO laws, regulations, and their principal impact are presented in Exhibit 3. This exhibit addresses the EEO laws and regulations that relate directly to the issue of discrimination in the private sector.

The Equal Pay Act of 1963

Some feel that the passage of the **Equal Pay Act of 1963** marked the evolutionary starting point of the EEO movement in the United States. This act was passed as an amendment to the Fair Labor Standards Act of 1938; it requires that men and women working for the same organization be paid the same rate of pay for work

Exhibit 3   Major EEO Laws and Their Implications

EEO Law	Major Implication
Title VII of the Civil Rights Act (1964)	Bars discrimination on basis of race, sex, religion, color, and national origin.
Age Discrimination in Employment Act (1967)	Bars discrimination against people over 40. Involuntary retirement prohibited.
Vocational Rehabilitation Act (1973)	Bars discrimination against otherwise qualified people with disabilities.
Pregnancy Discrimination Act (1978)	Prohibits discrimination against pregnant women.
Immigration Reform and Control Act (1986)	Prohibits recruiting and hiring of aliens not eligible for U.S. employment.
Americans with Disabilities Act (1990)	Prohibits workplace discrimination against people with disabilities. Reasonable accommodations required to make workplace accessible for all qualified employees.
Family and Medical Leave Act (1993)	Provides opportunity for employees to take up to 12 weeks unpaid leave for birth, adoption, care for elderly or ill parent, spouse, or child, or to undergo treatment. Applies to employers with 50 or more employees. Affects 40% of employees and and 5% of employers. Executives excluded.

that is substantially equal. Because of continuing disparities in pay between the sexes, this issue is the focus of many court cases and employment discrimination charges.

Title VII of the Civil Rights Act of 1964

Title VII of the Civil Rights Act of 1964 applies to employers with 15 or more employees and prohibits unfair employment discrimination based on race, color, sex, religion, and national origin. Employers with fewer than 15 employees may still be subject to state antidiscrimination laws that are similar to the federal Civil Rights Act.

There are two possible defenses for charges of discrimination brought under the Civil Rights Act of 1964: business necessity and bona fide occupational qualifications (BFOQs).

The **business necessity** defense is very limited and narrow. To succeed, the employer must show that the practice is essential to its business. For example, an airline that prohibited pregnant flight attendants from flying probably would not be violating Title VII if it could show that grounding the attendants was essential to its business. The business of an airline is to transport passengers safely. If the airline could show that the pregnant employees were a safety hazard because premature, sudden, or unexpected labor or birth could endanger the flight, it would probably have a successful business necessity defense.

Bona fide occupational qualifications (BFOQs) permit some legal discrimination and are based on the need to hire certain types of people for specific jobs. Under this provision, discrimination based on sex, religion, and national origin is acceptable if a bona fide occupational qualification makes it necessary. Examples of bona fide occupational qualifications include:

- Female attendants in a women's locker room

- Male models for a men's clothing line

- Native-Hawaiian performers for a Hawaiian luau

- Roman Catholic employee to take care of the altar at a Roman Catholic church

In each of these cases, bona fide occupational qualifications are based on the assumption that the qualification is truly mandatory. One exception would invalidate the entire BFOQ defense. For instance, it would be acceptable for a French restaurant to require that all of its guest-contact personnel speak French. However, if a single employee is hired for a guest-contact position who does *not* speak French, the BFOQ status is lost. The burden of proof that a BFOQ is required rests with the employer.

Seniority systems and seniority are also permitted under Title VII, as are systems based on merit or incentive—as long as differences are not the result of an intention to discriminate. In a seniority system, for example, employees with more seniority would retain their jobs while others with less seniority in the same position would be laid off. In a merit-based system, raises or other pay increases are contingent on employee performance.

Pre-employment inquiries involving matters that might be construed as discriminatory (sex, national origin, and religion) are acceptable as long as they can be shown to be job-related. Acceptable examples would include those we used to illustrate BFOQs. For instance, asking applicants to indicate their sex on an employment application is acceptable if the position is for a female attendant in a women's locker room.

Testing of ability is allowed if it can be shown that the test is truly required—and if it is not used to discriminate unfairly. For example, it could be allowable to require applicants for a cook's position to perform a cooking test, to ask applicants for a typist position to take a typing test, and to require applicants to take computer or other equipment familiarity tests if knowledge of such equipment is mandatory for the job.

Veterans preference rights and national security clearances relate only to public employee environments and are not discussed here.

Finally, employers are not required to extend preferential treatment to individuals or groups on the basis of race, color, national origin, sex, or religion. They also do not have to give special treatment to such groups to correct the imbalances of past practices. Some preferential treatment provisions *are* mandated under affirmative action guidelines for public employers (state and federal government) or for companies with federal contracts.

Violations of Title VII. There are two theories of discrimination under Title VII: disparate treatment and disparate impact. If an employer treats one individual differently from others because of the person's race, sex, color, religion, national origin, or other protected characteristic, that is **disparate treatment**. If an employer doesn't intend to discriminate, but does something that disadvantages more members of one group than another, that employer may be guilty of **disparate impact.** For example, consider what might happen if a restaurant requires dishwashers to have a college degree. By enforcing this standard, the restaurant excludes a larger proportion of African American applicants than white applicants. Furthermore, having a college degree is not really necessary to perform the job. In this case, the restaurant might be guilty of violating Title VII under the disparate impact theory of discrimination. On the other hand, if an employer hires white applicants who do not have a high school education but does not hire African Americans with the same or higher qualifications, the employer is guilty of disparate treatment.

A recent legal case in Mississippi illustrates how convoluted decisions over such issues can become. In this case, an employee of Barden Mississippi Gaming filed a lawsuit claiming that he lost his job at a casino in Tunica, Mississippi, because he was white. The employee alleged, and the court held, that the company had replaced him, a white human resources employee, with an African American employee who had less human resources experience. The court ruled in the employee's favor and required the company to pay $312,000 in damages to him.[12]

Policies intended to perpetuate an image are generally seen as overtly discriminatory, even though a company deems them necessary. For instance, a restaurant that hires only young people because it wants to create a youthful image is guilty of discrimination; there is no bona fide occupational qualification that prevents older employees from working in the restaurant.

The uniforms that some hospitality companies require their employees to wear may constitute a violation of the Civil Rights Act. For instance, requiring female servers to wear revealing costumes could be a violation since male servers are not required to wear the same attire. Such a policy can even be viewed as reinforcing an environment conducive to sexual harassment if the uniforms consistently lead to unwanted advances. The argument does not end here. Uniforms do not have to be skimpy or suggestive to be considered discriminatory. For instance, some religions prohibit their members from wearing slacks or certain types of clothing. Hospitality companies cannot require a female employee to wear slacks if the employee's religion prohibits such attire; to do so would be viewed as religious discrimination.

Age Discrimination in Employment Act of 1967

The **Age Discrimination in Employment Act (ADEA)** prohibits employment discrimination on the basis of age against people 40 years old or older. As a result, the EEOC views employees who are 40 or older as a protected group. All employment actions—hiring, recruiting, appraisals, promotions, advertising, and so on—affecting employees who are 40 or older are subject to scrutiny under the ADEA.

All private employers with 20 or more employees and all unions with 25 or more members must comply.

Examples of age discrimination include passing employees over for promotion for reasons other than ability, providing different benefit programs for different age groups of employees, and forcing older employees to retire. The ADEA will affect hospitality companies more and more in the future as a result of the overall aging of the work force and the industry's increasing reliance on older workers.

Vocational Rehabilitation Act of 1973

The **Vocational Rehabilitation Act of 1973** requires all employers holding federal contracts of $25,000 or more to employ "qualified" individuals with disabilities and to make "reasonable accommodations" as needed. If a company holds federal contracts of $50,000 or more, it must also file a written affirmative action report annually with the EEOC that outlines its program of compliance with this act.

According to the provisions of the act, a person is considered to have a disability if he or she has either a physical or mental impairment, has a record of such impairment, and/or is viewed by others as having such an impairment. This law stipulates that an employer cannot refuse to hire or otherwise discriminate against such employees or applicants simply because the company lacks the proper facilities to accommodate the individual's impairment.

The **Americans with Disabilities Act (ADA)** has a much wider impact on the hospitality industry. The ADA covers hiring and providing for individuals with disabilities much more extensively than does the Vocational Rehabilitation Act. A more thorough discussion of this act is provided later in this chapter.

Acts Affecting Veterans

The **Vietnam Veterans Readjustment Act of 1974** was designed to provide Vietnam veterans with protected group status for a period of four years after their discharge. Under this act, employers with $10,000 or more in federal contracts are required to take affirmative action to employ qualified Vietnam-era veterans. To qualify, a veteran must have served in the Armed Forces—not exclusive to Vietnam—between August 5, 1964, and May 7, 1975.

Hospitality managers must also meet the guidelines of the **Veterans Reemployment Act of 1942**. The act requires employers to rehire veterans—within 90 days of reapplication and with no loss of seniority—who leave a job for military service and then apply for reemployment upon completion of service. This act also requires employers to give employees time off, without pay, to maintain active reserve status. This time off is in addition to normal vacation time. The act also protects veterans who saw either active or reserve duty during the Gulf War in the Middle East during 1990 and 1991.

In December 2004, President G. W. Bush signed into law the Veterans Benefit Improvement Act of 2005, which made two main revisions to the Uniformed Services Employment and Reemployment Rights Act of 1994. One of the changes requires all employers to notify employees of their rights and responsibilities under USERRA.[13]

Pregnancy Discrimination Act of 1978

Before the enactment of the **Pregnancy Discrimination Act of 1978**, an employer could require an employee to take pregnancy leave for a stipulated period or at a specific time in her pregnancy. This is no longer the case. Under this act, employers cannot stipulate the beginning and ending dates of a pregnant employee's maternity leave. In addition, this act prohibits employers from refusing to hire pregnant applicants as long as they can perform the major functions of the job. The act does not force employers to provide health and disability programs if none previously existed, nor does it require employers to provide health coverage for abortions except in cases where the life of the mother is endangered. It does, however, prohibit employers from providing health insurance that does not cover pregnancy or that imposes high costs for this type of coverage.

Other forms of discrimination are also prohibited, including limiting pregnancy benefits to married workers and discriminating between men and women regarding employee benefits. Employers who provide pregnancy benefits are required to provide the same benefits to spouses of employees. In 1993, Congress enacted the Family and Medical Leave Act, intended to establish a national leave policy.

Such programs are also mandated by state law in at least 21 states. In some cases, state laws are even more stringent than the federal law. Some states have passed laws that require employers to provide unpaid leaves of absence to women for pregnancy or childbirth. This has caused an equal treatment/special treatment debate because some states do not require employers to provide the same leaves to men. In the 1987 case *Geduldig* v. *Aiello*, the Supreme Court upheld a California law requiring maternal leaves on the basis of "biologistic reasoning"—meaning that pregnancy was a unique physical condition. The Supreme Court upheld the California law again in the same year in *California Federal Savings and Loan Association* v. *Guerra*. In this case, the court found that Title VII of the Civil Rights Act of 1964 as amended by the Pregnancy Discrimination Act of 1978 did not preempt a state statute, and that the narrowly defined leave policy served the goal of sex equality. The California law in question requires that pregnancy leaves be granted for as long as four months.

This act substantially affects the hospitality industry, whose workforce is predominantly female. In addition to increasing the cost of employer-controlled health benefits, the act specifically prohibits employers from discriminating against pregnant women on the basis that these women may not fit the image the company wants to project. As a result, a hospitality employer cannot require an employee to take a leave of absence simply because her appearance no longer reflects the company image. At the same time, employers cannot force a pregnant employee to perform duties other than those that she normally does. For instance, a hotel could not reassign a front desk clerk to a back-of-the-house position during her pregnancy.

One provision that the Pregnancy Discrimination Act of 1978 does not cover is the right of employers to bar pregnant or potentially pregnant applicants from jobs in which hazards could potentially harm a fetus. In March 1991, the U.S. Supreme Court ruled in *Auto Workers* v. *Johnson Controls* that an employer can lawfully keep a woman out of a job only when "her reproductive potential prevents her from performing the duties of the job," or when a woman becomes physically unable to do the job because of her pregnancy. This case came about because Johnson Controls had prevented women from working in their battery plants for fear that lead poisoning might pose a health threat to a fetus if an employee became pregnant. The court ruled, however, that parents alone are responsible for making decisions about the welfare of their future children. Employers, on the other hand, are responsible for making employees aware of the potential hazards.

Companies still seem neither to completely understand nor equally apply the provisions of this law. For instance, a lawsuit filed in Texas by hotel manager Laura Taylor, employed with Bigelow Management, Inc., alleged that she was twice demoted after becoming pregnant. The company originally sought to dismiss the case, but the U.S. District Court, Northern District of Texas, denied that motion, citing the inappropriate comments made by Taylor's supervisor when he learned about her pregnancy. In the ruling, the court wrote, "Stray remarks may be sufficient evidence of discrimination in the event comments are related to the protected class of persons [to which] the employee belongs, close in time to the adverse employment action, made by an individual with authority and related to the employment decision." This case shows how stray comments can directly affect the outcome of a case against an organization. Advice for managers, then, would be to curb their tongues before speaking.[14]

Retirement Equity Act of 1984

The **Retirement Equity Act of 1984** requires companies to count all service since the age of 18 in determining vesting in retirement benefits, plus all earnings since age 21, even if there are breaks in service of up to five years. This act is considered a milestone for women since they typically start work at younger ages than men and often interrupt their careers to raise children. However, like other employment laws, this act applies to both sexes. As a result, both men and women will accrue larger benefits. This law also states that pension benefits may be considered a joint asset in divorce settlements and that employers must provide survivor benefits to spouses of fully vested employees who die before reaching the minimum retirement age.

Immigration Reform and Control Act of 1986

The **Immigration Reform and Control Act of 1986 (IRCA)** was designed to regulate the employment of aliens in the United States. Under this act, employers with four or more employees are prohibited from discriminating against applicants on the basis of citizenship or nationality. The act mandates that employers must verify citizenship status on all employees hired after November 6, 1986. Aliens who were hired before the enactment of the IRCA are not affected by the act.[15] This places the burden on employers for ensuring that aliens work lawfully in the United States.

All employers—no matter how small—must verify that applicants are authorized to work in the United States. This verification must take place within three days after hire by completing the Employment Eligibility Verification Form—commonly called the **I-9 form**. A sample I-9 form is shown in Exhibit 4.

Illegal workers tend to work in fields that require relatively few skills. In some cases, this includes hospitality positions. Approximately 31 percent of illegal immigrants in the United States work in the hospitality industry. Illegal workers most commonly hold positions as dishwashers, housekeepers, and cooks, in which 23 percent, 22 percent, and 20 percent, respectively, of all workers are illegal immigrants.[16]

Under the IRCA and under regulation of the Department of Homeland Security, employers may rely on several documents to establish an employee's identity and authorization to work. An applicant can verify his or her citizenship status by showing such items as a U.S. passport, certificate of nationalization, birth certificate, or a Social Security card.

Applicants also may be eligible to work if they possess a valid foreign passport and a U.S. employment authorization or receipt from an alien registration form. This receipt is commonly referred to as a green card. Employers who fail to verify an alien's authorization to work in the United States are subject to both civil and criminal penalties.

While the IRCA does not permit employers to discriminate, it does permit employers to choose or show preference to U.S. citizens or nationals over aliens. However, discharges and layoffs cannot be based on these preferences.

In addition, this act requires that employers provide a working environment that prohibits ethnic slurs and verbal or physical abuse related to an individual's national origin. As is the case with sexual harassment, the employer is responsible for providing a workplace free of such acts by supervisors, other employees, and nonemployees.

Employee Polygraph Protection Act of 1988

In the past, it was fairly common for employers to require employees and all applicants to submit to polygraph tests in a number of situations. The **Employee Polygraph Protection Act of 1988** prohibits the use of polygraphs in about 85 percent of the employment situations in which they were previously used. Under this law, employees are protected from dismissal, discipline, and discrimination solely on the basis of their refusal to submit to a polygraph exam. Employers can request polygraph tests under a very narrow exception. This exception permits employers to use polygraph tests to investigate economic loss or injury when they have reason to believe an employee was involved, and if they afford the employee other protection. Federal, state, and local governments and firms that perform sensitive work for the U.S. Department of Defense, FBI, or CIA are exempt from this law.

Drug-Free Workplace Act of 1988

Drug and alcohol abuse cost American businesses approximately $176 billion in lost productivity, health claims, and compensation in 1995 alone, according to the U.S. Chamber of Commerce. While many employers believe that this problem does

Exhibit 4   Form I-9: Employment Eligibility Verification

Department of Homeland Security
U.S. Citizenship and Immigration Services

OMB No. 1615-0047; Expires 03/31/07

Employment Eligibility Verification

Please read instructions carefully before completing this form. The instructions must be available during completion of this form. **ANTI-DISCRIMINATION NOTICE:** It is illegal to discriminate against work eligible individuals. Employers **CANNOT** specify which document(s) they will accept from an employee. The refusal to hire an individual because of a future expiration date may also constitute illegal discrimination.

Section 1. Employee Information and Verification. To be completed and signed by employee at the time employment begins.

Print Name: Last	First	Middle Initial	Maiden Name

Address (Street Name and Number)	Apt. #	Date of Birth (month/day/year)

City	State	Zip Code	Social Security #

I am aware that federal law provides for imprisonment and/or fines for false statements or use of false documents in connection with the completion of this form.

I attest, under penalty of perjury, that I am (check one of the following):
☐ A citizen or national of the United States
☐ A Lawful Permanent Resident (Alien #) A
☐ An alien authorized to work until _____
(Alien # or Admission #) _____

Employee's Signature	Date (month/day/year)

Preparer and/or Translator Certification. (To be completed and signed if Section 1 is prepared by a person other than the employee.) I attest, under penalty of perjury, that I have assisted in the completion of this form and that to the best of my knowledge the information is true and correct.

Preparer's/Translator's Signature	Print Name

Address (Street Name and Number, City, State, Zip Code)	Date (month/day/year)

Section 2. Employer Review and Verification. To be completed and signed by employer. Examine one document from List A OR examine one document from List B and one from List C, as listed on the reverse of this form, and record the title, number and expiration date, if any, of the document(s).

List A	OR	List B	AND	List C
Document title:				
Issuing authority:				
Document #:				
Expiration Date (if any):				
Document #:				
Expiration Date (if any):				

CERTIFICATION - I attest, under penalty of perjury, that I have examined the document(s) presented by the above-named employee, that the above-listed document(s) appear to be genuine and to relate to the employee named, that the employee began employment on (month/day/year) _____ and that to the best of my knowledge the employee is eligible to work in the United States. (State employment agencies may omit the date the employee began employment.)

Signature of Employer or Authorized Representative	Print Name	Title

Business or Organization Name	Address (Street Name and Number, City, State, Zip Code)	Date (month/day/year)

Section 3. Updating and Reverification. To be completed and signed by employer.

A. New Name (if applicable)	B. Date of Rehire (month/day/year) (if applicable)

C. If employee's previous grant of work authorization has expired, provide the information below for the document that establishes current employment eligibility.   Document Title: _____   Document #: _____   Expiration Date (if any): _____

I attest, under penalty of perjury, that to the best of my knowledge, this employee is eligible to work in the United States, and if the employee presented document(s), the document(s) I have examined appear to be genuine and to relate to the individual.

Signature of Employer or Authorized Representative	Date (month/day/year)

NOTE: This is the 1991 edition of the Form I-9 that has been rebranded with a current printing date to reflect the recent transition from the INS to DHS and its components.

Form I-9 (Rev. 05/31/05)Y Page 2

not affect them, this is probably not the case. A 1996 study illustrates how pervasive the drug problem has become. The study determined that if drug use in New York City were reduced by just 20 percent, the city would save $520 million in inpatient hospital costs, 670 fewer New Yorkers would die of AIDS annually, 400,000 days of hospital care and 1,100 beds could be eliminated, and there would be approximately 7,600 fewer cases of child abuse. In total, substance abuse was found to cost New York City $20 billion annually, or 21 cents out of every tax dollar, or nine percent of the entire city product. Similar conditions exist in other cities.[17]

In 1995, it was reported that the United States, which has about five percent of the world's population, consumes 60 percent of the world's illegal drugs.[18] Although there is no evidence to prove substantial drug abuse in the hospitality industry, there are indications of its likelihood. For instance, the ages of typical hospitality employees correspond to the age groups most likely to experiment with or use drugs. The working hours demanded by typical hospitality jobs also provide employees with few after-work alternatives for entertainment or relaxation. If for no other reason, hospitality employers should be concerned about drug and alcohol abuse because of their potential liability for negligent hiring practices. For example, an employer may be liable for damages done by an employee who is using drugs or alcohol if the damages were a result of the employee's drug or alcohol use.

The **Drug-Free Workplace Act of 1988** does not mandate a drug-free work environment for all private employers. It does, however, require that federal contractors establish policies and procedures to prohibit drug abuse and make a good faith effort to sustain drug-free working environments. Federal contractors must publish company rules about drug possession and use of controlled substances, the establishment of drug awareness programs, and the administration of appropriate discipline for employees convicted under drug statutes.

The Civil Rights Act of 1991

The **Civil Rights Act of 1991** brought sweeping changes to employment law, but not because it expanded the scope of protection. Instead, the act precipitated changes in the area of costs and litigation. Prior to this law, employees could receive only back pay and equitable relief. Employees are now able to sue for damage awards. More specifically, the act permits individuals to request a trial by jury if they believe they have been discriminated against. If intentional discrimination is found, punitive and other damages can be assessed.

Another aspect of the act addresses "business practices." Criteria used by a business for hiring decisions must be "job related for the position in question and consistent with business necessity." Employers with fewer than 15 employees are exempt from payment of punitive damages, except in cases of intentional discrimination.

Family and Medical Leave Act of 1993

After eight years of debate, Congress passed the **Family and Medical Leave Act (FMLA)** in 1993. The act requires employers with 50 or more employees within a 75-mile radius to offer up to 12 weeks of unpaid (but job-protected) leave during a

12-month period for birth; adoption; care for an ill parent, spouse, or child; or medical treatment. To be eligible, a worker must have been employed for at least 12 months and have worked 1,250 hours (or about 25 hours per week). Employers are not required to provide these benefits to the highest paid 10 percent of executives.

The right to take leave applies to males and females equally. Employers who employ both husband and wife can limit their *total* to 12 weeks annually. Intermittent leave cannot be taken for birth or adoption, but is available for illness. Employers must continue health care coverage while employees are on leave. Penalties for violation are severe for employers: up to 100 percent of lost wages and benefits, plus attorney fees and various court-related costs.[19]

Since the act's passage, 24 million Americans have taken advantage of its provisions. Statistics from the FMLA provide interesting facts about where the law is headed: [20, 21]

- 29 percent of all FMLA leaves are to care for family members, primarily aging parents.

- The median leave has been two months.

- Several states offer longer leave periods, specifically for "bonding" with new children. Twenty percent of the FMLA leaves to date are taken for this purpose.

Research on those who have taken FMLA leaves shows:

- Leave-takers are 18 percent less likely to be promoted than their peers.

- Leave-takers receive eight percent less in salary increases.

- There is a correlation between the length of leave and the decrease in raises and promotions awarded to leave-takers.

- Leave-takers have gotten lower performance evaluation scores.

Moonlighting while on FMLA leave is apparently not illegal. Company policies may specifically prohibit this, but most don't. There are no regulations about exactly how much time employees must spend daily working with their child or ill parent, and many have taken moonlighting jobs to help pay costs.[22]

A report from the Employment Policy Foundation (www.epf.org) notes that lost productivity, continued benefits coverage, and replacement labor cost employers an estimated $21 billion in 2004. The report's conclusions came from a survey of 110 organizations employing about 500,000 workers. Other highlights of the report include the following:

- The survey showed that 14.5 percent of employees at responding companies took FMLA leave during 2004. Among these, 35 percent took more than one period of leave, and 15 percent took six or more covered leaves.

- Thirty percent of FMLA leaves reported by responding employers lasted less than five days. Twenty percent of such leaves amounted to one day or less. The average leave was 10.1 days long.

- Less than half of the individuals who used FMLA at the surveyed organizations provided notice before the day the leave started.[23]

Exhibit 5   Sample Steps in an Affirmative Action Plan

- Establish a company affirmative action statement or policy.
- Determine the most effective methods of communicating the policy.
- Widely circulate the policy or statement.
- Designate or assign EEO/AA responsibilities to appropriate personnel.
- Train personnel.
- Conduct utilization analysis to establish program objectives based on the company policy.
- Establish goals and timetables.
- Establish implementation procedures.
- Establish system for monitoring, evaluating, and reviewing the system.
- Identify and correct problem areas.
- Prepare documentation and reports for submission to EEOC.

At the time of this writing, the DOL was considering changes to the FMLA that would extend the number of days a person must be sick—from 3 to 10—in order to request this leave. Various groups are debating this change and the impact that it could have on employers and employees alike.

Other Employment Laws and Court Interpretations

Not all the legislation affecting employer-employee relations is directly addressed in the major federal employment acts. **Executive orders**, issued by the president of the United States, and rulings in court cases have also helped to shape the order of employer-employee relations over the past 40 years. The following section outlines important executive orders and court rulings.

Executive Orders and Affirmative Action

Thousands of companies have contracts with the federal government. Companies doing business with the U.S. government must obey the mandates of various employer-employee laws and the requirements of numerous presidential executive orders. Several executive orders require employers to hire, recruit, and promote women and minorities on an affirmative action basis. Exhibit 5 outlines sample steps toward establishing an affirmative action plan.

Let's consider *Executive Order 11246*, issued by President Johnson in 1965. This order paralleled Title VII of the Civil Rights Law of 1964 by prohibiting discrimination on the basis of race, color, religion, or national origin. However, the executive order goes beyond Title VII and requires employers with U.S. government contracts of $10,000 or more annually to engage in affirmative action; it requires those with 50 or more employees and $50,000 in contracts to develop affirmative action plans. These plans must include a set of specific, results-oriented goals designed to correct past discrimination against women and minorities in the workplace. *Executive Order 11375* issued in 1967 set the same guidelines—based on gender—for federal contractors.

In 1969, President Nixon extended the issue of civil rights in the workplace by issuing *Executive Order 11478*. This order mandated that all U.S. government agencies and contractors base employment policies on merit and fitness, rather than gender, race, color, or national origin. Other executive orders issued in the late 1970s apply to veterans, citizenship requirements, and federal employees with disabilities.

Executive orders are administered by the Department of Labor through its Office of Federal Contract Compliance Programs (OFCCP). This office is charged with monitoring the employer-employee workplace actions of federal contractors through annual reports filed by contractors. The OFCCP is also charged with gaining compliance through conciliation agreements or, if necessary, through action by the U.S. Department of Justice. Failure to adhere to affirmative action provisions outlined in executive orders can result in loss of government contracts, ineligibility for future contracts, and fines or penalties.

Major Cases and Interpretations

In *Griggs* v. *Duke Power Company*, 1971, the U.S. Supreme Court found that, by requiring a high school education or successful completion of an intelligence test as a condition of employment, the employer had unlawfully discriminated against African Americans. Since that ruling, educational and testing practices have been increasingly scrutinized for discriminatory elements.

Subsequent court actions increased the employer's responsibility. For instance, in *Steelworkers* v. *Weber*, 1979, the Supreme Court ruled that companies and unions could establish quotas to eliminate racial imbalance in the workplace. This was later modified by two more rulings. *Firefighters Union No. 1784* v. *Stotts, et al.*, 1984, ruled that a company could not interfere with an established seniority system to protect the rights of newly hired employees. In 1989, the *Martin* v. *Wilks* finding enabled employees adversely affected by affirmative action to sue on the basis of alleged discrimination. The Civil Rights Act of 1991 substantially modified *Martin* by strictly limiting circumstances under which plaintiffs can challenge affirmative action programs long after they have been established. (The Civil Rights Act overturned several 1989 decisions by the U.S. Supreme Court that had made it difficult to prove discrimination. The 1991 version also increased protection for women and minorities, including individuals with disabilities, against job discrimination and sexual harassment.)

Other significant cases that have affected the balance of employer-employee relations in the workplace include the 1983 *Newport News Shipbuilding and Drydock Co.* v. *EEOC*. In this case, the court ruled that employers must treat male and female employees equally when providing health benefit coverage for spouses. Also in 1983, *Arizona* v. *Norris* found that employer-sponsored retirement plans must pay equal benefits to men and women—despite actuarial tables that showed that women were likely to live longer than men and, thus, cost more in benefits. In 1987, the courts ruled through *Johnson* v. *Transportation Agency* that employers can implement affirmative action policies to correct gender discrimination.

While none of the major cases was based in a hospitality industry setting, the rulings apply to hospitality companies.

State Employment Laws

Nearly all states and many localities have EEO laws. In many cases these laws provide much broader protection than federal EEO legislation, which often limits coverage to companies meeting certain size requirements. Companies of all sizes are generally required to follow state EEO regulations.

Many states and municipalities have enacted laws that protect groups not included in the federal protection plan. For instance, some states protect the rights of homosexuals. In fact, "sexual preference" is now protected in some states. Other states and municipalities prohibit discrimination based on physical appearance, political affiliation, contagious diseases, and so on. Because these provisions can change so radically from state to state, employers should not assume that compliance with federal law is enough. Instead, employers should conduct a careful review of state and local EEO laws before establishing a business in any locale.

Major Areas of Abuse and Litigation in Hospitality Operations

Some describe the hospitality industry as a hotbed for EEO abuse, although few major court cases have alleged discrimination on the part of hospitality companies. The potential for such problems exists in the hospitality industry for several reasons:

- The hospitality industry is the largest employer of minimum-wage employees in the United States.

- While the hospitality industry has long provided employment for a large number of women, many hospitality companies have relatively poor records of promoting women to top-level management positions. This raises a "red flag" for potential charges of sex discrimination.

- The large number of female employees working for male managers creates situations conducive to sexual harassment charges.

- In the past, some segments of the hospitality industry have emphasized appearance as a condition of employment. As a result, these companies could be subject to charges of preferential selection, which involves hiring candidates on the basis of personal characteristics, such as appearance. Preferential selection constitutes illegal discrimination.

- The hospitality industry has a high incidence of illegal discrimination in recruitment advertising.

- Historically, the hospitality industry has placed sex designations on some jobs. Some companies have specifically prohibited individuals from performing specific jobs based on their sex.

Exhibit 6   Major Areas of EEO Abuse and Litigation

Recruitment	Reverse Discrimination
Selection	Employee Benefits
Business Necessity Issues	Sex Discrimination
Four-Fifths Rule	Religious Discrimination
Applicant Testing	Seniority
Age Discrimination	Recruitment Advertising
Wrongful Discharge	

Exhibit 6 highlights some of the major areas of EEO abuse and litigation in the hospitality industry.

Recruitment and Selection

Managers in the hospitality industry may be tempted to recruit and hire under-qualified candidates simply to fill vacancies.

Most managers already realize that such decisions can yield unproductive employees. What many managers may not know is that such hiring practices can be construed as discriminatory. For instance, if a restaurant has posted a job description for a server that specifically calls for "experience," it must not deviate from this condition for employment. If it does—even once—the employer can be viewed as practicing discrimination if an applicant is turned down later on for lacking experience.

As noted earlier, business necessity is a narrow defense against a charge of discrimination under Title VII. To date, most successful cases have involved safety issues, such as special training and experience for airline pilots, bus drivers, and so on. A hotel operator's desire to project a certain image to hotel guests by employing only certain age groups or races would not be considered a business necessity. The government deems such hiring practices as inconvenience or annoyance issues. Failing to hire female employees due to a lack of locker rooms, restrooms, or other appropriate facilities would also be considered an inconvenience issue. Other policies that would not be considered business necessities include:

- Refusing to hire women as hotel stewards because they cannot lift heavy objects

- Hiring only pretty or young employees as greeters in a restaurant because the company likes the impression they make on its guests

- Hiring only male servers because management views the image as more "professional"

Hospitality managers should also know about what the EEOC calls "the four-fifths rule." The **four-fifths rule** was established by the Uniform Guidelines on Employee Selection Procedures in 1978. Under this rule, also known as the 80 percent rule, the selection of any racial, ethnic, or gender group at a rate that is less

Sexual Harassment:
Preventing and Resolving Workplace Complaints

Sexual harassment takes many forms, some easier to distinguish than others. More and more managers and supervisors are learning that a wide range of activities can be labeled as sexual harassment. With sexual harassment, the single biggest mistake a manager or supervisor can make is to fail to take every complaint seriously. All complaints must be carefully considered and investigated.

Basically, sexual harassment can occur when:

- Employment decisions are made based on an individual's acceptance or rejection of sexual conduct.

- A person's job performance is adversely affected by sexual conduct.

- Sexual conduct creates an intimidating, hostile, or offensive work environment for an individual.

- An employee is subject to unwanted sexual conduct from nonemployees and the employer fails to exercise control over the work environment to stop the improper behavior.

As this list reveals, sexual harassment does not necessarily involve sexual contact or overt sexual advances or suggestions. Harassment can occur when one employee stares provocatively at another, makes off-color remarks or jokes, or for many other reasons. In fact, sexual harassment can occur even when victims appear to be willing participants. For instance, an employee can participate in telling off-color jokes and later successfully claim that he or she was sexually harassed. The defense would be that the others involved expected the employee to participate in the joke-telling and that his or her failure to do so would result in workplace hostility. Courts have also considered pinups, calendars, graffiti, vulgar statements, abusive language, innuendoes, and references to sexual activity to be aspects of sexual harassment.

The basic point is that unwanted, abusive conduct toward one gender and not the other can constitute sexual harassment in the workplace. Sexual harassment that creates a hostile or offensive work environment for one gender is considered a barrier to sexual equality. Sexual harassment is essentially sex discrimination and is thereby prohibited by Title VII of the Civil Rights Act of 1964. As such, sexual harassment charges are filed by employees with the Equal Employment Opportunity Commission (EEOC), the government agency that enforces Title VII.

Companies wishing to establish strong policies against sexual harassment should follow these guidelines:

- Issue a strong policy statement against sexual harassment.

- Make it easy for employees to file harassment charges.

- Take every complaint seriously.

- Do not allow the person who makes a sexual harassment charge to walk away frustrated.

- Take remedial action to correct past sexual harassment.

(continued)

When conducting a sexual harassment investigation, a company should:

- Take every complaint seriously. Failure to do so can lead complainants to take action outside the company and can send a message to employees that the company does not care.

- Conduct the investigation promptly.

- Set a professional tone for each interview that is part of the investigation.

- Treat each allegation as a separate incident.

- Keep the facts and other information concerning the issue private.

- Obtain statements from the accuser and the accused regarding what took place.

- Clearly identify the relationship between the accuser and the accused, and determine whether or not this relationship had a bearing on the alleged harassment. For instance, determine if the harassment involved a supervisor and employee and if work responsibility issues could have been involved.

- Gather facts. Do not prejudge.

- Get detailed answers to the who, what, when, where, and how questions that are specific to the investigation. The company should follow up on these questions and answers until all the facts are clearly established.

- Interview witnesses and obtain statements from each regarding their knowledge of what took place.

The EEOC may become involved if the incident cannot be resolved by the company. When the EEOC intervenes in a sexual harassment charge, the following sequence of actions and events will likely take place:

- **Filing the Charge.** The individual will file charges with the EEOC by mail, by telephone, or by visiting an EEOC office. In most cases, the time limit on EEOC charges is 180 days from the date of harassment.

- **Serving the Charge.** Within 10 days after receiving the charge, the EEOC will contact the employer by serving a copy of the charge. At this time, the EEOC will request that the employer reply, in writing, about the alleged incident. Employers generally have from 10 to 30 days to respond.

- **Conducting a Fact-Finding Hearing.** The EEOC will plan an on-site visit or require the employer to attend a fact-finding hearing in which the employee charging harassment meets face-to-face with the employer. If an on-site visit occurs, an EEOC investigator will visit the workplace and collect information regarding the event.

- **Arranging a Negotiated Settlement.** In many cases, the EEOC assists the parties involved in negotiating a settlement. Employers typically agree to provide the employee with relief appropriate to the charge. This relief could include reprimanding or removing the harasser, reinforcing the company's sexual harassment policy, or providing for back pay, front pay, and attorney's fees.

> - **Issuing a Letter of Determination.** If a negotiated settlement is not reached, the EEOC will issue its findings through a letter of determination. This letter notifies the complainant of his or her right to sue. The same information is provided to the employer. The right to sue gives the complainant notice that he or she has 90 days in which to engage a lawsuit in federal district court.
>
> _____
>
> Adapted by the Educational Institute of the American Hotel & Lodging Association from the *Sexual Harassment Manual For Managers and Supervisors*, 1991, printed and copyrighted by Commerce Clearing House, Inc., 4025 West Peterson Avenue, Chicago, Illinois 60646.

than 80 percent of the group with the highest selection rate is regarded as strong evidence of adverse impact.

To illustrate this rule, suppose a new hotel opens and hires 60 of 120 white applicants and only 20 of 60 African American applicants. The white applicant hire rate is 60 out of 120, or 50 percent; the African American applicant hire rate is 20 out of 60, or 33 percent. The African American hire rate is only 66 percent of the white hire rate. These numbers fall short of the four-fifths rule and may indicate that the hotel's hiring practices have an adverse impact on African American applicants.

Applicant testing is a common area of selection discrimination. *Griggs* v. *Duke Power Co.* ruled that only those tests that test job-related ability are acceptable as bona fide occupational qualifications. This means that selection tests are considered illegal if they measure issues not related to job specifications. In *Washington* v. *Davis*, the Supreme Court ruled that job-related tests were acceptable as screening devices even if they result in adverse impact. In this case, the Washington, D.C., police department used a verbal skills test to evaluate applicants for police positions. The verbal skills were deemed necessary for the job and, therefore, allowable.

Discrimination in selection can also occur when recruitment is based on employee referrals. For instance, the case could be made that such referrals among an all-white staff could discriminate against other races.

Selection based on arrest records can also be problematic; being accused of a crime is much different from committing a crime. Employers can discriminate on the basis of an applicant's criminal conviction record, but not on the basis of accusations. However, even this is not an absolute. For instance, unless the conviction is directly related to the type of work, a manager might be guilty of discrimination if he or she refuses to hire someone based on a conviction record.

Age Discrimination

As the overall age of baby boomers increases, so will the overall age of the work force. It stands to reason, then, that the number of age discrimination cases will increase.

As we discussed earlier, the ADEA regards both applicants and current employees 40 years of age or older as a protected group. The ADEA specifically prohibits discrimination against this group in all employment conditions: hiring, discharge, compensation, and so on. Some provisions are made for business necessities, particularly in lines of work where health and safety are paramount, such as police work and air travel. For the most part, image is not considered a business necessity.

While many hospitality companies have made great strides in overcoming the perception of hiring only young, attractive employees, others have not. As a result, these companies are more likely to find themselves involved in age discrimination cases as the working population gets older. Refusing to put older workers in training programs, not promoting older employees, and forcing older employees to retire or to move to less desirable positions all represent age discrimination according to the provisions of the ADEA.

Reverse Discrimination

Reverse discrimination generally occurs when an employer attempts to rectify past human resources practices by hiring or promoting applicants or employees from a protected group over those who do not fit this description. In the past, granting preferential treatment to such groups has been considered reverse discrimination. However, since *Steelworkers* v. *Weber* in 1979, preferential treatment can be given to members of protected groups to eliminate what the Supreme Court termed "manifest racial imbalance" in jobs historically dominated by whites. No quotas are allowed. Preference is allowed based on race, gender, or some other protected characteristic if the intent is to attain a certain percentage of employees with that characteristic—but only if that preference is one factor among many. On the other hand, employers can follow seniority on such issues as layoffs and promotions, even when there is an adverse impact on recently hired or promoted minorities or women.

Employee Benefits and Sex Discrimination

In the past, employers sometimes offered one plan to men (deemed heads of the household) and another to women. Such practice was ruled illegal by the Pregnancy Discrimination Act of 1978. As a result, employers cannot discriminate on medical benefits, hospitalization, accident and life insurance, retirement plans, and so on.

As a result of the Pregnancy Discrimination Act, employers cannot discriminate against women because of pregnancy. As mentioned earlier, this act protects pregnant women regarding such issues as eligibility for employment and promotion.

Religious Discrimination

Title VII of the Civil Rights Act makes it illegal to refuse to hire someone simply because of his or her religious beliefs. It is illegal to refuse to hire individuals whose religious beliefs might prevent them from working at certain times. However, a company can refuse to hire someone because of his or her religious beliefs if it can prove that the company will incur undue hardship when the employee takes time off for religious reasons; the company must also show that the job cannot be performed by anyone else during such times. Hospitality companies may face other issues involving religious beliefs such as appearance, dress codes, and work schedules. In addition, employers must keep the workplace free from religious bias or intimidation by employees who attempt to impose their religious beliefs on others. The EEOC has issued religious discrimination guidelines to help employers comply with regulations regarding religious beliefs.

Seniority

Seniority has often been tested in court as it relates to Title VII and subsequent non-discrimination acts. The seniority debate often revolves around promotions and other benefits based on seniority systems, which may be inherently biased due to exclusionary hiring practices before the passage of Title VII. The U.S. Supreme Court has ruled that seniority systems are legal as long as they do not discriminate on the basis of race, color, religion, national origin, or sex. However, if it can be demonstrated that a seniority system has an adverse impact on women or minorities, it will be subject to challenge under Title VII.

What this ruling means for hospitality is that employers or unions can legally discriminate on the basis of seniority. According to the ruling by the Supreme Court, it is discriminatory to lay off employees with seniority simply to protect the jobs of recent hires who belong to protected groups.

Recruitment Advertising

Unfortunately, hospitality companies are guilty of breaking discrimination laws in their employment advertising more often than employers in any other industry. Ads that specify sex or age are still the most common abuses. As in other discrimination cases, the burden of proof lies with the employer, not with the applicant.

Hospitality firms can be forced to prove that their advertising is not discriminatory. This process can be both costly and time-consuming. Sex discrimination occurs in advertising when sex-specific terms such as "girl," "man," "maid," "waiter," or "hostess" are used instead of generic terms such as "server," "busperson," or even "waiter/waitress." Another form of discrimination is used in ads that specify or imply certain ages, such as "excellent opportunity for college student" or "part-time position for retiree." These ads are discriminatory because they discourage applicants in other age groups. A sample comparison of discriminatory versus nondiscriminatory advertising is presented in Exhibit 7.

Wrongful Discharge

Most discrimination charges arise over the dismissal of employees. Employers are often uninformed about legal standards regarding **wrongful discharge** and how to protect themselves from such charges.

Wrongful discharge is not the same as dismissal resulting from discrimination. Whereas Title VII applies only to employers of 15 or more employees, an employer of any size can be the target of a wrongful discharge suit. Also, discrimination suits

Exhibit 7   Sample Comparison of Classified Advertisements

Discriminatory	Non-Discriminatory
WAITRESS POSITIONS— Seeking young, energetic girls for full and part-time shifts. No college students please. Call Mr. Malcolm, 555-1234, evenings.	**SERVERS—**Full and part-time shifts available. Experience helpful, but will train. Call Ms. Jacobs, 555-1234, 10–2. We are an Equal Opportunity Employer, M/F.

must be based on race, sex, or some other protected characteristic, whereas wrongful discharge suits can be filed whenever an employee is dismissed for any reason.

There are two basic categories of wrongful discharge: contract theory and public policy theory. In contract theory, the employee might claim that a personnel manual, for instance, created a contract and that he or she was dismissed in violation of this "contract." In the public policy theory, the employee might claim that he or she was dismissed either for refusing to break the law or for insisting on obeying the law.

Fortunately, most employers can protect themselves from wrongful discharge complaints and lawsuits simply by establishing a discharge policy and sticking to its guidelines. Employers can follow one of two basic policies: employment at will and dismissal for just cause. **Employment at will** allows an employer to terminate employees with or without notice at any time for any reason. A **just cause** policy emphasizes fair and equal treatment and progressive discipline.

Employers can follow a set of relatively simple techniques to prevent charges of wrongful discharge:[24]

1. **Specify the rules.**

   - Clearly identify whether your company follows an employment at will or just cause policy. Failure to stick to the policy can result in a wrongful discharge suit.

   - Do not promise more than you are willing to deliver. Some courts have even viewed lengthy duration of employment as an "implied contract" of permanent employment.

   - If you adopt an employment at will policy, state up front in clear and conspicuous language that employment is "at the will" of the employer.

2. **Be candid with employees.**

   - In periodic evaluations, tell the truth about performance. Too many employers fail to note poor performance over a long period of time because they do not want to confront an employee.

   - Be specific about areas in which the employee needs to improve.

3. **Put employees on notice.**

- If you opt for dismissals based on a just cause only policy, establish and follow a progressive discipline program.

- Be sure to document and ask employees to sign any warnings or other disciplinary actions. However, don't force employees to sign anything. If an employee refuses to sign a document, simply indicate that fact in the file.

4. **Consider the options.**

- Discharge is rarely the only solution. Consider counseling, training, or returning employees to previous positions in which they performed well.

- Assist in outplacement whenever possible, or provide other benefits in exchange for a written release of claims against the company.

Title VII of the Civil Rights Act of 1964, the Immigration Reform and Control Act of 1986, the Age Discrimination Act of 1967, and the **Employee Retirement Income Security Act (ERISA)** all protect employees against wrongful discharge actions by employers, as do several state EEO regulations.

Issues in a Social Context

Even though Title VII and subsequent legislation made it illegal to discriminate in the workplace, it is wrong to assume that equality has been attained. This is especially true regarding two groups in the work force: women and senior citizens. Hospitality companies have made significant progress in their treatment of women and seniors. However, many feel there is still room for improvement.

Women in the Hospitality Work Force

Even though women fill a majority of the positions in many service industries, most hold what have commonly been referred to as "pink-collar jobs," working as servers, typists, secretaries, and room attendants.

On the average, jobs dominated by women pay less than those dominated by men. The hospitality industry has taken great strides toward correcting these abuses since the passage of Title VII, but there are still more steps to take. The hospitality industry continues to be one in which men typically supervise women.

Overtime Work Laws

In August 2004, the federal government issued new rules extending rights for overtime pay to more low-wage workers, but reducing or eliminating that protection for many white-collar and middle-income employees.

A draft of the rules in 2004 drew a strong reaction, with the DOL receiving more than 80,000 letters from workers fearing they would lose their overtime rights. The final rules are certain to further inflame opponents, including congressional Democrats and their organized-labor allies, who are seeking to overturn the restrictions. To temper the outcry, the administration boosted protections for low-wage workers in the final rules. They did this primarily by raising the salary floor below which workers are generally guaranteed the right to overtime. The previous floor, which hadn't been modified since the early 1970s, was as low as $8,000. Under the new FairPay rules, workers earning less than $23,660 per year ($455 per week) are guaranteed overtime protection. However, a new salary deduction exception in the FairPay regulation states that employees' salaries can be docked when they receive an unpaid disciplinary suspension of one or more full days for violating workplace conduct rules.

An interesting provision in this ruling states that if a hotel, restaurant, or other business closes temporarily because of a hurricane, or for any other reason, the property still must pay employees who are exempt from overtime a weekly salary to maintain their exempt status.

Most overtime rules date back to the passage of the act itself, in 1938, and changes to it are rare.[25]

Some states are reacting adversely to this new ruling. For instance, Maine finalized new regulations on the executive, administrative, and professional exemptions from the state's minimum wage and overtime law with the intention of preserving the status quo that prevailed before revised federal regulations went into effect August 23, 2004. (Similar moves are afoot in Michigan and Ohio, but so far neither of those efforts has gained much ground.) At the behest of Democratic Gov. John E. Baldacci, the Maine Department of Labor proposed rules that "any employee in a position that had or should have had the right to overtime under the U.S. Department of Labor regulations at 29 C.F.R. Part 541 [the so-called white-collar exemptions] in effect on August 22, 2004, will maintain that right."[26]

Impact of Unethical Business

Over the past few years, numerous companies have been charged with various forms of unethical business practices. Large organizations such as Adelphia, Enron, WorldCom, and others have seen their chief executive officers and others sentenced to long prison terms for their actions, including embezzlement of company funds and illegal reporting of assets on U.S. Securities and Exchange Commission (SEC) reports.

The hospitality industry has not been a focus of major SEC investigations to date. However, one ruling by the SEC is likely to affect many hospitality employers and concerns the employment of spouses and other family members. The series of new required disclosures is at least partially a by-product of the SEC's high-profile charges against Disney for failing to disclose family ties between its directors and company employees. Without admitting or denying that it broke the rules, Disney in December 2004 settled the SEC charges by agreeing to avoid future violations. Until the Disney case, some companies didn't disclose such relationships on the grounds that they didn't think the employment of an executive or director's family member represented a financial transaction that was covered under SEC Regulation S-K. That clarification has been strengthened to read that family members paid more than $60,000 must now be specifically disclosed on SEC reports. While this affects public companies only, the ruling could pertain to hospitality firms in which executive compensation includes salaries for spouses, children, or other family members.[27]

The SEC assumed in this matter that such salaries are merely methods of concealing real executive compensation and, as such, must be reported to shareholders and the SEC. This ruling applies not only to those living with the executive but also to "adults not living with the director or executive."

The Aging Work Force

In the hospitality industry, employees have typically been young. Hospitality has the reputation of being an industry that employees "just pass through" until they get their "real jobs." Some see this as evidence that the hospitality industry has failed to develop a career ladder for its employees, which, in turn, has created a negative image of the industry. However, in some cases, the industry has simply been responding to the demands of its guests.

In observance of discrimination laws, the hospitality industry is no longer able to use this rationalization for favoring younger workers. This presents real problems for hospitality managers torn between taking ethical and moral actions and responding to the demands of guests. For example, consider the dilemma of managers in an institutional food service environment where the clients ask the food service contractor to staff an executive dining room with youthful female employees. Even though the food service manager might like to respond to the request of the client, and feels a need to do so in order to retain the contract, he or she can't legally honor the request because of the ADEA.

The impact of EEO legislation on the hospitality industry will be magnified by the aging of the baby boom generation (born between 1946 and 1964). As baby boomers retire in large numbers during the next 10 to 20 years, the hospitality industry will face a new problem: how to cope with fewer experienced managerial personnel.[28] Hospitality will face an additional need: increased reliance on aging baby boomers to fill part-time positions. Not only will baby boomers retire in large numbers, but many will reenter the work force as part-time employees to supplement their pensions.

Employment Practices Liability Insurance

The evolution of employment practices liability insurance (EPLI) offers another example of industry adaptation.[29] In 1991, EPLI was offered by only five carriers in the United States and it focused only on large employers. By 2000, 70 companies offered such policies. What does an EPLI cover? The contract provides defense and indemnity protection against claims arising from the employer-employee relationship. It provides coverage for wrongful employment acts, wrongful termination, sexual harassment, or discrimination. Coverage is provided for the business entity itself as well as for senior officers and directors. Deductibles range from $2,500 to $25,000. When selecting an insurer for these policies, a business should ask the following questions:

- What is the carrier's EPLI experience?

- How will the insurer manage a claim?

- What is the scope of the coverage?

- What services does the insurer provide?

- What overseas coverage is provided?

Continuing Education

Many people choose at some point to continue their educations, and tax laws can have an impact on the decision. For example, the Master of Business Administration (MBA) degree has been popular for decades, symbolizing advanced competencies in business management. Costs for completing an MBA can exceed $100,000. The incentive is an average starting salary of approximately $75,000. From a legal perspective, it's important to remember that the costs of acquiring the degree are often tax deductible. For qualifying individuals, the tax savings are substantial. For self-employed individuals, the deduction lowers income subject to self-employment taxes, resulting in even greater tax benefits.

The allowance of the deduction for education expenses is included in Internal Revenue Code section 162 under the wide-ranging concept of "a deduction of all the ordinary and necessary expenses ... in carrying on any trade or business." Further analysis of this deduction reveals certain complexities in determining qualified education expenses.

Treasury Regulations section 1.162-5 (last revised in 1967) expands, explains, and provides examples related to the specifics of the deduction of education expenses. In general, the following must be met for the expense to be deductible:

- It is not required in order to meet the minimum educational requirements for qualification in employment, or other trade or business;

- It is not part of a program of study that will lead to qualification for a new trade or business; and

- It will maintain or improve skills required by the individual in employment or other trade or business; or

- It meets the express requirements of the individual's employer, or meets the legal requirements to maintain the individual's employment, status, or rate of compensation.[30]

Avoid Lawsuits (and Unionization)

It has become increasingly difficult to manage employees. Each year, new employment laws and regulations are issued that influence employers in hospitality. It is difficult, but of course necessary, to follow each of them to avoid costly litigation.

One legal expert who has worked with hospitality companies for more than 25 years recommends that the best way to avoid potential lawsuits (and the potential for formation of unions in your business) is simply to listen to employees, find out what they want, need, expect, and would like.[31] The company does not need a legal expert for this, just good, sound, caring management, according to the author. Low morale is usually caused by management actions that are unpopular with employees. Finding out what these are and anticipating the reaction of new employer rules can avoid much of the tension that leads up to lawsuits. To do this, you must listen to employees, either formally or informally. Whether through small group discussions or large employee opinion surveys, the results can help operators prevent litigation by understanding the employee's perspective better. One good first step is to ask an employee or employee group to participate regularly in employer decision-making. Providing this opportunity for employee input is often enough to ensure that employees will attempt to work problems out rather than take more drastic steps that affect businesses more adversely.

Using Credit Reports as Employment Checks

Since 2003, differing opinions have been voiced about how companies can use credit reports for employment checks. In response, the Federal Trade Commission issued a clarification as to how the Fair Credit Reporting Act (FCRA) can be used. According to these guidelines, employers must have written authorizations from employees or job applicants to obtain copies of their credit reports. If an employer takes an "adverse action" such as denying employment or promotion on the basis of information included in a consumer credit report, the employer must notify the applicant or employee and provide the name, address, and phone number of the agency that produced the report.

Employers conducting third-party investigations of suspected misconduct, such as sexual harassment, no longer need to comply with the notification requirements. Nonetheless, if an employer takes any adverse employment action during the investigation, it must provide the subject of the investigation with materials collected.[32]

Americans with Disabilities Act

On July 26, 1992, the Americans with Disabilities Act went into effect for many employers. This wide-ranging law dramatically affects the way hospitality companies relate to guests and employees. It also has a great impact on human resources management within the industry.

Background

President George Bush signed the Americans with Disabilities Act (ADA) in July 1990. This law forbids discrimination against people with disabilities. Many legal authorities see the ADA as the most sweeping piece of civil rights legislation since Title VII of the Civil Rights Act of 1964.

The ADA has five titles (or parts), as follows:

Title I   Employment

Title II   Public Services

Title III   Public Accommodations and Services Operated by Private Entities

Title IV   Telecommunications

Title V   Miscellaneous

Our discussion will focus primarily on Title I. Under the provisions of this title, it is unlawful to discriminate against people with disabilities in all employment and employment-related practices, such as:

- Recruitment

- Hiring

- Promotion

- Training

- Layoff

- Pay

- Termination

- Job assignments

- Leave

- Benefits

As a result of the ADA, protected group status is legally designated for citizens with disabilities in the United States. According to the American Association of People with Disabilities, or AAPD, a group dedicated to promoting economic self-sufficiency among its membership, there are more than 56 million people with disabilities in the United States—or about one out of every five people.

Still, according to the AAPD, of the 28 million people with disabilities of employable age, only about one-third has found work, suggesting that there remains a pool of people who are willing to work and capable of pitching in if given the opportunity.[33] Since 1995, the unemployment rate for women who are not disabled has been 19.94 percent, while for women with disabilities, the unemployment rate has been 66.94 percent. Since 1995, the unemployment rate for nondisabled men has been 5.04 percent, while for men with non-severe disabilities it has been just over 23 percent, and for men with severe disabilities, 76.8 percent. Additionally, for graduates of four-year colleges, the unemployment rate for both men and women who are not disabled has been 10.1 percent, while for graduates with disabilities, the unemployment rate grows to 49.4 percent. Not surprisingly, given these figures, the median household income for women with disabilities during this time was only $13,974, as compared to $28,518 for nondisabled women. Disabled men had a median household income of $15,275, compared to $31,068 for nondisabled men.[34]

Other civil rights regulations have provided certain protection for people with disabilities. The Vocational Rehabilitation Act of 1973 requires employers receiving more than $25,000 in federal contracts to actively recruit and accommodate people with disabilities. However, until the ADA, people with disabilities were not recognized as a protected class. Under the ADA, all employers, public or private, that employ 15 or more employees for each workday in each of 20 or more calendar weeks in the current or preceding year must adhere to the law. Exhibit 8 compares the Vocational Rehabilitation Act and the ADA.

Exhibit 8 Comparison of the Vocational Rehabilitation Act and the Americans with Disabilities Act

	Vocational Rehabilitation (1973)	ADA (1990)
Who is affected?	federal contractors and subcontractors	most employers
Terminology	handicapped	disabled
To prove discrimination	must show that decision was based "solely" on handicap	must show that decision was because of "disability"
Harm/risk to others	can discriminate if "substantial" risk is involved	can discriminate if "significant" risk is involved
Enforcing agency	Office of Federal Contract Compliance	Equal Employment Opportunity Commission
Lawsuits	cannot bring lawsuit	can bring lawsuit
Punitive damages	not allowed	punitive and compensatory allowed
Affirmative action required	Yes	No
Number of people protected	7 million	43 million
Disabilities included	short list	long list

The EEOC is the designated enforcement agency for the ADA. Charges of discrimination must be filed with the EEOC within 180 days of occurrence (except in states with approved enforcement agencies where charges may be filed up to 300 days later). After a complaint is filed, the EEOC has up to 180 more days to investigate the charge and either sue the employer or issue a right-to-sue letter to the complainant. Finally, after receiving such a letter, the complainant has up to 90 days to file a lawsuit. Depending on the circumstances and the state, an employee can file suit against a current or former employer for an event that happened up to 570 days (or more than 18 months) earlier. The same guidelines apply when a person is discriminated against by potential employers.

Companies that fail to comply with the ADA are subject to stringent penalties. For instance, the court can assess civil penalties against any employer to a maximum of $50,000 for a first violation and up to $100,000 for subsequent violations of the rights of individuals with disabilities. The ADA also provides for equitable remedies in job discrimination lawsuits; this includes job reinstatement, back pay, and even front pay for employees with disabilities who experience discrimination by an employer or potential employer. The Civil Rights Act of 1991 allows for recovery of compensatory and punitive damages up to $300,000 (depending on the number of workers employed) for intentional discrimination.

Exhibit 9   Highlights of the ADA

Effective July 26, 1992, for businesses with 25 or more employees.
Effective July 26, 1994, for businesses with 15 or more employees.

Defining disability: Any individual who has a physical or mental impairment that substantially limits one or more major life activities, has a record of such an impairment, or is regarded as having such an impairment is legally considered to have a disability.

Penalties of up to $50,000 for first violation; $100,000 for subsequent violations. Provides for equitable remedies in job discrimination lawsuits, including back pay, reinstatement, and even front pay.

Will affect workplace rights of approximately 43 million Americans.

Protected groups: orthopedically impaired (users of wheelchairs, walkers, and so on); speech, vision, and hearing impaired; people with mental retardation or emotional illnesses; individuals with disease such as cancer, heart disease, palsy, epilepsy, multiple sclerosis, arthritis, asthma, diabetes, and AIDS. Other groups include people with drug and alcohol problems who are in supervised rehabilitation programs.

The EEOC is the designated enforcement agency.

Much like Title VII, an employer is considered in violation of the ADA if employment practices are used that discriminate against people with disabilities regardless of whether the discrimination is intended. This resembles the adverse impact aspect of Title VII, which has provided the grounds for many of the discrimination suits filed since 1964. According to this provision, even employment practices that appear neutral can be considered discriminatory if they adversely affect people with disabilities. For example, adverse impact occurs under Title VII if the selection rate for a specific protected group is lower than 80 percent of the selection rate for the group with the highest selection rate, even if the employer does not intentionally discriminate. Exhibit 9 highlights some of the major points of the ADA.

Defining Disability

Under the ADA, an individual is considered to have a disability when he or she: (1) has a physical or mental impairment that substantially limits one or more major life activities, (2) has a record of such an impairment, or (3) is regarded as having such an impairment. Major life activities include seeing, hearing, speaking, walking, breathing, performing manual tasks, learning, caring for oneself, and working.

The ADA protects people with disabilities that involve speech, vision, and hearing, as well as disabilities caused by mental retardation, a specific learning impediment, and mental illness. In addition, people with diseases such as cancer, heart disease, cerebral palsy, epilepsy, multiple sclerosis, arthritis, asthma, and diabetes are protected, as are people with HIV and AIDS. Drug and alcohol addiction is considered a disability if a person participates in a supervised rehabilitation program or has undergone rehabilitation and is not currently using drugs or alcohol. The ADA also protects people who are regarded as having a substantially limiting disability. For instance, the ADA would protect a severely disfigured person from being denied employment because the employer feared the "negative reaction" of others. Other conditions covered under the ADA include autism, Alzheimer's disease, head injury, and brain injury. The act also encompasses general categories of impairment such as orthopedic, neurological, psychological, and respiratory disorders.[35]

Qualifying for Work

Under the ADA, people with disabilities are considered qualified if they can perform the **essential functions of the job** with or without **reasonable accommodation**. These two issues are critical for employers to understand. "Essential functions" are job tasks that are fundamental. For instance, cooking skills would be considered fundamental for a cook. However, the ability to hear orders called by servers to a cook might not be considered fundamental, since other means exist for communicating orders. As a result, an operation might be required to make reasonable accommodation so that cooking positions are open to people with auditory disabilities.

"Reasonable accommodation" refers to what employers must do to make the workplace accessible to people with disabilities. As a general rule, employers are required to accommodate people with disabilities unless doing so imposes an *undue hardship* on the employer. The EEOC believed that approximately 50 percent of people with disabilities would not require reasonable accommodation to be made by employers. Recent research conducted by the Matrix Research Institute in Philadelphia found that, on average, accommodations cost less than $500, or far less than the cost of replacing an employee.[36]

The following efforts are considered reasonable accommodations by the EEOC unless particular issues in a specific case deem them otherwise:

1. Making facilities accessible—constructing wheelchair ramps, widening aisles, raising a cashier station on blocks for a person in a wheelchair, etc.

2. Restructuring jobs to eliminate nonessential functions.

3. Reassigning a person to a vacant job—moving someone to another job if he or she becomes unable to perform in an existing job.

4. Modifying work schedules to allow for medical and other related appointments.

5. Modifying or acquiring equipment—this may include special equipment that a person with a disability needs to perform essential job functions.

6. Providing readers or interpreters for people who cannot read or have visual impairments.

The provisions for reasonable accommodations basically stipulate that employers must make the workplace accessible and barrier-free so that employees with disabilities can be hired and can access their work stations. Physical barriers such as stairs, curbs, escalators, and narrow doorways have to be modified to accommodate employees with disabilities. Elevators must have audio cues and Braille buttons for people with visual impairments.

Under the ADA, employers are prohibited from discriminating against employees and job applicants because of disability only if employers are aware that the disability exists. This means that employers are not liable for conditions they are unaware of. However, employers must anticipate issues of reasonable accommodation because cases will arise in which employees contend that their employer should have known that they needed such accommodations.

ADA: The First Years

The ADA has led to changes in many areas of hospitality management. For instance, the U.S. Department of Justice is currently inspecting hotel construction projects for compliance with the ADA. Why? Because hotels commit the same errors again and again. The first example of failure to comply is in hotel entrance doors. To comply, doors must have a 32-inch-wide clearance. The same is true for most other doorways, including guestrooms, bathrooms, kitchens, connecting rooms, and so on. With the door opened at a 90-degree angle, there must be 32 inches of clearance from the face of the door to the door jamb. The second common error is that accessible rooms are not dispersed among the different types of hotel rooms. Hotels and motels must offer accessible rooms among various types—standard rooms, suites, ocean-front, and so on. In addition, there must be connecting rooms as well as smoking and non-smoking rooms. Hotels with 50 or more rooms often lack accessible rooms with roll-in showers. The number required increases with the number of overall rooms.

Also, many hotels are not building rooms with accessible alarms. People with hearing disabilities cannot hear fire alarms, ringing phones, knocking at doors, and so on. Hotels must provide accessible rooms with visual strobe alarms connected to the hotel's fire alarm system as well as visual alarms to let guests know when the phone is ringing.

Many faucets, lamps, drapery controls, air conditioning controls, heating controls, and similar devices fail to meet ADA standards. These are inaccessible primarily because they require tight grasping or pinching. To test the accessibility, use the closed fist test. If you can operate the mechanism with a closed fist, it's accessible. Some signage is also in violation. To be accessible, signs must be clear and contrasting (black on white, or white on black), and Braille signs must also be provided.[37]

In some cases, the hospitality industry is affected by the ADA in unique ways. For instance, hospitality has long relied on employing people with pleasant appearances. In the past, some states enacted legislation that allowed hospitality companies to hire "pleasant-looking people." Prior to passage of the ADA, for example, employers in Tennessee could seek people with pleasant or pleasing appearances if the employees were to engage in meeting the public. Under the conditions of the ADA, such "cosmetic" hiring practices are considered discriminatory.

Another example of the direct impact of the ADA on hospitality involves the treatment of employees who are infected with HIV or who have AIDS. Hospitality leaders lobbied for an amendment to the ADA to permit operators to assign employees with contagious diseases to nonfood-handling jobs. This amendment was defeated, primarily because there is no evidence that AIDS can be transmitted via food handling or casual contact.

Communicable Diseases

Late in 2004, the EEOC issued explanatory guidelines that pertain specifically to restaurants. In these guidelines, the EEOC confirmed that in some cases employees with communicable diseases must be afforded disabled status when it affects their ability to work. Specifically mentioned in the new guidelines were four communicable bacterial agents: *Salmonella typhi, Shigella, E. coli,* and hepatitis A virus. When an employee is diagnosed with one of these four infections, he or she must not work in the restaurant. In this ruling, the EEOC informs restaurants that they must not categorically eliminate the employee from employment. In some cases, reasonable accommodations must be made instead, because the infected employee should be viewed as having a disability. This generally applies to cases in which employees contract these illnesses on a long-term basis.[38]

Endnotes

1. Eric Krell, "Under the Radar," *HR Magazine* 51, no. 1 (2006): 60.

2. Edie Weiner and Arnold Brown, "A Right-of-Way Strategy," *Strategy and Leadership* 33, no. 6 (2005): 22.

3. Caren Chesler, "Wall Street's Catch 22: Its Managers Keep Tripping over Their Own Feet in Female/Minority Hiring and Firing," *Investment Dealer's Digest*, 19 Sept. 2005: 1.

4. Erin J. Shea, "Handling Harassment," *Restaurants and Institutions* 5, no. 11 (2005): 54–55.

5. "Valentino-Vegas Settles Harassment Lawsuit," *Nation's Restaurant News* 39, no. 46 (2005): 104.

6. Scott A. Carroll and Steven R. Miller, "Focus on EEOC: Chair Shares Views on the Future of the Workplace," *Employment Relations Today* 31, no. 4 (2005): 59.

7. Morgan D. Hodgson and David C. Kresin, *Employment Relations Today* 32, no. 3 (2005): 77.

8. S. Plous, "Ten Myths about Affirmative Action," *Journal of Social Issues* 52 (Winter 1996): 25–31. Also available on the Internet at http://www.socialpsychology.org/affirm.htm.

9. "Getting Even: Why Women Don't Get Paid Like Men and What to Do About It," *Publishers Weekly* 252, no. 30 (2005): 53.

10. Barbara Hagenbaugh, "Women's Pay Suffers Setback," *USA Today,* http://www.usatoday.com/money/workplace/2004-08-26-women_x.htm.

11. Roger Wilkins, "Racism has its Privileges: The Case for Affirmative Action," *The Nation* (May 1995): 409–410, 412, 414–416.

12. "Race Discrimination Claim Costs Casino $312K," *Hospitality Law* 20, no. 6 (2005): 1–6.

13. Scott A. Carroll and Steven R. Miller, *Employment Relations Today* 32, no. 2 (2005): 77–86.

14. *Hospitality Law* 20, no. 6 (2005): 4.

15. Verifying an employee's eligibility to work in the United States is a complex process that involves several acceptable types of documentation. For more detail, consult Jack P. Jefferies, *Understanding Hospitality Law,* 4th ed. (Lansing, Mich.: Educational Institute of the American Hotel & Lodging Association, 2001).

16. "Where Illegal Immigrants Work," http://www.msnbc.msn.com/id/12208467/.

17. "Substance Abuse Costs New York $20 Billion a Year, Study Says," *Columbia University Record* 21 (8 March 1996): 1.

18. Robert Stutman, "Substance Abuse in the Workplace," Itasca, Illinois, Seminar (November 20, 1995).

19. "CORE Inc. Releases New Research: Complex Family and Medical Leave Act Regulations Could Pose Serious Burdens to Employers," *Wall Street Journal* (15 May 2000). NOTE: CORE is the largest provider of turnkey disability reinsurance in the United States.

20. "Media Briefing: Work-Family Policy Examined by Employment Foundations," *Wall Street Journal* (April 21, 2000).

21. "Career Prospects May Be Dimmer for Unpaid-Leave Takers," *HR Focus* 77, no. 4 (2000): 8–10.

22. "Moonlighting While on FMLA Leave May Not Be Illegal," *Managers' Intelligence* Report (2000): p. 14.

23. *HR Focus* 82, no. 6 (2005): 2.

24. These techniques are adapted from Andrew B. Kaplan, "How to Fire Without Fear," *Personnel Administrator* (September 1989): 74–76.

25. John D. McKinnon and Kimberly Pierceall, "U.S. Plans to Issue New Set of Rules on Overtime Pay," *Wall Street Journal,* 20 Apr. 2004, Eastern edition.

26. Margaret M. Clark, *HR Magazine* 49, no. 12 (2004): 33.

27. David Enrich, *Wall Street Journal,* 16 Mar. 2005, Eastern edition, p. 1.

28. For more information on this topic, see Robert H. Woods and Glenn Withiam, "The Great Retirement Caper, or, Bye-Bye Boomer," *Cornell Hotel and Restaurant Administration Quarterly* 33 (June 1992).

29. Fred Holender, "Employment Law Creates a Range of Insurance Products," *Business First* 15, no. 42 (2000): 19.

30. Cynthia Bolt-Lee, *The CPA Journal* 75, no. 9 (2005): 50–54.

31. "Avoid Labor Woes By Listening To Employees," *Hospitality Law* 17, no. 6 (2002): 7.

32. *HR Focus* 82, no. 2 (2005): 2.

33. Robin Lee Allen, "Hiring Disabled Workers Won't Handicap Business," *Nation's Restaurant News* 40, no. 12 (2006): 25.

34. Center for an Accessible Society, http://www.accessiblesociety.org/topics/economics-employment/labor2001.htm.

35. "Cumulative ADA Charge Data—Receipts: July 26, 1992–September 30, 1999." (July 2001). U.S. Equal Employment Opportunity Commission. http://www.eeoc.gov/stats/ada-receipts.html.

36. E. Gleich, "Mental Adjustment: How Far Should Employers Go to Help Someone with Mental Disorders?" *Time* (19 May 1997): 63.

37. Julie Hofius, "Compliance with ADA Lacking in Many Hotels," *Charlotte Business Journal* 15, no. 5 (2000): 40–41.

38. Carroll and Miller.

39. Paul Taylor, "Test Your Knowledge of Current Employment Law," *Charlotte Business Journal* 13, no. 26 (2000): 37–40.

Key Terms

adverse impact—A possible result of selection or employment practices in which members of one group or class are much more negatively affected by the practice than members of another group or class.

affirmative action—Policy that establishes obligation for federal employers or federal contractors to take positive steps to ensure that members of a protected group or class receive treatment that will help overcome past discriminatory practices.

Age Discrimination in Employment Act of 1967 (ADEA)—Legislation that made it illegal to discriminate on the basis of age. U.S. citizens age 40 and over are protected by this act.

Americans with Disabilities Act (ADA)—Legislation that requires commercial operations both to remove barriers to persons with disabilities in the workplace and to provide facilities for customers with disabilities. Called the "Bill of Rights" for persons with disabilities because it prohibits job discrimination against people with disabilities.

bona fide occupational qualifications (BFOQs)—Qualifications on which employers are allowed to legally discriminate during selection and promotion.

business necessity—Discrimination allowed by Title VII of the Civil Rights Act of 1964 as a legal reason for choosing one employee over another. To date, most of the acceptable cases have involved job-related safety issues such as special training or experience.

Civil Rights Act of 1964—Legislation that established the Equal Employment Opportunity Commission and provides regulations against discrimination in the workplace.

Civil Rights Act of 1991—Legislation that provides for both compensatory and punitive damages to those discriminated against.

disparate impact—An employer does not intentionally discriminate yet does something that gives one group an advantage over another.

disparate treatment—An employer treats one individual differently from others because of that person's race, sex, color, religion, national origin, or other protected characteristic.

Drug-free Workplace Act of 1988—Legislation that requires federal contractors to establish policies and procedures that prohibit drug abuse and to make a good faith effort to sustain a drug-free working environment.

Employee Polygraph Protection Act of 1988—Legislation that protects employees from dismissal, discipline, or discrimination solely on the basis of their refusal to submit to a polygraph (or "lie detector") exam.

Employee Retirement Income Security Act (ERISA) of 1974—Legislation that establishes reporting requirements, fiduciary responsibilities, and guidelines for participation, vesting, and funding for retirement and pension plans.

employment at will—An employer may terminate an employee with or without notice, at any time, for any reason.

Equal Employment Opportunity Commission (EEOC)—Created by the Civil Rights Act of 1964, this federal commission is responsible for enforcing non-discrimination laws in the United States.

Equal Pay Act of 1963—Legislation that establishes federal policy of equal pay for both men and women who do the same job with the same employer.

essential functions of a job—Language in the Americans with Disabilities Act that specifies that people with disabilities must not be barred from work if they can perform the "essential functions of the job." In the case of a cook, essential functions would include cooking skills.

executive order—Method by which equal employment opportunity provisions have been added to existing laws. Executive orders are made by the President of the United States.

Family and Medical Leave Act of 1993—Legislation that requires employers with 50 or more employees to provide 12 weeks of unpaid leave for employees after the birth or adoption of a child; to care for a seriously ill child, spouse, or parent; or in the case of the employee's own serious illness.

four-fifths rule—Rule established by the Uniform Guidelines on Employee Selection Procedures in 1978 that states selection or promotion of any racial, ethnic, or sex group must occur at a rate of at least 80 percent (four-fifths) of the rate of the group with the highest selection rate.

Immigration Reform and Control Act of 1986—Legislation designed to regulate the employment of aliens in the United States, and to protect employees from discrimination on the basis of citizenship or nationality.

I-9 forms—Forms used to verify citizenship of applicants and employees as required by the Immigration Reform and Control Act of 1986.

just cause—A policy that focuses on fair and equal treatment, and progressive discipline.

Pregnancy Discrimination Act of 1978—Civil rights legislation that prohibits discrimination by the employer on the basis of pregnancy.

reasonable accommodation—Language in the Americans with Disabilities Act that defines the workplace changes that must be made to satisfy the requirements of the act. Reasonable accommodations include such items as widening work aisles, lowering countertops, and installing ramps.

Retirement Equity Act of 1984—Legislation that requires companies to count all of an employee's service since the age of 18 in determining vesting in retirement benefits, and all earnings since age 21—even if the employee has breaks in service of up to five years. Other provisions of the act are that pension benefits are considered a joint asset in divorce settlements, and employers must provide survivor benefits to spouses of fully vested employees who die before reaching the minimum retirement age.

reverse discrimination—Discrimination against a member of a majority group in favor of a minority solely on the basis of race, color, religion, sex, age, disability status, or national origin.

Title VII (of the Civil Rights Act of 1964)—Legislation that prohibits discrimination on the basis of race, color, religion, sex, or national origin.

Veterans Re-Employment Act of 1942—Legislation that requires employers to rehire veterans who left for military service within 90 days with no loss of seniority, if the veteran re-applies. The act also requires employers to give employees time off, without pay, to meet active reserve status.

Vietnam Veterans Readjustment Act of 1974—Legislation that made Vietnam veterans a protected group for a period of four years upon their return to the private sector. This legislation also provided guidelines for employers regarding treatment of veterans from all wars.

Vocational Rehabilitation Act of 1973—Legislation that made it illegal for public sector employers to discriminate against individuals with disabilities. Legislation also applies to companies that hold federal contracts.

wrongful discharge—Charge brought against an employer for terminating employees without due process or without substantial efforts to first call an employee's attention to improper work habits and to help the employee change; terminating an employee's employment without sufficient reason.

Review Questions

1. The equal employment opportunity laws enacted by the U.S. Congress since 1964 have focused on what four areas?

2. How do affirmative action and equal employment opportunity laws differ?

3. What are bona fide occupational qualifications?

4. What is the four-fifths rule? How might it apply to hospitality companies?

5. What does adverse impact mean? How might this apply to hospitality companies?

6. Why is wrongful discharge such a sensitive employment issue?

7. *Griggs* v. *Duke Power Co.* is often cited as a critical case in the legal history of equal employment. Why?

8. Companies can be exempted from some employment laws by using a defense known as *business necessity.* Describe what this means, using a hospitality company as an example.

9. Many people say that EEO laws have affected the hospitality industry more than many others. Would you agree with this statement? Why or why not?

10. What are the central features of the ADA? How might the act influence the way hospitality companies select employees?

Internet Sites

For more information, visit the following Internet sites. Remember that Internet addresses can change without notice. If the site is no longer there, you can use a search engine to look for additional sites.

Americans with Disabilities Act
www.usdoj.gov/crt/ada/adahom1.htm

Equal Employment Opportunity Commission (EEOC)
www.eeoc.gov/

Immigration Reform and Control Act of 1986
www.eeoc.gov/

Occupational Safety and Health Administration (OSHA)
www.osha.gov/

Pregnancy Discrimination Act of 1978
www.eeoc.gov/facts/fs-preg.html

Sexual Harassment Hotline Resource List
www.feminist.org/911/harass.html

Society for Human Resource Management
www.shrm.org

Title VII of the Civil Rights Act of 1964
www.eeoc.gov/policy/vii.html

U.S. Department of Labor
www.dol.gov/

Mini Case Studies

The ADA in Action

The following mini cases ask you to apply your knowledge of the ADA to potential situations in hospitality settings.

Mini-Case One: Megahotels has been conducting drug tests as part of its pre-employment screening process. An applicant has charged that this is illegal under the provisions of the ADA. Is it?

Mini-Case Two: An applicant charges that your company has failed to comply with the provisions of the ADA because you discriminated against him for a room attendant position. Selection criteria for this position stipulated that an applicant must be able to successfully make beds, wash out sinks and bathtubs, and vacuum floors. The applicant believes that the employer is required to rewrite the job description so that some parts of this job, which are not actually essential functions, can be performed by others. Is he correct? Why or why not?

Mini-Case Three: A visually impaired guest in your restaurant has asked for a Braille menu. Do you have any options aside from providing a menu in Braille? If so, what are they?

Mini-Case Four: Megahotels has established a policy of hiring disabled over nondisabled people in order to correct past practices that discriminated against the disabled. Is this legal? Why or why not?

Mini-Case Five: You contend that the ADA applies to selection procedures. An employee who has recently become disabled contends that the law also covers all employees with at least five years' tenure. Which contention is correct?

Mini-Case Six: Your company has established a policy of nondiscrimination on the basis of disability for individuals applying for jobs and for employees being considered for promotion. However, the company still ties its compensation policy to the ability of each employee to perform every function of a job. Is this illegal? Why or why not?

Mini-Case Seven: Part of your application process is a test used to determine the speed that an applicant for a cook's position can plate orders. The test favors applicants who can more quickly plate the orders once the orders are cooked. Is this test discriminatory? Why or why not?

Mini-Case Eight: Jennifer is 35 and has multiple sclerosis. She has applied for the position of cashier in your food service establishment. Your advertisement for the job reads: "able-bodied female to perform cashier responsibilities." You explained to Jennifer that the job requires a great deal of stamina, but she insisted on filing an application. Even though Jennifer was among the first applicants, she was not hired. Are you liable under the ADA? Why or why not?

Mini-Case Nine: John is a recovering alcoholic who is currently enrolled in a rehabilitation program. John applied for a sales position with Megahotels and received a favorable review by the human resources manager during his interview. In fact, when he left the interview, John had the distinct impression that the job was his. However, a week passed and he heard nothing from the company. John called the hotel and was finally referred to the director of sales. The conversation went like this: "John, we are not going to hire you. Quite frankly, even though your sales experience fits our needs, we are afraid that the pressure you would feel on this job might knock you off the wagon. We do not want to be responsible for that." Does John have a case under the ADA? Why or why not?

Mini-Case Ten: Mary applied for the position of room attendant at Megahotels. She has experience as a room attendant and has good references. Mary was not hired for the position. When she asked why she was not hired, Mary heard this from the housekeeping manager: "You indicated on your application that you had a bad back. We are afraid that you might hurt your back while on the job and then take disability leave. We just can't take the chance." Has Mary been discriminated against under the ADA? Why or why not?

Test Your Employment Law Knowledge: Try to determine whether or not the employer is liable in the following cases.

- A woman accepts a position with a company engaged in international business. She is slated to go to China. However, she becomes pregnant. While the woman believes she can still go, her boss, who has been to China, believes it is too dangerous. Because there are no other jobs available in the company, the woman is terminated.

  (Answer: The woman sued under the Pregnancy Discrimination Act and was awarded $66,000.)

- Several female lifeguards file suit against their employer, claiming that the male lifeguards have been harassing them. The employer says the female lifeguards never complained and that all employees go through sexual harassment training.

  (Answer: The court ruled that the female lifeguards should have objected to the treatment prior to filing suit.)

- A football assistant coach is charged with drunken driving and reckless driving for driving backward on a one-way road. The university fired him because of the negative media coverage that ensued. The coach sued under ADA, saying that he was protected by a disability—alcoholism. Who won?

  (Answer: The court ruled for the employer, saying that employers must be allowed to discipline employees. Since the coach was not in an alcohol treatment program, he was not covered by ADA.)

- A woman works for a company where her "essential responsibility" as described in her job description is answering phone calls, which she must do about 100 times a day. After a car accident, the woman develops panic attack syndrome and panics each time the phone rings, and cannot answer it. The company dismisses her. Can the woman win a lawsuit?

  (Answer: No. The court ruled that because the "essential functions" of the job specifically included answering the phone, the company cannot be sued under ADA.)

- A female worker in a business started wearing a large (2-inch wide) button with the words, "Stop Abortion" and "They are Forgetting Someone" and a picture of an unborn fetus on it. She vowed to wear it until abortion laws were changed. Coworkers complained that she was hard to work with, was always politically motivated and espousing her beliefs, and that her performance had suffered since she started wearing the button. The boss gave the employee three choices: (1) don't wear the button at work, (2) cover it while with others, (3) wear a different button with the same message but no picture of a fetus. She refused to comply and was terminated. She sued and claimed the manager infringed on her religious beliefs.

(Answer: The court ruled that the three options provided by her boss were reasonable and that discrimination laws do not allow employees to submit coworkers to what she had referred to as religious beliefs.)[39]

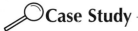

Case Study

Old-Timer Makes Waves

Caleb, the human resources manager at the Edgeway Hotel, scowled as his phone rang for the third time in ten minutes. "Human Resources," he answered, setting aside the stack of performance evaluations.

"Caleb, good morning. This is Jenna. I have a letter for you to look at."

Caleb immediately focused his attention on the call from corporate headquarters—if the senior vice president of operations had a letter for him to look at, these evaluations would have to wait. "Oh? What's it about?"

"It appears one of your front desk supervisors—who just happens to have worked with our president in the good old days when he was a front desk clerk—has a complaint," Jenna explained. "She feels she's being forced out because of her age. I'm faxing you the letter. She sent it directly to her 'old buddy' Mr. Alvarez. He's asked me to pass it on to you to take care of. Let me know what happens."

"All right. Who is it? I'll pull her file before the fax gets here."

"Sally Fenders. Call me when you resolve this. Goodbye," Jenna said, hanging up the phone.

Sally, Caleb mused, I know her; she's been here forever and a day. In fact, next month will be her 20th anniversary with the hotel. Caleb opened up the file cabinet and pulled Sally's thick folder. He opened her file and reviewed the past several years. After a quick reading, his notes highlighted key items in Sally's file:

1995	
September	Performance review, 5.0 average
	(Performance scale: 1 Probationary; 2 Below Standards;
	3 Meets Standards; 4 Exceeds Standards; 5 Outstanding)
December	Named Employee of the Year
1996	
May	Medical leave for hip surgery, out three months
September	Performance review, 4.0 average
1997	
February	Complimentary letter from a guest

September	Performance review, 3.85 average
1998	
March	Medical leave, out seven weeks
August	New supervisor
September	Performance review, 3.33 average
December	Sally reprimanded for sleeping on the job
1999	
September	Performance review, 3 average
October	New supervisor
2000	
January	Customer complaint about gruffness
March	Three customer complaints about service
September	Performance review, 2.8 average
November	Transferred to night shift
2001	
January	New supervisor

Caleb's secretary brought in the fax from Jenna. He sighed as he read the letter and then put in a call to Francine, the new rooms division manager, and asked her to meet him as soon as possible. Within a half hour, Francine arrived. "Hi, Caleb. I have about 10 minutes free. Will this take long?"

"I'll take the 10 minutes, Francine. It may take longer, but we can get back together later in the day. It's about Sally Fenders."

"Her!" Francine harrumphed. "I've been pressuring the front desk manager, Sydney, to start the counseling process with her. We can't carry folks like her—not and stay competitive. She refuses to change. She thinks we can treat a meeting planner who's bringing in $400,000 worth of business the same way you treat the little old lady who stays here once a year with a Discovery coupon!"

"Well, she's feeling the pressure," Caleb said. "Take a look at this." He handed Francine the letter.

Dear Mr. Alvarez:

Last year, the company threw a big party celebrating my 50th birthday and now it's trying to force me out. I've been transferred to night hours and I have a manager that complains about everything I do. He's constantly watching me and writing up everything I do. I think he wants to hire someone younger that he could pay less. Normally I'd wait him out—these front desk managers change every few years anyway—but I think he's trying to get rid of me.

I'm not the only one who feels this way. While I don't speak for everyone, there are quite a few of us old-timers who just don't know what's going on in this hotel. We used to know everything—customers, prices, and service levels. I don't know any of that anymore. I want to do the right thing, but I can't figure out what it is.

I'm not doing anything differently than I have for the past 20 years, but all of a sudden I'm not any good. How is it that I'm Employee of the Year in 1995, but now I'm worthless? I went to the awards dinner you held last year and was recognized as the employee with the longest service record. You said that I was a positive example and that the hotel celebrated the type of commitment and dedication that I had.

I remember when you were just a front desk clerk and I taught you how to use a room rack. I've never asked you for anything before, but I will now. Please stop this harassment. I have two kids in college and a sick husband. I still have a lot of good years in me. I've given my life to this hotel, and I shouldn't be pushed out because some hotshot manager wants to get cheap labor in.

I know I can count on you. I'd hate to hire a lawyer when I've been loyal to the company for 20 years.

Sincerely,
Sally Fenders

Francine put the letter down in disgust, "Isn't that convenient? Buddy-buddy with our president, is she? Notice how she neglects to mention that she's gruff with the customers, or that we've caught her dozing off on the night shift several times. I can't believe that she'd just go over my head like this. Sydney and I have put in a lot of time and effort with this lady. We've coached her, worked with her, given her extra training and support. It angers me that she'd send a letter like this. If I could get away with it, I'd fire her for that."

"Has the quality of her work changed?" Caleb asked.

"No, but that's the problem. We're in a newly competitive environment. She's been told, along with everyone else, that we have a new market segment and are taking on guests who demand a higher level of service. She hasn't been willing to make that change with us. The 'same old' doesn't cut it anymore. We've tried to get her to change. I even had Sydney send her to training. Nothing has worked."

"What sort of training did you send her to? Did she receive training on something she didn't know how to do? Did Sydney follow up with her so that she knew what she was supposed to learn?"

"I don't know, but I'll find out. But, training aside, you're the one always telling us that we can't carry employees indefinitely and she's become a high-maintenance employee. This isn't age discrimination—it's attitude discrimination. She doesn't have the right attitude for today's business."

Discussion Questions

1. What recent changes at the Edgeway Hotel precipitated the problem with Sally?
2. Is it an issue that Sally didn't follow the chain of command?
3. What are the roles and responsibilities of the management team in dealing with this situation?
4. Does Sally's length of service and past performance warrant special treatment by management in handling her current situation?

The following industry experts helped generate and develop this case: Philip J. Bresson, Director of Human Resources, Renaissance New York Hotel, New York, New York; and Jerry Fay, Human Resources Director, ARAMARK Corporation, Atlanta, Georgia.

Chapter 2 Outline

Job Analysis
    Select Jobs for Analysis
    Determine What Information to Collect
    Determine How to Collect the
        Information
    Determine Who Collects the
        Information
    Process the Information
    Write Job Descriptions and
        Specifications
Job Design
Legal Issues
Classifications of Employees
Staffing Guides
    Set Productivity Standards
    Determine Total Anticipated Sales and
        Guest Volume
    Determine Number of Employees
        Required
    Determine Total Labor Hours
    Estimate Labor Expense
Forecasting Sales Volume
    Trend Line Forecasting
    Moving Average Forecasting
    Seasonality
    Other Methods of Forecasting

Competencies

1. Explain the importance of job analysis and how to analyze jobs in the hospitality industry. (pp. 55–63)

2. Describe how the results of job analysis are used in job descriptions and job specifications. (pp. 63–65)

3. Explain the function of job design, and describe how managers apply techniques of job design. (pp. 65–68)

4. Describe the classifications of employees that make up an organization's labor force. (pp. 69–72)

5. Explain the importance of a staffing guide and identify the steps involved in developing a staffing guide. (pp. 72–76)

6. Apply trend line and moving average techniques to forecast business volume and labor needs. (pp. 77–78)

2

Job Analysis and Job Design

This chapter was co-authored by Tom Schrier, Ph.D. candidate,
University of Nevada, Las Vegas.

IMAGINE THAT YOU'VE BEEN SELECTED to open the first hotel for a new company. Among your earliest assignments is designing the jobs that people will do. You've had some experience in this area and know that before you can identify jobs, you have to identify some basics of hotel operation. Sitting down with a pen and paper, you start writing out questions you'll need to answer:

- What is the content of each job?

- How many jobs are necessary?

- How will the jobs fit together so that two people don't end up doing the same thing?

- What qualifications will people need in each job?

- What should each person be trained to do in each job?

- How will you know when people are doing a good job? How should you measure their performance?

- How much should you pay people for doing each job?

What you've just done as an imaginary consultant is to draw up questions you could answer through **job analysis** and **job design**. Job analysis is the process of determining what will be done in a job.

The process takes some time and effort, and, when completed, job analyses are rarely used in their entire form.[1] Given these factors, many hospitality companies make the mistake of not completing a job analysis for each position. What these companies don't know is that, while the analysis itself is rarely used, the information the analysis contains has a variety of uses. Job analysis reveals the tasks, behaviors, and personal characteristics needed to do a job. In many cases, it tells a company *why* specific abilities and skills are required for a job.

While job analysis determines *what* will be done on a job, job design determines *how* the job will be done. Job design involves defining the combination of tasks and responsibilities associated with a job.

The importance of job analysis and job design should not be underestimated. Training programs, job evaluation and compensation planning, and performance appraisals all depend on a complete and comprehensive job analysis. The results of job analysis can be used in human resource planning, recruitment, selection, placement, promotion, career path planning, and safety issues related to jobs. Job

Exhibit 1   Job Analysis: The Most Basic Human Resource Management Tool

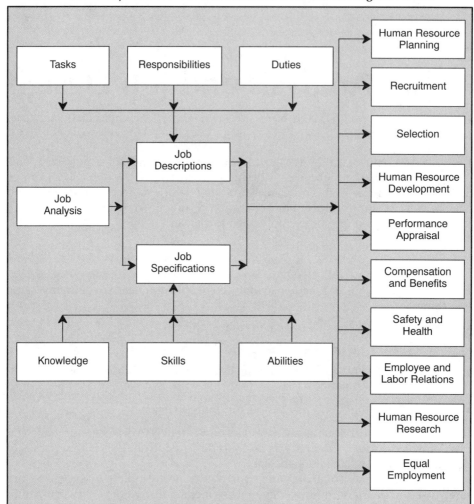

analysis can also be a company's frontline defense against charges brought by the Equal Employment Opportunity Commission. Job analysis may reveal that the business has a bona fide legal reason for certain types of discrimination in selection and promotion decisions. Exhibit 1 illustrates many uses for job analysis.

Some managers believe that once a job is designed and described in an employee manual, it never changes. Good hospitality managers know that analyzing and designing jobs is a continual process.

Job Analysis

As Exhibit 2 shows, managers must make several decisions in completing a job analysis. Each of these decisions will be discussed in the following sections.

Exhibit 2   Steps in Job Analysis

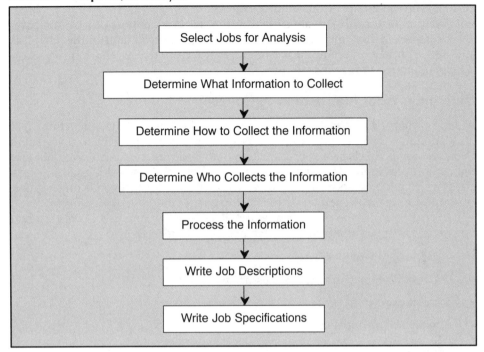

- Select Jobs for Analysis
- Determine What Information to Collect
- Determine How to Collect the Information
- Determine Who Collects the Information
- Process the Information
- Write Job Descriptions
- Write Job Specifications

Select Jobs for Analysis

A new hotel or restaurant requires a complete analysis of each job. But in an established operation, that might not be the case. Selecting which jobs to analyze is the first step in completing a thorough job analysis. Some companies analyze each job in the organization once per year; others use a rotation system and analyze each job every three years. How often the job is analyzed depends primarily on the degree of change associated with the position.

Both internal and external factors can affect the frequency of analysis. For instance, managers may need to analyze cooking jobs each time new items are added to a menu to ensure that no cook is overburdened. Adding or assigning new duties to a job or individual may call for a thorough job analysis. A good manager will analyze the "new" job to make certain that duties are equitably distributed and that productivity does not decline.

Assigning new duties is not the only internal factor that affects the frequency of job analysis. New technology in the workplace likely will require job analysis. For instance, automated check-in and check-out systems require that front desk positions be thoroughly analyzed to ensure the even distribution of work and efficient use of employees. Job analysis may be required even when a new employee comes on board. Consider the impact of hiring a new night auditor. If the auditor has substantial experience, the hotel could assign additional responsibilities to this position and redesign other duties. The opposite would be true if the night auditor has limited experience. Properties may wish to compare the skills of the new night auditor with those of previous night auditors.

External factors also create situations that require analysis of jobs. Increases and decreases in customer demand, seasonality (discussed later in this chapter), and new competition are examples of external factors that would require a hospitality operation to reanalyze its jobs.

Determine What Information to Collect

American corporations have a poor history of job design. Most managers think that it's a good idea to break jobs down into their smallest components to understand them. However, this is probably a function of their desire for control over jobs and their employees more than an understanding of job analysis or design. Breaking a job down to understand what goes on and how it can be improved is much different from simply breaking it down in order to control employee behavior.[2]

The different kinds of information collected in job analysis serve different functions. The types of information that need to be collected are:

- Actual work activities

- Tools, equipment, and other necessary work aids

- Job context

- Personal characteristics

- Behavior requirements

- Performance standards

The kind of information collected depends on the ultimate use of the data, the time allowed for collection, and the budget. For instance, if information from the job analysis will be used to write new or updated job descriptions, the information gathered should focus on one of the first three categories: work activities, equipment used, or job context. If the information will be used to create job specifications, the focus should be on personal characteristics.

Determine How to Collect the Information

Several methods of collecting information are available and widely used. Some are more useful for specific purposes. The matrix in Exhibit 3 suggests the most useful methods for certain areas.

Since hospitality jobs vary considerably from the front of the house to the back of the house and from property to property, managers will want to use several different methods of data collection. The following sections discuss each method as well as its advantages and disadvantages.

Observation. The simplest and least expensive method of collecting job analysis information is observation. With this method, managers simply watch employees at work and make detailed notes of the tasks and behaviors each performs. However, the observation method does not come problem-free. For instance, it is

Exhibit 3   Methods of Collecting Job Analysis Information

Method	Method Useful for:				
	Job Description	Job Specifications	Interview Development	Performance Evaluation	Training
Observation	X	X	X		
Interviews	X	X	X	X	X
Questionnaires	X	X	X	X	X
Critical Incidents	X	X	X	X	X
Performance Evaluations					
By supervisor		X	X		
Self-evaluation		X	X		
Diaries	X	X	X		

difficult to observe "normal" work performance, since employees typically perform better when they know they are being watched.

This result—or, as some consider it, phenomenon—is known in management research circles as the **Hawthorne Effect**. The Hawthorne Effect got its name from a study conducted at the Westinghouse Hawthorne Relay Assembly Works Plant in Chicago. In this study, researchers observed employees at work to determine (among other things) whether changing lighting levels would improve productivity. Researchers found that productivity improved when the lighting level was increased. To their surprise, however, they detected similar improvements in productivity when the lighting was dimmed. After much research, the observers concluded that the improvements in productivity were related to the fact that someone was paying close attention to the employees.

The observation method has other problems. For one, an observer may harbor certain biases toward specific employees. Second, observers may experience difficulty watching employees work without being obtrusive or getting in the way. Observers may also have problems selecting which employees to observe. For instance, should they watch the best, the worst, or the average employee? Finally, observers may find themselves in a quandary when deciding how to observe work that is not task oriented. The observation method is not very useful when analyzing a manager's job, simply because much of a manager's time is spent thinking and solving problems—duties difficult to observe. If observation is used, it is very important to watch several employees to arrive at an average of the work performed. The method is often improved when the person collecting the information actually does the job at some point to get a personal feel for what the work entails.

Perform the Job. One of the best ways to understand the intricacies of a job is to actually do the job. By performing the job functions, the person responsible for analyzing the job can better understand the skills, knowledge, physical requirements, personality type, and so on required to successfully do the job. A major advantage of this method is that it gives the analyst credibility with employees, since they see the analyst as someone who has experienced the job and actually knows what its demands are. This can create better relationships with employees and can lead them to cooperate more with the analyst during the information-collection process. However, if the job is highly technical or requires a great deal of training, this method could be impractical, since the time required to learn and efficiently perform the job could be too great.[3]

Interviews. Another popular method of compiling job analysis information is interviewing the employees who do the job. Many researchers swear by interviews. They say that no one can know a job better than the person who does it. However, the employee's own view of the job can bias this method of gathering information. For instance, people naturally tend to overstate the importance of their work and their qualifications. And, when interviewed, most people are susceptible to what is known as the **Heisenberg Effect**, which describes the tendency of people to subconsciously give answers they think the interviewers want to hear. Interviewers can reduce the impact of overstatement and the Heisenberg Effect by simply being aware that these problems exist and conducting interviews more carefully. Interviewers will find a second safeguard in collecting interview information from several employees.

Questionnaires and Checklists. Questionnaires and checklists often ask employees to rate their work on a predetermined scale. These scales are generally designed to evaluate the difficulty, frequency, and importance of the job and the relationship of one job to another. The ratings provide a useful method of quantifying jobs if the questionnaire is completed by a large group of employees who do the same job. The **position analysis questionnaire (PAQ)** is a structured questionnaire that quantifies job elements. It is completed by employees familiar with the job being examined and then is studied by a job analyst. The PAQ consists of a checklist of 194 job elements divided into six job dimensions:

- Information input (the employee gets information on how to do the job)

- Mental processes (reasoning, planning, and problem solving involved in the job)

- Work output (physical activities associated with the job)

- Interpersonal activities (relationships with other persons)

- Work situation and job context (physical working conditions and social aspects that affect the job)

- Miscellaneous characteristics

There are several questionnaires designed to help managers develop job descriptions using standardized questionnaires. One is the **management position description questionnaire (MPDQ)**, which collects information about management work in 13 different categories. A second is the **Minnesota job description questionnaire (MJDQ)**, one of the more popular one-size-fits-all job design systems. A study on the practical applicability of this multi-method questionnaire has shown that the MJDQ does not do a very good job. The likely reason for this, and the reason most off-the-shelf systems fail, is that jobs, like the people who do them, are unique. This explains why transferring the requirements from a job at one company to a similar, but not exactly the same, job at another company does not work. Complete, thorough, and effective job analysis and design requires a company to consider itself and its jobs unique, and to analyze each appropriately. While this may take longer than using a standardized questionnaire, the results are much better.[4] The federal government designed the Occupational Information Network system (or O*NET) to help employers with recruitment, training, and other workforce development programs. Information on O*NET is available online at http://online.onecenter.org.

Critical Incidents. The **critical incident** method involves observing and recording actual events. A critical incident might read like this:

> On June 27, 2001, Mr. Jones, a bellperson, observed a guest fretting over how to get through a strong rain to his car, parked in a lot several hundred yards away. Without hesitation, Mr. Jones provided the guest with his own umbrella.

Over time, a large enough number of such critical incidents can form a fairly clear picture of a job's actual requirements. The disadvantage of this method is that it takes a considerable amount of time to compile the critical incidents needed to draw a complete picture of the job. The advantage is that this method is an excellent way to develop training materials that show employees how services should be provided.

Performance Evaluations. Performance evaluations provide an excellent opportunity to collect job analysis information. For instance, a manager conducting a performance evaluation with a room attendant might learn that the work could be completed more effectively if the employee were given the chance to clean the same rooms each day. Most performance evaluation methods include open-ended discussions between managers and the employee being evaluated. The discussion should be two-sided. Managers should give the employee feedback on his or her performance and should listen to the employee's suggestions for improvement. Suggested improvements may relate to personal behavior or to the way a job is done.

Diaries. Some companies compile job analysis information by asking their employees to keep a diary or daily log of their activities during a specific period. This method is a cost-effective, comprehensive way to gather information. Diaries also encourage employees to think about the work they do and, therefore, to do a better job. However, this method requires employees to dedicate a substantial amount of time to writing the events in their journals. Employees may also try to bias their supervisor's view of them by writing about incidents or actions that did not take place. Also, some employees may not read or write well enough to keep a diary. Finally, job analysts must spend a substantial amount of time reading each journal and gathering information to completely portray the job.

Multiple Methods. As previously mentioned, the jobs within a hospitality firm can vary greatly. Therefore, it may be inefficient to use the same method of collecting information for every job within a property, or from property to property within a chain. Likewise, using a variety of methods may be the most efficient way to achieve a complete understanding of a single job. For example, to collect information for a front desk position, an analyst might use observation followed by interviews and/or questionnaires.[5]

Determine Who Collects the Information

The purpose, time constraints, and budget generally will determine who collects job analysis information. A trained professional is usually the best choice if the purpose is to design job specifications that will withstand close investigation by the EEOC. This professional can be from either inside or outside the company. Sometimes it is better to employ a third party since: (1) this person can often be more objective about the positions analyzed, and (2) the objectivity shown by an outsider can be important when presenting unusual or narrow job specifications to the EEOC. A disadvantage of using an outside consultant is that he or she may be unfamiliar with the job requirements.

There are advantages to using current or past supervisors or current employees to conduct a job analysis. Current supervisors and employees have the most insight into what actually goes on in the job. As a result, their analysis may include subtle tasks and skills that others overlook. Using in-house personnel is usually more cost-effective than hiring outside analysts. One disadvantage of using either current supervisors or employees is that the opportunity for bias increases. Also, employees sometimes refrain from reporting certain tasks so that they won't be required to perform those tasks when new job descriptions are written.

By using former supervisors, the company may avoid the personal or job-related bias that sometimes is evident in analyses performed by people close to the job. Because a former supervisor is no longer responsible for employee promotions, performance appraisals, and disciplinary action, there is less reason to suspect that personal issues might cloud his or her analysis.

Many organizations have begun using teams to analyze jobs. Such teams comprise employees who work in the position under analysis (or in lateral positions) and supervisors. This approach often provides the best overall view of a position. Before using teams for this purpose, it is likely you will need help developing the team. Chain operations have one more element to consider: consistency in job descriptions and specifications from unit to unit. As a general rule, a job analysis conducted by current supervisors or employees reflects local operational considerations. Such an analysis is less standardized and thus less useful to other operations in a chain.

One caution to managers before engaging in job analysis and design: unions are often opposed to any job analysis and design programs. One of the main reasons for this is that re-design is often accompanied by changes in compensation. Another reason is that job analysis breaks the job down into the smallest components for analysis, and this threatens the unions' ability to negotiate and/or control what each job consists of. However, union opposition to job analysis is often only a case of fearing the unknown. Making it known in advance that the objective is not reducing compensation or taking control from the unions—but, rather, helping workers and unions identify the important elements of a job and what exactly should be done in it—usually eliminates the opposition. In fact, unions may realize that completed job analyses and descriptions actually help by clearly establishing between management and employees exactly what work is to be done.[6]

Job elimination is one aspect of job analysis that managers often fail to empower their employees to do when asking them to analyze a job. At their heart, job analysis and design both strive to eliminate unnecessary parts of an employee's job. Asking job analysts to consider this while conducting the evaluation will often lead to better results.[7]

Process the Information

Data collection often yields more data than necessary. Using several different methods of data collection doesn't mean you'll get different information; sometimes you simply get the same or similar information from different sources. In addition, data collection can yield data that is peripheral to the actual job. As a result, managers need to *process* information after it is collected.

Information processing is a simple but time-consuming task. The goal is to identify data that will be most useful in defining and describing the work and how to do the job. Content analysis—or the process of identifying topics and arranging information found in collected data—is one of the most effective methods of processing information. A thorough content analysis can be completed by first reading through the collected data and identifying important topics, then arranging this data in appropriate categories. Content analysis can help eliminate repetition of tasks or responsibilities.

Write Job Descriptions and Specifications

Job analyses are rarely used in their completed form. Instead, information contained in the job analysis is used to create other management tools used regularly in hotels and restaurants.

The two managerial tools most commonly derived from a job analysis are **job descriptions** and **job specifications**. Job descriptions summarize the duties, responsibilities, working conditions, activities of a specific job, and qualifications of the prospective employee. For instance, a job description for an assistant director of human resources might include such responsibilities as recruiting, maintaining employee files, and so on.

In addition to describing the job, job descriptions are used for:

- *Recruiting.* Job descriptions help hospitality managers develop media ads to recruit employees.

- *Selection.* Job descriptions help managers develop selection requirements and interview questions.

- *Orientation.* Job descriptions serve as an excellent guide for familiarizing a new employee with the requirements of the job.

- *Training.* Comparing an employee's job skills with the requirements outlined in a job description helps managers determine what kind of training an employee needs and how it should be accomplished.

- *Employee evaluations.* Performance appraisals are often developed directly from job descriptions, which provide a basis for evaluating employee performance.

- *Promotions and transfers.* Job descriptions provide information required for determining if a current employee can perform the functions of a new job.

Key Elements. While specific formats used in job descriptions can vary substantially from company to company, content usually includes the following key elements: job identification data, a **job summary**, job duties, job specifications, minimum qualifications, and the date the job description was last revised (to be used as a guide for scheduling rewriting).

- *Job identification data.* This data consists of the job title, work unit, title of immediate supervisor, pay grade, the last time the job description was written or revised, and so on.

- *Job summary.* The job summary is usually a brief general statement that highlights the common functions and responsibilities of the job. In many job descriptions, the summary is called the "general statement of duties." For instance, a job summary for a hotel's assistant director of human resources might read:

  > Perform complex technical work in recruitment, examination, classification, wage and salary administration, training, and other functions of a human resources program.

  A job summary for a server might read:

  > Responsible for gracious and proper service to all guests in his or her station during the assigned shift. Also responsible for appearance of entire station area, including tables, walls, floor, and so on.

- *Job duties.* This portion of the job description usually lists tasks and responsibilities associated with the job. Typically, each statement in this section begins with an action verb and briefly states what this portion of the job accomplishes. Examples of action verbs commonly used are administer, assist, collect, conduct, prepare, furnish, and maintain. For instance, the job duties of a busperson in a food and beverage operation might be:

  - Move dirty dishes to the dishwashing area.

  - Assist server in serving guests.

  - Deliver water and beverages to guests.

  - Set tables before opening and reset during operations.

  - Maintain adequate supply of condiments at server stations.

- *Job environment.* A description of where the employee works and the surrounding environment.

- *Job specifications.* This element of a job description (sometimes referred to as knowledge, skills, and abilities, or KSA) often is used as a stand-alone document. Job specifications describe the qualifications required to perform the job. Employers may outline qualifications related to training or education, skills, and experience, as well as mental, physical, and personal characteristics. For instance, job specifications for a bell captain might include the ability to lift objects weighing up to 50 pounds repeatedly during an eight-hour shift, to coordinate other bell staff, and to learn room locations. Job specifications for the assistant human resources director position may include knowledge of personnel practices, experience with testing methods, and knowledge of EEOC guidelines. Responsibilities and qualifications are determined by a thorough analysis of the job.

- *Minimum qualifications.* The final part of a job description is the minimum qualifications, also referred to as minimum requirements. These are the fundamental qualifications a candidate must have to be considered for the position. To avoid any legal issues such as discrimination, it is important that the requirements in this section have a direct link to the candidate's ability to successfully perform the job. For example, five years of experience in food service and demonstrated leadership ability may be necessary requirements for the position of food and beverage director. On the other hand, it may be difficult to prove that a high school diploma is required for a janitorial position.

A sample job description is presented in Exhibit 4.

Job Design

According to a 1997 national study of the changing workforce by the Families and Work Institute, jobs are the biggest stressors in most people's lives. Findings like this have led to a movement to redesign jobs so that they are less stressful. This does not mean eliminating necessary elements of a job; it simply means determining which elements are necessary and which are not—and making the necessary ones more palatable.

One way to accomplish thorough job design is through flowcharting. After breaking a job down into its basic steps, managers should encourage employees to consider how each step relates to other aspects of their workplace or to other people's jobs. Flowcharting also allows the job analyst to more accurately determine what aspects of each job could be changed.[8]

Poor performance and low productivity are not always due to poor training, inadequate supervision, underdeveloped employee skills, or poor work habits. Sometimes employees are ineffective because the job is designed poorly. Job design and organizational design have perhaps the greatest influence on whether or not a job holder does his or her job well.[9] Poorly designed jobs can lead to unnecessary stress and low job satisfaction, which in turn lead to low motivation, high employee turnover, and high rates of absenteeism.

Exhibit 4   Job Description: Assistant Director of Human Resources

Title:	Assistant Director
Department:	Human Resources
Job Analyst:	Bob Smith
Date Analyzed:	12/01/2005
Wage Category:	Exempt

Reports to: Director of Human Resources

Subordinate staff: 2–5 staff members of the Human Resources Department

Other internal contacts: CEO, Vice President, department managers, and staff members of other departments

External contacts: Government agents, vendors, staff members of strategic partners

Job Summary:

Perform complex technical work in recruitment, examination, classification, wage and salary administration, training, and other functions of a human resources department.

Job Duties:

1. Recruitment—25%
   a. Prepares open position announcements
   b. Screens applications for qualifications
   c. Prepares offer of employment documents
   d. Maintains recruitment and selection records

2. Classification of job and employees—20%
   a. Prepares employee exit documentation
   b. Processes employee promotion paperwork
   c. Keeps records of employee advancement activities

3. Wage and salary administration—20%
   a. Computes employee wage changes
   b. Maintains records of payroll activities
   c. Verifies proper execution of payroll procedures
   d. Creates reports of payroll activities

4. Training—35%
   a. Conducts general orientation program for new hires
   b. Obtains materials for special training sessions as need arises
   c. Assists with departmental training
   d. Conducts follow-up training reviews
   e. Maintains documentation of employee completion of orientation and training programs

Exhibit 4 *(continued)*

Job Environment:

1. Primarily in an office setting

2. Recruitment conducted in locations such as:
   a. Schools, colleges, and universities
   b. Churches and synagogues
   c. Apartment complexes
   d. Youth, senior citizen, and community group environments

Job Specifications:

1. Knowledge of the principles of human resource administration

2. Knowledge of examination processes and job evaluation methods and techniques

3. Knowledge of statistics

4. Ability to conduct statistical analysis

5. Ability to organize and present effective oral and written reports

6. Ability to establish and maintain effective working relations with employees, department heads, officials, and the general public

Minimum Qualification:

Some experience in human resource management recruitment, examination, classification, and pay administration. Experience in training and other human resource functions of the professional level or equivalent also desired.

Based on the layouts in: Jeffrey S. Hornsby and Donald F. Kuratko, *The Human Resource Function in Emerging Enterprises* (Mason, Ohio: South-Western/Thomson Learning, 2002), 70–72, and Luis R. Gomez-Mejia, David B. Balkin, and Robert L. Cardy, *Managing Human Resources*, 4th ed. (Upper Saddle River, N.J.: Prentice Hall, 2004), 69.

Job design focuses on how work is to be done. Five techniques—**job simplification, job enlargement, job enrichment, job rotation,** and **team building**—are widely used in designing jobs. Job simplification involves breaking down jobs into their smallest components and assessing how work is done in each of these components of the whole job. It is sometimes called *time and motion analysis.* Job simplification is useful when the skills required to perform the tasks are not extensive and/or do not require a great deal of managerial involvement. For example, a position in which the only tasks assigned to an employee are to load/unload a dishwasher and shelve the dishes may have resulted from job simplification.

Job enlargement is the process of broadening jobs by adding tasks together. Typically, tasks involving similar skills and abilities are combined. Adding similar tasks in this way is sometimes called *horizontal job expansion* because the jobs require the same or similar skills and abilities. In some ways, job enlargement is the opposite of job simplification. An example of job enlargement would be to add cutting carrots and tomatoes to the duties of a prep assistant who primarily cuts lettuce for salads. Job enlargement can help to motivate employees who perceive increased responsibility as a step toward advancing their careers. However, some employees may be unwilling to take on additional tasks—especially if additional tasks are not accompanied by additional compensation. Others may simply feel that they are now performing two boring tasks instead of one.

In job enrichment, also called *vertical job expansion*, responsibilities are added to an employee's job that are not extremely similar to the tasks the employee performs. For example, we could enrich our prep cook's job by making him or her responsible for rotating the stock he or she uses, ordering the food products required for the job, or making finished salads with the products he or she chops up.

The distinction between job enrichment and job enlargement can sometimes get blurred. Both require an employee to perform additional tasks. The difference is that job enlargement gives the employee additional levels of responsibility.[10]

Job rotation is often used to alleviate some of the boredom that employees face when performing the same job over and over. Under a job rotation system, the prep cook responsible for cutting lettuce, carrots, and tomatoes would do this job only for a specific period. After this period, the prep cook would be rotated to another kitchen position with different job responsibilities. This system requires that employees be cross-trained in several different jobs.

Another widely used approach to job design is team building. At its heart, team building views employees as members of work groups rather than as individuals. Goals and rewards are directed toward team efforts rather than toward individual efforts. For example, the California-based HMS Group has developed a team-building experience involving building chocolate creations. Originally designed for the Culinary Institute of America, the "Chocolate Box Challenge" is an edible, hospitality-focused adaptation of the more familiar group-bungee-jump and shoot-your-boss-with-a-paint-pistol exercises.[11]

In another team-building exercise, participants organize and deliver a banquet together. While this exercise is perhaps not new to many hospitality managers, it helps participants develop quickly into teams.[12]

Team building encourages employees to work well together and to assist one another. A disadvantage is that it often requires several training sessions to get a team-building program started. Another disadvantage is that team building can sometimes lead to counterproductive competition among groups.

Legal Issues

It is sometimes implied that the human resources department is the recordkeeper for the entire company. With that in mind, it should be no surprise that human resources management would be concerned with determining and documenting specific responsibilities and duties of employees with job analyses and job descriptions. The overall purpose of performing a job analysis should be to find ways to make the company more productive and efficient through restructuring existing jobs or creating new jobs to fill any gaps. However, before employees are hired for the newly created or redefined jobs, legal issues must be considered.

Legality is an important issue for any company, not just those in the hospitality industry. This section will touch upon human resources laws that are directly related to job analysis and design, as well as staffing, which is covered later in this chapter.

Discrimination. When writing a job description, it is extremely important to consider what employee qualifications are truly required to perform the functions of the specific job. To prevent intentional discrimination, a manager must be aware of the issues addressed in Title VII of the Civil Rights Act of 1964. One of the most important aspects related to Title VII in creating a job description is the concept of *bona fide occupational qualifications (BFOQ)*. The courts have been leading the way when it comes to laws regarding BFOQs. For example, in the case of *Gerdom* v. *Continental Airlines,* Inc., 1982, the U.S. 9th Circuit Court of Appeals found that flight attendant weight restrictions were discriminatory due to the fact that they applied only to women. Despite the airline's claims that its customers preferred flight attendants to have a certain appearance, the court upheld the ruling that customer preferences are not a factor in performing the functions of the job.[13]

Americans with Disabilities Act (ADA). People with disabilities are considered qualified for a job if they can perform the essential functions of the job with or without reasonable accommodations. This has a huge impact on designing jobs, because it forces a firm to consider what each job's "essential functions" are. The use of the job simplification method previously described can help a firm determine if some of the tasks and responsibilities of a job can be eliminated or redistributed in order to accommodate an employee with a disability. "The ADA, Job Analysis, and Job Design" sidebar in this chapter more fully explains how the ADA is related to job analysis and design.

Occupational Safety and Health Act (OSHA). The Occupational Safety and Health Act requires that job descriptions explain "elements of the job that endanger health, or are considered unsatisfactory or distasteful by the majority of the population."[14]

Labor Laws. The U.S. Department of Labor regulates most of the laws regarding employment issues. The scope of the department is far too encompassing to discuss here. However, the legal issues the agency oversees are wages, discrimination, and working conditions, to name just a few. More information about the U.S. Department of Labor is available on the Internet at http://www.dol.gov.

Classifications of Employees

Once the various jobs have been analyzed and designed with job descriptions written and the legal issues worked out, people actually need to be hired to perform the jobs. The question then arises as to what type (or classification) of employee best fits the organization's needs. The answer to this question is complex. Various issues must be considered, including the following:

- What size is the organization?

The ADA, Job Analysis, and Job Design

In the past, many people would picture a person with a disability as someone who used a wheelchair, walker, or cane. Today, many people realize that disabilities cover a wide spectrum and may not be noticeable to a casual observer. The **Americans with Disabilities Act** is making people more aware of what constitutes a disability and what the rights of a person with a disability are.

This sidebar will look at the ADA in relation to job analysis and job design.

* * *

Under the ADA, people with disabilities are considered qualified for a position if they can perform the **essential functions of a job** with or without **reasonable accommodation**. Essential functions are tasks that are fundamental to the position. For instance, cooking skills would be considered fundamental for a cook. However, the ability of a cook to hear orders called by servers (for a person with a hearing impairment) or of a room attendant to read written room cleaning assignments (for a person with a developmental or cognitive disability) might not be fundamental. In such cases, operators must make reasonable accommodations to ensure that cooking and room attendant positions are open to people with such disabilities.

From a job analysis standpoint, employers need to identify the essential and non-essential activities of each job. Applicants who can perform the essential functions cannot be discriminated against because they cannot perform the non-essential functions. In addition, the ADA stipulates that employers may have to restructure jobs to eliminate the non-essential functions for these employees.

Unless it imposes an undue hardship, employers will also be required to make reasonable accommodations so that the workplace is accessible to people with disabilities. Among the accommodations considered reasonable by the Equal Employment Opportunity Commission are constructing wheelchair ramps, widening aisles, raising cashier stands, and modifying work schedules and equipment.

Both the essential functions provision and the reasonable accommodations provision of the ADA will dramatically affect how jobs are designed in some operations. For instance, employers may be required to rethink how work is done. Consider how a bellperson's position often involves carrying heavy bags to rooms for eight or more hours per day. That could change under the ADA. For example, hotels may be required to provide carts so that employees with disabilities would not be required to carry bags for long distances. In addition, frequent breaks for bell staff who cannot work for eight hours at a time may be viewed as a reasonable accommodation.

Managers need to take a number of actions to meet ADA requirements. At a minimum, managers should:

1. Review their methods of job analysis to ensure that essential and non-essential functions are appropriately designated.
2. Review job descriptions; specify essential and non-essential aspects of each position.
3. Review job specifications to ensure that applicants are not being excluded on the basis of non-essential functions.
4. Maintain records of accommodations made to comply with the ADA.

5. Create and maintain records of people with disabilities currently on staff to ensure that reasonable accommodations are made for these people.

6. Review the application process—especially portions that include medical exams or other issues that may infringe on the rights of people with disabilities.

7. Revise application forms to exclude generic questions about disabilities and health issues. Many application forms commonly used in the past are not acceptable under the ADA.

8. Create and maintain records of personnel with disabilities; records should include the accommodations made for these individuals in compliance with the ADA.

9. Post compliance statements in prominent locations.

- What is the corporate culture of the organization?

- What type of image does the organization wish to project?

- What is the labor market like?

The labor force of an organization can be broken down into two main categories: **permanent employees** and **alternative employees**. Permanent employees are the main staff of the organization. They typically work at least 30–40 hours per week, are on the regular company payroll, and often receive benefits. Alternative employees often work part-time or on a temporary basis. These employees often do not have regularly scheduled shifts or are employed at the hospitality company only for a short period of time. Alternative employees can be grouped into three classifications: temporary employees, part-time employees, and outsourced employees.[15]

Temporary employees. Temporary employees, often referred to as temps, are not actually employed by the hospitality organization. They are employees obtained from an employment agency. The agency charges a fee to the hospitality company, the employee, or both, which can be thought of as a "finder's fee." Temporary employees work only for a designated time period, which can last only one day or as long as several months. Temporary employees are useful for occasional events such as banquets, or during seasonal demands to fill positions for which hiring full-time employees would not be cost effective.

Part-time employees. Part-time employees generally work 20 hours or less per week. In many organizations, they do not receive benefits, medical or otherwise. While it varies from property to property, most part-time employees do not work regular shifts. They are extremely valuable for covering time periods of daily/weekly peaks in business, such as during check-out times at a hotel or during weekends at a restaurant.

Outsourced employees. Like temporary employees, outsourced employees are not actually employed by the hospitality organization. They work for a separate company that the hospitality company pays for the services the outsourced employees provide. Outsourced employees usually do not perform their jobs while they are physically at the hospitality business. Most never even set foot on the hospitality property. While it is obvious that outsourced employees would not be useful at a hotel front desk, they can quite effectively perform, for example, reservation call center functions or human resources tasks.

Staffing Guides

Staffing guides are scheduling and control tools that enable management to determine the number of labor hours and employees required to operate smoothly. They help managers control employee productivity and performance. Many managers also use staffing guides to estimate labor expenses for their labor budgets by multiplying the hours required by the pay rates of each employee. Staffing guides are very important tools for use in achieving profitability, which often depends on the degree to which managers control variable expenses such as labor.

To understand the development and use of staffing guides, managers must know the meaning of several key terms:

- **Productivity** is the amount of work output by an employee during a specific period of time.

- **Productivity standards** are the criteria that define the acceptable quantity of work to be completed by employees.

- **Performance standards** establish the required levels of quality in the work performed.

- **Labor forecasting** is any method used to anticipate the amount of work required in a specified period of time.

In addition, managers should recognize the two types of labor costs in hospitality companies: **fixed labor expenses** and **variable labor expenses**. Fixed labor expenses are those costs associated with the minimum number of employees required to operate a hotel or restaurant. Variable labor expenses are those costs that vary according to the amount of business. Managers have more control over variable labor expenses.

The following section provides a step-by-step example of how managers would develop a staffing guide. Our example will be based on a hypothetical operation: the Good Food Restaurant. Developing a staffing guide involves the following steps:

1. Set productivity standards.
2. Determine the total anticipated sales and guest count.
3. Determine the number of employees required.
4. Determine the total labor hours.
5. Estimate the labor expense.

Set Productivity Standards

The first step in developing a staffing guide is to set productivity standards. Efficient staffing requires that productivity standards be met through scheduling. If

Exhibit 5   Productivity Needs Assessment Form

Shift: ___Dinner___

Dates: Beginning ___1/1___   Ending ___1/7___

	Mon	Tues	Wed	Thurs	Fri	Sat	Sun	Average
Guest count	250	250	250	350	400	350	250	300
Position				Hours Worked				
Servers	18	18	18	24	28	24	18	21.1
Greeters	4	4	4	6	6	6	4	4.9
Bartenders	6	6	6	6	6	6	6	6.0
Busperson	3	3	3	4	5	4	3	3.6
Prep cook	6	6	6	6	6	6	6	6.0
Broiler cook	6	6	6	6	6	6	6	6.0
Sauté cook	5	5	5	5	6	5	5	5.1
Dishwasher	5	5	5	5	6	5	5	5.1

productivity standards have not already been established for each position, the manager can determine these standards by creating and evaluating a historical profile of labor required over a period of time. Exhibit 5 provides an example of a portion of a productivity needs assessment form. Since single shifts can be influenced by a variety of factors, such a form should be completed over a period of time to thoroughly evaluate the operation's staffing needs.

Once a productivity standards assessment has been completed, a manager can use the data to establish productivity standards for each position in the operation, as shown in Exhibit 5. Typically, such standards are based on labor hours required, although some operations base estimates on the number of employees required. The advantage of basing the standards on labor hours is that such standards more accurately portray exact scheduling needs.

The final step in determining the correct standard productivity levels for each operation is to compare the estimated needs to actual labor hours worked. Exhibit 6 provides a sample comparison form some managers use. The comments section of this form is used to note extraordinary events that affect labor costs (weather, sales related to certain activities, and so on). This form also lets managers know how much the actual hours worked were over or under their budgeted labor hours for a given period. In Exhibit 6, for example, budgeted labor hours were exceeded in six out of eight positions. To calculate how much this overage cost, managers should multiply the average salary for each employee category by the number of hours over budget in each category. For example, if servers average $5.25 per hour, a total of $6.30 more per day was expended in this category than was budgeted.

When productivity standards are used to anticipate employee staffing levels, the end result is a ratio of employees to guests. In other words, establishing

Exhibit 6 Labor Comparison Form

Shift: Dinner

Dates: Beginning 1/1 Ending 1/7

(Budgeted Hours / Hours Worked)

Position	Mon	Tues	Wed	Thurs	Fri	Sat	Sun	Average
Servers	18 / 20	18 / 19	18 / 20	24 / 23	28 / 30	24 / 25	18 / 19	21.1 / 22.3
Greeters	4 / 5	4 / 4	4 / 4	6 / 6	6 / 7	6 / 7	4 / 3	4.9 / 5.1
Bartenders	6 / 6	6 / 6	6 / 5	6 / 7	6 / 6	6 / 7	6 / 6	6 / 6.1
Busperson	3 / 2	3 / 2	3 / 3	4 / 4	5 / 5	4 / 4	3 / 3	3.6 / 3.3
Prep cook	6 / 7	6 / 7	6 / 6	6 / 7	6 / 7	6 / 6	6 / 7	6 / 6.7
Broiler cook	6 / 7	6 / 7	6 / 6	6 / 7	6 / 7	6 / 7	6 / 7	6 / 6.9
Sauté cook	5 / 5	5 / 4	5 / 4	5 / 6	6 / 6	5 / 5	5 / 5	5.1 / 5
Dishwasher	5 / 6	5 / 6	5 / 5	5 / 5	6 / 7	5 / 6	5 / 6	5.1 / 5.9

Comments:

productivity standards provides the manager with one-half of the equation required to correctly schedule employees. The other half of the equation is derived by estimating the anticipated guest volume per shift.

Determine Total Anticipated Sales and Guest Volume

Accurate labor use predictions require managers to anticipate business volume for each day of an upcoming period. The best source of information is previous sales for similar periods. Usually, managers maintain records of the sales for each previous meal period. This forms a historical record of sales over time that managers can use to estimate potential sales in the future. Given this anticipated total sales volume, a manager can determine the number of guests that the restaurant will serve by dividing the sales volume by the average per-person guest check.

If the average sales on Friday nights at the 150-seat Good Food Restaurant is \$6,000, and the average per-person guest check is \$15.00, we know that the average number of guests served is 400 (\$6,000 ÷ \$15).

Exhibit 7   Labor Requirements Per Hour

Hours of Operation	Anticipated Covers	Labor or Staffing Requirements
6:00 P.M. - 7:00 P.M.	80	4
7:00 P.M. - 8:00 P.M.	120	6
8:00 P.M. - 9:00 P.M.	100	5
9:00 P.M. - 10:00 P.M.	100	5

While this method is acceptable in many circumstances, more complex forecasting methods can better anticipate business volume. The most common forecasting methods are discussed later in this chapter.

Determine Number of Employees Required

After forecasting potential sales, a manager must determine how many employees are required to serve the estimated number of customers. Productivity standards are used to determine this requirement. Continuing with our example, let's assume that the productivity standard for this restaurant calls for one server for every 20 guests per hour of operation. If the restaurant is open for four hours on Friday nights, this would tell us that five servers are required (400 guests ÷ 4 hours of operation ÷ 20 guests per hour). However, what this calculation does not tell us is that some periods will be busier than others. Exhibit 7 provides a breakdown of the number of guests served per hour on an average Friday night at the restaurant.

As Exhibit 7 indicates, the restaurant will need six servers for one time period on Friday and only four or five for the others, since the business volume is not spread evenly throughout the evening. Rather than schedule the entire night to meet the peak demand (six servers), the manager could reduce labor costs for this shift by staggering schedules. Note that some servers will need to arrive early to set up, while others will need to stay late to clean up. In this example, scheduling all servers to arrive early and leave late would be the worst use of labor dollars. Note that, while the employees' schedules in our example fit perfectly with the anticipated need, this is not always the case in actual practice. Factors such as variation from hour to hour in demand, employee availability, and labor laws can cause overlaps or gaps in the actual number of employees scheduled compared to the desired number.

Determine Total Labor Hours

To determine total labor hours, a manager could multiply the number of hours each server is scheduled (an average of 4.0 hours in this case) by the number of servers scheduled (six). See the sample schedule worksheet presented in Exhibit 8.

Estimate Labor Expense

Labor expense for the Good Food Restaurant for the Friday night in question can be estimated by multiplying the average hourly wage paid to each server by the total

Exhibit 8   Sample Schedule Worksheet

Day: Friday		Estimated Guests:	A.M.	P.M.	Department: Food Service
Date: 8/1/00				400	Position: Server
Shift: P.M.					

Position/ Employee	6:00 a	7:00 a	8:00 a	9:00 a	10:00 a	11:00 a	12:00 p	1:00 p	2:00 p	3:00 p	4:00 p	5:00 p	6:00 p	7:00 p	8:00 p	9:00 p	10:00 p	11:00 p	12:00 a	1:00 a	2:00 a	3:00 a	4:00 a	5:00 a	6:00 a	Planned Total Hours
Joe																										3.0
Sally																										5.0
Phyllis																										4.0
Mary																										4.0
Jim																										4.0
Tom																										4.0
Total																										24.0

Position: Server

number of labor hours scheduled. Managers must consider the time that servers are scheduled to assist in setting up before the shift and/or cleaning up after the shift. If we assume that each server is paid an hourly wage of $5.25, the total *estimated* cost for servers on Friday night is $126 (24 hours × $5.25). Not all servers will work the exact number of hours scheduled, of course, so this remains an estimate.

To complete the staffing guide for the Good Food Restaurant, managers must make similar calculations for each position with variable labor costs.

There are many types of computer software programs that can automatically calculate the anticipated labor hours and labor costs with minimal user effort as well as perform sales prediction functions (discussed in the next section). The output and user-friendliness of these programs vary greatly, along with the price. New consumer software is constantly being developed. If you are interested in using some type of forecasting software, the best way to start your search for a product that fits your needs and budget is simply to use an Internet search engine to find all of the available options.

Forecasting Sales Volume

The staffing guide just discussed is based on a sales forecast for a single Friday night; this forecast is also based on past business levels for Fridays. Most hospitality organizations develop monthly, ten-day, and three-day forecasts of business volume.[16] Typically, managers develop monthly forecasts first and then revise the forecast for ten-day and three-day periods, depending on any special circumstances. These forecasts are used to determine the business volume component for upcoming scheduling periods. Exhibit 9 provides a sample form that food and

Exhibit 9   Sample Ten-Day Volume Forecast—Food

TEN-DAY VOLUME FORECAST—FOOD

Motor-Hotel _____
(Location)

Date Prepared _____
Week Ending _____

DATE																						
DAY	THUR		FRI		SAT		SUN		MON		TUES		WED		THUR		FRI		SAT		Totals	
	Previous Week																					
FOOD DEPARTMENT	F	A	F	A	F	A	F	A	F	A	F	A	F	A	F	A	F	A	F	A	F	A
Dining Room																						
Breakfast																						
Lunch																						
Dinner																						
Total D.R. Covers																						
Coffee Shop																						
Breakfast																						
Lunch																						
Total C.S. Covers																						
Banquet																						
Breakfast																						
Lunch																						
Dinner																						
Total Banquet Covers																						
Room Service																						
Total R.S. Covers																						
TOTAL FOOD COVERS																						

SPECIAL COMMENTS
(i.e. types of groups—V.I.P. etc.)

F = Forecast
A = Actual

Source: David L. Balangue, "Payroll Productivity (Part IV: Staff Planning)," *Lodging* (November 1978): 39.

beverage managers can use to develop a ten-day forecast. A sample three-day revised forecast form is presented in Exhibit 10.[17]

Trend Line Forecasting

The simple forecast used in the Good Food Restaurant example presented earlier was based on business volume for previous Friday nights. This method of forecasting is known as **trend line forecasting**. Trend line forecasting involves graphing the sales from similar periods and fitting a line to the average sales projected for past periods. Fitting a line is much like connecting the dots, although the objective is to establish a straight line through the dots rather than a jagged one from dot to dot. Statistically, the "fitted line" is created by determining the midpoint between the jagged points.

While this simple method of forecasting is useful, it is often misleading. Trend line forecasting does not account for any unusual events that may have taken place

Exhibit 10   Sample Three-Day Revised Forecast—Food and Beverage

Three-Day Revised Forecast—Food and Beverage			
	Yesterday	Today	Tomorrow
Day			
Date			
Guest Count			
Forecasted Guest Count			
Comments			

during a given period. A forecasting method that helps avoid this problem is called **moving average forecasting**.

Moving Average Forecasting

Sales are never as consistent as we hope they will be. Instead, sales in hospitality are characterized by a series of peaks and valleys. Some of these peaks and valleys result from special events in the area that may detract from or add to business volume. Weather and other events also create peaks and valleys in sales volume.

Moving average forecasting "smooths out" the data collected from a specific time period. Mathematically, the moving average forecast can be expressed as:

$$\text{Moving average} = \frac{\text{Activity in previous } n \text{ periods}}{n}$$

where n is the number of periods in the moving average.

As new weekly sales results become available, they can be added to the moving average forecast model; the oldest week is then dropped. In fact, the method is known as a "moving" average since it involves continually adding new results and dropping the oldest week off the model.

Seasonality

Many hospitality organizations are subject to variations in business depending on the season. **Seasonality** must be taken into consideration when forecasting anticipated business volume. Many restaurants, for instance, are busier just before and during the December holiday season and slower during summer months. Of course, restaurants in summer resort areas have just the opposite experience.

Hotels are also subject to seasonal adjustments. Downtown hotels, which usually depend on business travelers for their business, often experience substantial dips during some periods of the month or the year. For example, hotels in New York City and other large cities often see declines in business travel during January, February, and the summer; business travel is at its highest level in New York during the spring and fall. While some of the loss in business during the summer is made up by vacationers, hotels must adjust their schedules to reflect the needs of such travelers.

The simplest method of anticipating seasonal business variations is to use historical data from similar seasonal periods. For instance, when estimating sales for the month of June, operators will likely find that sales from June of the previous year provide the most accurate comparative data. A form of "seasonality" can also be used to prepare weekly business volume estimates. In fact, our Good Food Restaurant example used this format by basing sales estimates on previous Friday nights instead of on other days of the week.

Other Methods of Forecasting

Hospitality managers use a variety of forecasting methods to anticipate business levels; these levels, in turn, determine personnel levels. For instance, yield management is a system that attempts to manage the supply of rooms in a hotel over time by lowering and raising rates to maximize revenue. Other methods that are popular with hospitality managers are cited in Exhibit 11. Explanations of how to use these forecasting methods are beyond the scope of this book.[18]

Endnotes

1. James P. Clifford, "Job Analysis: Why Do It, and How It Should Be Done," *Public Personnel Management* 23 (Summer 1994): 324.

2. Dick Barton, "Changing the Job Mix to Encourage Latent Talent," *People Management* 2, no. 14 (1996): 23–25.

3. Jeffrey S. Hornsby and Donald F. Kuratko, *The Human Resource Function in Emerging Enterprises* (Mason, Ohio: South-Western/Thomson Learning, 2002), 49.

4. Jeffrey R. Edwards, Judith A. Scully, and Mary D. Brtek, "The Measurement of Work: Hierarchical Representation of the Multi-Method Job Design Questionnaire," *Personnel Psychology* 52, no. 2 (1999): 305–335.

5. R. Wayne Mondy and Robert M. Noe, *Human Resource Management,* 6th ed. (Upper Saddle River, N.J.: Prentice Hall, 1996), 99.

6. John Garen, "Unions, Inventive Systems and Job Design," *Journal of Labor Research* 20, no. 4 (1999): 589–604.

7. D. Keith Denton, "I Hate this Job," *Business Horizons* 37, no. 1 (1994): 46–53.

8. Shari Caudron, "Job Stress Is in Job Design," *Workforce Management* 77, no. 9 (1998): 21–23.

9. Dick Barton, "Changing the Job Mix to Encourage Latent Talent," *People Management* 2, no. 14 (1996): 23–25.

10. Mondy and Noe, 112–113.

11. "Training That Melts in Your Mouth," *Workforce Management* 78, no. 2 (1999): 34–35.

Exhibit 11   Summary of Lodging Industry Short-Term Sales Forecasting Approaches

	Rooms	Food	Catering
Major purposes of forecast:	Staffing (98%) Motivating personnel (25%)	Staffing (100%) Order food (72%) Motivating personnel (19%)	Staffing (82%) Order food (72%) Motivating personnel (16%)
Methodology:	Room reservations plus estimated walk-ins (93%)	Prior period sales adjusted based on intuition (46%)	Booked catered events plus estimate of additional sales (90%)
	Prior period sales adjusted based on intuition (7%)	Meal reservations and estimate for walk-ins (28%)	Prior period sales adjusted based on intuition (10%)
		Capture ratios related to the rooms forecast (26%)	
Expression of S-T forecast:	Daily number of rooms sold (80%)	Total covers (79%)	Total sales dollars (70%)
	Daily sales dollars (55%)	Total sales dollars (61%)	Total covers (67%)
	Daily number of rooms by type (35%)	Food covers by meal period (60%)	Sales dollars by catered event (47%)
	Daily sales dollars by type of room (20%)	Sales dollars by meal period (44%)	Covers by catered event (47%)

Source: Raymond S. Schmidgall, *Hospitality Industry Managerial Accounting*, 5th ed. (Lansing, Mich.: Educational Institute of the American Hotel & Lodging Association, 2002), 415.

12. Howard Prager, "Cooking Up Effective Team Building," *Training and Development* 53, no. 12 (1999): 12–16.

13. *Gerdom* v. *Continental Airlines, Inc.*, 692 F.2d 602, 9th Cir., 1982.

14. Mondy and Noe, 110.

15. Luis R. Gomez-Mejia, David B. Balkin, and Robert L. Cardy, *Managing Human Resources*, 4th ed. (Upper Saddle River, N.J.: Prentice Hall, 2004), 71–72.

16. Raphael R. Kavanaugh and Jack D. Ninemeier, *Supervision in the Hospitality Industry*, 3d ed. (Lansing, Mich.: Educational Institute of the American Hotel & Lodging Association, 2001), 138–140.

17. For more information on developing staffing guides in hotels, see Kavanaugh and Ninemeier, 133–137.

18. For more information on forecasting methods, see Raymond S. Schmidgall, *Hospitality Industry Managerial Accounting*, 6th ed. (Lansing, Mich.: Educational Institute of the American Hotel & Lodging Association, 2006).

**Key Terms**

alternative employees—Part-time or temporary workers. These employees often do not have regularly scheduled shifts or are employed at the company only for a short period of time.

critical incident—Job analysis technique based on capturing and recording actual events that occur at work which, when combined, form an accurate picture of a job's actual requirements. Useful in describing how services should be performed. Also used in training and as a measurement in certain performance appraisal systems.

fixed labor expenses—Labor costs associated with the minimum number of employees required to work for a function.

Hawthorne Effect—Management theory describing the positive effect that "paying attention" to employees has on workplace productivity.

Heisenberg Effect—Management theory stating that people being interviewed are likely to subconsciously give answers they think interviewers want to hear.

job analysis—Process of determining the tasks, behaviors, and characteristics essential to a job.

job description—A written summary of the duties, responsibilities, working conditions, and activities of a specific job.

job design—Process of defining how a job will be done.

job enlargement—Process of broadening components of a job by adding similar tasks or responsibilities to the job. Incorrectly used by managers in an attempt to make jobs more interesting to employees. Sometimes called horizontal job expansion.

job enrichment—Process of improving a job by adding responsibilities that require different skills. Sometimes called vertical job expansion.

job rotation—Process of moving employees from one job to another, or of changing employee responsibilities, in order to enhance job interest or to cross-train.

job simplification—Process of breaking down jobs into their smallest components, to assess how work is done in each of those components. Sometimes called time and motion analysis.

job specification—A written description of the personal qualities required to perform a job.

job summary—A brief general statement that highlights the common functions and responsibilities of a job.

labor forecasting—A forecasting method that uses business trends and volume, turnover, and other labor statistics to anticipate job vacancies.

management position description questionnaire (MPDQ)—Structured questionnaire used to collect information about management work in 13 different categories. Used in job analysis.

moving average forecasting—Forecasting method, based on past sales, that attempts to "smooth out" the peaks and valleys businesses experience, to project anticipated sales.

performance standard—A required level of performance.

permanent employees—The main staff of an organization. They usually work at least 30–40 hours per week, are on the regular company payroll, and often receive benefits.

position analysis questionnaire (PAQ)—A structured questionnaire consisting of 194 job elements used to define work. Used in job analysis.

productivity—The amount of work an employee accomplishes in a specific period of time.

productivity standards—The criteria that define the acceptable quantity of work to be completed by employees.

seasonality—A concept used in forecasting that describes the highs and lows of business sales on the basis of seasonal demand for products or services. Example: the demand for Caribbean cruise ship rooms is higher during the winter than in the summer.

staffing guide—A system used to establish the number of workers needed.

team building—A process of designing jobs that views employees as members of work groups rather than as individuals.

trend line forecasting—A simple forecasting method that estimates future sales on the basis of sales made during similar past periods.

variable labor expenses—Labor costs that vary according to the amount of business.

Review Questions

1. If a job analysis is never used in its entirety, why is its completion so important?

2. What are the different methods hospitality managers can use to collect job analysis information?

3. What are the major advantages and disadvantages of the different methods of collecting job analysis information?

4. Who should collect job analysis information and why?

5. How do job descriptions and job specifications differ?

6. What are the advantages and disadvantages of job enlargement, job enrichment, and job rotation?

7. What are some of the legal issues that hospitality managers must consider when designing a job and writing a job description?

8. What are the basic steps involved in developing a staffing guide for a hotel?

9. How would you establish productivity standards for a particular position?

10. What is the difference between trend line forecasting and moving average forecasting?

Internet Sites

For more information, visit the following Internet sites. Remember that Internet addresses can change without notice. If the site is no longer there, you can use a search engine to look for additional sites.

Job Analysis and Personality Research
http://harvey.psyc.vt.edu

U.S. Bureau of Labor Statistics
www.bls.gov

Office of Disability Employment Policy
www.dol.gov/odep

U.S. Department of Labor
www.dol.gov

Mini Case Study

Zippy Airline Catering—a small, independent company—was recently purchased by a large hospitality company in Guam. At the time, this operation had only eight full-time employees and a single manager, and produced a single product: prepared meals for three airlines that flew out of the Guam airport. Each meal was prepared individually by a single employee. To package a meal, an employee would sit at a long table where he or she would place a portion cut of meat, potato, and a vegetable in a ceramic tray. The ceramic tray was then covered with aluminum foil and placed in an oven. When finished, the employee took the tray out of the oven and packed it into catering boxes for transfer onto an airline.

To meet the tremendously increased demand brought about by additional flights into the airport, the hospitality company that purchased Zippy Airline Catering decided to re-engineer the preparation process. A conveyor belt was installed and each employee was assigned a single task in the meal preparation. Employees now sat along either side of the conveyor and placed only a single item—meat, potato, or vegetable—on the tray. Essentially, the individual preparation method had been thoroughly converted to a production-line approach. The speed of the conveyor belt had been calculated by the engineers who designed the system. The engineers estimated that each employee would be able to put his or her item on a tray before it passed beyond reach.

To encourage teamwork, the company instituted a group bonus plan that rewarded the employees for the total number of meals produced. According to this simple plan, the more trays produced, the more bonus earned.

Discussion Questions

1. Are the changes made by the hospitality company significant redesigns of the work done? Why or why not?

2. What do you think will happen as a result of this redesign?

3. What steps would you have taken before initiating substantial changes in the way work is done at Zippy Airline Catering?

Chapter 3 Outline

Competencies

3

Planning and Recruiting

This chapter was co-authored by Rodney Jordan, M.S., University of Nevada, Las Vegas (UNLV); Elfrida Tang, M.S., UNLV; and Angella Kyung, M.S. candidate, UNLV.

AN OLD SAYING STATES, "If you don't know where you are going, any road will take you there." In hospitality, operations that don't know where they are going—that is, that don't plan—take the road to high recruitment costs, high training costs, and low productivity.

To staff a hospitality operation, you must know the critical steps in the human resource planning process, which include identifying potential employees, encouraging potential employees to apply for a position, and selecting the right applicants for the job. Without completing these steps, hospitality operations are simply leaving their employee selection to chance.

While the process of recruiting and selecting employees is an expensive one, it is considerably less expensive than the alternative: processing unqualified staff. Ultimately, selecting unqualified employees results in repeating the same process over and over. What would happen, for instance, if a new hotel didn't develop a strategic human resource plan before advertising positions, interviewing applicants, and hiring employees? Most likely, the hotel would not hire the right people—or even the right number of people—for the given positions. The same applies to any ongoing business. Unless management takes the time to establish a plan before recruiting, interviewing, and selecting employees, it is leaving the results to chance.

Planning Human Resources

The human resource planning process involves anticipating an organization's business demands and providing the staff to meet these demands. Human resource planning involves two critical factors: the supply and the demand for staff. *Supply* represents the number of potential employees that are available to a hospitality company; *demand* represents the number and nature of the jobs the company needs. Supply and demand are affected by conditions both within and outside the organization—or by internal and external factors. Since both internal and external factors affect recruiting, both should be studied.

Factors that Affect Planning

Today, the work force is undergoing a major transformation, and managers need to be aware of the external factors that are likely to influence planning and recruiting. The following is a list of the trends that are likely to influence managers.[1]

- The work force is becoming smaller and less sufficiently skilled.

- It is becoming increasingly global.

- It is becoming vastly diverse.

The size of the working population is decreasing as the middle-aged population segment shrinks and mature-aged workers are not only retiring, but are also encouraged by favorable pension plans and growing affluence to retire early.[2] It is estimated that, by the year 2010, the number of job openings in the United States will exceed the number of workers by 10 million.[3] On the other hand, the developing world's middle-aged population is booming. Subsequently, worker migration is expected to increase competition in the labor market. Moreover, the Generation Y group (those born between 1977 and 1994) continues to enter the work force at an early age as education becomes more expensive and consumerism grows. As the work force becomes more youthful and consequently less skilled, the demand for skilled labor will likely rise.

Employers cannot assume that applicants today will possess the necessary tools to work competently in the industry. In fact, many potential employees may need training designed to make them eligible for work. Many programs that accomplish this are also considered good social responsibility activities.

Included in the items that employers want to develop to attract more potential employees to their workplace (and to make them more useful once hired) are:

- On-site math and reading skills training

- ESOL (English for Speakers of Other Languages)

- Sponsoring employees in trade and technical schools

The creation of a global labor market by looser economic barriers and technological advancement means that workers are now finding it increasingly easy to market themselves to employers almost anywhere in the world. The mobility of workers is contributing to a more diverse work force in terms of age, gender, ethnicity, and life pursuits; changes in birth rates, migration patterns, and cultural norms are contributing as well.

The growing number of women in the labor force has also contributed to the changing needs of employees. According to the International Labor Organization, it is estimated that, by 2015, women will make up 48 percent of the work force in the United States.[4] Areas of concern to this group of potential employees often include child care resources, job sharing, flexible hours, and equal pay for equal work issues.

Internally, human resources must be seen as linked to an organization's business strategy, and must be involved in the business planning process to ensure that the organization has the right people in the right roles at the right time.[5] In addition, before engaging in recruitment activities, managers should consider the following internal factors:[6]

- What do we need to deliver to the company to achieve the business strategic objectives? Think in terms of culture, recruitment, compensation, benefits, training and organizational development, and outside competition.

- What specific competencies are required?

- How are we going to address competency gaps?

- How should we develop our succession plan?

- What performance objectives do we need to establish, and how will they be measured?

- How will we reward employees?

- How will we communicate to employees their progress and success?

The Demand

Labor demand is the need for human resources in a particular labor market. For the most part, pinpointing labor demand is a matter of predicting anticipated sales. This chapter will emphasize how to predict staffing needs over a long period. In fact, most effective human resource planning programs anticipate the demand for employees over a period of a year or more.

The Supply

In an ideal business world, the people already on staff would exactly meet that company's needs for current and future positions. However, ideal worlds never exist. Instead, a hospitality organization must function in real world settings where there are either too many or too few employees with the skills required to meet the needs of the business. Because of this, hospitality managers must attempt to maintain an accurate estimate of the supply of labor available to their organization.

The **labor supply** available to hospitality managers comes from two principal sources. These two sources are the *internal* and *external* supply for labor. The external supply is influenced by factors beyond the control of hospitality managers: changes in demographic trends, addition of competitors to their marketplace, governmental regulations, and so on. While hospitality managers cannot control the external sources of labor, they can anticipate how these sources will affect their organization.

For example, let's look at the tight labor market facing hospitality today. We'll see that external forces in the economy have created a unique situation for hospitality: there are more jobs available in hospitality than there are people to fill them. Several factors have combined to create this situation, including overbuilding, the aging of the work force, and competition from other industries. Under such circumstances, a hospitality manager can anticipate that the traditional labor pools will be far too small to meet the demand of his or her organization. Later on in this chapter, we will examine how to more accurately forecast the labor supply. But, first, we need to understand how to forecast demand.

Forecasting Demand

The goal of forecasting is to accurately match the demand for employees and skills with the available supply. Hospitality managers use two general types of forecasting. The first type—normally called **bottom-up forecasting**—is the process of asking managers within an organization to estimate their needs for the upcoming period. This method of forecasting is intuitive; it is based solely on the experience of the managers. Although it is common, bottom-up forecasting is not necessarily the best method available. Let's look at an example.

Managers in a typical hotel will have various levels of expertise. Some managers—those with several years of experience—can anticipate and accurately estimate their labor needs for the coming year. These estimates are based on their personal knowledge of what has happened in the past. Other managers—typically those with less experience—probably cannot anticipate all the factors that will influence their labor needs. For instance, a newer food and beverage manager may not realize that his or her department will lose a large number of people at the end of the school year when employees leave for summer jobs, family vacations, and so on. In addition, this manager will not intuitively know how a change in hotel technology will affect the demand for employees. Consider what could happen when a hotel adopts an automated check-out system. Could you expect a new manager to be able to anticipate the effect the technology will have on front desk staff? Probably not. What you could expect, however, is that the entire human resource planning program would be jeopardized by the inaccurate estimates of this new manager.

Top-down forecasting eliminates the extent of inaccurate intuitive estimates when forecasting demand for human resources. Generally speaking, top-down forecasting relies on quantitative or statistical approaches.

Trend Analysis

Trend analysis is one method commonly used to forecast human resources demand. As we mentioned, competition, demographics, and changing government regulations can influence the demand for human resources. The key to trend analysis is selecting the single factor that most accurately predicts demand. This factor should relate directly to the nature of the business. No empirical evidence exists to prove that a single factor totally predicts employee demand in the hospitality industry. However, evidence does suggest that *occupancy rate* can be a good predictor. Since this is the case, we'll use occupancy rate as our factor in the following example on using trend analysis in the hospitality industry. The example is based on a hotel with 1,000 rooms.

Trend analysis consists of six steps. These steps are indicated by a number and boldface type; explanatory text appears directly below in the form of an example.

Step 1:   **Identify the appropriate business factor that relates to the number of personnel required.**

Example: Managers select occupancy rate as the single factor on which to base employee demand predictions.

Exhibit 1   Sample Chart: Occupancy and Employee Demand

Year	Occupancy Rate	Number of Employees	Labor Productivity Ratio
2002	60%	900	
2003	61	824	
2004	64	1,024	
2005	65	943	
2006	65	975	

Exhibit 2   Sample Chart: Projected and Adjusted Room Occupancy

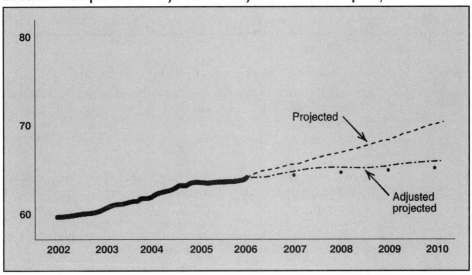

Step 2:   **Chart the historical record of how that factor relates to the size of the work force.**

Example: Managers collect and itemize occupancy figures for previous years, as well as information about the number of employees the company had on staff for those years. See Exhibit 1.

Step 3:   **Chart the trend in room occupancy.**

Example: Managers plot gathered information on a graph and draw a line from point to point for the previous years; the future trend is computed by extending the line. This projected trend is computed by adding all historical occupancy rates together and dividing by the number of years. (In this example, the answer is 63.) The adjusted rate represents the midpoint between straight-line forecast (67) and average forecast (63). See Exhibit 2.

Exhibit 3   Sample Projection of Labor Demand

Year	Average Daily Occupancy Rate	Average Daily Rooms Sold	Number of Employees	Labor Productivity Ratio
2002	60%	600	900	1.5 employees per occupied room
2003	61	610	824	1.35
2004	64	640	1,024	1.6
2005	65	650	943	1.45
2006	65	650	975	1.5
2007	65	650	975	1.5
2008	65	650	975	1.5
2009	65	650	975	1.5

Years 2006–2009 projected.

Step 4:   **Compute the average labor productivity for the company.**

Example: By examining historical employment records, the manager can establish a ratio of employees per hotel room sold. For example, a 65 percent occupancy rate in our hypothetical hotel (650 rooms) called for 975 employees. Therefore, 975 employees ÷ 650 rooms = 1.5 employees per room.

Step 5:   **Use the historical employee ratio to project future labor demand.**

Example: Managers estimate labor productivity at 1.5 employees per occupied room. See Exhibit 3.

Step 6:   **Make adjustments in the trend based on unusual events—past or present—that may influence the estimate.**

Example: Managers may find that they need to adjust their trend forecast because of high turnover in certain departments or because of additions to the staff.

A real hotel might have many more adjustments to make. For instance, if a counter-service coffee shop changes to a full-service restaurant, managers would need to add several servers—a factor that the historical information did not anticipate. Other examples might include the impact that changes in technology or conventions have on hotel services.

The adage "garbage in, garbage out" finds new life when describing the accuracy of trend analysis. If good information is provided for the computation, hospitality managers should expect estimates to be within five to ten percent of real needs. On the other hand, when poor information is used in the formula, predictions are worthless.

Hospitality operations should make predictions for each department before predicting the labor needs for the entire property. As hospitality managers know, different departments have very different histories. For instance, housekeeping and food and beverage departments have notoriously high employee turnover rates. The trend analyses for these departments must reflect the high turnover these areas experience.

Forecasting Supply

Forecasting the supply of human resources involves an analysis of the internal labor supply and an estimate of the external labor supply. Obviously, it is much easier to forecast the internal supply.

The Internal Supply

Forecasting the internal supply of labor begins with a careful inventory of the present staff and their current skills. Managers should also anticipate the ability of current employees to acquire new skills. Even though a hotel has filled particular positions with qualified people, other employees may be able to acquire—through training—the necessary skills to do the job. What makes this relevant to the forecast is that employees may acquire these skills *within the time frame* of the prediction. This means that the hotel may actually have a higher number of skilled employees than it realizes. The use of skills inventories helps managers anticipate such eventualities.

Skills Inventories

Skills inventories list each employee's current skills, ability to learn new skills, qualifications, and career goals. Many hospitality operations today compile and maintain skills inventories in computerized Human Resource Information Systems (HRISs). Some businesses still maintain skills inventories manually. Using an HRIS allows inventories to be maintained and updated continually, which is more difficult to do in a manual system.

To be effective, skills inventories must meet two criteria: (1) they must be regularly updated, and (2) both managers and employees must agree on the information included in the inventory.[7] Skills inventories for managers are often called **management inventories**. Unlike skills inventories, these inventories generally emphasize problem-solving skills and examine an individual's management track record.

Promotions, Layoffs, and Retirements

Predicting the supply of employees available to a hospitality operation is easier when policies are established for promotions, layoffs, and retirements. In unionized properties, these policies are typically included in the union contract to establish the relationship between employers and employees. Such policies also help properties forecast supply, since they establish what a property must do when an employee is promoted, laid off, or retired. Managers in non-unionized properties need to develop comparable policies.

Replacement and Succession Charts

Two types of charts are useful in predicting employee supply. Exhibit 4 shows a sample **replacement chart** that can help estimate the internal supply of employees

Exhibit 4   Sample Replacement Chart

Classification: Room Attendant				
Source of Recruits	**Number**	**Current Level**	**Losses**	**Number**
Transfers	3	25	Resignations	6
Promotions	2		Discharges	2
New Hires	5		Demotions	1
			Retirements	0
			Transfers	4
			Promotions	2
Total	10		Total	15

Current level	25		
Recruits	+10	Needed	5
Losses	−15		
Total	20		

Exhibit 5   Sample Succession Chart

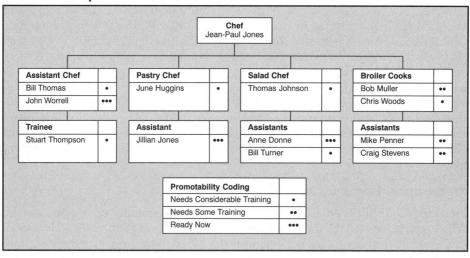

in a particular position. This chart depicts the various human resources activities and decisions that affect the room attendant position in a hotel; it also itemizes the effect these activities and decisions have on the supply of employees.

Succession charts can be used to plot anticipated successions in an organization by position. The sample chart in Exhibit 5 demonstrates which kitchen employees the organization considers promotable if certain degrees of training and experience are achieved.

Exhibit 6   Sample Succession Form for Managers

Probability of Vacancy		Date _____
Within 6 months	•	
Within 1 year	••	
Within 18 months	•••	
Within 2 years	••••	

Name		Comments: Training, Experience Needed
Jim Thomas	••	Requires interpersonal skills, management training
Bill Jones	•••	Housekeeping, front desk, valet service, room service
Ann Shanahan	•	Seminar in accounts receivable, payable
Gloria Cavanaugh	••••	Hired without prior experience, 6-4-97 Kitchen, front desk, bell captain

Succession Planning

The replacement and succession charts we applied at the line level in Exhibits 4 and 5 can also be applied at the management level. To prepare succession charts for management positions, hospitality companies often begin by completing and regularly updating a **management succession plan form**. A sample succession form for managers is shown in Exhibit 6.

A management succession plan form quantifies the information in a management succession or replacement chart. Hospitality operations that use such charts can plan thoroughly for management turnover rather than simply guess about availability and future management staffing needs. Research shows that management turnover in hospitality is often as high as 50 to 100 percent or more annually; given this fact, businesses may find succession charts extremely useful in quickly filling management vacancies.[8] Moreover, succession planning will play an increasingly important role for companies as they anticipate the retirement of baby boomers from key positions in the near future.[9]

Recruitment

It has become so common to post "help wanted" or "now hiring" signs in hospitality businesses that we hardly even notice the signs anymore. Recruitment is the process of attracting a pool of qualified job candidates from which the organization may select individuals to best meet its job requirements.[10] Recruitment is difficult to begin with—but predictions are that the process will get even harder. These facts alone set the stage: the annual growth rate of the United States population is only one percent—while the growth rate of the hospitality job market is nearly 18 percent.

To top off the complications, guests demand service more now than ever before. Guests know what they want—and expect it. Despite all these difficulties, the hospitality industry still puts too little emphasis on recruiting and selecting the right service-oriented people and too little emphasis on training. Once again, the adage "garbage in, garbage out" holds true. If the industry hires employees who provide poor service, guests will get poor service.

Not all hospitality operations are caught up in the "warm body" syndrome, quickly hiring readily available personnel. In fact, this is far from true. Many hospitality businesses already realize how important it is to recruit and hire the right employee. As a result, these operations are quickly gaining an edge over their competitors. The Ritz-Carlton Company, for example, has developed a four-faceted program to improve customer satisfaction. Each of the following four facets also helps employee recruitment, selection, and retention.

- Hire the right people.

- Provide orientation.

- Teach necessary skills.

- Instill appropriate behaviors.[11]

Similarly, a study conducted by PricewaterhouseCoopers shows that companies that are most successful at filling high employee needs because of rapid company growth are those that concentrate their human resources efforts on recruitment, career development, culture orientation, and communications. Hospitality companies were included in this study. The PricewaterhouseCoopers study also noted that these methods are especially significant for companies concerned about high employee turnover and retention costs. The study also noted that crucial strategic HR areas include leadership skills, orientation, values, rewards and recognition, image, communication, and employee participation.[12]

Progressive properties recognize recruitment as a process that involves identifying qualified employees and encouraging them to apply for open positions. The process begins by reconciling the demand for labor with the supply.

The Pre-Recruitment Process

As Exhibit 7 shows, a great deal of recruiting actually takes place before any ads are placed in newspapers or notices are posted in employee lounges. The **pre-recruitment process** consists of a number of interrelated steps, beginning with defining job requirements and ending with evaluating reruiting methods. The following section summarizes important considerations of the pre-recruitment steps outlined in Exhibit 7. More detail will be provided on some of these steps later in the chapter.

- *Define job requirements.* To define the job and its requirements, a manager needs to understand the primary responsibilities and tasks involved in the job, the background characteristics needed to perform the job, the personal characteristics required, the key features of the organization's culture, and the manager's managerial style.[13]

Exhibit 7   The Pre-Recruitment Process

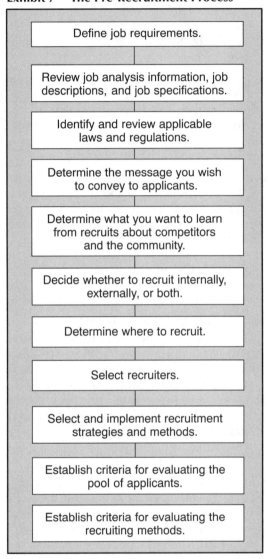

Define job requirements.

Review job analysis information, job descriptions, and job specifications.

Identify and review applicable laws and regulations.

Determine the message you wish to convey to applicants.

Determine what you want to learn from recruits about competitors and the community.

Decide whether to recruit internally, externally, or both.

Determine where to recruit.

Select recruiters.

Select and implement recruitment strategies and methods.

Establish criteria for evaluating the pool of applicants.

Establish criteria for evaluating the recruiting methods.

- *Review job analysis, job descriptions, and job specification information.* Managers should check that these tools are current, applicable, and complete. Changes and additions should be made when necessary.

- *Identify and review applicable laws and regulations.* Many issues associated with recruitment, selection, and promotion are subject to federal and state regulations. Managers should review such regulations before recruitment begins.

- *Determine the message you wish to convey to applicants.* The introduction of your business and the position are a critical part of recruitment. Many applicants are attracted to companies by recruitment advertising only to find that there is a considerable difference between the job in the ad and the job in the actual workplace. Businesses that carefully consider the message they want to send, and present the situation realistically, establish conditions that encourage long-term success.

- *Determine what you want to learn from recruits about competitors and the community.* While identifying potential applicants is the primary purpose of recruiting, it is not the sole purpose. Recruiting also gives managers a great opportunity to learn about the outside world. Applicants from other companies can provide valuable information about how your operation compares with the competition—as well as about how your operation is perceived.[14]

- *Decide whether to recruit internally, externally, or both.* Some companies, such as Delta Airlines, have successfully established programs in which only entry-level employees are recruited from the outside. In these companies, all supervisory and management positions are filled by internal applicants. Such internal recruitment programs are designed to create career ladders that encourage personnel to remain with the company longer. Other companies have successfully established programs for the external recruitment of both managers and entry-level personnel. The advantages and disadvantages of internal and external recruitment are discussed later in this chapter.

- *Determine where to recruit.* Managers should determine sources for both internal and external recruiting. For external recruiting, managers must determine the sites with the most potential for applicants—schools, competitors, apartment complexes, churches, and so on. Managers must also identify productive sites for internal recruiting. Consider such efforts by a chain hotel that is searching for housekeeping supervisors. This property might find more success recruiting from the housekeeping departments of other hotels in their chain than from departments within their own property.

- *Select recruiter(s).* The impression that many applicants may form about your operation is based on how they perceive the recruiter. Selecting the right recruiter is critical to attracting the right applicants. In addition, managers should consider that the employee they choose as the recruiter can be affected in a positive or negative way. An employee with doubts about his or her role may find that recruiting is exactly what he or she needs to rekindle a flame for the organization. Unfortunately, the opposite also may be true. For these and other reasons, selecting the right recruiter is paramount to the recruitment process.

- *Select and implement recruiting strategies and methods.* Recruitment can take many forms. In some cases, word-of-mouth may work best; in others, it may be better to recruit through the mass media (radio, television, newspapers, and magazines). Different approaches reach different markets. For that reason, the choice of approach is crucial to the recruiting process.

- *Establish criteria for evaluating the pool of applicants.* Too often, managers simply toss out a recruiting net to see what they can catch. This approach can have two outcomes—both unproductive. First, while the right applicants may be caught in the net, others may be too. These others, however, may be unsuitable "catches" who waste management time on interviews. Second, this approach may not "catch" any applicants who really fit the criteria. In some cases, recruiters may think that they should select the most promising applicants from this pool—simply to justify the cost of recruitment. To avoid these pitfalls, establish clearly defined evaluation criteria at the outset of recruiting.

- *Establish criteria for evaluating the recruiting methods.* Costs, costs per hire, number of contacts made, acceptance-offer ratios, and salary-requested rates all vary depending on the type of method used. Before beginning a recruiting program, hospitality operations should establish acceptable rates for each of these and other evaluation criteria.

As part of the pre-recruitment process, managers should also consider whether their personnel needs will be best met by internal or external sources of employees. The ultimate goal for a human resource practitioner is to balance internal promotions and external hires.[15] To do so, managers need to understand the advantages and disadvantages of the sources derived from **internal** and **external** **recruiting**.

Internal Recruiting

As we mentioned earlier, some companies like Delta Airlines generally recruit only entry-level employees from external sources; all supervisory and management positions are recruited internally—or, as some say, are "hired from within." Many hotel and restaurant companies do the same. Companies reap several benefits through internal recruiting. Internal recruiting:

- Improves the morale of the promoted employee.

- Improves the morale of the staff who see opportunities for themselves.

- Provides managers with a better assessment of the abilities of internal recruits since their performance has been observed over time.

- Results in a succession of promotions for supervisory and management positions—meaning that one promotion is necessary to fill each job vacated by a promotion. These successions help reinforce the company's "internal career ladder."

- Is lower in cost than external recruiting.

- Reduces training costs since training for entry-level positions is generally less expensive than training for management positions.

Internal recruiting also has its disadvantages. For instance, this method may:

- Promote inbreeding; after time, the flow of new ideas into the company diminishes.

- Cause morale problems among those employees who are skipped over for promotion.

- Have political overtones; some employees attribute promotions to friendships and relations with managers and supervisors.

- Create a critical gap in one department when personnel are used to fill a gap in another.

External Recruiting

External recruiting—or hiring from outside sources—is usually easiest at the entry level since managers can readily evaluate the skills and abilities required for such jobs. The factors that influence external recruitment strategies are all focused on the labor market, which consists of individual candidates who possess the knowledge, skills, attitudes, and abilities that meet the standards for employment within the organization.[16] External sources also include competitors. Experienced HR practitioners are always looking for talented individuals employed at other companies.[17]

Even though it costs more than internal recruiting, external recruiting has some distinct advantages. Among its major benefits, external recruiting:

- Brings "new blood" and new ideas into the company.

- Gives recruiters an opportunity to see how things are on the outside by talking with applicants from both direct and indirect competitors.

- Provides a fresh look at your organization, which sometimes reinforces the reasons current employees work in your company. Consider, for instance, the value of a recruit saying something like: "You keep your kitchen much cleaner than they do where I currently work," or "The light from the atrium certainly makes this a more pleasant place to work."

- Is sometimes cheaper than training.

- Avoids many of the political problems associated with internal recruiting.

- Serves as a form of advertising for the company. Newspaper ads, posters, bulletin board notices, presentations, and so on remind the public of your products and services.

Like internal recruiting, external recruiting has its dark side. Hospitality managers should be aware that sometimes:

- It is more difficult to find a good "fit" with the company's culture and management philosophy through external recruiting.

- Morale problems can develop if current employees feel that they have no opportunity to advance in the organization.

- Job orientation for external recruits takes longer than it does for internal recruits who already know the goals of the company, how the payroll system works, and so on.

- External recruiting can lower productivity over the short run, since, in some cases, new employees cannot produce as quickly or as effectively as internal recruits.

- Political problems and personality conflicts can result when employees believe that they could do the job as well as the external recruit.

- External candidates may not prove to be as they first appear. Any external candidate is still an unknown quantity. Managers will invariably know more about an internal applicant.[18]

Recruitment Sources

All too often, managers recruit through the most common methods available. By doing so, they may reach few viable applicants. We can't deny that recruitment today is more difficult than in the past. Even though the aging of the baby boomers means that the industry can no longer rely on the traditional job pool of 16- to 24-year-olds for the bulk of recruits, there are still many options left for creative managers to explore. This section discusses some of those options.

Internal Sources

Internal recruitment strategies often include career planning, skills inventories, and internal job-posting systems.[19] Maintaining adequate skills inventories and replacement and succession charts makes internal recruiting easier; doing so gives managers a better idea of who has the skills for an open position and who might be interested in taking the job. These inventories and charts should be viewed as critical—especially in organizations that stress internal recruiting. So that current employees know about openings, many businesses:

- Post notices or actual **job postings** on bulletin boards or announce current job openings in newsletters. Typically, postings or announcements include a job description and job specifications to inform employees of the responsibilities and skills required on the job. **Job bidding** results when employees sign a list indicating that they are interested in applying for posted positions.

- Use employees as referral sources. Some companies successfully use current applicants as sources of information on external recruits. This method has the advantage of locating the friends and acquaintances of current employees who often have more realistic views about the advantages and disadvantages of the organization. In addition, employees tend to refer only those friends who they believe would really make good employees; they realize that referring poor applicants reflects on their own judgment. Although many companies report that they use employee referrals to find new applicants, a study released in 1999 contends that they may not be doing this as much as they think or say they are—even though this can be one of the most cost-effective methods of recruitment today. For instance, this study found that too many managers do not know how to effectively recruit using referrals. Providing incentives, rewarding employees with promotions, and targeting employees for future promotions are all effective ways to make referral recruiting better.[20] Using referrals as the only source for recruiting can have unpleasant legal ramifications since this method may tend to discriminate against some protected groups. For instance, a hotel or restaurant located in a predominantly white neighborhood may naturally recruit or hire more white employees. If this company relied solely on employee referrals for recruitment, its policies might be construed as discriminatory.

External Sources

While local circumstances determine sources for external recruiting, we can supply a partial list of representative outlets. Sources that may be of value to hospitality operations include the following:

- Employment agencies—state and private
- Schools—high school job fairs, managers as guest speakers in classes, notices with guidance counselors, personal contact with teachers and coaches, participation in work-study programs
- Colleges—job fairs, contact with placement counselors, guest speakers, contact with teachers and coaches, participation in work-study programs, contact with campus social and professional clubs, hospitality management programs, dormitory counselors
- Churches and synagogues
- Youth groups
- Apartment complexes—laundry room bulletin boards, "doorknob announcements"
- Apartment newsletters
- Local sports teams (sponsorship)
- Women's groups
- Child-care centers
- Professional and trade journals
- Craft centers
- Exercise centers
- Senior citizen groups
- Governmental division-on-aging unit
- Agencies for people with disabilities[21, 22]
- Student organizations—Future Homemakers Association, Future Farmers of America, Distributive Education Clubs of America, and so on
- Sales, supply, and machinery representatives
- Community events
- Urban League and other agencies that provide skills training and job placement—Vietnam Refugee Fund, Mexican-American Opportunity Foundation, and so on
- Government rehabilitation agencies

- Government veterans agencies
- Chamber of Commerce
- Social/health organizations such as YMCA or YWCA
- Social service organizations such as the American Red Cross or the Salvation Army
- Volunteer groups—League of Women Voters, homeless shelters, health agencies, and so on
- Welcome organizations—Welcome Wagon, Hello Club, Newcomers, and so on
- Military agencies—reserve and active units of the local National Guard
- Open job fairs
- Employees at other hospitality companies or service-oriented organizations that you meet while dining out, shopping, or doing other day-to-day activities
- State American Hotel & Lodging Associations
- State restaurant associations
- Local and state assistance programs—for example, clothing and food drives for those in need
- Ads in local "pennysaver" and other low- and no-cost papers

Another source to consider is employees at same-chain properties who may be laid off during seasonal slowdowns. For instance, two Sonesta Hotels—one on Sanibel Island, Florida, and another in Cambridge, Massachusetts—have worked out an arrangement to transfer employees during slow seasons.[23]

Retired employees of the operation may be happy to help out and can provide an immediate source of expert knowledge during staff shortages or in other times of need. Likewise, former employees in good standing and current part-time employees might be available to fill in on a short-term basis.[24]

Other methods used successfully by small businesses that could work for hospitality managers include:

- Telerecruiting
- Talent scout cards
- Point-of-sale messages
- Direct mail campaigns
- Database recruiting
- Government funded programs
- Information seminars
- Referral incentives
- Sign-on bonuses[25]

Creative Recruiting Tactics

Several hospitality companies have developed creative ways of overcoming their labor shortages. For instance, Marriott has developed a program for recruiting and training homeless people. The National Restaurant Association and the American Hotel & Lodging Association have developed creative programs. One such program, called the Hospitality Business Alliance (HBA), focuses its efforts on finding and motivating high school students eager to develop skills that will enable them to become effective hospitality employees and supervisors. A key element in the HBA is the recruitment of industry employers who can provide school-to-work partnerships and guidance.[26] The Employer Group, an alliance of three hospitality companies and 25 other major employers, has also developed a collaborative approach to recruitment.[27]

In addition, some companies have found that keeping up with the times in recruitment can take on unusual aspects today. For instance, while it may sound like New Age propaganda, paying attention to employees' "mind, body, and spirit" can actually produce significant bottom-line results. This approach to employee management, which concentrates on transferring life skills, quality of life, and personal interest planning, has taken hold at traditional and nontraditional companies alike, where higher recruitment and retention rates are the payoff.[28]

Online Recruiting

Recruiting through cyberspace is becoming more popular. Many companies recruit nationally through either online recruiting agencies or their own Web sites. Several studies have been conducted to determine which Web sites are most effective. The measures most commonly used to assess Web site quality include an examination of the site's readability and the organization's effectiveness in promoting itself to potential customers and to potential employees. If you view every potential visitor as a possible client or employee, as some Web sites do, it is imperative to include job announcement information on your Web site. This approach started with high-tech companies but has rapidly spread across the spectrum. As a result, today potential applicants can learn about specific jobs, the company's potential for growth, orientation and compensation programs, and other factors that might influence them to apply with a specific company. Good Web sites include online applications or links to application sites.

In addition to company-specific recruiting sites, the World Wide Web is replete with headhunter, job posting, and job referral sites. Monster.com, BizBuyer.com, Aquent Partners, www.futurestep.com, employment911.com, careercentral.com, internweb.com, FutureCollegeGrads.com, job.sleuth.com, careermag.com, and many other sites offer complete job posting and résumé posting services.

Employers wishing to learn more about other aspects of employee recruitment—for instance, outsourcing of staff—can easily find answers on the Internet as well.

The Internet even provides information for those unfamiliar with certain aspects of recruiting. At sites such as askme.com and webhelp.com, employers can pose questions (to real people) about how best to recruit employees. These services and others like them usually refer the inquiring employer to Web sites that serve as resources. If those approaches are not sufficient, employers can also place ads in newspapers around the world through single Web sites. At advertise123.com, for instance, an employer can place recruitment ads in virtually any newspaper in any major U.S. city.

Finally, the Internet also provides ample opportunities to purchase or rent applicant tracking software, human resource information system software, and so on. Exhibit 8 provides an Internet glossary.

One of the advantages of Internet job posting is the potential for rapid response. Because information transfer on the Internet is virtually instantaneous, possible applicants can know about and apply (sometimes also by Internet) almost immediately. In addition to these recruiting resources, many hospitality organizations offer direct contact with applicants through their own home pages. Addresses for these home pages can be found through a Net search. Exhibit 9 provides an assortment of electronic recruitment tools.

Advertising

Regardless of the outlets targeted as sources for recruits, a property must first identify the legal ramifications of advertising through these sources and identify the types of people its advertising will attract.

In many locations, a property must obtain permission before distributing job notices and bulletins to outside sources. To avoid unlawful discrimination, properties must also pay special attention to how their advertisements are worded.

Finally, before recruiting from any external source, a property should conduct a job analysis and write job descriptions and specifications. Doing so can help ensure that the right people are identified, recruited, and hired.

One example of how successful online recruiting can be is offered by Marriott International, with over 131,000 employees. Marriott has found that using its Web site (http://marriott.com) is a cost-effective method of encouraging both current and potential employees to look at recruitment options. Like many other companies, Marriott also uses on-campus recruiting to locate many potential management candidates. Unlike some companies, however, Marriott likes to target universities with large international populations in order to attract students from other countries who may be employable back in their home country after graduation. Marriott is also developing regional recruitment centers in cities such as Washington, Phoenix, and Boston. These centers, located in downtown retail settings and on the ground floor where many potential employees pass by daily, offer one-stop shopping for potential job applicants.

Marriott has also reported that its Pathways to Independence—a program in which Marriott offers basic skills and workplace assimilation training to welfare recipients—has proven to be a very effective recruiting tool. This program enables many potential employees to become more eligible for employment. Marriott has reported that employees who undergo this type of training have an 80 percent

Exhibit 8   Internet Glossary

Internet Glossary			
Flame	Insulting, cruel, and derogatory messages sent via email or posted to the UseNet newsgroups.	Netiquette	Etiquette that is expected from users in the way that they communicate on the Internet using email or post to newsgroups.
ISP	Internet Service Provider: the company that conects you to the Internet.	Search engines	Sites on the World Wide Web that index the information found on the Web, enabling users to search for information of interest in a systematic way.
Listservs	List servers: the machines and software that allow for automated email lists to operate.	Thread	All of the articles posted to a UseNet newsgroup associated with an initial posting (including the initial posting).
Lurk	To read messages posted to email discussion groups and newsgroups without sending or posting any messages yourself while getting acclimated to the list's cultural norms and code of conduct.	Unmoderated list	Any email list that operates on a fully automated basis. Although there may be a list owner, he/she does not actively review messages received by the list prior to their being distributed to the list.
Moderated list	An email list that has an active moderator(s) that reviews and/or approves requests to become a subscriber to the list. The moderator(s) may also review the content of the messages to screen emails prior to their being distributed back out to the list.	URL	Uniform Resource Locator: the address used for linking and visiting sites on the Web.
		UseNet	Users' Network: the area of the Internet where newsgroups and electronic bulletin boards are found.

Source: Eric R. Wilson, "Zapping Your Recruitment Strategies," *HR Focus* (November 1996): 7.

graduation rate, a 90 percent retention rate after 90 days, and a 55 percent retention rate after one year. Marriott uses the same type of approach in the technical hospitality skills high school that it champions and supports in the Washington, D.C., area.[29]

Exhibit 9   Electronic Recruitment Tools

Electronic Recruitment Tools

☑ **Online Career Center.** This résumé database and job-posting site is supported by Hallmark, GTE, AT&T, Apple and other firms. You can search the résumé database or post an unlimited number of job ads on the electronic hub free of charge. Or, join the nonprofit group for a one-time fee and get a homepage logo and graphics. For more information, call (317)293-6499 or visit www.occ.com.

☑ **America Online Career Center.** AOL's Career Center targets job seekers, but companies can post recruitment ads or advertise for specific jobs. Contact AOL at (703)448-8700.

☑ **E-Span, Inc.** This advertising service sells a job-search tool that lets you research electronic résumé databases and surf the entire Net. Its software also comes with a fill-in-the-blank employment ad. To find out more, call (317)469-4535.

☑ **CareerMosaic.** You can post job ads with this service, provided by Bernard Hodes Advertising Inc. There's also a career resource center for job seekers. For more information, call (212)758-2600.

☑ **CHRIE HOSTEUR Network.** Résumé bank for hospitality. For more information, call the International Council on Hotel, Restaurant, and Institutional Education at (804)747-4971. http://www.chrie.org

---

Source: *HR Focus* (June 1996): 13.

Marriott successfully fills supervisory and managerial positions by emphasizing internal recruiting, effectively "growing its own" managers. Each hotel has a Management Candidacy Review Board composed of a department head and a member of the executive committee. The focus of this board is to review employees who may be near the level needed to train for management positions. If employees show managerial talent, the committee looks for opportunities for the employee to develop skills within the company. Marriott's Supervisor in Training and Manager in Training programs complement this activity by offering participants workbooks in which they record their learning experiences. The workbooks are later reviewed with mentors or coaches. These programs have proven so successful that each year approximately 30 to 40 percent of successful managerial applicants come from within Marriott's employee ranks.

Evaluating Sources and Methods

A critical determinant of recruiting success is the rate of applicants hired from each source per dollar spent on the process. Unfortunately, no such general information is available on different recruiting methods in the hospitality industry. Such data is easy to capture, however. Managers must maintain files on each method used in order to conduct an assessment of different recruiting methods. The file should

Exhibit 10   Recruitment by Table-Service Restaurants

Percentage of Table-Service Restaurants Choosing Recruiting Methods, by Size of Guest Check				
Recruiting method	Less than $8	$8-$14.99	$15-$24.99	More than $25
Employee referrals	54%	62%	62%	56%
Walk-in	40	43	41	37
Newspaper ads	45	43	38	44
Colleges/ schools	26	23	35	38
Job fairs	22	16	15	26
Targeted minority recruiting	16	12	13	22
Recruitment firms	18	13	26	16
Government employment office	26	23	16	16
Internet	16	11	15	13

Source: National Restaurant Association study of preferred recruitment methods, as cited in Bruce Grindy, "Hooking and Keeping Employees," *Restaurants USA*, October 1998, 24.

contain information about costs (both in terms of dollars and recruiting time), and about the recruits attracted. From an applicant's point of view, research reveals that applying directly to an employer is among the most effective ways to secure a job. Answering local newspaper ads, going through private or state employment agencies, or conferring with school placement offices are also valuable job search methods.[30]

No study to date actually defines the relative effectiveness of different recruiting methods used in the hospitality industry. However, some studies have examined specific recruiting efforts. Some things to consider when choosing recruitment tactics are the findings from studies on the productivity of each method. For instance, a study of small businesses (which many hospitality properties are) found that running newspaper ads and using past applications (people who had previously applied) resulted in significantly fewer hires than did providing internal employees with information on the possibility of promotion. Internal recruitment was twice as successful as external recruitment when measured by days-to-fill.[31]

The National Restaurant Association conducted a study at the end of 1998 to determine which recruiting methods their members prefer. Exhibit 10 depicts the results. One study examined older workers as a possible employee pool for hospitality operations. One finding was that older workers were generally rated in a positive way on several performance criteria. They were rated above average on factors such as dependability, attitude, maturity, and quality of work. Older workers were also regarded as exceptionally good at developing rapport with guests and other employees, and in such areas as self-confidence, analytical and leadership abilities, assertiveness, perseverance, and creativity.[32]

However, a sociological study of recruitment and selection practices in the restaurant industry, done in 1999, found the following:

- The industry distrusts traditional sources of labor.

- Employers are often passive or reactive in their recruiting efforts.

- Employers do not use educational credentials as hiring criteria.

- Employers do not use work experience as hiring criteria.

And that employers:

- Develop unusual methods of recruitment.

- Like to try to depict their business as totally different from other restaurants (and thereby nullify the need for comparisons between past job performance).

- Make selection decisions primarily on whether they believe an applicant can be motivated to work.[33]

Recruiting from the Applicant's Viewpoint

Managers should understand recruiting from the applicant's viewpoint for two reasons. First, an applicant's point of view can provide managers with information on how other recruiters function. Second, managers themselves have been—or may be—recruits at some point in time. The following discussion puts you in the recruit's shoes by examining what recruiters look for, how to prepare for an interview, and what questions recruiters typically ask.

What Recruiters Look For

Some years ago, two professors conducted a study of hospitality recruiters on college campuses to identify the factors that most influenced their choice of graduates. Not surprisingly, these researchers from the University of New Hampshire Hotel and Restaurant Administration Program discovered that recruiters were influenced the most by personal factors. Appearance, first impressions, and personality all rated very high with recruiters.[34] Jones, Izzolo, and Christianson found essentially the same results in their study of 43 hospitality firms.[35] To many outsiders, this confirmed the intense personality-orientation of industry recruiters.

Rest assured: recruiters are also interested in factors other than personality and appearance. For instance, one study indicated that recruiters on college campuses are interested in learning about candidates' strengths and weaknesses and in determining how these characteristics served as advantages or liabilities in previous jobs.[36] Many experts suggest that the key to performing well in interviews is preparation.

Because a job interview is a communication process, a job candidate's skills will become more polished over time. It is helpful if job candidates remember the following:

- The job candidate should speak clearly and enthusiastically about job experiences and skills. The job candidate should be professional, but unafraid to let his or her personality shine through. The candidate should be himself or herself.

- The candidate should listen carefully. He or she will want to remember the information the interviewer provides about the job, and will certainly want to answer questions the interviewer asks.

- The candidate should be positive. Employers do not want to hear a litany of excuses or bad feelings about a negative experience. If the interviewer asks the job candidate about a low grade, a sudden job change, or a weakness in his or her background, the candidate should not become defensive. Instead, the job candidate should focus briefly on the facts and what he or she learned from the experience.

- The candidate should pay attention to his or her nonverbal behavior, looking the interviewer in the eye, sitting up straight with both feet on the floor, controlling nervous habits (cracking knuckles, drumming fingers, and so on), and smiling when greeted.

- The candidate should not be afraid of short pauses. He or she may need a few seconds to formulate answers to questions, or the interviewer may need time to phrase an appropriate question. It is not necessary to fill up every second with conversation.

Preparing for Recruitment Interviews

Many candidates go to job interviews with little information about the company. More often than not, this is a big mistake. For a first interview, it behooves a candidate to do some preliminary research. Candidates should find out what fields the company currently operates in, any recent developments within the company, in which direction the company is headed, and how it is perceived by stock analysts. The convenience of the Internet has allowed candidates to easily access a wide variety of company and industry information. Candidates can find the latest industry news on Web sites such as hospitalitynet.org and ehotelier.com, while more company-specific information is usually available through the company's Web site. As a candidate's list of companies narrows, the research should become more intensive.

A great deal of information about hotel companies is also available in trade journals such as *Lodging Hospitality, Lodging, Hotels, Hotel and Resort Industry, Resort Development and Operations*, and *Resort Hospitality*. Similar information about restaurant companies is available from *Restaurants USA, Restaurants and Institutions, Restaurants Business, Restaurant Hospitality*, and *Nation's Restaurant News*. Trade journals and associations also supply information about other segments of the hospitality industry. For instance, information about club management is available in the trade journal *Club Management* and through the Club Managers Association of America (CMAA).

Information about convention and conference center management is available in *Associations and Meetings, Meetings and Conventions,* and *Meetings Management*. In addition, *Airline Business* offers information about the airline segment, and *Ski Area Management* offers information about companies in the skiing-related resort industry. Many of these companies have garnered the attention of business magazines and newspapers such as *Fortune, Inc., Wall Street Journal, Forbes, Barrons,* and *Business Week*. Recruits can find additional information on hospitality companies in a variety of other published sources. Librarians at colleges and universities can help identify sources for information on most hospitality companies. Statistical and business periodical indexes, corporate research reports, international and national business directories, and compilations of industry surveys are among the valuable resources at the fingertips of many local librarians.[37]

What Recruiters Ask

Recruiters—no matter where they are from—typically ask the same series of questions. Although their delivery may vary, recruiters typically request the same general information. Exhibit 11 lists some of the more common questions posed by recruiters.

Unfortunately, some recruiters can be swayed by personal biases. A study of pre-screening factors considered by recruiters preparing to interview college students revealed the following percentages of recruiters interested in specific characteristics.

- Work experience (25.7 percent)
- Willingness to relocate (15.1 percent)
- Extracurricular activities (13.9 percent)
- Grade point average (10.1 percent)

These percentages indicate that recruiters consider other factors more important than grades.[38]

Recruiters have indicated that excellent interview skills are very important in their hiring decisions. The following are a few interviewing tips geared toward job seekers:

- Job candidates should be prepared to market their skills and experiences as they relate to the job. They should attempt to position themselves in the interviewer's mind as individuals with a particular set of skills and attributes. Employers have problems that need to be solved by employees with particular skills; job candidates should strive to describe qualifications appropriately.

- Candidates should plan to arrive for interviews 10–15 minutes before the appointed time. Arriving too early confuses the employer and creates an awkward situation, while arriving late creates a bad first impression. It is wise to ask for directions when making arrangements for the interview.

- Candidates should carry a portfolio notepad or, at the very least, a manila file folder labeled with the employer's name. Candidates should take extra résumés and a list of questions to ask. They may refer to the list of questions to be

Exhibit 11   Sample Interview Questions

Relevant Job Background
- What were your gross and take-home wages?
- Did you regularly work 40 hours a week? How much overtime did you get?
- What benefits did you have? How much did you pay for them?
- What salary are you looking for? What is the lowest amount you can accept?
- Which days of the week work out best for you?
- Have you ever worked weekends before? Where? How often?
- Which shift do you enjoy working the most? Which shift can't you work?
- Do you regularly have to be somewhere besides work at a certain time?
- How many hours a week would you like to work?
- Are you a morning person or a night person?
- How will you get to work at that hour?
- Is your transportation reliable?
- How many days a year do you think is normal for a person to be absent or late?
- What position did you hold when you started that job? When you left?
- What was your starting salary there? What were you making when you left? How did you get increases?
- How many people gave you orders there?
- What were the most important duties of your job?
- What three things do you want to avoid on your next job?
- What do you expect from a supervisor?
- Why did you choose this line of work?

Education and Intelligence
- What subjects did you like best/least?
- Do you think your grades are a good indicator of your overall abilities?
- What accounted for your good grades?
- Have you ever thought about continuing your schooling?
- Why did you choose that school/major?
- Is it a good school? Why or why not?
- If you had to do it all over again, would you make the same decisions? Why or why not?
- What is the most important thing you've learned in the past six months?
- Do you like to read? What do you like to read?

Physical Factors
- What do you like to do in your spare time?
- How many times were you absent or late on your last job? Do you think that's normal? What were the reasons?
- On your last job, were they tough on absenteeism and lateness? Do you think their policy was fair? Did they ever talk to you about it?
- What do you consider a good night's sleep?

Personal Traits
The following are more suitable for younger people without much work background.
- What does your family think of your working as a cook?
- How old were you when you got your first job?
- What was the first job you ever had?
- What was your first boss like?
- How did you get your first job? Your most recent job?

(continued)

Exhibit 11　*(continued)*

The following are general questions about personal traits. Change the job title to meet your needs.

- Who has the greater responsibility—a desk agent or a reservations agent?
- Do you feel that food servers are too competitive among themselves?
- Do you find that a lot of guests are leaving smaller tips these days?
- How would you handle a guest who never tips?
- Have you ever had to deal with a guest who is angry or complaining about everything? How did you calm the person down?
- Were you ever chewed out or criticized unjustly?
- What do you consider to be the main reasons cooks quit their jobs?
- What do you consider to be the most important responsibilities for a good desk agent? Why?
- Why is the housekeeper's job so important?
- Suppose your supervisor insisted you do a certain thing in a certain way, when you definitely know there's a better way. What would you do?
- Have you ever had a supervisor "play favorites"? What did you do about it?
- Which company did you like working for the most/least? Why?
- What would you change if you managed that department? Did you try to change it?
- What was your biggest accomplishment or contribution at that job?
- Would you go back and work there again? Why or why not?
- Who was the best/worst supervisor you ever had?
- What can you do for us that other applicants can't do?
- What made you stay at that job for so long?
- Did your last company have a good product?
- How much notice did you give when you left your last job? Why?
- Have you ever had to "stick your neck out" and make a decision on your own? How long did it take you to decide, and what did you consider before you decided?
- How would your former boss and fellow employees describe you?
- What areas did your last performance review say you needed to improve on?
- What was the most important thing you learned on that job?
- What are your three strongest assets?
- What are the three areas in which you would most like to improve yourself?
- Are you happy with your present status and income? Do you think it's in line with your peers?
- What one thing have you done of which you are the proudest?
- Where would you like to be five years from now? Ten years from now? What are you doing to make it happen?
- What's the funniest thing that ever happened to you?

Questions for Managers

- When you left, who replaced you?
- What type of training program did you have for your employees?
- What have you done in the last twelve months to improve your department and/or customer base?
- What do you think are the most important attributes of a manager?
- Who were your biggest competitors? What were their strengths/weaknesses?
- Did you ever have to take an unpopular stand?
- How would your employees describe you as a supervisor?
- Why do you think people today are hard to motivate?
- How many people did you have to fire on your last job? For what reasons?

Source: David Wheelhouse, *Managing Human Resources in the Hospitality Industry* (Lansing, Mich.: Educational Institute of the American Hotel & Lodging Association, 1989), 90–91.

sure they have enough information to make a decision. Candidates should not be preoccupied with taking notes during the interview.

- In many career fields, the lunch or dinner included during the interview day is not only employer hospitality, it is a significant part of the interview process. Candidates should brush up on etiquette and carry their share of the conversation during the meal. Often social skills are part of the hiring decision.

- After the interview, job candidates can take time to write down the names and titles (making sure to check the spelling) of all the interviewers, their impressions of the operation, remaining questions they have, and information they obtained. If candidates are interviewing regularly, this will help them keep employers and circumstances clearly defined.

Finally, job candidates should follow up each interview with a thank-you letter. Employers regard this as evidence of the candidate's attention to detail, as well as an indication of his or her final interest in the position.

Human Resource Information Systems (HRISs)

By definition, a Human Resource Information System (HRIS) is a method of collecting, maintaining, organizing, analyzing, and reporting information on people and jobs. Managers should remember that an HRIS is basically another recruiting tool. These systems are designed to make the storage and retrieval of information easier, faster, and more cost productive; HRISs can also make it easier to access information for analysis. The key, of course, is using an HRIS to produce information that you really need.

Only a decade or so ago, most HRISs involved the use of large computers and specially trained personnel. Today, HRISs must, by nature, incorporate both internal networks (intranets) and Internet connections with recruitment sources. Those companies that are the most visionary in this area already have well-established "virtual workforce" connections that speed their recruitment, selection, and succession planning processes.[39]

The type of data typically stored in an HRIS includes:

- *Personal data.* Name, Social Security number, gender, date of birth; names, ages, and genders of dependents; marital status; minority classification; address and telephone number; names of relatives or other persons to contact in case of emergency; and so on.

- *Recruiting data.* Date of recruiting contact, responsible recruiter, source of candidate, names of supervisors or managers referred to for interviews, dates of interviews, dates of offer and acceptance, outline of offer, and date added to payroll; if rejected, reasons for rejection or for candidate's rejection of employment offer; test scores; and so on.

- *Work experience data.* Names and locations of supervisors, employment history, job skills, training received, and dates and types of disciplinary action.

- *Compensation/Work assignment data.* Salary or wage history, date of next forecast pay consideration, amount of next forecast pay consideration, title, hours worked weekly/monthly, appraisal reports, and dates for next appraisal.

- *Benefit plan data.* Medical/life benefit plan information (self and family), pension plan information, vacation plan information, specialty benefit plan information, and so on.

- *Exit interview data.* Date removed from payroll, reason cited for removal, forwarding address, name and address of new employer, eligibility for rehire, reason for departure, and so on.

Data in an HRIS has many purposes. For instance, information kept in a typical HRIS can be used in operational reports, regulatory reports, and analytic reports. Operational reports in a hotel might include such items as job vacancy information, wage reports, or recruiting reports. Preparing regulatory reports—such as required annual reports to the EEOC and OSHA—is much easier when information is collected, stored, and compiled in an HRIS. Many people feel one of the best applications of an HRIS is analytical reporting. For instance, a hotel may wish to compare a method of recruiting to turnover activity. By using the information stored in an HRIS, the operation can prepare this report quickly and effectively. Without an HRIS, a similar report would take hours of manual labor to produce.

These systems do have problems. Hotels may tend to store "nice-to-know" information in the HRIS database and produce far too many "interesting" reports that have little usefulness. Because the information is readily available, some HRIS managers may overuse the system's capability and mire the organization in paper.

While the Federal Privacy Act of 1974 limits only information collected and stored in federal agencies, it provides some indication of where limits may someday be placed in private industry. Operators employing HRISs should review and be aware of the three specific rights of individuals under this act: (1) individuals have the right to review, copy, and amend reports about themselves kept in any personnel file—including an HRIS, (2) individuals have the right to prevent information about them from being used for any purpose other than that for which it was collected, and (3) individuals have the right to sue for damages as a result of any action that violates their rights. From a hospitality manager's point of view, the best protection in this area of potential litigation is also threefold: (1) set up specific policies regarding the collection and use of information, (2) inform employees of these policies, and (3) require employees to read and sign a statement acknowledging these policies. By doing so, the organization protects both the individual and itself.

System Errors

Many of the mistakes associated with an HRIS are related to the system the business chooses. Research indicates that managers most commonly err when they anticipate the system's cost. As a rule of thumb, total systems implementation will cost approximately eight times the software and hardware costs. For example, if the software and hardware costs are $10,000, the total implementation costs will approximate $80,000.[40]Aside from cost considerations, any property considering an HRIS should keep the following points in mind:

- Managers and users should be active participants in installing the system. All too often, systems are installed and installers leave before really teaching the staff how to use the system effectively.
- Data collection should focus on "need-to-know" information.
- Reporting needs should be analyzed thoroughly before choosing a system. Typically, this can be accomplished through a five-step process:

    1. Development of needs analysis (What does the system need to do?)
    2. Vendor evaluation (What suppliers does the company have to choose from? What are their reputations?)
    3. Customization (What degree of customization is required for the system?)
    4. Technical testing (What tests should be run before making a choice?)
    5. Acceptance testing (How much assistance does the vendor provide during initial stages of implementation?)[41]

Like the various methods of forecasting, inventories, and planning charts, managers should understand the purpose behind an HRIS to achieve the best results.

Outsourcing

Another way to fulfill recruiting needs is to outsource either some or all services. Many hotels look outside their organizations for concierge and other professional guest services.[42] Others use programs that "lease" employees. These programs remove recruiting responsibilities from managers and remove recordkeeping responsibilities from the hiring company and place it on the leasing company.

According to an article by Murthy and Murrmann, the hospitality industry has improved its employee leasing programs and, with careful selection, hospitality companies can identify competent and viable leasing firms. The article offers insights into how to find leasing firms and when to consider using them.[43]

One way in which hotels are outsourcing is through agreements with restaurant companies to provide major food and beverage services. Columbia Essex, for instance, opened Radisson Properties with onsite T.G.I. Friday's restaurants to serve as their principal food and beverage facility.[44]

 ## Endnotes

1. E. Tucker, T. Kao, and N. Verma, "Next Generation Talent Management Insights on How Workforce Trends are Changing the Face of Talent Management," *Business Credit* 107 (July/August 2005): 7.

2. Tucker et al.

3. Tucker et al.

4. Tucker et al.

5. B. Macaleer and J. Shannon, "Does HR Planning Improve Business Performance?" *Industry Management* (January 2003).

6. Adapted from Macaleer and Shannon.

7. For more information on skills inventories, see Paul Sheiber, "A Simple Selection System Called 'Jobmatch,'" *Personnel Journal* 58 (1979): 26–29.

8. For more information on turnover in the hospitality industry, see Robert H. Woods and James F. Macaulay, "Rx for Turnover: Retention Programs that Work," *Cornell Hotel and Restaurant Administration Quarterly* 30 (May 1989): 78–90.

9. "As Baby Boomers Reach Retirement and Companies Face a Labor Shortage, Developing Current Employees Should Be the Answer," New York: Catalyst, June 6, 2005, www.catalystwomen.org.

10. Norma D'Annunzio-Green, Gillian A. Maxwell, and Sandra Watson (eds.), *Human Resource Management: International Perspectives in Hospitality and Tourism* (London: Continuum, 2002), 17.

11. Stephen Brewer, "Luxury Hotels," *Lodging Hospitality* 50 (June 1994): 58.

12. Pamela F. Weber, "Getting a Grip on Employee Growth," *Training and Development* 53, no. 4 (1999): 87–91.

13. *Harvard Business Essentials: Hiring and Keeping the Best People* (Boston: Harvard Business School Press, 2002), 2–3.

14. For more information on what can be learned from others during recruiting, see Robert I. Sutton and Meryl R. Louis, "How Selecting and Socializing Newcomers Influences Insiders," *Human Resource Management* 26 (Fall 1987): 347–361.

15. D.V. Tesone, *Human Resource Management in the Hospitality Industry: A Practitioner's Perspective* (Upper Saddle River, N.J.: Pearson/Prentice Hall, 2005), 106.

16. Tesone, 105.

17. Tesone, 107.

18. L. Dean Webb and M. Scott Norton, *Human Resources Administration: Personnel Issues and Needs in Education*, 4th ed. (Columbus, Ohio: Merrill/Prentice Hall, 2003), 264.

19. D'Annunzio-Green et al., 17.

20. "Maximizing Employee Referrals," *HR Focus* (January 1999): 9–10.

21. Julie Fintel, "Looking for Help in All the Right Places," *Restaurants USA* (November 1990): 31.

22. For more information on the effectiveness of people with disabilities in hospitality employment, see Jeff Weinstein, "Ready and Able," *Restaurants and Institutions* (28 November 1990): 68.

23. For information on this project, see Megan Rowe, "The Industry Cries Out for Help," *Lodging Hospitality* (September 1990): 58.

24. Webb and Norton, 265.

25. Catherine D. Fyock, "Resourceful Recruiting," *Small Business Reports* 17 (April 1992): 49–58.

26. Milford Prewitt, "High School Training Programs Offer Solution for Labor Shortage," *Nation's Restaurant News,* 18 March 1996, 70.

27. Robert Klara, "In the Struggle for Labor, Some Find Strength in Numbers," *Restaurant Business,* 10 June 1996, 24.

28. "Maximizing Employee Referrals," *HR Focus* (January 1999): 9–10.

29. "Marriott's Welfare-to-Work Program, Pathways to Independence, Reaches 10-Year Milestone," The Timeshare Beat, Inc., online forum for the International Association of Timeshare Professionals, December 19, 2000, http://www.thetimesharebeat.com/archives/2000htl/htldec75.htm.

30. Carl Rosenfeld, "Job Seeking Methods Used by American Workers," *Monthly Labor Review* (August 1985): 40.

31. HG Heneman and RA Berkley, "Applicant Attraction Practices and Outcomes Among Small Businesses," *Journal of Small Business Management* 371 (January 1999): 53–74.

32. Frederick J. DeMicco and Robert D. Reid, "Older Workers: A Hiring Resource for the Hospitality Industry," *Cornell Hotel and Restaurant Administration Quarterly* 29 (May 1988): 58.

33. D.B. Bills, "Labor Market Information and Selection in a Local Restaurant Industry: Tenuous Balance Between Rewards, Commitments and Costs," *Sociological Forum* 14, no. 4 (1999) 4: 583–607.

34. Mel Sandler and David Ley, "Corporate Recruiters: What Do They Really Want?"*Cornell Hotel and Restaurant Administration Quarterly* 29 (August 1982): 42–45.

35. T. Jones, A.W. Izzolo, and D. J. Christianson, "Campus Recruitment: A Four-Year Program Profile," *FIU Hospitality Review* 2 (1993): 73–79.

36. Ellen Kaplan, "College Recruitment: The View from Both Sides," *Personnel* (November 1985): 44–48.

37. Readers can find a list of information sources on businesses and associations in *MBA Field Studies: A Guide for Students and Faculty,* edited by Raymond Corey (Boston: Harvard Business School Publishing Division, 1991).

38. Michael I. Sciarini, Robert H. Woods, and Phillip Gardner, "A Comparison of Faculty, Recruiter, and Student Perceptions of Important Pre-Screening Characteristics," *Hospitality and Tourism Educator* 7 (Winter 1995): 21–25.

39. "Which HRIS Technologies Best Support the Virtual Workplace?" *HR Focus* (February 2000): 6–9.

40. R. B. Frantzreb, "The Micro-Computer Based HRIS: A Directory," *Personnel Administrator* 31, no. 9 (1987): 67–100.

41. Cynthia D. Diers, "Personnel Computing: Make the HRIS More Effective," *Personnel Journal* (May 1990): 94.

42. Carol Sue Ravenel, "A New Way to Satisfy Guests," *Lodging Hospitality* 48 (May 1992): 32.

43. Bvsan Murthy and Suzanne K. Murrmann, "Employee Leasing: An Alternative Staffing Strategy," *Cornell Hotel and Restaurant Administration Quarterly* 34 (June 1993): 18–23.

44. Megan Rowe, "If You Can't Beam 'em, Join 'em," *Lodging Hospitality* 49 (December 1993): 57–59.

Key Terms

bottom-up forecasting—Forecasting technique based on estimates made by managers in each department. These estimates are combined to create an estimate of human resources needs for the entire property.

external recruiting—Process of seeking applicants from outside the property to fill open positions.

human resource information system (HRIS)—Computerized method of collecting, maintaining, organizing, analyzing, and reporting information on human resources and positions in an organization.

internal recruiting—Process of seeking applicants from inside the property to fill open positions.

job bidding—Process of posting a list internally for employees to sign when they are interested in open positions.

job posting—Internal or external notice of a job opening.

labor demand—The need for human resources in a particular job market.

labor supply—The supply of human resources in a particular job market.

management inventory—A list of the problem-solving and management skills of current managers and management candidates that is used to identify candidates for internal recruitment.

management succession plan—A written plan that identifies readiness or skills required for managers to move up in the organization.

pre-recruitment process—Sequence of recruiting steps that take place before advertising positions or posting notices.

recruitment—Process of attracting a pool of qualified job candidates from which an organization may select individuals to best meet its job requirements.

replacement chart—A management tool that estimates the internal supply of employees for a particular position.

skills inventory—A list of skills, abilities, qualifications, and career goals of current employees that is used to identify candidates for internal recruitment.

succession chart—Management tool used to plot anticipated successions in an organization by position.

top-down forecasting—Forecasting techniques for human resources based on quantitative and statistical approaches.

trend analysis—Forecasting technique for predicting the future based on past performance.

Review Questions

1. What are the steps in the pre-recruitment process?

2. What are the basic steps involved in forecasting labor demands?

3. What are the purposes of replacement and succession charts?

4. What is bottoms-up forecasting? What are the advantages and disadvantages of this method?

5. What is top-down forecasting? What are the advantages and disadvantages of this method?

6. What are the advantages and disadvantages of internal recruiting?

7. What are the advantages and disadvantages of external recruiting?

8. What are the three most common types of reports generated by an HRIS? What are their uses?

9. What privacy issues should hospitality managers be concerned with when considering implementation of an HRIS?

 **Internet Sites**

For more information, visit the following Internet sites. Remember that Internet addresses can change without notice. If the site is no longer there, you can use a search engine to look for additional sites.

Cornell Hotel and Restaurant Administration Quarterly
http://hotelschool.cornell.edu/publications

International Council on Hotel, Restaurant and Institutional Education
www.chrie.org/

Information about specific companies and their recruiting programs can be found at their home pages on the Internet.

Mini Case Study

During the 1980s, a hotel chain in the Midwest instituted a recruiting plan based on referrals from current employees. This system worked, primarily because the operation had a strong, competent staff during that period. However, problems began to develop in the 1990s as fewer and fewer people applied to fill the increasing number of positions at the hotel.

Despite a shrinking pool of applicants for an expanding number of jobs, the human resources manager continued to rely on the employee referral system for his labor supply. He justified this decision by saying, "Even though fewer employees are available, the employee referral method brings employees into our chain who know about our work and our expectations. That's because these people have friends working here. In the long run, this knowledge will help us keep training and orientation costs down."

Unfortunately, the manager's program is failing miserably. The hotel is desperately short of staff. To acknowledge the problem, the hotel chain developed a new position: director of recruiting. You have been hired for this position. You are asked to prepare a recruitment plan that taps labor supplies that your chain has failed to develop over the past several years. Your first problem, however, is convincing the human resources director of the need for such a recruitment program.

What arguments can you use to convince the human resources director of the need to establish new recruiting methods and strategies?

Chapter 4 Outline

Competencies

4

Selection

This chapter was co-authored by Tatiana Poliakova, M.S. candidate,
University of Nevada, Las Vegas.

WHEN CONDUCTED PROPERLY, **selection** provides an organization with the personnel it needs to excel and to leave its competition far behind. But when conducted improperly, selection leads to wasted time and effort by management and employees and to guest discontent. In 2003, the Employment Management Association's estimated cost of hiring an employee was $4,263. Moreover, according to the Association, in a competitive industry, the hiring cost may reach 30 percent of an employee's annual salary.[1]

Selection is one of the most critical tasks a manager undertakes; it is not something to delegate to untrained managers or employees. Peter Drucker, perhaps the greatest management theorist of our time, calls selection decisions "the most long-lasting decisions and the most difficult to unmake." The best managers bat only about .333, or make the right decisions about one-third of the time. The other 67 percent are either minimally effective or dismal failures.[2] Successful selection does not tolerate shortcuts; it requires comprehensive planning dedicated to human resources issues. Effective job analysis and design, recruiting, job descriptions and specifications, and attention to various legal and social requirements determine whether the right person is found and selected for the job.

Like managers everywhere, hospitality managers often hastily select employees in reaction to some type of "crisis"—personnel shortages, too little time to devote to an applicant, and so on. Managers who react to situations in this way do not become leaders in their field. Managers who take selection seriously succeed.

This chapter will focus on educating managers in correct and effective techniques to use in the selection process. Among the issues discussed will be validation of the selection process, selection steps and techniques, employment and pre-employment tests, and interviewing skills and techniques.

Does Selection Really Work?

There is little question that good employee selection practices definitely affect overall performance. In a study that matched human resources practices with stock market performance, G. H. Harel and S. S. Tzafrir found a conclusive link between the two.[3] In addition, according to a 2005 study on job performance, within an organization, human resources practices also affect collective commitment, operational performance, expenses, and profits.[4]

When done properly, selection is *legal* discrimination among job candidates. Its goal is to choose the candidates who are likely to succeed in the job. Selection practices should be both reliable and valid. Reliability refers to the consistency and dependability of a selection process over time; validity refers to the accuracy of the selection process in assessing a candidate.

Reliability

Reliability refers to the degree to which a selection method *consistently* produces the same results. A selection method is reliable if it consistently leads an employer to the same selection decisions, regardless of who is actually applying the method. If it does not do this consistently, the method is not reliable. Reliability is extremely important. Whether the selection method is a physical or mental test, an observation, or an interview, it must be reliable.

Validity

Validity is the degree to which a selection process really measures or predicts what it is intended to measure or predict. The key in any selection process is to develop measures that validate the likelihood of success for each candidate. The selection process commonly uses two types of strategies to test for validity: criterion-related validity and content validity.

Criterion-Related Validity. The purpose of validation is to measure how well the predictor used in selection works. Predictors measure the relationship between performance during the selection process and performance on the job. This makes choosing a predictor a very important decision.

Criterion-related validity is concerned with the relationship between the predictor and the criterion scores. For the most part, the criterion in our discussions will be job performance. There are two types of criterion-related validity: predictive and concurrent.

Predictive validity uses a predictor to ascertain whether good performance is likely on the job. While many organizations base their decisions on predictors, few take the time to validate whether predictors actually measure what is intended. As a result, there may be little correlation between performance on the predictor and performance on the job.

To validate a predictor, a hospitality company should subject all applicants to that predictor. Once tested using the new predictor, applicants are selected on some other basis, such as the strength of their résumé or previous experience. Once employees are hired, however, their performance can be tracked over time. After a certain period, performance can be compared to pre-hiring test scores. A strong correlation between scores on the exam and job performance establishes validity for the predictor. Managers can then use this testing method as a predictor in future selection processes.

Because predictive validity tests how employees might perform in the future, it is sometimes called the future employee method. Concurrent validity—sometimes called the current employee method—differs from the predictive method in two ways: (1) choice of time frame in which the predictive and criterion data are collected and (2) choice of subjects. Typically, concurrent validity tests the ability of current employees to perform a certain job. For instance, servers in a food and beverage operation might be asked to complete some type of exam.

To use the concurrent validity approach in selection, a hospitality company would first conduct a thorough job analysis to determine which characteristics were most desirable in a specific job. The company would then develop a test to measure these characteristics. After that, the test would be administered to a group of current employees. Finally, a statistical comparison would be made between the predictor and the actual success of the employees on the job. If the correlation is strong, managers could say they identified an accurate predictor.

One example of how this works comes from research conducted on the Five-Factor Model. In this research, scholars found a very high level of significance between the predictability of some factors to actual performance on the job.[5]

On the other hand, practice has shown that the traditional staffing agency's selection criteria, such as training and experience, work poorly in predicting employee performance.[6] To facilitate job selection, the U.S. Department of Labor has developed the Occupational Information Network (O*NET), a computerized base of data on modern occupations. The research on potential O*NET applications provides examples of how organizations can use the data gathered through analysis of contemporary jobs in developing content- or criterion-related selection strategies.[7]

Content Validity. By using the criterion-related validity approach, a hospitality company can determine if a test measures the performance required in a job, but the company still may not know if an applicant can perform the entire job. **Content validity**, however, measures the overall ability of an applicant to perform the *entire* job. Unlike the predictive and concurrent methods, the content validity approach relies on the opinions of experts.

Content validity usually requires five steps:

1. Completion of a job analysis

2. Development of a test

3. Presentation of the test to a panel of experts for verification

4. Additions to or deletions from the test by the experts

5. Verification of validity and completeness of the modified test with current employees

To better understand this process, let's look at an example:

> XYZ Hotels is advertising for a server position. The position requires servers to greet guests, suggest products, take orders, and serve guests. Four people have applied. Since Jessica makes a great first impression, she would be excellent at greeting guests. Kate excels in describing products and taking orders. John is great at serving guests and attending to their needs during the meal. Colleen is good at each of these tasks but not as good at any single task as any of the other three. Which one should you hire?

You create a test to measure the probability of success as a server. If that test emphasizes making a strong first impression, you will likely hire Jessica. If it measures the ability to sell the hotel's products and take orders, you will probably hire Kate. If the test measures service during the meal, John will likely get the best score. However, since each of these three applicants have skills limited to certain parts of the job, they will probably be poor hires. Colleen, on the other hand, whose skills are second-best for each individual part of the job, is the best overall. However, Colleen will not be hired *unless* the test measures overall ability. This measure of overall ability is known as content validity.

The validity of tests or assessment devices used in personnel selection is usually evaluated in terms of the correlation between scores on a test and scores on some performance measure. There have literally been thousands of studies on the validity of selection.[8] The key to usable validity is determining whether the device is a good determinant of performance. While many different forms of validity assessments are available, some are quite complicated. A good measure of validity is something that measures at the 95 percent confidence interval (meaning there is only a five percent chance that something else could happen by accident).[9] Robertson and Smith's meta-analytical study on the theory and practice of selection indicates that an increased validity of procedures represents the most significant change that has lately occurred in the field of personnel selection.[10] Research indicates that personality assessment, as a method of selection, is especially vulnerable to validation errors due to a plethora of personality tests that the contemporary market offers to organizations.[11]

A Reminder

While reliability and validity sound like academic concepts, in reality, they are not. Both are critical issues in determining the best selection procedures for a situation. Some companies are very sophisticated in determining the reliability and validity of their selection methods; they make and regularly update statistical correlations to pinpoint the extent to which their techniques work. Companies that do little to ensure that their methods are reliable and valid will probably have higher turnover rates and legal problems related to their selection process. Turnover can result from hiring the wrong person for the job; legal problems can develop from trying to terminate that wrong person.

Selection Steps ———————————————————————

Many hospitality organizations now have human resources departments complete with managers who plan and develop effective selection systems. In addition, these human resources professionals may actually conduct much of the selection process. In the majority of hospitality organizations, however, selection still falls to the line manager for whom the employee will eventually work.

Effective selection is one of management's most important functions. Managers should observe four principles when selecting employees:

- *Explicitness.* Be sure that everyone involved has a clear picture of the desired employee. Whether selecting two or ten people, the criteria should not change

Exhibit 1   Basic Steps in Filling a Job

1.	Identify the opening.
2.	Review job description for clarity and responsibilities.
3.	Review job specifications for qualifications.
4.	Identify sources for applicant recruitment.
5.	Review applications.
6.	Select interviewing environment.
7.	Select interviewing strategy.
8.	Develop interview questions.
9.	Conduct interview.
10.	Close interview.
11.	Evaluate candidate.
12.	Check references.

along the way. The more explicit the criteria, the more likely you are to find who you want.

- *Objectivity.* The entire hiring process must be quantifiable, from start to finish. Whenever possible, give the applicants numerical scores to let them know how they are faring in the process compared to your criteria for selection. Using an evaluation technique that is not totally objective can lead to poor employee selection and to legal problems.

- *Thoroughness.* All selection processes must be thorough. All should include three phases: initial screening, interviewing and testing, and a meeting with the primary decision-maker.

- *Consistency.* A continuity of people, purpose, and procedures throughout the selection process will produce much better results. In addition, this consistency will allow the company to make selections based on valued criteria and to avoid potential legal pitfalls by keeping the process fair and unbiased.[12] A 2004 study on criterion-related validity of the multiple hurdles strategy (see the next section) provides mathematical formulas that allow users to overcome validation restrictions known as self-selection bias, and attrition.[13]

Selection also involves a complex series of steps. Exhibit 1 shows the basic steps involved in filling a job vacancy. Not every person who applies for a job goes through all these steps; some applicants are weeded out along the way. Legally, hospitality companies must accept and dutifully consider every application for employment. Companies, too, have a legal right to establish policies that curtail selection if an applicant is deemed unsatisfactory at any reasonable point in the process.

The selection method a property uses will determine the length of the selection process. Many hospitality companies use two common approaches to the selection process: the multiple hurdles strategy and the compensatory strategy.

Multiple Hurdles Strategy

The **multiple hurdles strategy** is so named because it allows for elimination of applicants at any stage of the selection process. For example, a job posting for a front desk agent may stipulate that applicants: (1) have experience with the hotel's computerized lodging system, (2) work evenings, and (3) have a working knowledge of Spanish since the property caters to many Spanish-speaking guests. Applicants without experience in the computerized lodging system are disqualified at the first hurdle, those who cannot work evenings are disqualified at the second hurdle, and those without a working knowledge of Spanish are disqualified at the third hurdle. This process is based on the belief that all requirements are critical for job success.

When using multiple hurdles or other selection strategies, managers must prove that the requirements they outline are job related. If they cannot, a company can face illegal discrimination charges. If Spanish-speaking abilities were not truly job related in our scenario, it would be discriminatory to require job applicants to possess the skill. In *Lanning* v. *Southeastern Pennsylvania Transportation Authority*, a 2002 case, a transportation patrol provider was challenged in court for screening out candidates who would not meet a minimum qualification requirement of running 1.5 miles in 12 minutes. Although this requirement adversely affected women, the appellate court upheld that the selection strategy was valid because, while patrolling a transportation site, an employee needs to be able to cover a substantial distance swiftly enough to provide timely support to a fellow patroller.[14]

Compensatory Strategy

Hospitality companies sometimes decide that positions can be filled by candidates who can combine various skills and abilities. Properties with this philosophy may use a **compensatory strategy** during selection. As the name implies, this method is based on the assumption that a candidate's strengths may compensate for weaknesses in other areas.

Let's apply the concept to our previous example at the front desk. Under a compensatory strategy, an applicant for our front desk agent position may be acceptable even though she does not have a working knowledge of Spanish because she speaks another language, has demonstrated the ability to quickly learn languages, and is currently enrolled in a Spanish class. Managers should remember, however, that substituting one skill for another must be done within the legislative guidelines for discrimination. For instance, it would probably be discriminatory to hire a non-Spanish-speaking applicant over another applicant who met each of the listed requirements.

Companies that take a compensatory approach to selection should make provisions to identify such skills as *desirable* qualities rather than *requirements*. This allows for more discretion in selection decisions. As in most discrimination issues, the critical ingredient is the extent to which any practice is followed consistently. For instance, a company could not refuse to hire a candidate who doesn't meet *all* the listed qualifications, then turn around and hire another candidate who meets only compensatory qualifications.

Necessary vs. Sufficient Qualifications

Many hospitality companies make the mistake of identifying only one or a few qualifications for a job. As a result, a candidate might have the necessary qualifications but still fail to meet the needs of the organization for other reasons. Legally, this is a very dangerous issue that can often lead to charges of selection discrimination. To avoid this problem, hospitality companies should meticulously identify all the required and desired qualifications for the position during the job analysis process.[15] Again, consider our front desk agent example. Here, an applicant met two of the qualifications exactly and met the third by virtue of her ability to speak French and to learn languages easily and because of enrollment in a Spanish class. If such qualifications are allowable, the hospitality company must identify them.

Selection Techniques

After determining a selection philosophy, a company can begin to apply selection techniques. While the exact methods and applications of selection techniques vary from organization to organization, most effective selection processes include several techniques. These techniques or stages involve filling out applications, conducting interviews, and making reference checks.

Application Blanks

The purpose of an **application blank** is to learn what applicants have done in the past. Application blanks typically ask a person to report on previous work experience, educational background, employment history, work references, personal references, and other personal data. By collecting information on an applicant's past, an organization assumes it can predict what an applicant will do in the future.

Two important points stand out in a discussion of application blanks. The first concerns the issue of *needed* versus *desirable* information. Application blanks can be too long or too short. Excessively long or complex applications can discourage potential applicants; they also raise concern over whether the issues on the form are truly job related. On the other hand, application blanks that are too short can fail to collect the information needed to assess an applicant's qualifications to do the job.

Throughout the selection process, companies should limit questions to what are known as *bona fide occupational qualifications*. At issue is limiting questions to areas that are job related. A study of 151 Fortune 500 companies found that 98 percent of the application forms used included illegal or questionable items. Another study of 50 national companies found that 48 used forms asking inappropriate questions. The most common errors in both cases involved questions about arrest records, physical disabilities, military records, and education.[16] Generally speaking, questions about marital or family status, age, sex, sexual preferences, race, birthplace, religion, military records, convictions or arrests not related directly to the job, specific types of references (religious or military, for example), and requests for photographs are potentially illegal.

The issue of bona fide occupational qualifications became particularly important after July 26, 1992, when the Americans with Disabilities Act (ADA) became law. In the past, many application blanks included questions such as: "Do you have any handicaps?" "Do you suffer from any permanent ailment or disease?" or "Have you ever suffered a serious accident while on the job?" Some application blanks included sections that asked applicants to identify any disabilities (loss of hearing, sight, and so on). These types of questions are not allowed under the ADA. You may, however, ask about a person's ability to perform the essential functions of the job.

Many hospitality organizations rely on managers to subjectively evaluate the information contained on the application blank; this is unnecessary. Two types of application blanks—weighted application blanks and biographical information blanks—help make evaluation more objective.

Weighted Application Blanks. Weighted application blanks (WAB) attempt to identify issues that are important to actual performance on the job. In that sense, weighted application blanks are predictors of job performance. Creating a WAB begins with a thorough analysis of each job. The purpose of this analysis is to determine which characteristics are required to effectively perform each job. Normally, this process is confirmed by what amounts to trial and error. After completing a job analysis to determine the characteristics and aptitudes an employee needs, a WAB is created that reflects the most desirable qualifications. After using the form for some time, a company tracks the work history of each new hire to determine the relationship between actual performance on the job and the performance predicted by the weighted application. In this way, the weighting on the application blank can be validated, and changes can be made on subsequent forms.

Biographical Information Blanks. While weighted application blanks emphasize work experience, **biographical information blanks (BIB)** identify factual material, attitudes, life experiences, and social values that may make an applicant more desirable. Typical biographical information blanks—also known as biodata blanks—include a series of multiple-choice questions designed to elicit such information. Because the courts consider hiring decisions based on attitudes, life experiences, and social values to be subjective, BIBs should be used with caution and only with the advice of competent legal counsel.

While general and weighted application blanks produce verifiable information, biographical information blanks produce unverifiable responses. Nonetheless, many biodata approaches have been very successful predictors of performance on the job. For instance, the single question, "Did you ever build model airplanes that flew?" was nearly as good a predictor of success in flight training during World War II as was the entire battery of psychological and other selection tests used.[17] And, while unproven to date, a question such as: "Did you enjoy cooking with your mother or father as a child?" could be a strong predictor of success in a cook's position.

Another example of biodata that appears to work is high school grade point average (GPA) as a predictor of grade success in college; those with high GPAs in high school are more likely to earn high GPAs in college. Fiedler's Least Preferred Co-Worker (LPC) test provides us with a third example. This approach tests situational leadership styles and can work as a predictor in certain situations.[18]

In Fiedler's LPC test, managers describe their "least preferred co-worker"—or the employee they would least like to work with. Fiedler's theory is that managers who describe least preferred co-workers in *favorable* terms have great concern for human relations. According to Fiedler, these managers are most likely to have strong, positive, supportive, and caring emotional bonds with their employees. On the other hand, those managers who describe least preferred co-workers in *unfavorable* terms are most likely to display weak human relations skills, to adopt more authoritative or autocratic managerial roles, and to place task demands over employee needs or preferences.

Both weighted application blanks and biographical information blanks must conform to guidelines of the Equal Employment Opportunity Commission (EEOC). The key "test" of these guidelines is how accurately the application blank predicts performance on the job. The company or organization must also ensure that applications do not cover issues that can be construed as illegally discriminatory.

Pre-Employment Tests

Tests are an attractive selection method because they allow candidates to be compared easily. For instance, a candidate who scores 90 on a paper-and-pencil test designed to evaluate applicants would appear more attractive than a candidate who scores 80. Tests were used widely in the 1950s and 1960s as selection devices. General intelligence and mechanical comprehension tests were especially popular during this period. However, using tests to evaluate job applicants can often lead to serious charges of discrimination.

Tests became the focus of many discrimination suits after the passage of Title VII of the Civil Rights Act in 1964. Specific guidelines for testing were established through the *Uniform Guidelines on Employee Testing*, set forth as part of Title VII. One of the more important guidelines pertains to test validity. All selection procedures must demonstrate a strong relatedness to the actual work done. Tests are no exception. Companies must be able to show that the tests they use are valid for the application. In many court cases, firms using tests as selection devices could not prove that the results were valid predictors of job success.

Discrimination is the second overriding issue in testing. Tests can inadvertently discriminate against certain protected groups. Hospitality employers should be particularly careful to avoid discrimination since women and minorities constitute a large percentage of hospitality job applicants.

Regardless of past problems, tests can sometimes be a practical way to legally determine the best applicant. The next section describes several tests that may apply in different hospitality settings.

Paper-and-Pencil Tests. Paper-and-pencil tests require written responses to either written or oral questions posed to a job candidate. Both multiple choice and essay formats have been used successfully. While some companies still hire psychologists to develop and validate tests specifically designed for their own work environments, many companies simply purchase standardized paper-and-pencil tests. The most popular tests of this type today measure cognitive abilities: general intelligence, abstract reasoning, numerical ability, verbal ability, clerical ability, and mechanical aptitude. Because courts have focused on such selection devices in the past, hospitality companies should pay careful attention to the tests they use and how they use them. Also, some states prohibit or regulate the use of these tests. Companies can evaluate the characteristics of a published test by answering five questions:[19]

1. Does the test measure aptitudes and abilities needed for the job?

2. Are the tests reliable?

3. Are proper test development procedures used in the design?

4. Are the tests easy to administer?

5. What is the past success of the test (especially regarding EEOC proceedings)?

Honesty Tests. Because workplace theft amounts to tens of billions of dollars per year, many employers are interested in testing the honesty of each job candidate. This is especially true in industries where ample opportunity exists for employee theft. Many consider hospitality a theft-prone industry since employees have chances to steal both products and money almost every day.

Some **honesty tests** measure attitudes toward honesty by posing a hypothetical situation in which the potential employee makes a value judgment. For instance, a common follow-up question to a situation involving money that is lost by a guest and then found by an employee might be: "Do you think it is wrong to keep the money?" Another form of honesty testing evaluates a candidate's candor—or, more appropriately, lack of candor—and propensity to lie. In some of these tests, the principal method involves posing either negative statements that are true about most people or positive statements that are false about most people; then the candidates are asked to identify how often their behavior mirrors that described. For instance, a question might be: "Do you ever have bad thoughts that you would not want to tell others about?" Statistically speaking, most people do. The theory is that a candidate who responds "no" is probably lying and has a low propensity toward candor. However, an honesty test means little if it is not job related.

Some researchers, educators, and managers feel that honesty tests are effective. Believe it or not, these sources say, many people *will* admit to theft or other dishonesty when asked about it directly.[20] These tests are relatively easy to interpret, which makes them attractive to some companies. However, like paper-and-pencil tests, some states prohibit or regulate the use of honesty tests.

Another common form of honesty testing is the polygraph exam, also known as the lie detector test. This exam is reliable in 60 to 70 percent of its applications. Polygraph tests were popular in the hospitality industry in the mid-1980s. Their popularity has since waned due to unreliability and possible legal ramifications.

Much of the debate surrounding polygraphs was muted on December 27, 1988, when the U.S. Congress passed the Employee Polygraph Protection Act. This act prohibits polygraphs in about 85 percent of employment situations. Generally speaking, polygraph tests are now allowed only when applicants are applying for state, local, or federal government positions or for positions with companies under contract with the Department of Defense, the FBI, or the CIA. Employers may still request polygraph tests under a very narrow exception that permits employers to investigate economic loss or injury in cases when reasonable suspicion of an employee is involved and the employee is afforded other protections. Even under these conditions, examinees have the right to refuse tests and to discontinue a test after it has begun; they also have the right to prohibit the disclosure of test results to unauthorized persons.

Physical and Motor Ability Tests. In the past, employers could subject applicants to physical exams as a part of the selection process. However, due to potential discrimination against people with disabilities, the ADA eliminates most of the conditions in which exams are allowed. Some **physical and motor ability tests** that are specifically job related (for instance, the ability to lift objects for bell staff) may still be admissible.

Body Fluid Tests. According to the U.S. Chamber of Commerce, drug and alcohol abuse cost the country approximately $246 billion per year in lost productivity, or $965 for every man, woman, and child in the U.S. Of this, alcohol ($148 billion) accounts for a larger share of losses than illegal drugs ($98 billion).[21] Even though the cost is high, many companies have decided not to compromise on efforts to curtail drug abuse. Currently, some companies are addressing the issue of drug abuse in the workplace by using **body fluid tests.**

Most companies use drug testing during the selection process. In 1987, approximately 21 percent of U.S. companies tested for drug use.[22] In 2004, 72 percent of companies conducted drug tests. The number of drug tests that turn up positive has declined steadily, from 13.6 percent in 1988 to 4.5 percent in 2004, and to 4.3 percent in the first half of 2005.[23] More than 50 percent of all positive tests conducted by testing lab Quest Diagnostics during the first half of 2005 turned up marijuana. In second and third place in the Quest Index, respectively, were cocaine (15.2 percent of all positive tests conducted for the total U.S. work force) and amphetamines (10.6 percent), which includes methamphetamine or "meth." Depending on location, company culture, and other factors, meth and cocaine vie for second place in popularity within the United States.[24]

Meth use has increased quickly in the United States. According to recent statistics, more than 12 million Americans have tried it, and 1.5 million use it regularly. Police have found meth-making operations in all 50 states; in Missouri, police seized more than 8,000 labs, equipment caches, and toxic dumps between 2002 and 2004. Nationwide, 58 percent of police said meth is their biggest drug problem; 19 percent said cocaine is; 17 percent cited marijuana; and 3 percent, heroin.[25]

The Drug-Free Workplace Act of 1988 requires federal contractors to establish policies and procedures to ensure their organizations are free of drug abuse and to make good-faith efforts to sustain drug-free working environments. Among the requirements are publication of company rules about drug possession and use of controlled substances, establishment of drug awareness and drug abuse prevention programs, and administration of appropriate discipline for employees convicted of drug charges. This act does not require all employers to follow these guidelines. However, given the mood of the country toward drug abuse—and the realization by employers of the cost of such abuse—it is likely that federal and state legislation providing for drug-free work environments will be passed in the near future.

Drug testing is costly. Although urine tests are relatively inexpensive ($15 to $20 per exam), they have a high rate of failure. According to the *Los Angeles Times* news service, a study of 161 prescription and over-the-counter medications showed that 65 of them produced false positive results in the most widely used urine test. The number of false positive results averaged about 32.2 percent. Included in these 65 medications were painkillers, cough medicines, nasal sprays, night-time cold medicines, anxiety drugs, and other commonly available drugs.[26]

More reliable tests are available. Gas chromatography-mass spectrometry tests are almost 100 percent accurate. These tests detect the molecular "fingerprint" of drugs. However, their cost is fairly high ($50 to $100 per test). Employers must ask themselves a big question: Is the cost of the test worth the potential loss they could suffer if they hired a drug user?

Companies should exercise great care before implementing any drug testing program. Drug testing carries serious potential for discrimination. Consider what could happen if a company tested only certain groups of employees it considered "high-risk." If a company implements drug testing, it must test *all* applicants.

The National Clearinghouse for Drug and Alcohol Information suggests that employers use the tip sheets shown in Exhibit 2 for information on drug programs.

Work Samples. By definition, **work sample tests** measure a candidate's ability to perform the skills and tasks associated with a specific job. The most commonly used work sample test requires a candidate for a clerical position to take a typing test. Work sample tests are one of the most reliable predictors of success on the job because applicants are asked to perform or simulate specific tasks they would do on the job.

Such tests can be extremely useful in many areas of the hospitality industry. Consider the case of a Southeastern college that manages a lodging facility. In its advertisement for a chef, the college specified that the applicant would need to demonstrate cooking skills. Later, each applicant was actually asked to prepare a meal for the search committee.

Companies must consider two issues when using work sample tests. First, the test must have content validity. This means that the test must measure job performance skills that are actually useful on the job. Second, it can be difficult to establish acceptable standards for work sample tests. Companies should conduct a thorough job analysis to determine exactly what level of competence is required on the job before subjecting any applicants to a test.

While work sample tests are often predictive of success, they can be misused. As a result, such tests can come under close scrutiny by the EEOC. Employers who

Exhibit 2   Alcohol and Drug Information Tip Sheets for Employers

Name of Tip Sheet	What It Does
1. Why Should You Care About Having a Drug-Free Workplace?	Describes the reasons for and benefits of a drug-free workplace program
2. The Components of a Drug-Free Workplace Program	Provides a brief overview of the components of a drug-free workplace program
3. Hallmarks of Successful Drug-Free Workplace Programs	Suggests ways to ensure successful implementation of your program
4. Drug-Free Workplace Programs. Are They Worth the Time? What Are the Risks, Costs, and Benefits?	Helps employers assess the costs, risks, and benefits of starting a program
5. Creating a Drug-Free Workplace Policy	Explains the basics of developing a policy that is tailored to your organization's needs
6. Employee Education	Suggests ways to provide alcohol and other drug abuse education in the workplace: who, what, when, where, and why
7. Supervisor Training	Provides guidelines for training supervisors and outlines their roles and responsibilities
8. Employee Assistance Programs (EAPs)	Describes options for developing an EAP and gives tips for finding a qualified EAP provider
9. Drug Testing	Provides information and guidance to help develop a sensible and reliable drug testing program
10. Outside Help and Consultants: Do You Need Them? How To Find Them...What They Cost	Discusses options for enlisting the help of consultants as well as ways to find them
11. Avoiding Problems With Alcohol, Tobacco, and Other Drugs: Making Prevention Work	Provides 13 action steps toward preventing alcohol and other drug use in the workplace
12. Evaluating Your Program	Shows ways to evaluate the success of your drug-free workplace program

The National Clearinghouse for Alcohol and Drug Information. www.health.org:80/govpubs/workit/tip.htm.

choose this method of selection should give all applicants the same tests, under the same conditions, and should not discriminate against any protected group. Employers must also review their legal liability before administering such tests. Work sample tests can sometimes place applicants at risk of physical injury—for example, an applicant for a cook's position is at risk when demonstrating chopping skills with a knife.

Assessment Centers. Assessment centers were originally designed by the U.S. Office of Strategic Services and the British War Office during World War II to assess candidates for high stress assignments. Because of their cost, assessment centers are typically used to predict managerial performance rather than line-level employee success.

The idea behind **assessment centers** is to place applicants in a series of real-life situations in which they make decisions and take action. Typically, observers watch the performance of each candidate and make subjective evaluations of their performance. In most cases, the assessment center approach takes from one to two-and-a-half days to conduct. This is part of the reason for the high cost. Applicants complete in-basket exercises (exercises that ask applicants to rank, order, and respond to items in a "to-do" file), work in leaderless groups, complete computer simulations, role play, attend problem-solving meetings that emphasize creativity and other leadership traits, and so on—much as they would do at work.

Three to five observers are usually required to implement an effective assessment center. These observers take notes on the performance of each person. After the participants finish, the observers meet and compare their notes. Many times, observers work as a group to rank attributes they observe in each candidate.

Each term, the School of Hotel Administration at Cornell University puts a group of graduate students through the assessment center approach to identify both good and bad qualities in these future managers. Students find the method effective—even if they do not perform well—since they each receive individualized feedback. Even if a student is not chosen for a particular management assignment, the evaluation process itself provides helpful goals to work toward. Once again, job-relatedness and validity are important issues to consider when using assessment centers to evaluate applicants.

Reference Checks and Recommendations

Checking references and recommendations is an integral part of the selection process. There are numerous reasons for collecting and verifying information. For instance, some sources claim that as many as 30 percent of the résumés in the United States include at least one major fabrication. Many of these fabrications involve education, work experience, or equipment use. One retired FBI DipScam (diploma scam) task force expert estimated that diploma mills generate more than $500 million dollars per year in revenues. Further, it is likely that more than one million Americans have purchased, and probably use, fake credentials.[27] Those numbers have increased with the growth of the Internet and globalization. It is now about as easy to set up a fake university as it is to set up a Web site.[28]

Ways to Find, Hook, Land, and Keep Employees

The National Restaurant Association conducted a survey at the end of 1998 on what the major challenges of restaurants were. At that time, all segments of restaurants listed their top challenge as "finding qualified labor." Prior studies had determined such challenges as "competition" and "maintaining business volume." The decline in unemployment nationwide has caused some of this problem, of course. However, there are also fewer and fewer applicants for hospitality jobs because these potential employees choose other fields in which to work.

According to the study by the National Restaurant Association, operators had preferred the following methods of selecting employees.

Average Guest Check Size

Selection method	Less than $8	$8.00-14.99	$15-24.99	$25 and more
Written application	97 %	94 %	97 %	95 %
Structured interview	91	93	96	5
Reference check	86	85	87	94
Background check	60	56	53	67
Personality tests	28	26	23	26
Skills tests	18	15	21	43
Job simulation	21	18	18	19
Drug test	8	11	8	20
Assessment center	6	5	4	8

Source: Bruce Grindy, "Hooking and Keeping Employees," *Restaurants USA*, October 1998, pp. 22–27.

References can be personal or professional. While many companies still collect personal references, many companies see it as a waste of time. These companies feel that since little is known about the references, information from them would likely be of minimal value. However, professional and educational references are a different story.

Professional references relate directly to the work history of an applicant. While most of these references will report only employment dates and position responsibilities, this information is often valuable in creating a profile of the applicant. However, this information is offered with a caution. In 1995, there were over 2,000 claims of defamation of character in California, based on information given in reference checks.

Exhibit 3 shows an example of one form to use when compiling reference checks.

What Type of Information to Release

A survey by the Society for Human Resource Management revealed that most of the information released on **reference checks** relates to employment dates (96

Exhibit 3   Sample Employment Reference Release

Employer Tip Sheet

I acknowledge that I have been informed that it is [Your Business's] general policy to disclose in response to a prospective employer's request only the following information about current or former employees: (1) the dates of employment, (2) descriptions of the jobs performed, and (3) salary or wage rates.

By signing this release, I am voluntarily requesting the [Your Business] depart from this general policy in responding to reference requests from any prospective employer that may be considering me for employment. I authorize employment-related information that [Your Business], in its sole discretion and judgment, may determine is appropriate to disclose, including any personal comments, evaluations, or assessments that [Your Business] may have about my performance or behavior as an employee.

In exchange for [Your Business's] agreement to depart from its general policy and to disclose additional employment-related information pursuant to my request, I agree to release and discharge [Your Business] and [Your Business's] successors, employees, officers, and directors for all claims, liabilities, and causes of action, known or unknown, fixed or contingent, that arise from or that are in any manner connected to [Your Business's] disclosure of employment-related information to prospective employers. This release includes, but is not limited to, claims of defamation, libel, slander, negligence, or interference with contract or profession.

I acknowledge that I have carefully read and fully understand the provisions of this release. I further acknowledge that I was given the opportunity to consult with an attorney or any other individual of my choosing before signing this release and that I have decided to sign this release voluntarily and without coercion or duress by any person.

This release sets forth the entire agreement between [Your Business] and me, and I acknowledge that I have not relied upon any representation or statement, written or oral, not set forth in this document.

Signed:_____ Date:_____
       (Employee)

Reference Check Control Form

Applicant Name:_____ Position:_____

Personal references checked:

Name:_____ Relationship:_____

Address:_____

Telephone:_____ Date Contacted:_____ Method of Contact_____

Notes:_____

Name:_____ Relationship:_____

Address:_____

Telephone:_____ Date Contacted:_____ Method of Contact_____

Notes:_____

Exhibit 3 *(continued)*

Employment references checked:	
Name:_____	Employer:_____
Relationship:_____	Dates of employment:_____
_____	Pay:_____

Address:_____

Telephone:_____ Date Contacted:_____ Method of Contact_____

Would you rehire:_____ Reason for termination:_____

Notes:_____

Name:_____ Employer:_____

Relationship:_____ Dates of employment:_____

_____ Pay:_____

Address:_____

Telephone:_____ Date Contacted:_____ Method of Contact_____

Would you rehire:_____ Reason for termination:_____

Notes:_____

Records Checked:

School records (date requested:_____) Notes:_____

Criminal records (date requested:_____) Notes:_____

Driving records (date requested:_____) Notes:_____

Credit records (date requested:_____) Notes:_____

Source: http://client.lycos.com/cch/tools/rfrncrel.rtf.

percent) or position-responsibility issues (89 percent).[29] Much lower response rates occur for issues that could be more valuable to employment selection decisions. Such issues and the corresponding response rates include salary information (43 percent), reason for leaving (30 percent), performance evaluation information (six percent), medical history (one percent), and rehire eligibility (three percent).

The reasons for this are obvious—we live in a litigious society. Many employers are reluctant to report on an employee's past performance for fear of someday ending up in court with that person. Some suggest that the safest route to take is to report information only on dates of employment, job title, absentee record, promotions and demotions, compensation, and stated reasons for termination—and only if the express written permission from the former employee is on file. Unfortunately, even such factual information can lead to an unforeseen legal entanglement.

Regardless of these problems, companies should ask applicants to sign waivers that grant permission to contact references, check court records, and verify educational histories and other credentials. These waivers should include a statement about releasing all involved from any liability. While they may not be lawsuit-proof, such waivers can be very helpful.

Some companies use outside agencies to check applicant references. Most reference checks can be completed within 24 hours for a reasonable sum.

Credit Reference Checks

Many companies use **credit reference checks** to evaluate the character of job applicants. The company simply calls the credit bureau and gives the Social Security number the applicant provided. Many application blanks include a clause granting the company permission to check on an applicant's credit, and may include space for applicants to list credit references. However, employers should know that this practice has come under close scrutiny for its potential to violate individual privacy provisions of the Fair Credit Reporting Act. Also, the subject of the credit check must be notified, given a copy of the credit reference report, and allowed a chance to correct any discrepancies.

Third-Party Reference Checks

Third-party pre-employment background checks can cost as little as $75, depending on the depth of information required. Many businesses in the United States now use outside agencies to conduct reference checks. While many hotel managers view reference checking as a necessary evil, such work is the principal function of these agencies, which conduct reference checks with professional expertise.

Negligent Hiring

Failure to conduct a thorough reference check can leave an employer open to litigation for **negligent hiring**—commonly defined as an employer's failure to exercise reasonable care in the selection of its employees. *Restaurants USA* reports that it is becoming increasingly common for employers to be sued for not taking reasonable precautions to protect their guests from the actions of employees. Restaurant delivery companies have been sued, for instance, for criminal acts committed by delivery drivers. Hotels have been successfully sued for actions taken against guests by maintenance and other employees with access to guestrooms and other secluded settings. Such cases can be very costly. A Texas taxicab company lost $4.5 million in a lawsuit involving a cab driver who picked up a woman and her small children, drove them to a deserted area and raped and assaulted the mother. The cab driver had a record of assault and battery; the courts ruled that the cab company should have known the driver was a risk.[30]

A Florida law, which became effective in October 1999, allows a legal presumption in favor of an employer in "negligent hiring" cases. The law does this by clarifying steps employers should take for background checks when hiring. The key in negligent hiring cases, of course, is that the employer "should have known." In effect, this tort reform package allows an employer to utilize a presumption against negligent hiring in a civil action regarding death, injury, or damage to a third person caused by an "intention tort" of an employee. Intention torts are claims such as battery, assault, false imprisonment, and invasion of privacy. To take advantage of this presumption, the pre-employment background investigation must include:

- a criminal background investigation

- a reasonable effort by the employer to contact references and former employers concerning the suitability of the applicant

- completion of a job application form that includes questions about whether the applicant has ever been convicted of a crime (including details of the crime)

- obtaining, with written permission from the applicant, a check of the driver's license record of the prospective employee

- interviewing the prospective employee

According to the Florida statutes, when employers take each of these steps in their effort to properly select the right employees, they are afforded a valuable defense in any potential negligent hiring cases involving the employee in the future.[31]

Methods of Collecting Reference Information

Telephone inquiries, written recommendations, and personal interviews represent the principal methods of collecting reference information. Each method has advantages and disadvantages.

Telephone Reference Checks. Telephone contact is the simplest—but least successful—method for checking references. Many references are reluctant to provide information over the telephone to someone they do not know. A prospective employer can partially overcome this problem by asking applicants to alert former employers that a telephone reference check may be conducted on a designated date. Exhibit 4 shows a form that managers can use in conjunction with a telephone reference check.

Written Reference Checks. Written reference checks can be initiated by either the applicant or the prospective company. Generally, reference forms include a portion for verifying an individual's strengths and weaknesses. Most forms also include a waiver of an individual's Privacy Act rights to view the report. Applicants complete this portion before the form is mailed to references.

While written reference checks take a manager little time to process, such inquiries are frequently not answered. Many former employers are leery about responding in writing to requests for information on former employees since these files are potentially open to employee inspection. Exhibit 5 shows a sample employment verification form.

Personal Interviews. The most infrequently used method of collecting information about an applicant is the face-to-face personal interview with an applicant's references. While some government agencies use this method extensively, the time and cost of such an approach prevents many private sector employers from using the method except in important or unusual circumstances.

Exhibit 4 Sample Telephone Reference Form

TELEPHONE EMPLOYMENT VERIFICATION

Date _____ *25 March 20XX* _____

Applicant's name _____ *Jerry Hannah* _____

Company ____ *Seasons Resort* _____

Dates employed: From: _____ *09/XX* _____ To: _____ *Present* _____

Position ____ *Room Attendant* _____

Reason for leaving ____ *Pending move to the area* _____

Would you rehire? ____ *Yes* _____

Person verifying ____ *Emily Crawford* _____

Telephone number of company ____ *(921) 555-1212* _____

Comments ____ *Able to start after giving a two-week notice* _____

The Right to Privacy

Throughout a reference check process, employers should maintain a genuine concern for the applicant's privacy. In fact, a number of states have legitimized this concern by attempting to protect an employee's or potential employee's right to privacy. As a general rule, employers should review the appropriate state legislation regarding privacy before undertaking any action.

Employers should always get permission from former employees before releasing any information about them. The best rule of thumb is to secure written permission from individuals for the release of specific information and to limit responses to those areas for which permission has been granted. Individuals have gained the right to know what is contained in their personnel files maintained by the federal government (Privacy Act of 1974), as well as the nature and substance of their credit reports (Fair Credit Reporting Act). In addition, students may now inspect education records, and universities are prohibited from disclosing information about students without written consent. As a result, postsecondary institutions will release student information (grades, etc.) only to the student unless the student instructs otherwise in writing.

Trends clearly point toward more open disclosure laws. In the near future, it is likely that employees will have the right to inspect any files kept on them by

Exhibit 5   Sample Employment Verification Form

EMPLOYMENT VERIFICATION

I hereby authorize the Seasons Resort to verify my employment history with your company.

_____
Signature
Jerry Hannah
_____
Print Name
123-456-7890
_____
Social Security Number

Employed from _____ to _____

Job Title: _____

How would you rate this employee?_____

_____

_____

Why did this employee leave your company?

_____

_____

Would you rehire? [   ] Yes   [   ] Questionable   [   ] No

If questionable or no, please explain_____

_____

_____

Comments _____

_____

Signed _____

Title _____   Date _____

---

employers in the private sector and will be able to respond to negative or derogatory information contained in them. Many states already have statutes to this effect. If the private sector becomes subject to legislation similar to current federal laws, employers will be prohibited from collecting any information that is not directly related to job performance.

Employment Interviews

The overall goal of an employment interview is the attraction, selection, and retention of a highly competent employee. Attraction is achieved when the organization creates or enhances a positive image of the company. Selection is carried out when the company predicts who is and who is not likely to succeed in a job. Retention is enhanced when a company projects an accurate first impression of the position, including a clear description of job objectives and responsibilities.

While employment interviews are by far the most common method of evaluating applicants—and for predicting success—there is also reason to believe that they are the most unreliable. While several problems are associated with interviews, the most notable is the lack of **inter-rater reliability**. What this means is that if two people interviewed the same candidate, they would probably not make the same conclusions. Both might agree on general issues, on overall assessments such as "outstanding" or "poor," and on factual issues such as past performance, but probably would not agree on more subjective issues such as likelihood of success in the job.

Not all experts concur on this appraisal of employment interviewing. Some researchers believe that the reliability of the interviewing process has increased significantly since managers are more aware of and educated about how to interview properly and effectively. In addition, when interviewers are aware of internal and external factors that can distort an interview, they can better prevent them, thereby increasing the probability of a successful interview.

Problems with Interviews

The distortion associated with employment interviews often results from the variable conditions under which interviews are conducted. Interviewers vary in their approaches. Even the best-trained interviewers operate under constraints that range from organizational to situational.[32] Some feel that one way to improve the reliability of interviews is to standardize or structure interview techniques. However, as one expert notes:

> …(the) interview context is more than the standardization of interview content. It also includes interviewer and organizational efforts, conscious or unconscious, that alter the context within which the interview is conducted (e.g., allotted interview length, relative importance of candidate attraction and/or selection, decision accountability).[33]

The following sections outline some of the problems associated with interviewing reliability.

Similarity Error. Interviewers are likely to make **similarity errors;** that is, they are likely to be attracted to candidates who are similar to them in terms of outside interests, personal background, and even appearance. In addition, interviewers are often negatively disposed to people who are different from them. Even similarities and dissimilarities that are not job related can result in an interviewer's selective opinions about candidates.

Contrast Error. It is common to interview several candidates for the same position and to compare the candidates with one another, either consciously or subconsciously. However, candidates should be compared not to one another, but to the standards a company has established for the successful candidate. Assume that two poor applicants are followed by an average candidate. Because of the contrast between candidates, the average applicant may incorrectly be viewed as excellent. This type of misevaluation is called a **contrast error.**

Overweighing Negative Information. Unfortunately, we are more likely to note negative rather than positive information. This means that when we examine a résumé or an application, we tend to look for the negative—not the positive. This also occurs in interviews; an interviewer is more likely to notice and remember the negative than the positive.

Race, Sex, and Age Bias. Because of the similarity error, interviewers are more likely to be positive toward candidates who are the same race, sex, and age as themselves in some cases. However, a 1999 study on this has shown there is no existing racial bias exhibited by either black or white decision-makers.[34]

First Impression Error. Many interviewers form a strong first impression of a candidate that they maintain throughout the interview. This **first impression error** can be based on first appearance and even on the information they have about a candidate before they actually meet.

Halo Effect. Sometimes an interviewer's impression of a single positive dimension about a candidate—appearance, performance in a single task, or background—can substantially color the interviewer's overall impression. The **halo effect** occurs when an interviewer views everything that a candidate says or does in this favorable light.

Devil's Horns. The opposite is true with **devil's horns**. A single negative trait or impression often causes interviewers to see everything a candidate says or does in an unfavorable light.

Faulty Listening and Memory. Interviewers do not always hear what is said in the way that it was intended, nor do they remember everything that was said. In fact, even immediately after an interview, the interviewer may have forgotten as much as 75 percent of what was said. This phenomenon is generally rooted in poor listening habits, failure to take notes during the interview, and preoccupation with what comes next. Taping an interview can reinforce memory but should be done only with the applicant's permission.

Recency Errors. Recency errors relate to the most recent actions of an applicant. An interviewer is likely to remember the most recent behavior or responses of an applicant rather than the behaviors or responses that occurred earlier in the interview. Recency can be a particular problem when interviewing a current employee for a different position within the company. Because the interviewer often has personal knowledge of the applicant, he or she often remembers certain behaviors the candidate has displayed. Typically, the more recent the behavior, the more likely it will be remembered.

Exhibit 6   Common Interpretations of Nonverbal Communication Cues

What You Do and What It Says

Nonverbal Message	Typical Interpretation
Making direct eye contact	Friendly, sincere, self-confident, assertive
Avoiding eye contact	Cold, evasive, indifferent, insecure, passive, frightened, nervous, concealing something
Shaking head	Disagreeing, shocked, disbelieving
Patting on the back	Encouraging, congratulatory, consoling
Scratching the head	Bewildered, disbelieving
Smiling	Contented, understanding, encouraging
Biting the lip	Nervous, fearful, anxious
Tapping feet	Nervous
Folding arms	Angry, disapproving, disagreeing, defensive, aggressive
Raising eyebrows	Disbelieving, surprised
Narrowing eyebrows	Disagreeing, resentful, angry, disapproving
Wringing hands	Nervous, anxious, fearful
Leaning forward	Attentive, interested
Slouching in seat	Bored, relaxed
Sitting on edge of seat	Anxious, nervous, apprehensive
Shifting in seat	Restless, bored, nervous, apprehensive
Hunching over	Insecure, passive
Erect posture	Self-confident, assertive

Source: Diane Arthur, "The Importance of Body Language," *HR Focus* 72 (June 1995): 23.

Interviewer Domination. Information should flow both ways in an interview. In some cases, the interviewer so dominates the process that the applicant fails to collect the information he or she needs to remain interested in a job.

Nonverbal Communication. Nearly 70 percent of communication is nonverbal. Many researchers have shown that nonverbal cues such as clothing, smiles, speech patterns and habits, and appropriate eye contact substantially influence an interviewer's impression of a candidate. A study of recruiting within the hospitality industry shows that interviewers often make up their minds about whom to hire based almost solely on a candidate's attire and demeanor. Interviewers must make a conscious effort to project the right image and other appropriate nonverbal messages; otherwise, they can unfairly influence an applicant's responses. Exhibit 6 demonstrates typical interpretations of some common nonverbal messages.

Premature hiring decisions based on characteristics such as appearance or demeanor alone represent a lack of objectivity associated with interviewing. Other possible problems include a lack of uniformity in the interview process and a lack of training for the interviewer and the interviewee. Despite its problems, interviewing is still the most common selection method. Interviews will likely remain popular because of their widespread use and because they are easy to do. It makes more sense to attempt to improve the reliability of the process than to change the method that so many companies use for selection. One method of improving the process is to use an Applicant Rating Form for each interviewee (see Exhibit 7). This form can help managers determine which applicants excel in the interview areas that matter most. The next few sections provide suggestions for improving the reliability of interviews by addressing how managers can prepare for, choose, and approach various types of interviews.

Preparing for Interviews

Collection of information during an interview can be enhanced substantially by following a few simple rules. The four basic rules are:

1. Do your homework before the interview.

2. Establish the appropriate setting.

3. Establish a rapport.

4. Know the job.

The first rule is to always do your homework *before* meeting with an applicant. Nothing is more distracting than reading from a candidate's résumé during an interview. Lack of knowledge about the candidate sends signals that you either did not care enough to prepare in advance or that you are unorganized. Generally, interviewers should block out whatever time is needed to conduct the interview and create an environment in which the focus is solely on the candidate and the interview. Interruptions (phone calls, walk-ins) are extremely distracting and inappropriate during an interview. The third rule—establish a rapport—is necessary to get the applicant talking. By putting the candidate at ease, the interviewer will learn more during the process. The fourth rule—know the job—calls for a thorough review of the job analysis before an interview. Many might argue that this fourth rule is the most important; they might add that it is impossible to find the right candidate unless the interviewer fully understands the job requirements in advance.

Types of Interviews

Interviews fall into three categories, depending on the interviewer's latitude in the process. The three types are commonly known as unstructured interviews, semi-structured interviews, and structured interviews. These types are also known as non-directive, mixed, and patterned interviews, respectively.

Unstructured Interviews. In **unstructured interviews,** questions are not planned in advance. Instead, the interviewer directs the interview down whatever path seems appropriate at the time. By doing so, the interviewer achieves very little similarity between interviews. This means that interviews with different candidates will likely cover entirely different subjects.

Opinions vary on the value of unstructured interviews. Some experts believe that these interviews have little merit because of the low inter-rater reliability they

Exhibit 7   Sample Applicant Rating Form

APPLICANT RATING FORM

This form can be used to more effectively compare one applicant to another. It is important to capture your impressions of a candidate immediately after interviewing.

Candidate's Name _____

Job Title _____   Date _____

Selection Criteria	Rating										Weighted score	
	Below acceptable level					Acceptable	Good	Outstanding			weight	total
	10	20	30	40	50	60	70	80	90	100		
1. Physical appearance, neatness, grooming												
2. Salary needs												
3. Composure												
4. Dependability												
—Attendance												
—Work habits												
5. Communication ability												
6. Cooperation												
7. Responsibility and initiative												
8. Work experience												
—Experience with similar work												
—Knowledge of tools												
—Knowledge of procedures												

Total _____   Weighted Total _____

achieve. Additionally, those same experts believe that the unstructured method is most likely to skip over important job-related issues and to result in illegal questions. Other experts believe that skilled interviewers can use this method to achieve a better understanding of the candidate since areas can be explored that both structured and semi-structured approaches would miss. Proponents of both perspectives agree that training is essential for interviewers who use a non-directive approach.

Even though there is some question about the validity of the unstructured interview, it is likely the most common method used. Sometimes, interviews are unstructured for the wrong reasons; managers who are poorly prepared often take an unstructured approach to interviewing.

Semi-Structured Interviews. Another type of interview involves preparing or planning the issues to be explored but allowing for flexibility during the process. This structure has been called a "cone" approach—meaning that the interviewer prepares very *broad* questions that relate to *specific* important issues. For example, interviewers might explore a candidate's beliefs about the team approach to work performance versus the individual approach, or about performance on a recent job. Once these "cones" are introduced, the interviewer encourages the candidate to speak more freely about each topic. In this way, the **semi-structured interview** allows for elaboration as well as structured responses.

A critical feature of both unstructured and semi-structured interviews is the use of open-ended questions to elicit additional responses from the candidate. For instance, the closed-ended question, "Did you enjoy your previous job?" requires only a "Yes" or "No" response. The open-ended question, "What aspects of your previous job did you like best?" engages the interviewee and promotes a more comprehensive response.

Structured Interviews. In **structured interviews,** questions are prepared in advance and are asked in the same way and at the same time during the interview. Very little flexibility is allowed. Flexibility is reserved for a period of follow-up questions that an interviewer can ask if a candidate fails to fully address patterned questions.

The structured interview results in answers that are comparable between candidates. As a result, some experts believe that structured interviews provide more reliable and valid information. On the other hand, this approach tends to produce information that is arguably narrower or shallower. Some experts believe that this type of interview is less worthwhile because an interviewer can fail to learn important strengths and weaknesses about a candidate.

Three variations of the structured interview exist. The first is the traditional patterned interview. This type tends to focus on past work experiences, goals, education, and so on. Typically, questions asked during a patterned interview would be something like: "What are your long-term plans?" "What are your strengths and weaknesses?" or "What do you hope to be doing five years from now?"

The situational interview is a variation of the structured interview that uses three types of questions. The first type is situational ("What would you do if your cook failed to show up on a Friday night?" or "What would you do if a guest complained that his or her room was not acceptable?"). The second type of question relates to job knowledge. For instance, a candidate might be asked to define certain terms ("What do we mean by rack rate?") or to explain a procedure. The third type of question relates to a candidate's willingness to perform the work that is necessary on the job ("Are you willing to move to another city?" "Can you work weekends?" "Can you stay on your feet for hours at a time?" and so on).

Another type of patterned interview is called the behavioral description interview. In this method, an interviewer begins by establishing an area of discussion. For instance, he or she might ask an applicant for a front desk position to respond to a question or statement such as: "Tell me about the most difficult shift you worked in your last job." This question would be followed by another that elicits more information on the types of behaviors a candidate is likely to exhibit on the job. Common questions might be: "Why was this shift so difficult?" or "How did you handle the problems that you faced?" The objective of the behavioral description approach is to link past behavior with likely behavior.

Other types of interviews used in certain circumstances include panel or board interviews (also known as group interviews) and **stress interviews**. The first type requires a candidate to be interviewed by a panel or group of interviewers. Group members later compare their notes to arrive at a group decision about the applicant. Stress interviews create a highly charged emotional setting in which a candidate is literally challenged by the interviewer. When using this approach, an interviewer might challenge an applicant's response to a seemingly standard question. Chastisement, belittlement, and even contradiction on the part of the interviewer are common in stress interviews. This approach is useful only for simulating the type of stress applicants might face on the job, for it provides an example of how they may respond under pressure.

Regardless of the interview method, interviewers must know what topics and questions to avoid. Exhibit 8 lists sample lawful and unlawful pre-employment inquiries. Since laws and their interpretation vary from state to state, an attorney should review a property's application and interview procedures to ensure that discriminatory practices do not occur.

Approaches to Interviewing

As well as choosing the general structure of an interview, managers must decide on the general tone they want to set for an interview. There are three common approaches to interviewing. Each might be the best in different situations.

Direct Approach. In the direct approach, interviewers typically ask specific questions that require only yes or no responses. While useful in situations where the exact response is required, this approach leaves little room for learning much about a candidate. Interviewees may also tend to use only "canned" responses that they know interviewers want to hear.

Non-Direct Approach. With this approach, the interviewer encourages the applicant to talk freely about his or her experiences in former jobs, goals for the future,

Exhibit 8   Guide to Pre-Employment Inquiries

INTERVIEW QUESTIONS: WHAT YOU CAN AND CANNOT ASK		
SUBJECT	**PERMISSIBLE INQUIRIES**	**INQUIRIES TO AVOID***
NAME	"Have you ever worked for this company under a different name?" "Is any additional information concerning change of name, use of an assumed name or nickname necessary to enable a check on your work and education record? If yes, explain."	Inquiries about preferred title: Miss, Mrs., Ms. Inquiries about name which would indicate applicant's lineage, ancestry, national origin or descent.
MARITAL & FAMILY STATUS	Whether applicant can meet specified work schedules or has activities, commitments or responsibilities that may hinder meeting attendance requirements. Inquiries concerning duration of stay on job or anticipated absences which are made to both males and females alike.	Any inquiry indicating whether an applicant is married, single, divorced, engaged, etc. Information on childcare arrangements. Any questions which directly or indirectly result in limitation of job opportunities.
AGE	Requiring proof of age in the form of a work permit or a certificate of age if a minor. Requiring proof of age by birth certificate after being hired. Inquiry as to whether or not the applicant meets the minimum age requirements as set by law and requirement that upon hire proof of age must be submitted in the form of a birth certificate or other proof of age. If age is a legal requirement: "If hired, can you furnish proof of age?" or a statement that hire is subject to verification of age.	Requirement that applicant state age or date of birth. Requirement that applicant produce proof of age. The Age Discrimination in Employment Act of 1967 forbids discrimination against persons who are age 40 or older. Avoid any advertising that contains expressed or implied age-based limitations. The EEOC and the courts will determine if the advertisement has the effect of discouraging people aged 40 or older from applying, or if it limits or discriminates on the basis of age in any way.
SEX	Sex of the applicant may be requested (preferably not on the employment application) for affirmative action purposes but may not be used as an employment selection criterion. Inquiry or restriction of employment is permissible only where a bona fide occupational qualification (BFOQ) exists. (This BFOQ exception is	Sex of the applicant. Any other inquiry which would indicate sex of the applicant. For example, a statement which says, "Miss, Mrs., or Mr." Sex is not a BFOQ because a job involves physical labor (such as heavy lifting) beyond the capacity of some women; nor

(continued)

Exhibit 8 *(continued)*

SUBJECT	PERMISSIBLE INQUIRIES	INQUIRIES TO AVOID*
SEX (continued)	interpreted very narrowly by the courts and the EEOC.) The burden of proof rests on the employer to prove that the BFOQ does exist and that all members of the affected class (e.g. females) are incapable of performing the job.	can employment be restricted just because the job is traditionally labeled "men's work" or "women's work." Applicant's sex cannot be used as a factor for determining whether or not an applicant will be satisfied in a particular job. Employers may not request information from female applicants that is not requested from males (such as marital or family status). Sexual harassment is prohibited by Title VII. Unwelcome sexual advances, requests for sexual favors and other verbal or physical conduct of a sexual nature constitute sexual harassment when: 1) submission to such conduct is made either implicitly or explicitly a term or condition of employment; 2) submission to or rejection of such conduct is used as the basis of employment decisions affecting that person; or 3) such conduct substantially interferes with a person's work performance or creates an intimidating, hostile or offensive work environment.
DISABILITY	The Rehabilitation Act of 1973 permits employers to "invite" applicants to indicate how and to what extent they are disabled. Applicants must be informed of the following: 1) compliance with the invitation is voluntary; 2) the information is being sought only to remedy discrimination or provide opportunities for people with disabilities; 3) the information will be kept confidential; and	An employer must be prepared to prove that any physical and mental requirements for a job are due to "business necessity" and the safe performance of the job. Except in cases where undue hardship can be proven, employers must make "reasonable accommodations" for the physical and mental limitations of an employee or applicant, which includes alteration of

Exhibit 8 *(continued)*

SUBJECT	PERMISSIBLE INQUIRIES	INQUIRIES TO AVOID*
DISABILITY (continued)	4) refusing to provide the information will not result in adverse treatment. The Rehabilitation Act and ADA permit all applicants to be asked about their ability to perform job-related functions and whether they can be performed in a safe manner.	duties, alteration of work schedule, transfer to a vacant position, alteration of physical setting and provision of job aids. The Rehabilitation Act and ADA generally forbid employers from asking job applicants general questions about whether they are disabled or asking them about the nature or severity of their disability. Such inquiries, however, are allowed when they can be shown to be job-related and consistent with business necessity.
RACE & COLOR	General distinguishing physical marks (such as scars, etc.) to be used for identification purposes. Race may be requested (preferably not on the employment application) for affirmative action purposes but may not be used as an employment criterion.	Applicant's race. Color of applicant's skin, eyes, hair, etc., or other questions directly or indirectly indicating race or color.
ADDRESS OR DURATION OF RESIDENCE	Applicant's address. Inquiry into length of stay at current and previous addresses. "How long have you been a resident of this state or city?"	Specific inquiry into foreign address which would indicate national origin. Names and relationship of people with whom the applicant resides. Whether applicant rents or owns home.
PLACE OF BIRTH	"Can you, after employment, submit a birth certificate or other proof of U.S. citizenship?"	Birthplace of applicant. Birthplace of applicant's parents, spouse or other relatives. Requirement that applicant submit a birth certificate before employment. Any other inquiry into national origin.
RELIGION	An applicant may be advised by job announcements and advertisements	Applicant's religious denomination or affiliation, church, parish,

(continued)

Exhibit 8   *(continued)*

SUBJECT	PERMISSIBLE INQUIRIES	INQUIRIES TO AVOID*
RELIGION (continued)	concerning normal hours and days of work required by the job to avoid possible conflict with religious or other personal convictions. However, except in cases where undue hardship can be proven, employers and unions must make "reasonable accommodation" for religious practices of an employee or prospective employee. Reasonable accommodation may include voluntary substitutes, flexible scheduling, lateral transfer, change of job assignments or the use of an alternative to payment of union dues.	pastor or religious holidays observed. Any inquiry to indicate or identify religious denomination or customs. Applicants may not be told that any particular religious groups are required to work on their religious holidays. The use of such pre-selection inquiries as "What days and hours are you available for work?" that determine an applicant's availability may be considered by the EEOC to be unlawful unless the employer can show that it: 1) did not have exclusionary effect on the applicant; or 2) was otherwisej ustified by business necessity. Generally, this ban on religious discrimination does not apply to religious institutions.

*These inquiries should be avoided as selection criteria unless it can be proven that a bona fide occupational qualification (BFOQ) or a business necessity is involved (i.e., the inquiry must be job-related).

Source: "What Employers Can Ask," *HR Focus* (June 1995): 4–5.

expectations at work, and so on. The objective is to gain more personal information about candidates. Open-ended questions are used exclusively.

Eclectic Approach. This approach emphasizes both yes/no and open-ended questions. Yes/no questions are used to learn specific background information while open-ended questions are used to allow the candidate to expound on certain topics or areas of interest. The eclectic (or mixed) approach requires interviewers to have more skill than the direct approach since it relies on the use of open-ended questions. Conversely, less skill is required in the eclectic approach than in the non-direct approach since the latter uses only open-ended questions.

Making the Right Impression

Interviewers represent their companies. An interviewer is frequently an applicant's sole contact with a company. In this case, the interviewer represents the type

How to Identify High Performers

Everyone wants high performers. They work harder than average employees. The problem is, how do you find them? You start by envisioning what a high performer would be in your company. It's useful to make two lists—one of low performers and one of high performers—and then compare the two. It's even more useful if both managers and employees are in on this list-making process. After making the list, write down employees' names at the top of the columns. These employees exemplify the qualities of high and low performers. Then hire in the image of the high performers. To make sure you have the right items on the high performers list, you may wish to compare your list to the list prepared below:

- *Examine records carefully.* The application should tell you a lot about the applicant. If it doesn't, don't rule the applicant out. Not everyone can complete an application expertly. Instead, if an application appears incomplete, ask probing questions.

- *Make sure applicants can read.* Up to 40 percent of Americans cannot read at all or are functionally illiterate. Reading tests can come from local newspaper stories. If you like an applicant who cannot read, make sure you refer him or her to a literacy program.

- *Check applicants' math skills.* Most jobs require basic math. However, many applicants cannot perform at this level. Including a basic addition, subtraction, multiplication, and division test in your applicant review process can determine who can and cannot complete basic math problems. However, remember: an applicant who cannot perform math calculations at the level you need is not necessarily a bad hire. She may simply need remedial training to become a high performer.

- *Put assertiveness to the test.* How much do applicants appear to want the job? Are they assertive about their skills and their interest in the job? If so, they may make good customer-contact personnel who can sell your products and services. Remember, you might find that life has thrown an applicant a few curves and he may need self-assurance training or counseling to become a high performer.

- *Verify problem-solving skills.* Give each applicant a problem to solve. Keep it simple but listen to the applicant's reasoning as to how she would attack the problem. Ask applicants how to determine whether their solution would work.

- *Evaluate interpersonal skills.* Begin with whether or not the applicant smiles; observe body language. Does it send positive or negative signals which future customers might observe?

- *Check out social skills.* Does the applicant have good posture, a firm handshake, and good demeanor? Some experts say that if the applicant's handshake is wimpy, so will he be on the job.

- Look for proof of second-mile performance. Ask applicants for instances when they have gone "above and beyond the call of duty." These instances can be at work or in their leisure time. Both are indicators of second-mile performance and a person who is likely to go beyond the minimum requirements of a job.

How to Identify High Performers *(continued)*

- *Be as tough as nails.* Don't be a pushover. Tell the applicant exactly what you want and expect. When you ask a reasonable question, expect a reasonable answer and probe for more if you don't get it.

- *Hire the first good hire.* Even though you may have many applicants to interview, if you have followed guidelines of good management selection and interviewing, hire the first applicant who convinces you he or she is a high performer. Don't lose the chance to hire this person.

This list was adapted from an article by Lewis C. Forrest, Jr., "Hiring High Performers," *MRW Today,* January 1998, pp. 15–18.

of people who work for a company, their behavior, actions that are acceptable and not acceptable, and so on. As a result, a company should be particularly careful in choosing an interviewer.

There are two schools of thought on this subject. The first—and most obvious—claims that since an interviewer sets the image of success for a candidate, only the *best* representatives should be interviewers. This sounds logical. However, a second school of thought suggests that interviewing can also encourage personnel to improve their performance. This theory suggests that, since interviewers are required to project a positive impression of the company, the interview process can prompt an employee to rethink why he or she joined the company. Since interviewers often learn as much about the "outside" as they provide to an applicant about the "inside," the comparison can sometimes help current employees whose performance is mediocre to recognize the value of their jobs and promote improved performance.

Establishing a realistic impression is a second crucial factor during an interview. Since interviews are actually the initial stage of orientation for an applicant who comes on staff, it is critical to communicate what the job really entails. For instance, telling an applicant that a front desk agent's position can lead to exciting opportunities to travel and see the world obviously does *not* establish a realistic perspective of the job. Nor would telling an applicant for a management trainee position that he or she would make important decisions about room rates, property locations, or other higher management issues.

We've examined several different approaches to selection and interviewing in this chapter. Some companies may find that they can best identify successful employees by using a combination of skills tests and direct interviews. Others may find that combining paper-and-pencil tests with non-direct interviews works best. Regardless of which methods are used, managers must take care to ensure that the methods they choose accurately predict which applicants will perform best on the job.

Endnotes

1. "The Total View," The Chrysalis Corporation, a Full-Service Consulting Firm, www.chrysaliscorporation.com/tv_hiring_costs.htm.

2. Peter Drucker, "Getting Things Done: How to Make People Decisions," *Harvard Business Review* 63 (July–August 1995): 22.

3. "The Effect of Human Resources Management Practices on Market Performance," *HR Management* 38, no. 3 (1999): 185–199.

4. Patrick M. Wright, Timothy M. Gardner, Lisa M. Moynihan, and Mathew R. Allen, "The Relationship Between HR Practices and Firm Performance: Examining Causal Order," *Personnel Psychology* 58, no. 2 (2005): 409–447.

5. F. DeFryt and I. Mervielde, "RIASEL Types and Big Five Traits as Predictors of Employment Success," *Personnel Psychology* 52, no. 3 (1999): 701–727.

6. Shawn Zeller, "The Perfect Candidate," *Government Executive* 37, no. 1 (2005): 40–46.

7. P. R. Jeanneret and M. H. Strong, "Linking O*Net Job Analysis Information to Job Requirement Predictors: An O*Net Application," *Personnel Psychology* 56, no. 2 (2003): 465–492; and Patrick D. Converse, Frederick L. Oswald, Michael A. Gillespie, Kevin A. Field, and B. Bizot, "Matching Individuals to Occupations Using Abilities and The O*Net: Issues and an Application in Career Guidance," *Personnel Psychology* 57, no. 2 (2004): 451–488.

8. For more on these tests, see F.J. Landy, L.J. Shankstar, and S.S. Kohler, "Personnel Selection and Placement," *Annual Review of Psychology* 45 (1994): 261–296.

9. Kevin R. Murphy and Ann Harris Shiarella, "Implications of the Multidimensional Nature of Job Performance for the Validity of Selection Tests: Multivariate Frameworks for Studying Test Validity," *Personnel Psychology* 50, no. 4 (1997): 823–855.

10. Ivan T. Robertson and Mike Smith, "Personnel Selection," *Journal of Occupational and Organizational Psychology* 74, no. 4 (2001): 441–473.

11. Because relying on personality instruments for selection is a common practice in hospitality (Marriott International and Sands Group are among the users), Eric Krell's eight questions to prospective instrument vendors concerning validity and reliability may represent an asset for the industry. See Eric Krell, "Personality Counts," *HR Magazine* 50, no. 11 (2005): 46–53.

12. These principles are adapted from an article by William Cottringer, "Selecting the Best of the Bunch," *Security Management* 398, no. 10 (1995): 21–23.

13. J. L. Mendoza, D. E. Bard, M. D. Mumford, and S. C. Ang, "Criterion-Related Validity in Multiple-Hurdle Designs: Estimation and Bias," *Organizational Research Methods* 7 (2004): 418–442.

14. Maury A. Buster, Philip L. Roth, and Philip Bobko, "A Process for Content Validation of Education and Experienced-Based Minimum Qualifications: An Approach Resulting in Federal Court Approval," *Personnel Psychology* 58, no. 3 (2005): 771–800.

15. Eric Felsberg's list of elements to consider for analyzing jobs may be helpful in this process. See Mendoza et al.

16. Stephen J. Vodanovich and Rosemary H. Lowe, "They Ought to Know Better: The Incidence and Correlates of Inappropriate Application Blank Inquiries," *Public Personnel Management* 21 (Fall 1992): 363–364.

17. Cynthia Fisher, Lyle D. Schoenfeldt, and James B. Shaw, *Human Resource Management* (Boston: Houghton Mifflin, 1990), 253.

18. For a succinct description of Fiedler's Least Preferred Co-Worker approach, see John R. Schermerhorn, Jr., James G. Hunt, and Richard N. Osburn, *Managing Organizational Behavior*, 4th ed. (New York: Wiley, 1991), 469–472.

19. Fisher, Schoenfeldt, and Shaw, 260.

20. Ed Bean, "More Firms Are Using Attitude Tests to Keep Thieves Off the Payroll," *Wall Street Journal*, 27 February 1987.

21. Alan I. Leshner, "U.S. Costs of Alcohol and Drug Abuse Estimated at $246 Billion," (13 May 1998), National Clearinghouse for Drug and Alcohol Information.

22. Donald J. Petersen, "The Ins and Outs of Implementing a Successful Drug-Testing Program," *Personnel* 64 (October 1987): 47.

23. Joel Ceausu, "Drug-taking Workers Cost the US 500 Million Working Days a Year," *Personnel Today*, 24 Jan. 2006, p. 8.

24. Michael Gray, *Security Management* 50, no. 2 (2006): 50–58.

25. David J. Jefferson, "America's Most Dangerous Drug," *Newsweek* 146, no. 6 (2005): 41–49.

26. Ronald Siegel, MD, *L.A. Times* News Service, 23 March 1995.

27. News release, Committee on Education and the Workforce, September 23, 2004. www.house.gov/ed_workforce/press/press108/second/09sept/diplomamill 092304.htm.

28. GAO Report on Diploma Mills, *Techniques: Connecting Education and Careers* 78, no. 3 (2003): 7.

29. David Steir, "Many Ask, But Don't Give References," *HR News* 8 (February 1990): 2.

30. Caleb S. Atwood and James M. Noel, "New Lawsuits Expand Employer Liability," *HR Magazine* 50 (October 1990): 74.

31. Erik C. Gabrielle, "New Law Protects Employers When Employees Go Berserk," *South Florida Business Journal* 20, no. 9 (1999): 71A.

32. Robert W. Eder, "Contextual Effects on Interview Decisions," in R. W. Eder and G. R. Ferris, eds., *The Employment Interview: Theory, Research and Practice* (Newbury Park, Calif.: Sage Publications, 1990).

33. Eder.

34. M. Rotundo and P. R. Sackett, "Effect of Rater Race on Conclusions Regarding Differential Prediction," *Journal of Applied Psychology* 84, no. 5 (1999): 815–882.

Key Terms

application blank—A form used by companies to solicit information from prospective employees about their knowledge, skills, abilities, and needs.

assessment center—A selection tool that places applicants in simulated real-life situations where observers watch their performance to determine the extent to which the applicants would fit the company's needs.

biographical information blank (BIB)—A pre-employment form that collects information about an applicant's attitudes, life experiences, and social values.

body fluid test—A pre-employment test used to determine whether applicants are using or have been using drugs.

closed-ended questions—A type of question that requires only a "Yes" or "No" response.

compensatory strategy—A selection approach that emphasizes an applicant's specialized abilities or strengths over his or her weaknesses.

content validity—A test to determine whether the selection measure used assesses the overall ability of an applicant to perform a job.

contrast error—An error in a performance appraisal or interview that results when a manager or interviewer consciously or subconsciously compares one employee or applicant to another.

credit reference check—A selection test that measures an applicant's credit history. Some experts feel that an applicant's credit history is a good predictor of job performance.

criterion-related validity—The degree to which the predictor relates to the criterion (such as job performance).

devil's horns—An impression based solely on one undesirable quality that an applicant may possess. Opposite of the halo effect.

first impression error—An error made by a manager or interviewer who bases his or her entire opinion of an applicant on the first impression that person makes.

halo effect—An impression based solely on a single positive dimension of an applicant such as appearance or performance. Opposite of devil's horns.

honesty tests—A type of test that measures attitudes toward honesty by posing hypothetical situations about which a potential employee makes a value judgment.

inter-rater reliability—The degree to which observations made by different interviewers about the same applicant agree.

multiple hurdles strategy—A selection approach stipulating that applicants must clear each stage of the selection process before being hired. In other words, applicants must "clear every hurdle" before being accepted.

negligent hiring—A practice commonly defined as an employer's failure to exercise reasonable care in the selection of its employees. Lawsuits over actions by employees are often based on an employer's failure to protect guests because of negligent hiring practices.

open-ended questions—A type of question that requires a respondent to elaborate on an issue.

paper-and-pencil tests—A selection device that requires written responses to either written or oral questions posed to applicants.

physical and motor ability tests—Selection tests that subject applicants to physical exams. Only those physical and motor tests that measure specific job-related skills or abilities are acceptable under the Americans with Disabilities Act.

predictor—A measure used to predict performance on the job.

recency errors—A type of error in a performance appraisal or interview that results when managers or interviewers base employee ratings primarily on the most recent events or behaviors.

reference check—An inquiry made by prospective employers of past employers to learn about and verify an applicant's work history.

reliability—The degree to which a selection method consistently produces the same results.

selection—The process of choosing the right person for a job out of a pool of recruited candidates.

semi-structured interviews—An interview style that allows both planned and unplanned questions. Typically, the unplanned questions allow interviewers to ask more specific questions about broad issues raised by structured questions.

similarity errors—A type of error in a performance appraisal or interview that results when a manager or interviewer is attracted to an applicant because of personal or professional similarities.

stress interview—An interviewing style that creates an emotionally charged setting in which the applicant is challenged by the interviewer to see how he or she performs under stress.

structured interview—An interview style in which questions are totally prepared in advance and are asked of each applicant in the same order.

unstructured interview—An interviewing style in which no questions are planned in advance. Instead, an interviewer directs the interview down whatever path seems appropriate at the time.

validity—The degree to which a selection process really measures what it is supposed to measure.

weighted application blank (WAB)—An application form in which points are accumulated for different types of work experience. Typically, weighted application blanks emphasize the most desirable qualifications of applicants.

work sample test—Selection test that measures a candidate's ability to perform the skills and tasks associated with a specific job. For instance, an applicant for a typing position may be asked to type.

Review Questions

1. Why is the issue of validity so important in the selection process?

2. What are the features of the multiple hurdles strategy and the compensatory strategy?

3. Why would weighted application blanks produce information that is more useful in predicting performance on the job than unweighted blanks?

4. What are the advantages, disadvantages, and possible pitfalls of paper-and-pencil tests, honesty tests, physical and motor ability tests, body fluid tests, work sample tests, and assessment centers?

5. Under what circumstances would telephone reference checks provide more useful information than written reference checks? Why?

6. What are the common problems associated with interviewing reliability?

7. What are the four basic rules to remember in preparing for interviews?

8. What are the advantages and disadvantages of structured, unstructured, and semi-structured interviews?

9. What are the features of direct, non-direct, and eclectic approaches to interviewing?

10. Would you recommend using the best manager or a mediocre manager as an interviewer? Why?

Internet Sites

For more information, visit the following Internet sites. Remember that Internet addresses can change without notice. If the site is no longer there, you can use a search engine to look for additional sites.

HR Hub
www.hrhub.com/

HR Online
www.hronline.com/

Privacy Act of 1974 (2000 Edition)
www.usdoj.gov/foia/1974intro.htm

Title VII of 1964
www.eeoc.gov/policy/vii.html

U.S. Chamber of Commerce
www.uschamber.com/

U.S. Department of Labor
www.dol.gov/

U.S. Equal Employment Opportunity Commission (EEOC)
www.eeoc.gov/

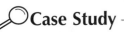

Case Study

Turning Around the Turnaround

Ashcroft Hotels, a mid-size chain with an outstanding track record of turning around underperforming properties, recently acquired the Lincoln Hotel. The Lincoln posed a considerable challenge—even for the Ashcroft chain. The transition began with corporate executives deciding to replace the Lincoln's general manager with Martin Wood, the most experienced and successful manager of the chain's turnaround team. Martin would be responsible for assessing the current staff at the Lincoln Hotel and making the necessary changes to improve the property's performance.

The only restriction was that Martin had to replace the current food and beverage director with Theo Waters, a rising star at the corporate flagship hotel. Joanne Landis, Ashcroft's vice president of food and beverage, insisted that now was the time for Theo's big test.

Martin expressed some concern. He felt that turning around the Lincoln Hotel posed enough of a challenge. He didn't need the additional burden of mentoring some hotshot who never faced serious problems and always had the resources available to help him succeed.

Joanne understood Martin's concerns and took full responsibility for Theo's placement. "You'll see," Joanne said, "Just turn him loose and he'll turn it around." Unconvinced, Martin gave in to the demand, but insisted that Theo had to be part of the management team at Lincoln. Joanne readily agreed that Theo, like the other managers, would be accountable to Martin. Her last comment was, "I don't want to interfere with your responsibilities, Martin. I only want to give Theo a chance to shine at another property. I'll have HR send you a copy of his file this afternoon."

Theo Waters was indeed a rising star at Ashcroft. He had bused tables and was a food server in college while he earned his hospitality degree. After graduation, he entered Ashcroft as a management trainee at the flagship hotel. He was soon promoted to assistant restaurant manager. His first department head position was as the room service manager. Most recently, he was the fine dining restaurant manager. He learned the chain's standards and procedures at the finest and best-run hotel in the chain. Even in this environment, he helped fine-tune an already profitable, smoothly running operation into an even more profitable one. In addition, he was instrumental in launching the company's new award-winning fine dining concept, which the company planned to roll out to other properties, like the Lincoln.

The next week, Theo arrived at the Lincoln Hotel. At an hour-long meeting, Martin welcomed Theo as the first new member of the high-performance team that would turn the hotel around.

"Theo," Martin began, "it's important that we start things off right. Change is always difficult, but at underperforming hotels, like the Lincoln, change is often resisted, especially if managers and employees perceive changes as personal attacks."

"I understand," responded Theo, "changing procedures at the flagship wasn't easy, you know. But once we let the staff know how serious we were, people straightened up and we moved ahead."

Martin paused and momentarily regretted giving in to Joanne. "Yes, Theo. You did a fine job there. But we're not just changing procedures here—we're challenging and changing a whole culture of work."

"Sure. It's a bigger job. What are some of the immediate problems?" asked Theo.

Martin handed Theo a short list of several areas that needed immediate improvement:

- First off, the restaurant is operating at a loss. Profitability must be restored as soon as possible.

- The inventory levels are too high, as are costs, but the staff also complains of frequent stockouts of critical items.

- Food production is often of inconsistent quality and portion size and food items are late coming out of the kitchen for waiting guests.

- Sanitation levels are often unacceptable both in the kitchen and in the dining areas.

- Table linens sometimes come back from the in-house laundry with stains still on them, and employee uniforms are dated and poorly maintained.

- A couple of ovens in the kitchen are not working properly and most of the appliances are old and need some sort of maintenance, but complaints to engineering just seem to pile up.

- Guests often complain about poor service. The hotel's director of sales is reluctant to bring potential clients to the hotel's own restaurant because of the service, which has embarrassed her too often before.

- There are scheduling problems, especially (but not only) during high occupancy periods, when the restaurant is often understaffed to meet the demand.

Martin continued, "As you can see, there are problems with the management team as well as with the line staff. I suspect that the director of sales and the rooms director are understating forecasts so they can always exceed them. This puts staffing in the restaurant at risk—you're always short-handed. I don't know what the deal is with engineering, but I'll find out."

"I'm sure I can tackle my area's problems right away," Theo offered.

"Theo, for the next 30 days I'm going to be focused on several critical areas of the hotel. But don't be the Lone Ranger. I'm here for support and advice, so don't hesitate to meet with me. This has to be a team effort."

Theo began by calling a restaurant department meeting, during which he made it very clear that the level of performance that had been acceptable in the past would no longer be tolerated. "I intend to make this restaurant's service rival that of our flagship property," he announced.

He distributed a new procedures manual that he recently helped revise in his previous position and insisted that everyone read it thoroughly and begin following its contents. Theo pointed out, "There will be no more eating in production or service areas of this restaurant—that's why we have a break area."

Theo continued, "I'm bringing in a leading customer service training program that guarantees to increase the restaurant's average check and total revenue. This training program will also address the top ten guest complaints and give the servers responses and tools that will help them satisfy unhappy guests." He banned the servers' current practice of pooling tips: "I don't believe that pooling tips encourages the kind of superior service we want at this restaurant," he declared.

A few days later, Theo unveiled a new work schedule with major changes on it in a deliberate attempt to upset underperformers. When some staff members complained, he responded, "There are a lot of restaurants in this town. If you don't like it here, a person has to do what a person has to do."

Over the next couple of weeks, Theo was kept busy putting out one fire after another. He disciplined the chef for allowing cooks to give servers food prepared by mistake. He found a group of servers still pooling tips and threatened to fire them. It seemed like every time he turned around, the staff was doing all it could to ignore his directives and undermine his authority.

One day, near the end of the month, things just blew up. The restaurant was very busy because of high occupancy at the hotel. As Theo walked through the dining room, he heard a guest complain angrily that his food was taking forever to arrive. Theo went to the kitchen and asked the chef what was causing the delay. The chef explained that he was not prepared for this business volume. "My cook was swamped and burned the first plate, which had to be redone."

Theo returned to the waiting guest and, as he comped the meal, another guest at the next table complained that she had been sitting for several minutes and no one even brought her water to drink. Theo rushed to the kitchen and accused Beth, that table's server, of failing to take a guest's order within the time frame set out in the procedures manual. Beth lost her composure and let Theo have it. "I'm working a double station. How am I supposed to keep up according to your standards? Why don't you get off people's backs. We're working awfully hard to cover up for your stupid new schedule. What do you expect when we're always understaffed?"

Theo pitched in and began helping servers get the food out. In the dining room he noticed the director of sales leaving with a client. She called him over and privately said, "This is exactly the kind of service that always embarrasses me when I'm with clients." Theo snapped back, "If you didn't sandbag your occupancy projections, we could schedule staff appropriately and this wouldn't happen!" As Theo walked away, another server rushed up to him and said he couldn't get the cappuccino machine to work properly. After comping another meal, Theo struggled to control his emotions. "Engineering has known about the cappuccino problem for days. Why doesn't anything ever get done right?"

By the end of his first month, despite increased customer counts, the restaurant's revenue performance had not noticeably improved. Moreover, Theo had managed to alienate not only the restaurant staff, but also most of the hotel's management team. Even the controller, who had cautiously supported Theo initially, started to doubt his "superstardom" because she saw a lot of comped checks and no increase in net revenue. Her willingness to cooperate with Theo was beginning to ebb.

Martin called Theo into his office for an end-of-month progress report.

Discussion Questions

1. Do you agree with corporate's decision that Theo is an excellent candidate for this new position? What about his background and experience would help prepare him to succeed at the Lincoln Hotel? Why did Martin Wood have misgivings about Theo's abilities? What about Theo's background and experience would hinder his ability to succeed at the Lincoln Hotel?

2. What did Theo do well in approaching his new assignment? Why did Theo's efforts to create change fail? What could Martin Wood have done to avoid the end-of-month situation?

3. At the end-of-month meeting, what is Martin likely to say to Theo? How might Theo respond? What are the next steps that Theo should take in his effort to turn his department around?

Case number: 3564C

The following industry experts helped generate and develop this case: Philip J. Bresson, Director of Human Resources, Renaissance New York Hotel, New York, New York; and Jerry Fay, Human Resources Director, ARAMARK Corporation, Atlanta, Georgia.

Part II

Human Resources Development

Chapter 5 Outline

Orientation Goals
Planning Orientation Programs
    General Property Orientation
    Specific Job Orientation
    Orientation Kits
    Approaches to Avoid
    Approaches to Take
    Orientation Follow-Up
Socialization
    Planning Socialization Programs
    Approaches to Socialization
    Who Should Socialize Newcomers?

Competencies

1. Explain the purpose of an orientation program. (pp. 169–170)

2. Distinguish between a general property orientation and a specific job orientation. (pp. 171–173)

3. Identify approaches to orientation that managers should avoid, and others that they should take. (pp. 174–175)

4. Explain the purpose of a socialization program. (pp. 175–179)

5. Identify specific socialization strategies and approaches. (pp. 179–182)

5

Orientation and Socialization

This chapter was co-authored by Ellie H. Park, M.S. candidate, University of Nevada, Las Vegas (UNLV); Ju-hee Kang, M.S. candidate, UNLV; and Itsuko Miyoshi, M.S. candidate, UNLV.

EMPLOYEE TURNOVER IN THE HOSPITALITY INDUSTRY often averages as much as 200 to 300 percent per year. Statistically speaking, this means that the entire staff of a hospitality operation turns over two to three times per year! Fortunately, this rarely happens. Instead, the percentages reflect extremely high turnover rates for employees in their first 30 days, combined with diminishing rates for other employees.[1] More times than not, the employees who resign within 30 days of hire just got off to a poor start. For many, the stress of starting a new job is simply too great.

On the first day of a new job, employees face new surroundings, work rules, responsibilities, bosses, and co-workers. At best, this combination of new things may make an employee feel insecure; at worst, it may provoke anxiety that compels the employee to resign. In such cases, all the time and money spent by the company to locate, recruit, select, and hire that employee is lost.

Orientation programs are designed to reduce the stress that employees feel when beginning a new job. However, many orientation programs compress huge amounts of information about managerial philosophies, company history, policies, and procedures into a very brief period and the new employee is overwhelmed. In theory, orientation provides new employees the information they need to succeed in a company. But, in practice, unless orientation is carefully managed, too much new information at one time just increases the anxiety new employees experience.

New employees who receive orientation training tend to stay longer. This is especially true when orientation stresses what is important to the newcomer, not what is important to the company. Inadequate orientation programs can be financially damaging to a company because they may reduce the new employee's effectiveness for the first few weeks on the job and may contribute to job dissatisfaction and turnover.[2] A company should focus on employee-centered orientation, instead of regulation-mandated training, to help newcomers cope with the stress of starting a new job.[3]

Orientation Goals

New employees have many questions about their jobs and their new organization. These questions must be answered quickly and effectively to get employees off on the right foot. Research has found that it is natural for new employees to engage in

Exhibit 1   Questions New Employees Might Ask

1. What exactly is the organization's mission?
2. Why does the organization exist?
3. What are the exact duties of my job?
4. What are my rights as an employee?
5. What are the limits to what I can and cannot do without getting permission?
6. What positions can I advance to within the organization?
7. How do I fit in the organization?
8. What performance standards must I meet to succeed in the job and the organization?
9. What general and specific benefits am I eligible for?
10. Who will I work for?
11. How will I "fit in" with co-workers?
12. What can I do to establish a good relationship with the people I will work and interact with?
13. What type of training will I receive, both immediately and later on, to help me prepare for this and future jobs within the organization?

Source: Adapted from Raphael R. Kavanaugh and Jack D. Ninemeier, *Supervision in the Hospitality Industry*, 3d ed. (Lansing, Mich.: Educational Institute of the American Hotel & Lodging Association, 2001), 116–119.

activities such as information and feedback seeking, relationship building, job-change negotiating, and positive framing of new surroundings and circumstances. Exhibit 1 provides some questions new employees might ask.

Hospitality companies must develop well-designed orientation programs that address the questions employees have about their jobs. The information included in these programs falls into three general categories:

- Information about job-related issues such as company standards, management expectations of employees, and policies and procedures

- Information about cultural issues such as acceptable norms of conduct, definitions of acceptable and unacceptable behavior, management philosophies, traditions, and strategic beliefs

- Information about specific job responsibilities and technical aspects of the job, such as what is contained in the job description, what kinds of equipment operation is required to perform the job, and how performance is evaluated

Planning Orientation Programs

About 85 percent of companies with 100 or more employees offer orientation programs.[4] Proper planning of an orientation program ensures that all the pertinent topics are covered without duplication. Key considerations in orientation planning are included in Exhibit 2.

Exhibit 2   Key Considerations in Orientation Planning

- Program goals
- Range of topics to be considered
- Timing and duration of orientation sessions
- Company topics vs. departmental and job topics
- Identification of specific training to be conducted by the human resources department
- Identification of specific training to be conducted by managers and supervisors
- Technical vs. social aspects of orientation
- Methods for encouraging employee discussion sessions and feedback
- Training required for human resources representatives before the orientation program
- Training required for managers and supervisors before the orientation program
- Checklist of topics to ensure follow-up by the human resources department and managers
- Review and update of the employee handbook
- Program flexibility to accommodate differences in employee education, intelligence, and work experience

Source: Adapted from Wayne F. Cascio, *Managing Human Resources: Productivity, Quality of Work Life, Profits* (New York: McGraw-Hill, 1989), 228.

Some properties divide orientation into two programs. The first focuses on **general property orientation,** and the second focuses on **specific job orientation**.

General Property Orientation

One of the first steps a property takes to orient a new employee is to acquaint that employee with the organization and with the property as a whole. This stage of orientation covers such topics as the organization's mission statement and management philosophy, general policies and procedures, insurance and benefits, personnel forms, guest and employee relations, and the role of employees in meeting organizational goals.

At large properties, general property orientation is typically conducted by a representative from the human resources department. At smaller properties, the general manager usually presents the information.

Orientation plays a valuable role in reducing turnover, which can be expensive. In fact, turnover costs in the leisure and hospitality industry were $6,803 per employee in 2004.[5] Other benefits that employees and the organization can derive from general property orientation are listed in Exhibit 3.

One researcher who has studied orientation measured the extent to which those employees who attended voluntary programs were actually more or less acculturated to the company. What he learned was that, even though the program was voluntary, employees attending the orientation were significantly more socialized on the goals/values, history, and people of the company. The people attending orientation programs also showed significantly higher levels of organizational commitment than non-attendees. This was very desirable, of course.[6]

Exhibit 3   Benefits of General Property Orientation

Benefits to the Company:

- Provides a consistent message to all new employees
- Helps employees know that they are working for a great company
- Introduces management
- Provides a memorable first impression of the company
- Builds a strong foundation of company values and philosophy
- Presents business goals and priorities
- Provides an opportunity to succeed
- Introduces the team approach at all levels in the organization
- Lowers turnover

Benefits to the Employee:

- Provides an understanding of the company's expectations about employee performance
- Helps employees understand the value of their positions
- Builds self-esteem
- Helps employees realize that they are important to the operation
- Provides structured learning about the company and the job
- Establishes early commitment to being a member of the team
- Builds a foundation for employee motivation

Source: Raphael R. Kavanaugh and Jack D. Ninemeier, *Supervision in the Hospitality Industry,* 3rd ed. (Lansing, Mich.: Educational Institute of the American Hotel & Lodging Association, 2001), 120–121.

Specific Job Orientation

During specific job orientation, the focus shifts from organizational and departmental topics to those directly related to job performance. Employees are introduced to the responsibilities outlined in their job description, portions of the handbook relating to their job, the work environment and location of equipment, and their department's relationship to other departments. New employees are taken on a tour of the property and their department and are introduced to people with whom they will work and interact. The department's policies and procedures are discussed, including those related to work hours, time clock operation and payroll, breaks, smoking, employee dining, and so on. Managers and supervisors involved in a specific orientation program identify potential career tracks so that new employees understand their promotional opportunities and limits. Specific job orientation programs are designed to familiarize employees with their job responsibilities and work environment. Exhibit 4 outlines some additional benefits of this method of orientation.

Orientation Kits

Well-organized managers should prepare **orientation kits** that new employees can take home. Orientation kits enable employees to review material discussed

Exhibit 4   Benefits of Specific Job Orientation

Benefits to the Department:
- Provides consistency in employee training and development
- Maintains currency of resources
- Helps employees ensure quality service and meet guest expectations
- Ensures that required standards will be maintained
- Provides consistency in staff performance
- Ensures staff capability
- Helps the department run more smoothly

Benefits to the Employee:
- Teaches the employee how to do the job correctly
- Builds self-esteem due to feeling of accomplishment
- Builds high morale
- Creates team fellowship and cooperation
- Helps employee become productive more quickly

Source: Raphael R. Kavanaugh and Jack D. Ninemeier, *Supervision in the Hospitality Industry*, 3rd ed. (Lansing, Mich.: Educational Institute of the American Hotel & Lodging Association, 2001), 122.

during the day and share information with their families or friends. Since the first day of orientation may overwhelm a new employee with information, orientation kits enable them to reflect on the information and think about questions to ask the human resources department or manager the following day. Exhibit 5 provides a list of sample items to include in an orientation kit. Hospitality companies should consider including the following items in their orientation kits in addition to those listed in Exhibit 5:

- Copies of EEOC notices and company policies regarding compliance
- Recent company newsletters
- Names and telephone numbers of other employees in the department
- Schedule for the remaining portions of orientation and training
- Information regarding social activities of the department and/or company
- Current organizational chart
- Projected organizational chart (illustrating succession)
- Map of the facility
- Key terms unique to the industry, company, and the job
- Copy of specific job goals and descriptions
- Schedule for the remaining portions of orientation and training
- Information regarding social activities of the department and/or company

Exhibit 5   Items Commonly Found in Orientation Kits

Remaining employment and benefit enrollment forms to be completed

Explanations of:

- Hours of work, meal and break periods
- Attendance policy
- Safety procedures
- Sanitation procedures
- Uniform or dress code requirements and personal appearance and grooming standards
- Emergency procedures
- Performance evaluations
- Disciplinary rules and actions
- Promotion policy
- Harassment policy
- Payroll procedures
- Vacation, sick, and other leave policies
- Holiday schedule
- Group health insurance policy
- Pension/savings plan
- Important telephone numbers and when to use them
- Available or required training programs
- Employee assistance programs (if applicable)
- Union policies (if applicable)

Approaches to Avoid

Unfortunately, many managers do not take orientation seriously. Instead of seizing this opportunity to get a new employee off to a good start, many managers simply delegate orientation to the closest available employee. By handing over orientation, managers lose one of their best opportunities to directly influence employee behavior.[7]

There are five approaches to orientation that managers should avoid:[8]

- *Emphasis on paperwork.* When too much emphasis is placed on human resources paperwork, employees may feel like they are not really part of the company.

- *Mickey Mouse approach.* When new employees are assigned easy jobs so they can "get the feel for the work," they may believe that they are not really considered capable or important. (This is so-called because of the laxity of the program—it does not refer to the Disney approach.)

- *Sketchy overviews.* When new employees are given vague or incomplete information and then are tossed into jobs to sink or swim, they often sink.

- *Suffocation.* When new employees are given too much information, they often feel overwhelmed.

- *Unrealistic job previews.* Research has shown that employees who receive realistic job previews that communicate the real advantages and disadvantages of a position are much more likely to remain with a company.

We could add one more approach to this list that is particularly common in the hospitality industry. The "follow-Mary-around" approach turns the entire orientation over to an employee. While it is a good idea for employees to take new employees on tours and introduce them to co-workers, turning orientation over to an employee is not a good idea because the new employee will learn both the good *and* bad habits of the employee conducting the orientation.

Approaches to Take

We also suggest some orientation approaches to take. Each of the following will help new employees start work in a positive way.[9]

- Welcome the new employee. Arranging a welcome party may be a good way to reinforce the new hire's excitement.

- Help the employee develop positive impressions about the employer. The supervisor's direct involvement, such as at lunch on the employee's first day, suggests to the new hire that the employer cares about him or her.

- Confirm the employee's decision to take the job. Help the employee see that he or she made the right choice about the job and the company.

- Put the new employee at ease. Make him or her comfortable with the workplace and with colleagues.

Exhibit 6 discusses ten steps to incorporate into an effective new-employee orientation.

Orientation Follow-Up

Orientation should be followed by a period of close supervision. During this time, managers should closely observe and assist the new employee in learning the new job. Managers can spend less time watching and helping a new employee as the employee's performance improves.

Orientation should have an end point. For example, orientation at Marriott, which lasts about three months including mentoring and refresher courses, ends with a banquet for each "class" that has been with the hotel for 90 days.[10] Managers can define an orientation end point by setting a date to meet with a new employee to answer questions. This meeting usually is scheduled a few days to a week after orientation and training begin. During this meeting, the manager can appraise the employee's progress to date and establish goals and objectives for the employee to meet before the first formal performance appraisal. Some companies also schedule one-, two-, and three-month reviews with employees for similar purposes. Others, like Marriott, have developed mentoring or "buddy" programs for new employees that provide continual close contact with experienced

Exhibit 6   Ten Steps in a Well-Designed Orientation

The following ten steps should be included in a successful orientation.

1. **Introduction to the company.**
   The key is to make the new employee feel good about the company, beginning to instill the pride of belonging and being a part of the company.

2. **Review of important policy and practice.**
   Include standards of conduct, performance standards, the introductory period of employment, discipline policy, and safety.

3. **Review of benefits and services.**
   This review of benefits is crucial. Employees need to appreciate the cost of benefits. Discuss services that employees might not consider benefits, such as credit union, parking, food, medical care, discount, and social and recreational services.

4. **Benefit plan enrollment.**
   Complete necessary benefit enrollment forms. Allow the employee time to discuss plan options with a spouse before making a commitment.

5. **Completion of employment documents.**
   Complete payroll withholding, emergency information, picture releases, employment opportunity data, and other relevant and appropriate documents.

6. **Review of employer expectations.**
   Related to Step 2, this deals more with employer-employee relationships. Use of a performance appraisal form makes a good topical outline for a discussion of employer expectation on teamwork, working relationships, attitude, and loyalty.

7. **Setting of employee expectations.**
   If employees meet the employer's expectations, what can they expect in return?
   Detail training and development, scheduled wage and salary reviews, security, recognition, working conditions, opportunity for advancement, educational assistance programs, counseling, grievance procedure, and other relevant expectations.

8. **Introduction to fellow workers.**
   Use of nametags and buddy system are helpful.

9. **Introduction to facilities.**
   Provide a standard tour of the facility. It is more effective to break it into several tours, starting with the immediate work area on the first day.

10. **Introduction to the job.**
    Be prepared to have the new employee involved in the work flow.

Source: Ronald Smith, "Employee Orientation: 10 Steps to Success," *Personnel Journal* (December 1984): 48.

employees for the first few months on the job. These mentoring approaches to socialization have been extremely effective during the first six months after hiring.

Individualized socialization by mentors was found to be much more productive in a study of union commitment as well.[11]

DuPont has developed an even more sophisticated program that appears applicable to the hospitality industry. The DuPont orientation process, called "orienteering," has three parts, or tiers. In the first tier, orienteering coaches help newcomers gain a clear sense of their work units, direction, objectives, resources, and company values. In the second tier, scheduled 30 to 90 days after hiring, newcomers are helped to understand how both their work and their team or unit work fits into the attainment of company goals. In the third tier, which is 30 to 60 days after the second tier, employees are taught to develop strategies for contributing to the organization over the long haul.[12]

To determine whether newcomers are adequately oriented (or socialized) to their new surroundings, managers may want to give a short test. One effective technique involves taking a recent speech delivered by the CEO of the company and blocking out 10 to 12 key words in the text of the speech. New employees are then asked to insert each correct word. One researcher who studied this method found out that employees who were adequately oriented and socialized were, in fact, able to supply each word correctly, while those who were not were unable to do so. Managers may want to replicate this type of test to make sure that the messages they intended to deliver during orientation and/or socialization have been completely mastered by new employees.

Socialization

Orientation is introductory instruction concerning a new environment or organization. The orientation period is especially important since it can help relieve the anxiety many new employees experience. However, simply orienting employees to their new environment is not enough. New employees also must be introduced to the **values**, **norms**, and **behaviors** consistent with success in the organization. This process is known as **socialization** or cultural orientation. Socialization is an *ongoing* process of learning the social culture of the organization and how to get along with others in the organization.[13] While orientation typically occurs in a new employee's first week to month on the job, socialization takes much longer. Rushing new employees into their work without attending to the socialization process is not effective. Moreover, it makes employees feel unprepared, unsupported, overwhelmed, and less than appreciated. Organizations can use several ways to ensure that new employees are appropriately socialized into their new positions.

> The socialization of new employees can be difficult because of their anxiety ("Will I be able to handle it?" "How will I get along with my boss?" "Where do I start?"). With these issues in mind, Texas Instruments conducted a classic experiment in which one group of new workers (control group) were given the normal first-day orientation, consisting of a two-hour briefing by the personnel department on hours of work, insurance, parking, and the like. Then, as was customary, the new employees met a friendly but very busy supervisor, who provided further orientation and job instruction. A second (experimental) group received the same two-hour personnel department orientation followed by a six-hour anxiety

reduction session. There individuals were told that there would be no work the first day, that they should relax, sit back, and use this time to get acquainted with the organization and each other and ask questions. The following points were emphasized during this phase: (1) the high probability of success on the job as evidenced by statistics disclosing that 99.6 percent of all new employees are successful on the job; (2) what new employees should expect in the way of hazing and unfounded rumors from older employees designed to intimidate them about their chances of success; (3) encouragement of new employees to take the initiative in asking their supervisors questions about their jobs; (4) information about the specific personality of the supervisor to whom they would be assigned. This innovative orientation program had a remarkable impact: The experimental group exceeded the control group in terms of learning rate, units produced per hour, absentee rate, and tardiness. Although this research was conducted years ago, it clearly shows the beneficial effects of reducing the anxiety of new workers.[14]

Certainly, this research suggests that socialization activity to reduce anxiety should be included in all employee orientation programs.

Organizational socialization has been described as the process by which newcomers come to understand and appreciate the values, abilities, expected behaviors, norms, and social knowledge essential for assuming an organizational role and for participating as an organizational member.[15] While socialization to the entire culture of a company may take months, newcomers tend to experience and incorporate the more perceptible and concrete parts of the culture, like acceptable behavior or norms, immediately. Research indicates that new employees who are effectively socialized to the organization are more productive more quickly than those who are not. Researchers contend that socialized employees quickly learn the values that are critical to the organization and can integrate those values into their jobs. For example, new employees who learn that service is a key value of their hotel are more likely to reflect that value in their work. In addition, employees who are effectively socialized are more productive for longer periods than employees who are not.

The effects of socialization were first noted in a study of civilian and military prisoners of the North Korean Communists during the Korean War. Researchers noted that, through intensive indoctrination, Americans could be "converted" very quickly to partially reflect the values of their Communist captors. Researchers noted that the "occupational indoctrination" that students received upon entering the work world had a similar effect; in a relatively short time, many of the values students held were easily converted by the companies they worked for.[16] Gradually, this process of socialization became known as "organizational socialization" or, in some circles, simply "learning the ropes."

The faster employees "learn the ropes," the faster they will become effective, productive members of an organization. With some employees, exposure alone enables them to learn specific values, norms, and behaviors. Some employees, however, will never learn the ropes unless they receive assistance and guidance.

In short, proper orientation and socialization can help reduce unwanted turnover—especially turnover that occurs within an employee's first 30 days. Effective orientation and socialization programs can help organizations in other ways. For instance, effective cultural socialization can contribute to reduced absenteeism and higher productivity. Finally, researchers have linked effective cultural socialization to other benefits, including profitability,[17] employee performance, and loyalty. Further, failing to develop and deliver good orientation and socialization programs can have an opposite effect. In a study conducted on socialization, for instance, newcomers reported on how many negative versus positive impressions they received. During the first day, the negative impressions outweighed the positive by 71 percent to 29 percent. Over the first week, 59 percent of the impressions the newcomer received were negative, and over the first month, 54 percent were negative. After six months, the newcomers reported that overall, 56 percent of the impressions they received about the company and their coworkers were negative. When newcomers took orientation and socialization programs, on the other hand, the figures were reversed and nearly 70 percent reported positive impressions about the first month. These still held after six months, as well. [18]

Planning Socialization Programs

The socialization process generally consists of these stages: (1) welcoming activities; (2) understanding the organizational history, values, and purpose; (3) implementation of a realistic orientation program that addresses the stress new employees feel; and (4) immediate connection to a person in a similar role or to a mentor.[19]

Adding welcoming activities can help employees feel appreciated at work. Some organizations create welcome baskets for this purpose. The baskets may include items with the organization's logo and mission on them (such as T-shirts, coffee mugs, pens, and balloons); survival items (such as chocolate bars, coffee, and gift cards); or items, such as a bouquet of flowers, that are designed to say "We are glad you are here" and "You are now part of our team." It is also common for organizations to plan a welcome dinner or lunch for new employees.[20]

New employees need to feel connected to the organization to act in accordance with the organization's purpose and mission. During the initial introduction to their new job and roles, it is important that the new hires learn about the organization's history, values, and purpose.

Thus, managers must first identify what they are trying to socialize employees to do. To do this, managers need to understand the critical cultural values of their organizations before beginning a socialization program.

Few managers or employees can simply describe the key values of their **organizational culture** to an outsider. Organizational cultures are usually very complex and, for that reason, difficult to articulate. In addition, organizational members are generally too close to their cultures to easily identify the critical values, beliefs, and norms.

Many organizations hire culture consultants to help identify the critical values of their companies. This is the first step in teaching values to employees, with the hope that they will project these values more frequently on the job. Insiders find it difficult to be effective consultants because they cannot divorce themselves sufficiently from the culture to be objective. Sociologists might describe this phenomenon by suggesting that insiders are "too native to study the local customs."

Companies wishing to identify their organizational cultures should follow ten rules to find an effective culture consultant:[21]

- *Rule 1:* Find a consultant who will treat your company as unique. Each company already has a unique culture; that's what makes it different. Generic questionnaires do not help a manager find out what is important in his or her company.

- *Rule 2:* Find a consultant who will not stereotype your company. This follows the advice in Rule #1: each company is different. Your company culture does not fit a mold (entrepreneurial, chauvinistic, bureaucratic) of any kind.

- *Rule 3:* Hire a consultant who will admit that you—the manager or owner—cannot "control" your culture. You *can* facilitate, manage, and direct your culture, but you *cannot* control it.

- *Rule 4:* Find a consultant who believes that what your employees think and do is important. There is often a lot of difference between "the way things should be" and "the way things are" in a company. What you want to know is what your employees believe in and will work to support.

- *Rule 5:* Definitely do not listen to someone who suggests that you either need to or can "get," "buy," "create," or "borrow" a culture. You already have a culture. You do not want someone else's. No amount of money can buy one.

- *Rule 6:* Hire someone who thinks that cultures are hard to learn about, who doesn't generalize. Certain things are easy to see about your culture. For instance, symbols, ceremonies, stories, rites, rituals, and norms are all part of your culture, but are not as important as the shared values, beliefs, and assumptions.

- *Rule 7:* Hire someone who refuses to label your culture as "weak," "strong," "good," or "bad." Cultures can be all these things at different times.

- *Rule 8:* Take a long-term view. There is no such thing as a "quick fix" for cultural ineffectiveness. Cultural change takes time, and it can be painful, both personally and for the corporation.

- *Rule 9:* Make sure you find a consultant who thinks of your culture as many-faceted. Companies generally have many subcultures, each playing a role in the whole.

- *Rule 10:* Find a consultant who will teach your managers how to manage your culture effectively. Remember that managers should play three important cultural roles: assessor (find out what the culture stands for), spokesperson (spread the culture), and change agent or facilitator (effect cultural changes). A good consultant should teach your managers how to play these roles long after he or she is gone. Otherwise, you will have to hire the consultant to perform each of these tasks repeatedly.

Once the culture has been effectively identified, managers can begin to develop a socialization program to teach these values to their new employees.

Exhibit 7   Socialization Strategies

1. *Formal vs. Informal.* In formal strategies, newcomers are segregated from other organizational members. In informal strategies, newcomers are included with members; much of the learning takes place in their natural environments.

2. *Individual vs. Collective.* Newcomers either go through socialization alone or as part of a group.

3. *Sequential vs. Non-sequential.* Newcomers either go through identifiably different stages or the process is one single transitional stage.

4. *Fixed vs. Variable.* Fixed strategies have specific timetables for certain types of training; variable have no timetables.

5. *Tournament vs. Contest.* In tournaments, newcomers win to move on to next stage; in contests, newcomers are given multiple opportunities to succeed.

6. *Serial vs. Disjunctive.* Serial strategies involve current members teaching newcomers to "act as we act"; disjunctive strategies allow for new behaviors.

7. *Investiture vs. Divestiture.* In investiture, the process is one of "giving" information to newcomers; in divestiture, the process is one of taking old habits away.

Source: Adapted from John Van Maanen, "People Processing: Strategies of Organizational Socialization," *Organizational Dynamics* (Summer 1978): 240–259.

It is critical in the socialization process to offer a realistic orientation program designed to reduce new employee stress.[22] For example, a research-based program called ROPES (Realistic Orientation Programs for new Employee Stress) serves this purpose. The ROPES program also is designed to provide realistic information about the job to new employees and encourage them to stay in their jobs. It is important to let new employees know that they will likely encounter common experiences that cause stress, but that this is a by-product of orientation. Crossing any organizational boundary, whether entering or leaving a job, causes stress. It is important that new employees know that feeling fear, frustration, disappointment, and sometimes even anger in their new positions is common and in fact is expected, and that these feelings will likely disappear in time. Giving new employees opportunities to discuss such issues with current employees can help reduce feelings of fear, anxiety, and so on that new employees might have.

Approaches to Socialization

There is no single best way to socialize employees. Managers must choose from a variety of socialization approaches and decide which are best for the company and its employees. Managers must make seven choices when designing socialization programs. These choices are listed in Exhibit 7.

At first glance, these strategies might sound too academic or theoretical to actually work. However, the strategies listed are currently used in many different types of organizations. For example, organizations practice sequential socialization by training employees to perform many different functions before allowing them to manage. Hospitality companies often use this sequential method.

Similarly, most American high schools "track" students by preparing them to enter either college or the work force immediately after high school. This is an example of a "tournament" socialization strategy; once students score poorly on an achievement test, they are tracked out of college prep courses. If it were a "contest" socialization strategy, all students would be allowed to try all courses. The Marine Corps, fraternities, religious cults, and many elite schools practice divestiture to eliminate newcomers' unwanted or bad habits. Many companies divest newcomers of what they know in order to begin with a "clean slate."

Different strategies work for different companies, depending on the organizational goals. If a company wants to produce a relatively high degree of similarity in the thoughts and actions of newcomers, a combination of formal, serial, and divestiture strategies works best. If a company believes that dissimilarity is best, informal, disjunctive, and investiture strategies may work best.[23] A hospitality company that wishes to teach newcomers to behave and perform like current employees within a specific time frame should choose a formal-sequential-fixed-serial combination. Companies that want employees to learn more on their own should choose an informal-variable strategy.

Research has shown that different approaches influence different socialization factors. For instance, the investiture-divestiture tactic has been found to have significant impact on self-change in individuals. On the other hand, fixed-variable tactics have a significant impact on whether newcomers attempt changes in the mechanics of their jobs early on.[24]

Who Should Socialize Newcomers?

Most managers would say that the best managers and employees should teach newcomers what is important in an organization because these employees best exemplify the behaviors that managers like. This may be true in many cases, but not in all cases. Socializing newcomers can also be done by marginal employees. In fact, research suggests that it may be better to have marginal employees socialize newcomers. Often, the performance of marginal employees improves at the same time new employees are socialized.[25] This happens because the underachievers must prepare for the job of socialization; doing so sometimes helps reinvigorate their attitudes about the organization. Newcomers can also provide employees with positive views of the organization by comparing their new job to their past jobs. For instance, consider the effect of a newcomer who notes that the kitchen has much better lighting than the one he or she worked in before, or who says that he or she heard a lot of nice things about the people who work here, or who claims that the employee meals seem much better than at other companies. Such feedback helps refresh current employees' perspectives on their own jobs. Research also has indicated that newcomers socialized by teams are more likely to learn the ropes faster.[26]

Endnotes

1. Raphael R. Kavanaugh and Jack D. Ninemeier, *Supervision in the Hospitality Industry*, 3rd ed. (Lansing, Mich.: Educational Institute of the American Hotel & Lodging Association, 2001), 116.

2. Kenneth N. Wexley and Gary P. Latham, *Developing and Training Human Resources in Organizations*, 3rd ed. (Upper Saddle River, N.J.: Pearson Education, 2002), 168.

3. Sheryl A. Larson and Amy S. Hewitt, *Staff Recruitment, Retention, and Training Strategies for Community Human Services Organizations* (Baltimore, Md.: Brookes Publishing Co., 2005), 107.

4. Nancy K. Austin, "Giving New Employees a Better Beginning," *Working Woman* 20 (July 1995): 20.

5. Janemarie Mulvey, "Employee Turnover Rises, Increasing Costs," Employment Policy Foundation (22 March 2005), www.epf.org/pubs/factsheets/2005/fs20050317.pdf.

6. H. J. Klein and N. A. Weaver, "The Effectiveness of an Organizational-Level Orientation Training Program in the Socialization of New Hires," *Personnel Psychology* 53, no. 1 (2000): 47–66.

7. Robert H. Woods, "When Servers Meet Customers: An Analysis of the Roles of Restaurant Servers," *Hospitality Research Journal* 14 (1990): 539–552.

8. W. D. St. John, "The Complete Employee Orientation Program," *Personnel Journal* (May 1980): 373–378.

9. Wexley and Latham.

10. Ronald Henkoff, "Finding, Training, and Keeping the Best Service Workers," *Fortune* 130 (3 October 1994): 110.

11 Clive Fullagar et al., "Impact of Early Socialization on Union Commitment," *Journal of Applied Psychology* 80 (February 1995): 147.

12. Carol S. Klein and Jeff Taylor, "Employee Orientation Is an Ongoing Process at Dupont Merck Pharmaceutical Company," *Personnel Journal* 73 (May 1994): 67.

13. Larson and Hewitt, 108.

14. Wexley and Latham, 172.

15. Meryl R. Louis, "Surprise and Sense Making: What Newcomers Experience in Entering Unfamiliar Organizational Settings," *Administrative Science Quarterly* 25, no. 1 (1980): 226–251.

16. Edgar H. Schein, "Organizational Socialization and the Profession of Management," *Sloan Management Review* (Fall 1988): 53–65 (reprinted version of article that originally appeared in the *Sloan Management Review* in 1968).

17. Karen H. Tidball, "Creating a Culture that Builds Your Bottom Line," *Cornell Hotel and Restaurant Administration Quarterly* 29 (May 1988): 63–69; Richard D. Normann, *Service Management: Strategy and Leadership in Service Businesses* (New York: Wiley, 1984); Jay Barney, "Organizational Culture: Can It Be the Source of Sustained Competitive Advantage?" *Academy of Management Review* 11 (1986): 656–665.

18. Craig C. Lundberg and Cheri A. Young, "Newcomer Socialization: Critical Incidents in Hospitality Organizations," *Journal of Hospitality and Tourism Research* 21, no. 2 (1997): 58–74.

19. Larson and Hewitt, 111–112.

20. Larson and Hewitt, 112.

21. The rules for choosing a culture consultant are adapted from Woods, "Ten Rules for Culture Consultants," *The Consultant (FCSI)* 23 (Summer 1990): 52–53.

22. Larson and Hewitt, 113.

23. John Van Maanen, "People Processing: Strategies of Organizational Socialization," *Organizational Dynamics* (Summer 1978): 258.

24. J. Stewart Black and Susan J. Ashford, "Fitting In or Making Jobs Fit: Factors Affecting Mode of Adjustment for New Hires," *Human Relations* 48 (April 1995): 425.

25. Robert I. Sutton and Meryl Reis Louis, "How Selecting and Socializing Newcomers Influences Insiders," *Human Resource Management* 26 (Fall 1987): 347–361.

26. Lisa K. Gundry and Denise M. Rousseau, "Critical Elements in Communicating Culture to Newcomers: The Meaning Is the Message," *Human Relations* 47 (September 1994): 1064.

Key Terms

behavior—The manner in which a person conducts himself or herself; the response of an individual or group to an action, stimulus, or environment.

general property orientation—A formal program presented by an employer to introduce the organization's mission and values to employees; usually conducted shortly after hiring.

norm—A pattern or trait that is considered typical behavior of an individual or group.

organizational culture—The dominant culture or personality of the organization.

orientation—The process of introducing new employees to their work and the environment in which their work is completed.

orientation kit—The package of information provided by employers to new employees during orientation to help new employees understand and get acquainted with the organization's policies, procedures, and facilities.

socialization—The process in which employees learn what is expected of them at work; includes both written and unwritten rules of behavior.

specific job orientation—The process of introducing new employees to the specific tasks and behaviors of their job.

turnover—The rate at which employees leave a company or work unit.

values—A set of beliefs, often socially and culturally defined, which attempt to guide the behavior of an individual or group.

Review Questions

1. What are the broad goals of an orientation program?
2. What are the three general categories of information provided in orientation?
3. How does general property orientation differ from specific job orientation?
4. What items should be included in an orientation kit?
5. What approaches to orientation should managers avoid?

6. How does orientation differ from socialization?
7. What are the purpose and some of the benefits of socialization?
8. What is organizational culture? Why is it important in designing socialization programs?
9. What are the ten rules involved in hiring culture consultants?
10. Who should socialize newcomers? Why?

Mini-Case Study

Before opening his new restaurant, Bob Borich spent two weeks training his personnel. While the money spent on employee salaries and other training costs added substantially to the pre-opening costs, Bob justified the expense by noting the large number of restaurants that failed in their first year because of inadequate service. Bob believed that in the long run, his training costs would be viewed as money well spent.

Six months after opening, Bob experienced a turnover of about 50 percent. As a result, he found himself hiring new employees weekly. Because Bob was busy with the operation of the restaurant—particularly since he had started cooking three shifts a week to ensure food quality—he turned orientation over to a group of employees who had been with him from the start. He reasoned that since these employees had been through the full training program and had displayed their loyalty, they would provide just the type of orientation that he would—if he had the time.

Unfortunately, although the new employees seemed perfectly suited for their jobs, turnover increased dramatically. Within three months after starting the orientation program, Bob was experiencing turnover in excess of 100 percent annually. While still below the national average for his industry, Bob was dissatisfied with the high rate of turnover. Sitting down with a cup of coffee, Bob thought over his problem at the end of a particularly frustrating week.

Discussion Questions

1. What advice would you give Bob Borich?
2. How unique do you believe Bob Borich's current situation is?
3. What parts of orientation should be turned over to employees to conduct?

Chapter 6 Outline

Competencies

1. Identify and explain the stages of the training cycle. (pp. 188–190)

2. Explain how a training needs assessment is developed and conducted. (pp. 190–196)

3. Describe various training methods and how to select one. (pp. 196–208)

4. Explain how to implement and evaluate training programs and activities. (pp. 208–212)

6

Training and Development

This chapter was co-authored by Kelly Phelan, M.S., University of Nevada, Las Vegas; Ph.D. candidate, Purdue University.

JOBS ARE EVOLVING AT an increasingly rapid pace. Estimates are that more than 50 percent of the jobs currently being performed in the United States did not even exist a half-century ago. Hospitality is not exempt from this evolution. If anything, the rate of job growth and job change in hospitality is among the most rapid of any field. Think of how much guest registration has changed. Many hotels and motels used manual check-in and check-out systems well into the 1980s. Today, many hotels offer some form of automated check-in and check-out. The work of hospitality employees will continue to change as new technology develops.

While employee recruitment and selection are crucial to an organization's success, they do not guarantee that employees will perform well. Organizations must provide training to new employees to transform their high potential into high performance. In the hospitality industry, service and quality determine the success or failure of a property. Not surprisingly, the employees determine the level of service provided, and, thus, the overall quality of the guest experience. Therefore, well-considered, adequate training should be provided to ensure guest satisfaction and, ultimately, increased profits.[1] Teaching managers and employees how to adjust to the new jobs they do is the primary focus of this chapter.

Training Expenditures Today

United States businesses spend roughly $62 billion a year on training.[2] On average, $826 is spent annually to train each employee, an increase of nearly $200 over the past five years.[3] Fourteen percent of training is delivered by computer, while most training, 73 percent, is still delivered in a conventional classroom setting. American businesses spend considerably less than international companies on training. The largest companies in the United States spend an average of two percent of their total work time on training. Companies in Germany and Japan, for instance, spend five times as much time on training.[4]

How is all this money spent? *Training* magazine reports that the largest portion of the money—approximately 68 percent—is spent on the salaries of training personnel. Other large expenditures include facilities overhead (nine percent), the cost of seminars and conferences (seven percent), hardware used in training (five percent), outside services such as consultants and speakers (four percent), customized materials (four percent), and off-the-shelf materials used in training (three percent).

Many people debate whether the money spent on hospitality training is spent effectively. Some analysts feel that service in the United States has never been worse.[5] While employees may know how to perform the skills associated with their positions, far too often they do not know—or are not interested in—how to deliver the services. Some say this points out the need for more behavioral training in the hospitality industry. Hospitality companies are responding to this call by increasing training.

A study conducted by the American Society for Training and Development showed that employer-provided training is on the rise in terms of the amount of money invested and the percentage of employees being trained. Yet, there is still a gap between leading-edge companies and the average organization. The training leaders are different in the amount of training they provide, the resources they invest in employee development, the practices they use, and the means of training delivery. Generally, to be leading edge, a company has to spend more money on training employees, especially in human performance work practices such as self-directed teams, and on innovative training practices such as mentoring. Not only must organizations provide more training, they must also provide training to more employees—at least 86 percent to be leading edge. The average organization trains about 74 percent of its employees.[6]

Most research continues to link employee training with increased productivity and supports the theory that trainees reach full productivity levels sooner than new employees who don't receive structured training.[7] Considering this, one would expect hospitality companies to at least consider spending more money on training. However, at a recent Council of Hotel and Restaurant Trainers conference, several top industry executives admitted spending less than two percent of their company budgets on training.[8]

It is not enough for hospitality employees simply to know how to perform the tasks required in their jobs. Since most hospitality employees work with the public, they must also know how to demonstrate behaviors associated with good service. Skills training and behavior training require different approaches. This chapter will discuss both.

The Training Cycle

Most experts agree that training should be viewed as a continuous cycle rather than as a single event. As Exhibit 1 shows, the **training cycle** begins with a **needs assessment**, or identification of a problem. This problem usually results from a discrepancy between a *desired* outcome and what really happens.

In a hospitality company, this discrepancy can take many forms. Guest complaints about service, room cleanliness, or the amount of time it takes to check in are all examples of a discrepancy between the desired outcome and reality. Unfortunately, few guests tell us when a problem exists. Most training programs do not result from guest complaints, but from discrepancies identified by managers or employees.

The second stage in the training cycle is the identification of **training objectives**. In this step, managers establish the goals of a training program. Objectives

Exhibit 1   The Training Cycle

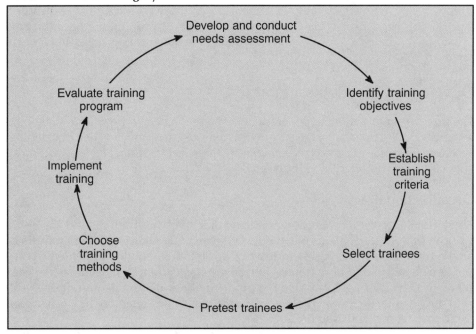

vary with the circumstances. Some objectives aim to improve the service delivered to customers; others may aim to improve productivity or reduce costs.

The third stage in the training cycle process is the establishment of **training criteria**. Training criteria are the benchmarks hospitality managers set to measure effectiveness. In effect, these benchmarks become the standards that participants should reach in their training. Once achieved, these benchmarks tell managers that the learning of a particular training topic is complete.

The fourth stage is selection of trainees. Trainees can be new or potential employees or current employees. In both cases, managers should be careful to select employees who will benefit from the training. Too often, training programs are too simple or too complex for the trainees. Both extremes result in ineffective training.

The fifth stage is **pretesting** employees to establish the baseline of knowledge, skills, or abilities for the training. By testing the employees' current knowledge, skills, and abilities before beginning a training program, managers have a base for evaluating the program's effectiveness later on.

The sixth stage is choosing the proper training methods and techniques. As we show later in this chapter, methods and techniques vary substantially depending on the objectives of the training program, the criteria developed for evaluating learning, and the current level of employee performance.

The seventh stage is implementation of the training program itself. The key to this stage is following the format derived through planning. Managers should be sure to follow the methods identified in previous stages of the training cycle.

The eighth, and final, stage in the training cycle is **training evaluation**. Unfortunately, many hospitality managers—even those who are good at identifying training needs, selecting the proper approach to training, and conducting training—fail to effectively evaluate whether or not training goals have been achieved.

Developing Needs Assessments

The first step in any training program is to assess the need for training. In human resources circles, this first stage is known as a needs assessment. When developing needs assessments, experts typically identify three factors to analyze: the organization, tasks and behaviors, and individuals.

Organizational Analysis

Every training program affects the specific unit receiving training and the organization as a whole. An example often used to explain **organizational analysis** is drawn from the manufacturing industry. Consider what might happen when one team on an assembly line is trained to perform its task at a 25 percent faster pace. While this change might improve the productivity of this single unit, it does not help the organization as a whole because the rest of the assembly line is not prepared to meet the increased production pace.

The same holds true for hospitality. Consider what might happen when servers are trained to write guest checks in a new way. While training might teach servers a more effective way to write guest checks, it could be detrimental instead of helpful unless the cooks who read the checks are also trained in this new method. The same would be true if front desk agents were trained to prepare guest folios in a new way. Unless the night auditor received the same training, the program would not be effective.

These examples illustrate task-oriented training approaches. However, organizational analysis also exists on another important level. Consider issues such as management philosophy and organizational culture. To be effective, each company must incorporate its own management philosophy into its training programs. Consider the suitability of a training program that teaches employees to make decisions for themselves in a company that encourages employees to turn problems over to managers. For the most part, training programs are unsuccessful when they conflict with the management philosophy and organizational culture of a company. For example, assume that an important ingredient in your organizational culture is "teamwork." A training program that teaches employees to work better individually would be incompatible.

These examples illustrate the need for consistency among training objectives and organizational goals. In the 1960s, many organizations experimented with sensitivity training to help employees grow as individuals and become better listeners and to teach them to generate new ideas. Unfortunately, many of the organizations that these employees returned to after training did not embrace these goals. Reward systems did not support these goals and management styles at the time promoted a more dictatorial approach. Consequently, the training was wasted.

Task and Behavior Analysis

Every job consists of several different tasks and behaviors. The objective in **task and behavior analysis** is to determine which tasks and behaviors are required for each specific job. The first step in this process is to conduct a thorough job analysis. The second step is to prepare complete job descriptions and job specifications.

Job analyses, descriptions, and specifications identify three critical elements for managers to consider before beginning any training program. These elements encompass the knowledge, skills, and abilities necessary to complete the various tasks and behaviors associated with a job. These three—often called **KSAs** (knowledge, skills, and abilities)—provide the information managers need to determine which duties and responsibilities to feature in training programs.

Individual Analysis

An **individual analysis** identifies the strengths and weaknesses of the employee performing the job. The purpose of individual analysis is to specifically determine which employees require what types of training. Sometimes, training programs are designed for entire departments. Other times, only individual employees receive training.

For example, a restaurant manager may conduct a thorough needs analysis and find that his or her employees need training in wine sales and service. That manager should then assess whether all restaurant employees should receive the same training. Some employees will know nothing about wine, while others will know quite a lot. Under such circumstances, a training program on the basics of wine identification and service would be useful to some employees, but unnecessary for others. From a managerial perspective, training employees who already have this knowledge represents a waste of training dollars. To prevent such waste, managers should assess the individual KSAs of each employee before beginning any training program.

Conducting Needs Assessments

Now that we've identified some reasons for performing needs assessments, we can examine methods for conducting them. This section will examine 12 methods of conducting needs assessments and the advantages and disadvantages of each method. These methods are listed in Exhibit 2. Unfortunately, no single method can be recommended for all circumstances or environments. Instead, each method may be effective in different situations. When choosing a method or combination of methods, it can be helpful to review the skill levels of job applicants and employees (see Exhibit 3).

Advisory Committee

Typically, an **advisory committee** consists of managers who review job skill and behavior demands and compare these to the current level of employee

Exhibit 2   Needs Assessment Methods

```
 1. Advisory committee
 2. Job descriptions and job specifications
 3. Work sampling
 4. Job performance measurements
 5. Attitude surveys
 6. Performance appraisals
 7. Skills tests
 8. Performance documents
 9. Guest feedback
10. Questionnaires
11. Exit interviews
12. Critical incidents
```

performance. This method of needs assessment often benefits from employee representation on the committee. An effective advisory committee in a housekeeping department may include the assistant housekeeping manager, a manager from the front desk, a manager from reservations, and employees from each department. One advantage of advisory committees is that, often, they can establish desired outcomes that are well suited to organizational needs. A disadvantage is that employee participation is sometimes limited by a reluctance to disagree with their managers. This obstacle can be overcome by establishing an open-meeting, full-participation policy from the outset.

Job Descriptions and Job Specifications

A second method of conducting an effective training needs assessment is to compare the KSAs identified in current job descriptions and specifications to current job performance. The effectiveness of this type of needs assessment, typically conducted by managers in charge of a given unit, can be enhanced by an advisory committee.

Work Sampling

Work sampling is conducted by a trained analyst who systematically observes and reviews actual work performance. The analyst only observes the work; he or she does not participate. The advantage of work sampling is that the analyst *sees* the work actually being done instead of just seeing the results or hearing recollections of each person doing the work. Disadvantages include the cost of hiring an analyst and the time involved. To accurately assess current performance, the analyst must watch a relatively large number of employees at work. Unless all employees are observed, work sampling is ineffective for identifying individual employee needs.

Job Performance Measurements

Job performance measurements are much like work sampling because both involve an analyst. The major difference is that, for job performance

Exhibit 3 *Nation's Business* **Poll of Readers: Skill Levels of Job Applicants and Workers**

What level of skills are workers bringing to jobs in your business?

Very good	5%	Adequate	37%
Good	16%	Deficient	42%

How has the skill level of job applicants you see changed over the past three years?

Improved	7%	Declined	46%
About the same	47%		

What is the most common shortcoming of job applicants you see?

Lack of specific technical skills	17%
Lack of basic reading and math skills	16%
Inability to communicate well, orally and/or in writing	19%
Poor attitude and work habits	43%
Lack of previous work experience	5%

How much negative financial impact has there been on your business because of inadequately trained workers?

Little or no impact	21%	Heavy impact	17%
Moderate impact	62%		

How much retraining/education do you offer your current employees each year?

None	17%	Six to 10 days	15%
Less than a day	9%	More than 10 days	26%
Two to five days	33%		

Who should have the primary responsibility for educating and training workers?

Businesses	26%
Public and private schools (including community colleges)	67%
Government agencies	1%
Outside suppliers and consultants	1%
Industry/trade associations or local chambers of commerce	5%

Who should pay for training workers?

Businesses seeking the skilled workers	37%
State or local government	13%
Federal government	3%
Workers themselves	47%

Which of these would best improve education/training programs at the local level?

Publicly funded vouchers for government or private-sector training	23%
One-stop education/training and referral centers	27%
Increased flexibility of state/local use of federal funds	37%
No changes needed	13%

Source: *Nation's Business* (October 1995): 93.

measurements, the analyst actually performs each job in addition to observing employee performance. This direct involvement can result in identification of KSAs that other methods do not. However, when assessing jobs that require special skills (many cooking jobs, for instance), it is often difficult to find an analyst who can perform all the necessary tasks without advanced training.

Job performance measurements can require a substantial time commitment, especially in cases that involve unusual or infrequent job responsibilities. Many experts view this method as one of the least cost-effective because of the time it takes an analyst to observe and participate in each job. In addition, extensive training, which increases costs, is sometimes required to prepare the analyst for each position. Although costly, this method is one of the most thorough.

Attitude Surveys

Not all training focuses on improving task completion. Many hospitality companies recognize the importance of employee attitudes and behavior toward guests. **Attitude surveys** can provide an effective means of determining when training is required to improve the behavioral side of service. Attitude surveys are also useful in pinpointing what employees like and dislike about their jobs, fellow employees, and managers. These surveys can be useful in developing training programs that increase employee satisfaction and thereby can help reduce unwanted employee turnover. The principal disadvantage of surveys is their relative inability to determine the need for either skills or task-related training.

Performance Appraisals

When used properly, regular performance appraisals help identify individual employees in need of training. Consistent task- or behavior-related problems indicate the need for additional training. However, because many managers do not know how to conduct performance appraisals effectively, this method often identifies training needs incorrectly.

Skills Tests

The use of skills tests is one of the most common methods of assessing training needs. These tests measure an employee's ability to perform a certain task in a certain way. For example, a manager might ask an employee to demonstrate the proper method of opening and serving wine to determine whether that employee needs training. While this method is useful in determining the need for skills-related training, it is not useful for identifying training needs for certain behaviors or more complex tasks.

Performance Documents

Reports pertaining to absenteeism, sales, guest complaints, commendations, and productivity are some of the **performance documents** useful for pinpointing individual training needs. Documents such as turnover or waste reports are useful in determining department training needs. Since such data is often collected during the normal course of business, the use of performance documents represents a low-cost approach to assessing training needs, as well. However, this method is not useful for identifying behavioral training needs because the focus is on data or statistics rather than on behavior.

Guest Feedback

When asked, owners and managers of small hospitality businesses might say they know that their employees need training when guests complain. However, research shows that guests rarely complain. Instead, guests simply do not return. Worse yet, they may tell others about their disappointing experience. As a result, guest feedback is not useful for assessing training needs unless the hospitality organization actively collects information from a large number of guests. Active guest feedback collection does have one advantage: it demonstrates a property's commitment to service.

Questionnaires

Questionnaires are useful for gathering training needs information because of the large amount of data that can be collected easily and cheaply. For example, a company might ask employees and managers throughout a hotel to complete a special questionnaire to determine the training needs of housekeeping staff. Questionnaires can also provide an effective means of identifying managerial training needs; experts might collect information from several companies to determine the training needs for managers in a specific hotel.

Exit Interviews

Employees or managers leaving an organization are often willing to share information and experiences that can help managers determine training needs. When properly collected, this information can give managers useful insight into issues that they sometimes cannot see, particularly into those issues that relate to turnover. Some companies even require employees leaving the organization to participate in **exit interviews** before receiving their final paycheck.

However, research indicates that employees rarely give accurate information in exit interviews unless anonymity and confidentiality are ensured.[9] Few employees want to "burn their bridges" since they may someday need a recommendation from the company they are leaving. Employees are also likely to have friends still on the job who might be hurt by their comments. And, frequently, an employee's reason for leaving may relate to disagreements with the very managers who conduct the interviews.

Exit interviews generally provide a useful method of needs assessment when interviews are conducted either by third parties (someone not associated with the hospitality company) or by computerized surveys that collect data while providing employee anonymity.

Critical Incidents

The **critical incidents** method requires observers (managers or outsiders) to notice and record specific incidents that are examples of either good or poor employee performance. This method is particularly useful when the intended training technique involves **case studies,** since the incidents themselves provide the cases to use in training.

When collected over a period of time, critical incident observations identify training needs. There is a drawback, however: such incidents rarely occur when you want them to. As a result, managers can spend considerable time waiting for critical incidents to happen.

While each of these methods is useful and necessary, management should not overlook the basic training needs of its employees. A *Harvard Business Review* article illustrates how basic skills training—focusing on reading, writing, and arithmetic—produces some of the greatest productivity gains.[10]

Designing the Training Program

Effective training programs do not create themselves. To ensure that employees are well prepared for the jobs they are expected to perform, management must train them properly. First, managers must articulate training objectives. Then, they must establish criteria to meet those objectives. Finding the right trainees is vital to a firm's success. Selecting employees and assessing their skills before training is important so that managers can evaluate the success of the training program upon its completion.

Steps in designing the training program include establishing training objectives, establishing training criteria, selecting employees to train, and pretesting the trainees.

Establishing Training Objectives

Training objectives typically fall into four general categories: reaction-based, learning-acquired, on-the-job behaviors, and results-oriented.

Objectives that are based on a trainee's reaction to a training program relate to how the trainees view the process. In some cases, a training program objective might simply be to enhance employee regard for the company. Training programs designed to teach employees to read or write, to quit smoking, or to lose weight are examples of programs with reaction-based objectives. In each case, while the achievement of the training objective would benefit the company indirectly, it would benefit the participant directly. Reaction-based assessment should be a part of every training program, not just those that benefit employees directly.

The second category of objectives involves the learning acquired during the training program. In some training programs, knowledge acquisition is the ultimate objective. This was the gist of the wine service testing example used earlier, which measured employee knowledge of specific skills. This type of training objective is also quite common in management development programs and in education classes.

The third type of training objective relates to on-the-job behaviors. For instance, quality of service is often measured in terms of the degree of sincerity or friendliness displayed by guest-contact personnel. As a result, hospitality companies commonly develop training programs that emphasize positive behavior toward guests as the principal objective.

The most common type of objective is the results-oriented objective. In a results-oriented program, the goal is to improve measurable outcomes of an individual or group. Programs that train employees to use cash registers, check in guests more quickly, reduce waste in kitchens, or increase the number of repeat guests are all examples of training programs with results-oriented objectives.

While many training programs are based on one type of objective, many use multiple objectives. An example might be a program for training current employees to perform some task or behavior that qualifies them for merit pay increases. In this case, objectives would be reaction-based, results-oriented, and focused upon on-the-job behaviors.

When developing training objectives, it is important that managers identify what they hope to accomplish in clear and measurable terms. Objectives such as "improve employee job satisfaction" fail because they are too vague. However, "reduce turnover" (as a measure of improving job satisfaction) would be a recognizable and measurable objective. Well-designed objectives can be stated using action verbs such as "describe," "complete," "make," "define," "identify," "participate in," and so on.

Establishing Training Criteria

A training program that correctly assesses needs and clearly identifies objectives is useful only if the criteria for success are clearly outlined. Such criteria establish a benchmark for measuring what will be learned or gained from the training process. For example, in a training program developed for a Virgin Islands resort hotel, the criteria for each session related to subject matter knowledge and to the ability to perform tasks or demonstrate desired behaviors correctly and consistently. During a session devoted to food service training, knowing how to set, bus, and serve a table efficiently was established as a criterion for success. To measure accomplishment, trainers required each participant to perform these tasks independently within a specific time frame. Other criteria could be established to measure behavioral, reaction-based, or learning-acquired objectives.

Selecting Trainees

Employees who participate in training ultimately determine whether a program is successful or not. Selection can be ongoing for training programs that involve several steps or multiple stages.

An example of an ongoing selection process can be drawn from a training program at the Virgin Grand Hotel in St. John, U.S. Virgin Islands. The objective of this program was to train Virgin Islanders for front-line service positions in the hospitality industry. None of the participants had any hospitality training experience. The program was funded partially by the U.S. government through a Partners in Commerce (PIC) program.

The training program was organized in several stages, each related to a different skill or behavior useful to hospitality employees. The eight-week program enlisted specialists to instruct each of the one-week sessions, which ran from

8:00 A.M. until 4:00 P.M. Since the number of participants was fairly high (about 100), several classes were offered each week to accommodate participants on a rotating basis.

At the end of each week, instructors from each class met with the local training program director and property managers to evaluate the progress of each participant. After instructors arrived at a consensus, the training director met privately with each participant to discuss individual progress during the week and to establish goals for the following week. Participants who were not progressing were advised—in writing—of their goals for the following weeks. If they did not meet these goals, participants were dropped from the program. As a result, only 75 of over 100 original participants eventually graduated from the program.

Pretesting Trainees

Many managers begin training after completing a needs assessment, determining objectives, identifying criteria, and selecting participants. These managers, however, are missing a step: they're failing to establish what their employees currently know. Because no baselines of KSAs are identified before implementing training, it is difficult to compare performance before and after training. As a result, it is impossible to evaluate the success of a training program.

Ideally, a hospitality manager should identify two separate groups during pretesting. One group is tested before and after training. The other group is also tested before and after the program, but does not receive training. This second group is called the control group. This type of testing is called pretest-posttest design with a control group.

By measuring both groups—the group that receives training and the group that does not—managers can clearly assess the impact of a training program. Pretesting can be conducted easily after trainees are divided into two groups.

If it is impossible to break the trainees into two groups, managers should test employees both before and after training. While this method allows managers to assess KSAs both before and after training, it does not yield definite conclusions about the value of the training program because other factors introduced during the training period can affect the KSAs displayed during the posttest.

Unfortunately, some managers simply test their employees' KSAs after training. When no pretest is used, all these managers really know are the employees' KSAs at the time of testing, which provide little information about a training program.

Choosing Training Methods ————————————————

Because of rapid advances in technology, new training techniques are created almost every year. Just a few years ago, only the most sophisticated training programs used computers. Today, computers are used in many training programs, both alone and in conjunction with various other media. For instance, what a user sees on a computer terminal can be displayed to an audience through the use of a projector screen. Touch-screen systems also allow trainees to work at their own pace by linking computers with compact videodisks. This creates interactive videodisk training that enables trainees to access a wide variety of sounds and images.

While many of these new training methods apply to the hospitality industry, just as many older methods remain useful. Deciding among methods usually depends on the type of training intended, the trainees selected, the objectives of the training program, and the training environment. Experts say that no single training method is right for every situation. Instead, training is situational; some objectives can be more easily accomplished with one method, while other objectives are more easily achieved with another method. Some general guidelines should be followed in choosing appropriate training methods. For example, adults learn in specific ways. Exhibit 4 presents some of the general concepts about adult learning that are useful to remember.

This section discusses most of the popular training methods used today. These methods are grouped in these categories: training for managers, training for nonmanagers, and training for all employee levels.

Training for Managers

The methods appropriate for training managers include:

- Case study training
- In-basket training
- Conference training
- Behavioral modeling

Case Study Training. Case studies typically detail a series of events—either real or hypothetical—that take place in a business environment. This method challenges participants to sort through provided data to identify problems and then propose solutions to these problems. Researchers have referred to this type of training as "Aha! Learning" because, at some point during case analysis or discussion, participants often suddenly realize—"Aha!"—what is and what is not important. Exhibit 5 shows that case studies can be particularly useful in training that involves problem-solving skills.

Experts often cite one disadvantage of this approach: cases take place in a vacuum, while decisions are made in "real time." In other words, managers in "real life" don't face just a single issue as they do in case studies. Instead, "real life" managers face that issue plus many others at the same time. Participants may tend to approach case studies too analytically. In a real hospitality environment, problems generally come in all shapes and sizes, not in neatly packaged case studies.

In-Basket Training. In-basket training generally presents participants with a wide array of problems similar to those found in their in-basket at work. As a training tool, in-basket training has three objectives: (1) to train participants to identify which issues require the most immediate response; (2) to teach participants how to delegate those problems that do not require their personal attention; and (3) to instruct employees how to work on several problems simultaneously.

Exhibit 4   General Learning Concepts

- Behavior that is rewarded (reinforced) is more likely to recur.
- This reinforcement, to be most effective, must immediately follow the desired behavior and be clearly connected with that behavior.
- Mere repetition, without reinforcement, is an ineffective approach to learning.
- Threats and punishment have variable and uncertain effects on learning. Punishment may disturb the learning process.
- The sense of satisfaction that stems from achievement is the type of reward that has the greatest transfer value to other situations.
- The value of an external reward depends on who dispenses the reward. If the reward giver is highly respected, the extrinsic reward may be of great value; if not, it may be without value.
- Learners progress in an area of learning only as far as they need to in order to achieve their purposes.
- Individuals are more likely to be enthusiastic about a learning situation if they themselves have participated in the planning of the project.
- Autocratic leadership has been found to make members more dependent on the leader and to generate resentment in the group.
- Overstrict discipline tends to be associated with greater conformity, anxiety, shyness, and acquiescence; greater permissiveness is associated with more initiative and creativity.
- Many people experience so much criticism, failure, and discouragement that their self-confidence, level of aspiration, and sense of worth are damaged.
- When people experience too much frustration, their behavior ceases to be integrated, purposeful, and rational.
- People who have met with little success and continual failure are not apt to be in the mood to learn.
- Individuals tend to think best whenever they encounter an obstacle or intellectual challenge that is of interest to them.
- The best way to help people form a general concept is to present an idea in numerous and varied situations.
- Learning from reading is aided more by time spent recalling what has been read than by rereading.
- Individuals remember new information that confirms their previous attitudes better than they remember new information that does not confirm their previous attitudes.
- What is learned is more likely to be available for use if it is learned in a situation much like that in which it is to be used, and immediately preceding the time when it is needed.
- The best time to learn is when the learning can be useful. Motivation is then at its strongest peak.

Source: R. Wayne Mondy and Robert M. Noe, *Human Resource Management* (Englewood Cliffs, N.J.: Prentice-Hall, 1996), 235.

Exhibit 5   Relative Effectiveness of Training Methods

Method	Knowledge Acquisition Rank	Changing Attitudes Rank	Problem-Solving Rank	Interpersonal Skills Rank	Participant Acceptance Rank	Knowledge Retention Rank
Case Study	2	4	1	4	2	2
Conference (Discussion)	3	3	4	3	1	5
Lecture (W/Questions)	9	8	9	8	8	8
Games	6	5	2	5	3	6
Role Play	7	2	3	2	4	4
Movies/Films	4	6	7	6	5	7
Programmed Instruction	1	7	6	7	7	1
Sensitivity Training	8	1	5	1	6	3
Lecture Television	5	9	8	9	9	9

Scale: 1 = Best; 9 = Worst

Source: Stephen J. Carroll, Jr., Frank T. Paine and John J. Ivancevich, "The Relative Effectiveness of Training Methods," *Personnel Psychology* 25 (1972): 495–509.

In-basket training is sometimes used as a selection process for identifying potential managers. When used as a selection tool, in-basket training may test how applicants prioritize problems and how well they delegate authority. Research has shown that this method effectively predicts future job behavior.

Conference Training. This form of training is essentially one-on-one discussion between the trainer and trainee. Conference training permits virtually any issue to be explored in-depth. For instance, a non-commercial food service manager might use this type of training to explain to a cashier why it is necessary to maintain accurate records of each transaction. The obvious advantage is the reinforcement provided by close contact between trainer and trainee. Disadvantages include the time and cost of individualized training.

Behavioral Modeling. Social learning theory claims that people learn most behavior by observing others, meaning that most people model their behaviors after others' behaviors. Modeling takes advantage of that theory by giving participants the chance to actually see how a model acts in a certain situation, rather than by simply instructing participants how to act. A sequence of steps must take place to implement modeling:

- A specific interpersonal skill is introduced, usually through lecture.
- A model acts out the skill either on video or in person.

- The trainer highlights key points in the model's portrayal.
- Trainees practice the skill through role-playing.
- The trainer and other participants provide feedback on the role-playing.

For modeling to work, the trainee must be able to relate to the model. A model who is the same age and sex as the participant is likely to have more credibility than a model with different traits and views. The advantage of modeling is its emphasis on "doing" rather than on "telling." Managers can be shown how to delegate, communicate, conduct a meeting, interview an applicant, or discipline an employee. The role of the facilitator in this process is to coach participants to follow the modeled behaviors more closely. Most research shows that this form of training is a good way to teach effective interpersonal skills to supervisors and others.

The disadvantages of this approach are that the training method is limited to behavioral issues and that the training facilitator must be adept at conducting sessions. However, since hospitality management involves behavioral and interpersonal skill issues, this method often represents an excellent form of training, especially for managers and supervisors.

Training for Nonmanagers

Training methods suitable for nonmanagement employees include the following:

- On-the-job training
- Job instruction training
- Lectures
- Coaching/mentoring
- Programmed instruction

On-the-Job Training. On-the-job training (OJT) can be a very effective method of learning; unfortunately, it is often conducted incorrectly. Typically, one employee is simply asked to teach another some desired skill. In far too many cases, trainers are assigned not because they can teach, but because they can perform tasks or behaviors well. Being good at a job does not necessarily make someone an effective trainer.

When supervisors or trained trainers are involved, OJT can be very effective and cost-efficient because training can be conducted during business operations in actual work settings. To a degree, OJT resembles modeling, a fairly good method for hospitality training.

Like most methods, OJT has its disadvantages. As noted earlier, training assignments can be inappropriate or ineffective. In addition, training can interfere with normal business. Because the training is fast-paced, trainers generally have little or no time to provide feedback or to reiterate important steps. Finally, this type of training perpetuates the status quo because trainees are very likely to perform in the same way as their trainers, right or wrong.

Job Instruction Training. Job instruction training (JIT) is a structured approach to training that requires trainees to proceed through a series of steps in a sequential

Exhibit 6   Steps in Job Instruction Training

Step 1: Prepare the Employee
- Put employee at ease
- Arouse interest in training

Step 2: Present the Task or Skill
- Tell
- Show
- Explain
- Demonstrate
- Allow time for questions and repeat steps if necessary

Step 3: Try Out the Performance
- Allow employee to try on his or her own
- Have employee explain key points
- Correct errors
- Re-instruct if necessary

Step 4: Follow-Up
- Allow employee to perform on his or her own
- Check on employee frequently
- Gradually reduce assistance

pattern. The pattern is outlined in Exhibit 6. This type of training is good for task-oriented jobs, such as operating equipment and preparing foods.

Lectures. Perhaps the most common form of **off-the-job training** is the oral presentation of information to an audience. The advantage of a lecture is that large amounts of information can be delivered in a relatively short period of time to a large number of people. As a result, the lecture method is very cost-effective.

One disadvantage of the lecture method, however, is the lack of two-way communication. In addition, no allowance is made during lectures for the varying levels of understanding among participants. Some participants may find lectures boring and slow while others in the same audience may have trouble keeping up. Recent research shows that the "MTV generation" of today is inclined to learn from other, more participative methods.[11]

Coaching/Mentoring. Both coaching and mentoring have gained favor in recent years because these methods often produce desirable behavioral results. By using a form of conference training and/or modeling, coaches and mentors often concentrate on improving the skills of subordinates. Many managers are better described as coaches or mentors because they play a greater role than just that of manager. Coaches and mentors are concerned with the overall professional development of their protégés. As a result, they encourage their protégés' skill and leadership development rather than take the narrow-minded approach of just making sure employees know how to do their immediate job tasks. Mentors encourage protégés to work toward greater aspirations.[12]

Programmed Instruction. Programmed instruction enables trainees to learn at their own pace. Originally, programmed instruction was accomplished through paper-and-pencil tests that evaluated whether trainees had learned enough to proceed to the next stage. Today, computers have generally replaced papers and pencils. Self-programmed and self-directed instruction is becoming more popular, partially due to the Internet and to long-distance education programs. Research on the effectiveness of such programs has generally been very positive. It appears that many employees prefer to learn at their own pace and they actually learn and retain more. In fact, one study showed approximately 94 percent of the participants in a self-directed learning program both learned more and enjoyed the program more.[13]

Computerized training programs are sometimes referred to as computer-assisted instruction (CAI) or computer-components. After reviewing each component, the trainee is asked to respond to a series of questions about the material. When the trainee passes the test on this material, he or she moves on to the next section. Managers using programmed learning for training should realize that different trainees may be working at different levels in the same room.

Interactive videodisk programs are the most sophisticated approach to programmed learning used today. These programs combine computer and video technology, enabling trainees to proceed at their own pace. This high-tech training uses a computer that is often connected to a touch-screen monitor and a videodisk player. Individual trainees or groups can watch a video segment that simulates a particular situation, then respond via computer to corresponding questions.

Interactive technology is rapidly becoming a major training component as U.S. companies and individuals invest billions annually in computer-based training. Laser disks, CD-ROMs, interactive voice systems, Internet-based training, satellite training, and other methods are revolutionizing training. Hospitality companies such as Holiday Inn are investing millions in multimedia training. Much has been written about the advantages and uses of these training methods in hospitality today and in the future.

E-learning has become an attractive alternative to the classroom because of the amount of time and money saved. Some experts believe the first-year potential savings of an e-learning program can be as high as 50 percent due to the reduced travel, classroom, and instructor expenses. It is likely that e-learning will soon account for at least half the money spent on corporate training and education.[14] The principal disadvantage of interactive technology is the start-up cost. Properties may need to invest thousands of dollars, depending on the equipment selected.

Training for All Employee Levels

Methods of training suitable for all employee levels include the following:

- Job rotation
- Role-playing

- Vestibule training

- Business games

- Sensitivity training

- Basic skills training

- Team training

- Diversity training

Job Rotation. Job rotation involves moving trainees from one job to another. This training method is widely used in training hospitality managers, many of whom spend a certain number of weeks in each job before assuming their managerial duties. An advantage of job rotation is that trainees can see how work is performed in many different jobs. Trainees also get to know the employees in each position.

When used to train line-level employees, job rotation actually becomes a method of cross-training that affords employees the knowledge and skills to do different jobs. However, the success of this type of training depends on how information is presented at each step of the process. If on-the-job training is used in each assignment—often the case in hospitality—very little learning takes place.

Role-Playing. Role-playing enables participants to experience real or exaggerated work situations. For instance, consider the use of role-playing in a training session designed to help participants improve their interpersonal skills. A trainer might ask one participant to role-play a hospitality manager and another to role-play an employee. The purpose is to allow each participant to experience what it "feels like" to be in that role.

Hospitality trainers often ask participants to play the roles of guests and servers to experience what guests see and feel. Other common role-plays include role reversal for a man and woman, assuming the role of a person with a disability, and so on. The intent in each case is to give trainees the opportunity to see what it's like to face the barriers or obstacles others may face.

Gaining the opportunity to step into another person's shoes is a principal advantage of role-playing, a method of training that generally evokes emotions and frustrations. And because four principles of learning are involved—active participation, modeling, feedback, and practice—role-playing often results in a high level of learning when used properly. Trainers should encourage involvement, since learning depends on each participant's involvement in his or her roles. A 1999 research project found that work-related learning objectives can sometimes be more readily transferred through role-plays.[15] According to the Center for Workforce Development, employees learn only about 30 percent of the information and skills needed for their jobs through formal training, and the other 70 percent on the job and from watching co-workers.[16]

Vestibule Training. Vestibule training—or simulation—involves the virtual duplication of the work environment in an off-site setting. The advantage of using a duplicated environment rather than the actual workplace is that training can take place without interrupting the normal flow of business. While vestibule training usually results in a fairly high level of learning, it is also regarded as an expensive way to accomplish some training objectives, primarily because of the cost of duplicating the workplace environment. Some hospitality training is well suited for this method. For instance, training employees to use electronic equipment such as cash registers or check-in systems can be accomplished through vestibule training by simply setting up the necessary equipment in an empty room.

Vestibule or simulation training is also useful in training managers and employees how to make decisions in specific environments. The theory is that if managers or employees have faced similar situations—even if they were simulated—they will be more likely to make the right decisions. Many business games on the market allow participants to simulate workplace environments. In some of the more complex simulations, participants create and operate simulated organizations for brief periods. Other simulations allow participants to experience what it feels like to be placed in a specific situation. Two simulations that can work in classes and in seminars are *Bafá Bafá* and *StarPower*. The objective of Bafá Bafá is to create an environment in which participants learn what it feels like to visit another culture; in StarPower, participants learn how to manage power.[17]

Business Games. Business games are another form of simulation through which participants learn how to deal with a variety of issues in a mock business environment. Commercial forms of this training approach are available from many sources. The advantages of business games are threefold: games are fun, they provide a setting that simulates reality, and many issues can be introduced using a single game. A disadvantage is that participants sometimes become engrossed in winning and forget that the goal is to learn.

Sensitivity Training. A training method often used to enhance interpersonal skills is **sensitivity training**. Also called T-Group or laboratory training, this method helps participants become more aware of their own behaviors and of their behaviors toward others.

First developed by Kurt Lewin and other scholars, sensitivity training is usually conducted in small groups of four to ten participants. Typically, each participant is confronted about his or her behaviors by other group members. Each participant then has the opportunity to express his or her feelings about the group process. The training facilitator's role is critical because of the deep emotional reaction some participants may experience during the process. The advantage of sensitivity training is that it enables participants, in a constructive way, to see how others see them. The principal disadvantage is that, unless expertly facilitated, the process can become dangerously personal.

Basic Skills Training. Nearly 90 million adults in the United States are considered functionally illiterate, meaning they can barely read labels, and so on. Employees' lack of basic skills results in an estimated $60 billion loss in productivity for American companies each year.[18] Considering this statistic, investing in employees' basic skills such as reading, writing, computing, and English as a second language is potentially very worthwhile. At MGM Grand in Las Vegas, more than 85 percent of all housekeepers do not speak English as their native language. In an effort to make their jobs easier and their interactions with guests more smooth, all new housekeepers go through six weeks of training. During each day of training, they attend English classes in the morning, and then learn housekeeping policies and procedures in the afternoon.

Team Training. In the hospitality industry, working together is an everyday occurrence; however, team training is virtually nonexistent. Instead, the us-versus-them mentality has a tendency to serve as an easy defense mechanism. Some companies have enlisted the expertise of professional team-building programs such as Outward Bound to instill a sense of cooperation and team spirit through adventurous challenges. Companies can choose from a variety of other team-building techniques. For instance, Shandwick International sent eight public relations executives to a restaurant for a team-building exercise called "recipes for success." The participants worked in teams on specific tasks to help them increase their conflict-resolution skills and become more comfortable giving orders.[19]

Managers can develop their own successful team training programs if they keep the following points in mind:

- Team building is a complex and challenging process. Expecting a quick team mentality is unrealistic. The most successful teams are ones that developed over time.

- Team development does not always fit nicely into the "forming, storming, norming, and performing" model. Training can help work through each stage, but lapses may occur; team members and managers must be aware of this.

- New members must be quickly brought up to speed. Throwing a new team member in with the group without giving him or her comprehensive training would be detrimental all around.

- Active, hands-on experience yields the best results. Teaching conflict resolution via lecture robs team members of the opportunity to reflect and exchange ideas.[20]

Diversity Training. As the work force becomes more and more multicultural, companies are increasingly adding diversity-training programs for employees. This type of training is often necessary to educate employees to be more sensitive to their co-workers' needs, as well as to treat guests respectfully. After numerous discrimination lawsuits, Adams Mark Hotels instituted diversity-training programs for almost 11,000 employees. Each employee is required to attend an all-day seminar designed to teach racial and religious sensitivity.[21]

Hospitality managers should follow several guidelines to choose the best method for any particular training program. To be effective, the training method should:[22]

- Motivate trainees to improve their performance.
- Clearly demonstrate desired skills.
- Provide for active trainee participation.
- Provide an opportunity to practice new skills.
- Provide timely feedback on trainee performance.

- Provide some means for reinforcement while trainees learn.

- Structure tasks from the simple to the complex.

- Be adaptable to specific problems.

- Encourage positive transfer of knowledge and skills from training to the job.

Implementing the Training Program

Appropriate implementation is just as important to the success of any training program as the appropriate selection of methods, trainers, and trainees. Even though managers plan their training programs thoroughly, far too often they fail to implement those programs as planned. In many cases, managers simply implement the easiest training program possible. This defeats the purpose of planning. Careful follow-through on all planned details is critical in the implementation stage, the stage during which trainees actually undergo training.

Implementation can involve a variety of approaches, and sometimes creativity generates the best solutions. For example, Bankers Trust in New York developed a computer game designed to train its managers and staff about banker strategy and financial rules. Employees were playing solitaire on the company computers anyway; instead of wasting their time, they could learn valuable skills while having fun with the company game.[23] The same approach could work in hospitality. For instance, a front desk clerk could benefit from playing a hotel management game on a computer terminal during slow times.

One thing to remember when designing and delivering training programs is that you must be aware of people with disabilities and how effective your program will be for them. Research has shown that when training is more suitable and better structured for people with disabilities, a greater transfer of information takes place. Working with disabled people to develop training and orientation programs is one of the most effective ways to be sure their needs are met.[24]

Anticipate Resistance to Change

Both employees and managers may be resistant to change. Such resistance may be linked to negative experiences or to a fear of lost employment. So many U.S. companies have been downsizing, rightsizing, outsourcing, and reengineering that even if you have not personally experienced job loss, you may have friends who have or you have read about it in the press. Actually, jobs in the United States have been increasing, not decreasing, often even at companies known for downsizing. For instance, a study of U.S. companies found that, while 64 percent had eliminated jobs in the previous 12 months, 86 percent had created and filled new positions. As a result, 46 percent had more workers than they did a year before (another 22 percent remained constant).[25] In spite of this, many now consider jobs more temporary than in the past. Some even believe that the "job" is a social artifact and that the future of work may be more like a concert tour than a permanent position. For instance, the "Rolling Stones Voodoo Lounge" tour earned $300 million, but it carried only six full-time employees. A majority of the tour's workers were temporary and went on to something else after the tour.[26]

This threat of change often disrupts social groups and leads to different social relationships. Before implementing any training programs, managers should build the trust and confidence of their employees, open communication lines to dispel rumors, and, whenever possible, allow employees to participate in change-making decisions.[27]

Evaluating Training

Simply having a training program is not enough. Considerable evidence suggests that a substantial part of organizations' investment in training is often wasted due to poor learning transfer and trainee relapse.[28] One of the most important steps in training is program evaluation. Unfortunately, this is the step that receives the least attention and, all too often, is ignored altogether. As a result, many companies do not really know what effect a training program has had on employees or on the organization.

There are several logical reasons managers fail to follow through on training by completing evaluations. If they see some change in one or more employees, managers often simply assume that the training has had an effect. Managers also tend to assume that training works—with or without observed changes—just because it was conducted. In addition, managers often take ownership for training programs because they were the force behind the program. In some cases, managers simply do not want to go through objective evaluations because they might discover that a program was not worthwhile.

Perhaps the most common reason managers fail to evaluate their training programs is that they do not know how. This section provides models that managers can use to evaluate their training programs by highlighting critical points in the evaluation process.

It is important to remember when reading this section that the success of the overall training program will likely rest on whether or not you effectively evaluate the process as a whole. Managers are more likely to look at the results-based outcomes and sometimes neglect the personal issues involved in training. However, training participants who feel like they were more involved in the developmental feedback process (or evaluation) have reported much higher levels of satisfaction and learning. In addition, those participants able to voice their concerns about training issues also showed greater acceptance and learning.

In one study of learners' responses to training, researchers found out that there were four problems with their training process: 1) participants wanted more training, 2) they were concerned that some biases might influence peer evaluations, 3) there was too little time and attention paid to evaluation of the training programs, and 4) criteria used for evaluation did not always take employee reaction into consideration effectively.[29]

Measuring Change

The principal goal of any training program is change. Managers should ask two questions during an evaluation: Did change occur? Did this change result from the training? Managers need to know if the training caused the change. Even if managers can answer both questions positively, they still may want to ask several more: Do the changes benefit the entire organization? Will the same program work again in the future? Should it be altered? It is important to remember that responses to change can be varied. Therefore, it is preferable to measure training outcomes in terms of change from pretest to posttest, rather than merely through attainment (posttest only) scores.[30]

Earlier in this chapter we referred to four categories of training objectives: reaction-based, learning-acquired, on-the-job-behaviors, and results-oriented. One more objective should be added to training today. This is the increase in the amount of training designed to improve optimism among employees. Sometimes it is not enough for employees to simply be motivated to want to learn. They also need to have optimistic expectations of the learning itself. Too many employees have been caught up in what psychologists call "learned helplessness," a condition in which people simply give up on controlling their own lives and let others control. This is particularly acute in the workplace, where many workers have never had the right to make decisions for themselves. All of that is changing now, and businesses want employees who are self-starters and who can make decisions.

Creating optimistic expectations among trainees is one way to help bridge the gap between learned helplessness and effective training. Without this, researchers believe that trainees might enter a training program with the expectation to fail. Since expectations sometimes control outcomes, this may become a self-fulfilling prophecy. Setting both quantitative and qualitative expectations for trainees, with their participation, is also useful in overcoming this problem.[31]

These five types of objectives form the basis for evaluating training programs. A good evaluation should measure all five. This section presents questions related to the five objectives and common methods of ascertaining the answers.

Reaction. Reaction refers primarily to the views of trainees regarding the training program. Did they like the program? Did they like the methods used? Can they recommend other methods to address the same issues? Can they recommend changes that would improve the program? What did they think of the trainers and the facilities used in the training process? Finally, would the trainees recommend that the program be implemented again? Typically, managers can learn the answers to all these questions through questionnaires, posttraining interviews, or a combination of both.

While reaction is important, sometimes it only provides ratings of the trainer or the course design. More important to the trainee and the organization are whether or not trainees learned from the process, whether their on-the-job behaviors display this learning, and whether the training produced desirable productivity results.[32]

Learning. Managers should ascertain whether or not the trainees learned anything from the program. A variety of methods are available for evaluating acquired learning. These include tests (oral, written, or performance) and observation of work progress and simulations.

Let's refer to our earlier example that involved training servers about wine. This example can be used to illustrate how observing a simulation is a useful method for evaluating learning. For instance, after the wine training, servers could be asked to show what they learned. By grading these simulations, managers have an effective method of evaluating how much the servers learned.

On-the-Job Behaviors. Evaluating on-the-job behaviors in connection with a training program is not the same as evaluating on-the-job behaviors through performance appraisals or employee evaluations. For instance, companies that conduct performance appraisals on a regular basis evaluate an employee's behaviors as part of that employee's progress and professional development.

Evaluating an employee's behavior immediately after a training program is an effective method of evaluating the program. These appraisals might be conducted by an employee's supervisor, peers, any staff he or she supervises, guests, or a combination of any of these four groups. This type of evaluation gauges behaviors the employee learned during training. Employee attitude surveys are also a good method of measuring the effectiveness of programs designed to improve on-the-job behaviors.

Results. The ultimate test of a training program is its effect on an organization or department. Good programs have a positive effect. To determine a program's effect, managers should evaluate any measurable criteria. For instance, managers can look at turnover rate to measure the effectiveness of training designed to encourage employee satisfaction. Productivity would provide a measurable criterion for evaluating training programs designed to reduce the time it takes to perform a given task, such as checking in a guest or preparing a meal. Quality can be measured using guest evaluations of goods and services. For instance, directly after room attendants complete a training program on improving guestroom cleaning, guests can be asked to evaluate the cleanliness of their rooms. Cost is also an obvious measurable criterion. Are costs lower than they were before the training program? Has waste been reduced or eliminated? Are employees working fewer hours to complete tasks now than before training? And, finally, are profits higher as a result of the training program?

Identifying the Cause

Simply identifying change is not enough; effective evaluations of training programs must also identify whether the changes resulted from training. If this is not determined conclusively, managers cannot assume that the training was the cause; other factors could have influenced the change that managers are observing. The most effective method of determining whether a training program caused the changes is to create a pretest-posttest control group environment (as described earlier in this chapter).

Troubleshooting Program Failures

Not all training programs work. While managers assume that training will yield the desired results, in many cases the training does not. However, when a training program fails, it may not be due to poor design. For instance, the trainer may have presented the material inappropriately for the trainees. Trainees may not have understood the material. It is also possible that training needs were improperly assessed or that the wrong training method or site was chosen. Finally, training objectives or criteria may have been unsuitable.

The point is that training programs themselves are not always to blame when desired change is not achieved. When this occurs, managers should focus on identifying the *cause* of the problem. Again, the five objectives of training success—reaction, learning, on-the-job behaviors displayed, results, and optimism—should help isolate the *source* of training program problems.

The Training Payoff

There is ample evidence that training dollars, when properly invested, provide excellent returns. If a company takes the time to conduct needs assessments, establish objectives and criteria, and select the right trainers and methods, training can be one of the best investments a company can make.

The Walt Disney Company is a prime example of a hospitality company that takes training seriously. All new employees go through "OrientEARing," a training program lasting several days in which new employees learn the history of the company, quality standards, traditions, and even a special Disney language (employees are "cast members," who, when they are working, are "on stage," and wear uniforms called "costumes"). During training, new cast members are always reminded of the company they have chosen to work for, since reminders are everywhere: training takes place at Disney University, classrooms have pictures of famous graduates like Mickey Mouse and Goofy, and television clips of Walt Disney himself are shown throughout as reminders of his vision of the company and its humble beginnings. This company-wide training takes place before new recruits even step foot in their new departments. Though it may seem like overkill to the outside observer, this form of training has certainly proven successful for Disney. Annually, Disney has a turnover rate of only 15 percent, compared to the 60 percent attrition rate in the rest of the hospitality industry.[33]

One of the most vivid examples of positive training results comes from Motorola, which spends about $150 million annually to deliver a minimum of 40 training hours to each of its 132,000 employees (more than four percent of its payroll, far above the average one percent spent by American industry). The results are astounding. Since the program began, Motorola's annual sales have increased by 18 percent, earnings by 26 percent, and productivity by 139 percent. Altogether, Motorola employees can choose from over 600 courses offered at 14 sites, and the company intends to expand its training to 80 to 100 hours per employee per year.[34]

Using Technology for Training

It's not enough anymore to run the best in-house or external training programs. Today, the computer and the Internet are changing how businesses train. As we discussed earlier in this chapter, computer-based training (CBT) of any kind is essentially programmed instruction in the sense that workers train at their own pace. However, there is a lot to learn about this subject. The overview that follows is designed to introduce readers to the most important concepts on using technology for training. Much more information is available on this topic, and more is becoming available every day. An Internet search using the search terms "employee (or management) training" should turn up additional information.

Both Internet and intranet (internal net) are hot topics in training today. While most of this information is on external networking, it is important to remember that many companies have gone internal by setting up extensive intranets. It's not hard to understand why intranets are so popular in corporate America. By applying technology developed for the Internet to internal information functions, companies and other organizations can greatly facilitate both static and dynamic communications. Company data, employee benefits and training, job postings, and telephone directories are but a few of the many areas suitable for an intranet. Before plunging ahead, however, organizations should carefully weigh the pros and cons, including expense and support needs, to be sure an intranet is appropriate for their needs.[35]

It is also important to consider the potential limits of Internet-related training. A conversation between former Secretary of Labor Robert Reich and Daniel Coleman, the author of *Working with Emotional Intelligence*, highlights this problem. Coleman made the case that there is too much emphasis on technical-skills training and too little on emotional-intelligence skills such as adaptability, self-confidence, and motivation. Technical skills may get you in the door, he says, but emotional-intelligence skills get you ahead. Reich agreed with this statement and made the point that he is very concerned by the disparity in training improvements among the leading-edge companies and others. Reich also noted that companies need to start thinking of their employees as assets, not costs, to make the real leap to effective training. To do this, financial analysts should concentrate more on developing a return on investment (ROI) for training programs, noted Reich.

One of the areas in which companies have made significant improvements in using technology for training is in the use of CD-ROMs. According to Barbara A. Worcester in *Hotel and Motel Management*, 45 percent of the lodging properties in the United States now have this capability but may not be using it effectively.[36] Most use CD-ROMs for: 1) check in/out training (27.6 percent), 2) guest services training (20.4 percent), and for 3) reservations training (22 percent). After that, the use drops significantly: 4) yield management training (5.8 percent), and 5) motivating employees (5.4 percent). One of the advantages of Internet or CD-ROM–based training is that it allows participants to learn in bite-size chunks rather than sitting for hours in a classroom. In addition, this type of training has the advantages of:

- Accessibility—either time or distance can separate trainees from trainers.

- Cost—training is less costly, after investment in capital hardware.

- Updates—corrections, additions, and changes can be readily accomplished. CD-ROMs are easy to print and distribute.

- Frequency—work with CD-ROM whenever you want it.

- Pace—the student learns at his or her own pace.

- Instruction—the technology leverages the abilities of top instructors to more students.

- Participation—everyone in training participates; some students in classrooms do not.[37]

Another form of training that is gaining in popularity and very likely to grow with great speed in the future is web-based training (WBT). In *Training and Development*, Margaret Driscoll provided a step-by-step overview of how to get a WBT program underway. Her 12-step strategy for planning and implementing WBT is presented below.

1. Clarify the purpose of the pilot—the initial program.

2. Identify and enlist the support of a high-level champion—GM or president.

3. Form a core team and identify extended team members—most core members are involved in a pilot cross-functional team essential to providing the needed resources.

4. Create a set of evaluation criteria. Ask each member to create a list of items that will indicate whether the project has gone well. For example:

   Training: 85 percent of leaders participate in program; 95 percent of participants achieve mastery; courses can be developed quickly.

   MIS: less than 7 percent call for help; software conforms to company standards.

   Field managers: reduces time spent on busy-work; increases flexibility in schedule.

   Learners: 70 percent believe system is easy to use.

5. Develop a plan to gather data. Know where to get the information you need.

6. Match technology to the topic. Define in clear and simple terms and work up from there. Choose technology that is compatible with company systems, attains educational goals, has technical assistance, has low-cost maintenance, and so forth.

7. Implement an off-the-shelf program or self-develop.

8. Prepare for rollout—test with small group, fix and test again, fix, then roll out.

9. Conduct a dry run—let anyone who wants to play with it.

10. Deliver the program. Establish start and stop dates and let learners know. Encourage everyone to complete the first stage.

11. Gather data.

12. Summarize the experience and make recommendations.[38]

One reason WBT is so popular is that its cost is often much lower than other methods. Human resources author Jack Wilson noted this and also identified four other reasons companies are flocking to WBT. Internet training provides five key benefits to today's business: 1) Cost savings—more than 45 percent of traditional training costs are travel-related. 2) Increased productivity—employees learn more efficiently because they absorb information in smaller doses. Employees are happier and more productive. 3) No fear—employees fear sitting in a classroom because they don't want to look foolish. This is self-directed. 4) Fun—Internet teaching captures the learners' attention. People retain 80 to 90 percent of what they do, and only 10 to 15 percent of what they hear. Web-based training is doing. 5) Continuous traced learning—maintains your progress and costs.[39]

An example of the effectiveness of this type of training is described in the case of Days Inn, a company that turned to WBT very early on. Days Inn turned to interactive WBT because, with its 18,000 employees in 1800 locations and turnover at about 100 percent, it was constantly training. Web-based training cost 50 percent less than classroom training. Computer-based training saved about 20 percent in the first year (after capital costs) and 50 percent thereafter.[40]

Career Development

Training devoted to developing managers is generally called either career development, management development, or career planning. These terms all refer to the same issues: increasing managerial performance; enhancing job satisfaction; improving knowledge, skills, and abilities; and identifying managerial strengths, weaknesses, and interests (see Exhibit 8).

Managers typically progress through developmental career stages. From an organizational perspective, the most common stages are organizational entry; the reality-shock experienced when a manager realizes that this is his or her life and career; mid-life or middle-career syndrome; the approach of retirement; and finally, retirement. Helping managers cope with these stages is the focus of most management development programs.

Different types of programs fit the different stages. During the organizational entry stage, many companies focus management development training on socialization, learning how to adjust to the hospitality business world, and how to become an effective manager. Training programs that stress managerial role theory, leadership styles, interpersonal skills, assessment centers, role playing, modeling, and management style training are common during this stage.

During the reality-shock period, companies generally focus management development on promoting responsibility and growth to reassure managers that there is a place for them in the organization. Since mid-life or middle-career syndrome is often characterized by boredom with the job, the emphasis here should be on new challenges and objectives. Achievement and motivation are important issues.

When managers approach retirement, training emphasis often shifts to issues associated with mentoring and passing information on to younger generations of managers. Coaching, understudy assignments, and modeling are good training methods to implement at this stage. Since many managers also face a loss of identity with the loss of their jobs, additional training might focus on exploring self-identity and leisure activities.

Exhibit 8   What Is Career Development?

In today's world, the term *Career Development* is taking on a new definition. Career Development no longer refers to upward or vertical movement in organizations; it no longer means only the process of grooming employees for management positions.

Today, the term Career Development means *continued growth, performance, and reward for all employees who are motivated to develop their potential and performance.*

However, even if we accept the idea that career development does mean something different today, we often are plagued with many traditional assumptions about career development that seem to get in the way of constructive action. Let's look more closely at some traditional assumptions and emerging views about career development:

Traditional View	Emerging View
There is only one right career and it peaks in mid-life.	Rapid change in technology, work force, economy, and values has changed the appropriateness of the "one right career." Employees must be challenged and rewarded throughout their working lives to maximize their contributions. Therefore, multiple careers are frequent, mutually beneficial, and rewarding to the individual and society.
Moving up the management ladder is the only way to experience career fulfillment and development.	Employees can continue to build skill and knowledge without moving up the corporate ladder. *Flat career profiles have characterized the career of successful doctors, lawyers and scientists for decades.* Management should consider more carefully their organization's need before ruling out other career "ladders." Employees' expectations also are moving toward quality of life issues. People are more satisfied with broadening experiences.
Senior employees should not be expected to expand their knowledge and skills.	Retiring on the job does little for the individual or the organization. Senior employees have much to contribute and should have opportunity for continued challenge and growth. Learning and development can and do occur in all age groups and at all career stages.
Development occurs in classrooms and in formal training programs.	Development occurs largely on the job for most professional employees. Supervisors, subordinates, peers, and job expectations have strong impact on development. Formal trainers and change agents are not always in the best position to provide developmental experiences for these employees.
Development pays off only for young or new employees.	Development of early, mid- and late career employees benefits the organization. Development means preparing for present needs and preventing future problems.
There is little that can be done to enrich most jobs.	Most employees, when given the opportunity, can offer realistic suggestions for enriching current jobs. Jobs can be enriched by increasing the employee's personal control of responsibilities. Opportunities for learning new skills and knowledge enrich jobs. An increased understanding of the relationship of tasks to the overall mission makes work seem more meaningful. Change and variety of tasks as well as a better sense of closure and impact can be enriching. The amount of support, the facilities, and the tools provided can affect the nature of the job as well as the visibility and inclusion of the employee.

Source: ©Worklife Pty. Ltd. 1995, The Centre for Worklife Counseling, Mosman N.S.W. Australia.

Endnotes

1. John P. Walsh, "Employee Training Leads to Better Service, Increased Profits," *Hotel & Motel Management* 19, no. 1 (2004): 14–15.

2. Sally Roberts, "Training Starting to Click," *Business Insurance* 34 (January 2000): 21.

3. "Employee Training Expenditures on the Rise," *The American Salesman* 49 (January 2004): 27.

4. Wesley S. Roehl and Skip Swerdlow, "Training and Its Impact on Organizational Commitment Among Lodging Employees," *Journal of Hospitality and Tourism Research* 23 (May 1999): 176–194.

5. Keith Naughton, "Tired of Smile-Free Service?" *Newsweek* 135, no. 10 (2000): 44–45.

6. L. J. Bassi and M. E. Van Buren, "Sharpening the Leading Edge," *Training and Development* 53, no. 1 (1999) 1: 23–27.

7. Andrew Eaglen, Conrad Lashley, and Rhodri Thomas, "Modeling the Benefits of Training to Business Performance in Leisure Retailing," *Strategic Challenge* 9, no. 5 (2000): 311–326.

8. Dina Berta, "Funds for Training Top Discussion at CHART Confab," *Nation's Restaurant News* 37 (August 18, 2003): 20.

9. For information on using exit interviews correctly, see Robert H. Woods and James F. Macaulay, "Exit Interviews: How to Turn a File Filler into a Management Tool," *Cornell Hotel and Restaurant Administration Quarterly* 28 (November 1987): 39–46.

10. Regina Fazio Maraca, "Looking for Better Productivity: Don't Forget the Three R's," *Harvard Business Review* 74 (August 1996): 9.

11. Alexandra Rand, "Technology Transforms Training," *HR Focus* 73 (November 1996): 11.

12. Michael H. Shenkman, "Manage for Today, Mentor for Tomorrow," *Nonprofit World* 23 (Sept/Oct 2005): 28–30.

13. Lynnette M. Godat and Thomas A. Brigham, "The Effect of a Self-Management Training Program on Employees of a Mid-Sized Organization," *Journal of Organizational Behavior Management* 19, no. 1 (1999): 65–83.

14. "The Pay-offs of E-learning Go Far Beyond the Financial," *HR Focus* 80 (October 2003): 7.

15. Robert F. Poell, Ferd J. Van der Krogt, Danny Wildemeersch, "Strategies in Organizing Work-Related Learning Projects," *Human Resource Development Quarterly* 10, no 1 (1999): 43–61.

16. "Training Experts," *The Controller's Report* (April 2003): 14.

17. For a full description of *Bafa Bafa* and its usefulness in hospitality training, see Robert H. Woods, "Lessons from *Bafa Bafa*," *Cornell Hotel and Restaurant Administration Quarterly* 31 (August 1990): 115–119.

18. George Bohlander and Scott Snell, *Managing Human Resources* (Mason, Ohio: Thomson/South-Western, 2004), 270.

19. Jeff Barbian, "New Work Cooking," *Training* (February 2001): 26.

20. Bohlander and Snell, 273.

21. "Adams Mark Hotel & Resorts Launches Diversity Training Program," *Hotel & Motel Management* 216, no. 6 (2001): 15.

22. Wayne F. Cascio, *Managing Human Resources: Productivity, Quality of Work Life, Profits* (New York: McGraw-Hill, 1989), 251.

23. Alan Greenberg, "Bankers Trust Markets Corporate Gameware for Training," *Infoworld* 17 (24 April 1995): 28.

24. Stefan Gröschl, "Current Human Resources Practices Affecting the Employment of Persons with Disabilities in Selected Toronto Hotels: A Case Study," *International Journal of Hospitality & Tourism Administration* 5 (October 2004): 15–30.

25. Barbara Ettore, "HR's Shift to a Center of Influence," *HR Focus* 73 (June 1996): 16.

26. Ettore: 16.

27. R. Wayne Mondy and Robert M. Noe, *Human Resources Management* (Englewood Cliffs, N.J.: Prentice-Hall, 1996), 228–230.

28. Lisa A. Burke and Timothy T. Baldwin, "Workforce Training Transfer: A Study of the Effect of Relapse Prevention Training and Transfer Climate," *Human Resource Management* 38, no. 3 (1999): 227–234.

29. Donald B. Fedor, Kenneth L. Bettenhausen, Walter Davis, "Peer Reviews: Employees' Dual Roles as Raters and Recipients," *Group & Organization Management* 24, no. 1 (1999): 92–120.

30. Peter Warr, Catriona Allan, Kamal Birdi, "Predicting Three Levels of Training Outcome," *Journal of Occupational & Organizational Psychology* 72, no. 3 (1999): 351–375.

31. Peter Schulman, "Applying Learned Optimism to Increase Sales Productivity," *Journal of Personal Selling & Sales Management* 19, no. 1 (1999): 31–37.

32. Nancy M. Dixon, "Training: Meet Training's Goals Without Reaction Forms," *Personnel Journal* 73 (September 1994): 51.

33. Randolph Cirilo and Brian H. Kleiner, "How to Orient Employees into New Positions Successfully," *Management Research News* 26 (2003): 16–27.

34. Linda Grant, "A School for Success: Motorola's Ambitious Job-training Program Generates Smart Profits," *U.S. News and World Report* (22 May 1995): 53.

35. Uma G. Gupta, Frederic J. Hebert, "Is Your Company Ready for an Intranet?" *S.A.M. Advanced Management Journal* 63, no. 4 (1998): 11–15.

36. Barbara A. Worcester, "CD ROM Training On the Rise," *Hotel and Motel Management* (June 15, 1998): 49–50.

37. Gary Weidner, "Interactive Training: Is It In Your Future?" *Plant Engineering* 53, no. 7 (1999): 50–54.

38. Margaret Driscoll, "How to Pilot Web-Based Training (WBT)," *Training and Development* 52, no. 11 (1998): 44–60.

39. Jack Wilson, "Internet Training: The Time is Now," *HR Focus* 75, no. 3 (1999): 6–7.

40. Bill Roberts, "Training Via the Desktop," *HR Magazine* 43, no. 9 (1998): 98–103.

🔑 Key Terms

advisory committee—Committee composed of managers who review the job skills and behavior demands of the organization and compare these skills and behaviors with current levels of employee performance.

attitude survey—A needs assessment method designed to determine when behavioral training is required; also a questionnaire or other information-gathering tool designed to determine how employees feel about work issues.

business game—A training method in which trainees learn how to deal with a variety of issues in a simulated business environment.

case study—A training method in which employees are confronted by a series of events—hypothetical or real—and asked to solve the problems presented in each scenario.

conference training—A training method that consists of one-on-one discussions between a trainer and a trainee.

critical incident—Job analysis technique based on capturing and recording actual events that occur at work which, when combined, form an accurate picture of a job's actual requirements. Useful in describing how services should be performed. Also used in training and as a measurement in certain performance appraisal systems.

exit interview—Meeting conducted between an employer and an employee leaving the organization that attempts to identify specific training needs or other work-related problems.

in-basket training—A training method in which employees confront a wide array of problems similar to what they might find in their in-basket when they come to work.

individual analysis—Process that helps managers identify specific training needs for the person performing a particular job.

job instruction training (JIT)—A structured approach to training that requires trainees to proceed through a series of sequential steps.

job performance measurements—A needs assessment method in which a trained analyst performs each job to get a personal feel for the knowledge, skills, and abilities needed.

job rotation—Process of moving employees from one job to another, or of changing employee responsibilities, in order to enhance job interest or to cross-train.

KSA—Acronym for knowledge, skills, and abilities.

modeling—A training method designed to encourage employees to behave as role models behave.

needs assessment—The first stage in the training program, in which an organization assesses the need for training.

off-the-job training—Training in which trainees learn job procedures in an environment other than the actual work environment.

on-the-job training—Training in which trainees learn job procedures while watching, talking with, and helping an experienced employee.

organizational analysis—The process in which the entire organization's need for training is assessed; generally includes an assessment of the effect that training will have on the organization.

performance document—Document relating to absenteeism, sales, guest complaints, or guest compliments that identifies a need for training.

pretesting—A testing process that establishes what employees currently know and what they need to be trained for; conducted before training implementation.

programmed instruction—A training method in which employees learn at their own pace. Originally a paper-and-pencil method; now mostly computer-oriented.

role-playing—A training method that allows trainees to assume roles and act out parts in a realistic situation or setting.

sensitivity training—A training method designed to make employees more aware of behavioral or interpersonal training needs.

task and behavior analysis—A process that determines which tasks and behaviors are needed for each job.

training criteria—Benchmarks for training success.

training cycle—A continuous series of steps involved in the training process.

training evaluation—A step in the training cycle that determines whether or not the training program is working.

training objective—A measurable end result of a training program. Training objectives are typically classified as reaction-based, learning-acquired, on-the-job behaviors, and results-oriented.

vestibule training—An off-the-job training method that simulates the workplace and asks employees to perform or display knowledge, skills, or abilities similar to those required at work.

work sampling—A needs assessment method of individual analysis in which a trained analyst observes and reviews an employee's work to determine training needs.

Review Questions

1. Why is training referred to as a "cyclical process"?
2. What are the steps in the training cycle?
3. What are the 12 methods of needs analysis?
4. When are attitude surveys an effective method of analyzing training needs? When are skills tests an effective method?
5. How are exit interviews useful to training efforts?
6. What is the difference between training objectives and training criteria?
7. When are case studies an appropriate training method?

8. When is modeling an appropriate training method?

9. What type of situations could benefit from in-basket training?

10. What are the differences between organizational analysis, task and behavior analysis, and individual analysis?

Internet Sites

For more information, visit the following Internet sites. Remember that Internet addresses can change without notice. If the site is no longer there, you can use a search engine to look for additional sites.

American Society for Quality
www.asq.org

Centre for Worklife Counselling,
Australia
www.worklife.com.au

National Skill Standards Board
www.nssb.org

The American Society for Training
and Development
www.astd.org

Thinq and Training Server®
www.trainingserver.com/index.htm

The Internet also offers several work placement services under career development. Search for sites using words "career development."

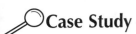

Case Study

"I Never Wanted to Be a Supervisor Anyway"

John is a food server at the Lakeside Inn, a 200-room hotel with a coffee shop and a full-service restaurant called Hummingbirds. Two years ago, John started out as a busperson in the coffee shop, but because of his outstanding performance he was quickly transferred to Hummingbirds and made a food server.

John's excellent record continued in his new position. John was always on time, was great with the customers, and was a real team player. When the buspersons fell behind, he helped them catch up without being asked. When another server needed help, John was always willing to take on tables in addition to his own. He even got along with the cooks. Within weeks at his new position, he knew everyone's name and was usually the center of attention in the employee breakroom. As time went by, he won employee of the month so many times it became somewhat embarrassing.

Phil Brown, the dining room supervisor at Hummingbirds, was John's boss. Because John got along with the staff so well, Phil asked John to fill in for him every Wednesday—Phil's day off and the slowest day of the week for the restaurant. John seemed to do a good job in this role. Serious problems seldom came up on Wednesdays, and if one did, John would tell Phil about it on Thursday morning so Phil could take care of it.

When Phil was made restaurant manager of another hotel in the chain, he encouraged John to apply for his position. "I think you'd make a great supervisor.

The job will be posted internally for three days, and I'm not sure who's going to apply, but you can count on me for a glowing recommendation." Phil not only thought this would be good for John, but knew that the company encouraged promotion from within and it would be a feather in Phil's cap if one of his employees took over his position.

At first, John was not enthusiastic about the supervisor job—"I really enjoy what I'm doing," he told Phil—but, bolstered by Phil's confidence in him, he finally decided to apply. His interview was with three people: Phil; Phil's boss, Alan, the restaurant manager; and Susan, the hotel's human resources director. John was outgoing and personable during the interview, and after John left the room, Phil cited John's initiative, high energy level, leadership skills, and high quantity and quality of work as reasons John should get the nod. Although Alan and Susan were concerned about John's lack of formal supervisory training, they decided, given John's excellent record, to give him a chance.

The next day, John went with Phil to Phil's new restaurant and spent a week in training. At the beginning of the week, Phil went over a checklist of supervisory skills John needed to acquire and gave him some training materials to study. Throughout the week, Phil helped John fill out the paperwork a dining room supervisor must deal with. At the end of the week, Phil wished John good luck, gave him a pep talk, and told him to call anytime he had a problem.

John reported for work at Hummingbirds the next morning, uncomfortable in his new suit and tie but feeling confident and determined to do a good job. It didn't take him long to discover that the biggest adjustment he faced was in relating to his former coworkers. When he was a food server, everyone was his friend and he had enjoyed all the during-work and after-hours socializing the employees did together. But now he was left out. In this and many other ways, his former co-workers made him feel that he wasn't "one of the gang" anymore. That was bad enough, but he began to suspect that his friends, now his employees, were taking advantage of him. For one thing, they didn't really treat him as a manager. When Alan walked through the kitchen, all the servers and cooks snapped to attention; when John walked through, they just looked around—"Oh, hi John"—or didn't acknowledge him at all and continued casually chatting. Because they knew John so well, they constantly asked him for favors: "Can I trade nights with Lisa?" "Can I have tomorrow off?" "Can Sam and I switch table assignments?" "You remember I'm a bowler, right? Could you please not schedule me Thursday nights? The league's starting up next week." The requests went on and on. John soon learned that, try as he might, he couldn't write a schedule that pleased everybody or didn't have to be changed constantly. The few times he couldn't give employees the day off they wanted, some of them called in sick. John wondered if they were lying, of course, but he couldn't prove anything and he didn't want to think they would treat him so badly. All he knew for certain was that he felt abused and taken advantage of by the very people he used to be so close to.

Despite these feelings, John wanted to preserve his relationships with his staff, and he wanted to please his new boss, too. So he didn't let Alan know about the pressures he was feeling, and he granted almost every employee request. This often meant that John found himself doing his old job of serving customers, busing tables, even filling in for dishwashers, while his employees either called in with an excuse and didn't show up, or didn't put forth the effort John thought they should. Too many times John found himself waiting tables, fretting about the mountain of paperwork on his desk, and watching other servers working at what he considered half speed.

As the first few weeks went by, he also became disappointed in Martha's performance. Martha was the senior server on the staff, and she had inherited John's old role as the "head server," the person John counted on to be a team leader and fill in for him on his day off. But Martha never did the little things that would have really helped him out, never went the extra mile for anyone. Why couldn't she just volunteer and pitch in like he used to do?

That Monday morning started out like most Monday mornings at Hummingbirds—extremely busy. The normally big breakfast crowd swelled even larger by several busloads of sales executives who had just arrived at the hotel for a four-day meeting. John was at his desk, hurrying through some reports he had promised Alan would be finished yesterday. He knew it was only a matter of time before he'd be called into the dining room. His three six o'clock servers were trying to take care of the rapidly increasing crowd, and Janice, one of his three seven o'clock servers, had called him the night before to tell him she wouldn't be in till eleven— her basement had flooded and she had to meet with a cleaning crew and an insurance adjuster in the morning. So today of all days he would have to serve the breakfast crowd one server short.

When John's telephone rang right at 7:00, his heart sank. Sure enough, Sally, another of his seven o'clock servers, was calling to say she was sick and wouldn't be coming in. She was a good employee who had never called in sick before, so he fought back his feeling of panic and told her to take care of herself and not worry about a thing. He no sooner thanked her for calling and hung up when the phone rang again. It was Rich, the third seven o'clock server, calling in sick, too. This was the fourth time Rich had called in sick in the two months John had been supervisor, and John knew that Rich had a habit of drinking too much on the weekend—in fact, John used to help Rich think of excuses to tell Phil back when Phil was the supervisor. But he really did sound sick this time, so John put aside his suspicions and told Rich to come in later if he felt better.

John gave up all thoughts of catching up on his reports and grabbed the schedule. The only people he might be able to call in were Wendy and Maria. No answer at Wendy's house. Maria was home, but she couldn't come in because she was a chaperon that morning for her daughter's sixth-grade field trip. She was very sorry.

"That's okay," John said wearily, and with exaggerated carefulness placed the receiver back in its cradle. It was all he could do to keep from throwing the phone across the room. Instead of six servers for the morning, he was down to three, with a bigger crowd than usual and no one he could turn to for help. Even Alan was unavailable—he was in a staff meeting with the hotel's general manager. John grimly straightened his tie and headed for the dining room.

Hurrying through the kitchen, he was assaulted by the sounds of a staff under pressure: cooks yelling orders, dishes clattering violently, oven doors slamming.

He charged through the double swinging doors into the dining room just in time to see Steve, one of his buspersons, heading for the restaurant's entrance, holding a towel tightly wrapped around his right hand.

"What happened to him?" John asked Martha.

"He was hurrying too much, broke a coffee cup and cut himself. I sent him to the doctor—looks like he'll need stitches."

Great, John thought as he surveyed the situation. Every table was packed, and the roar of a hundred conversations made it almost as noisy in the dining room as it had been in the kitchen. John couldn't remember the restaurant ever being so crowded, and there was a line of guests extending from the restaurant's entrance into the hotel lobby, waiting for a table.

Taking a deep breath, John threw himself into the fray. He tried to be everywhere at once, waiting tables, pouring coffee, seating guests, running the cash register, all the while trying not to notice the frowns from guests angry at the inevitable delays in service. Each guest complaint muttered within earshot—"What kind of a place is this?" "Great service around here!"—hit him like a lash. John fought down the waves of helplessness and frustration he felt and threw encouraging words at harried staff members whenever he rushed past one of them. He was in the middle of yet another long apology to an irritated guest when, out of the corner of his eye, he saw Martha at the cash register, standing on tiptoe and waving to him furiously above a long line of guests waiting to pay their bills.

He excused himself with a strained smile and hurried over to Martha. "What's the problem?"

"I don't know," Martha said breathlessly, "the register just stopped working."

John stared in frustration at the silent machine; he didn't have a clue about how to get it working again. "What did you do?" he barked at Martha.

"I didn't do anything!" Martha wailed. "It's not *my* fault."

"It's not *my* fault either," John snapped. "Damn it, think! Did you do something just before it quit?"

"Hey!" one of the guests back in the middle of the line called up to John, "I had to wait for my food, wait for my check, and now I have to wait to give you my money? Come on, do something!"

"I'm trying to do something, sir," John said through clenched teeth.

"Well, do it now, 'cause I'm tired of this crap." There was a murmur of agreement from the other guests in line.

John grabbed Martha by the arm much harder than he intended and half shoved her toward the kitchen. "Go to my office and get my calculator."

Martha pulled her arm away. "I don't know where it is."

John slammed his fist down on the counter. "Damn it, do I have to do everything myself?!" he shrieked.

A hush fell over the restaurant. Everyone froze; all eyes turned toward John. Martha blinked back tears and was starting to say something when her gaze shifted past John's shoulder and her eyes widened. John turned around to see his boss, Alan, looking around the restaurant incredulously. "What in hell is going on here?" he demanded.

Later that day…

Alan looked across his desk at John and sighed. What could have gone so wrong? This morning's incident was just the latest in a series of problems he'd had with John ever since John took the dining room supervisor's job. John didn't seem to understand budgets and was not keeping up with the administrative part of the job—late reports, botched purchase orders, unsigned invoices—the list was rather lengthy. John didn't even seem to be handling the people-skills part of his job very well. Several employees had come to Alan with complaints that John was playing favorites when it came to scheduling. And grabbing Martha this morning—Alan just hoped she didn't cause the hotel any headaches over that.

It had taken a while, but Alan had gotten Hummingbirds under control again with the help of George, the coffee shop manager. After the crisis was past, Alan had left George in charge of the restaurant and had taken John up to his office for a long-overdue counseling session. But now he wasn't sure where to begin.

"John," he said finally, "what happened? I couldn't believe my eyes when I saw you ranting and raving in front of a room full of guests."

"Look," John said defensively, "I had my hands full. You weren't around, we were working short-handed, the register went dead—I didn't know what to do. I was doing the best I could. I was never trained for that kind of situation."

"But John, you had training. You spent a week with Phil; he said you were ready. You worked in the restaurant for two years. I don't know what else we could have done for you."

"You never prepared me for an emergency like that."

"But no one could have foreseen what happened this morning!" Alan exclaimed. "Besides, managers are supposed to be able to cope with all the crazy things that go wrong. That's why we put you in that position; we thought you could handle it."

"Well, maybe you were wrong," John blurted out, "maybe you shouldn't have promoted me in the first place." John looked down at his feet and mumbled, "I never wanted to be a supervisor anyway."

Discussion Questions

1. Did Phil and Alan make a mistake in promoting John? Why or why not?

2. What should Alan do about John?

3. Assuming Alan decides to keep John on as supervisor, what are the immediate steps Alan should take with John?

4. If John stays on as supervisor, what are the immediate steps Alan and John must take with other people affected by John's outburst?

Case number: 3566CA

The following industry experts helped generate and develop this case: Philip J. Bresson, Director of Human Resources, Renaissance New York Hotel, New York, New York; and Jerry Fay, Human Resources Director, ARAMARK Corporation, Atlanta, Georgia.

Chapter 7 Outline

Competencies

1. Describe general performance appraisal issues and summarize the functions of performance appraisals. (pp. 227–233)

2. Identify and discuss potential problems with performance appraisals. (pp. 233–237)

3. Describe the principal types of rating systems used in appraising employee performance. (pp. 237–239)

4. Describe commonly used methods of appraising performance. (pp. 239–247)

5. Identify who should evaluate performance, and discuss objectives for programs that train managers and supervisors to conduct performance appraisals. (pp. 247–254)

6. Discuss how often performance appraisals should be conducted, identify legal issues relating to performance appraisals, and summarize keys to developing an effective employee appraisal system. (pp. 254–258)

7

Evaluating Employee Performance

This chapter was co-authored by Bruce Ollstein, M.S., M.B.A., University of Nevada, Las Vegas (UNLV); and Lisa Young, M.S. candidate, UNLV.

EVALUATING THE PERFORMANCE of an employee or manager is always difficult. One expert has compared performance appraisals to telling someone: "Here's what I think of your baby."[1] No matter what you say during a performance appraisal, employees on the receiving end will frequently see you as a heel. Performance evaluations generate significant anxiety and concern in some employees. When these evaluations are improperly managed, an environment of resentment and resistance can develop, leading to numerous organizational problems.

It is not new for American businesses to use some form of performance appraisals. One of the earliest forms was applied at the Henry Ford car assembly plant shortly after the company was founded. In this system, when employees were finished with their day's work, they walked past a wall filled with individual cubby holes, one for each worker, and each containing a blank piece of paper. These blank pieces of paper were their daily performance reviews. If they received a white slip of paper, it meant they were invited back for another day of work. However, if they received a pink piece of paper, it meant that they were fired. This is the origin of the term "pink slip."[2]

According to one estimate, more than 97 percent of all organizations in the United States use some sort of performance evaluation or appraisal system.[3] These appraisals are used for many purposes. However, many managers fail to use performance appraisals accurately, so often the systems fail to achieve their intended purpose. Performance appraisals fail for many reasons. Some of these failures can be traced to how managers view the system to begin with.

According to one survey, 70 percent of employees say that performance appraisals do not provide them with a clear picture of what is expected of them. In addition, only about 10 percent of employees felt the performance appraisal system was successful.[4] Most employees felt more confused after their appraisals than before.

David Hoenemeyer, vice president and assistant general manager of Harrah's Las Vegas and former director of operations at Hard Rock Hotel and Casino, Las Vegas, sees performance evaluations as an important but frustrating tool:

> We must have a fair and objective means to evaluate our team members. Our system at Harrah's is one of the best I've seen. But there will always

be certain individuals who get misrated, for various reasons, either too high or too low. Employees and managers have many informal channels of communication. When someone has a bad experience with the appraisal process, it can become a morale issue very quickly. It is absolutely in management's best interest to constantly tweak the formal appraisal system for subtle improvements. The hospitality industry is all about people, and the competition is getting better all the time. Our rating processes need to be given greater priority now more than ever.[5]

Some companies realize that their performance appraisal systems are not working. For instance, one survey found that 51 percent of companies believed their current system offered little or no value to the organization.[6] A 2005 survey of over 48,000 employees, managers, and CEOs from 126 U.S. firms determined that only 13 percent of employees and managers—and only 6 percent of CEOs—consider their firm's performance evaluation system useful.[7]

Does this mean that managers should junk the system and not appraise employees on their performance? The answer is clearly "no." A manager's role is to get the best performance from his or her employees. To do so, a manager needs some system of evaluating how well employees are doing.

Performance appraisals are subject to human emotions, human judgments, and, therefore, human errors. Not only do many managers fail to see that it is impossible to attain an absolutely unbiased and objective evaluation of an employee's performance, they also fail to see that they wouldn't want to achieve such a perfect evaluation. Humans are not machines. Exact behavior is not only impossible, but undesirable. While managers should conduct performance appraisals as effectively as they can, they must also realize that they cannot perfect the process. Managers and employees will always be subject to human conditions that affect performance appraisals.

Sometimes managers use performance appraisals to motivate. When this is so, managers concentrate on finding the good in an employee's performance. At other times, managers may be influenced by political considerations. For instance, if a manager considers it advantageous to the organization to keep raises and promotions to a minimum, that manager may give an employee a marginal appraisal.

The cost of performance appraisals has been estimated at between $1,945 and $2,200 per employee. Most managers don't realize performance appraisals cost so much, because most costs, including temporary productivity dips following reviews, are not tracked.[8] Given these high costs, it is easy to see why it is important to conduct effective performance appraisals.

The goal of this chapter is to teach managers how to use performance appraisals, not to recommend a right way. On the contrary, our objective is to teach managers the ins and outs of performance appraisal so that they can keep the performance appraisal systems in their organizations flexible, responsive, and, most of all, fair.

The thing to remember when reading this chapter is that appraisals are important. Regardless of the type of approach or method used, appraisals serve a valuable purpose in hospitality.[9] This is confirmed by the study illustrated in Exhibit 1.

Exhibit 1   Importance of Appraisals

Impact on Performance	Hotels	Clubs	Restaurants	Other Industries
Very Important to Success	59.4%	48.3%	38.1%	53.7%
Somewhat Important	35.4%	38.5%	43.7%	41.2%
No Opinion	1.2%	5.7%	10.3%	2.2%
Of Little Importance	3.5%	6.7%	4.8%	2.2%
No Importance to Success	.5%	.8%	3.2%	.8%
	100%	100%	100%	100%

Source: Robert H. Woods, Michael P. Sciarini, and Jack D. Ninemeier, "The Use of Performance Appraisals in Three Segments of the Hospitality Industry: A Comparative Study," *Journal of Hospitality and Tourism Education* 10, no. 3 (1998): 59–63.

Functions of Performance Appraisals

If you were to ask managers why their companies use a certain performance appraisal system, you would probably get a lot of different answers. Performance appraisals fill many different needs in organizations. Most of these needs fall into one of two categories: improving work performance or making work-related decisions.

Managers may use performance appraisals to provide feedback to employees. The primary purpose of an appraisal in this case is to reinforce or encourage performance, or to help employees develop in their careers. Appraisals help to support human resources decisions by separating poor performers from good ones. Performance appraisals can aid promotion, discipline, training, or merit-increase decisions. Appraisals can also help establish goals or objectives for training programs, assess training needs, validate selection (and other processes), or diagnose organizational or departmental problems.

In most industries, these uses are somewhat evenly applied. For instance, about 28 percent of managers in all industries combined use performance appraisals for compensation decisions, while another 28 percent use them to establish employee objectives. Another 24 percent of managers use appraisals for establishing training needs, while 17 percent use them for promotions.

However, the hospitality industry does not follow suit with these other industries. Instead, hospitality managers use performance appraisals for a variety of purposes, often at the same time. For instance, Exhibit 2 illustrates how appraisals are used in three different hospitality industry segments.

Exhibit 2   Uses of Performance Appraisals

Use	Lodging	Restaurants	Clubs
Compensation Decisions	86.4%	90.7%	72.2%
Employee Objectives	78.1%	82.6%	77.6%
Establish Training Needs	73.3%	80.2%	60.5%
Promotions	65.0%	77.9%	47.8%

Source: Robert H. Woods, Michael P. Sciarini, and Jack D. Ninemeier, "The Use of Performance Appraisals in Three Segments of the Hospitality Industry: A Comparative Study," *Journal of Hospitality and Tourism Education* 10, no. 3 (1998): 59–63.

As we can see from Exhibit 2, different segments of hospitality use performance appraisals for different purposes. What is interesting about this exhibit is that there is such variation among managers in these three segments.[10]

Since performance appraisals can be used for so many purposes, it is probably impossible for one appraisal system to fill all the needs of an organization. Appraisals should be designed with a specific purpose in mind. For instance, a hotel company may wish to determine which employees need training. Could a performance appraisal system designed for this use also serve as a tool to determine which employees to promote or to terminate? Probably not. A company will very likely have several different performance appraisal systems in use at the same time, each serving a different purpose. Consider the uses outlined in the following sections.

Performance Feedback

One of the most common uses of a performance appraisal is to provide **performance feedback**. Typically, feedback is intended to reinforce or help improve performance. Employees normally want to know how well they are doing; if they don't receive regular feedback, they may not have a realistic grasp of their performance. For instance, when managers don't speak directly to employees about performance, employees may think their work is just fine or they may worry that their work is poor. Regularly scheduled performance appraisals enable managers to keep employees informed about their performance.

Clearly, most supervisors can do better in the area of performance feedback. In a 2002 survey of 25 organizations in and around Chicago, conducted by Andersen Consulting, over 50 percent of respondents claimed that the feedback they received from supervisors was insignificant and of little value.[11] One international study, surveying over 10,000 individuals, found that more than 50 percent of respondents felt that their supervisor was "not clear, frank, or complete" in discussing the employees work performance, 17 percent did not know or were unsure of what the manager thought of their work, and 22 percent were unsure of or did not know the objectives they were expected to achieve; 33 percent reported that their manager supplied little or no assistance in improving their performance, and had failed to initiate any type of formal discussion of their performance. Perhaps most interesting of all, 90 percent of respondents claimed to be enthusiastic about an opportunity for "real dialogue" about their performance.[12]

Todd Haushaulter, casino administrator at Wynn Las Vegas, is a vocal advocate for keeping employees "in the loop" about their performance:

> I have found that the formal evaluation is a great way to force supervisors to tell their employees what is good and what needs fixing. But for any of those comments to resonate with the employee, the once- or twice-a-year formal sit-down session cannot represent the first time she has heard about her performance. I try to give useful feedback on a regular basis throughout the year. Sometimes I correct mistakes and explain the standards for behavior. Other times, I just give someone a compliment on a great job in order to keep them motivated. If I am concerned about a pattern of unacceptable behavior, I keep formal documentation and discuss it with the individual so he has a chance to make corrections and improve. But the key point is this: when someone sits down with me for a formal performance appraisal, there is absolutely no chance that anything he hears will be new information. I have kept that person "in the loop" and they know where they stand before they come to that meeting. The nice thing about the formal process is that it reinforces the standards and gives me another chance to say either "fix this now" or "great work, your contribution really means something." Luckily, at Wynn Las Vegas our selection process is usually validated by our performance evaluations. Most of my subordinates leave their feedback sessions with smiles and just a little extra internal motivation to make sure they give their next customer one-hundred-and-ten percent.[13]

In addition to Haushaulter's insights, comments from various hospitality professionals suggest that performance feedback sessions should include:

- No surprises—employees should already have a good idea of how they are doing
- Employee involvement—encourage employees to express ideas and feelings
- Primarily objective data—measurable factors are more useful and effective than subjective opinions

Employee Training and Development

Appraisals can help identify the employees or managers who need additional training or those who don't and are ready to move on. Appraisals can also be used to determine training needs on a department basis. For instance, front desk agents may need additional training after a new, computerized folio system has been installed and in place for a while. Managers can determine the need for training by conducting training-oriented performance appraisals with the front desk agents in the department.

Technology and Performance Appraisals

Employees of hospitality companies are now facing greater scrutiny of their individual job performances, thanks to software that helps firms more efficiently measure service-sector output.

New Web-enabled employee performance software packages help managers measure everything from front desk processing time to customer-complaint resolution and even time spent in the break room. All of this information is now finding its way into performance appraisals.

One employee performance software program now on the market is Wing-Span, offered by SilkRoad Technology (www.silkroadtech.com). This software helps managers gather performance data from multiple rater assessments and provides all the information needed for a productive performance appraisal. It also helps managers align corporate strategy with day-to-day employee activity. The WingSpan program measures reported individual competencies against predefined professional standards, and it provides supervisors with "accurate, comprehensive, and timely data for employee reviews."

Halogen eAppraisal (www.halogensoftware.com) automates and simplifies employee appraisals. It handles document routing, so that documents get "to the right people at the right time," helps managers with the actual writing process, notifies key personnel of deadlines, and allows for easy oversight by senior management. This software helps make employee evaluations a simple, ongoing process rather than a stressful once-a-year event.

Siebel Hospitality offers software that integrates reward programs with employee performance and evaluations. When integrated with one of the employee performance measurement systems just mentioned, Siebel's software helps a firm manage all of its appraisal/performance needs.

For small hospitality companies that are on a tight IT budget, new low-cost employee performance software is now available. Two possible choices are Performance Now (www.knowledgepoint.com) and Employee Appraiser (www.successfactors.com). Both of these applications help managers organize employee performance evaluations and identify potential legal concerns in addition to offering writing assistance.

In addition, appraisals can be useful aids in establishing career goals or long-term employee development plans. Armed with an employee's record of previous performance appraisals, managers can provide effective employee guidance and career counseling. An internal study by Marriott determined that its employees were very concerned about the development of career paths.[14] Effective employee appraisals may help an organization in the career development of individuals, and this may create greater employee satisfaction.

Decision-Making Tool

When used as a decision-making tool, performance appraisals provide an effective way to link rewards and discipline to performance. Employees who are performing well may receive favorable evaluations that can lead to merit pay, promotions, career development assignments, or transfers. Those who consistently receive poor evaluations can be legitimately identified for discipline, demotion, or discharge from the company.

Performance appraisals provide a basis for compensation, promotion, transfer, grievance, or discipline decisions. Merit pay, for instance, should relate directly to an employee's performance on the job. Performance appraisals help managers decide who should receive merit pay increases and who should not. Some performance appraisals give managers the opportunity to evaluate how employees perform when they are given more authority. Such assessments provide guidelines for promotion decisions. Many of the same performance appraisals used in promotion decisions are useful when making decisions about transfers. In discipline, discharge, and grievance cases, performance appraisals can provide useful background information. Effective employee performance documentation can protect an organization involved in a grievance, lawsuit, or equal-employment-opportunity discrimination charge.

Evaluation of Training, Policies, or Programs

Performance appraisals can be used to measure the effectiveness of training. Evaluating personnel before and after training measures the effectiveness of a training program. The close contact during an appraisal provides an opportunity for managers and employees to discuss the goals and problems associated with specific policies or programs. During an appraisal, managers may learn from employees that certain policies or programs do not work as designed. In that sense, appraisals can serve as an evaluation for new policies.

Validation of the Selection Process

The goal of selection is to predict which job candidates will perform best and fit best in the organization. Predictions should be tested to determine whether the selection system works effectively. Performance appraisals provide an excellent opportunity to do just this. For instance, when performance appraisals identify recently hired employees who are not performing well, managers may have evidence of a selection system that does not work correctly.

On the other hand, appraisals may indicate that the selection system works by showing that many recently hired employees are meeting the organization's standards. Performance appraisals can also justify selection decisions. When used in conjunction with selection, performance appraisals may help establish the **predictive validity** of selection methods.

Potential Problems with Performance Appraisals —————

Performance appraisals are subjective and are influenced by many factors. Several research projects have indicated, for instance, that males are more negative raters than females, overall.[15] This section outlines some of the problems associated with inaccurate performance appraisals. These problems include validity and reliability errors as well as bias or fairness errors. A manager's motives may also adversely affect the performance appraisal process. Understanding the factors that increase the likelihood of error can help managers conduct fair and accurate performance appraisals.

Validity and Reliability Problems

Validity and reliability are important to performance appraisals. Some of the errors that can occur during appraisals and damage their validity and reliability include:

- *Construct validity*—Performance appraisals must measure what they claim to measure. For instance, does measuring "service" actually measure the service delivered?

- *Content validity*—Performance appraisals must measure the entire issue, not just a portion or part. For instance, a performance appraisal that measures guest service at a front desk cannot simply measure the speed in which guests were served, since service involves many other issues.

- *Inter-rater reliability*—When two or more raters agree on the same rating, inter-rater reliability is high. If one rater rates a food server very high while another rater rates the same server very low, inter-rater reliability is low.

- *Consistency*—It is important to look for consistency when evaluating an employee, and not just focus on one or two particular points in time. For instance, if sales-per-person is used to measure the productivity of a food server, the appraiser should record several instances over time rather than a single instance, which may be unusually high or low due to factors beyond the server's control.

Bias

Legally, performance appraisals are free from bias if they meet the requirements of Title VII of the Civil Rights Act of 1964 and are fair to all employees. However, it is difficult for managers to make unbiased decisions at all times. Sometimes, managers commit **leniency errors, severity errors, central tendency errors, recency errors, past anchoring errors,** and **halo errors** when making decisions. Let's examine the first three types first:

- *Leniency errors*—Some managers give more lenient ratings to employees than they deserve. If a large enough sample were taken, we would expect that employee ratings would approximate the shape of a bell curve; this is not the case with all managers. For example, if all employees were rated on a scale of 1 to 5 (1 = excellent, 5 = very bad), we would expect the majority of employees to land near the midpoint of the scale. Since lenient managers rate more employees closer to 1 than to 5, overall ratings would be more favorable than normal.

- *Severity errors*—Some managers give more severe ratings than is normal. This is the reverse of the leniency error. As a result, more employees would be rated near the lowest point on the scale (5) than near the highest point (1).

- *Central tendency errors*—Many managers tend to rate everyone, regardless of their performance, near the midpoint on a scale. In this case, many more employees would be rated near the midpoint (or 3) than is normal.

These three errors create problems for two principal reasons. First, because managers in the hospitality industry tend to change jobs a lot, employees are often rated by new managers. If one manager was lenient and the second severe, an employee's performance could appear to be declining. On the other hand, a severe rating the first year followed by a much better rating given by a more lenient manager the second could lead others to conclude—erroneously—that an employee had improved and possibly deserved a raise or promotion.

The second reason that leniency, severity, and central tendency errors create problems is that employees' ratings may depend on who rates them, not on their performance. Employees in one department, for instance, may be passed over for promotions or career development assignments because their manager tends to be more severe. In another department, however, employees may receive promotions or assignments simply because their manager is more lenient.

Assume that a 1 to 5 scale is used for evaluation, and that a rating of "1" is equal to "exceptional" and that "5" is equal to "unacceptable." Some managers view this scale as comparable to grades in school. In that case, 1 = A, 2 = B, 3 = C, 4 = D, and 5 = E. Since some managers are reluctant to give low grades, they assign most employees either 1 or 2 (A or B). This leads to leniency errors. Other managers may view 1 as almost unattainable, 2 as exceptional, 3 as very good, 4 as good, and 5 as poor. These managers are likely to rate employees lower. The result is a severity error. Managers who commit central tendency errors tend to bunch all employee ratings around "average"—usually 3 on a 1 to 5 scale.

Managers can make three more common types of errors in the performance appraisal process:

- *Recency errors*—People tend to remember recent things over those that occurred earlier. For instance, a manager is more likely to remember things employees did a few weeks or a month before the performance appraisal than to remember things employees did six or eight months earlier. Unless managers keep a record throughout the year, they are likely to judge employees on recent performance only.

- *Past anchoring errors*—Managers tend to rate employee performance similar to previous ratings. For example, if past ratings were high, managers tend to rate employees high again, even if they deserve lower ratings.

- *Halo error*—This type of error is the result of judging an employee primarily on the basis of a single positive trait, behavior, or action. While people usually perform some tasks well, others poorly, and others about average, the halo effect often causes managers to see all actions as good.

Other Reasons for Inaccurate Appraisals

Each of the errors just discussed results from the way people think and the way they react to others. Therefore, each error is recognizable and explainable in behavioral terms and is probably unintentional. Other unintentional errors that lead to inaccurate ratings are as follows:

- Attractiveness (especially of female ratees) leads to higher ratings overall by both male and female raters.

- Men who display typically masculine traits and women who display typically feminine traits receive higher ratings overall.[16]

- Personalities are rated rather than performance.

- Managers allow employee backgrounds to influence ratings.

- Managers see everything about an employee as bad simply because of a single negative trait or behavior (called the "devil's horns" error).

- A performance appraisal lacks clear standards of evaluation.

- Managers don't observe employee performance adequately (either for a specific amount of time or in the appropriate environment).

- Managers compare one employee to another (called the "contrast effect") rather than to a performance standard.

- Some managers view the process as bureaucratic and are more interested in regulation, containment, and legal protection than in employee development. This is only true in organizations that do not effectively use the performance appraisal process.[17]

- Fewer middle managers (because of downsizing) means more appraisals must be conducted by each manager who remains. This can lead to manager overload, which can lead to rushed appraisals and errors.

- Increasing task complexity often means that employees have multiple supervisors, each of whom may desire behaviors and outcomes that are in conflict with the wishes of other raters.

- The increase in technology applications in the workplace means less personal interaction. This decreases effective communication of standards and increases the potential for misunderstandings.

- The increased career mobility of both supervisors and employees means less time is available to gain real and meaningful insights into an individual's true level of performance.[18]

Research shows that a rater who has not conducted an employee's previous ratings is more likely to give a rating similar to previous appraisals. A rater who has conducted an employee's previous ratings is more likely to give a lower rating on a subsequent appraisal.[19] Except when an overall rating is very high, negative attributes appear to be more heavily weighted than positive attributes in all other cases.[20]

Managers also inaccurately or unfairly rate employees for intentional reasons. In one survey, more the 70 percent of the raters admitted to intentional and unethical inflation or deflation of subordinates' appraisals.[21] Exhibit 3 shows that managers have a variety of motives for rating employees inaccurately or unfairly. Some

Exhibit 3   Rating Errors and Manipulative Rating Behavior

		Inflated Ratings	Deflated Ratings
Rater's Motive	**Positive**	• Keep the employee motivated • Maximize the merit pay increase • Avoid creating damaging permanent records • Reward good recent performance • Assist an employee with personal problem • Reward effort • Like the employee personally	• Scare better performance out of employee to prevent eventual termination • Build a stronger case against the employee who is destined to be terminated
	Deviant	• Avoid hanging out dirty laundry • Make themselves look good • Avoid conflict or confrontation with employee • Promote a problem employee up and out of manager's department	• Punish an employee • Encourage an employee to quit • Minimize merit pay increase • Comply with organizational edict to keep ratings low

Source: Clinton Longnecker and Dean Ludwig, "Ethical Dilemmas in Performance Appraisal Revisited," *Journal of Business Ethics* 9 (December 1990): 966.

motives can result in higher ratings than employees deserve; others result in lower ratings. Either way, such actions undermine the performance appraisal system and are regarded as manipulative behavior on the part of the manager. It is precisely because of this type of manipulation that unions have traditionally shown a distrust of management and often attempt to structure pay increases and promotions around seniority rather than performance appraisal results.[22]

Principal Appraisal Rating Systems

When developing a performance appraisal system, managers must first determine the type of behavior they will rate. The three principal types of ratings used are trait-based, behavior-based, and results-based ratings.

Trait-Based Ratings

Trait-based ratings are used primarily to assess the personal characteristics of employees. These ratings rely on factors such as company loyalty, communication skills, attitude toward supervisors, ability to work as part of a team, and decision-making ability. Trait-based performance appraisals seldom stand up in court because they often base ratings on characteristics instead of on job performance.

Behavior-Based Ratings

Behavior-based ratings assess employees on their behaviors, rather than on personal characteristics. For instance, such appraisals may rate employees on their friendliness toward guests, helpfulness, how often they thank guests for their patronage, and so on. Hospitality operations often emphasize an employee's behavior toward guests and other employees as much as that employee's actual ability to perform specific tasks. As a result, behavior-based ratings are fairly common in hospitality companies.

Behavior-based performance appraisals are more defensible in court than trait-based appraisals because they rate behaviors that directly relate to acceptable job performance. However, these rating systems do have problems. Managers often find that a behavior-based system accepts many behaviors that are each very different from one another. Managers may also discover that the system allows for little variation of those behaviors. For example, a company appraisal system may define some behaviors as more acceptable than others—in other words, define behaviors that employees must display in order to succeed at that company. Consider a manager's dilemma when rating a food server who displays many behaviors that are not consistent with the rating scale, yet is regularly requested by a large number of guests. Although the server's behavior does not exactly meet company standards, guests seem to like the server. If the manager follows the rating system exactly, this employee would receive a low rating even though guests appreciate the server's work.

Results-Based Ratings

The employee we just described would receive a very different performance appraisal in a **results-based rating** system. Even though this server doesn't display desired behaviors, he or she does receive a lot of compliments from guests. Consequently, since the server's results are good, a high ranking would be in order under a results-oriented system. While this seems to makes sense, results-oriented appraisals are not problem-free.

Some managers may focus too much on results at the cost of behaviors or characteristics. Consider how an appraisal system for front desk agents might evaluate the number of guests an agent checks in during a specific time period. If the system evaluates only results, a front desk agent who checks in many guests during this period would be rated higher than one who checks in fewer. However, working under pressure to check in a great number of guests, an agent may fail to make a good impression, alienate guests, and lose future business for the hotel.

Restaurant managers will also find a common problem with results-oriented evaluation. Is a server who serves the most people during a given shift necessarily better than other servers? How do you compare the server to others? If the results-oriented rating is based simply on total sales, the server who serves the most guests will likely be rated the highest.

Deciding which type of rating system to use is a complex decision. In some cases, managers will find that the job dictates the type of system. For instance, some properties may determine that cooks should be evaluated with a results-oriented

Exhibit 4   Types of Appraisal Systems Used

Type	Lodging	Restaurants	Clubs	All Industries
Graphic Rating Scale	28%	35.1%	52.5%	24%
Management by Objectives (MBO)	49%	37%	21.4%	31.8%
Narrative Essay	37%	24.7%	12.1%	33.9%
Behaviorally-Anchored Rating Scales (BARS)	41%	19.4%	3.9%	NA
360-Degree Feedback	0	26.4%	8.2%	NA
Other	9%	4.6%	1.9%	10.3%

Source: Robert H. Woods, Michael P. Sciarini, and Jack D. Ninemeier, "The Use of Performance Appraisals in Three Segments of the Hospitality Industry: A Comparative Study," *Journal of Hospitality and Tourism Education* 10, no. 3 (1998): 62.

system. In other cases, a combination of trait-based, behavior-based, and results-oriented approaches works best.

Methods of Appraising Performance

Several methods of performance appraisal are in use today. Exhibit 4 compares the hospitality industry's use of selected appraisal systems with the rate of use across all industries. Each method has different advantages and disadvantages. This section presents the most commonly used methods and the strengths and weaknesses of each.

Ranking Methods

Three ranking methods are commonly used. Each method eventually results in ranking employees from best to worst, or from first to last. The three methods are (1) simple or straight ranking, (2) alternative ranking, and (3) paired comparisons.

Simple ranking requires an appraiser to rank all employees from best to worst. This method has the advantage of providing a simple order for consideration. At the end of the appraisal process, each employee is ranked individually on a continuum from best to worst. However, simple ranking has considerable disadvantages, not the least of which is the choice of criteria against which to rank employees. Simple ranking does not distinguish between different aspects of job responsibilities. As a result, appraisers typically consider only one responsibility, or perhaps a few. Appraisers can improve the simple ranking method by identifying job responsibility criteria and ranking each employee on this separate scale.

Exhibit 5   Example of Paired Comparisons Ranking

Employees to be ranked: Macaulay, Simpson, Taylor, Nathan

Macaulay is better than Simpson
Simpson is better than Taylor
Nathan is better than Simpson
Macaulay is better than Taylor
Macaulay is better than Nathan
Nathan is better than Taylor

Macaulay is ranked #1
Nathan is ranked #2
Simpson is ranked #3
Taylor is ranked #4

Unfortunately, though, there is no standard method of measurement, so different raters may have different perceptions of the span between consecutive numbers such as 3 and 4. Some may think there is a great deal of difference, while others view consecutive numbers as very close together.

Alternative ranking closely resembles straight ranking in terms of its advantages and disadvantages. The difference between the two methods lies in how the ranking is determined. When using alternative ranking, the appraiser lists each employee on a separate sheet of paper and then chooses the best first, the worst second, the second-best third, the second-worst fourth, and so on until the list is exhausted.

The **paired comparison** method involves directly comparing employees to each other on each job criterion. Exhibit 5 shows an example of this method. The simplest way to compute final rankings using the paired comparison method is to count the number of times an employee's name appears on the left side of the ranking chart. The employee whose name appears most often is ranked highest; the one whose name appears the least is ranked lowest.

From an appraiser's point of view, simple ranking, alternative ranking, and paired comparisons clearly identify the most valuable and least valuable employees on staff. However, these methods cannot determine *why* one employee is more valuable than another, or how much more valuable one employee is than another to an organization.

Forced Distribution

Forced distribution relies on the assumption that, under normal circumstances, the final rankings of all employees would conform statistically to a bell-shaped curve. This method assumes that roughly 5 percent of employees are exceptional, 10 percent are outstanding, 15 percent are above average, 40 percent are average, 15 percent are below average, 10 percent are poor, and 5 percent are very poor.

Exhibit 6   Forced Distribution Scale

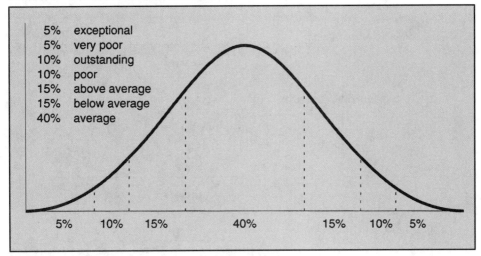

5%	exceptional
5%	very poor
10%	outstanding
10%	poor
15%	above average
15%	below average
40%	average

5%   10%   15%   40%   15%   10%   5%

Forced distribution eliminates some leniency and severity problems by creating a central tendency. It can, however, result in dissatisfaction among employees who resent being categorized at the low end of the curve. Exhibit 6 shows a sample forced distribution scale.

A famous anecdote pertaining to forced distribution involves Jack Welch's aggressive leadership style as the new CEO of General Electric in 1981. Welsh wanted to disrupt the entrenched establishment, so he demanded that his executives identify the top 20 percent of managers and the bottom 10 percent. The one group was positioned for promotion, the other for termination. The subsequent success of GE, eventually becoming the highest market-capitalization firm in the United States, encouraged many executives to embrace a forced distribution concept.[23]

Graphic Rating Scale

The **graphic rating scale** is used most widely for hourly employees. Using the graphic rating scale, appraisers typically rank employees on 10 to 15 criteria using a scale that ranges from 1 to 5. The criteria used generally cover such items as work characteristics, quality of work, quantity of work, dependability, attendance, interaction with people, job knowledge, and attention to detail. Ratings on each criterion are then added together to arrive at a composite score for each employee. A sample section of a performance appraisal using a graphic rating scale is shown in Exhibit 7.

This appraisal method is simple to use; it also provides scores that are readily understandable. However, this method is the most susceptible to rating pattern errors such as leniency, severity, and the halo effect because appraisers may find it difficult to determine the exact meaning of many criteria. For instance, what does "dependability" mean? Does it mean the same thing to all appraisers?

Exhibit 7   Example of a Graphic Rating Scale

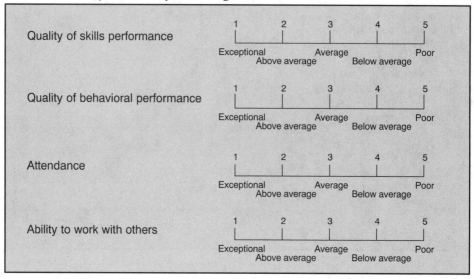

An additional problem with a graphic rating scale is the variability in importance of the different criteria. Appraisers typically apply different levels of importance to different criteria. For example, one appraiser may view attendance as extremely important and rank employees differently on this factor than on a factor considered less important. The level of importance that appraisers assign to each criterion can make a substantial difference in final composite scores. Management can overcome this problem partly by pre-weighting scales based on the importance assigned to each criterion. As a result, final scores can be influenced by multiplying each item by a different weight before the total is calculated.

Regardless of the problems associated with graphic rating scales, this is still one of the most popular rating methods used. However, use of the graphic rating scale dropped from a high of 50 percent of total appraisals in 1988 to 24 percent in 1996.[24] This drop occurred for two reasons: (1) it does not provide clear and descriptive data for evaluating employees, and (2) it has not proven to be as defensible in court as methods that include written assessments of performance. Ironically, the graphic rating scale grew in popularity in the 1980s because managers thought it was more defensible in court. But times change; scales that include accounts of critical incidents, essays evaluating performance, etc., are more defensible.[25]

Behaviorally Anchored Rating Scales (BARS)

Like the graphic rating scale, **behaviorally anchored rating scales (BARS)** require appraisers to rate employees on a scaled continuum. In this case, appraisers rate the specific actions or dimensions of an employee's work based on **critical incidents**. This method relies less on an appraiser's opinion of what is good and what is bad than other methods do. The critical incidents provided on a BARS appraisal form provide specific examples of what are considered to be good and bad behaviors.

Critical incidents are work-related events that managers observe and record to form an accurate picture of a job's requirements. Normally, the critical incidents used on BARS scales are developed by a committee of employees and managers. Since employees participate in determining the criteria for ranking, the BARS method is often more acceptable to employees than other methods of performance appraisal.[26] In addition, the BARS method often provides more accurate ratings of overall performance.

The major weakness of the BARS method is the amount of time and the expense required to develop the system. Each job requires a totally different appraisal system, since critical incidents are different for each. As a result, development can be a very time-consuming and costly process. Exhibit 8 provides an example of a behaviorally anchored rating scale.

Behavioral Observation Scales (BOS)

Behavioral observation scales (BOS) were developed in response to criticism about the BARS method. Because the BARS method allows only one measure of each employee on a specific scale, some researchers thought that it could not provide a fair assessment of employees who sometimes performed well and sometimes performed poorly. Instead of using critical incidents as the measurements, the BOS method establishes critical incidents as the behavior to be observed and asks appraisers to evaluate how often employees behave in this way. For example, a rater could be asked to rate an employee from "always" to "never" based on the number of times he or she "works well with other employees as a team." Exhibit 9 provides an example of Behavioral Observation Scale (BOS).

A 2000 study involving 96 police officers found that ratees' satisfaction with the performance appraisal process was highest when using BOS, rather than BARS or the graphic rating scales. Additionally, ratees' perceptions of performance goals were most favorable under BOS. A separate analysis of the same data by other experts showed that performance improvement goals for the officers rated using the BOS method were judged to be the most observable and specific.[27]

Narrative Essays

Raters using **narrative essays** simply write essays that describe the employees they are rating. Ideally, raters should take the time to write essays that present a good picture of employee performance. When carefully written, these essays are very useful in filling gaps left by more quantitative methods. Also, narrative essays should provide written suggestions on how employees can improve. However, essays rarely turn out this way. Managers typically do not take the time to write careful essays that describe the performance of their employees.

Critical Incidents

Managers who conduct appraisals using critical incidents as performance criteria keep individual logs on employees that focus on an employee's behavior in

Exhibit 8   Example of a Behaviorally Anchored Rating Scale

Rating	Scale	Sample Actions
Communicates effectively with staff members and attends meetings frequently	7.00	This manager calls a meeting to explain why the hotel will be cutting back on staff. Employees are permitted to ask questions and discuss why certain positions in the hotel are being eliminated
	6.00	During a busy expansion program, this manager increases the frequency of policy-committee meetings to improve communication about and coordination of the project.
	5.00	About once a week this manager invites several line employees into his or her office for an informal talk about hotel activities.
Communicates satisfactorily with staff members and attends some meetings	4.00	This manager neglects to discuss with his front-office manager the problem of overstaffing among the bell staff during certain periods of the day, but expresses concern to the resident manager.
	3.00	This manager misses department meetings and fails to visit with subordinates individually, but leaves memos around the hotel with instructions on what should be done.
Experiences difficulty communicating with staff members and attends meetings infrequently.	2.00	During executive-committee meetings this manger dismisses subordinates' comments as stupid.
	1.00	

Source: Robert H. Woods, Michael P. Sciarini, and Deborah Breiter, "Performance Appraisals in Hotels," *Cornell Hotel and Restaurant Administration Quarterly* (April 1998): 25–29.

specific situations. This method may be particularly applicable in many hospitality companies, since the behaviors managers usually focus on are exceptionally desirable or undesirable.

For instance, consider a parking attendant who lends his umbrella to a guest during a rainstorm. Such a critical incident provides an excellent example of how that company feels employees should behave. The advantage of this method is that it provides information that is readily useful in performance appraisals. For example, a manager could recall a specific incident involving an employee and either

Exhibit 9   Example of a Behavioral Observation Scale (BOS)

	Consistently friendly with guests				
1.	1	2	3	4	5
	almost never			almost always	

	Consistently helps other servers				
2.	1	2	3	4	5
	almost never			almost always	

	Consistently sells extras				
3.	1	2	3	4	5
	almost never			almost always	

	Consistently easy to work with				
4.	1	2	3	4	5
	almost never			almost always	

commend or reprimand that employee based on what happened. The critical incident method also creates symbolic goals or stories that depict behaviors to emulate. A training video, for instance, might show a bellperson making a special trip to a guestroom to deliver a teddy bear that he saw a guest's child drop in the lobby. This type of critical incident portrays the behavior—attention to guest service—that the property desires.

A disadvantage of this method is that managers must keep careful logs of each critical incident they observe. Even when accurate logs are kept, it is unlikely that managers will capture enough incidents to fairly assess the unexceptional or normal behaviors of each employee.

Management by Objectives (MBO)

Unlike other methods, **management by objectives (MBO)** involves meetings between employees and managers (or between managers and their supervisors) in which joint goals are established. Specific plans for achieving each goal are also established, as are the means for measuring progress toward goal achievement. Typically, an MBO system requires regular meetings to assess progress toward established goals; ultimately, employees are rated on their achievement of the goals. Exhibit 10 outlines the steps involved in establishing an MBO program; Exhibit 11 presents a sample MBO appraisal form.

Exhibit 10   Steps in Establishing an MBO Program

1. Employee proposes goals for upcoming evaluation period.
2. Employee and manager discuss goals, modify as necessary, and reach an agreement on specific goals—which are established and agreed to in writing.
3. Employee and manager agree on specific action plan to attain goals.
4. Manager encourages goal attainment informally during evaluation period.
5. At the end of the period, employee and manager meet again to discuss accomplishments and agree on extent to which goals were attained.
6. Process is repeated.

Exhibit 11   Sample MBO Appraisal Form

Hotel _____   Name of manager _____

Review Period _____   Reviewer _____

Performance goals	Measures of results	Results
(1) Market share	Room-nights	Increase by 3 percent
(2) Guest service guest comments	Ratio of positive to 94 percent	Increase from 90
(3) Room-department profit	Room-department income percentage	Increase by 1 percent
(4) Employee morale	Grievance rate	Decrease by 5 percent
(5) Employee development training completions	Number of	Increase by 10 percent
(6) Helath and safety conditions	Number of accidents	Decrease by 10 percent
(7) Hotel external relations	Number of leadership positions	No change

Source: Robert H. Woods, Michael P. Sciarini, and Deborah Breiter, "Performance Appraisals in Hotels," *Cornell Hotel and Restaurant Administration Quarterly* (April 1998): 25–29.

Some managers and scholars believe very strongly in the MBO approach; they see it as a viable means of performance appraisal as well as a good management philosophy.[28] However, others see some shortcomings; they see the emphasis that many managers place on setting easy-to-achieve goals in order to build a good record and, subsequently, positive performance appraisals. This approach creates a culture of "yes-men" who damage organizations because they fail to examine tough-to-achieve alternatives carefully. Critics point out that the MBO system stresses the accomplishment of short- rather than long-term goals.[29] In an environment in which all opinions are the same, there is less incentive to ask for opinions; therefore, opinions become less valuable. It is also difficult to evaluate the accomplishment of different goals by different employees under the MBO system. Some employees set more difficult goals than others. This provides appraisers with yet another challenge when ranking employees by comparison. In spite of these deficiencies, use of MBOs grew from 29.5 percent of appraisals in 1981 to 31.8 percent in 1996.[30] This growth occurred in part because federal, state, and local government agencies began to use and recommend the MBO method more frequently.

In the hospitality industry, an MBO system is often tied to the process of customer-based goal setting. For example, if a hotel restaurant wants to improve the speed of delivering service, it might tie the restaurant manager's performance appraisal to some form of speed goal. If the desired speed goal is achieved, that manager's performance appraisal would reflect that positive result.[31] Specific goals aside, it is important that MBO standards be challenging but realistic. The supervisor and the employee must work together to establish solid objectives. If that process is given a half effort, the MBO appraisal will have minimal utility. Harold Johnson, General Manager of the Mt. Charleston Hotel in Nevada, is adamant about spending the necessary time to establish specific objectives:

> The MBO process is daunting to a lot of managers and employees because it requires a certain level of trust. I like to sit down with a new employee and make it clear to him that I am on his side. I want him to succeed, and I am going to help him succeed. The MBO process is not just an empty exercise. It is a fantastic tool to help set clear objectives that everyone can understand and attain. It is also important that the objectives have some "stretch" aspect that forces the individual to really put forth more than just a token effort. When you find the right balance, it can be very empowering for the employee. He knows what needs to be done and he has the freedom to make it happen as he sees fit. But unless you take the time at the outset to really sweat out the specifics with fairness and balance, you can get yourself into a disappointing exercise in just paperwork.[32]

Peer-reviewed research suggests that the MBO process increases the performance level of employees and overall firm productivity. When upper management was truly committed to the process and directly participated in key details, productivity gains were even greater.[33]

Who Should Evaluate Performance?

Most managers will find it simple to determine the line of responsibility for performance appraisals. The immediate supervisor is responsible for performance appraisals 93 percent of the time. However, this person may have little actual contact with the employees he or she evaluates. In fact, researchers have found that managers spend as little as five to 10 percent of their time with any single employee in a given week; even then, the contact may take place in a number of settings or may involve minimal interaction.[34] In these cases, a manager must ask whether the time spent with employees is enough to adequately evaluate their performance. On the other hand, an employee's immediate supervisor may be the person best-suited to evaluate that employee's performance in relation to departmental or organizational goals.

One issue is fairly certain: immediate supervisors make vastly superior assessments when compared with those of a second-level supervisor. The "boss's boss" is normally unaware of a given employee's abilities and/or performance, and tends to give ratings that are highly inflated and less accurate. These ratings tend to show less distinction across rating criteria and across employees.[35]

Raters can be influenced by many factors. Age discrimination in employee performance appraisals can be a very sensitive issue. In Age Discrimination Employment Act (ADEA) cases involving performance appraisals, a company is more likely to win if the employee/plaintiff is between the ages of 40 and 49 because juries are more sympathetic to people over 50.[36] Research on another age-related factor—the age of the rater—shows that older managers are more likely to give favorable overall ratings and younger managers tend to give higher ratings on interpersonal skills.[37] These factors emphasize the importance of training raters to be more objective and less biased.

Scholarly research has shown that bosses in a bad mood are more likely to issue negative performance appraisals. Research also confirms that the subconscious stereotypes that managers hold regarding race, age, attractiveness, and other attributes directly affect their appraisals. Because of these issues, companies have continued to tinker with different systems for conducting performance evaluations. What follows is a sample of some of the more popular methods in use today in the hospitality industry.[38]

Peer Evaluations

Some researchers contend that peer evaluation is the best appraisal method, due to regular peer contact and the importance of teamwork in the hospitality industry. In fact, research shows that managers often interact with some of their employees only to resolve problems, while employees constantly interact with their peers. Although this makes a strong case for peer evaluation, such appraisals are best used as part of a system that involves appraisals by managers. In most cases, agreement among peer and supervisory ratings is very high.[39]

Research has indicated that employees may, indeed, provide excellent evaluations. In one study, researchers found high levels of correlation between employee evaluations of guest service delivered in their hotels to the evaluations guests themselves provided.[40]

One recommendation for the use of peer evaluations comes from operators who have used peer reviews in their performance appraisal systems. According to these operators, peer reviews often are as valid as reviews by other persons, and they have the added advantage of easing conflicts among co-workers.[41]

Staff Evaluations of Managers

A restaurant company in Seattle has established a policy of allowing employees to evaluate each new manager after the manager's first six months on the job. This idea is often referred to as a 180-degree appraisal, since the traditional direction of evaluation has been reversed.[42] These appraisals are taken so seriously that a poor rating can lead to a manager's dismissal. While few companies have gone so far as to link employee-driven appraisals directly to manager job retention, there is good reason to use this method of appraisal for management development. Employees typically know the extent of a manager's interpersonal skills. They also know how well that manager delegates authority and leads others. A big plus for staff appraisals is that, in the short run, they have proven to be good predictors of performance success.[43]

Staff appraisals depend on the level of trust among employees, managers, and the organization. Unless the appraisal is strictly quantitative, it may be impossible to do, since managers will know exactly who said what. And in some—if not most—situations, managers ultimately hold reward and punishment power over employees.

Self-Appraisal

The notion that we are always harder on ourselves than on others may not be true when it comes to performance appraisals. Some research indicates that self-appraisals tend to be less critical than appraisals by others.[44] However, research findings indicate that this may be true only when employees with high self-esteem rate themselves.[45] Self-appraisals can be inflated by self-serving bias. Individuals tend to give themselves extra credit for successes, and they tend to blame others for failures. Another problem with this form of assessment involves inflation due to "blind spots." Individuals have a tendency to guess high when they lack reliable insight or facts about themselves. Even more troubling, self-appraisals can be unfair to women and minorities, because both of these groups self-assess more negatively than what is found on average in the larger population.[46] Nevertheless, when used with other appraisal methods, self-evaluations provide a good basis for establishing goals and objectives, especially for training and development.

Guest Appraisals

At first, hospitality managers may think that guest appraisals are the best method of employee evaluation, since the ultimate goal of any service organization is guest satisfaction. They can certainly help determine training needs. Unfortunately, collecting accurate information from guests is difficult. Many guests do not fill out items such as guest comment cards unless they are extremely pleased or passionately dissatisfied. As a result, guest appraisals tend to stress the extremes rather than the average. Also, it can be difficult to correlate guest appraisals to exact job responsibilities, which means these evaluations may not stand up in court. When used with another system, however, guest appraisals provide a good means of assessing performance.

Multiple Rater Evaluation Systems

Using more than one rater can increase the accuracy and perceived fairness of a performance appraisal. Hilton Grand Vacations Club on the Las Vegas Strip uses a multiple rater evaluation system to motivate its sales staff and create sales superstars. Managers see their multiple rater system as a big reason for the company's success. Julie Benson, director of sales in-house, explains:

> Each sales professional sets monthly personal and professional goals as part of their overall plan to achieve their annual sales targets. At these monthly performance reviews, each salesperson receives feedback from every one of the nine sales managers. The benefits of the team approach are two-fold: it creates a winning atmosphere where sales management is held accountable for the overall success of the sales team, and each manager can fine-tune employee sales performance based on his or her unique area of expertise. From these monthly review sessions, the managers identify training issues, which are then incorporated in our weekly sales meetings.[47]

Multiple rater evaluation systems also provide higher-quality management information for selection decisions and better equal employment opportunity documentation, and may reduce overall costs by consuming less management time. One multiple rater method that has gained popularity is called the 360-degree appraisal.

360-Degree Appraisals. The 360-degree appraisal approach is so named because it includes a wide variety of raters in an appraisal. Supervisors, subordinates, coworkers, employees from other departments, and even customers and suppliers may participate. Depending on how their use is measured, such appraisals are used in 13 percent[48] to 26 percent[49] of all U.S. companies. (Thirteen percent represents companies that use four or five of the above categories of raters; 26 percent represents companies that use at least three of the categories. Some experts call using a limited number of raters a "partial-360 approach.") Fully 90 percent of Fortune 500 companies use 360-degree appraisals.[50] The 360-degree appraisal approach is growing in popularity in part because it is highly valued in team environments. Many industries have moved toward self-managed teams, also known as self-directed work forces. As these teams grow in importance, the 360-degree appraisal is likely to develop even greater popularity.[51]

In a 360-degree appraisal system, between four and ten raters provide feedback to each ratee. Generally, both objective and narrative/essay comments are included. Often, ratees are required to rate themselves, and then a copy of their self-evaluation is included in a packet other raters use. Unlike other rating systems, 360-degree feedback is anonymous. While you don't know who your raters are, you may know their positions in the company, i.e., co-worker, supervisor, subordinate, etc. Many who use 360-degree feedback believe the system makes a difference and is useful. While slanted scores can still occur, the wider range of raters reduces the chance that discrimination or bias will significantly affect the overall appraisal results. Such appraisals may therefore be more defensible in lawsuits.

The following are some recommendations for implementing a 360-degree appraisal system: [52]

- Feedback must be anonymous and confidential, although it is acceptable to identify the appraisers' levels in the company

Seven Guidelines for Improving the Performance Appraisal Process

The following seven guidelines can help managers improve the performance appraisal process where they work:

1. *Involve both managers and employees in the design of the performance appraisal process.* Involvement in the design of the performance appraisal process helps participants take ownership of the process and increases their satisfaction with it.

2. *Clearly establish performance appraisal objectives in advance, and place proper emphasis on each objective.* Managers and employees must agree—in advance—on exactly what is being appraised, to ensure that employees know exactly what is expected of them.

3. *Focus feedback during the appraisal on observable, job-related results and performance.* Managers often get in big trouble, both legally and otherwise, by commenting on non-job-related issues during a performance appraisal.

4. *Avoid personal feedback.* A formal performance appraisal is neither the time nor the place for this.

5. *Listen first; talk later.* Let employees begin, and encourage them to talk as long as they wish. This often sets the stage for better communication and understanding.

6. *Be positive first.* Focus on good things first, then discuss negative issues in a constructive manner.

7. *Probe first and describe later.* Give employees a chance to criticize their own performance before offering your input. As a general rule, follow the initiate-listen-focus-probe-plan pattern during the appraisal process.

- Consider how long the ratee has held the position; some "history" among appraisers and ratee is necessary.

- A feedback expert should interpret the data for accuracy.

- Follow-up is essential; developing a plan of action after receiving feedback makes it all work.

- Be sure to combine narrative ratings with numerical ratings. Numbers alone don't say much.

- To avoid fatigue and overwork, don't evaluate everyone all at once when you implement the new 360-degree appraisal system.

Although it is growing in popularity, the 360-degree appraisal approach has some disadvantages. The use of multiple raters can lead to conflicting opinions, the process is time-consuming and administratively complex, and it requires managers and employees to learn a new system, which raises training costs.

A 2001 study by Watson Wyatt Consulting, the Human Capital Index, found that companies using 360-degree appraisals were associated with a 10.6 percent decrease in shareholder value (on average) when contrasted with similarly-situated companies using more traditional reviews.[53] Although Watson Wyatt viewed the 360-degree system as a useful tool, they noted flaws that included excessive time and training issues and a tendency for individuals to form "rating alliances" that disrupt the integrity of the system.[54] According to Dr. John Sullivan, San Francisco State University, "there is no data showing that [360-degree feedback] actually improves productivity, increases retention, decreases grievances or is superior to forced ranking and standard performance appraisal systems. It sounds good, but there is no proof it works."[55]

A word of caution relates to the implementation of anything new. Any new approach is likely to create a "Hawthorne Effect," i.e., temporary improvement in productivity that results from the change itself.[56] Therefore, to see how a new system really works, be sure to use it for a while. Despite the fact that some researchers are questioning the utility of 360-degree feedback, many firms that are using this system believe it to be a superior system overall that provides incomparable data for determining merit raises, promotions, and terminations.

Performance Appraisal Training

When training managers and supervisors to conduct performance appraisals, seven issues are important. Trainees should complete training with:

- An understanding of rating errors

- An understanding of how to process observed information

- An understanding of how to establish a frame of reference for what is observed

- A familiarity with the performance appraisal system in use

- The experience of having observed a performance appraisal

- Practice in effective interviewing techniques

- Practice in conducting a performance appraisal

To be effective managers, appraisers must be familiar with the rating errors discussed earlier in the chapter. One way to gain such knowledge is to read materials that describe problems associated with these errors (such as this chapter). Managers and supervisors can be trained to process information through accurate recordkeeping and to more carefully observe employees at work. Recordkeeping training, for instance, can emphasize the importance of noting behaviors and actions throughout the observation period to avoid recency problems.

Appraisers can be trained to become better observers if they're taught how to identify rating criteria and focus on those behaviors and actions. A frame of reference for desired behaviors and actions can be established using examples of critical incidents or films and observations of employees at work. These illustrations help appraisers identify standards of comparison.

Trainees can learn about the performance appraisal system their property uses by listening to a current appraiser or experienced manager discuss appraisal at a training session. Observation of an actual performance appraisal provides the trainee with a real-life example. Interview technique training also provides future raters with the opportunity to hone their interview skills.

Interviewing should emphasize the problem-solving approach to performance appraisals, which generally encourages employee participation. Interviewers should actively listen to and work with employees to set mutually agreeable goals.

While the problem-solving method of interviewing is recommended, managers also sometimes use the "tell and sell" or "tell and listen" approaches. The "tell and sell" approach emphasizes managerial control over the interview and generally recommends that managers tell employees their findings, then attempt to sell employees on the implications of the findings or on goals for improvement. Using the "tell and listen" approach, a manager tells employees about his or her findings, then asks employees to discuss the implications of the appraisal and recommend goals for improvement.

Practice is the final step in training future managers to conduct effective performance appraisals. Role playing with current appraisers is an excellent means of training, because it provides trainees with immediate feedback on how to conduct appraisals. This final training step provides appraisers with valuable experience in conducting performance appraisal interviews.

When discussing performance appraisal training, customer service consultant Emily Huling recommends the classic book *The One Minute Manager*, by Kenneth Blanchard and Spencer Johnson. These authors believe that supervisors should continuously practice one-minute praising and one-minute reprimanding. By doing so, the supervisor will not see the formal performance review as an overwhelming task.[57]

Special Training Considerations

There are two factors that should be taken into consideration when developing a performance appraisal training program: cultural differences among workers in the global marketplace, and the phenomenon of "virtual workers."

Cultural Implications of the Global Marketplace. Anytime performance evaluations are executed in an international environment, there are cultural implications that need to be considered. In Western societies, a performance-oriented appraisal is both expected and accepted by the individuals involved. Traditionally collectivist societies that are only beginning to accept capitalism or those that have a more Eastern philosophy will emphasize harmony, personal relationships, and organizational integration in their employee-evaluation systems.[58]

Certain cultures may also be less likely to embrace modern two-way appraisal systems. For example, in China, where there is great respect given to authority and age, it may be unreasonable to expect a functional staff-evaluation process; the resistance to the idea of subordinates evaluating managers might be too great.[59] In India, where "fatalistic rationalization" is often referred to when the issue of substandard performance is addressed, the ideas that impact effective rating systems are different than those in the United States. Individuals often demonstrate an external locus of control that does not lend itself to traditional U.S.-style performance evaluations.[60]

The bottom line is that today's diverse work force and global hospitality environment demand sensitivity to the feelings, needs, and values of employees who have different belief systems. Effective hospitality managers will need to remain flexible and open-minded if they are to maximize the utility of performance evaluations in an international environment.

Virtual Workers. Many modern firms are allowing individuals to work from home. Ninety-five percent of Fortune 1000 companies are allowing some of their workers to be part of a telecommuting program.[61] According to the Department of Labor, nearly 20 million U.S. employees work from sites outside their employer's place of business.[62] These off-site workers pose challenges to their supervisors who have the task of issuing appraisals on individuals they seldom see. Some sales force team members, individuals who are always on the go and rarely check-in with headquarters, also call attention to this problem. The hospitality industry has many workers that fit this description: convention and group sales representatives, various back-of-the-house number crunchers, and even employees that work the graveyard shift (they stay on property, but often find themselves rated by bosses who work the day shift).

One director of human resources for an international firm recommends the following policies for setting up performance appraisals with virtual workers:[63]

1. Establish clear goals—make certain everyone is on the same page.

2. Evaluate by the bottom-line; results and performance are what count. But don't forget, accessibility to team members and clients is part of performance. If the person cannot be reached, you have a problem, and the appraisal should reflect that.

3. Set up a monitoring or accountability procedure with periodic face-to-face meetings and required deadlines for results reporting.

4. Express trust throughout the process, but be objective in the final analysis of the employee's performance.

Although some researchers have hypothesized that distance (or separation by scheduling) between rater and ratee will degrade the effectiveness of the appraisal process with virtual workers, so far there are no conclusive findings on this issue.[64]

Frequency of Performance Appraisals

Research consistently shows that once or twice a year is far too infrequent for performance appraisals. Despite these findings, this is the norm. In fact, believe it or not, a national survey of employers revealed that December 24 is the most popular time for managers to conduct annual performance reviews.[65] The problems with annual or semiannual performance appraisals relate to the appraiser's ability to remember events and behaviors that occurred as long as 12 months ago. Appraisers can minimize—but not eliminate—this problem by keeping thorough notes throughout the year. Our memory is seldom good enough to recall details associated with behaviors and actions that occurred far in the past. While it may be impractical to provide feedback every day, managers should give feedback as frequently as possible.

In the hospitality industry, rapid managerial turnover causes an additional problem regarding annual or semiannual appraisals. Because managerial turnover in many companies is 50 percent to 100 percent (and sometimes more), employees may actually work under several managers during a single appraisal period. Unless extremely good records are kept, severe distortion can result in appraisals.

If at all possible, hospitality companies should strive for quarterly performance appraisals, and should schedule them more often if managerial turnover is a problem. An alternative is to conduct employee appraisals on specific assignments. After an employee completes a training program, for instance, an appraisal should be conducted to establish performance criteria and to set goals. Employees working on special projects should also have appraisals conducted immediately upon completion or termination of the project.

Performance appraisals are most effective when used often. Nevertheless, most segments of the hospitality industry tend to use annual reviews. If this method is used, it is best to conduct all appraisals during the same time period, rather than staggering them. With staggering, some employees may get rated in the first quarter and others in the third, for example. The reason for avoiding the staggering approach is fairness. Suppose one employee's appraisal is conducted with the company facing a significant court ruling in two weeks that has every manager on edge. Now imagine that a different employee has the benefit of being evaluated six months later, after a record quarter of earnings that puts every manager in a good mood. As a ratee, which situation would you rather be in?[66]

Exhibit 12 reports how frequently appraisals are used in three segments of the hospitality industry. In this exhibit, we see that restaurants probably use performance appraisals most effectively, because they use them most often. Clubs use them least effectively, relying on annual reviews for 80 percent of their employees.[67] Most employees want more frequent appraisals, because this approach provides them with more immediate feedback on their performance.

Appraisals and the Law

Because performance appraisals directly influence employment decisions, they come under close scrutiny to ensure that they are not discriminatory. Typically, the key issues in investigations are **job relatedness** and objectivity. Performance appraisals must relate directly to the responsibilities of the job. Objectivity has been found to be a problem in some companies.

According to noted researchers, a valid performance appraisal system demonstrates a high correlation between the system and the company's established, objective measures of performance and accurately predicts future job success. These authors suggest that managers should submit their performance appraisal system to ten tests to determine whether it meets the minimum legal requirements for any appraisal system. Five of these tests relate to content (job-related) issues

Exhibit 12   Frequency of Hospitality Performance Appraisals

Frequency	Lodging	Clubs	Restaurants	All Industries
Quarterly	5.6	1.1	11.7	3.6
Semi-annually	18.2	16.5	27.3	15.6
Annually	67.1	80.1	41.6	62.9
Other	9.1	2.3	19.5	18.0

(Numbers are percentages of the sample studied.)

Source: Robert H. Woods, Michael P. Sciarini, and Jack D. Ninemeier, "The Use of Performance Appraisals in Three Segments of the Hospitality Industry: A Comparative Study," *Journal of Hospitality and Tourism Education* 10, no. 3 (1998): 61.

while the other five relate to process requirements (due process issues). The five content issues are:[68]

- Performance standards must be based on an analysis of job requirements.
- Evaluation should be based on specific dimensions of job performance rather than on a single broad measure.
- Performance standards should be objective and observable.
- Ratings should be documented.
- The validity of the appraiser's ratings should be assessed.

  The five process issues are:

- Performance standards must be communicated to and understood by employees.
- Specific instructions for appraisals should be put in writing.
- More than one appraiser should be used whenever possible (to create inter-rater reliability).
- Appraisers should carefully review results with employees.
- Each company should establish legitimate, formal appeal procedures and inform employees of such procedures.

Two more items should be added to this list: periodic system evaluation and ample documentation of all issues related to performance appraisals. Documentation should include appraiser findings, interview notes, and employee-signed results. The system should be periodically evaluated and overhauled, if necessary, to meet the job-relatedness requirement. Job responsibilities change, which means performance appraisals must change. Documentation provides the paper trail required to argue a company's case successfully in court, if that becomes necessary. Above all, managers must be sure that appraisals are consistent. Too often, employees are fired in spite of good appraisals. This is called "pretext" (as when a false reason conceals the truth) and can supply grounds for losing many wrongful discharge lawsuits.[69]

Performance evaluations are often important evidence in court cases involving the termination of an employee. In one hospitality industry case, *Steiner* v. *Showboat Hotel and Casino*, the 9th Circuit Appeals Court considered testimony that revolved around low marks on an employee's evaluations. The plaintiff claimed that these low ratings were an intentional retaliation against her for other non-job related reasons. But in examining the evidence, the court disagreed with this point and found that the appraisals had merit and were a fair analysis of the individual's objective performance.[70] The outcome of the case turned on other issues, but the point is clear: employee performance appraisals will be subject to legal scrutiny if they are disputed by an individual.

In *Hillstrom* v. *Best Western TLC Hotel* (U.S. Court of Appeals for the 1st Circuit), an employee's mistakes were tracked by management using a critical incident log. Although the employee sued for various forms of discrimination and for violations of the Family and Medical Leave Act, the court found that the hotel had not acted inappropriately. Evidence of sound procedures for inputs into the critical incident log made an impact on the court's decision.[71]

In *Willis* v. *Harrah's Illinois Corporation*, the 7th Circuit Appeals court looked at the potential wrongful discharge of a former coatroom attendant who had been promoted to retail supervisor in the casino's gift shop. Following promotion, the employee proved to be "offensive" to customers and "hard to deal with." The newly minted supervisor "missed an entire shift" and "failed to properly handle a payroll report." Harrah's documented the employee's behavior and placed the individual on a 30-day corrective action program. Despite the apparent inconsistency of firing an employee soon after a promotion, the case was decided in favor of the casino. Procedures and protocols had been followed in terms of performance evaluations and critical incident reports, and the company was found to be justified in its termination decision.[72]

In *Bauer* v. *Metz Baking Company*, a district court in Iowa looked at a case involving age discrimination issues at a hospitality supplier. Various supervisors had issued numerous performance evaluations of an elderly worker over a number of years. These appraisals were deemed to be "somewhat uneven" in their assessment of the employee's performance. Despite this documented inconsistency, the hospitality supplier was able to get the case dismissed. This firm had taken the time to document numerous incidents of sub-caliber work performance by the individual, and it had followed up these warnings with training sessions and coaching. Since the firm appeared to act in good faith to help the worker fix the work-related problems, the firm was ultimately vindicated.[73]

The U.S. case law that involves hospitality companies and performance appraisals is constantly evolving. Although there is no single antidote that will keep a hospitality firm out of court, it is a good idea to keep rigorous documentation on all evaluation activities, and it makes good sense to consistently treat employees fairly and compassionately so that the firm's intentions and actions stand up to significant scrutiny. While litigation over performance appraisal methods and results is not uncommon, concern over it should not deter managers; the advantages of performance appraisals far outweigh their possible disadvantages.

Final Thoughts on Evaluating Employee Performance

While there is no single performance appraisal system that works best in all circumstances, it is possible to develop a good system that meets an individual company's or manager's needs. The keys to developing a successful employee evaluation system can be derived from the main topic headings in this chapter:

- Identify the functions the performance appraisal will serve (reinforce or improve performance, motivate, determine career progress and set goals, validate the selection process, and so on).

- Develop sound criteria for the system (make sure it is valid, reliable, and job-related) to avoid potential problems with inaccuracy.

- Identify the types of performance to measure (traits, behaviors, results).

- Choose the method of appraisal (graphic rating scales, narrative essays, critical incidents, and so on) that will work best for the situation.

- Determine who will conduct appraisals and train those appraisers.

- Determine the frequency of performance appraisals.

- Make sure the system meets all legal requirements.

- Periodically evaluate the appraisal process to ensure that each function still meets the intended purpose.

While it is difficult to design and implement an appraisal system to evaluate employee performance, it is far better to make the effort than to have no system at all.

Endnotes

1. Berkley Rice, "Performance Ratings—Are They Worth the Trouble?" *Psychology Today* (September 1985): 30.

2. Tom Moffit, "Origin of the Pink Slip," *HR Focus* 72, no. 6 (1995): 15.

3. Brien N. Smith, Jeffrey Hornsby, and Roslyn Shirmeyer, "Current Trends in Performance Appraisals: An Examination of Managerial Practices," *SAM Advanced Management Journal* 61 (Summer 1996): 10–15.

4. James Goodale, "Improving Performance Appraisal," *Business Quarterly* 57 (Fall 1995): 65–71.

5. Interview with David Hoenemeyer, Vice President and Assistant General Manager of Harrah's Las Vegas, October 25, 2005, Las Vegas, Nevada.

6. Donald J. McNerney, "Improved Performance Appraisals: Process of Elimination," *HR Focus* 72 (July 1995): 1–4.

7. D. Brown, "Performance Management Systems Need Fixing: Survey," *Canadian HR Reporter* 18, no. 7 (2005): 5.

8. Bob Filepczak et al., "What to Do with an Egg–Sucking Dog," *Training* 33 (October 1996): 17–21.

9. Robert H. Woods, Michael P. Sciarini, and Jack D. Ninemeier, "The Use of Performance Appraisals in Three Segments of the Hospitality Industry: A Comparative Study," *Journal of Hospitality and Tourism Education* 10, no. 3 (1998): 59–63.

10. Woods, Sciarini, and Ninemeier: 61.

11. D. Brown, "Re-Evaluating Evaluation," *Canadian HR Reporter* 15, no. 7 (2002): 5.

12. L. Pickett, "Transforming the Annual Fiasco," *Industrial and Commercial Training* 35, no. 6 (2003): 237-238.

13. Interview with Todd Haushaulter, Casino Administrator at Wynn Las Vegas Hotel and Casino, late October 2005, Las Vegas, Nevada.

14. Robert H. Woods and James F. Macaulay, "Retention Programs that Work," *Cornell Hotel and Restaurant Administration Quarterly* 30, no. 1 (2001): 84.

15. Neil Brewer, Lynne Socha, and Rob Potter, "Gender Differences in Supervisors' Use of Performance Feedback," *Journal of Applied Social Psychology* 26 (May 1996): 786–804.

16. Lisa M. Drogosz and Paul E. Levy, "Another Look at the Effects of Gender, Appearance, and Job Type on Performance Decisions," *Psychology of Women Quarterly* 20 (1996): 437.

17. Delores McGee Wanguri, "A Review, Integration, and Critique of Cross Disciplinary Research on Performance Appraisals, Evaluations, and Feedback 1980–1990," *Journal of Business Communication* 32 (July 1995): 277.

18. The last four bullet points in this list were adapted from James E. Neal, Jr., *The #1 Guide to Performance Appraisals: Doing It Right!* 4th ed. (Perrysburg, Ohio: Neal Publications, Inc., 2003), 16.

19. H. Canan Sumer and Patrick A. Knight, "Assimilation and Contrast Effects in Performance Ratings: Effects of Rating the Previous Performance on Subsequent Performance," *Journal of Applied Psychology* 81 (August 1996): 436–443.

20. Yoar Ganzach, "Negativity (and Positivity) in Performance Evaluation: Three Field Studies," *Journal of Applied Psychology* 80 (August 1995): 491–500.

21. J. E. Pynes, *Human Resources Management for Public and Nonprofit Organizations,* 2d ed. (San Francisco, Calif.: Jossey-Bass, 2004), 211.

22. Pynes, 199.

23. K. Clark, "Judgment Day," *U.S. News & World Report* 134, no. 1 (2003): 1-1. Retrieved 11/21/2005 from the Academic Source Primer database.

24. Smith, Hornsby, and Shirmeyer: 11.

25. Wanguri: 267–293.

26. For a description of the development of a BARS scale, see Donald P. Schwab and Herbert G. Heneman III, "Behaviorally Anchored Rating Scales," in Herbert G. Heneman and

Donald Schwab, eds., *Perspectives on Personnel/Human Resource Management*, rev. ed. (Homewood, Ill.: Irwin, 1982), 73–74.

27. A. Tziner, C. Joanis, and K. R. Murphy, "A Comparison of Three Methods of Performance Appraisal with Regard to Goal Properties, Goal Perception, and Ratee Satisfaction," *Group & Organization Management* 25, no. 2 (2000): 175.

28. See George S. Odiorne, *Management by Objectives: A System of Managerial Leadership* (Belmont, Calif.: Fearon, 1965), or Karl Albrecht, *Successful Management by Objectives: An Action Manual* (Englewood Cliffs, N.J.: Prentice–Hall, 1978).

29. For a discussion of problems associated with MBOs, see Jeffrey S. Kane and Kimberley A. Freeman, "MBO and Performance Appraisal: A Mixture that's Not a Solution, Part I," *Personnel* (December 1986): 26–36.

30. Smith, Hornsby, and Shirmeyer: 11–12.

31. Kathleen M. Iverson, *Managing Human Resources in the Hospitality Industry: An Experiential Approach* (Upper Saddle River, N.J.: Prentice Hall, 2001), 179.

32. Interview with Harold Johnson, General Manager of the Mt. Charleston Hotel, November 8, 2005, Las Vegas, Nevada.

33. D. A. DeCenzo and S. P. Robbins, *Fundamentals of Human Resource Management*, 8th ed. (Hoboken, N. J.: Wiley, 2005), 257.

34. D. L. DeVries et al., *Performance Appraisal on the Line* (New York: Wiley, 1981).

35. M. R. Edwards and A. J. Ewen, *360° Feedback; The Powerful New Model for Employee Assessment and Performance Improvements* (New York: AMACOM, 1996), 40.

36. C. S. Miller, J. A. Kaspin, and M. Schuster, "The Impact of Performance Appraisal Methods on Age Discrimination in Employment Act Cases," *Personnel Psychology* 43 (1990): 555–578.

37. Wanguri: 277.

38. Clark: 1-1.

39. Wanguri: 277.

40. Carol A. King and Jenene G. Garey, "Relational Quality in Service Encounters," *International Journal of Hospitality Management* 16, no. 1 (1997) 1: 39–63.

41. Ali Cybulski, "Conflict Resolution: People's Court: Peer Review Eases Conflicts," *Restaurant Business* 96, no. 18 (1997) 43–44, 48.

42. D. V. Tesone, *Human Resource Management in the Hospitality Industry: A Practitioner's Perspective* (Upper Saddle River, N. J.: Pearson Education, 2005), 155.

43. Wanguri: 277.

44. L. M. Shore and G. C. Thornton, "Effects of Gender on Self- and Supervisory Ratings," *Academy of Management Journal* 29 (1986): 115–129.

45. Wanguri: 275.

46. Edwards and Ewen, 38.

47. Interview with Julie Benson, Director of Training, Hilton Grand Vacations Club, November 23, 2005, Las Vegas, Nevada.

48. Don L. Bohl, "Mini-Survey: 360-Degree Appraisals Yield Superior Results," *Compensation and Benefits* 28 (September/October 1996): 16–19.

49. Mary N. Vinson, "The Pros and Cons of 360-Degree Feedback," *Training & Development* 50 (April 1996): 11–12.

50. F. Carruthers, "Nothing But the Truth," *Australian Financial Review,* 14 November 2003, 78. Note that this reference is talking about U.S. companies, not Australian.

51. Tesone: 155.

52. Vinson: 12.

53. B. Pfau, I. Kay, K. M. Nowack, and J. Ghorpade, "Does 360-Degree Feedback Negatively Affect Company Performance?" *HRMagazine: On Human Resource Management* 47, no. 6 (2002): 55.

54. Clark: 1-1.

55. Pfau, Kay, Nowack, and Ghorpade: 57.

56. Bohl: 19.

57. E. Huling, "Bad Management Can Have High Costs," *Rough Notes* 145, no. 10 (2002): 48.

58. S. Groeschl, "Cultural Implications for the Appraisal Process," *Cross Cultural Management* 10, no. 1 (2003): 69.

59. Groeschl: 71.

60. Groeschl: 72.

61. C. Bogdanski and R. J. Setliff, "Leaderless Supervision: A Response to Thomas," *Human Resource Development Quarterly* 11, no. 2 (2000): 197.

62. G. Manochehri and T. Pinkerton, "Managing Telecommuters: Opportunities and Challenges," *American Business Review* 21, no. 1 (2003): 9.

63. "Performance Appraisals for Virtual Workers," *Getting Results for the Hands-on Manager* 42, no. 12 (1997): 3.

64. G. E. Thomas, "Leaderless Supervision and Performance Appraisal: A Proposed Research Agenda," *Human Resource Development Quarterly* 10, no. 1 (1999): 92.

65. Timothy D. Schellhardt, "Mr. Cratchit, Let's Have a Word Before You Go Home Tonight," *Wall Street Journal,* 24 December 1996, B1.

66. Barbara L. Steiner, Plaintiff-Appellant, v. Showboat Operating Company, d/b/a Showboat Hotel & Casino, Defendant-Appellee. No. 92-16882. (U.S. Court of Appeals for the Ninth Circuit 1994) Retrieved 11/22/2005, from LexisNexis.

67. Woods, Sciarini, and Ninemeier: 61.

68. Umbreit, Eder, and McConnell: 62–63.

69. Jonathan Segal, "Evaluating the Evaluators," *HR Magazine* 40 (October 1995): 46–50.

70. Pynes: 199–200.

71. Roy Hillstrom, Plaintiff-Appellant, v. Best Western TLC Hotel, Defendant-Appellee, 03-1972 1 (U.S. Court of Appeals for the First Circuit 2003). Retrieved 11/22/2005, from LexisNexis.

72. Shirley F. Willis Plaintiff-Appellant, v. Harrah's Illinois Corp. Defendant-Apellee. 98-2655 1 (U.S. Court of Appeals for the Seventh Circuit 1999). Retrieved 11/22/2005, from LexisNexis.

73. Judy A. Bauer, Plaintiff, Vs. Metz Baking Co. Defendant. C 98-4058-MWB 1 (U.S. District Court for the Northern District of Iowa, Western Division 1999). Retrieved 11/22/2005, from LexisNexis.

Key Terms

alternative ranking—Rating system in which an appraiser lists all employees and then chooses the best, worst, second-best, second-worst, and so on.

behavior-based rating—Rating system based on the behaviors of employees

behavioral observation scale (BOS)—Rating system in which appraisers identify how often an employee displays desired behaviors.

behaviorally anchored rating scale (BARS)—Rating system in which appraisers rate employees on specific behaviors displayed.

central tendency error—An error in a performance appraisal or interview that results when managers or interviewers rate all or most employees as average.

critical incident—Job analysis technique based on capturing and recording actual events that occur at work which, when combined, form an accurate picture of a job's actual requirements. Useful in describing how services should be performed. Also used in training and as a measurement in certain performance appraisal systems.

forced distribution—Evaluation method in which a manager ranks employees on an exact bell-shaped curve.

graphic rating scale—Rating system in which appraisers rate employees on specific measurable criteria.

halo error—An error in a performance appraisal or interview that results when managers or interviewers rate employees based on a single positive attribute.

job relatedness—The extent to which a rating system actually relates to the work done.

leniency error—An error in a performance appraisal or interview that results when managers or interviewers rate employees too positively.

management by objective (MBO)—Performance appraisal system in which a manager meets with each employee and sets specific goals to attain; both the manager and employee meet later to assess the extent to which these specific goals were reached.

narrative essay—Rating system in which appraisers write a narrative essay that describes the strengths and weaknesses of each employee.

paired comparison—a method of evaluating performance that involves comparing the performance, behaviors, skills, or knowledge of each employee with each other employee.

past anchoring error—An error in a performance appraisal that results when managers or interviewers rate employees on the basis of previous ratings.

performance appraisal—A meeting held between a manager and an employee for the purpose of evaluating the performance, behaviors, knowledge, and skills of that employee.

performance feedback—Feedback provided by the manager to an employee during a performance appraisal.

predictive validity—The extent to which a measurement predicts future behavior.

recency error—An error in a performance appraisal or interview that results when managers or interviewers base employee ratings primarily on the most recent events or behaviors.

results-based rating—Rating system based on measuring the extent to which employees accomplish results.

severity error—An error in a performance appraisal or interview that results when managers or interviewers rate employees too severely.

simple ranking—Method of ranking all employees in a single list. Also called straight ranking.

trait-based rating—Rating system based on an employee's personal characteristics.

 Review Questions ————————————————————————————————

1. What are the basic functions of performance appraisals? How might each of these functions be used?

2. How do construct validity and content validity differ? Why is each important to consider when establishing performance appraisal systems?

3. Why is job relatedness such an important issue in performance appraisals?

4. What are four types of common rating errors?

5. What are the principal differences between graphic rating scales and behaviorally anchored rating scales?

6. What are the advantages of using the narrative essay approach to appraisals? What are some of the problems?

7. What are the advantages of using peers and guests as raters in performance appraisals? What are some of the problems associated with using these groups as raters?

8. What objectives should be included in a training program for appraisers?

9. How frequently should a property conduct performance appraisals? Why?

10. How do the content issues and process issues managers should consider when assessing whether or not their performance appraisal system meets legal requirements differ?

Internet Sites ──────────────────────────

For more information, visit the following Internet sites. Remember that Internet addresses can change without notice. If the site is no longer there, you can use a search engine to look for additional sites.

Legal Information Institute, Cornell
Law School
www.law.cornell.edu/

U.S. Department of Education
www.ed.gov

National Performance Review
http://govinfo.library.unt.edu/npr/
default.htm

Case Study ──────────────────────────

Raising the Performance Bar

Just 30 days ago, Laverne Wilson was excited when she started her new position as executive housekeeper at the spectacular Melrose Hotel. The Melrose had enticed her away from a competing property with the promise of higher pay, greater prestige, and, of course, more responsibility. With her eye for detail, however, Laverne immediately noticed major housekeeping oversights at the hotel. In fact, on her first day at the Melrose, she was greeted by an overflowing trash can near the main entrance and cigarette butts on the lobby floor.

As Laverne reviewed guest comment cards and the results from guest satisfaction surveys, the problems seemed to multiply. Guest complaints ranged from stained linens to crumpled and soiled stationery in the guestrooms. Worst of all, guest property had been reported missing from rooms on a number of separate occasions, without resolution. To top it off, guest satisfaction reports over the last six months showed consistently low ratings for the housekeeping department and its services.

The real challenge emerged as Laverne read through the past year's performance appraisals of the housekeeping staff. Performance ratings were based on a scale of 1 to 5 (5 = outstanding, 4 = exceeds expectations, 3 = meets expectations, 2 = needs improvement, and 1 = unsatisfactory). Laverne was surprised to find that virtually every housekeeping employee had received the highest performance rating. "How on earth," she wondered, "could the staff in this department receive such high ratings when the performance of each unit is absolutely substandard?"

Since she was a newcomer to the management team at the Melrose, Laverne decided to tread lightly. She first met with the general manager and asked for advice. He had been aware of the performance problems for some time and was anxious to work with Laverne to correct them. He knew the hotel would suffer financially in the long run if things didn't change, so he gave Laverne the go-ahead to shake things up. While speaking with the GM, Laverne also learned of important incentive changes. To complicate her task, salary increases and bonuses would now be based on the performance not only of individual employees, but of entire units. In fact, each department's share of bonus pool funds would now be based on its overall performance. As the meeting ended, the GM added that guest satisfaction ratings would play a bigger role than ever in determining salary increases.

Laverne felt overwhelmed. How could she convince the various units in her department to improve their performance, particularly when they had been following the same routine for years? She was the new kid on the block and no one in her department would be very pleased with her for rocking the boat. Later in the day, Laverne sat down with the human resources director, Rodney Ramirez, to express her concerns.

"Rod," Laverne began, "I have a problem. Certain units in my department are underperforming, yet the employees have been getting stellar ratings on their annual performance evaluations. I need to meet with the unit supervisors, but before I do, I thought I would get your input. How can I encourage supervisors to evaluate their staff more realistically and get them to make the necessary improvements in their units? I don't expect them to be happy with this news, but if things don't change, my department will be in big trouble."

Rod thought about the situation for a moment and then responded. "Yes, you're in a tough spot, especially when you're trying to upset the status quo. It's going to be difficult and you can expect resistance, but we hired you because we knew you could handle the situation. Let's work together on this. I could prepare some refresher training programs for your units, but the bottom line is that different departments in this hotel have been using performance reviews in different ways and for different purposes. In order to make performance reviews work in the future, you need to recalibrate them. Competencies and evaluation criteria should be consistent throughout your department. To some degree, you're being tougher on your employees but you're also being fairer. Keep in mind that all the changes you make will benefit our guests."

Laverne thanked Rod for his time and helpful advice and thought about what to do next. She scheduled a meeting with the supervisors from the three most problematic units in her department: Melika Chinoy, a room inspector; Susan Duvall, the laundry supervisor; and Clarence Patterson, the public space supervisor. After a few days of preparation, she was ready to face the fire.

When they all met the following week, Laverne got right to the point. "Thank you for meeting with me today. I think you all must be aware of some problems facing our department. I called you here today because the problems all seem to point to your units. Let me ask you, What do you think are trademarks of quality housekeeping?" Laverne sat back in her chair with her arms crossed and glared at each supervisor as she waited for their responses.

Melika was the first to speak up, "It's obvious. Clean rooms and linen, attention to details."

Clarence added, "A nice-looking lobby and clean bathrooms."

"Right," Laverne affirmed. "So tell me why all of these guest comment cards say only bad things about the hotel? Look at this one. A guest says that the room she stayed in was filthy. Here's another complaint about stained sheets. Here's someone else who complained of a foul odor in the lobby. What are you going to do about this?"

Laverne paused. Susan's back straightened in the chair and her face seemed to harden. Melika and Clarence looked at each other. No one offered to speak.

"I want to see improvement in these areas," continued Laverne, "but, oddly enough, when I look at the performance evaluations of your staff, everyone has received a resounding ovation. How can every individual in your units receive a top rating, yet housekeeping underperforms as a department? We are only here to serve the guests of this hotel. If customers aren't satisfied—and judging from the number of complaints we've received, they aren't—then we aren't doing our jobs."

Laverne paused again to observe the threesome's reactions. Melika and Clarence were visibly agitated, while Susan appeared unmoved.

Laverne decided to continue. "Prior to the upcoming annual performance reviews, each of you must reconsider your methods of appraising employees. We need consistent evaluation guidelines that must be closely followed without exception. In other words, it's your responsibility to reevaluate your employees and I want to see concrete improvement in their performance within the next two months. We can no longer gloss over the staff and hope for the best. You should also be aware that next year's bonuses and salary increases will be based on overall departmental performance. We get nothing if this situation doesn't improve. Now I'll listen to your comments."

Susan Duvall, the laundry supervisor, was the first to respond. "With all due respect, Ms. Wilson, you haven't been here very long. I have been here twelve years and, although I agree with some of the problems you've mentioned, your predecessors never approached us in this way. We have always aimed for a cooperative work environment and I think it is totally unfair that you point the finger at us. This employee reevaluation stuff may be an opportunity for improvement and change, but what about the other units in the department? Aren't they part of the problem too?"

Melika chimed in. "I think re-evaluating our employees is stupid. Like it or not, I need to keep my workers. It's a tight job market. People aren't lined up trying to get a job here. My unit will suffer if I lose people. It's easier to give them a high rating and then encourage them to do their best. I just ain't gonna change the way I've always done things. I've got to think about my people."

Clarence, who had never been one to let his opinions go unspoken, was the most outraged. "I've been at this darn hotel for ten years and things have been going great, up to now. What the heck do you expect me to do? We've got lousy equipment and this hotel isn't up to the most modern standards, you know. The employees I work with are my friends. Why, I've known old Frank since I started here. Now I'm his supervisor and you want me to tell him his work isn't up to snuff? Forget it. Then you tell us we won't get a raise if we don't work harder? We don't get paid enough as it is!"

Discussion Questions

1. How could Laverne have approached the supervisors differently?

2. What steps should Laverne now take with each supervisor to ensure that he or she improves employee performance in each respective unit?

Case Number: 3567CA

The following industry experts helped generate and develop this case: Philip J. Bresson, Director of Human Resources, Renaissance New York Hotel, New York, New York; and Jerry Fay, Human Resources Director, ARAMARK Corporation, Atlanta, Georgia.

Part III

Compensation and Labor Issues

Chapter 8 Outline

Major Influences of Compensation Plans
 Cost of Living
 Labor Market Influences
 Union Influences
 Government Influences
Motivating Employees
 Content Theories
 Process Theories
Determining Job Worth
 External and Internal Equity
 Job Evaluation Methods
Establishing Pay Structures
 Competitive Pay Policies
 Pay Grades
 Determining Pay Within Grades
 Two-Tier Wage System
 Skill-Based Pay
 On-Call Pay
 Team-Based Pay
Current Issues in Compensation
 Administration
 Pay Secrecy
 Wage Compression and Expansion
 Comparable Worth
 Wage and Hour Audits

Competencies

1. Describe types of compensation and outline the major influences on compensation plans. (pp. 271–275)

2. Describe major content and process theories of motivation and their application to compensation plan design. (pp. 275–283)

3. Outline methods of determining job worth and describe the advantages and disadvantages of each. (pp. 283–288)

4. Describe the steps and identify options for establishing pay structures. (pp. 289–293)

5. Describe current issues in compensation administration. (pp. 293–298)

Compensation Administration

This chapter was co-authored by Keepyung Kim, M.S. candidate, University of Nevada, Las Vegas (UNLV); Angella Kyung, M.S. candidate, UNLV; and Hojin Lee, M.S. candidate, UNLV.

WHEN MOST PEOPLE HEAR THE WORD "compensation," they think about the wages or salaries that people earn in return for work. However, wages and salaries represent only part of the total compensation employees receive. An effective compensation program consists of both cash and non-cash rewards. Neither are randomly chosen. Instead, both are intended to support the company's compensation philosophy, to motivate and reward performances that are in line with company objectives, and to provide a positive rate of return on investments.

A company's compensation philosophy articulates where the company wants its pay policies to be in the marketplace. It also articulates how the company will reward and motivate employees.[1] All the methods including cash, equity, and benefits that employers use to pay for the work of employees are called the *total reward* program. The elements of the total reward program are *monetary compensation* and *nonmonetary compensation*. Nonmonetary compensation is basically the cultural aspect of the organization. This chapter concentrates on monetary compensation.

Monetary compensation is commonly divided into *direct compensation* and *indirect compensation*. These two kinds of compensation are sometimes further categorized as either *immediate compensation* or *deferred compensation*. Although some elements of compensation are easy to categorize, the complexity of today's compensation options occasionally produces forms of compensation that defy easy or definitive categorization.

In general, **direct compensation** involves an employer's payment of money to an employee—either in the present or at some future date—in exchange for that employee's productive work. Direct *immediate* compensation includes base pay, merit pay, incentive pay, bonuses, piece rates, shift differentials, and so forth. Direct *deferred* compensation includes money earned in one period that is not paid until a later period (as is the case with some executive compensation plans that encourage retention by granting bonuses for a given year, but paying them only if the executive is still with the company a given number of years later—one form of the so-called "golden handcuffs").

Most employees also receive indirect compensation. In general, **indirect compensation** is compensation that is given as a condition of employment rather than in direct exchange for productive work. For example, if a non-exempt employee works overtime one week, the employee's direct compensation (wages) will reflect that extra work; however, the employee will not receive "more" health insurance coverage (an indirect form of compensation) for that week. Indirect compensation includes various protection plans, pay for time not worked, assorted savings plans, and various services and perquisites. Protection plans include medical insurance, life insurance, disability insurance, Social Security, unemployment insurance, and workers' compensation insurance. Pay for time not worked includes vacation, holidays, sick leave, jury duty, and so forth. Savings plans include 401(k) plans and various "*deferred* compensation" plans (this being a term used to refer to specific tax-advantaged programs that allow employees to set aside money—with or without employer matching—and allow it to grow on a tax-deferred basis). Perks might include company cars, travel allowances, and discounts on company products and services. Generally, indirect compensation is *immediate* when it applies to a current employee. It is *deferred* when it continues to be available to employees after retirement or severance. Exhibit 1 shows a basic (but far from exhaustive) diagram of various types of compensation.

Major Influences on Compensation Plans

While many people think that compensation programs relate directly to the amount or type of work done, this is rarely the case. Instead, the rate of compensation is affected by many factors in most hospitality companies. Some influences relate to economic conditions in the company or the community, while others relate to internal or external labor market conditions. Other factors that affect compensation include employee perceptions of pay and union and government influences. Even employee satisfaction and motivation can influence a company's compensation practices. This section discusses some of the various influences on compensation.

Cost of Living

Cost of living refers to the real dollar value of a worker's purchasing power for ordinary necessities such as food and clothing. The **consumer price index** is generally the best overall indicator of the real value—or purchasing power—of wages or salaries. Basically, the consumer price index is a measurement of changes in the retail prices of goods and services. It is computed by comparing the cost of these goods and services at a fixed time with the cost at subsequent or prior times. The U.S. Consumer Price Index is issued monthly by the Bureau of Labor Statistics, an agency of the Department of Labor.

The consumer price index varies according to many different environmental and economic factors. As the consumer price index goes up, the value of money goes down. For instance, a consumer price index of five percent means that an item that used to cost $1.00 now costs $1.05. The consumer price index is often referred to as inflation. In times of high inflation, the value of a dollar goes down rapidly. As a result, increases in compensation rates must be larger. In low inflationary times, the value of a dollar goes down more slowly. As the value or purchasing price of the dollar changes, companies must adjust their compensation rates to remain competitive.

Exhibit 1   Compensation System

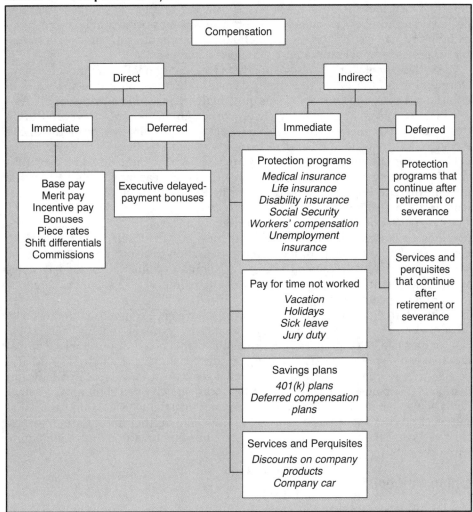

Compensation is also influenced by the cost of living in different regions. For instance, a $25,000 salary in Muskogee, Oklahoma, would command much more *real income* (or purchasing power) than the same salary in Minneapolis, Minnesota. By the same token, a job that paid $30,000 in New Bern, North Carolina, would provide much more real income than a job paying the same amount in New York City. Job location can greatly influence the rate of compensation.[2]

Labor Market Influences

The number of workers available in the labor market varies on both national and local or regional scales. For instance, when the unemployment rate is high on a national level, the number of workers available and willing to work is greater. Conversely, when the unemployment rate is low, the number of available workers declines. The number of available workers also varies by occupation. The hospitality industry may face a shortage of potential workers at the same time other industries experience an overabundance of potential employees.

Availability of workers also depends on local or regional economic conditions. During much of the 1980s, the unemployment rate in the oil-producing states of Louisiana, Texas, and Oklahoma was quite high because of low prices for oil. As a result, there was an abundant supply of workers in this region. However, during this same period, unemployment in New England was quite low, primarily due to the region's increasing number of technology-related jobs. Because of the increases in high-tech employment, hospitality companies in New England had a very difficult time finding interested workers. In fact, Four Seasons Hotels had such a difficult time finding room attendants for its Boston location that they imported workers from Texas and converted hotel rooms into employee dormitories.

Compensation rates must vary according to the availability of workers. In the previous 1980s scenario, hospitality companies in New England were forced to increase both immediate and deferred compensation to attract employees. At the same time, high unemployment rates in Oklahoma and other oil-producing states allowed hospitality managers in these states to maintain or, in some cases, reduce former rates of compensation.

The internal conditions of a company also influence compensation rates. The most obvious example is company profitability. A company making high profits can compensate its employees better than one that is not very profitable. Companies that can respond quickly to changes in the consumer price index should also be able to react rapidly to labor market changes. For instance, research indicates that hotel companies can react to inflation more quickly than companies in other fields because of their ability to raise room rates on a daily basis.[3] Companies that can react quickly should also be able to raise compensation rates for employees. Doing so keeps the company in a competitive position for attracting and retaining employees.

Union Influences

Unions influence compensation rates through their emphasis on seniority. While non-union companies typically reward individual employees for their performance, skills, knowledge, or abilities, union contracts generally call for the same pay for all employees who perform the same job. For instance, a room attendant in a hotel in New York City (where most hotels are unionized) is compensated on the basis of his or her rank, not on his or her contribution to the organization. In contrast, a room attendant in a non-union hotel would likely be rewarded based on his or her contribution.

In the short run, unions typically raise overall compensation rates. However, it is unclear whether compensation rates are always higher in union hotels over the long run. Compensation in union properties depends as much on the skills of the union negotiation team as it does the performance of the employees themselves. A strong negotiation team can provide its union members with compensation rates that exceed their actual worth in the marketplace. In contrast, a weak team can bring about just the opposite.

One aspect of union contracts that typically results in higher compensation rates over the long term is the cost-of-living adjustment clause. This adjustment became standard in most union properties during the 1970s and 1980s. Under this provision, employees receive increases in their compensation rates according to increases in the consumer price index. In other words, increases in the consumer price index produce consistent increases of union wages, which enable employees to maintain their living standards despite increases in inflation.

Government Influences

Since the early 1930s, the U.S. government has played a big role in how private enterprise compensates its employees. Laws that mandate minimum wage, wage rates, overtime pay, child-labor restrictions, retirement benefits, equal employment opportunity, comparable worth, and other issues all greatly affect the rate at which companies compensate their employees. Exhibit 2 highlights the major federal laws that affect how private businesses compensate their employees.

Not all employees in an organization are protected by the laws outlined in this exhibit. For instance, employees who work for companies that are not involved in interstate commerce, who are engaged in seasonal industries (20 consecutive weeks or less), or who are classified as executives, administrators, professionals, or outside sales people are exempt from minimum wage and overtime provisions. This group of employees is known as **exempt employees**. **Non-exempt employees** are protected by minimum wage and overtime laws.

Motivating Employees

Motivating is stimulating employees to work as the company desires. Compensation programs must motivate individual employees to work. Unfortunately, not all employees have the same wants and needs. As a result, not all compensation programs work for all employees. While it is easy to assume that money is the principal motivator for employees, this is rarely the case. Only some employees are motivated by money; others are motivated by other needs. As a result, compensation programs rarely succeed when they base motivation solely on monetary rewards.

Motivation theories fall into two principal types: content theories and process theories. Content theories propose that all people are motivated by certain common needs. The various content theories identify and categorize these needs in different ways. In contrast, process theories identify the factors in any given situation that determine whether an individual will become motivated or not.

Content Theories

The best-known content theories are Maslow's Hierarchy of Needs Theory, Alderfer's ERG Theory, Herzberg's Two-Factor Theory, and McClelland's N-Achievement Theory.

Exhibit 2   Federal Laws Affecting Compensation

Law	Major Provisions
Davis-Bacon Act (1931)	Requires that workers be paid the prevailing wage for the local area.
Walsh-Healy Act (1936)	Requires overtime pay (time and one-half) for work beyond 8 hours per day and 40 hours per week. Applies only to government contractors.
Fair Labor Standards Act (1938)	Establishes minimum wage rates; establishes overtime pay for all work over 40 hours per week; establishes child labor standards (for people under 16).
Social Security Acts	(1935) Retirement program (1939) Income to family of deceased worker (1956) Disability program (1965) Medicare
Equal Pay Act (1963)	Prohibits discrimination on basis of gender.
Consumer Credit Protection Act (1968)	Provides guidelines for wage garnishments and makes it illegal for employer to terminate employee over a single debt.
Employee Retirement Income Security Act (ERISA) (1974)	Establishes standards of funding, responsibilities, vesting, and eligibility for retirement programs. Protects employee retirement programs.
Federal/State Child Support Enforcement Program (1975)	Allows automatic mandatory wage withholding for child support payments.
Child Support Program Enforcement Amendment (1984)	Employers cannot discipline, discharge, or refuse to hire employees over child support issues.
Consolidated Omnibus Budget Reconciliation Act (COBRA) (1985)	Provides employees and families option of purchasing health insurance after death, disability, or voluntary or involuntary termination (except for gross misconduct).
Tax Reform Act (1986)	Regulates taxation of employee benefits.

Other federal and state laws affect how companies compensate their employees. For instance, workers' compensation and unemployment insurance both have a significant impact on compensation policies. In addition, several civil rights acts influence compensation practices.

A fifth theory, Economic Man Theory, emphasizes money as the reason people work for paychecks.

Economic Man Theory. The idea that money is the only important goal that people work for is embedded in Economic Man Theory. This theory simply states that people work for paychecks to buy food and clothing, the basic necessities of

Exhibit 3 Maslow's Hierarchy of Needs

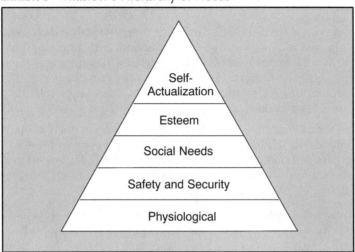

life, that there are employees whose primary motivator for the job is the money it pays. This theory corresponds to the first stage of Maslow's Hierarchy of Needs Theory, which is discussed next. Critics of this theory say that money as the motivator would not affect the productivity of the employee performing the job in the long run.

Maslow's Hierarchy of Needs Theory. Maslow's Hierarchy of Needs Theory contends that individuals have five basic needs (see Exhibit 3). This theory states that all people experience these five needs at different times, depending on individual priorities. Maslow's theory assigns an order of priority—or *hierarchy*—to these five needs. The theory further states that an individual will be motivated to fulfill a higher-level need only when a lower-level need is satisfied or nearly satisfied. According to this theory, if a manager can identify the stage an employee is at, the manager can effectively motivate the employee. Maslow's theory identifies the following five categories of needs:

1. *Physiological needs*—This group includes basic and essential needs, sometimes called biological needs. Examples of these needs include heat, light, food, and comfort.

2. *Safety and security needs*—Once the physiological needs are met, Maslow contends, individuals are most influenced by safety and security needs, such as the need to protect oneself from danger, harm, threat, injury, loss, or deprivation. In organizations, this level of need might include an employee's need for job security, seniority, safe working conditions, benefits, insurance and retirement plans, and severance pay.

3. *Social needs*—After satisfying physiological and safety and security needs, individuals seek to fulfill their social needs. These include the need for companionship, love, and belonging. In organizations, such needs may be met

through formal and informal work groups, teams, and company-sponsored activities.

4. *Esteem needs*—After fulfilling the lower needs, individuals turn to their personal ego needs. Self-esteem—or satisfaction with oneself—involves one's sense of worth, accomplishment, achievement, competence, maturity, independence, and self-respect. In organizations, esteem needs might involve personal reputation, recognition, titles, praise, status symbols, responsibility, promotions, and appreciation.

5. *Self-actualization needs*—After the other four levels of need are satisfied, Maslow contends, individuals have a need to focus on self-fulfillment. Seeking to realize one's full potential, increase knowledge or skills, be creative, or simply "be the best I can" are manifestations of this need in both personal and professional life.

According to Maslow, an individual at the safety and security level might be motivated the most by pay. But once that person meets his or her safety and security needs, the amount of pay becomes less important than opportunities for self-esteem or self-achievement. Maslow's theory is supported by numerous studies that show that employees and managers want incentives other than pay.[4] The theory does have application problems, however. Managers may have a difficult time assessing where employees are in terms of needs, then anticipating changes in their needs. Another problem is that not all employees feel the same needs at the same times. Managers make a grave mistake when they assume that all employees in a restaurant, for instance, are at the safety and security level. Some may be at this level while others may be at much higher levels. While Maslow's theory does not provide a solution for creating compensation plans, it does provide some insight into employee motivation.[5]

Alderfer's ERG Theory. Alderfer agrees with Maslow that individuals have basic needs that could be arranged in order of priority, that there are basic distinctions among those needs, and thus those needs need to be classified. However, whereas Maslow's theory divides the needs into five categories, Alderfer's theory divides them into only three:

1. Existence—These needs are satisfied by such factors as food, air, water, pay, and working conditions. These needs are similar to Maslow's physiological and safety needs.

2. Relatedness—Relatedness needs are satisfied by meaningful social and interpersonal relationships. These needs are similar to Maslow's social needs.

3. Growth—These needs are satisfied when an individual makes creative or productive contributions. Growth needs are similar to Maslow's esteem and self-actualization needs.

The biggest difference between Maslow's theory and Alderfer's theory is that the ERG theory adds a frustration-regression model. That is, like Maslow's theory, the ERG theory states that an individual will be motivated to fulfill a higher-level need when a lower-level need is satisfied. However, unlike Maslow's theory, the

ERG theory also states that an individual will be motivated to fulfill a lower-level need when he or she has continuously failed to satisfy a higher need.[6]

Herzberg's Two-Factor Theory. According to Herzberg, employees have two distinct types of needs: **hygiene factors** and **motivators**. This first set of needs has also been called *maintenance factors* or *dissatisfiers*, while the second set has been called *satisfiers*.

Herzberg's theory contends that hygiene factors alone cannot lead employees to feel satisfied with the work environment; employees expect such factors to be present. On the other hand, if hygiene factors are lacking, employees may feel dissatisfied. Hygiene factors include company policies on pay, relationships with peers and other employees, personal life, status, and security.

In contrast, motivators can make employees feel satisfied and motivated to work. Examples are achievement, recognition, responsibility, and the opportunity to advance. Herzberg's theory states that the presence of motivators can lead to employee satisfaction, while their absence leads to either dissatisfaction or to no satisfaction at all. Some authors call motivators that lead to satisfaction **intrinsic rewards**. Hygiene factors can also be called **extrinsic rewards**.[7]

According to the Herzberg theory, money is not a motivator. Instead, employees expect pay for the work they do. While some research has failed to prove the Herzberg theory, many companies have successfully applied it through job enrichment programs. Because they are basically motivators or satisfiers that help employees feel satisfied and motivated to work, job enrichment programs should be considered part of the compensation package.

McClelland's N-Achievement Theory. McClelland's N-Achievement Theory contends that people have three needs: achievement, power, and affiliation. According to this theory, all employees have some combination of these three needs. The theory also contends that companies can predict employee performance by identifying each employee's needs. In addition, the McClelland theory contends that people with a high **need for achievement** make good managers. These individuals tend to exhibit moderate levels of risk-taking, a desire for concrete performance feedback, problem-solving responsibility, and a tendency to set moderate goals. They may also possess strong organizational and planning skills. To motivate these employees, companies must create opportunities for them to initiate, conduct, and complete jobs.

The McClelland theory portrays the **need for power** as a desire to assume leadership. For many companies, such a need is perceived as a positive attribute. The **need for affiliation** reflects a desire for close, cooperative, and friendly relations with others. According to the theory, people with a high need for affiliation tend to succeed in jobs that require strong social interaction skills, or in which interpersonal skills are highly valued.

McClelland identifies three types of managers: institutional managers, personal-power managers, and affiliation managers. Institutional managers have greater needs for power than for affiliation and tend to exhibit high levels of self-control. Personal-power managers have a greater need for power than for affiliation, but are open to social interaction. Affiliation managers tend to have a greater need for affiliation than for power and are open to social interaction. Research by McClelland and others has shown that personal-power managers and institutional managers typically are more productive because of their greater need for power.[8]

Process Theories

Process theories of motivation are used to explain how employees can be motivated to work. In a sense, these theories help teach managers how to manage motivation. These process motivation theories are widely acknowledged: **expectancy theory** (Victor Vroom), **equity theory** (J. Stacey Adams), **goal setting theory** (Edwin A. Locke), and **reinforcement theory** (B. F. Skinner).

Expectancy Theory. According to expectancy theory, motivation is related to an individual's perception of three factors:[9]

- Expectancy—The probability that effort will lead to performance.

- Instrumentality—The probability that performance will lead to certain outcomes (positive and negative). A single "performance" can lead to several outcomes.

- Valence—The value attached to each outcome.

From an employee's perspective, this can be restated as three questions: "If I try to perform a certain task or at a specified level, am I likely to succeed? If I succeed, what are the likely results? Do I like or dislike those results?" If an employee believes that working harder will lead to higher performance, the expectancy is strong. If an employee sees no connection between effort and performance, the expectancy is weak. For example, if an employee lacks the knowledge, training, or equipment needed to perform a task, simply working harder is not likely to lead to the desired performance, and therefore the motivation to work harder will be low.

The next element is the individual's perception of whether performance will lead to certain outcomes. An employee might believe that performing at a specified level will lead to praise, higher pay, promotions, and/or job security. On the other hand, this performance level may also cause resentment among co-workers who see the employee as a rate buster. If an employee believes that a given outcome or result is likely, the instrumentality is strong. For example, if an employee works in an organization that clearly ties pay to performance, the employee will perceive that higher performance is likely to lead to higher pay. If there is no clear relationship between performance and certain outcomes, the low instrumentality will weaken motivation.

The third element necessary for motivation is **valence**, which is the individual's opinion of or desire for the likely outcomes. A desired outcome has motivational force, while an undesired outcome weakens or destroys motivation.

The strongest motivation occurs when an employee believes that he or she can perform at a specified level, that doing so will clearly lead to specific outcomes (or rewards), and that those likely outcomes (rewards) are desirable. Motivation will be low if an employee sees no relationship between effort and performance, or

Exhibit 4   Equity Theory

$\dfrac{\text{Personal Outcomes (pay, benefits, job satisfaction)}}{\text{Personal Inputs (education, knowledge, experience, effort)}}$ $=$	$\dfrac{\text{Other's Outcomes}}{\text{Other's Inputs}}$	EQUITY
$\dfrac{\text{Personal Outcomes}}{\text{Personal Inputs}}$ $<$	$\dfrac{\text{Other's Outcomes}}{\text{Other's Inputs}}$	INEQUITY (UNDER-REWARDED)
$\dfrac{\text{Personal Outcomes}}{\text{Personal Inputs}}$ $>$	$\dfrac{\text{Other's Outcomes}}{\text{Other's Inputs}}$	INEQUITY (OVER-REWARDED)

between performance and rewards, or if the reward is not considered valuable or desirable.

Managers and organizations can address motivation problems at each of these three stages. For employees to be motivated to perform at a given level, they must believe that they can in fact perform at that level if they try. Organizations that select and train employees effectively and give employees the tools and equipment needed to perform their jobs strengthen their employees' belief that effort will lead to performance. To further strengthen motivation, organizations should clearly tie their reward systems to desired performance. Finally, organizations should ensure that the rewards they offer are in fact valued by employees. Many organizations simply assume that the rewards they offer are valued. When they are wrong, the effect on motivation is unfortunate.

Equity Theory. The equity theory relates to whether an employee believes he or she is being fairly treated in comparison to another person perceived as being in a similar position. This theory is based on the assumption that all employees ask two questions about their work:

- "What do I receive in return for what I give?"

- "What do others receive in return for what they give?"

The equity theory contends that employees create mental ratios about their work situations in order to answer these two questions. Exhibit 4 depicts these ratios. Note that it is the employee's *perception* of whether equity exists that affects motivation.

As the exhibit shows, equity occurs only when employees believe that the ratio of their outcomes received (pay, benefits, job satisfaction) to their input given (education, knowledge, experience, effort) is equal to the same ratio of a "comparison other" (who may in reality be like or unlike the employee). On the other hand, inequity occurs either when employees believe they are receiving less (under-reward) or more (over-reward) for their efforts than the comparison other. According to this theory, balance is important to people; most workers are uncomfortable with either of these two imbalances.

When imbalance is perceived, employees might:

Exhibit 5   Skinner's Reinforcement Theory

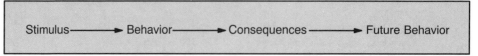

Stimulus ———► Behavior ———► Consequences ———► Future Behavior

- Work less hard because they believe others are overcompensated
- Work harder because they believe they are overcompensated in relation to others
- Convince others to work less hard in order to restore equity
- Convince others to work harder to restore equity
- Reassess their perception of equity
- Change their comparison other

This sense of equity relates to fellow employees in the company (**internal equity**) and to workers in similar positions in other companies (**external equity**). For instance, an employee will feel a sense of imbalance if he or she believes that employees in other hotel companies are rewarded more for similar work. As a result, that employee may ask for more money or may go to work for another hotel company.[10]

Goal Setting Theory. Goal Setting Theory, proposed by E.A. Locke, states that setting specific goals motivates better performance. It explains that ambiguous goals like "do our best" cannot motivate individuals to produce more output. Specific and challenging goals will result in higher levels of performance if individual employees accept the goals.[11]

According to the theory, the following factors are needed to bring higher levels of performance from specific and challenging goals:

- Ability—Although a difficult goal could result in better performance, a manager should consider the ability of the individual employee who will aim for the goal before setting the goal. If a manager sets a difficult goal and an employee lacks the ability to achieve it, there will be no goal achievement.

- Goal Commitment—Employees commit to a goal when they accept it. That is, the more accurately a person understands a goal, the easier it is to achieve it.

- Feedback—To promote performance, managers should provide feedback, which will help employees to understand whether they can achieve the goal.

After goals are achieved and employee performance is evaluated, outcomes (rewards) are allocated. In the same manner as in the expectancy theory, employee motivation will be high if rewards are valuable or desirable.[12]

Reinforcement Theory. B.F. Skinner's reinforcement theory is based upon the assumption that people are *conditioned* to respond to stimuli. In the work world, reinforcement theory suggests that an employee's behavior can be shaped by past experience. The simple four-step model in Exhibit 5 illustrates the theory.

Skinner's reinforcement theory suggests that, if a manager wants to elicit a desired behavior or response from an employee, the manager must reinforce that behavior. The type of reinforcement used can elicit different responses. This theory leads to four possible managerial actions in response to employee behavior:

- *Positive reinforcement*—A manager can encourage desired behavior by rewarding that behavior.

- *Negative reinforcement* (also called *avoidance*)—A manager can encourage desired behavior by removing a punishment or unpleasant stimulus (such as criticism of an employee's performance) when the desired behavior finally occurs.

- *Extinction*—A manager can ignore a behavior to discourage it.

- *Punishment*—A manager can punish an employee's undesired behavior to discourage the employee from performing that way again.

Managers who want to apply Skinner's theory should consider the following:

- Be certain that *only* the desired behavior is reinforced (reward for performance). A company will get the behaviors it rewards. If a poorly designed compensation or reward system does not in fact reward the behaviors a company wants, the reward system will undermine rather than support company goals.

- Extinction, which does not necessarily indicate what a desired response *should* be, can affect both desired and undesired behaviors. If a manager fails to reinforce a desired behavior, an employee may not exhibit that behavior again because it was not reinforced.[13]

The reinforcement theory has been successfully adapted by other behavioral scientists and consultants to comply more fully with workplace needs. For instance, Ken Blanchard espouses most of this theory in his best-seller, *The One-Minute Manager*. In these books, Blanchard emphasizes positive rewards as the best method of eliciting desired performance in employees. Managers who want to try this method should make it a practice to "catch someone doing something 'good'" and then praise that employee. Blanchard encourages public praise to make employees feel good about their behavior and to set examples for others.[14]

Determining Job Worth

Every organization must develop some method of determining job worth. Some companies rely on comparisons with other organizations in the same marketplace, while others use internally focused methods. This section presents the various methods of evaluating job worth as well as the advantages and disadvantages of each method.

External and Internal Equity

Managers can apply the concepts of external and internal equity when evaluating and determining job worth. External equity relates to pay variations among similar properties in a particular market, while internal equity relates to pay variations within a particular company.

To determine appropriate pay levels, some organizations conduct formal or informal surveys of their competitors. Organizations that do not have personnel with the expertise to conduct or analyze such surveys often hire college professors or consultants who specialize in these areas.

Conducting pay surveys is complex. A thorough analysis of external equity conditions must consider many factors, including overall compensation levels in other organizations, union influences, demographic information on the workers employed, labor market and economic conditions, and financial conditions of the external organizations surveyed and the company conducting the analysis.

It is also important to examine the manner in which jobs are designed in surveyed organizations. In most cases, compensation and salary consultants compare what are known as **compensable factors**, or the common elements of jobs. Doing so eliminates any bias when comparing—across companies—jobs that have dissimilar or unusual tasks and behaviors. Compensable factors that are acceptable to an organization's management and employees raise satisfaction levels. In addition, wage and salary surveys must be carefully constructed and pretested to establish their accuracy as predictors.

Government agencies can provide some useful information for establishing external equity. For instance, the Bureau of Labor Statistics of the U.S. Department of Labor provides statistics on employment fields and occupations that can be helpful to an external equity analysis. Private organizations such as the Society for Human Resource Management can also provide useful information. However, in many cases, this information is either too generic or not industry-specific enough to base an entire compensation program on its merits.

A thorough external equity analysis depends on direct collection of information from competing organizations in the market. Meaningful results are also dependent on a skilled analysis of the collected data. For instance, most survey results include mean salaries and wages, median salaries and wages, modal (most common) salaries and wages, pay percentiles and pay distributions, or the **pay range** for various jobs. After a properly conducted survey, the information is compared with compensable factors to determine a true picture of the external equity of job pay.

As pointed out earlier, internal equity relates to pay variations within a single organization. Job survey results on external equity typically include an analysis of pay ranges within job descriptions. The same is true for internal analyses. In addition, an internal analysis answers the question of how much variation should exist between the pay for one job and that of another.

In the hotel industry, internal equity is considered when determining pay differences between room attendants and bell captains, daytime room attendants and night-shift room attendants, or lunch cooks and dinner cooks. Careful analysis of different positions enables employees to realize a sense of equity when comparing the work they do with the work of others.

Internal equity analysis depends on establishing meaningful compensable factors and developing and implementing a thorough **job evaluation** system. The next section discusses different approaches to the development and implementation of job evaluations.

Job Evaluation Methods

The four most widely employed methods of conducting job evaluations are the:

- Ranking method
- Classification method
- Point method
- Factor comparison method

However, other methods are also useful in designing pay scales. A fifth method, **skill-based pay**, is becoming popular in many industries and may be ideally suited for some hospitality companies. Skill-based pay will be discussed later in this chapter.

The Ranking Method. The **ranking method** usually uses a team of managers—or an evaluation committee that may include employees—to rank jobs. This team or committee typically collects examples of all job descriptions used in the organization and ranks these descriptions on a continuum. The scale ranges from hardest to easiest, from most skilled to least skilled, or from most important to least important to the organization.

On the surface, this method seems to provide a simple, fast, and inexpensive means for determining which jobs should be paid the most. However, this approach is much like comparing apples to oranges. Generally, few jobs have similar compensable factors, so comparisons can be inaccurate. In addition, it is not possible to establish the distances between jobs on the continuum. For instance, while this method might determine that a cook's job is more important and more difficult than a dishwasher's job, it still does not reveal how much more important or difficult one job is than the other. Finally, in all but the smallest organizations, it is difficult to assemble a team of managers with the expertise to evaluate *every* job in the company.

The ranking method can be improved by using the **paired comparison method**. When this approach is used, each job is compared by job criteria on a one-to-one basis with every other job and then ranked. A comparison of each job with all other jobs provides a more complete picture of job worth than does a simple ranking. However, the distance on the continuum between jobs and the subjectivity of each comparison is still a problem.

The Classification Method. Sometimes called job grading, **the classification method** compares each job to a predetermined grade or class. The U.S. government and many state governments use this approach to job evaluation. For instance, the GS (General Scale) ratings of federal government jobs relate to the comparison of each job within a predetermined class or grade. The federal government uses 18 grades (although the top three pertain only to senior-level executives). In this system, grades 1 through 15 pertain to:

- Clerical and non-supervisory personnel (GS 1 to GS 4)

- Management trainees (GS 5 to GS 10)

- General management and highly specialized jobs (GS 11 to GS 15)

This system also identifies the length of service within each grade. For instance, a GS 7-4 would have more time in rank than a GS 7-1. These additional classifications refer primarily to salary and promotion.

While this approach seems to solve the problem of how to evaluate each position, it has some drawbacks. Creating an effective scale can be both costly and time-consuming. In addition, each advance in technology that changes a job's importance can render the scale obsolete. The diversity of tasks required by each job can also make classification extremely difficult. Perhaps the greatest disadvantage of the classification method is its emphasis on written job descriptions. Because classification depends on job descriptions, managers, supervisors, and employees may believe that wages can be increased simply by rewriting job descriptions. One distinct advantage of this approach, however, is that new jobs can easily fit into the classification scheme as they are developed.

The Point Method. The **point method** is probably the most widely used method of job evaluation. A point system assigns a point total to each job on the basis of several clearly defined criteria. Jobs are then placed in job grades according to their point totals. Creating a point system is a fairly complex task that often calls for help from outside consultants. Few companies have the expertise to design a point system in-house. Once designed, however, a point system is easy to understand and use.

The point method involves three basic elements: determining compensable factors, weighting the relative importance of each compensable factor, and creating degrees within each compensable factor.

The first step, determining compensable factors, begins with job analysis of all (or at least representative) jobs in the company. The goal of this analysis is to group similar types of jobs into "families" that will each constitute or fall into a separate job structure. For example, some companies put all administrative employees in one job structure, all clerical employees in another, all service employees in yet another, and so on. To avoid unnecessarily complex compensation structures, however, most companies place all jobs into as few job structures as they sensibly can. Once these job families have been selected, the compensable factors for each family are identified. Compensable factors are those factors that a company values and chooses to pay for. They must be demonstrably related to the actual work performed to be credible and acceptable to the people affected by the system. They also need to support the company's culture and values. Compensable factors might include such elements as education, experience, skills, effort, analysis and problem solving, autonomy, responsibility, interactions with others, working conditions, and any number of other possibilities. Overlapping factors should be avoided because they disproportionately reward or penalize certain job elements.

Compensable factors are all valuable to a company, but they are not necessarily *equally* valuable. Once the compensable factors are identified, they must be

Exhibit 6   Compensable Factor: Use of Equipment

Definition: This factor addresses the types of tools and machines used by employees to perform the essential duties of this position.

Explanation: Responsibilities involving equipment use range from working simple machines to managing highly technical computer equipment. The ability to operate particular equipment coincides with assessing a skill level.

Degree	Job Requirements
1	Work requires no previous knowledge or training on specialized equipment. Skills can be acquired through on-the-job training.
2	Work requires use of advanced office equipment, such as a personal computer, but duties are limited to generating documents and files through standardized techniques, such as typing letters or entering data.
3	Work requires use of advanced office equipment to interpret and prepare documents, mainly through word processing capabilities. Training on PC is required.
4	Work requires significant use of advanced office equipment. Knowledge of additional PC capabilities, such as spreadsheets, software, and statistical manipulation, is necessary to perform job duties and generate information to be used by others.
5	Work requires a regular use of advanced office equipment. In addition, knowledge of software and spreadsheets is critical for analyzing, inputting, and revising data. Also interprets data generated from other sources.
6	Work requires operation of equipment for which extensive training, certification, and licensing are required and that affects the safety of the job holder and others.

weighted to reflect their relative importance. For example, the most important may be weighted at 25 percent.

While the compensable factors explain the components of work being considered when evaluating a job family, degrees within these factors are needed to provide a mechanism for differentiating between jobs. Compensable factors must be divided into degrees that represent the spectrum of jobs. Each degree should be described in narrative form. Exhibit 6 presents an example dealing with equipment use in an administrative/clerical job.

The next step involves simple calculation to determine the number of points assigned to each degree. To do this, an arbitrary point total for each job structure must be selected. The number of points selected is often between 600 and 1200. Once a total is chosen, it is multiplied by each factor weight to determine the maximum points available for each factor. For example, if a 1000-point plan is chosen and one factor is weighted at 25 percent, that factor qualifies for up to 250 points. This total is divided by the number of degrees to determine the point totals for those degrees. If this factor has five degrees, each degree is generally worth 50

Exhibit 7   Example of Determining Pay Rates

Benchmark Jobs	Physical Factor	Skill	Responsibility	Working Conditions	Interpersonal Skills		Prevailing Wage for Benchmark Job
Cook	2.75	2.75	2.75	2.25	1.00	=	11.50
Server	1.75	1.00	1.50	.75	2.50	=	7.50
Greeter	.50	1.50	1.50	1.00	2.50	=	7.00

Non-Benchmark Jobs	Physical Factor	Skill	Responsibility	Working Conditions	Interpersonal Skills		Prevailing Wage for Non-Benchmark Job
Dishwasher	2.25	1.00	.75	2.00	.25	=	6.25
Prep Cook	1.75	1.75	1.25	1.75	.25	=	6.75
Busperson	2.25	1.00	.75	1.25	1.00	=	6.25

points. After the points are allotted to each factor degree, it is a simple process to apply and total the points for each job. The jobs are then grouped into grades or levels based on their point totals.

The Factor Comparison Method. The **factor comparison method** entails identifying **key jobs**. Generally, the key jobs are those that the evaluation committee considers extremely important to the success of the organization. For instance, cook, greeter, and server might be considered key—or benchmark—jobs in a restaurant. When using the factor comparison system, the prevailing hourly wages for key jobs are used as a benchmark for comparing all other jobs. In this case, we will assume that the prevailing hourly wage for cooks, greeters, and servers in the market is $11.50, $7.00, and $7.50, respectively. Committee members then *work backward* from these totals to assign rates to each of the compensable factors identified as pertinent to the company. An example of this method is shown in Exhibit 7. The compensable factors used in the example are physical demand, skill, responsibility, working conditions, and interpersonal skills.

After pay rates for each of the compensable factors are assigned to key jobs, pay rates for non-benchmark jobs can be established on a factor-by-factor basis. The bottom half of Exhibit 7 shows an example of extending the wages of benchmark jobs to non-benchmark jobs.

Among its advantages, the factor comparison method provides a scale that is custom-made for the organization. This scale is also easy to apply. However, the method is ponderous, especially for developing pay rates for supervisory and management-level jobs. The method is also difficult to explain to employees because of its complexity. The example in Exhibit 7 considers only five compensable factors. In most situations, the number of compensable factors would be higher. As a result, it is difficult to distribute the total wage for each key job into compensable factors. In addition, choosing key jobs, determining prevailing rates for these jobs, and assigning rates to the compensable factors for non-benchmark jobs are all subjective decisions that can lead to employee dissension.

Establishing Pay Structures

Determining how to identify the value of different jobs is only part of the pay structure puzzle. Organizations must also determine the number of **pay grades** offered, how company pay will compare to that of competition in the market, and how compensation is determined within specific pay grades. The following section summarizes pay structure options.

Competitive Pay Policies

Each hospitality organization must decide how to position its pay policies in comparison to other companies in the market. Collecting information on pay and benefit packages offered by competitors and others in the hotel, restaurant, and tourism industries is critical to successful recruitment and retention. This becomes particularly significant when companies merge. When two companies merge, they likely are merging not only assets but compensation philosophies as well. One company may use one philosophy of paying its employees while the other uses another. This clash of cultures makes it mandatory for managers to collect competitive data on salaries and wages. If they do not, the company will likely run the risk of losing many valuable employees.[15] Generally speaking, a company can position itself in one of three ways:

- *Pay leaders*—pay more than the market average on the theory that better pay will attract better employees.

- *Pay followers*—pay below market average on the theory that less pay will equal greater profits.

- *Meet the competitors*—pay the prevailing wage in the market.

A survey of 341 of the Fortune 1000 companies found that 75 percent used hiring bonuses and an additional six percent were in the process of implementing such programs. Additionally, 45 percent of these companies used retention bonuses as a way to keep talented employees, while another 15 percent were considering this approach.[16]

Pay Grades

Each hospitality company must also determine the number of pay grades it will use. Typically, a company finds that whatever job evaluation method it uses will create information that can be easily converted to a chart. For instance, assume that a company uses the point method to evaluate pay for each job. This evaluation results in assigning a point value to each job on the basis of compensable factors. A completed chart might look like that depicted in Exhibit 8.

Assume that each dot in Exhibit 8 represents a job. This exhibit clearly shows where each job falls on the wage continuum. For instance, the job immediately above 110 points on the graph should command less pay than the one above 250 on the graph. However, the question is: How much less? By answering this question, a company can ascertain its appropriate number of pay grades and establish the range between each grade.

Exhibit 8 Determining How Jobs Fall into Pay Grades

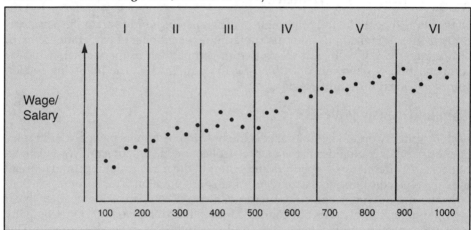

In Exhibit 8, the vertical lines depict pay grades. In this case, the sample company has six pay grades. If we assume that the lowest pay grade begins at minimum wage, what will be the highest pay for this grade? For instance, given a minimum wage of $5.15 per hour, does the pay for this grade range from $5.15 per hour to $5.65, or from $5.15 to $5.40, and so on? Normally, jobs on the lower end of the pay scale have narrower pay ranges than those at the top of the scale.

It is important to establish ranges of pay within each grade. This allows employees to receive raises without changing pay grades. For example, a range of pay for dishwashers allows a more experienced or senior employee in this category to make more money than a less experienced or junior employee.

The conventional wisdom is that performance pay must be high enough to effectively reward performance and that there must be observed differences in pay between people who make higher and lower contributions to the organization. However, a study by Bloom suggests that pay structures where there is a large differential can actually lead to lower organizational performance, especially in companies where teamwork and collaborative efforts are required.[17] In some cases, the ratio of pay differences from highest to lowest paid employees has reached as much as 200:1.[18] According to Bloom, large pay differentials can create feelings of injustice, and this can reduce cooperation, quality, and commitment to long-term success.

Determining Pay Within Grades

In the previous example of two dishwashers, one had more experience and seniority than the other. Seniority provides a good reason for establishing a range of pay within job grades or classifications, particularly in union environments. Most union contracts establish seniority as an important factor in determining employee pay. **Seniority-based pay** is also useful in non-union working environments, especially for employees at the low end of the pay scale.

Merit is typically the second determinant of pay within grades. Unions generally support increases in base pay over **merit pay,** a policy that has been longstanding. Many hospitality organizations link pay to performance. Merit pay policies are intended to create effective reward systems that motivate employees to try their best at all times. Some experts note that pay-for-performance systems are particularly effective in environments in which a high level of trust exists between management and employees, and in which management establishes a fair and ongoing evaluation of performance (such as regular performance appraisals).[19]

Two methods of determining pay scales are "broadbanding" and "careerbanding." Broadbanding is the elimination of all but a few, say three to ten, comprehensive salary and job classifications. The bands usually have minimum and maximum dollar amounts of pay that overlap and average no more than 130 percent from top to bottom. In broadbanding, for example, all managers might be grouped into one band, all clerical employees into another band, and all part-time employees into still another band. Broadbanding emphasizes titles, grades, and job descriptions. Careerbanding is similar to broadbanding, but it is more closely tied to career development. Instead of using minimums and maximums to establish pay scales, as in broadbanding, scales are determined by market surveys. For instance, a company might take a market survey to determine how competitors pay, and establish its rates based on what it learns.[20]

Two-Tier Wage System

Two-tier wage systems establish two distinct pay structures for employees. Two-tier systems are most common in union environments in which a union grants pay concessions to management in the form of future pay. These systems provide a higher pay structure for existing employees while a lower one is created for employees hired beyond a specific date. For instance, a union might agree to wage cutbacks that create a base minimum rate of $7.00 per hour for existing room attendants while the minimum rate paid to new hires might be $6.65. This policy must be explained to applicants during the selection process.

A two-tier wage system offers advantages to both current employees and management. The advantage for current employees is that they will be on the higher scale for as long as they work for the company. Management has the advantage of being able to cut back on wage expenses by paying new employees less. Eventually, employees on the old system will retire and the company will be left with only lower-wage employees.

Theoretically, this system offers an effective way for management to reduce labor costs. However, the two-tier system also creates equity problems among employees. As we discussed earlier in this chapter, when one employee perceives that he or she is working as hard as another employee but is receiving lower pay, a sense of inequity is likely to develop. As a result, productivity among those earning the lower rate is likely to decline. Evidence indicates that two-tier wage systems are on the decline.[21]

Skill-Based Pay

Another method of determining employee pay is to institute a skill-based pay system. Skill-based pay systems assume that a company can afford to pay more to people who do more. Determining pay by the number of skills an employee has is one way to do this. Seniority does not play a role.[22] According to this method, companies base pay on the knowledge or skills each employee acquires rather than the job to which the employee is assigned. Hypothetically, all employees start at the same level of pay. As an employee adds skills or knowledge, the company increases his or her rate of pay. The result is a compensation plan that is related directly to the number of different jobs an employee can perform.

Knowledge-based pay is a variation of a skill-based pay system in which pay is tied to knowledge rather than to skills. In such systems, employees can increase their pay by becoming experts at their current jobs.

One of the major attributes of a skill-based pay program is that employees often believe it is fairer than other systems. In a study of 600 organizations, researchers found that employees strongly agreed that skill-based pay programs take much of the subjectivity out of pay evaluations, and they perceive these systems to have more justice.[23] Another advantage of a skill-based pay program is that employees typically learn skills that are transferable to other jobs within the company. As a result, these employees can fill in when temporary labor shortages develop in different areas. In addition, skill-based pay provides an extra motivation for employees to learn. Such pay systems can be particularly useful when technological advancements create the need for new skills or knowledge. Skill- or knowledge-based pay systems also support the use of career ladders for certain jobs. Skill-based pay plans have the advantage of improving staff performance, reducing unwanted turnover, and improving a company's recruitment of new employees.[24] In effect, such systems create additional rungs on the career ladder for employees to climb.

Skill- and knowledge-based pay programs have been effectively employed in several service industries for employees with "short" career ladders. For instance, in the late 1980s, such pay programs were introduced to nurses in hospitals. Nurses had only two options before the introduction of such programs: move into management (and out of the hands-on, service-oriented or "caring" end of the profession), or remain in a nursing position. Skill- and knowledge-based pay programs provide a third option for nurses, enabling them to seek title changes or pay raises within the customer service end of their profession.

Some hospitality companies have had similar success with skill- or knowledge-based pay programs. For instance, TGI Friday's developed both skill- and knowledge-based programs during the late 1970s. According to TGI Friday's plan, employees who learned additional skills received both symbolic acknowledgments of their progress (uniform pins that denote expertise in certain skills much like merit badges do for Boy Scouts) and pay increases. In addition, employees who acquired additional skills under this system moved closer to being promoted to management if that was their goal.[25]

Like most other systems, skill- and knowledge-based programs have some disadvantages. One problem with skill-based pay systems is that they take some time to establish. If, for instance, a company decided to implement a skill-based pay system one year, evaluations related to pay probably could not be used until the following year, after employees have had an opportunity to develop or refine the skills included in the compensation program.[26] Another disadvantage is the increase in labor costs as employees learn additional skills. Another is that some employees learn all the skills assigned to their jobs, then "top out" with no place else to go within the organization. Also, such programs can create false expectations for employees who hope to use their new skills in permanent new jobs within the company only to be disappointed with temporary assignments. Companies that use such programs also face the problem of how to categorize and/or utilize skills that become outdated by technological or organizational change. Even considering these drawbacks, the advantages of such programs can far outweigh the disadvantages.[27]

On-Call Pay

A study of the use of "on-call pay," sometimes called "sleeper pay," showed that approximately 65 percent of the responding companies provide pay premiums to their on-call employees. These premiums usually amount to extra hourly pay if an employee is called in to work.[28]

Team-Based Pay

Organizations are increasingly depending on teams for their producing activities and processes that improve organizational performance. A team is made up of a small number of people with complementary skills who are committed to a common purpose, a set of performance goals, and an approach for which they hold themselves mutually accountable. Team members can interact with and be interdependent with each other. Teams are different from groups because group members are more likely to be working toward individual performance goals, whereas team members work toward a common goal. Also, groups have less autonomy and are more closely supervised than teams. Thus, pay systems that pay individuals may not properly fit organizations designed around teams.

Team-based pay rewards employees according to the outcome produced by the team. It has a greater emphasis on goal accomplishment of teams. An example of team-based pay is a commission shared among several members of a sales force that worked together to sell a real estate property.

Current Issues in Compensation Administration ────────

Compensation administration is a changing field. Only a few years ago, issues such as comparable worth and wage compression were not of major concern to hospitality managers. However, that situation has changed. Hospitality managers today must know about each issue that affects their compensation programs. This section highlights current issues in compensation administration: pay secrecy, wage compression and expansion, and comparable worth.

Pay Secrecy

One of the most basic problems a hospitality manager must contend with regarding his or her compensation program is whether or not to keep pay rates secret. This decision involves at least two issues. First, does the company make its pay grades and the pay ranges of those grades known to employees (or, in even greater openness, does it reveal the actual pay of individual employees)? Second, if the company prefers pay secrecy, does it attempt to prevent or forbid employees from discussing their pay with other employees?

Many people assume that full disclosure of salaries and wages creates employee dissatisfaction because they believe employees may see some situations as unfair. However, this may not be true. Full pay disclosure is the norm in most government systems at both federal and state levels. Most state universities readily disclose the salaries of professors and staff members.

Research indicates that when pay is kept secret, employees generally guess the pay of peers and managers incorrectly. Interestingly enough, employees generally guess low on the pay of managers rather than high. Most private enterprises still maintain policies of pay secrecy. In fact, according to the Bureau of National Affairs, only about 18 percent of companies in the United States maintain open pay information systems.[29] A 2001 survey of human resources directors yielded similar results, showing that only 13 percent worked in companies that allowed pay discussions.[30] However, this may change in the future. One survey indicated that 80 percent of the human resources directors in companies polled believed it might be a good idea to be more open about pay. This assumption was based on the belief that it would be better for employees to know the facts than to speculate about rumors.[31] Some managers see open pay policies as a way to promote employee morale, in that pay discussions offer a tangible demonstration of the ways in which performance is defined, measured, and rewarded.[32]

Given that most private U.S. enterprises still embrace policies that forbid or discourage employees from discussing their pay, it is particularly interesting to note that such polices are generally illegal in the United States. The National Labor Relations Board has repeatedly found such policies to be unfair labor practices in violation of employees' rights under the National Labor Relations Act to discuss the terms and conditions of employment in concert with other employees. The NLRB has repeatedly held that employees fired for discussing salary information with other employees must be reinstated. Many employers *wrongly* believe that NLRA rights and protections do not apply to non-union employees. It appears that enforced pay secrecy policies continue in the United States at least in part because employees are not aware of (or are reluctant to test) their rights under the NLRA.[33]

Wage Compression and Expansion

Wage compression results primarily from competition with other companies for new hires. Faced with a shortage of qualified applicants, many companies may increase the starting wages of new employees in order to compete. However, since competition for current employees is not as great as it is for new hires, current employees may not receive the same salary increases. Employers have several reasons for not increasing the wages of current employees at the same rates as for new hires. Generally, employers reason that current employees are less likely to leave a company once they begin gaining seniority and once their benefit packages start to accumulate.

As a result of wage compression, a company may find that employees with less seniority (sometimes even new employees) often earn as much as those who have been on staff for a significant period of time. The salaries of university professors provide a good example: starting salaries of university professors today are often much higher than were the starting salaries of current faculty members. This is due primarily to competition among universities for a smaller pool of qualified personnel. Even though current faculty members receive merit and cost-of-living pay increases, their salaries typically do not equal those of new hires. In effect, university faculty can command higher salaries by changing employers than by remaining in long-term positions.

In the long run, wage compression could lead to dissatisfaction among senior employees who see a shrinking gap between their salaries and those of new hires. Some would argue that current employees are worth more to a company because of their experience and expertise. However, competition for the limited number of new hires drives salaries and wages up faster than merit pay and cost-of-living increases do for current employees. Companies are caught in a trap of potentially losing senior employees because of the inequity these employees feel when comparing their salaries with those of new hires. While many employees cannot leave because they are tied to a benefit system, their productivity may decline as a result of wage compression.

Wage expansion occurs when companies raise the wages of current employees to keep their salaries in line with the higher wages of new hires. Theoretically, such programs can result in substantial increases in the overall wages of all employees, a result that many hospitality companies cannot afford. For instance, a hospitality company may have to increase the pay offered to new room attendants in order to attract new hires. But if the company increases the wages of *all* room attendants to maintain equity, the next higher group of employees will also want pay increases to maintain what they feel is the appropriate range between salaries. As a result, employers can be forced to successively increase the wages of *all* employees.

The best way to approach the problems created by wage compression and expansion is to analyze the total cost of each employee. It is interesting to note that employees with longer tenure typically cost more in benefits than do new employees. While replacing current employees with new hires at higher wages may appear to increase the overall compensation program, in reality it may not, primarily because the company pays less in *overall* compensation to new hires. Some companies may justify wage compression by a complete analysis of all compensation programs.

Comparable Worth

Many people confuse **comparable worth** with equal pay issues. These people typically cite the Equal Pay Act of 1963 as evidence that the U.S. government mandated the abolition of unequal pay on the basis of sex or race. However, comparable worth and equal pay are substantially different issues. The Equal Pay Act prohibits pay discrimination in the *same* job. Comparable worth deals with the issue of pay in *similar* jobs.

In the United States, men and women tend to work in different jobs. While this is changing, some jobs are considered predominantly female jobs and others are considered predominantly male. For instance, most secretaries are female, and most construction workers are male. Similar types of sex segregation of jobs exists in the hospitality industry. Most room attendants, for instance, are female, while most cooks are male. While exceptions certainly exist, many jobs are still predominantly single-sex jobs.

Comparable worth advocates cite the fact that pay is based on job classification rather than on the work that goes into a job. They might note that, while the work performed in a predominantly female occupation is as difficult and important as that performed in a predominantly male occupation, traditional "female professions" are paid only about two-thirds as much as traditional "male professions."

Numerous arguments have been made to explain salary differences for comparable jobs. For example, some suggest that the difference between wages for males and females is the result of seniority, not discrimination. According to this view, men typically have been on the job longer and, as a result, earn more. Others might say that differences occur because men and women tend to choose different jobs that command different salaries. Labor leaders and feminists generally counter these arguments with examples of how women or minorities are paid less even though the compensable factors in jobs may be equal.

Many labor experts believe that the issue of comparable worth is the most important labor problem businesses face. These experts typically cite examples such as the increasing number of women in the work force, the gradual dissolution of boundaries between male and female jobs, and court cases that uphold settlements for discrimination on the basis of comparable worth. Yet not everyone agrees. One thing is certain about this issue: if the courts find that businesses are discriminating on the basis of different pay for comparable jobs, the decision will greatly affect the manner in which hospitality companies pay their employees. In fact, since approximately 70 percent of the employees in the hospitality industry are women, such a decision could cause hospitality companies to alter their compensation programs completely.

Wage and Hour Audits

All pay policies and procedures must comply with the provisions of the Fair Labor Standards Act. Policies and procedures that are inconsistent with the act can result in fines for a company and back pay for employees.

As some managers know, the U.S. Department of Labor conducts wage and hour audits to determine whether companies are following the provisions of the Fair Labor Standards Act. Managers can prepare for such audits by learning and reviewing the issues that such investigations are likely to cover. Exhibit 9 presents a 17-point outline that managers can use as a guide. By conducting a self-audit,

Exhibit 9   Points Focused on by Wage and Hour Investigators

Managers may find it helpful to review the following 17 points in anticipation of any formal review by wage and hour investigators from the U.S. Department of Labor.

1. **Exempt vs. non-exempt employees**
   To meet exempt qualifications, employees must generally be either executive, administrative, or professional employees. Factors considered during an investigation include job descriptions, wage rates, methods of payment, and the functions employees actually perform.

2. **Time period covered**
   Non-exempt employees are entitled to overtime pay. In general, the Fair Labor Standards Act requires that employees be paid overtime for all work over 40 hours per week. A workweek is any consecutive seven-day period designated by the employer. Investigators check this and the "multiplication factor" used to calculate overtime.

3. **Hours worked**
   Investigators check how employees are informed about "signing in" and "signing out" procedures, and whether preliminary work activities such as cleaning up, prep work, and so on are included in work reported. Time sheets or cards are reviewed carefully for accuracy.

4. **Compensable time**
   During an investigation, the investigator will want to examine the hours during which employees are at work, but for which they are not compensated (such as breaks or lunch).

5. **Calculation of overtime rate**
   For some employees, the regular rate of pay and the hourly rate of pay differ. For instance, a bellperson may be paid $7 per hour, but receive an additional $1 per bag delivered. In this case, the regular rate of pay is $7 plus $1 for each bag. Overtime is calculated on the regular rate of pay, not on the hourly rate.

6. **Exemptions from the regular rate**
   Investigators check to see how employees earning commissions or service charges are paid, how such amounts are tracked, and how such compensation for these employees is identified (i.e., flat rate or hourly rate).

7. **Employees working more than one job**
   Employees working two jobs often receive two rates of pay. Overtime for these employees should be a weighted average of the two rates, not based upon the rate paid while incurring the actual overtime hours.

8. **Gratuity vs. service charge**
   Hospitality companies must keep accurate records of monies paid in service charges to employees for such items as banquet service or room service.

9. **Tip credit**
   Employers should create and maintain a list of employees who qualify for tip credit. This list should be periodically reviewed to determine whether the tip credit is actually being recovered by the employee.

10. **Tip pooling**
    Employers should document and maintain a list of employees included in any tip pooling, the percentages for tip pooling distribution, the employer's method for tracking tip pooling procedures, and management participation in the process.

11. **Discrimination**
    Hospitality managers must be careful not to discriminate with regard to pay. Pay between men and women in similar jobs has been a consistent problem and is a focus of many investigators. Managers should check to ensure either that pay is equal or that there are logical reasons for discrepancies, such as seniority or merit.

(continued)

Exhibit 9 *(continued)*

---

12. Policies and handbooks
Many courts hold that handbooks and policy manuals represent implied contracts between employers and employees. Investigators often examine these documents to determine if promises are made to employees that are not kept.

13. Recordkeeping
Hospitality companies must keep employee records for a specified period of time. Managers should review such records and ensure they are kept for appropriate periods.

14. Independent contractor
Some managers attempt to avoid recordkeeping and pay requirements by maintaining that some employees are independent contractors. Investigators examine records for written agreements between employees and employers that substantiate this. They also may investigate the nature of such contractual relationships.

15. Training time
Investigators check to ensure that trainees receive the proper rates of pay while training. Such pay rates vary, of course, depending on the job.

16. Payment procedures upon termination
Terminated employees generally must be paid at the time of termination. Investigators check to see if this pay is accurate and includes time for vacations and other accrued benefits.

17. I-9 documentation
Employers must maintain timely and accurate files on each employee, including completed and accurate I-9 forms when necessary. Employers should check that all forms are completed properly. One potential problem for employers is the type of documentation accepted on the I-9 form as proof of eligibility for work. Employers should read the instructions on the form carefully to make sure they comply with this important documentation.

Source: Adapted from Jay Krupin, "Wage and Hour Policies and Procedures Training Manual for Compliance with U.S. Department of Labor Regulations Affecting Hotels," presented at the Human Resources Executive Forum, Indian Wells, California, 5 February 1992.

managers can correct errors in policy or procedure before a visit from wage and hour investigators.

Endnotes

1. Valerie L. Williams and Stephen E. Grimaldi, "A Quick Breakdown of Strategic Pay," *Workforce* 78, no. 12 (1999): 72–76.

2. The cost of living indices for different cities and regions are reported annually and quarterly in several government documents. Private industry publications also report increases and decreases in this index and compare the costs of living in different regions to national norms. One publication that reports this information annually and rates the cost of living in hundreds of American cities is the *Places Rated Almanac: Your Guide to Finding the Best Places to Live in America,* by Richard Boyer and David Savageau (New York: Prentice-Hall Travel).

3. Avner Arbel and Robert H. Woods, "Debt Hitch-Hikers: The Paradox of Zero Cost of Capital in the Hotel Industry," *Cornell Hotel & Restaurant Administration Quarterly* 31 (November 1990): 103–109.

4. Robert W. Eder and N. Roth Tucker, "Sensitizing Management Students to Their Misperceptions of Five Worker Job Attribute Preferences," *The Organizational Teaching Review* 12 (1987–88): 93.

5. For a fuller description of Maslow's theory, see Abraham H. Maslow, *Motivation and Personality* (New York: Harper and Row, 1954). This topic is also discussed at length in Maslow's article, "A Theory of Human Needs," *Psychological Review* (1943): 370–396.

6. Clayton P. Alderfer, *Existence, Relatedness, and Growth: Human Needs in Organizational Settings* (New York: Free Press, 1972); and John M. Ivancevich and Michael T. Matteson, *Organizational Behavior and Management*, 6th ed. (Boston: McGraw-Hill, 2002).

7. For a complete description of Herzberg's theory, see Frederick Herzberg, "One More Time: How Do You Motivate Employees," *Harvard Business Review* (January-February 1968).

8. David McClelland and D. Burnham, "Power Is the Great Motivator," *Harvard Business Review* (March 1976): 100–110.

9. For a full discussion of expectancy theory, see Victor Vroom, *Work and Motivation* (New York: Wiley, 1964).

10. For further information on equity theory, see J. Stacey Adams, ed., "Inequity in Social Exchange," *Advances in Experimental Social Psychology*, vol. 2 (New York: Wiley 1977), 93–112.

11. E. A. Locke and G. P. Latham, *A Theory of Goal Setting and Task Performance* (Englewood Cliffs, N.J.: Prentice Hall, 1990).

12. Ivancevich and Matteson.

13. Adapted from W. C. Hamner, "Reinforcement Theory and Contingency Theory Management in Organizational Settings," in H. L. Tosi and W. C. Hamner, eds., *Organizational Behavior and Management: A Contingency Approach* (New York: Wiley, 1977), 93–112.

14. For a full description of how to use Blanchard's model, see Kenneth Blanchard and Stephen Johnson, *The One-Minute Manager* (New York: Morrow, 1982).

15. Mike Malley, "Surveying the Surveys," *Hotel and Motel Management* 213, no. 5 (1998): 24–26.

16. "Pay Raises to Remain Stable in 2000," *HR Focus* 77, no. 1 (2000): 16.

17. Matt Bloom, "The Performance Effects of Pay Dispersion on Individuals and Organizations," *Academy of Management Journal* 3 (1999): 25–50.

18. Tim Gardner, "When Pay for Performance Works Too Well: The Negative Impact of Pay Dispersion," *Academy of Management Executive* 13, no. 4 (1999): 101–104.

19. Nathan Winstanley, "Are Merit Increases Really Effective?" *Personnel Administrator* 4 (1982): 23–31.

20. Kathryn Tyler, "Compensation Strategies Can Foster Lateral Moves and Growing in Place," *HR Magazine* 43, no. 5 (1998): 64–71.

21. "Labor Letter," *The Wall Street Journal*, 16 June 1987, p. 1.

22. John L. Morris, "Lessons Learned in Skill-Based Pay," *HR Magazine* 41, no. 6 (1996): 136–141.

23. Cynthia Lee, Kenneth Law, and Philip Bobko, "The Importance of Justice Perceptions of Pay Effectiveness: A Two Year Study of a Skill-Based Pay Plan," *Journal of Management* 25, no. 6 (1999): 851–874.

24. Bobette M. Gustafson, "Skill-Based Pay Improves PFS Staff Recruitment, Retention and Performance," *Health Financial Management* 54, no. 1 (2000): 62–64.

25. For a thorough description of how some restaurant companies use this type of skill- and knowledge-based pay, see Robert H. Woods, "More Alike than Different: The Culture of the Restaurant Industry," *Cornell Hotel and Restaurant Administration Quarterly* 30 (August 1989): 82–98.

26. John L. Morris, "Lessons Learned in Skill-Based Pay," *HR Magazine* 41, no. 6 (1996): 136–141.

27. For a fuller description of the advantages and disadvantages of skill- and knowledge-based pay programs, see Fred Luthans and Marilyn Fox, "Update on Skill-Based Pay," *Personnel* (March 1989): 26–31.

28. Robert W. Thompson, "Executive Briefing: Strategic Intelligence," *HR Magazine* 45, no. 2 (2000): 12–13.

29. Bureau of National Affairs, *Wage Administration*, 21.

30. Kemba J. Dunham, "Employers Ease Bans on Workers Asking, 'What Do They Pay You?'" *Wall Street Journal*, 1 May 2001, p. B10.

31. "Employers Are Willing to Talk Pay More Often," *HR Focus* 71 (August 1994): 14.

32. "Tossing the Coin: Pay Secrecy." 2000. Online. Internet. 11 August 2001. Available http://www.themanagementor.com/EnlightenmentAreas/HR/HRcontent_tossingthe coin.ASP.

33. National Labor Relations Act, Section 7; *Service Merchandise, Inc.* (1990) 299 NLRB No. 160, 1989-90 CCH NLRB 16,274; *NLRB v. Brookshire Grocery Co. dba Super One Foods, #601* (5thCir 1990) 117 LC 10,466. See also http://www.workforce.com/archive/article/000/13/16.xcl, "Silencing Salary Talk Can Lead to Trouble."

Key Terms

Alderfer's ERG Theory—A theory that divides the individual's basic needs into three categories: existence, relatedness, and growth needs.

classification method—Job evaluation method based on grading jobs. Also known as job grading.

comparable worth—Issue of equal pay for men and women performing jobs that require essentially the same skills.

compensable factors—Elements common to each job on which compensation is based.

consumer price index—Measurement of changes in the retail prices of goods and services.

cost of living—Term used to refer to the real dollar value of a worker's purchasing power.

direct compensation—An employer's payment of money to an employee—either in the present or at some future date—in exchange for that employee's productive work; includes wages, salary, bonuses, piece rates, and so forth.

Economic Man Theory—A theory that states that money is the main reason employees perform an assigned job.

equity theory—A theory that relates to whether employees feel like they are being treated fairly or unfairly compared to others.

exempt employees—Executives, administrators, professionals, and outside salespeople who are exempt from overtime pay.

expectancy theory—A motivation theory that explains motivation as a process involving an individual's perception of three variables (expectancy, instrumentality, and valence).

external equity—Equity that exists with employees outside an organization.

extrinsic rewards—In Herzberg's Two-Factor theory, those factors that are expected by employees, and do not lead to satisfaction.

factor comparison method—Job evaluation method based on identifying key jobs as anchors and comparing others with those anchors.

Goal Setting Theory—A theory that contends that specific and challenging goals will result in higher levels of performance if the employee accepts the goals.

Herzberg's Two-Factor Theory—A theory that contends that some work factors influence satisfaction while others are expected by employees.

hygiene factors—In Herzberg's Two-Factor theory, those factors that are expected by employees, and therefore cannot lead to satisfaction. Also known as extrinsic rewards.

indirect compensation—Compensation not directly related to an employee's productive work, includes various insurance protection programs, pay for time not worked, savings plans, and perquisites.

internal equity—Equity that exists with other employees within an organization.

intriansic rewards—In Herzberg's theory, those factors that can lead to satisfaction.

job evaluation—Method of determining what jobs are worth.

key jobs—Jobs used in factor comparison method to anchor the scale of what each job is worth.

knowledge-based pay—Pay system based on the amount of knowledge each employee has.

Maslow's Hierarchy of Needs Theory—Motivation theory contending that individuals have five basic needs: physiological, safety and security, social, esteem, and self-actualization.

McClelland's N-Achievement Theory—Motivation theory contending that people have three needs: power, affiliation, and achievement. This theory also contends that companies can predict employee performance by determining the concentration of each need in individual employees. *See also* Need for Achievement, Need for Affiliation, and Need for Power.

merit pay—Pay based on an employee's performance over a predetermined period of time.

motivators—In Herzberg's theory, those factors that can lead to satisfaction. Also known as intrinsic rewards.

need for achievement—According to McClelland's N-Achievement theory, people with a high need for achievement are usually good managers.

need for affiliation—According to McClelland's N-Achievement theory, people with a high need for affiliation generally tend to do well in jobs that require high levels of social interaction or where interpersonal skills are highly valued.

need for power—According to McClelland's N-Achievement theory, people with a high need for power are usually seen as good leaders.

non-exempt employees—All employees who are due overtime pay when they work more than 40 hours in a week.

paired comparison—Method of job evaluation in which each job is compared on a one-to-one basis with other jobs to determine an overall ranking; also method of comparing performance, behaviors, skills, or knowledge of each employee to each other employee.

pay grades—Rates of pay for particular jobs in an organization.

pay range—Range between the highest and lowest pay for each job in an organization.

point method—Most widely used job evaluation method; calls for assigning points to each job based on specific tasks performed.

ranking method—Job evaluation method that involves ranking all jobs in a company by a group of experts, usually managers.

reinforcement theory—A theory proposed by B.F. Skinner that people are conditioned to respond to stimuli and that behavior can be guided through the use of various types of reinforcement.

seniority-based pay—Pay system based on employees' experience and seniority.

skill-based pay—Pay system based on the number of skills employees can perform.

team-based pay—A pay system based on the outcome produced by a team.

total reward program—All the methods including cash, equity, and benefits employers use to pay for the work of employees.

two-tier wage system—Pay system that establishes two distinct pay structures for employees. Most common in union environments. These systems typically establish one system for employees with seniority and another for new employees.

valence—In expectancy theory, the strength of an individual's preference for a particular outcome.

wage compression—Pay inequities based on levels of demand that result in higher pay for new employees than for current employees.

wage expansion—A condition that occurs when employers try to raise pay rates of current employees to keep salaries in line with higher wages of new hires caused by wage compression.

 **Review Questions**

1. Analyze the external and internal factors that may influence compensation programs in your market. What recommendation would you make to a manager intending to start a new hospitality company in the market?

2. How does motivation relate to compensation?

3. What is a total reward program?

4. What are the major content theories of motivation?

5. How does the equity theory relate to compensation in the hospitality industry? What about the expectancy theory?

6. Some experts criticize Skinner's Reinforcement Theory on the basis of its simplicity. Do you believe this theory has applicable value for hospitality managers? Why?

7. What are the four methods managers can use to evaluate the worth of jobs?

8. What limitations does the ranking method have?

9. What factors or policies should a company consider when establishing pay structures?

10. What are the principal differences between pay-for-performance and seniority-based pay systems?

11. Why is comparable pay such a hot issue for the hospitality industry? If the courts decide that jobs of similar value and skills *must* be paid equally, what effect do you believe it will have on the hospitality industry?

12. One of the issues discussed in this chapter was wage compression. How would you address this problem as a manager in the hospitality industry?

Internet Sites

For more information, visit the following Internet sites. Remember that Internet addresses can change without notice. If the site is no longer there, you can use a search engine to look for additional sites.

Consumer Information Center
www.pueblo.gsa.gov

Federal Wage and Labor Law Institute
www.fwlli.com

Hay Group
www.haygroup.com

STAT-USA
www.stat-usa.gov/

U.S. Bureau of Labor Statistics
stats.bls.gov

U.S. Census Bureau
www.census.gov

U.S. Government Employment Standards Administration (ESA)
www.dol.gov/esa/whd/

U.S. Government Printing Office
www.access.gpo.gov

U.S. Wage and Hour Division
www.dol.gov/esa/whd

Mini Case Study

Your employees have been incurring a lot of overtime lately for staffing special events. You cannot afford to pay time-and-a-half for overtime so you make a deal with your employees: if they work 50 hours this week, you will let them work 30 hours the next week and take a long weekend. They are happy and you are happy. Is this acceptable? What can happen if you get "caught" doing this?

Chapter 9 Outline

Competencies

9

Incentive and Benefits Administration

This chapter was co-authored by Erin Chou, M.S. candidate, University of Nevada, Las Vegas (UNLV), and David Tolman, M.S. candidate, UNLV.

Employers frequently combine incentives or benefits with wages or salaries to form a total compensation package for employees. Most employers recognize the direct link between performance and incentives. Pay and performance have been linked together by researchers since the early 1990s.[1] Researchers who study and write about organizational behavior theory agree with this approach. For instance, both equity theory and expectancy theory suggest that properly managed pay-for-performance systems encourage motivation and productivity. Other researchers note that both individual and group performance are higher when pay is linked to performance. The question most hospitality managers should ask is not whether to offer incentives: all companies should have them. The one to ask is how to structure such programs. This chapter discusses how managers can structure both incentive and benefit programs to encourage greater productivity and performance.

Effective Incentive Programs

Some hospitality managers who try incentive programs have little faith in their ability to improve performance. The likely reason for this lack of confidence is not the programs themselves, but in how the programs are administered. Nothing is more important for a manager to learn than how to effectively motivate employees to do better work.

Much research has been conducted on how managers can effectively develop and institute their own programs.[2] One way that managers can better relate to this important task is to consider the role of a coach (or manager) on a sports team and ask themselves whether that person's role is important to team and individual success. In most cases, managers will agree that there is a link between a coach's goal-setting and motivation and the team's performance. Research has confirmed this to be the case.[3] Like that favorite coach who seems to get the most out of players, managers must excel in the role of coach/motivator.

To be effective, incentive programs should have these critical characteristics:

- The programs must be directed toward attaining clear, specific goals that employees can understand.[4]

- Goals must be fair and easy to measure. All too often, managers establish incentives based on subjective measures. By so doing, managers create doubt in the minds of employees about how fairly a program is administered. Employees prefer incentives based on objective measures that both managers and employees can understand easily.

- There must be room for improvement in productivity or performance. Insisting that an employee improve, when he or she is already performing at a very high level, is de-motivating.

- Goals must be attainable. Employees must have some expectations of success or they will not attempt to achieve the goals.[5]

- Rewards must be substantial enough to encourage effort. Whether money or merchandise, the rewards must be desirable. Too often, managers set rewards that employees perceive as not worth their effort.[6]

- Increases in productivity and performance should be tied to other rewards such as advancement. Goals perceived to be linked to both long-term advancement and short-term rewards are more effective than goals linked only to short-term rewards.[7]

- Rewards must be linked to output, not to time invested. The basic principle of any incentive plan is that employees will produce more if the reward is linked to productivity.[8]

- Rewards should be administered quickly to reinforce the reason for the reward. For instance, incentive pay sometimes lags considerably behind regular wages. If incentive rewards lag too far behind, employees begin to feel that they are either being taken advantage of, or that the company is more interested in increased productivity than in achievements.[9] To understand this, simply put yourself in the employees' shoes, and ask whether you would want a reward to be given to you immediately or on a timely basis, or sometime later.

Advantages of Incentive Programs

Linking pay to performance can help hospitality managers accomplish four very important goals of their own:

- Retain quality employees.

- Increase productivity.

- Reduce labor costs.

- Increase employee focus on organizational objectives.

The first advantage often results from the long-term effect that incentive programs have on personnel. When companies link pay to performance, they often find that the employees who receive the greatest rewards are typically the best performers. These employees also feel the most encouraged to remain with the organization.[10] In contrast, employees who receive the smallest rewards are typically those who produce the least. As a result, low performers are more likely to leave the organization and go elsewhere where pay is not linked with performance. In this way, over time, companies that use incentives-linked pay programs can attain their own goal of having a staff of only high-performing employees.

The second advantage companies gain in linking incentives to performance is improved productivity. When pay is linked to performance, employees have a reason to work harder and to produce either more or better goods and services. Researchers have clearly established this link.[11]

The third advantage is the cost savings that many companies can realize. By linking pay to performance, hospitality managers can negate some of the effects of rising salaries and wages by establishing a relationship between organizational success and pay. Some organizations pay employees more when times are good and pay them less when times are bad. Employees tend to understand this good-times–bad-times relationship. Couching goals in those terms will help employees understand why salaries and wages are tied to performance.

Finally, pay-for-performance systems increase employee focus on organizational objectives. When incentives are properly linked to organizational objectives, all employees work toward common goals. As a result, organizations may be more successful in achieving their defined goals.[12]

While these four advantages would indicate that linking pay to performance is always best, not all companies can successfully carry this out. Managers will encounter several barriers to implementing pay-for-performance systems. For example, consider what might happen when:

- Rewards are set too low to produce an incentive (employee distrust, low performance).

- The link between rewards and performance is not clearly established because the measures for success are not clearly defined or outlined. (This can lead to employee mistrust of the company, failure of the company to achieve organizational goals, and employees perceiving inequity between how much they value their contribution to the company and how much the company values this same contribution.)

- Supervisors either resist performance appraisals or improperly administer such evaluations—resulting in feelings of unfairness among employees.

- The employee union (if the property is unionized) opposes the pay-for-performance system. Unions typically feel such programs undermine seniority and cost-of-living raise programs. (Unions depend on seniority-based systems for their success.)

Finally, the design and administration of pay-for-performance systems require careful attention to detail. Some companies are either unable or unwilling to devote the attention that such programs require. (Employees know when this is the case and have less respect for their managers' abilities. This results in all kinds of problems.)

Individual vs. Group Systems

Both individual and group incentives can play significant roles in improving productivity in hospitality organizations. Many organizations may want both types of incentive programs in place at the same time. Typically, **individual incentive programs** are most useful when the work involved is not too interdependent, or when individual improvement most benefits the organization. **Group incentive programs**, on the other hand, are most useful when cooperation and coordination are the program's goals, or when managers believe that teamwork is an appropriate part of the organizational goal. Group systems have become increasingly popular in recent years as more companies implement teamwork systems.

Individual Incentive Programs

There are six common types of individual incentive programs:

- Piecework incentive programs
- Standard hour programs
- Commission programs
- Bonus plans
- Pay for knowledge (or pay for skills)
- Merit pay[13]

Piecework Incentive Programs

Piecework incentive programs are based on the theory of rewarding employees who exceed established minimums of productivity. They are also based on the premise that if jobs involve simple tasks, the incentive plan would motivate workers to produce maximum results.[14] In such a case, the company's performance would prosper as a result. For instance, in a catering department where pay is based on piecework, employees might be expected to produce 500 plates in a specific period of time. If this were the case, employees should be rewarded if they produce more than 500 plates. Similarly, in manufacturing, employees might be expected to produce 50 widgets and rewarded for their production in excess of 50 widgets.

Piecework is still used widely in hospitality and other service industries. For example, a food service manager might establish a reward system based on the number of sandwiches a prep cook produces. Hotel housekeepers are sometimes paid on a piecework basis, too. For example, they might be paid on how many rooms they clean in a given period of time. Some argue that servers also work under a piecework incentive system: that is, servers receive a standard wage for providing service to their stations, plus a reward in the form of a tip for increasing sales in their stations.

Standard Hour Programs

Standard hour incentive programs are based on the number of units completed per hour (per day would be a *standard day program*). To establish such a program for housekeeping, a manager first determines how many rooms a housekeeper should clean per hour. The manager then divides the hourly wage by the number of rooms per hour to arrive at a benchmark for a standard hour program. For example, a manager might determine that it takes a room attendant an average of 30 minutes to clean one room; therefore, a room attendant should clean two rooms per hour. If the hourly wage for room attendants is $10.00 per hour, the manager might then decide to pay a fixed rate of $5.00 per room cleaned ($10.00 ÷ 2) instead of the hourly wage. Under such a system, room attendants who clean more than two rooms per hour receive more pay, while those who clean fewer make less money.

Before implementing such a standard hour incentive program, a manager should establish specific, objective methods for measuring employee success. In the above example, managers need to determine how to measure whether a room is "clean" or not. Managers also must consider whether employees are earning at least minimum wage, and how their wages compare with competitors in the market.

Commissions

Many hospitality employees who directly interact with guests are compensated under a **commission** arrangement, especially employees in food service operations where tipped employees receive an incentive commission based on sales, service, or both. Hotel sales departments often base their wages on commissions. Timeshare sales personnel work on this system, since their only income comes from commissions.

When setting up a commission program, a property should consider how incentives are structured. Typically, incentives should increase as sales increase. This structure provides a series of rewards for each goal attainment. In the case of hotel sales agents, for example, the higher the sales, the more the rewards. Graduated incentive programs provide sales agents with increased incentives for each level of productivity.

Bonus Plans

Bonus plans are based on a combination of base and incentive pay. Two types of bonus plans are common. In the first, all employees share in the achievement of organizational objectives. For instance, all employees in a hotel might receive bonuses when certain sales or profit goals are reached. Other bonus plans are linked to individual performance. Bonuses are becoming more popular as a result of the growing use of teams in the workplace. A survey found that 35 percent of U.S. employers reward employees with lump sum bonuses instead of raises. The advantage to the company, of course, is that the bonus does not carry over from year to year, while raises do.[15]

Typically, bonuses are rewarded when managers and employees attain predetermined goals. It is important that the goals be measurable and agreed-upon by both employer and employee. For example, a manager might receive a bonus for achieving a specific profit level, and the manager must have agreed to that goal in advance. Such programs are also effective with employees. For instance, room attendants might receive bonuses for achieving specified goals such as cleaning a certain number of rooms or applying a certain standard of quality to their work. Like piecework, standard hour, and commission incentives, bonuses add to organizational labor costs only when rewarded. Bonus plans have an additional advantage: they typically require little documentation and can be tailored to almost any situation.

Pay for Knowledge

Pay for knowledge, a method of determining employee base wages, is also useful in incentive programs. As an incentive, pay for knowledge bases rewards on the goals an employee reaches beyond those that are specifically required by the current job. Some believe that this represents the wave of the future. One researcher predicted that by the year 2015, pay will be 40 percent fixed while 60 percent will depend upon how much value the employee produces for the company.[16]

Merit Pay

Properties that reward through **merit pay** typically experience an increase in base wages at the end of a specific period. When implemented properly, merit pay systems clearly link rewards to performance. In other words, an employee's merit pay is based on his or her performance of predetermined tasks during a quarterly, semi-annual, or annual evaluation period.

The principal disadvantage is an increase in overall wages because rewards increase base pay. Additional challenges for the manager can result when the same employees consistently produce excellent results. For instance, a room attendant may consistently produce excellent results and, thereby, be in line for high levels of merit pay at the end of each evaluation period. Over time, the employee's pay can exceed the range approved for employees in that work category, or even exceed that of employees at higher grades. Managers should remember that each job has a theoretical cap (or maximum amount) on what the job is worth. Under a merit pay system, employees who excel during each rating period can become frustrated when they reach their cap and are not permitted to earn further rewards. At this point, those employees would likely have to be moved to other types of incentive pay programs. Additional problems arise when evaluations involve subjectivity errors such as the halo effect, recency, and leniency.

Disadvantages of Individual Incentive Programs

All incentive programs require administration. Managers will have to consider whether the cost of administration outweighs the value of improvement. Additionally, many incentives require substantial documentation and computation at the end of each reward period, and rewards that lag too far behind can become disincentives to employees, who may start to believe that the organization is taking advantage of their performance. In some cases, employees believe that incentives are not fairly administered or are simply used by management as an excuse to increase expected performance. For instance, employees who work particularly hard over a period of time to achieve specific incentives might feel that their increased performance will be used to measure normal performance in the future.

Group Incentive Programs

Group incentives are a good way to motivate employees to perform cooperatively. From a theoretical perspective, group incentives either increase profits or reduce costs by encouraging employees to work to attain an organization's goals. They also help develop a sense of cooperation and teamwork within a hospitality organization. The most common types of group incentives are generally characterized as **gainsharing programs**, although hospitality managers may never hear of or use this exact term.

Gainsharing programs are typically formula-based incentives that either increase profits, increase productivity, reduce costs, or, in some cases, attain all three objectives. The name "gainsharing" is derived from the practice of sharing a portion of the gains made by the company with employees. Three types of plans are most common:

- Cost-saving plans (Scanlon, Rucker®, Improshare®)
- Profit-sharing plans (Lincoln Electric Company)
- Stock ownership (used in many hospitality companies, including Marriott)

Cost-Saving Plans

Cost-saving plans are also known as cash-reducing plans since they reduce the amount of cash required to operate a business.[17] The most common cost-saving plan is the **Scanlon plan**, named after Joseph Scanlon, a labor union leader in the 1930s. Scanlon's plan was designed originally to promote employment, production, and profits during the Depression.

The Scanlon plan's underlying philosophy is based on assumptions that the organization should function as one integrated unit; that employees will contribute valuable ideas and suggestions if they have the opportunity; and that all employees recognize their vested interest in the organization's success.[18] The Scanlon plan is sometimes referred to as the "best industrial management idea that did not become popular."[19]

The Scanlon plan is based on the ratio of labor costs to the *sales value of production* (SVOP). The SVOP includes both sales revenues and the total value of goods in inventory. The Scanlon plan is particularly useful in "high touch labor" companies—such as hospitality operations where person-to-person contact is most important—because it rewards labor savings. A company needs historical data to implement the Scanlon plan. Usually, a company will track historical SVOP data over a period of five to ten years, then average the costs of production for that period by dividing labor costs by the SVOP. The ratio obtained establishes a benchmark that the company can use to evaluate performance of the entire work force in the future.

Essentially, the resulting ratio is a percentage of the total cost of labor compared to the revenue from goods and services produced by that labor. Assume, for instance, that the ratio is .33. This would mean that 33 percent of revenue historically has been spent on labor. Any period in which labor costs are less than .33 would result in contributions by the company to the Scanlon plan.

Typically, the contributions are distributed on the basis of 75 percent for employees and 25 percent for the company. Most plans are administered monthly, although some are administered quarterly. A key element of the Scanlon plan is the election of committees to oversee collection of data and distribution of the monies. These committees consist of employees from all levels and departments.[20]

Another cost-saving program, the **Rucker plan**, calls for dividing labor costs by the *share of production costs* (SOP). These costs include material, supply, and service expenditures used to produce finished products or services. The result of this division is called the *economic productivity index* (EPI). When the EPI is lower than historical costs, it means that employees carefully watched the costs of materials used in production, and should share in the money saved. In effect, the Rucker plan provides incentives for employees based on the difference between net sales (after cost of goods) and costs. Like the Scanlon plan, the Rucker plan requires good historical data and usually is monitored by employee committees.

A third type of cost-saving plan is called **Improshare**, for "improved productivity through sharing plans." Through an Improshare program, a company computes the standard cost of labor hours per unit of finished goods or services to establish a measure of employee productivity and efficiency. If current costs are below historical costs for the standard, employees get incentive bonuses. This system can work very well in hospitality companies as incentives for employees to reduce high labor costs. The program can run year-round or on a seasonal or quarterly basis to re-invigorate employees to save.

Profit-Sharing Plans

The theory behind profit-sharing plans is that if employees can improve profits by reducing costs or streamlining productivity, they should share in that profit. Technically, profit-sharing plans could include any plan that distributes a percentage of profits to employees based on their contribution to the organization's goals.

Some companies see profit-sharing plans as very useful ways to increase productivity and profits. In other companies, such plans have become just another hygiene factor; employees expect a percentage of profits regardless of their individual contributions.

Depending on the type, use, and design of the profit-sharing plan, no monies are expended unless profits are made or increased; some see this as an advantage. In addition, these plans sometimes make employees more aware of the overall operation costs, competitive market forces, and the fact that management is not always getting rich on the efforts of employees. However, in bad years, all employees go unrewarded regardless of their contributions to the company. Unless employee committees assist in developing and distributing such plans, employees may believe that managers are merely setting profits aside to cover long-term costs in order to avoid paying them their percentage of profits.

There are three common types of profit-sharing plans: cash plans (current distribution plans), deferred plans (deferred distribution plans), and combination plans. Each plan typically establishes an eligibility waiting period.

Cash Plans. Cash plans are also known as current distribution profit-sharing plans because payouts are typically made at or near the time profit is made. Under cash plans, the distribution of cash, stock, or some combination of the two is made based on the company's profitability. Usually, distribution is made on a quarterly basis, although some monthly plans are used.

The Lincoln Electric Company plan is among the most famous cash payout plans. In 1914, James Lincoln's employees promised to help increase profits if they could share in them. Lincoln used this plan until the 1970s; in many cases, employee bonuses exceeded salaries and wages because of the substantial contributions the employees made to profits. A key element of the Lincoln Electric plan is that it guarantees each employee a schedule of 30 hours per week for 49 weeks of work.

Deferred Plans. Deferred plans are also called deferred distribution profit-sharing plans. These plans are similar to cash plans except that a company places the employees' payout in escrow in deferred plans. The payout is then awarded later, generally when an employee's pension or retirement begins. Because employees do not receive distributions at the time of profit, the link between performance and incentive pay is less clearly defined.

Combination Plans. Combination plans blend attributes of both cash and deferred plans. Some funds are paid at the time profits are earned and some are set aside for pensions and retirement.

Employee Stock Ownership Plans

Employee stock ownership plans (ESOPs) establish an account for each employee in a company. Typically, the company distributes either cash or stock into employee accounts based on employee contributions to the company or its profits. Contributions continue until employees either retire or leave the company. Generally, ESOPs are managed by an employee stock ownership trust (ESOT).

Before the Tax Reduction Act of 1975, ESOPs were primarily for managers and executives. Since that time, such plans have been extended to include employees at all ranks. ESOPs increase employee commitment, company loyalty, and motivation. Studies have found that sales in companies with ESOPs grow faster than sales in those that do not have ESOPs.[21] Many hospitality operators with ESOPs also have discovered that such plans retain and motivate employees.[22]

There are two common types of ESOPs:

- *Ordinary ESOPs*—Under these plans, a company makes annual contributions to employee accounts. The contributions are then used to buy company stock that is credited to each employee's account. Employees receive assets of accounts upon retirement or termination.

- *Leveraged ESOPs*—Under a **leveraged ESOP**, the ESOP borrows money from a bank or other lending institution to help the company fund capital use projects. The company repays the ESOP, which repays the bank.

ESOPs have the potential to increase productivity and to reduce turnover, absenteeism, and costs. In addition, ESOPs provide a variety of tax benefits to all parties, and research shows that they lead at least short-term positive stock reactions. Unfortunately, not all such plans work. For example, an ESOP known because of its inadequate planning is the one adopted by United Airlines in 1994. It ended in 2002 when the company declared bankruptcy. According to some experts, United's plan was doomed from the start: It was adopted under duress, rejected by a major part of the work force (the flight attendants), and opposed by new management.[23]

Some experts believe that employees could reap higher returns by investing independently rather than in an ESOP. Owners, lenders, or employees should not let this criticism diminish the attractiveness of ESOPs, however. At the very least, ESOPs provide a way for employees to save money easily and, at their best, ESOPs provide strong incentives for all involved. For instance, the company can write off both the principal and the interest on the ESOP loan (limited to 25 percent of total annual payroll). The lender pays taxes on only half the interest earned on loans made to companies for ESOP purposes. Owners can defer taxes on their gains if the ESOP owns a minimum of 30 percent of the company stock. Finally, employees are not taxed on the company's contributions to their ESOP accounts until they receive cash or stock when they retire or leave the company.[24]

Although many companies enjoy the benefits of an ESOP, there are nevertheless negatives associated with the plans. Many economists point out the following issues, which can cause failure:[25]

- A "free rider" problem: even if employees as a group have an incentive to work harder and smarter, some individuals will slack off and let others do more of the work.

- Employees don't value ownership as much as it costs a company to provide the plan.

- If employee owners are in the majority and actually control the organization, workers will favor higher wages and other short-term benefits at the expense of investment in future growth and profitability.

When used as part of a pension plan, company stock can cause other problems. For instance, when too much company stock is purchased for the pension plan (which many companies tend to do to keep their stock prices up), employees are too heavily tied to the company's performance.[26] This happened in the case of Enron, where thousands of employees lost their entire life savings because they had invested all of their retirement savings in company stock on the advice of company officers. When the company went bankrupt, these employees were left with nothing.

Stock Options. Companies primarily offer stock options to their executives and top-level managers. As long as an individual is employed by the company, stock options give the holder the right to purchase stock at a price pre-set in his or her contract, even when stock prices are higher.

At one time, stock options were a principal method of attracting managers and providing an incentive for them to help generate profits and thereby increase stock prices. Since the Tax Reform Act of 1986, however, stock options have been viewed less favorably. This is because the gains on stock—when cashed—are treated as ordinary income rather than long-term capital gains. As a result, employee profits gained through a stock option may be taxed at higher rates than normal income. Companies still find stock options an attractive way to recruit new managers, however, by offering them as a basic part of the company's salary and benefits package.[27]

Managers must be careful to follow Sarbanes-Oxley Act guidelines for these activities. This act was passed in 2004 and was designed to curb unethical business practices in the United States by enhancing reporting requirements for companies and by requiring the companies and their executives to follow stringent ethical guidelines.

Which Works Best: Money or Merchandise?

Managers often wonder whether incentives should take the form of cash or other rewards such as merchandise or trips. Strong arguments can be made for either approach. Merchandise has a longer-lasting effect than money. Merchandise constantly reminds employees of the incentive for the reward. Each time they see the merchandise, employees are likely to think about how they can work harder to receive other rewards. Merchandise can be a source of pride for an employee, a tangible symbol of success. In addition, prizes can be purchased below retail rates, at a reasonable cost to a company.

Cash, on the other hand, can be spent easily. As a result, employees may be left with no identifiable link between performance and reward. However, cash has an advantage that merchandise does not. As two experts put it, "Nothing else can be used to satisfy as broad a range of needs as money."[28] An employee can use cash gained through an incentive program to purchase whatever goods or services are needed or desired. Cash awards may be particularly attractive to employees who have difficulty making ends meet on a regular basis. A merchandise award (such as a trip to Hawaii) may not be a motivator if an employee cannot use it. For instance, an employee's spouse may not be able to get off work, child care may not be available or affordable, the added costs of the trip may be too high, and so on. Basically, the incentive system a company chooses should reflect the goals of the organization and suit the needs of the employees.

Disadvantages of Group Incentive Plans

Individual incentive programs can backfire from the employee point of view. Sometimes, employees may work hard to achieve an incentive only to find that their employers come to expect that extra hard work as normal performance.

This disadvantage also applies to group incentive plans. Group incentives, especially the profit-sharing type, have additional problems. Even when employee performance exceeds expectations, employees will still suffer when the company has a bad year. Also, unless properly managed, group incentive plans can unfairly reward employees who perform at levels lower than the group as a whole.

Many experts think that individual incentive plans produce better results than do group incentive plans. Those who have studied the two types often say that group incentive plans result in an indistinct connection between pay and the individual efforts of each group member. They also say that group incentives can cause resentment. For instance, some employees always try to get a free ride on the performance of others. Employees who work hard to attain rewards perceive an inequity between their own inputs and outcomes and those of other group members.

Resentment and inequities can be overcome in different ways in different environments. In the classroom, resentment and inequities can be minimized if each group member is given an opportunity to evaluate the contribution of other group members. Peer evaluations also are useful in a work environment because they give group members an opportunity to control the disbursement of rewards. When peer evaluations are used, group members typically decide how much of the reward each group member should receive.

Employee Benefits

Benefits are generally thought to be an effective way to attract and retain personnel, motivate performance, and increase job satisfaction. Offering a great benefit package that involves high cost and obligation is an indication of commitment to the employees.[29] However, since benefits are not tied to performance, their value as a motivator or satisfier is debatable. Because benefits are so common in the U.S. industry, employees perceive many as expected compensation rather than as a motivator. According to the U.S. Department of Labor, employee benefits accounted for 30 percent of the total payroll costs for employers in 2004.[30]

As of March 2005, only 53 percent of employees participated in medical care plans offered by their employers.[31] The percentage of workers without health insurance in the hospitality industry is even higher.

Retirement benefits are very important as well. About 62 percent of the hospitality industry work force does not have retirement benefits. There are exceptions, however. For instance, Starbucks has been recognized by the President of the United States as being a model of ethical standards for business, partially because of its comprehensive benefits packages offered to all employees, even part-timers. Benefits for Starbucks employees include medical insurance, dental and vision care, mental health and chemical dependency coverage, short- and long-term disability, life insurance, sick time, paid vacations, 401(k) retirement savings, stock options (referred to as "Bean Stocks"), and a free pound of coffee each week.[32]

A study of United States restaurants found that most companies have increased their benefits packages to managers, primarily in order to attract and keep better managers. Among the items increased are salaries, bonuses, choice of work locations, days off, retirement plans (often the "golden handcuffs" kind linked to long-term employment), and stock equity purchase options. Exhibit 1 illustrates the cost of compensation packages (including benefits) compared to

Exhibit 1   How Does Compensation Affect Turnover in Restaurant Industry?

Segment	Average turnover	Average turnover costs per GM	Average cash value of compensation
Quick serve	38.3%	$26,944	$ 43,075
Midscale	32.6	24,500	65,100
Upscale casual	25.9	25,923	68,100
Fine dining	18.0	50,000	102,000

Source: Padma Patil and Beth G. Chung, "Changes in Multiunit Restaurant Compensation Packages," *Cornell Hotel and Restaurant Administration Quarterly* 39, no. 3 (1998): 45–53.

turnover rates in four segments of the restaurant industry. The far right column includes both salary and benefits.

Many benefits have become commonplace. For instance, most industries provide health insurance for all employees and most employees in the United States receive two or more weeks of paid vacation per year.

The benefits offered by most companies fall into four general categories:

- Mandatory benefits
- Optional—or voluntary—benefits
- Pension and retirement benefits
- Miscellaneous benefits

Managers should ask themselves several questions when evaluating and establishing benefits programs:

- What benefits am I required to offer?
- What optional benefits can I offer?
- How should I administer the benefits?
- How can I contain the costs of benefits?

The following sections put these questions in context.

Mandatory Benefits

Mandatory benefits are legislated by both federal and state governments. One required benefit is commonly known as Social Security, mandated by the Federal Insurance Contribution Act of 1935 (FICA). This program was established to protect employees and their dependents by providing retirement income, disability income, health care coverage (Medicare), and survivor benefits. Other examples of mandatory benefits include **workers' compensation** and **unemployment compensation insurance.**

Social Security. Social Security is designed to provide a form of financial security to employees and their dependents. It is an expensive program for employers.

Today, both employers and employees contribute 7.65 percent of the employees' paychecks per year (up to a total that changes yearly based on inflation) toward Social Security benefits; employees draw upon these contributions after retirement.

Unlike most insurance programs, Social Security uses current payments to pay benefits to retired employees. For example, employees working today pay for those employees who have retired. Social Security has filled a great need for many years and has provided financial security to many people at a low cost. Many experts agree, however, that a combination of factors is stressing the program. For example, more employees today are working at lower rates of pay; consequently, fewer dollars are put into the system. Second, baby boomers—people born between 1946 and 1964—are aging, which means that during the next 20 years, more employees than ever before will begin retiring. Retiring baby boomers will find themselves depending on the contributions of a smaller demographic group, the baby bust—people born between 1965 and 1980—for Social Security support. Fifty years ago, 16 workers paid into the system to support every beneficiary; today, 3.3 workers are contributing to each Social Security beneficiary.[33]

Current Social Security provisions permit former employees or their spouses to begin receiving income from this fund at age 65 with no penalty. They can opt to begin receiving income from Social Security at age 62, but with some substantial and permanent reductions in the amount they receive. These reductions will deepen in the future. Currently, an individual receives a 20 percent permanent reduction if funds are taken at age 62; by 2022, this reduction will be 30 percent. These changes reflect the government's efforts to try to salvage the Social Security system.

Other changes in the system include continual increases in the "normal" retirement age established by the U.S. Congress. When baby boomers begin reaching retirement age in 2009, the Social Security eligibility age will increase to 66. In 2027, it will increase again to 67. These changes affect anyone born after 1942.

Unemployment Compensation. Another benefit mandated under FICA includes unemployment compensation insurance (UCI). According to current provisions, a former employee who is out of work and actively seeking work can receive up to 80 percent of his or her normal pay—as long as that employee did not lose his or her job for reasons of misconduct. While mandated by federal legislation, state governments manage unemployment compensation insurance; provisions vary from state to state. The net federal unemployment tax is 0.8 percent of the first $7,000 paid to each employee. State contributions are based on the number of claims made against employers and may range from as low as one percent to as high as 10 percent of total salary costs.

Workers' Compensation. Workers' compensation provides compensation for employees who become disabled or who die at work, regardless of who is at fault. For that reason, it is known as a "no-fault" program. The program is usually funded by insurance paid for by employers; the rate of contribution is based on a company's injury history. Organizations with high injury records have higher costs than those with fewer recorded injuries. Benefits vary from state to state. Premiums for workers' compensation rose 50 percent nationwide between 2001 and

2004. The hospitality industry has historically been subject to disproportionate numbers of workers' compensation claims due to the volume of employees, high turnover, and lack of training.[34]

One way in which hospitality companies are trying to reduce their workers' compensation costs is to institute central call-in programs. With call-in programs, unit-level managers immediately report employee injuries to risk managers at toll-free phone stations instead of submitting forms. Companies that use such programs dramatically reduce filing mistakes that increase their costs.[35]

Hospitality companies also can reduce workers' compensation claims by addressing the problems that cause injuries. For example, slip-and-fall accidents account for over 40 percent of the total workers' compensation dollars spent in the U.S. hospitality industry. Each slip-and-fall claim averages approximately $5,400. Case studies have shown that the costs of these claims can be reduced by up to 90 percent if companies teach employees how to pick proper slip-resistant footwear.[36]

In the mid-1980s, Sky Chefs was losing 18,000 workdays annually, mostly due to back-related injuries. By instituting a training program to teach people how to lift properly and by setting up cash reward systems to encourage safe lifting, the company reduced lost workdays to 8,500 in 1994 and 5,000 in 1995. At an average of $25,000 per claim, this saved the company millions of dollars.[37]

Research on employees who claim workers' compensation has produced interesting results. The first is that 85 percent of the claims are filed by 15 percent of the employees. Of the 15 percent, 60 percent suffer from back trouble, often caused or worsened by stress outside work. RTW, a Minneapolis-based company that specializes in workers' compensation, has been able to reduce claims by 50 percent by proactively identifying these employees and by developing plans to put them back to work quickly. Companies like RTW can save employers thousands of dollars in claims annually.[38]

Voluntary Benefits

Organizations offer a wide range of voluntary benefits. However, some of these benefits have become so standard that now employees in most industries expect them. Health and life insurance benefits are among the voluntary benefits that employees often expect. Many hospitality companies excel at providing these benefits and offer innovative insurance programs to attract personnel; others lag far behind and fail to address these important needs.

Group Life Insurance. Group life insurance coverage is usually based on the annual earnings of the employee, although most plans provide employees the opportunity to purchase additional coverage. The typical rule of thumb for calculating life insurance coverage is to multiply the employee's annual earnings by two. Thus, an employee who earns $20,000 per year would be offered $40,000 in life insurance. Long-term disability insurance generally is offered in conjunction with life insurance.

Group Health Insurance. The rapidly rising costs of medical services have rendered group health insurance the most costly benefit offered to employees. A 2001 survey of employers, insurers, and health care providers showed that employers

---

COBRA Cost to Businesses Include:

Proof of COBRA training

Written COBRA procedures (manual with instructions)

Documentation of program design (1986 or 1987) and program updates (to present)

Documentation of program monitoring

Initial notification

Stacked event notification

Disability extension notification

Conversion notification (required if employer's group health plan has a conversion option)

Documentation of events reported to employer/plan administrator for divorce/ dependent events and disabilities

Open enrollment notice

Expiration notice (recommended—not a specific requirement)

Insignificant premium underpayment procedure (possible notice)

Premium billing procedures (optional—not a requirement)

Complete and accurate disclosure to health care providers

Cancellation procedures (voluntary and involuntary)

Verification of correct election

---

have been meeting rising costs with strategies such as raising premiums and increasing employee co-payments.[39]

Another substantial reason for the rapid increase in health care costs in recent decades was the passage of **COBRA (Consolidated Omnibus Budget Reconciliation Act of 1985)**. Under this act, following certain "qualifying events" such as termination, death, or divorce, employers must allow terminating employees and/or employees' dependents the opportunity to continue purchasing group health insurance under the company plan for up to 18 months (for employees) or 36 months (for employees' dependents). The ex-employee or the dependent must pay the employer the cost of the premiums for the coverage, and the employer is allowed by law to charge the ex-employee or dependent a two percent surcharge.

The surcharge does not begin to cover all the employer's costs, however. The costliness of COBRA is more than just taking care of those people "on COBRA"; it is a total process of notifying, tracking, and documenting all facets of compliance with this highly complex law. If sued or audited by regulators, an employer must be able to prove that it has properly complied with COBRA's rules. Beyond these administrative costs (which include postage, salaries, general overhead, and so forth), employers incur even greater costs both because of improperly continued health care coverage and because the health care claims of COBRA continues typically average 1.6 times those of active employees. The average cost to an employer of a person on COBRA is $7,021.[40]

Exhibit 2   Are You Getting the Discount?

Here's how a managed care plan might over- charge for medical services by failing to apply the negotiated discount:	
Hospital bill	$10,000
Negotiated discount of 25%	2,500
Actual Cost	**7,500**
Employee pays 20% of $10,000	2,000
Employee should pay 20% of $7,500	1,500
Employee overpays	**500**
Employer pays 80% of $10,000	$8,000
Employer should pay 80% of $7,500	6,000
Employer overpays	**2,000**

Source: Sedgwick Noble Lowndes, printed in *HRfocus* (January 1996): 7.

Health care costs are also rising for some employers and employees because fewer and fewer people are paying for the costs. For instance, approximately 75 percent of people who receive medical care pay less than full price for it. Some pay less than full price because of government-sponsored plans such as Medicaid and Medicare that require providers to provide services at low cost; others pay less because private associations such as Blue Cross/Blue Shield have made discount arrangements with providers; still others pay less because they have no insurance or other funds to pay for the costs. As a result, additional costs are paid by the remaining 25 percent who have full-cost coverage in the United States. In medical insurance coverage terms, this is known as *cost shifting*; the costs of health care are shifted from those who receive it to others more able to pay.

Employers also need to be careful to monitor costs to make sure they are receiving promised discounts. Some managed care plans pocket the discounts they have negotiated with hospitals and physicians rather than pass the savings along to sponsors and participants. Exhibit 2 offers a quick example of how much such abuse can cost an employer.

In addition, since employers are partners in the contract between managed care providers and their employees, they can be liable for overcharges.[41]

Alternative Health Programs. In response to the high costs of medical coverage, several alternative programs have become popular. Health maintenance organiza- tions, preferred provider organizations, and self-insurance illustrate what experts describe as efforts to reduce costs of health insurance in any way possible.

Health maintenance organizations (HMOs) offer medical coverage for a fixed annual fee. These organizations emphasize preventive care based on the theory that people who see their doctors regularly will develop fewer long-term disabilities. Since the Health Maintenance Act of 1973, employers with 25 or more employees have been required to offer HMOs as an alternative type of health coverage if such coverage is available in the local area. Under this act, employers must pay the same amount to HMOs that they would for employee insurance. If costs are greater than those for regular health insurance, employees pay the rest. Health maintenance organizations purport to lower the cost of care by regulating whom patients can see for healthcare and what treatments they receive. For example, HMO patients must be referred to a specialist by their primary HMO care physician for coverage to be in force.

Health insurance offered through **preferred provider organizations (PPOs)** is based on agreements made between employers and health care providers. Generally, PPOs agree to provide health services at reduced costs to participants. Patients may see only "approved" doctors who belong to the PPO network. The guarantee benefits both employers and medical providers. Employers receive medical insurance at a reduced cost while medical providers receive a guaranteed base of customers.

Some employers use **self-insurance** to reduce health care costs. With self-insurance, employers simply pay directly for their employees' health care costs rather than indirectly through insurance company plans. Companies with self-insurance plans take the risk that the costs they incur will be less than the costs they would incur by buying health insurance. In many cases, employers with self-insurance also negotiate with certain providers in the market to provide lower-cost medical coverage for their employees. Some hospitality companies—particularly larger ones—use self-insurance plans. Many hospitality companies have found self-insurance to be an effective means of containing health care costs.

An article in *Restaurant Business* many years ago indicated that self-insured restaurants (often participants in a plan offered by their state restaurant association) were saving significant amounts using self-insurance. For instance, in Louisiana, the cost for self-insurance was $4.83 per $100 in payroll costs versus $7.08 for commercial rates.[42] However, employers should carefully weigh their costs as research has shown self-insurance to be higher in most cases. As Exhibit 3 shows, the largest companies generally realize the greatest savings. Hospitality managers should check all the options, including contacting their state and national associations for advice, before adopting any self-insurance program. Savings may or may not be possible.

Other insurance programs include indemnity plans, such as Blue Cross/Blue Shield, that allow patients to visit the doctor and specialist of their choice. Indemnity plans tend to be more costly to companies. Another choice is the medical savings account (MSA). This offers an option funded by employees' pre-tax contributions, which are used to pay for routine medical care. These plans are paired with catastrophic medical insurance to cover the costs of serious illnesses.

Self-insurance, HMOs, and PPOs are not the only methods employers can use to contain health care costs. Some companies emphasize outpatient care rather than in-hospital care. These companies pay the full bill on outpatient care and establish co-pay plans for in-hospital care. Other companies have increased deductibles (the amount that each employee and family member must pay annually before health insurance payments begin) so that employees will pay the small costs

Exhibit 3   Self-Insurance: Higher Across the Board

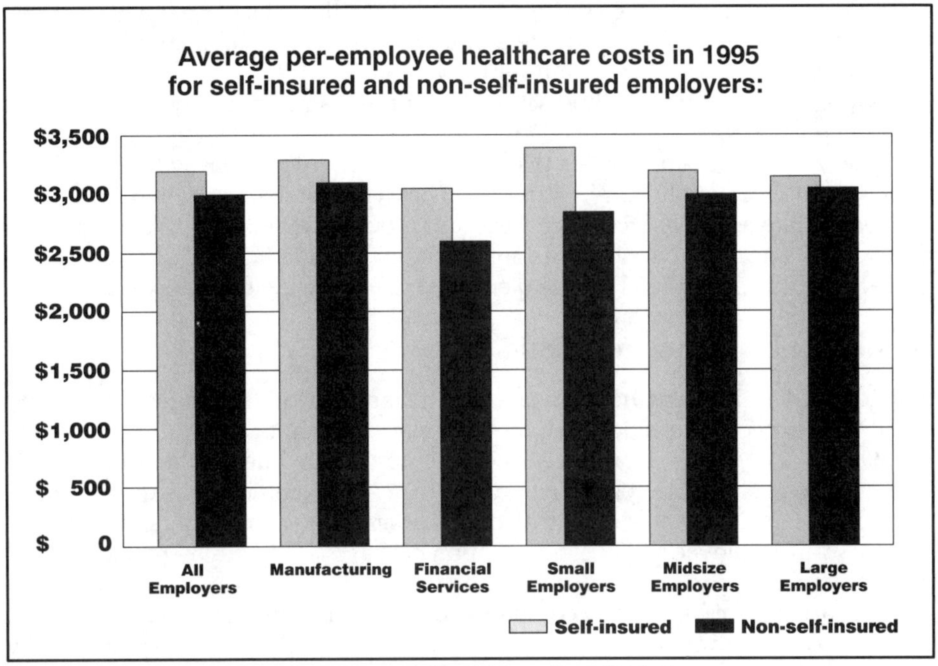

Average per-employee healthcare costs in 1995
for self-insured and non-self-insured employers:

Categories: All Employers, Manufacturing, Financial Services, Small Employers, Midsize Employers, Large Employers

Legend: Self-insured, Non-self-insured

Source: Business & Legal Reports, Inc., printed in *HRfocus* (June 1996): 7.

associated with health coverage. Another way companies contain costs is to develop co-pay programs in which employers and employees share the burden of health costs. In typical co-pay programs, employers pay from 80 percent to 90 percent of the costs of coverage while employees pay the remaining 10 percent to 20 percent. Some companies are also requiring employees to get second opinions for some services and procedures such as elective surgery.

Employers are also trying to reduce health care costs by encouraging employees to think more about their health. Many medical professionals support the idea that people can avoid or minimize certain health problems that require costly care by making and maintaining certain lifestyle changes. This concept is referred to as preventive health care. Some companies hold "health fairs" that are specifically designed to encourage employees to think about and practice preventive health care. Tufts, the third-largest HMO in New England, regularly offers preventive health care plans in its hotel-subscriber properties.[43]

Cafeteria plans, established by the Revenue Act of 1978, come in two basic forms: (1) premium-only plans (POP), the more popular type of plan, and (2) flexible spending accounts (FSA). Large companies may also be able to afford a "full cafeteria plan," which allows companies to allot a set amount of money for employees to pick and choose from a variety of benefits.

Premium-only plans allow employees to deduct their share of the premiums from pre-tax wages. The advantages of this type of plan is that it allows employees to spend pre-tax dollars, and therefore take home more money, and it allows the company to eliminate the 7.65 percent FICA and Medicare taxes on the wages used to pay for these plans. FSAs provide employees with a pre-tax method to pay for medical expenses and/or dependent care that is not covered by insurance. Employees choosing this method set aside a specific amount each year to be used for these purposes.

One way to cut benefit costs that is becoming more popular with many companies is to offer "voluntary" benefits. These programs are called voluntary because employees have access to a variety of types of benefits and choose the ones they want. Typically, these benefits are placed in a cafeteria plan (or more appropriately an IRS Section 125 Plan) and employees choose the ones they want.

Pension and Retirement Benefits

Pension and retirement benefits are additional optional benefits that many employees expect. These benefit programs vary substantially from company to company. In some cases, employers pay the entire cost, while in others, employees and employers share the costs. In all cases, the cost to employers is quite high. A study by the United States Department of Labor shows, on average, nearly four percent of an employee's total compensation package is for retirement and savings benefits.[44]

The principal reason many companies offer pension and retirement benefits is to develop a stable and reliable work force. On the surface, such plans seem ideally suited to help cure some of the problems faced by hospitality, including high turnover and the poor perception employees have of hospitality work. However, the industry has not adopted pension and retirement plans to the extent other industries have.

In 1997, Congress passed a law that allowed small businesses, especially family-owned businesses, to take advantage of more pension plans. This provision was part of the Small Business Jobs Protection Act. Under this plan, family-owned businesses can offer retirement benefits to all family members who work for the company. Previously, small businesses could offer only what were known as "aggregate plans" that prohibited family members from making full contributions to 401(k) plans. Under the previous plan, if a father/son or husband/wife wanted to make contributions to a 401(k) plan, their contributions were limited to an aggregate total, not individual totals. This substantially reduced the amount they could contribute.[45]

The restaurant industry championed a tax relief bill signed by President Bush in June 2001. The bill was designed to streamline the process for employers to set up pension plans for employees, and to make pensions more secure and more portable. The National Restaurant Association praised the bill as being "pro-employer/pro-employee" because it gave employers and employees more discretion in setting up retirement plans.[46]

One objective of most pension and retirement plans is to defer income tax costs from the present to the future or, basically, to the time when a person's income will be lower because of retirement. Each of the pension and retirement benefits programs discussed in this section meet the "qualification" requirements of the Internal Revenue Code for tax deferral. Interest and dividends earned by the pension fund are also tax deferred. Taxes are payable after retirement, when monies from the plan are withdrawn.

Employers use two principal types of pension and retirement plans. In **contributory retirement plans**, both the employer and employee contribute to retirement accounts (most popularly on the basis of 50 cents contributed by the company for every dollar contributed by the employee). In **non-contributory retirement plans**, only the employer contributes to employee retirement programs.

Defined Contribution Plans. Defined contribution plans are also known as "money purchase" or "profit-sharing" plans. An account is created for each employee into which fixed-rate contributions are made. Both employers and employees may contribute to such plans.

An Employee Stock Ownership Plan (ESOP) is a type of defined contribution plan. Benefits payable to employees on retirement include interest and accumulation of capital and dividends. This type of plan is popular because it emphasizes organizational growth and success. However, it provides less security than do plans that deposit funds into accounts serviced by outside companies.

Defined Benefit Plans. Under defined benefit plans, retirement benefits depend on the length of service and average earnings of employees during their employment. Employers generally service such plans by setting monies aside in escrow for the retirement benefits of their employees. With a defined benefit plan, employees have the advantage of knowing their exact retirement income in advance.

Employee Retirement Income Security Act of 1974. The Employee Retirement Income Security Act of 1974 (ERISA) established reporting requirements, fiduciary responsibilities and guidelines for participation, vesting, and funding for retirement and pension plans. It also established a federal insurance agency—the Pension Benefit Guaranty Corporation—to insure defined benefit retirement and pension plans so that employee pensions are protected if sponsoring companies go bankrupt. To qualify for coverage, employers must meet specific provisions and pay premiums of more than $15 per employee.

According to ERISA, any employee aged 21 years or older who has worked for a company for at least one year is eligible to enroll in retirement or pension plans provided by the company. The act also includes provisions to prevent employers from firing long-term employees just prior to vesting in pension plans.

At the time ERISA was legislated, Congress had two objectives: (1) to encourage employers to establish and maintain retirement income for their employees, and (2) to create legal protection for those employees to ensure that the retirement benefits being promised were actually there when they retired. ERISA has accomplished both goals very substantially. The growth in pension plans, both in terms of the number of participants and money contributed, has been phenomenal.

While ERISA has been in place, the greatest changes have come from two areas: (1) the shift from defined benefit (DB) plans to defined contribution (DC) plans, and (2) the growing emphasis and impact of ERISA on employer-provided health care.

The change from DB to DC plans has resulted in shifting the risk for poor investment performance from the sponsor (or the Pension Benefit Guaranty Corporation) to the individual employee. Now employees are more responsible for the performance of their own investments, thus shifting decision-making from sponsor to employee.

ERISA enactors did not expect such an increase in the cost of providing adequate health care coverage to current and retired employees. When ERISA was passed, the emphasis was on retirement, and few lawmakers foresaw the great increases in health care costs to come. To compensate for this oversight, Congress subsequently enacted both COBRA and HIPAA (Health Insurance Portability and Accountability Act) legislation. In the future, Congress will have to work harder to overcome some additional problems with ERISA, including the preemption clauses that have sometimes led to workers and retirees not receiving medical treatment for illnesses.[47]

Individual Retirement Account. Individual Retirement Accounts (IRAs) were originally established by ERISA for employees who did not participate in their employers' retirement plans. Over the years, many of these tax-deductible accounts became available to employees who already had retirement accounts with their employers. However, the Tax Reform Act of 1986 reimposed some of the original restrictions on IRAs. Contributions to traditional IRAs are tax deductible now only for lower-income taxpayers and for those without company-sponsored retirement plans. Other forms of IRAs have recently been developed. Because IRAs are *individual* funding vehicles (rather than an employer-provided benefit), they are outside the scope of this discussion.

Salary Reduction Plans (401(k) Plans). Salary reduction plans allow employees to make tax-deferred contributions to retirement accounts in company profit-sharing plans. These plans are also known as *401(k) plans* and *capital accumulation plans*. Until 2001, the annual limit on contributions to an individual's 401(k) plan was $10,500. Under the Bush tax relief plan of June 2001, the 401(k) contribution limit is gradually raised to $15,000.[48] Under these programs, taxes are deferred until the money is withdrawn after retirement.

Many companies encourage employees to participate in these plans through matching contributions. Many companies pay $.50 to $.60 on every dollar an employee puts into the plan, up to six to eight percent of their total salary.

Other Benefits

Employees can enjoy a wide variety of benefits offered through other company-sponsored plans. Among the most common are educational benefits, employee assistance programs, child and dependent care programs, cafeteria and flexible benefits plans, legal services, long-term care policies, and pay for time not worked.

Educational Benefits. Educational benefits have become very commonplace. Usually, companies reimburse employees for tuition when the employer approves of the course work. In some cases, tuition for spouses and children is also included. While some employers pay only tuition, some pay all the costs associated with education, including books and supplies. Some employers pay full tuition, while other employers cover only part. Passing grades are generally a requirement for receiving educational benefits.

Several hospitality companies have developed educational benefit plans. McDonald's has a well-known plan; so does Burger King. Employees enrolled in an approved educational program can be reimbursed for a certain percentage of tuition expenses. Chick-Fil-A, the first major fast-food company to institute a tuition reimbursement plan, found that the program engenders loyalty among employees and reduces absenteeism.[49]

Employee Assistance Programs. The number of U.S. employers providing **employee assistance programs (EAPs)** has rapidly increased, due, in part, to drug abuse prevention awareness. EAPs were introduced in the 1940s to combat alcohol-related work problems. Today, EAPs typically focus on drug- and alcohol-related problems, but can also provide counseling to employees for marital problems, personal finance, career concerns, and problems on the job. EAPs have become so widespread that more than 80 percent of the Fortune 500 companies today provide some sort of EAP program. Some companies establish in-house EAP programs, while others contract with referral systems to provide employees with professional EAP services.

Child and Dependent Care Programs. In 1981, Congress passed provisions that permit employers to exclude up to $5,000 from employees' taxable income to pay for child and dependent care expenses. As a result, employees can now pay for this type of care with pre-tax dollars, thus stretching their income. Before 1981, employees had to pay for child and dependent care out of after-tax earnings.

Research reveals that three out of four employees in the service industries need child-care services. On the average, employees miss about eight days of work per year because of child-care–related problems.[50] Given these figures, it clearly benefits hospitality companies to offer child-care programs to their employees.

Cafeteria and Flexible Benefits Plans. In the past, employers merely decided which benefits plans to offer and then offered them to *all* employees. This situation has changed substantially in most companies. Results of a national survey conducted by Opinion Research Corporation (ORC) suggest that a traditional uniform benefit program is unlikely to fully satisfy more than 20 percent of any given employee population. ORC also conducted a national poll that showed that only 50 percent to 55 percent of employees indicated they were satisfied with their current benefits. Clearly, it is important to allow employees to select the benefits that will best serve their needs.[51] Many employees today have a great deal of control over which company-sponsored plans they enroll in because of cafeteria and flexible benefits plans.

Although generally regarded as the same, cafeteria and flexible benefit plans are different. Technically, cafeteria plans offer either benefits or cash in lieu of benefits to employees; flexible benefits plans offer only benefits. Both offer the

Exhibit 4   Importance of Choice in Employee Benefits

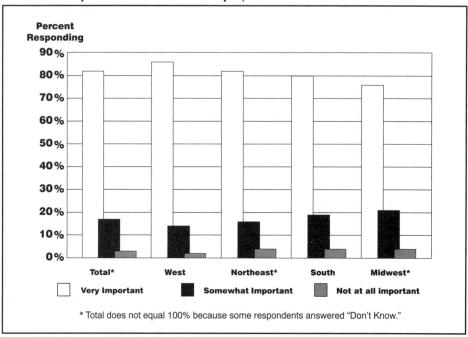

Source: Pulse Surveys of America, Inc., by the Colonial Life and Accident Insurance Company and The Employers Council on Flexible Compensation, 1992; printed in *HRfocus* (April 1995): 7.

employees choices. As Exhibit 4 shows, this choice is very important to most employees.

Cafeteria and flexible benefits plans offer substantial advantages to employees, especially those in households with two wage earners. For instance, if a married couple works for companies that provide cafeteria or flexible benefit plans, one wage earner can choose one set of benefits while another can choose a different set. Three types of benefit plans come under the general heading of cafeteria and flexible benefit: **core spending account** plans, **module spending account plans**, and **flexible spending account** plans.

- *Core spending account plans* provide a series of "core" benefits to every employee, plus a list of other benefits from which employees can choose.

- *Module spending account plans* offer a choice of preestablished "packages" of benefits to every employee. Employers determine the benefits included in each package.

- *Flexible spending account plans* provide a given amount of money that the company will spend on benefits for employees and allow each employee to decide which benefits are best for his or her personal needs. This program is similar to the core spending account plan, except that there are no designated "core" benefits.

Exhibit 5   Paid Leave Banks

Back to Work	
The effectiveness of each program in controlling absenteeism on a scale of 1 (most effective) to 5 (least effective):	
Paid leave bank	1.86
No-fault program	2.46
Discipline	2.53
Buy-back plan	2.59
Yearly review	2.81
Bonus	2.90
Personal recognition	3.37

Source: CCH, printed in *HRfocus* (December 1995): 9.

The advantages of cafeteria and flexible benefits are obvious: employees have more freedom to choose benefits. However, such programs also have disadvantages. The most common disadvantage is the increased amount of paperwork these plans generate.

Long-Term Care Policies. Another type of benefit that appears to be increasing in popularity rapidly is the long-term care policy. These insurance policies are designed to cover things that Medicare doesn't (Medicare covers only two percent of institutional care and less than one-half of nursing home costs). The number of long-term care policies will likely grow gereatly as baby boomers age. If interested, employees should apply before age 55, when costs go up substantially.

Pay for Time Not Worked. Pay for time not worked includes vacation pay, holiday pay, sick leave, dependent care leave, religious holiday leave, personal leave, bereavement leave, National Guard Duty, Reserve Duty, jury duty, and other time off during which the employer continues to pay employees. In many companies, full-time employees receive vacation pay after completing one year of service. Company policies vary substantially regarding pay for time not worked.

Some companies even offer their employees sabbaticals, or extended time off. McDonald's established a sabbatical program in 1977. Full-time employees with 10 years of service are eligible for an eight-week leave. After 20 years, employees can have 16 weeks off. The time must be taken all at once; in that way, it offers a long enough period to accomplish personal or professional goals.

Paid Leave Bank. Employee absenteeism and its associated costs are on the rise. One way for companies to curb absenteeism costs is to include all "time off" plans together and let the employee decide how to use the time. Exhibit 5 shows the effectiveness of paid leave banks in controlling absenteeism compared with other programs companies use.

Paid leave banks have two major advantages over other leave programs: employees bear the responsibility for managing their time off and they have the flexibility they desire. Paid leave banks—combined with accrued leave time plans—can help prevent the high incidence of vacations and sick days taken at the end of the year. The average employee takes four to seven sick days per year. Research has shown that by lumping vacation, personal, and sick days together in one paid time off category, the average number of employee days off is actually going down, not up.[52]

Flexible Work Schedules. A current trend is for companies to offer flexibility in employee work schedules. Employers are recognizing that people have responsibilities away from work and are trying to be more accommodating to individual needs. According to research, approximately 57 percent of employers offered flexible work schedules in 2005. Workplace flexibility has become a great benefit for employees seeking balance in their personal lives. Employees are given flexibility when they have an acceptable conflict, such as for health reasons, for child care, or for schooling. Workplace flexibility is wide in its range, from sick and FMLA leave to telecommuting, job sharing, compressed workweeks, and phased retirement.[53]

Maximum Work Hours. Jobs in the hospitality industry have traditionally required long hours, including nights, weekends, and holidays. One result of this is high turnover among entry-level salaried managers. Aaron Kennedy, founder and CEO of Noodles & Company, recognized the impact management-level turnover could have on his business operations. To encourage his managers to stay with the company, he surveyed them about what types of benefits they would enjoy most. What he discovered was that the managers valued their free time and wanted time to be with family and to enjoy their hobbies. The outcome of the survey is a generous package that includes the traditional health, retirement, and vacation in addition to gym memberships, leases on cars, guaranteed 45-hour work weeks, and free ski passes (the company is based in Boulder, Colorado). Noodles & Company currently has a 10 percent turnover rate among salaried managers, which is well below the industry average. Kennedy spends an average of $25,000–$30,000 on benefits per store, per year, but that far outweighs his costs of recruiting and training new managers.[54]

Endnotes

1. M. Singh, "Integrated Pay for Performance: The High-Tech Marriage of Compensation Management and Performance Management," *Compensation & Benefits Review* 37, no. 1 (2005): 18–25.

2. "Design Your Own Incentive Pay Plan to Improve Performance," *Receivables Report for American's Health Care Financial Managers* 16 (August 2001): 9–10.

3. C.M. Spray, C.K. Wang, and S.J. Biddle, "Understanding Motivation in Sport: An Experimental Test of Achievement Goal and Self Determination Theories," *European Journal of Sport Science* 6, no. 1 (2006): 43–51.

4. John Meyer, "Employee Commitment and Motivation: A Conceptual Analysis and Integrative Model," *Journal of Applied Psychology* 89, no. 6 (2004): 991–1007.

5. Gary Latham, "Goal Setting and Goal Orientation: An Integration of Two Different yet Related Literatures," *Academy of Management Journal* 47, no. 2 (2004): 227–239.

6. Larry Howard and Thomas W. Dougherty, "Alternative Reward Strategies and Employee Reactions," *Compensation & Benefits Review* 36, no. 1 (2004): 41–51.

7. Melissa S. Baucus and Caryn L. Beck-Dudley, "Designing Ethical Organizations: Avoiding the Long Term Negative Effects of Rewards and Punishments," *Journal of Business Ethics* 56, no. 4 (2005): 355–370.

8. Ken Bates, Hilary Bates, and Robert Johnston, "Linking Service to Profit: the Business Case for Service Excellence," *International Journal of Service Industry Management* 14, no. 2 (2003): 173–183.

9. Kelly C. Strong, Richard C. Ringer, and Steven A. Taylor, "The Rules of Stakeholder Satisfaction," *Journal of Business Ethics* 32, no. 3 (2001): 219–230.

10. Sara Rynes, Barry Gerhart, and Laura Parks, "Personnel Psychology: Performance Evaluation and Pay for Performance," *Annual Review of Psychology* 56 (2005): 571–600.

11. Angela G. Morgana and Annette B. Poulsenb, "Linking Pay to Performance Compensation Proposals in the S&P 500," *Journal of Financial Economics* 62 (2001): 489–523.

12. Steven Currall, Annette Towler, Timothy Judge, and Laura Kohn, "Pay Satisfaction and Organizational Outcomes," *Personnel Psychology* 58, no. 3 (2005): 613.

13. Casey Ichniowski and Kathryn Shaw, "Beyond Incentive Pay: Insiders' Estimates of the Value of Complementary Human Resource Management Practices," *Journal of Economic Perspectives* 17, no. 1 (2003): 155–180.

14. Thomas B. Wilson, "Is It Time to Eliminate the Piece Rate Incentive System?" *Compensation & Benefits Review* 24 (March/April 1992): 43–49.

15. "Taking Your Lumps," *HRFocus* (January 1996): 15.

16. Jude T. Rich, "Future Composition Shock," *Compensation & Benefits Review* 28 (November-December 1996): 27–33.

17. Mary Jo Ducharfme and Mark Podolsky, "Variable Pay: Its Impact on Motivation and Organizational Performance," *International Journal of Human Resources Development and Management* 6, no. 1 (2006): 68–76.

18. Kenneth W. Thornicroft, "Promises Kept, Promises Broken: Reciprocity and the Scanlon," *Employee Relations* 13 (1991): 12–20.

19. Chris Lee, "Best Idea That Got Lost in the Shuffle," *Training* 36, no. 2 (1999): 35–36.

20. For more information on Scanlon plans, see A. J. Geare, "Productivity from Scanlon Type Plans," *Academy of Management Review* 1 (1976): 99–108.

21. Corey M. Rosen and Michael Quarrey, "How Well Is Employee Ownership Working?" *Harvard Business Review* (September-October, 1987): 126.

22. John Tarras, "ESOP's Fable," *Restaurant Hospitality* 74 (September 1990): 40-41.

23. Cory Rosen, John Case, and Martin Staubus, "Every Employee an Owner. [Really.]," *Harvard Business Review* 83 (June 2005): 122–130.

24. Raymond S. Schmidgall and Christian Bechtel, "ESOPs: Putting Ownership in the Employee's Hands," *Cornell Hotel and Restaurant Administration Quarterly* 30 (February 1990): 81.

25. Rosen, Case, and Staubus.

26. Lisa Meulbroek, "Company Stock in Pension Plans: How Costly Is It?" *The Journal of Law and Economics* 48 (2005): 443–474.

27. For a discussion of the impact of the Tax Reform Act of 1986 on stock options, see Phillip C. Hunt, "Tax Reform: Its Impact on Compensation and Benefits," *Employment Relations Today* (Spring 1987): 39-52.

28. Wayne F. Cascio, *Managing Human Resources: Productivity, Quality of Work Life, Profits* (New York: McGraw-Hill, 1989), 440.

29. Angela Maas, "Small Companies, Big Rewards," *Employee Benefit News* (electronic version, February 2005).

30. United States Department of Labor, *Most Requested BLS Statistics* (November 18, 2005), http://data.bls.gov/cgi-bin/surveymost?bls.

31. United States Department of Labor, *News: Employee Benefits in Private Industry, 2005* (August 24, 2005), www.bls.gov/news.release/pdf/ebs2.pdf.

32. Ben Van Houten, "Employee Perks," *Restaurant Business* 96 (May 15, 1997): 85–87.

33. Paul Frumkin, "Industry Mulls Cost, Intricacy of Social Security Reform," *Nations Restaurant News* 39 (March 7, 2005): 1.

34. Gail E. Sammons, "Reducing Workers' Compensation Claims," *Hospitality and Tourism Education* 6 (Winter 1994): 43-46.

35. Susan Werner, "Call-in System Improves Injury Report Procedure," *Business Insurance* 25 (February 18, 1991): 53–54.

36. "Fighting Back Against Slips and Falls," *Lodging Hospitality* 59 (October 1, 2003): 15.

37. Mark. D. Fefer, "Taking Control of Your Workmans' Compensation Costs," *Fortune* 130 (3 October 1995): 131-135.

38. Nina Munk, "Can't Lift Boxes? Then Sweep Floors," *Forbes* 158 (November 4, 1996): 167-170.

39. Michael Prince, *Business Insurance* 35 (March 12, 2001): 22.

40. Michael Bond, "Using Health Savings Accounts to Provide Low-Cost Health Care," *Compensation & Benefits Review* 37, no. 2 (2005): 29–32.

41. "About Cobra Compliance Systems (CCS): We Are Here to Help," COBRA Compliance Systems, Inc. (August 11, 2001), www.cobracs.com/about.htm.

42. Steve Brooks, "Comp and Circumstance," *Restaurant Business* (1 March 1993): 62–68.

43. Christopher Kenneally, "Celebrating Health to Lower Stress Insurance," *New England Business* 13 (February 1991): 46–47.

44. United States Department of Labor. *News: Bureau of Labor Statistics* (USDL: 00-186) (June 2000), http://stats.bls.gov/echome.htm.

45. Paul Moomaw, "Nest-Egg Knowledge," *Restaurants USA* 17 (1998) 5: 9–12.

46. "National Restaurant Association Achieves Priorities in Tax Relief Bill," Restaurant.org (May 30, 2001), www.restaurant.org.

47. Sherwin Kaplan, "The Next 25 Years of ERISA—and How to Prepare for Them," *Employee Benefits News* 14 (April 1, 2000): 41-44.

48. Carter M. Young, "Major Tax Cut Provisions," *ABC News.com* (June 7, 2001), http://abcnews.go.com.

49. Todd Englander, "Chick-Fil-A: Not Just Chicken Fee," *Incentive* 163 (January 1989): 24–26.

50. Stephen LaJacono, "Mildly Ill/Backup Child Care: A Benefit for Employees and Employers," *Employee Benefits Journal* 25 (December 2000): 48–51.

51. Ministry of Manpower, *Flexible Benefits Plan* (October 29, 2005), www.mom.gov.sg/MOM/LRD/Publications/731_csflexiben.pdf.

52. Michael M. Markowich, "HR's Leadership Role in the Third Wave Era," *HR Magazine* 40 (September 1995): 92–100.

53. Leah Carlson, "Firms Balance Workplace Flexibility and Business Demands," *Employee Benefit News* (electronic version, April 2005).

54. Dina Berta, "Noodles & Company Proves Perks Are Key to Retaining Employees," *Nations Restaurant News* 34, no. 40 (2000): 18.

Key Terms

bonus plan—An individual incentive system based on a combination of base and incentive pay. Typically, bonuses are based on attaining preset goals.

cafeteria benefits plan—Benefit program that offers either a variety of benefits or cash in lieu of benefits to employees.

COBRA—Consolidated Omnibus Budget Reconciliation Act, passed in 1985. According to the provisions of this act, employers must offer health insurance coverage to terminated employees for up to 18 months after termination, and to employees who quit or retire for up to 36 months. Some coverages also apply to dependents.

commission—Payment made to an employee that is based on some measurable unit (usually sales volume).

contributory retirement plan—Pension and retirement program in which both the employer and the employee contribute.

core spending account—Benefit plan that provides a series of benefits to every employee plus a list of benefits employees may choose.

defined benefit plan—Pension and retirement program in which employers set aside amounts of monies at regular intervals to meet specific retirement benefits.

defined contribution plan—Pension and retirement programs in which contributions are made at a fixed rate for each employee. Both employers and employees can typically contribute.

employee assistance program (EAP)—Employer-sponsored counseling program designed to help employees deal with personal problems related to drug or alcohol abuse, stress, family tension, finances, career goals, or other situations that affect their work.

Employee Retirement Income Security Act (ERISA) of 1974—Legislation that established reporting requirements, fiduciary responsibilities, and guidelines for participation, vesting, and funding for retirement and pension plans.

Employee Stock Ownership Plan (ESOP)—Compensation plan that establishes an account in the employee's name to which the company makes contributions based on either employee contributions or on company profits.

flexible benefits plan—Benefit program that offers a variety of benefits for employees to choose from.

flexible spending account—Benefit program that provides employees with a specific amount of "money" to spend on benefits. Typically, employers provide a wide variety of benefits at specific costs and allow employees to decide how to spend the monies allotted to them for these benefits.

gainsharing program—Formula-based group incentive program in which a percentage of the gains made by the company is shared with employees.

group incentive program—Goal-based compensation system that links pay to group performance to improve productivity; reduces costs; motivates personnel; and attains other company objectives. Such programs include the Scanlon plan, Rucker plan, and Improshare.

health maintenance organization (HMO)—A voluntary health benefit program that offers medical coverage to employees for a fixed annual fee.

Improshare—Cost-saving group incentive plan in which a standard cost of production is established and the employees share in the cash savings of production costs under that amount.

individual incentive program—Goal-based compensation system that links pay to individual performance to improve productivity, reduce costs, motivate personnel, and attain other company objectives. Such plans include bonuses, pay for knowledge, and merit pay.

individual retirement account (IRA)—Retirement plan established by the Employee Retirement Income Security Act of 1974 that allows employees not covered by employer retirement accounts to set monies aside tax-free for use later in retirement.

leveraged ESOP—Plan that uses employee stock ownership account funds to provide capital to the company for projects the company may undertake.

merit pay—Pay based on an employee's performance over a predetermined period of time.

module spending accounts—Benefit programs that provide a choice of pre-established "packages" of benefits offered to employees.

non-contributory retirement plans—Pension and retirement programs in which only the employer contributes.

pay for time not worked—Vacation pay, sick pay, holiday pay, and so on.

piecework incentive—Incentive program based on pay for the number of work tasks completed.

preferred provider organization (PPO)—A health benefit program that offers medical coverage at reduced costs to participants.

Rucker plan—Cost-saving group incentive plan based on the ratio of labor costs to the share of production costs. This plan uses a standard measure called an economic productivity index.

salary reduction plan (401(k) plan)—Compensation plan that allows employees to make tax-deferred contributions from their paychecks to retirement accounts. Also known as a capital accumulation plan.

Scanlon plan—Cost-saving group incentive plan based on the ratio of labor costs to the sales value of production (SVOP).

self-insurance—Benefit program in which employers pay directly for the cost of employee health care rather than pay indirectly through insurance provided by an insurance company.

standard hour incentive plan—Incentive program based on the number of units completed per day.

unemployment compensation insurance (UCI)—Mandated benefit that requires employers to purchase unemployment insurance benefits that can be withdrawn as income by employees who are out of work. This benefit program is administered by individual states.

workers' compensation—"No-fault" benefit plan that provides for employees who become disabled or who die at work. The program is funded by contributions from the employer. Benefits vary by state.

Review Questions

1. Why do many researchers and industry personnel no longer view benefits as a motivating factor for employees?

2. What defines an effective incentive program? What are the advantages of such programs?

3. How do individual and group incentives differ?

4. How do the piecework, standard hour, and merit pay individual incentives differ? Which are more applicable to line-level employees in the hospitality industry? Why?

5. How do the Scanlon, Rucker, and Improshare group incentive plans differ?

6. What are the major mandatory benefits that employers must provide their employees?

7. What are the most common types of health care benefits offered by employers? How do these types differ?

8. What are the most common kinds of pension and retirement plans offered by U.S. companies? How do these plans differ? How did the Tax Reform Act of 1986 affect these plans?

9. Given what you know about the demographic makeup of hospitality employees, which types of benefit plans do you think would be most useful for hospitality companies?

10. What services are most commonly offered through employee assistance programs?

Internet Sites

For more information, visit the following Internet sites. Remember that Internet addresses can change without notice. If the site is no longer there, you can use a search engine to look for additional sites.

Academy of Management
www.aomonline.org

Cornell University ILR School
www.ilr.cornell.edu/CAHRS

ESOP (Employee Stock Ownership)

www.esopassociation.org

HMO Page
www.hmopage.org

HR Magazine
www.shrm.org/hrmagazine

Internal Revenue Service
www.irs.ustreas.gov

Reuters Health Information
www.reutershealth.com

Social Security Administration
www.ssa.gov

U.S. Dept. of Health & Human Services
www.hhs.gov

U.S. Government Department of Labor Occupational Safety and Health Administration
www.osha.gov

Workforce Online
www.workforceonline.com

Mini Case Study

You are an executive housekeeper at a mid-size property. You currently have a system in place whereby you pay your housekeeping staff by the hour. Recently, a group of employees approached the general manager about eliminating this compensation program and replacing it with a piecework system. The general manager asks you to develop a theoretical piecework system for room attendants and to analyze the advantages and disadvantages of such a system.

Chapter 10 Outline

Competencies

1. Describe the reasons employees join unions, and analyze the statistics and trends of union membership. (pp. 341–343)

2. Explain the goals and content of major U.S. legislation affecting labor relations. (pp. 343–350)

3. Define craft and industrial unions, and outline the sequence of events in organizing and certifying or decertifying a union. (pp. 350–356)

4. Describe how unions are adapting and changing as they look to the future. (pp. 356–360)

10

Labor Unions

This chapter was co-authored by William Werner, J.D., University of
Nevada, Las Vegas (UNLV); Ming-Lun Lee, Ph.D. candidate, UNLV;
and Tzu-Chu Chien, M.S. candidate, UNLV.

Management sometimes mistakenly believes that employees join unions just
because they want more pay. Pay is only one of the reasons that employees join
unions; in many cases, it is not a major reason at all.

Employees join unions primarily because they believe unions will help them
accomplish their goals. Economic security is one goal. Other goals are the assurance of safe and comfortable working conditions, respect, job security, and control
over their own work. Employees are also driven toward unions by poor dispute
resolution and communications systems, layoffs, inconsistent policy enforcement,
and unfair treatment by management.

Employees are more likely to want to join a union because they are dissatisfied with management—not because they are dissatisfied with pay. Employees
expect fair treatment, communication of policies and procedures, and job security.
When managers don't meet these expectations, employees often turn to unions.
They often believe, or at least hope, that union representation will increase their
control over the workplace and protect them from unfair and abusive managers. In
a sense, employees who vote for a union in their workplace are voting against
management as much as for the union.[1]

Statistics and Trends

Union membership peaked in 1945. At that time, 35.8 percent of the non-agricul-
tural work force in the United States belonged to unions. Since then, the percentage of the work force belonging to unions has steadily declined. By 1995, the
percentage of the work force belonging to unions had dropped to 15 percent, and
in 2004, the percentage of unionized workers, excluding government workers,
had fallen below 8 percent. Figures have ranged from a low of 4.2 percent union
workers in North Carolina to highs of 26.5 percent in Hawaii and 25.4 percent in
New York. In the hospitality industry, union membership ranges from 5.5 percent
to 8.9 percent.[2] The declining percentages do not mean that the *number* of union
members has dropped; in fact, the number of workers who belong to unions actually grew between 1945 and 1993—from 15 million to 17.6 million.[3] However, the
number of overall workers in the United States grew more rapidly than did union
membership.

The percentage of workers who belong to unions has declined in the United States for one principal reason: the shift from a manufacturing- to a service-based economy. In 1970, 23 percent of the total work force worked in the manufacturing sector. By 1990, only 16 percent of the total work force consisted of line-level employees in manufacturing, while 46 percent of the work force consisted of line-level positions in the service sector. For the most part, the remaining 38 percent of the work force held manufacturing- or agriculture-related jobs. Since unions have historically had their strongest base in manufacturing, the economic shift has resulted in a significant and gradual decline in union representation.[4] This trend may or may not continue. Statistics gathered by the United States Bureau of Labor Standards show that union membership, including government workers, leveled off at 13.9 percent in 1999, reversing a downward trend.[5] A *Newsweek* poll found that popular discontent with cost controls and wage cuts in U.S. businesses has led to the highest level of worker support (62 percent) of unions since the early 1960s.[6]

While the shift from a manufacturing to a service economy is the primary cause of declining union membership, it is not the only reason. Another significant factor has been the enactment of various pieces of legislation that protect employee rights. Laws regulating workplace health and safety, wages, equal employment opportunity, and employee benefits have diminished the need for union representation and "protection" by mandating workplace practices that were once likely to be achieved only through collective bargaining.

White-collar workers have offset some of the losses associated with manufacturing-based union membership. In 1970, only 21.8 percent of the union members in the United States were classified as white-collar. By 1978, this percentage had grown to 25.8 percent. By 1985, the total percentage of union members who held white-collar jobs had risen to 41 percent.[7]

Much of the increase in white collar membership has come from two sectors of the economy: public employees and teachers. Today, nearly half the unionized workers in the United States (7.1 million) work for local, state, or federal government. The largest public sector union, the American Federation of State, County and Municipal Employees (AFSCME) is now one of the largest, most influential unions in the United States. Before 1962, public employees were prohibited by law from joining unions. Executive Order 10988 changed that. Signed by President Kennedy in 1962, this order gave federal employees the right to be represented by unions and to bargain collectively with their employers. While this order did not allow federal government employees to strike over union-management disagreements, it did allow this large group of employees to unionize.

Since then, state government employees have also gained the right to organize and to bargain collectively. Over the last 30 years, the percentage of government employees belonging to unions has grown greatly[8] Increased unionization among teachers has also made a significant contribution to growth in union membership in the United States. In 1967, members of the National Education Association (NEA) voted to allow members to strike if collective bargaining negotiations broke down. Since that time, membership in this union has grown to 2.3 million (21 percent of teachers). The NEA is now the largest union.

The experience of hotel and restaurant unions has mirrored that of other industries. Membership in the Hotel Employees and Restaurant Employees Union (HERE), the most active union in the hotel and restaurant industries, dropped from a high of 507,000 members in 1970 to about 280,000 members in 1989 and rose again to 300,000 by 1998, but by 2004 had dropped again to 250,000.[9] This increase in the 1990s was partially due to the acculturation of Canada's union.[10] **Union certification** and **decertification** elections in the hotel and restaurant industries also indicate this decline is likely to continue; HERE is losing more elections than it wins. For this reason, the union has turned to a method to organize workers without an election: the voluntary recognition campaign discussed later in this chapter.

A principal reason HERE seems unable to effectively unionize large segments of the industry is that hotel and restaurant workers are not easy to organize. For instance, more than 40 percent of the employees in these two industries work less than 35 hours per week. In addition, hotel and restaurant workers tend to move frequently from job to job; many are not as interested in job security issues as are employees who plan to remain with the same employer for many years.[11] Unions have also been relatively unsuccessful in unionizing hotel and restaurant workers because many of these employees are women and minorities—groups that have traditionally resisted unionization.

Unionization in the hotel industry is most common in 12 states: California, Pennsylvania, New York, Nevada, Washington, Illinois, Ohio, Hawaii, New Jersey, Florida, Michigan, and Massachusetts. Unionization in the restaurant industry is most common in eight states: California, Pennsylvania, New York, Washington, Illinois, Ohio, Michigan, and Oregon.[12]

Labor unions in Philadelphia and other cities have also begun investing in hotels as a means both of making money off their investments and ensuring their own futures. Using members' pension funds, unions in Philadelphia have invested $200 million in new hotels and in renovations. At least $40 million of the funds have been invested in the Hyatt Regency at Penn's Landing. These investments are wise because they have a direct correlation to union members' jobs. As investors, unions increase their say in how the properties are managed.[13] The AFL-CIO is also financing hotels these days. With about $1 billion in assets, the union pension fund is allocating 10 to 15 percent of its annual investment assets to hotel properties. The money, from the Building Investment Trust of the AFL-CIO pension, comes with a hitch: the hotels must use union construction workers during construction or renovation and they must sign neutrality agreements, allowing unions easy access to the hotel's new employees for organizing. The hotel owner also promises to recognize the union if a majority of employees sign union cards, so no election would be necessary. Projects include the Hilton Garden Inn in Philadelphia, a Holiday Inn Express Suites in San Francisco, the Jacksonville Hilton Towers and the Radisson Suites in Champlain, Illinois.[14]

Legislation Affecting Labor Relations

Much of the U.S. legislation regulating unions resulted from the Depression. Before the Depression, Congress had passed the Railway Labor Act (1926). This act minimized the impact of railway labor disputes on the economy by providing a means for prompt disposition of disputes between railroads and their employees. This act also established the right of railway workers to unionize and created a mediation and arbitration system to settle labor disputes in railway companies. Among the reforms in Franklin Roosevelt's New Deal of the 1930s were attempts to regulate management-labor relations. It was theorized that government regulation of union-management relations could help stimulate the economy.

The success of the Railway Labor Act in reducing railroad strikes led Congress to attempt further regulation of labor relations between employers and employees. The Norris-LaGuardia Act (1932), passed during the New Deal, limited the use of court injunctions to break strikes. Before this act, employers regularly used federal court injunctions to prevent workers from striking or to break strikes. Under the Norris-LaGuardia Act, employers can secure injunctions only when they can prove that a strike will cause irreparable damage, violence, or harm to innocent parties. Even then, injunctions are allowed for only five days.

While the Railway Labor Act and the Norris-LaGuardia Act proved that the government could establish effective legislation regulating labor relations, they did not prevent employers from using tactics designed to break unions or punish employees who joined unions. Frequently, employers were still able to abuse employees because the employees were still vulnerable to being fired or retaliated against for union activity.

The Wagner Act of 1935

The first real effort to prevent mistreatment of employees by management came with the passage of the **Wagner Act of 1935**, also referred to as the National Labor Relations Act. The Wagner Act gave employees the legally protected rights to organize, to strike, and to engage in collective bargaining through an elected representative. Still enforced today, the Wagner Act plays a very significant role in union-management relations. For example, it requires all employers to **bargain in good faith** with employees in an attempt to settle labor disputes.

Provisions in the Wagner Act provided for the creation of the **National Labor Relations Board (NLRB)**. The Wagner Act empowered the NLRB to regulate the degree to which employers could attempt to prevent employees from organizing and from collective bargaining. The NLRB was also empowered to enforce their rulings through court orders, imprisonment, fines, and injunctions. Basically, the act stipulated five **unfair labor practices.** Employers were prohibited from:

- Interfering with or coercing employees to discourage them from forming or joining unions. Employers may not threaten employees or promise them additional benefits for the purpose of influencing their decision to unionize.

- Attempting to dominate or influence the operation of unions. Before the Wagner Act, employers sometimes entered into so-called "sweetheart" arrangements with union leaders by bribing them to force their membership to accept terms the company wanted in contracts.

- Discriminating regarding the hire or tenure of employees based on union membership or activity.

Exhibit 1   The National Labor Relations Board Administrative Process

How NLRB's Process Works

How the union's charges of unfair labor practices against the owners could move through the National Labor Relations Board administrative process:

▶ **Union files charges:** Dec. 27, the players union filed charges of unfair labor practices against owners with NLRB's regional office in New York, saying owners implemented their salary cap illegally, before a legal impasse was reached.

ISSUING AN INJUNCTION:

General Counsel Feinstein, with approval of five-member NLRB Board, could petition U.S. district court to issue a preliminary injunction. The court could order owners to rescind their salary cap and return to the old system while the NLRB processes the complaint. Owners could appeal the injunction to an appeals court. If an injunction is issued, the NLRB is required to speed processing of the case.

▶ **Regional director investigates:** Daniel Silverman, regional director, began investigating the charges immediately. Following investigation, which could take 4-6 weeks, general counsel Fred Feinstein will decide whether to issue complaint and whether to seek injunction.

▶ **If complaint is issued:** There will be a hearing before an administrative law judge.

▶ **What happens at hearing:** A full-blown trial, with sides presenting evidence. The ALJ will either uphold or dismiss complaint.

▶ **Losing side can appeal to NLRB Board:** The five-member NLRB Board in Washington, D.C., will review the case and issue a decision.

▶ Loser can then appeal to U.S. Circuit Court of Appeals.

▶ Loser can then appeal to U.S. Supreme Court, which would hear the case only if it so chooses.

Source: *USA Today,* 20 January 1995, 3C.

- Retaliating against employees who file unfair labor practice charges with the NLRB.

- Failing to bargain in good faith.

Members of the NLRB are appointed by the president of the United States and confirmed by the Senate for six-year terms. This manner of selecting members of the board is still the law. The NLRB appeals process is outlined in Exhibit 1. The case described in this exhibit deals with the 1994 Major League Baseball strike.[15]

Taft-Hartley Act of 1947

In 1947, the Wagner Act was amended and retitled the Labor-Management Relations Act, also known as the **Taft-Hartley Act**. The intent of this act was to balance power between unions and employers. As we noted in the previous section, the Wagner Act focused solely on employee rights and employer practices. Taft-Hartley attempted to balance the requirements of unions and employers by placing requirements on unions also. Provisions of this act:

- Prohibit closed shops, which meant that unions could not require union membership as a precondition of employment. Unions *can* require employees to join the union after a waiting period (usually 30 days) if specifically allowed in their contract with management. Such a contract provision is known as a **security agreement** and such workplaces are known as union shops.

- Establish the rights of states to enact **right-to-work laws**. Twenty-one states have subsequently enacted right-to-work laws. These laws ban union shops and "maintenance of membership" requirements in which employees must join unions for specified periods of time regardless of whether they continue to work in the job. Most right-to-work laws are found in sunbelt and southern states.[16]

- Establish unfair labor practice charges that could be filed *against* unions by union members and employers. These practices include coercing members to join unions or coercing employees to select a specific union during elections.

- Prohibit employers from discriminating against employees to influence union membership.

- Stipulate that unions must bargain in good faith with employers.

- Prohibit unions from conducting secondary boycotts, which are directed by a union against an employer with whom the union has no dispute. The objective is to "persuade" or pressure the neutral employer to discontinue business with another employer with whom the union is in dispute.[17]

- Prohibit unions from preventing suppliers from making deliveries.

- Stipulate that unions cannot prevent employees from crossing picket lines to go to work.

- Prohibit unions from "**featherbedding**," or requiring employers to pay for work not performed.

- Establish the Federal Mediation and Conciliation Service (FMCS) which helps unions and management reach agreements and provides mediators who help resolve labor disputes.

- Provide for civil suits against either employer or employee for failure to follow the terms of union contracts.

- Give the NLRB power to enforce cease-and-desist orders through court injunctions if either side engages in unfair labor practices.

- Give management the right to discuss advantages and disadvantages of unions with employees as long as management does not threaten to punish employees who join unions or promise to pay extra benefits to those who do not.

Sample NLRB forms regarding such charges appear in Exhibits 2 and 3.

Landrum-Griffin Act of 1959

The McClelland Committee on Anti-Racketeering uncovered abuses of power, unethical conduct, and corrupt practices in some unions. As a result of these

Exhibit 2   Sample NLRB Form: Charge Against Employer

FORM NLRB-501
(11-94)

FORM EXEMPT UNDER 44 U.S.C. 3512

UNITED STATES OF AMERICA
NATIONAL LABOR RELATIONS BOARD
CHARGE AGAINST EMPLOYER

DO NOT WRITE IN THIS SPACE	
Case	Date Filed

INSTRUCTIONS:
File an original and 4 copies of this charge with NLRB Regional Director for the region in which the alleged unfair labor practice occurred or is occurring.

1. EMPLOYER AGAINST WHOM CHARGE IS BROUGHT

a. Name of Employer	b. Number of Workers Employed

c. Address *(street, city, State, ZIP, Code)*	d. Employer Representative	e. Telephone No.
		Fax No.

f. Type of Establishment *(factory, mine, wholesaler, etc.)*	g. Identify Principal Product or Service

h. The above-named employer has engaged in and is engaging in unfair labor practices within the meaning of Section 8(a), subsections (1) and *(list subsections)* _____ of the National Labor Relations Act. and these unfair labor practices are unfair practices affecting commerce within the meaning of the Act.

2. Basis of the Charge *(set forth a clear and concise statement of the facts constituting the alleged unfair labor practices.)*

By the above and other acts, the above-named employer has interfered with, restrained, and coerced employees in the exercise of the rights guaranteed in Section 7 of the Act.

3. Full name of party filing charge *(if labor organization, give full name, including local name and number)*

4a. Address *(street and number, city, State, and ZIP Code)*	4b. Telephone No.
	Fax No.

5. Full name of national or international labor organization of which it is an affiliate or constituent unit *(to be filled in when charge is filed by a labor organization)*

6. DECLARATION
I declare that I have read the above charge and that the statements are true to the best of my knowledge and belief.

By _____   _____
(Signature of representative or person making charge)   (Title, if any)
Fax No. _____

Address _____
(Telephone No.)   Date

WILLFUL FALSE STATEMENTS ON THIS CHARGE CAN BE PUNISHED BY FINE AND IMPRISONMENT (U.S. CODE, TITLE 18, SECTION 1001)

Source: National Labor Relations Board, Washington, D.C.

findings, Congress enacted the **Landrum-Griffin Act of 1959,** which was designed to regulate how unions and management report their activities. This act is also referred to as the Labor-Management Reporting and Disclosure Act. The provisions against employers relate primarily to the practice of hiring consultants to

Exhibit 3   Sample NLRB Form: Charge Against Union

FORM NLRB-508
(6-90)

FORM EXEMPT UNDER 44 U.S.C. 3512

UNITED STATES OF AMERICA
NATIONAL LABOR RELATIONS BOARD
**CHARGE AGAINST LABOR ORGANIZATION
OR ITS AGENTS**

DO NOT WRITE IN THIS SPACE

Case	Date Filed

INSTRUCTIONS: File an original and 4 copies of this charge and an additional copy for each organization, each local, and each individual named in item 1 with the NLRB Regional Director of the region in which the alleged unfair labor practice occurred or is occurring.

1. LABOR ORGANIZATION OR ITS AGENTS AGAINST WHICH CHARGE IS BROUGHT

a. Name	b. Union Representative to contact

c. Telephone No.	d. Address (street, city, state and ZIP code)

e. The above-named organization(s) or its agents has (have) engaged in and is (are) engaging in unfair labor practices within the meaning of section 8(b), subsection(s) (list subsections) _____ of the National Labor Relations Act, and these unfair labor practices are unfair practices affecting commerce within the meaning of the Act.

2. Basis of the Charge (set forth a clear and concise statement of the facts constituting the alleged unfair labor practices)

3. Name of Employer	4. Telephone No.

5. Location of plant involved (street, city, state and ZIP code)	6. Employer representative to contact

7. Type of establishment (factory, mine, wholesaler, etc.)	8. Identify principal product or service	9. Number of workers employed

10. Full name of party filing charge

11. Address of party filing charge (street, city, state and ZIP code)	12. Telephone No.

13. DECLARATION
I declare that I have read the above charge and that the statements therein are true to the best of my knowledge and belief.

By _____
(signature of representative or person making charge)

_____
(title or office, if any)

Address _____

(Telephone No.)	(date)

WILLFUL FALSE STATEMENTS ON THIS CHARGE CAN BE PUNISHED BY FINE AND IMPRISONMENT (U. S. CODE, TITLE 18, SECTION 1001)
*U.S. GPO: 2000-464-640/29074

Source: National Labor Relations Board, Washington, D.C.

defeat unions in elections or to decertify unions. Under this act, such consultants are required to register and to submit reports to the U.S. Department of Labor.

The Landrum-Griffin Act was also designed to eliminate the influence of corrupt union leaders. Provisions of this act:

- Provide for a "Bill of Rights" for union members that gives members: the right to assemble, nominate candidates, vote, attend meetings, and participate in union business; the right to sue unions in civil court if employee rights are abridged; and the right of individual union members to get copies of collective bargaining agreements.

- Provide for union elections once every five years for national and international unions. Elections are either by secret ballot by members, or by ballots by delegates at union conventions if delegates are elected by secret ballot.

- Require unions to submit bylaws and constitutions to the U.S. Department of Labor.

- Require unions to file for elections within one month of organizational or recognitional picketing and to refrain from such picketing for 12 months if a vote goes against the union.

- Establish the right of unions to picket but not to keep employees from going to work if they want to cross picket lines.

- Regulate financial transactions involving union funds.

While the Landrum-Griffin Act eliminated much of the racketeering that was prevalent in unions at the time, some argue that it did not curtail the influence of organized crime. For instance, in 1985, the President's Commission on Organized Crime noted the substantial influence of organized crime in the Teamsters, Laborer's International, International Longshoreman's, and Hotel Employees and Restaurant Employees unions.[18] Criminal practices this commission noted included the extraction of "insurance" against strikes from some companies, "sweetheart" deals, and improper handling of union membership benefit funds.

The Landrum-Griffin Act also allowed for what has become known as the "financial core" membership in unions. Provisions of U.S. labor relations acts allow unions to require employees to pay dues and initiation fees within a reasonable period after joining the work force. However, unions cannot require employees to participate in union activities. The 3rd U.S. Circuit Court of Appeals upheld this provision by ruling that union members can change their membership to "financial core" and return to work during a strike after notifying the union. Members who choose to cross picket lines are immune from union discipline.[19]

Civil Service Reform Act of 1978

Government employees gained the right to organize and bargain collectively when President Kennedy issued Executive Order 10988 in 1962. Legal rights of government employees were further defined by the passage of the **Civil Service Reform Act of 1978**. This act:

- Established the Federal Labor Relations Authority to administer the act. This independent agency includes the Office of General Counsel, which is empowered to investigate and prosecute charges of unfair labor practices.

- Restricted the issues that management and labor could bargain over.

- Established binding arbitration to resolve disputes.

- Prohibited strikes by government employees.

In 1981, President Reagan reaffirmed the provision that prohibited strikes by government employees. He fired 11,301 federal employees who were members of the Professional Air Traffic Controller's Organization (PATCO) because they went out on strike.

Worker Adjustment and Retraining Notification Act of 1991

The most significant labor relations law passed in a while is the Worker Adjustment and Retraining Notification Act (WARN), which requires employers to give employees 60 days' notice of closings or mass layoffs. WARN covers employers with 100 or more full-time employees or 100 or more full- and part-time employees working a total of at least 4,000 hours per week. WARN can be triggered by the sale of a business if it leads to layoffs. The U.S. Supreme Court has ruled that employers who fail to provide 60 days' warning can be sued by employees for back pay or their union can sue on their behalf. Exactly who is and who is not protected by WARN is debatable as the courts continue to interpret the law and which industries it affects.[20] Exhibit 4 highlights the major acts affecting labor relations.

Union Structures and Organization

There are two principal types of unions: **craft unions** and **industrial unions**. Craft unions represent workers who essentially have the same skills or perform the same tasks. A union consisting solely of plumbers or electricians is a craft union. Industrial unions represent workers in given industries. A union consisting of auto workers, steelworkers, or hotel and restaurant employees is an industrial union.

Typically, unions are organized much like management. Responsibilities of the union stewards closely resemble those of front-line supervisors on the management side. Responsibilities of union business agents or chief stewards resemble those of department managers. Local union presidents are comparable to general managers in stature, while presidents of national or international unions are comparable to CEOs.

Unions differ from management by organizational structure and authority. Distinct relationships exist between local union chapters and national or international unions. Local unions are chartered either by national or international unions, which retain the authority to monitor activities of the locals to ensure that national rules are followed. According to the Landrum-Griffin Act, national unions also have the right to impose trusteeships or replace management in local unions if national guidelines are not met. In return, the national or international unions provide grievance, arbitration, and strike and political representation services to local unions.

Perhaps the most important information that managers should understand about unions is how unions organize workers. In all cases, unions must follow legal provisions for organizing, most of which were enacted by passage of the Taft-Hartley Act in 1947. Exhibit 5 shows a sample NLRB notice that informs employees of their rights regarding unionization and a pending organizing drive.

Exhibit 4   Legislation Affecting Labor Relations

Wagner Act (NLRA, 1935)

Purpose: To diminish labor disputes that burden or obstruct interstate and foreign commerce, and to create a National Labor Relations Board.

Major provisions

1. Established National Labor Relations Board.
2. Outlined unfair labor practices for employers.
3. Established the duty to bargain collectively through chosen representatives.

Taft-Hartley Act (LMRA, 1947)

Purpose: To amend the NLRA, to provide additional facilities for the mediation of labor disputes affecting commerce, and to equalize legal responsibilities of labor organizations and employers.

Major provisions

1. Banned closed shops.
2. Outlined unfair labor practices for unions.
3. Provided states with power to enact right-to-work laws.
4. Established national emergency impasse procedures.
5. Outlawed featherbedding.

Landrum-Griffin Act (1959)

Purpose: To protect employees' rights to organize, choose bargaining representatives, and protect the free flow of commerce by requiring labor organizations, employers, and their officials to follow ethical standards of conduct when administering their organizations.

Major provisions

1. Established bill of rights for union members.
2. Established union election guidelines.
3. Outlawed hot-cargo agreements [that is, agreements stating that a union does not have to handle cargo from an employer with whom the union is having a dispute].
4. Established reporting and disclosure procedures for unions and employers.
5. Established guidelines for trusteeships.

Civil Service Reform (1978)

Purpose: To protect all non-uniformed, nonmanagerial federal service employees and agencies.

1. Allowed employees the right to choose their own bargaining agent.
2. Established the right to bargain on non-economic and non-staffing issues.
3. Required that unresolved grievances be arbitrated.

Worker Adjustment and Retraining Notification Act   (1991)

Requires certain employers to notify their unions of a closure or large-scale layoff 60 days in advance.

Source: Adopted from Marc G. Singer, *Human Resource Management* (Boston: PWS-Kent Publishing Co., 1990), 393.

Exhibit 5   Sample NLRB Notice

NOTICE TO EMPLOYEES

FROM THE
National Labor Relations Board

A PETITION has been filed with this Federal agency seeking an election to determine whether certain employees want to be represented by a union.

The case is being investigated and NO DETERMINATION HAS BEEN MADE AT THIS TIME by the National Labor Relations Board. IF an election is held Notices of Election will be posted giving complete details for voting.

It was suggested that your employer post this notice so the National Labor Relations Board could inform you of your basic rights under the National Labor Relations Act.

YOU HAVE THE RIGHT under Federal Law

- To self-organization
- To form, join, or assist labor organizations
- To bargain collectively through representatives of your own choosing
- To act together for the purposes of collective bargaining or other mutual aid or protection
- To refuse to do any or all of these things unless the union and employer, in a state where such agreements are permitted, enter into a lawful union-security agreement requiring employees to pay periodic dues and initiation fees. Nonmembers who inform the union that they object to the use of their payments for nonrepresentational purposes may be required to pay only their share of the union's costs of representational activities (such as collective bargaining, contract administration, and grievance adjustments).

It is possible that some of you will be voting in an employee representation election as a result of the request for an election having been filed. While NO DETERMINATION HAS BEEN MADE AT THIS TIME, in the event an election is held, the NATIONAL LABOR RELATIONS BOARD wants all eligible voters to be familiar with their rights under the law IF it holds an election.

The Board applies rules that are intended to keep its elections fair and honest and that result in a free choice. If agents of either unions or employers act in such a way as to interfere with your right to a free election, the election can be set aside by the Board. Where appropriate the Board provides other remedies, such as reinstatement for employees fired for exercising their rights, including backpay from the party responsible for their discharge.

NOTE:

The following are examples of conduct that interfere with the rights of employees and may result in the setting aside of the election.

- Threatening loss of jobs or benefits by an employer or a union
- Promising or granting promotions, pay raises, or other benefits to influence an employee's vote by a party capable of carrying out such promises
- An employer firing employees to discourage or encourage union activity or a union causing them to be fired to encourage union activity
- Making campaign speeches to assembled groups of employees on company time within the 24-hour period before the election
- Incitement by either an employer or a union of racial or religious prejudice by inflammatory appeals
- Threatening physical force or violence to employees by a union or an employer to influence their votes

Please be assured that IF AN ELECTION IS HELD every effort will be made to protect your right to a free choice under the law. Improper conduct will not be permitted. All parties are expected to cooperate fully with this Agency in maintaining basic principles of a fair election as required by law. The National Labor Relations Board, as an agency of the United States Government, does not endorse any choice in the election.

NATIONAL LABOR RELATIONS BOARD
an agency of the
UNITED STATES GOVERNMENT

THIS IS AN OFFICIAL GOVERNMENT NOTICE AND MUST NOT BE DEFACED BY ANYONE

FORM NLRB-666 (5-90)

Source: National Labor Relations Board, Washington, D.C.

Organizing Drive

Unions can be certified as the legal representatives of employees in three ways. First, the employer can voluntarily acknowledge that a majority of the employees want the union and begin bargaining with the union. Second, the NLRB can hold a secret ballot election to determine whether a majority of employees want the union. Third, the NLRB can, in rare cases, certify a union without an election.

Union organizers can obtain an NLRB election when they can prove that a minimum of 30 percent of employees at a given business, or within a subgroup of employees, want a specific union to represent them. Union organizers prove this percentage by gathering employee signatures on **authorization cards**. While unions are required to obtain signatures for only 30 percent of employees to begin the election process, unions typically gather signatures for 60 percent to 65 percent of the employees during an **organizing drive** by contacting employees at home or at social gatherings. Unions can stimulate employee interest in signing authorization cards by placing leaflets on cars, distributing leaflets outside work, making telephone calls, and holding meetings. In some cases, unions mount media campaigns to win the public over to their causes and to persuade employees to sign authorization cards.

A 1995 U.S. Supreme Court ruling, *NLRB* v. *Town & Country Electric, Inc.*, also gave a boost to union organizing efforts. According to this ruling, the Court sanctioned the union practice of "salting" or sending union organizers to seek jobs at non-union companies specifically to persuade workers to join a union.[21]

In rare cases, when evidence indicates that an employer's unfair labor practices dramatically changed the outcome of a union organizing vote or election, the NLRB can certify a union without a ballot. Under these circumstances, the NLRB issues a **bargaining order** that certifies a union as the legal representative of the employees. However, this can be done only when the union can prove that at some time before the unfair labor practices, it enjoyed the support of a majority of employees. This can be proven with authorization cards.

Recently, unions have been using a new approach to organizing. This approach involves getting a majority of employees to sign authorization cards and then pressuring the company to "voluntarily" recognize the union without an election. The National Labor Relations Act does not prohibit this tactic, and, although a union might be able to pressure an employer into it, voluntary recognition is never required by law no matter how many employees sign authorization cards. In effect, the union is getting companies to force employees to join unions.[22]

This "card check" procedure has been successful in organizing the workers at Jacobs Field and the Browns Stadium in Cleveland, at the InterContinental Hotel in Cleveland, at the Staples Arena in Los Angeles, in Minneapolis, in Peoria (Illinois), at the MGM Grand Hotel and Casino in Detroit, at the Motor City Casino, and at Neyla's restaurant in Detroit. This tactic has also been used successfully at the Sheraton Premier in Tysons Corner (Va.), in Philadelphia, in Las Vegas, in Hawaii, and in various other locations. Workers in some Subway sandwich shops around the country have even organized using this method.[23]

Elections

The NLRB conducts union representation elections at the workplace during regular work hours. When circumstances prevent on-site elections (a snowstorm, for example), the NLRB may use a mail ballot. A secret ballot is required in all elections. Exhibit 6 shows a sample NLRB secret ballot.

Elections are initiated by the collection of 30 percent of employee signatures in favor of a single union. However, any number of unions can be on the ballot, provided each accumulates at least 10 percent of employees' signatures. When only one union is on the ballot, the only question posed is "Do you want to be

Exhibit 6   Sample Secret Ballot

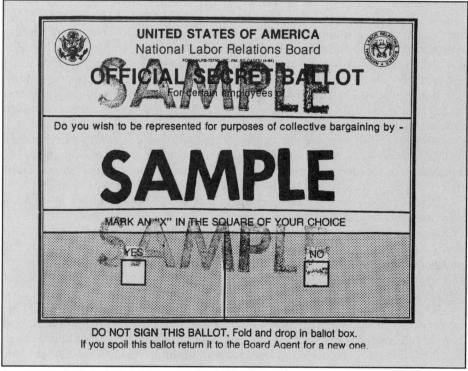

Source: National Labor Relations Board, Washington, D.C.

represented by this union?" A simple majority of the employees who vote determines the outcome. When more than one union is on the ballot, employees must identify which union they prefer. A majority is required for one union to become the workers' legal representative. If no single union receives a majority of the votes, a runoff election is held between the two options that received the most votes.

If a majority of the employees favor a specific union, the NLRB *certifies* the union as the legal representative of the **bargaining unit**, which is the specific group of represented employees. In such a case, the employer is bound by law to bargain in good faith with the union to attempt to reach a contract that details the relationship between employer and employees. Exhibit 7 summarizes the typical steps in a union organizing drive.

Decertification

Employees can also decide to *decertify* a union. Decertification is just the opposite of certification; it means that the employees do *not* want to be represented by their union any longer. Between 1977 and 1989, 120 decertification elections occurred in hotels and 275 in restaurants. Most of these elections occurred at properties organized by HERE. Overall, the unions lost the decertification votes in 70 percent of

Exhibit 7   Typical Steps in a Union Organizing Drive

```
                        ┌─────────────────┐
                        │ Employees meet  │
                        │   with union    │
                        └─────────────────┘

┌──────────────────┐                              ┌──────────────────┐
│ Look for evidence │                             │     Look for      │
│ of poor management│     ┌─────────────────┐     │  natural leaders  │
└──────────────────┘      │ Union organizers│     └──────────────────┘
                          │  join the drive │
┌──────────────────┐      └─────────────────┘     ┌──────────────────┐
│   Recruit more    │                             │    Talk with      │
│    employees      │                             │ fired employees   │
└──────────────────┘                              └──────────────────┘

                                                  ┌──────────────────┐
                                                  │ Collect data on   │
┌──────────────────┐                              │ company finances, │
│  Collect names of │     ┌─────────────────┐     │organizational     │
│  other employees  │     │  Employees help │     │charts, wages &    │
└──────────────────┘      │ union organizers│     │ benefits, etc.    │
                          └─────────────────┘     └──────────────────┘
┌──────────────────┐                              ┌──────────────────┐
│    Circulate      │                             │ Get signatures on │
│ printed materials │                             │authorization cards│
└──────────────────┘                              └──────────────────┘

              ┌──────────────────────────────────┐
              │ With 30% of employees signed up,  │
              │ union files petition for election │
              └──────────────────────────────────┘

              ┌──────────────────────────────────┐
              │ NLRB hearing on petition determines│
              │ bargaining unit and voter eligibility│
              └──────────────────────────────────┘

              ┌──────────────────────────────────┐
              │          Active union             │
              │        campaign begins            │
              └──────────────────────────────────┘

              ┌──────────────────────────────────┐
              │            Election               │
              └──────────────────────────────────┘

 Union defeated                              Union elected

┌──────────────────┐                       ┌──────────────────┐
│  No petition refile│                      │ Negotiations between│
│    for 1 year     │                       │ employer and union on│
└──────────────────┘                       │collective bargaining │
                                           │     agreement        │
                                           └──────────────────┘
```

Source: David Wheelhouse, *Managing Human Resources in the Hospitality Industry* (Lansing, Mich.: Educational Institute of the American Hotel & Lodging Association, 1989), 409.

the hotel elections and 83 percent of the restaurant elections.[24] Roughly the same trends occurred in other industries.

Decertification elections are called in the same way as certification elections. At least 30 percent of represented employees must express an interest in decertifying the union. However, a decertification vote cannot be called for 12 months after the original certification or during the term of a labor contract. To call for a decertification vote, a decertification petition must be filed with the NLRB, but the employer is not permitted to initiate or influence the process. A sample petition used for decertification and other actions appears in Exhibit 8.

Employer Strategies

The Wagner Act prevents employers from interfering with union organizing campaigns by coercing or restraining employees; employees have the right to join unions free of the employer's interference. Any action by management to take this right can be considered an unfair labor practice. Discharging union sympathizers, threatening to close operations, and offering extra benefits to employees who vote against unionization are all unfair practices, as is discriminating against employees in hiring or promotion decisions. Ensuring before they are hired that applicants will vote against unionization is an unfair labor practice as well.

Employers have found proactive and reactive measures to be useful tools in avoiding unionization. Proactive measures eliminate the need for unions. When employers establish fair pay policies, good working conditions, two-way communication, fair grievance procedures, and other good employer-employee practices, unions may have little to offer employees.

However, not all companies implement such policies; some companies take reactive measures. They might hire labor attorneys who specialize in organization and election campaigning, or consultants who specialize in training managers in effective resistance methods. Campaigns generated by outside consultants and attorneys typically emphasize the hardships that occur during strikes. They emphasize the rewards of current benefits and how employee-management relationships can change when a union takes over. Both proactive and reactive measures can accomplish desired results.

The Future of Unions

It is difficult to say whether or not unions will remain viable. Evidence supports both sides of the argument. A 1986 poll by the *Washington Post* showed that 56 percent of the Americans polled nationwide thought that employees were better off belonging to a union than not.[25] This poll also reported that about half (48 percent) of the participants believed that the United States still needs unions, although 61 percent felt that union leaders were out of touch with their membership. By 1994, only 41 percent of the U.S. population polled responded that they were favorably inclined toward unions, while 45 percent had unfavorable opinions.[26] While Americans still believe in unionism as an ideal, they tend to hold a negative view of union management and performance.

One bellwether of future union membership might be found in the results of studies of how teenagers view unions. In these studies, only about 35 percent of the teenagers support the union concept. Most of their support comes from male participants: females show little support.[27]

The assumption by management that unions are dead or that employees are no longer interested in unions could easily lead to unionization, both in the

Exhibit 8   Sample NLRB Petition

FORM NLRB-502 (5-85)	UNITED STATES GOVERNMENT	FORM EXEMPT UNDER 44 U.S.C. 3512

NATIONAL LABOR RELATIONS BOARD

PETITION

DO NOT WRITE IN THIS SPACE

Case No.	Date Filed

INSTRUCTIONS: Submit an original and 4 copies of this Petition to the NLRB Regional Office in the Region in which the employer concerned is located. If more space is required for any one item, attach additional sheets, numbering item accordingly.

The Petitioner alleges that the following circumstances exist and requests that the National Labor Relations Board proceed under its proper authority pursuant to Section 9 of the National Labor Relations Act.

1. PURPOSE OF THIS PETITION (If box RC, RM, or RD is checked and a charge under Section 8(b)(7) of the Act has been filed involving the Employer named herein, the statement following the description of the type of petition shall be deemed made.)   **(Check One)**

☐ **RC-CERTIFICATION OF REPRESENTATIVE** - A substantial number of employees wish to be represented for purposes of collective bargaining by Petitioner and Petitioner desires to be certified as representative of the employees.

☐ **RM-REPRESENTATION (EMPLOYER PETITION)** - One or more individuals or labor organizations have presented a claim to Petitioner to be recognized as the representative of employees of Petitioner.

☐ **RD-DECERTIFICATION** - A substantial number of employees assert that the certified or currently recognized bargaining representative is no longer their representative.

☐ **UD-WITHDRAWAL OF UNION SHOP AUTHORITY** - Thirty percent (30%) or more of employees in a bargaining unit covered by an agreement between their employer and a labor organization desire that such authority be rescinded.

☐ **UC-UNIT CLARIFICATION** - A labor organization is currently recognized by Employer, but Petitioner seeks clarification of placement of certain employees: (Check one)   ☐ In unit not previously certified.   ☐ In unit previously certified in Case No. _____

☐ **AC-AMENDMENT OF CERTIFICATION** - Petitioner seeks amendment of certification issued in Case No. _____ Attach statement describing the specific amendment sought.

2. Name of Employer	Employer Representative to contact	Telephone Number

3. Address(es) of Establishment(s) involved (Street and number, city, State, ZIP code)

4a. Type of Establishment (Factory, mine, wholesaler, etc.)	4b. Identify principal product or service

5. Unit Involved (In UC petition, describe **present** bargaining unit and attach description of proposed clarification.)	6a. Number of Employees in Unit:
Included	Present
	Proposed (By UC/AC)
Excluded	6b. Is this petition supported by 30% or more of the employees in the unit? * ___ Yes ___No *Not applicable in RM, UC, and AC

(If you have checked box RC in 1 above, check and complete EITHER item 7a or 7b, whichever is applicable.)

7a.☐ Request for recognition as Bargaining Representative was made on (Date) _____ and Employer declined recognition on or about (Date) _____ (If no reply received, so state).

7b.☐ Petitioner is currently recognized as Bargaining Representative and desires certification under the Act.

8. Name of Recognized or Certified Bargaining Agent (If none, so state)	Affiliation
Address and Telephone Number	Date of Recognition or Certification

9. Expiration Date of Current Contract, If any (Month, Day, Year)	10. If you have checked box UD in 1 above, show here the date of execution of agreement granting union shop (Month, Day, and Year)

11a. Is there now a strike or picketing at the Employer's establishment(s) Involved? Yes ___ No ___	11b. If so, approximately how many employees are participating?

11c. The Employer has been picketed by or on behalf of (Insert Name) _____, a labor organization, of (Insert Address) _____ Since (Month, Day, Year) _____

12. Organizations or individuals other than Petitioner (and other than those named in items 8 and 11c), which have claimed recognition as representatives and other organizations and individuals known to have a representative interest in any employees in unit described in item 5 above. (If none, so state)

Name	Affilation	Address	Date of Claim (Required only if Petition is filed by Employer)

I declare that I have read the above petition and that the statements are true to the best of my knowledge and belief.

_____
(Name of Petitioner and Affilation, if any)

By _____   _____
   (Signature of Representative or person filing petition)   (Title, if any)

Address _____   _____
   (Street and number, city, State, and ZIP Code)   (Telephone Number)

WILLFUL FALSE STATEMENTS ON THIS PETITION CAN BE PUNISHED BY FINE AND IMPRISONMENT (U. S. CODE, TITLE 18, SECTION 1001)

Source: National Labor Relations Board, Washington, D.C.

hospitality industry and elsewhere. These assumptions could cause management to ignore employee needs or to fail to develop proactive approaches to preventing unionization. Both alternatives open the door to unionization.

Unions have succeeded in organizing 7.1 million public employees in the United States since they were first permitted to do so in 1962. Unions today are also focusing on service industries in an attempt to gain new members. Information processing, communications, and computer manufacturing have all been recent targets of union organizing campaigns.[28] In 2001, the AFL-CIO reported organizing victories in the fields of home health aides, textile workers, graduate student employees, and private- and public-sector workers.[29] Unions that focus on hotel and restaurant employees have also begun aggressive campaigns. For instance, HERE has merged with UNITE and established several well-trained and well-financed project teams whose long-term goal is to establish effective strategic approaches to organizing.[30]

Central Florida is one of the areas targeted for union organizing activities. Because Florida is a right-to-work state, this market has traditionally been non-union. However, hotels within the Disney complex are unionized. Based on its success with Disney, the International Union of Operating Engineers targeted other area hotels. The union claims that employees in central Florida hotels are underpaid and mistreated. Other experts confirmed in 1991 that unionization efforts in central Florida were growing and that unions there were likely to succeed.[31] But while some hotel unions in Florida and other states were able to organize thousands of new members in the 1990s, their gains were almost entirely erased when the September 11 terrorist attacks resulted in thousands of job losses in the industry. Union organization efforts are likely to continue if not increase in the industry, but the percentage of hospitality employees represented by unions has not changed significantly from what it was 20 years ago.

Unions have gained some public favor by supporting social issues in some states. In San Francisco, for instance, HERE advocated that hotel developers help provide affordable housing to people displaced or otherwise affected by a new hotel development. The union claimed that new hotels drove up rents to levels unaffordable to people with low incomes. The union argued that developers should pay a fee to help offset the costs sustained by these individuals. Nikko Hotels, which opened a San Francisco property in October 1987, paid $778,562 into a housing fund for this purpose in 1988. The union submitted a plan to the San Francisco Planning Commission calling for a developer to pay fees of $1,400 per room.[32] In another case, HERE indicated that it would resort to militant tactics to help secure a prevailing wage and benefits policy for the Los Angeles Community Redevelopment project in downtown Los Angeles.[33] In 2000, HERE's membership topped 300,000, but by 2004 it was back down to 250,000.[34]

The overall tactics employed by unions to increase their membership have changed in the last decade or so, and there is evidence that the approach works. The AFL-CIO and most other unions now advocate a four-pronged approach that includes political involvement, salting, flooding the community, and corporate campaigns. Political involvement entails direct support of candidates at all levels who promise to help labor. Salting, or sending trained organizers into a company to promote unionism, has been very successful in many areas because the well-trained "salts" are much better at organizing than are regular employees. Community flooding sends lots of organizers into a community to target a particular business. Corporate campaigns include pressuring a company's financial institution and creditors to withhold loans or to demand payments, enlisting the support of local political and community groups, picketing the homes of the company's board of directors, initiating stock proxy challenges, sending letters to the editors of local papers, and filing charges with investigative or administrative agencies such as OSHA, the Department of Labor, and the NLRB. These corporate attacks are so all-consuming that companies often are hard pressed to defend themselves on so many fronts at once.[35]

Unions are still strong in the hospitality industry in certain geographic areas. Orlando, as we noted, has many union properties today, as do New York and San Francisco. However, Las Vegas, known to some as "the last great union town in America," may be the strongest, despite recent attempts by MGM Grand and others to break the union. On Memorial Day in 1994 it looked as though the dispute between the MGM Grand and Culinary Workers Local 226 might erupt into violence as 17,000 strikers demonstrated against MGM Grand's attempts to open with non-union labor. Since then, Local 226 has won unprecedented contracts guaranteeing employer neutrality and immediate union recognition if a majority of workers signed union cards. The first agreement was signed by Steve Wynn, owner of The Mirage, Treasure Island, and The Golden Nugget.[36]

Less than 10 percent of the private sector work force is currently organized, but experts disagree on whether that number will rise or fall. This does not mean unions are dead. That nearly 10 percent, in fact, may include more union members (in absolute numbers) than at the pre-World War II height of union power because of the increased number of workers overall. Union composition is changing, to be sure. Today, over half of union members are women, mostly from clerical and professional service industries that are likely to experience significant growth in the future.[37]

Signs of union strength include a dispute at the Radisson Hotel in Minneapolis that lasted eight years; a boycott of the New Otani Hotel and Garden in Los Angeles; and the mass demonstrations that occurred in Las Vegas when the MGM Grand announced it would be a non-union property.

In fact, the 50,000-member Culinary Workers Union, Local 226 in Las Vegas, is now the fastest growing union in the country. Union membership in hotels and restaurants in Las Vegas rose by 20,000 workers between 1990 and 2000. Included in that increase were 4,300 new workers at Bellagio Hotel and Casino.[37] This growth has helped Las Vegas replace Detroit as the quintessential union city in the United States. The union is so strong in Las Vegas that in 1997 a shop steward ran for the Nevada State Senate on a union-supported platform, garnered 64 percent of the overall vote, and unseated an incumbent Republican senator.[38]

While the percentage of the work force that is unionized has fallen over the years, the overall strength of unions may not be declining. New membership tactics have succeeded in gaining some public support and new members in recent years. As the unions become more white collar, public opinion about their ties to crime also appears to be changing. As a result, the public may approve of unions more in the future. Union membership growth in 1999 was the largest in 21 years, rising from 16.21 million to 16.48 million, an increase of 265,000, according to statistics gathered by the United States Bureau of Labor Standards. The percentage of United States workers in unions (public and private sector combined) remained steady at 13.9 percent, reversing a downward trend. Based on this and other evidence, unions are clearly still a significant force.

Endnotes

1. For more information on why employees join unions see, Jeanne M. Brett, "Why Employees Want Unions," *Organizational Dynamics* (Spring 1980): 47–59; W. Clay Hamner and Frank J. Smith, "Work Attitudes as Predictors of Unionization Activity," *Journal of Applied Psychology* 63 (August 1978): 415–421; and Daniel G. Gallagher and Charles Greer, "Determinants of Unionism: A Review of the Literature," in *Research in Personnel and Human Resources Management* 4, edited by Kendrith M. Rowland and Gerald R. Ferris (Greenwich, Conn.: JAI Press, 1986): 269–306.

2. www.dol.gov. U.S. Department of Labor homepage.

3. George J. Church, "Unions Arise," *Time,* 13 June 1994, 56–59.

4. Statistics used in this paragraph are drawn primarily from several articles that appeared in *Business Week* on May 16, 1988, which reflected the current and historical status of unions in the United States.

5. http://www.aflcio.org. AFL-CIO Web site.

6. Marc Levinson, "It's Hip To Be Union," *Newsweek,* 8 July 1996, 44–46.

7. *The Changing Situation of Workers and Their Unions: A Report by the AFL-CIO Committee on the Evolution of Work* (Washington, D.C.: AFL-CIO, February 1985): 15.

8. Charles Muhl, "Union Members in 1994," *Compensation & Working Conditions* 47 (February 1995): 14–20.

9. www.hereunion.org. Hotel Employees and Restaurant Employees Union.

10. Suzanne K. Murrmann and Kent F. Murrmann, "Union Membership Trends and Organizing Activities in the Hotel and Restaurant Industries," *Hospitality Research Journal* 14 (1990): 491. Other unions that represent smaller numbers of hotel and restaurant workers include the International Brotherhood of Teamsters, the International Union of Operating Engineers, Service Employees International Union, United Food and Commercial Workers, and the Retail Wholesale and Department Store Union.

11. Murrmann and Murrmann: 503.

12. Murrmann and Murrmann: 494.

13. "Unions Smart to Invest in Hotel Projects," *Philadelphia Business Journal,* 3 December 1999, 50.

14. Kathy Seal, "Union Pension Funds Fill Financing Void for Hotel Projects," *Hotel & Motel Management,* 6 March 2000, 15–16.

15. *USA Today,* 20 January 1995, 30.

16. States that have passed right-to-work laws include: Alabama, Arizona, Arkansas, Florida, Georgia, Idaho, Iowa, Kansas, Louisiana, Mississippi, Nebraska, Nevada, North Carolina, North Dakota, South Carolina, South Dakota, Tennessee, Texas, Virginia, Wyoming, and Utah.

17. Brent Zepke, *Labor Law* (Totowa, N. J.: Littlefield, Adams & Co., 1977), 125.

18. "Trade Unions: The Usual Suspects," *The Economist,* 4 May 1985, 29.

19. William E. Lissy, "Election of 'Financial Core' Union Membership," *Supervision* 51 (September 1990): 22–23.

20. Gillian Flynn, "The Unions' Power to Sue Is Growing," *Personnel Journal* 75 (September 1996): 135–138.

21. Constance B. DiCesare, "Salting," *Monthly Labor Review* 119 (April 1996): 29–30.

22. D. V. Yager, "Corporate Companies and Card Checks: Creating the Company Unions of the Twenty-First Century," *Employee Relations Law Journal* 24, no. 4 (1998): 21–56.

23. www.hereunion.org/newsinfo/orgvictory/

24. Murrmann and Murrmann: 500.

25. "Washington Post Poll," *Washington Post*, 13 September 1987, 1.

26. "Union Members: Demographic Change, Differences," *Campaigns and Elections* 15 (September 1994): 55–57.

27. Brian Heshizer, "Gender Differences in the Attitudes of Teenagers Toward Unions," *Mid-American Journal of Business* 2, no. 2 (1997): 47–56.

28. "Unions Today: New Tactics to Tackle Tough Times," *The Bureau of National Affairs* (Washington, D.C.: The Bureau of National Affairs, Inc., 1985): 1.

29. www.aflcio.org

30. Murrmann and Murrmann: 503.

31. Russell Shaw, "Unions Eye Central Florida Hotels," *Hotel & Motel Management,* 10 June 1991: 2, 66.

32. Kathy Seal, "Union Wants Input from New Hotels for Housing Fund," *Hotel & Motel Management,* 10 June 1991, 2, 46.

33. Kathy Seal, "Wage Policy Delays Ritz-Carlton Project for Downtown L.A.," *Hotel & Motel Management,* 29 April 1991, 3, 22.

34. www.hereunion.com

35. John E. Lynchecki and John M. McDermott, "Unions Employ New Growth Strategies," *HR Focus* 73 (September 1996): 22–24.

36. Mike Davis, "Armageddon at the Emerald City: Local 226 *vs.* MGM Grand," *The Nation,* 11 July 1994, 46–51.

37. www.hereunion.org

38. Diane E. Lewis, "Hotel Union Gains Clout for Labor Movement in Las Vegas," *The Boston Globe*, 7 October 1999.

🔑 Key Terms

authorization cards—Petitions or individual cards signed by employees that call for union recognition and/or certification elections.

bargain in good faith—A practice mandated by the Wagner Act of 1935 whereby management and unions must attempt to reach agreement on disputed issues through negotiation but are not required to reach an agreement.

bargaining order—An order issued by the National Labor Relations Board that certifies a specific union to represent employees. The order occurs only when the NLRB has evidence that unfair labor practices during the election process influenced the outcome of the vote.

bargaining unit—The specific group of employees represented by a union, as determined by the National Labor Relations Board.

Civil Service Reform Act of 1978—Legislation that established the right of federal employees to select their own bargaining agents, and that established the policy for resolving disputes through arbitration.

craft union—Union that represents workers who have essentially the same skills or who perform the same tasks, for example, plumbers or electricians.

decertification—The process that employees can use when they no longer want to be represented by a specific union.

featherbedding—A union practice of requiring employers to hire more workers than are needed, or to limit production so that workers are paid for full shifts but only work partial shifts. Requiring payment for work not done is prohibited by the Taft-Hartley Act of 1947.

industrial union—Union that represents workers in specific industries such as the automobile or hospitality industry.

Landrum-Griffin Act of 1959—Legislation that outlined legal responsibilities of unions and forced unions to follow specific election procedures and ethical standards. Sometimes called the "Bill of Rights" for union members.

National Labor Relations Board—Independent federal agency created by the Wagner Act of 1935 to administer and enforce the act. This agency supervises management-union relationships and is empowered to levy fines, order imprisonment, and issue court orders and injunctions against parties that engage in unfair labor practices.

organizing drive—A period in which union organizers collect signatures of employees on authorization cards in an attempt to force a union election.

right-to-work law—Legislation passed by some states to allow each employee of a unionized company to choose to join the union or not.

security agreement—A policy in a union contract with management that allows a union to require employees to join the union after a waiting period (usually 30 days).

Taft-Hartley Act of 1947—Legislation that banned closed shops, outlined unfair labor practices for unions, empowered states to choose to enact right-to-work laws, outlawed featherbedding, and established national emergency impasse procedures. Amended the Wagner Act of 1935.

unfair labor practices—Labor practices specifically prohibited by federal and state laws; in particular, those laws regarding either collective bargaining or application of company regulations.

union certification—Election process that identifies a single union as the legal representative of the employees.

Wagner Act of 1935—Legislation that outlined the responsibility of management to bargain collectively with unions, and that defined unfair labor practices for management. Also called the National Labor Relations Act.

Worker Adjustment and Retraining Act of 1991—Law that requires some employers to provide 60 days' advance warning of layoffs or business closures.

Review Questions

1. What are the main provisions of the Wagner Act?

2. What are the main provisions of the Taft-Hartley Act?

3. What are the main provisions of the Landrum-Griffin Act?

4. What are the main provisions of the Civil Service Reform Act?

5. Why were the PATCO strikers legally fired by President Reagan in 1981?

6. What are the differences between craft unions and industrial unions?

7. What percentage of the employees in a company must sign authorization cards before a union certification election can be called?

8. What are the steps in the union decertification process?

9. What are some of the demographic reasons that unions have not been very successful in organizing hotel and restaurant employees to date?

10. What types of activities have unions engaged in recently to help improve their public image?

Internet Sites

For more information, visit the following Internet sites. Remember that Internet addresses can change without notice. If the site is no longer there, you can use a search engine to look for additional sites.

AFL-CIO News
www.aflcio.org/

Information on WARN
www.doleta.gov/programs/factsht/warn.htm

LaborNet
www.labornet.org/

National Labor Relations Board
www.nlrb.gov

Library of Congress
www.loc.gov/

The Internet provides excellent coverage of labor unions in countries throughout the world. Search "labor unions" and browse the displayed links for contacts.

Mini-Case Study

You heard that some employees in your hotel have been trying to persuade others to join them in promoting a union. To find out for yourself, you eavesdrop on employee conversations during a company-sponsored softball game. In doing so, you hear three employees trying to talk others into signing authorization cards for a union election.

The next morning at work, you call the three employees you heard talking about the union into your office. You confront them directly. Two of the employees admit that they were trying to talk others into joining a union; the third denies the charge. To eliminate this union "threat," you reduce all three employees to part-time jobs and start scheduling them for weekends only. You also call an all-employee meeting in which you openly discuss what you have heard. You tell employees that if they refrain from signing authorization cards you will grant them an extra holiday per year. You also promise to increase their health insurance coverage. Two weeks later, a representative from the National Labor Relations Board appears in your office and charges you with unfair labor practices. Are you guilty? Why or why not?

Chapter 11 Outline

Competencies

1. Identify mandatory, voluntary, and illegal collective bargaining issues and common economic and non-economic reasons behind bargaining. (pp. 367–370)

2. Describe how managers should prepare for collective bargaining, choose a negotiation team, and select a bargaining strategy. (pp. 370–374)

3. Differentiate between mediation and arbitration and explain how they may affect negotiations. (pp. 374–375)

4. Describe the role of strikes in collective bargaining, define various types of strikes, and outline possible management responses to strikes. (pp. 375–377)

5. Identify major sources of grievances, describe typical grievance procedures, and outline how to prevent grievances at union properties. (pp. 377–383)

6. Explain how non-union properties can address grievance procedures. (p. 384)

11

Negotiation and Collective Bargaining

This chapter was co-authored by William Werner, J.D.,
University of Nevada, Las Vegas.

Labor legislation such as the Wagner and Taft-Hartley Acts requires both management and unions to bargain in good faith over "mandatory" bargaining subjects. Failure to bargain in good faith over mandatory issues can result in an unfair labor practice charge. It is important to keep in mind, however, that an employer can fulfill its duty to bargain in good faith without ever agreeing with the union on any subject.

By definition, mandatory bargaining subjects are those that directly affect the employment relationship: wages, benefits, work rules, hiring and firing, and working conditions. Only mandatory issues require bargaining. Other issues can be either **voluntary bargaining issues** or **illegal bargaining issues**. This chapter will elaborate on these and other issues involved in collective bargaining. It will also examine strategies for negotiating agreements between management and unions.

Issues in Bargaining

Federal regulations for **collective bargaining**—the negotiation process between unions and management during which contracts are developed—originated during a time when strikes were common in the United States. The intent of the regulations was to encourage or to force management and unions to hash out their differences at the bargaining table, thereby reducing the number and duration of crippling strikes in the nation.

The National Labor Relations Act of 1935 (the Wagner Act) declared it unfair labor practice for an employer to refuse to bargain with employee-selected representatives. The act created the National Labor Relations Board (NLRB) to administer its provisions. In 1947, the act was amended and retitled the Labor-Management Relations Act, also known as the Taft-Hartley Act. This act continues to be the fundamental labor law regarding union organizing and collective bargaining in the United States.

The NLRB established specific guidelines based on the Taft-Hartley Act for determining whether each side at the bargaining table bargains in good faith. Under these guidelines, either side can be found guilty of failing to bargain in good faith if they: (1) fail to provide relevant information; (2) surface bargain (just go through the motions without any intent of settlement); or (3) refuse to compromise at the outset of negotiations (take a "take it or leave it" stance). The previous bargaining history of both sides also helps determine failure to bargain in good faith.[1]

Collective bargaining is a complex process that can be best understood through actual experience. Some simulation exercises can approach real-life situations that managers face in bargaining; many educators feel this is good practice for the real thing.[2]

Managers with experience in collective bargaining note that there are three types of issues typical to bargaining: mandatory, voluntary, and illegal. Only mandatory issues require management and unions to bargain in good faith. Either side can decide not to bargain over voluntary issues if they wish. Both sides are prohibited from bargaining over illegal issues.

An **impasse** can be declared if both sides maintain a consistent effort to bargain in good faith, but cannot reach agreement. When an impasse occurs, some method of mediation or arbitration may be used, but the employer then gains the option to unilaterally implement its last best offer. Impasses can be declared only over mandatory issues.

Mandatory Issues

Mandatory bargaining issues include issues that relate directly to the relationship between employer and employee. Labor legislation, however, does not provide an exclusive or exhaustive list of what constitutes mandatory bargaining issues. The question of whether an issue is mandatory is sometimes litigated by one party. This means that new issues may be declared mandatory by a court decision. The most common mandatory issues include:

- Wages
- Hours of work
- Incentive pay
- Overtime
- Employee layoffs and recalls
- Union security clauses
- Management rights clauses
- Grievance procedures
- Seniority
- Safety
- Benefits (insurance, time off, and so on)
- Retirement (stock options, pension plans, and profit-sharing)
- No-strike clauses
- Drug testing

Voluntary Issues

Voluntary bargaining issues can be discussed if both sides want to do so. These issues are sometimes called permissive bargaining issues. Neither side is required by law to discuss these issues. Some voluntary bargaining issues are:

- Supervisory compensation
- Supervisory discipline
- Performance bonds for union or management
- Contract ratification process
- Company price or product issues

Illegal Issues

During the process of collective bargaining, both sides are restricted from bringing illegal, or prohibited, issues to the bargaining table. Such issues include:

- Any practice that violates Equal Employment Opportunity laws (discriminatory hiring or promotion practices, for instance)
- Closed-shop agreements
- Featherbedding
- Union or agency shop clauses in states with right-to-work laws

Reasons Behind Bargaining

Collective bargaining negotiations occur for both economic and non-economic reasons. When bargaining occurs for economic reasons, it generally focuses on wages or benefits. These areas are the source of most disagreements between unions and management. Economic reasons for bargaining include:

- Wages
- Pay ranges for different jobs
- Management discretion in pay ranges
- Wage adjustments due to inflation (cost-of-living increases, back pay, raises)
- Profit sharing
- Bonus plans
- Pensions
- Insurance coverage and benefits
- Holidays, vacations, personal days, or sick pay

Unions sometimes want management to clarify specific pay issues. Unions want pay ranges standardized to eliminate management discretion. Unions also want the terms of raises clearly spelled out. For instance, unions want management to specify in a contract how raises are awarded: up front, at the end of a year, or evenly throughout the year.

Recently, non-economic issues have become more important to both unions and management. Management may want **management rights clauses** in contracts to ensure that management has the right to control the types of products and services the company makes or delivers. These clauses also ensure that management has the right to determine the method and implementation of employee discipline. Unions want contracts to include **just cause clauses**. These clauses limit management's right to discipline or discharge employees. Just cause clauses spell out specific forms of discipline that can be meted out for breaking specific company rules or regulations. In addition, just cause clauses specify reasons for which employees can be fired.

Among the non-economic issues important to both union and management are:

- Quality of work life issues (such as workplace safety, training, benefit packages, educational opportunities, and child care)

- Union security (primarily seniority and "just cause" vs. "management rights" to discharge and discipline)

- Work rules (rules that specifically outline how work will be done)

- Size of work crew (number of employees assigned to each task)

- Types of work that can and cannot be done by various employee groups (assurance that management does not assign union work to non-union employees or eliminate employee groups by combining their jobs with those of other employees)

- Grievance and arbitration procedures (the process by which employees can complain about work issues and resolve them through mandatory arbitration)

Preparing for Negotiation

Most of the progress in collective bargaining occurs during the primary bargaining stage of negotiations. At this point, both sides are more likely to make concessions, to debate issues openly, and to attempt to resolve their disputes without a strike. Both sides should avoid threatening behavior and refrain from issuing ultimatums. Union and management representatives should carefully discuss and develop proposals and counterproposals. It is critical to make progress during the primary bargaining stage, since both sides can become more entrenched and steadfast in their positions as negotiations continue, making a final resolution less likely.

Successful negotiations depend on complete preparation. They also depend on management's complete understanding of the current contract, pending issues, and why these issues are important to the union members. To be effective during this early stage of negotiation, management should carefully prepare its arguments in advance and study the potential impacts of the union's demands.

In preparing for negotiations, management should establish objectives for bargaining. Management should also prepare several proposals and set limits for concessions. Most experts suggest that management thoroughly analyze employee demographics, grievances filed during the current contract period, and the wages and benefits offered by the company and its competitors.

Preparations for bargaining usually begin months or even years before the opening of negotiations. In fact, many experts believe that management should begin preparing for the next collective bargaining sessions immediately after a contract is approved.

Some experts suggest that there are several critical activities involved in successfully preparing for collective bargaining negotiations. Management should:[3]

- Identify management objectives and approve the negotiation plan.

- Conduct an audit and analysis of grievances filed under the existing contract.

- Compare the contract to other contracts in the industry and review union demands in previous negotiations.

- Analyze the wages and benefits paid by others in the industry and community.

- Analyze the compensation packages paid by its own operation.

- Designate a bargaining team.

- Designate a coordinating committee to develop bargaining guidelines.

- Establish communication with other employers in the industry or with employees in related industries to identify any necessary replacement workers.

- Develop a contingency plan for a possible impasse in negotiations.

- Develop a communications plan to inform workers of the progress of contract negotiations.

- Analyze the contract to determine issues to discuss and identify issues for the union to present for discussion.

- Refine the bargaining strategy.

- Establish bargaining guidelines for top management approval.

- Finalize the plan in writing.

- Brief directors on the entire preparation plan.

Choosing a Negotiation Team

The union negotiation team usually consists of the business agent, some employees and stewards, a lead negotiator, and an officer of the local union. The management negotiation team typically consists of the head of the human resources department, an attorney, and often a consultant trained in collective bargaining negotiations. The management team should include experts skilled in written and oral communications, labor and benefit cost analysis, and estimating. The team should also include a member who is well-informed on the legal issues

Exhibit 1   Preparing for Negotiation

Negotiation Checklist

A systematic way to ensure you are well-prepared before your next negotiation.

☑ *Item accomplished*

    A.   About You
☐ 1.   What is your overall goal?
☐ 2.   What are the issues?
☐ 3.   How important is each issue to you?
        Develop a scoring system for evaluating offers:

     ☐ (a)   List all of the issues of importance from step 2.
     ☐ (b)   Rank order of all the issues.
     ☐ (c)   Assign points to all the issues (assign weighted values based on a total of 100 points).
     ☐ (d)   List the range of possible settlements for each issue. Your assessments of realistic, low, and high expectations should be grounded in industry norms and your best-case expectation.
     ☐ (e)   Assign points to the possible outcomes that you identified for each issue.
     ☐ (f)   Double-check the accuracy of your scoring system.
     ☐ (g)   Use the scoring system to evaluate any offer that is on the table.
☐ 4.   What is your "best alternative to negotiated agreement" (BATNA)?
☐ 5.   What is your resistance point (i.e., the worst agreement you are willing to accept before ending negotiations)? If your BATNA is vague, consider identifying the minimum terms you can possibly accept and beyond which you must recess to gather more information.

    B.   About the Other Side
☐ 1.   How important is each issue to them (plus any new issues they added)?
☐ 2.   What is their best alternative to negotiated agreement?
☐ 3.   What is their resistance point?
☐ 4.   Based on questions B.1, B.2, and B.3, what is your target?

    C.   The Situation
☐ 1.   What deadlines exist? Who is more impatient?
☐ 2.   What fairness norms or reference points apply?
☐ 3.   What topics or questions do you want to avoid? How will you respond if they ask anyway?

    D.   The Relationship Between the Parties
☐ 1.   Will negotiations be repetitive? If so, what are the future consequences of each strategy, tactic, or action you are considering?
☐ 2.   ☐ (a) Can you trust the other party? What do you know about them?
          ☐ (b) Does the other party trust you?
☐ 3.   What do you know of the other party's styles and tactics?
☐ 4.   What are the limits to the other party's authority?
☐ 5.   Consult in advance with the other party about the agenda.

Source: Tony Simons and Thomas M. Tripp, "The Negotiation Checklist: How to Win the Battle Before It Begins," *Cornell Hotel and Restaurant Administration Quarterly* 38 (1997): 14–23.

involved in labor-relations negotiations to ensure that the employer does not commit unfair labor practices during negotiations.

Each side designates a chief negotiator. The chief negotiator has the final authority during negotiations. While the management negotiator should have the authority to accept or reject binding agreements, the chief negotiator for the union does not have this authority.

Confidentiality is important during collective bargaining negotiations. Issues discussed in the negotiating room should remain private until it is appropriate to discuss them publicly. As a result, the size of the team becomes an issue; it should be small enough to protect confidentiality.

Negotiation Strategies

Bargaining can take several forms during negotiations. The form bargaining takes influences the strategy of the bargaining team.[4]

Distributive Bargaining

Distributive bargaining occurs when management and the union conflict over a major issue. Often, each side presents a proposal in which one side "wins" and one side "loses." Proposals with such clear win-lose outcomes are said to be zero-sum issues. Proposals involving wage disagreements are good examples of this. If the union is granted $10 more in wages, then the company must, by definition, lose $10.

Integrative Bargaining

Integrative bargaining occurs when the two sides are not in direct conflict over an issue. Integrative bargaining often involves quality of work life issues. Both sides have something to gain from the resulting decision. Unlike zero-sum issues, integrative bargaining issues do not always have a clear winner and loser. Instead, issues of this type call for more collaborative bargaining.

Attitudinal Structuring

During negotiations, both sides may try to establish impressions of friendliness, trust, respect, and cooperation in order to influence or manipulate one another. This type of bargaining is known as **attitudinal structuring**. Attitudinal structuring also occurs when one side attempts to create a negative impression of the other side.

Intraorganizational Bargaining

Negotiators have to "sell" the agreements they reach to their own constituents. For example, union negotiators must sell their agreements to members to gain favorable votes for ratification. Negotiators for management must also sell their side on the issues they negotiate. This type of bargaining is called **intraorganizational bargaining** and can occur before, during, or after actual bargaining.

Boulwarism

General Electric developed **boulwarism** during the 1960s in response to collective bargaining negotiations with its unions. (Boulwarism was named after Lemuel Boulware, General Electric's Vice President of Public and Employee Relations at that time.) With boulwarism, management presents the final offer early in negotiations and refuses to vary from it, while directly influencing the employees to accept it. In most cases, boulwarism has been ruled an unfair labor practice because it manifests the employer's intention to refuse to bargain in good faith. Even if this strategy is not declared unfair, it is generally unsuitable for negotiations because of its cost. Companies using this strategy find that negotiations generally take much longer to conclude and increase the likelihood of a strike, thereby resulting in more time and money being spent.

Mediation and Arbitration

Mediation and arbitration use third parties to help unions and management reach agreement during collective bargaining negotiations. The difference between mediation and arbitration rests primarily in the amount of power given to the third party. Both mediation and arbitration require the voluntary support of unions and management, except in cases of court-ordered mediation or arbitration.

Mediation

A mediator is a third party who attempts to help both sides reach an agreement. Mediators can make recommendations, but they cannot force agreement. Reliable mediators can be contacted through the **Federal Mediation and Conciliation Service**, the National Mediation Board for airlines, or through various state mediation services. Workplace mediation usually passes through four phases: (1) introducing the process to the parties involved, (2) collecting information and defining the issues, (3) developing understanding and seeking alternatives, and (4) reaching agreement.[5]

Arbitration

Arbitrators can be contacted through the same sources as mediators or through the American Arbitration Association or the National Academy of Arbitrators. Unlike mediators, arbitrators have the power to force agreements on both sides during negotiation. Arbitrators review all the information available from both sides and dictate an agreement, often one they perceive to be near the middle ground. Sometimes one or both sides take extreme positions before arbitration begins in order to gain as much ground as possible. This problem can be avoided by using **final offer arbitration.** In final offer arbitration, an arbitrator chooses one side's offer over the other. Both sides try to propose agreements as close to the middle ground as possible. By moving toward the center, unions and management can often reach agreement without the use of an arbitrator.

Mediation-Arbitration

In some cases, unions and management agree to use the services of a mediator-arbitrator. This person first mediates to bring the two sides closer together, then arbitrates or forces a decision.

Like mediators and arbitrators, mediator-arbitrators are available through the Federal Mediation and Conciliation Service, the American Arbitration Association, the National Academy of Arbitrators, or through state mediation and arbitration agencies.

Strikes

Strikes and management lockouts are used as last resorts in negotiations because of their severe economic effect on both sides. Before agreeing to strike, union members must decide if they can sustain the economic losses incurred during a strike period, especially loss of wages, depletion of the union's strike fund, and possible loss of their jobs. Management must carefully consider the effect of strikes or lockouts. The loss of business, alienation of clientele, and disruption of normal business can add up to great economic losses. Management should consider other hardships, such as slowdown and start-up costs, shareholder losses, reduced profits, reduced employee morale, and the development of harsh feelings on both sides. Strikes can break down lines of communication and teamwork that sometimes take years to develop. Strikes often last much longer than either side anticipates, which means that costs are usually greater than anticipated.

Types of Strikes

Not all strikes are the same; there are six major types. The differences relate to the legality of the strike and the amount of protection afforded union members during the strike.

Economic Strike. Economic strikes can result when sides reach an impasse during the negotiation of such mandatory issues as wages or working conditions. During economic strikes, management has the right to hire replacement employees, work in employee positions themselves, or use employees who cross picket lines. If a company hires replacement employees, the NLRB cannot order the company to replace these workers with its permanent employees when the strike ends. However, the NLRB can stipulate that permanent employees be rehired as the replacement employees leave the company. Striking workers cannot be discharged while on economic strike.

Unfair Labor Practice Strike. Union members can strike over management's unfair labor practices, such as refusal to bargain, interference with organizing activities, or denial of union recognition. If an unfair labor practice strike occurs and the employer hires replacement workers, the NLRB has the right to order replacement workers off the job and to reinstate striking employees.

Jurisdictional Strike. A jurisdictional strike involves a dispute between two or more unions and an employer over which union has the right to represent certain employees. Such strikes can occur if a collective bargaining agreement does not carefully outline which union represents employees. Jurisdictional strikes are illegal under the Taft-Hartley Act.

Wildcat Strike. Wildcat strikes are not officially sanctioned by union leadership or by a majority of union members. Wildcat strikes can occur when one group of employees believes that it is being singled out for discipline or that it is being treated unfairly. Striking employees can be legally replaced during wildcat strikes and the employer can sue the union for damages unless there is a non-suability clause in the union's collective bargaining agreement.

Sitdown Strike. A sitdown strike is declared when employees simply stop working, yet remain at the workplace. This type of strike is illegal because employees have the right to be on company property only to work. Management can order sitdown strikers off company property.

Secondary Strike. A secondary strike is waged against an employer who does business with another employer whose workers are on strike. Such actions were declared illegal by the Taft-Hartley Act. For instance, the employees of a hotel supplier cannot strike against their own employer simply because the hotel's employees are on strike. Secondary strikes are different from boycotts, in which union members refuse to purchase a company's products or services while that company's employees are on strike.

Management Approaches During Strikes

Both unions and management must follow specific rules of conduct during strikes. Both sides must allow people having business with the company to pass through picket lines. Both sides must refrain from using profanity in public, violence, or threats, and from fighting or perpetrating assault and battery during strikes. Unions must keep doorways and other entrances open to traffic and allow vehicles to move in and out of the property.

Management must be careful not to engage in unfair labor practices during strikes. Such practices include:

- Offering extras to strikers who return to work

- Threatening strikers with loss of jobs or other discipline

- Promising nonstrikers benefits to remain on the job

- Discharging employees who take part in legal strikes

Each of these activities constitutes a violation of the Wagner Act of 1935.

Strikes in the United States and Around the World

The number of strikes in the U.S. and around the world has declined steadily since World War II. Work stoppages during 1990 to 1995 cost countries in the Organization for Economic Cooperation and Development (OECD) an average of 100 working days per 1,000 employees per year. This compares to 145 days per 1,000 employees per year in the 1980s.

Exhibit 2   When the Work Stops

Maintaining a strong employee relations program goes a long way toward preventing walk-outs and other unexpected job actions. Here are some tips from Frederick Preis, Jr., a labor lawyer whose firm, McGlinchey Stafford Lang of New Orleans, represents some of the largest restaurant chains in the U.S.

- Adopt a management philosophy that offers fair, considerate and consistent treatment of employees.
- Hire productive, quality employees.
- Implement an effective communications program.
- Hire capable and people-oriented supervisors.
- Use a positive approach to discipline.
- Handle complaints effectively.
- Institute equitable and competitive pay practices.
- Offer reasonable employee benefits.
- Recognize employees for their efforts.
- Make sure sensitive data is secure.
- Get involved in community relations.
- Evaluate the employee relations performance of supervisors.
- Evaluate all employees at regular intervals.

Source: Paul B. Hertneky, "How to Deal with a Walk-Out," *Restaurant Hospitality* (February 1995): 65–66.

Work stoppages are very damaging and employers should guard against letting working conditions decline. Human resources consultants regard walk-outs as symptoms of deep-seated problems. Generally, hospitality owners will not forgive managers who allow labor problems to interfere with business. Exhibit 2 offers concrete suggestions for building a healthy employee relations program that will help prevent walk-outs.[6]

Grievances

Reaching a collective bargaining agreement is only the first step in creating a viable and enduring relationship between union employees and employers. While both management and union are bound by the agreement, each side may differ dramatically in its interpretation of the agreement.

Consider a hotel in which a manager has previously determined—through a set of union-approved written rules and regulations—how work should be done. While a *new* manager is bound by the agreement, he or she may attempt to interpret the way that work can be carried out. Let's say that the new manager decides to revamp the weekend schedule for room attendants. He or she decides that instead of scheduling 20 room attendants on Saturday and 10 on Sunday, it would be better to schedule 15 room attendants for both days. The new manager reasons that since many of the dirty rooms aren't needed until Monday, housekeeping could spread room cleaning out over the weekend. Employees might grieve that decision because, while the amount of work they are asked to do does not change, the dates and times they work do.

Exhibit 3   Typical Union Grievance Procedure

Stage 1 Employee complains to a frontline supervisor about an issue. No written report is required. About 75 percent of grievances are resolved at this stage.

Stage 2 Employee complains to department head or personnel office with the aid of a steward or other union official. Generally, the employee is required to submit the grievance in writing.

Stage 3 Union official presents the written grievance to company president.

Stage 4 Written grievance is presented for arbitration.

Source: Adapted from Dan R. Dalton and William D. Todor, "Antecedents of Grievance Filing Behavior: Attitude/Behavioral Consistency and the Union Steward," *Academy of Management Journal* 25 (1982): 1258–1269.

Most contracts include provisions for settling such grievances through a process known as the grievance procedure. Exhibit 3 outlines a typical grievance procedure.

Sources of Grievances

Many grievances result from disagreements between union and management over contract terminology. Grievances also can pertain to union security, compensation practices, working conditions, what the union views as improper administration of the contract, ambiguous terms in the contract, employee disregard for rules, and discipline practices. Alteration of a contract itself is never grievable, meaning that neither party can use the process to change the existing agreement. Issues related to alteration of the contract are left until the next bargaining session, when the current contract expires. The next few sections outline the most common types of grievances filed by unions.[7]

Security. Job security is a critical union issue. Unions are on constant watch for management attempts to diminish the security of a union or its members. For that reason, discipline, layoffs, and seniority issues are often grounds for grievances. Many grievances, if not most, are about the discipline or discharge of an individual union employee. How overtime pay is allotted is another prime grievance issue. For example, a union or its members may feel their security is threatened if a manager attempts to hire new employees to perform additional work instead of paying overtime to current union employees.

Compensation Practices. Grievances over compensation practices can take many forms. The most typical compensation grievance involves the allocation of overtime (who receives it and under what circumstances). Unions also file grievances related to job evaluations (especially those linked to compensation) and pay range classification.

Working Conditions. Disagreements over work rules, workloads, seniority, layoffs, safety and health, management versus union control, and hiring practices frequently lead to working-condition-related grievances. Many working-condition grievances are based on past practice. Most collective bargaining agreements recognize that traditional management practices establish certain expectations of employees. Grievances generally recognize past practices as contractual.

Ambiguous Terms. Many grievances arise simply because of unclear language in the contract. When contract language is ambiguous, unions and management often attempt to interpret it to fit their own needs.

Employee Disregard for Company Rules. The largest single grievance area involves how management exercises its right to discipline employees when they disregard company rules. Management typically wants to retain the right to discipline employees for offenses such as absenteeism, insubordination, dishonesty, and incompetence. Unions, however, consider it a primary responsibility to protect their members and consider any type of employee discipline as potentially grievable. Basically, unions want to ensure that management does not abuse its right to discipline employees.

The basic disagreement here arises from the inherent conflict between management and unions. Management sees the "reasonable" exercise of discipline as its right, often referred to as *managerial prerogative*. Unions, however, perceive "just cause" as the chief criterion for discipline.

Some fired employees now challenge their terminations by filing charges with the NLRB, claiming a violation of the "protected concerted activity" provision of the National Labor Relations Act (NLRA). This act stipulates that an employee who acts on behalf of other employees in complaining about wages, hours, and working conditions, or attempting to force collective bargaining is protected by Section 7 of the NLRA. If discharged under such conditions, an employee must be reinstated.[8]

The Grievance Procedure

Grievances are complaints or concerns filed by employees against management. Nearly all contracts contain a specific procedure for resolving grievances. Earlier in the chapter, Exhibit 3 outlined the four steps involved in most grievance procedures. This exhibit shows how the people involved change at each stage. At the first stage, the grievance involves only the employee, union steward, and immediate supervisor. In the final stage, however, most grievances also involve an arbitrator.

Most grievances are resolved before arbitration, partly because arbitration costs the union and management a lot of money and time. One attractive alternative to a formal grievance process is an employee-based grievance system. In this system, employees participate or even conduct grievance hearings. Generally, employees view this system as more fair than the formal grievance process because their peers conduct the grievance evaluation.[9] Management, too, appears to appreciate this process because it places some of the decision-making burdens on the union.

Grievances are not limited to union properties, of course. Many companies use established grievance procedures to reduce employee desire for unionization. Research by the U.S. General Accounting Office indicates that 90 percent of businesses in the United States use such procedures.[10]

Grievance Arbitration. If a grievance cannot be resolved by negotiations between the union and management, it is typically turned over to an arbitrator for final resolution. This process is referred to as binding arbitration. In most cases, the contract stipulates that the cost for arbitration be split equally between the union and management. This cost can be substantial. Arbitration can cost between $2,000 and $15,000. Arbitrators are selected on the basis of their track record in previous settlements, the predictability of their decisions, and the fairness they display. When selecting arbitrators, each side presents to the other a list of potential arbitrators. Each side then alternately strikes one name from the combined list until only one name is left. That person is chosen as the arbitrator for that particular grievance.

Arbitration Evidence. The arbitration process begins by allowing each side to present its case. Presentations may include testimony, witnesses, documents, and so on. The best evidence is factual. A good arbitrator will allow both sides to fully disclose their evidence. Failure to do so can result in unfair labor practice charges. The NLRB can overturn arbitration decisions if it decides that an arbitrator has a conflict of interest in a case. Arbitration decisions can also be overturned if the NLRB determines that an arbitrator has grossly neglected his or her duties by not hearing all the information, or has acted unfairly. The grounds for overturning an arbitration decision are very narrow; arbitrators are rarely overruled.

Preventing Grievances

Many grievances can be prevented if management follows a policy of fair and consistent management practice and selects, hires, and trains employees properly in the first place. However, managers in union properties can expect to face grievance situations from time to time.

Since many grievances involve employee discipline, it is critical to establish and adhere to a specific discipline policy and associated procedures. Exhibit 4 presents an excerpt from a corporate policy on the employee appeals process.

Each property should also develop and post in a conspicuous location a set of "house rules" or major rules for all employees to follow. These rules establish the guidelines by which management can enforce disciplinary actions.

Documenting Incidents. The most critical step in winning a grievance is clear, complete, and accurate documentation of facts. Any time an action occurs requiring discipline, a manager should first document the facts in their entirety, including a thorough description of what happened. The description should also include dates and times of the event, names of people involved, names of any witnesses, and any other pertinent facts.

Progressive Discipline. All employees need to know they will be treated fairly. An important aspect of fair treatment is the establishment and use of a progressive discipline policy.

Most progressive discipline policies are based on McGregor's four "Red Hot Stove" rules, which illustrate what happens when you touch a red hot stove. According to McGregor's rules, learning must be (1) immediate, (2) with warning, (3) consistent, and (4) impersonal. Rule 1 means that managers should exercise

Exhibit 4   Sample Discipline Policy: Employee Appeals Process

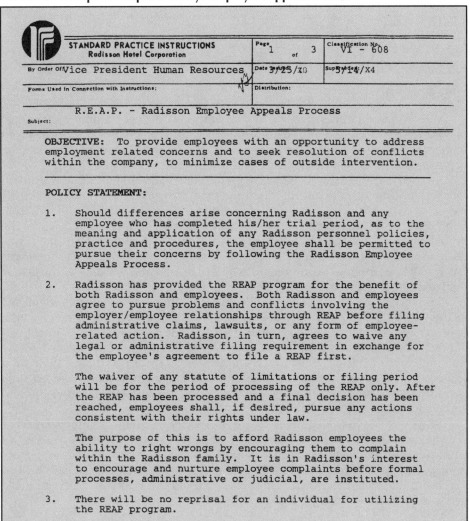

STANDARD PRACTICE INSTRUCTIONS Radisson Hotel Corporation	Page 1 of 3	Classification No. VI - 608
By Order Of Vice President Human Resources	Date 3/25/10	Supersedes 5/14/X4
Forms Used in Connection with Instructions:	Distribution:	

Subject: R.E.A.P. - Radisson Employee Appeals Process

OBJECTIVE: To provide employees with an opportunity to address
employment related concerns and to seek resolution of conflicts
within the company, to minimize cases of outside intervention.

POLICY STATEMENT:

1.   Should differences arise concerning Radisson and any
     employee who has completed his/her trial period, as to the
     meaning and application of any Radisson personnel policies,
     practice and procedures, the employee shall be permitted to
     pursue their concerns by following the Radisson Employee
     Appeals Process.

2.   Radisson has provided the REAP program for the benefit of
     both Radisson and employees. Both Radisson and employees
     agree to pursue problems and conflicts involving the
     employer/employee relationships through REAP before filing
     administrative claims, lawsuits, or any form of employee-
     related action. Radisson, in turn, agrees to waive any
     legal or administrative filing requirement in exchange for
     the employee's agreement to file a REAP first.

     The waiver of any statute of limitations or filing period
     will be for the period of processing of the REAP only. After
     the REAP has been processed and a final decision has been
     reached, employees shall, if desired, pursue any actions
     consistent with their rights under law.

     The purpose of this is to afford Radisson employees the
     ability to right wrongs by encouraging them to complain
     within the Radisson family. It is in Radisson's interest
     to encourage and nurture employee complaints before formal
     processes, administrative or judicial, are instituted.

3.   There will be no reprisal for an individual for utilizing
     the REAP program.

Courtesy of Radisson Hotel Corporation, Minneapolis, Minnesota

disciplinary action immediately to stress the connection between unacceptable behavior and discipline (if you touch a red hot stove, you get burned). Rule 2 instructs managers to warn employees in advance about the consequences of breaking the rules (like warning a child about the dangers of touching a red hot stove). Rule 3—consistent enforcement—and Rule 4—impersonal enforcement of discipline—illustrate the need for equal discipline at all times for everyone (anyone who touches a red hot stove at any time will get burned). Managers must enforce rules consistently, without bias. Inconsistency leaves employees without a clear understanding about following rules.

Most progressive discipline policies have a minimum of four steps:

- Oral warning

- Written warning

- Suspension

- Discharge

As the name implies, oral or spoken warnings do not require managers to provide the employee with written documentation. This does not mean that management is relieved of documentation; on the contrary, managers should keep complete records of any disciplinary actions they take.

Written warnings should include a request that the employee sign a document that outlines the offense and the disciplinary action taken. This proves that the employee saw the document. A sample written warning document is provided in Exhibit 5. This form documents the nature of the problem, when and where the problem occurred, when and where the warning took place, and what action was taken as a result of the warning. The form also documents whether the employee has received a previous warning and whether the current warning is the last or final warning the employee will receive.

In many cases, an employee will refuse to agree with the events identified in the warning; he or she may also refuse to sign the warning. In such cases, managers should sign the warning notice and include a note with the form indicating that the employee had the opportunity to sign the warning and refused. Many warning forms include a space for employees to record and sign their own responses to an incident. Managers should encourage employees to record such statements; this provides another way to document employee acknowledgment and obtain signatures.

Suspension is basically a final warning. The action "shows" employees what will happen if their behavior does not improve. A suspension provides an employee with a realistic experience of what it would be like to lose his or her job. A suspension also shows family members or friends that the employee is having severe trouble at work and, in some cases, provides the impetus the employee needs to get back on the right track.

Union Rights During Investigatory Interviews. Under most union contracts, union members have the right to have a union representative present during investigatory interviews. These are interviews during which management examines facts surrounding an event, not interviews in which disciplinary action is taken. While managers are not bound to advise employees of this right, they must honor this right when requested. If an employee requests that a union representative be present during an investigatory interview, managers should accommodate the request or delay the interview until a union representative can be present. Managers should never refuse the request and proceed with the interview; unions view such conduct as another reason to file a grievance over the disciplinary action. Managers are not required to negotiate with union representatives during investigatory interviews. A union representative's role in

Exhibit 5   Sample Employee Warning Notice

EMPLOYEE WARNING NOTICE

EMPLOYEE NAME_____ DEPARTMENT_____

DATE OF PROBLEM_____ TIME OF PROBLEM_____

NATURE OF PROBLEM
(Please Check)

[   ] Absence / Lateness   [   ] Carelessness   [   ] Work Performance

[   ] Violation of Safety Rules   [   ] Conduct   [   ] Breaking Hotel Rules

[   ] Attitude   [   ] Insubordination   [   ] Other

EXPLANATION REGARDING THIS WARNING (BE SPECIFIC: STATE EXACTLY WHERE,WHEN, WHAT, INCLUDING DATES, ETC.)

_____

_____

_____

_____

_____

ACTION TAKEN:_____

_____

_____

PREVIOUS WARNING?   [   ]No [   ]Yes   If Yes, Date_____

[   ] FINAL WARNING: The employee has been told that any further violation of this type, or any other infractions of company policy may result in termination.

NOTE TO EMPLOYEE: Employees who have a problem affecting job performance are encouraged to seek help on a confidential basis by contacting the Employee Assistance Center at_____ , or the Personnel Office at_____ , for additional information about the program.

I HAVE DISCUSSED THIS MATTER WITH THE ABOVE EMPLOYEE ON

_____ at _____ Signature:_____
   Date   Time   Supervisor

YOUR SIGNATURE ON THIS FORM INDICATES ONLY THAT YOU HAVE BEEN ADVISED OF THIS WARNING NOTICE. IF YOU FEEL THAT THE WARNING IS UNFAIR, YOU ARE ENCOURAGED TO TALK TO THE PERSONNEL OFFICE.

_____
                        Employee Signature

this process is limited; he or she may not interfere with the interview, but is allowed some involvement in the process. The applicable labor contract may also set guidelines for union participation in interviews.

Exhibit 6   Sample Grievance Procedure: Non-Union Property

1. Employee makes complaint to supervisor
2. Employee makes complaint to any manager in any department
3. Employee takes complaint to grievance committee composed of employees and management representatives
4. Grievance committee formally posts grievance and results in a conspicuous place for all employees to see

Concerns of Non-Union Properties

Most hotels and restaurants are non-union properties. Even in non-union properties, management still has a responsibility to establish and post rules. In fact, many managers have developed grievance procedures in non-union properties expressly to decrease the likelihood that employees will unionize.

Establishing Non-Union Property Grievance Procedures

Many employers establish grievance procedures even in the absence of any threat of union organization. One reason for such procedures is to eliminate the need that employees may feel for union protection. Grievance procedures in non-union settings differ from those in union settings because no union representatives are involved. A typical non-union property grievance procedure is outlined in Exhibit 6.

The success of non-union grievance procedures depends on fairness and management support. For such a system to work, managers must inform employees of their opportunities to complain about work-related issues, provide the avenue for such complaints, and support the system. Managers who undermine or disregard grievance committee decisions send the wrong message to their employees. Such behavior demonstrates that managers do not believe in the system and will not abide by its findings. In such cases, the system can cause more harm than good, since it shows employees that managers do not follow the rules. This sets a poor example for employees and damages (or corrupts) the system, and may lead employees to look to unions for better protection.

Endnotes

1. For more information on collective bargaining history and data from collective bargaining, see *Monthly Labor Review* 123, no. 2 (2000): 53–58.

2. A good example of a collective bargaining simulation is described in James R. Pickworth, "An Experiential Approach to Collective Bargaining," *Cornell Hotel and Restaurant Administration Quarterly* 28 (August 1987): 60–66.

3. Adapted from R. L. Miller, "Preparations for Negotiations," *Personnel Journal* (January 1978): 36–39.

4 Richard E. Walton and Robert B. Kersie, *A Behavioral Theory of Labor Negotiations* (New York: McGraw-Hill, 1965).

5. Sybil Evans, "Doing Mediation to Avoid Arbitration," *HR Magazine* 39 (March 1994): 48–51.

6. Paul B. Hertneky, "How to Deal with a Walk-Out," *Restaurant Hospitality* (February 1995): 65–66.

7. Suzanne K. Murrmann and Kent F. Murrmann, "Characteristics and Outcomes of Grievance Arbitration Decisions in Hospitality Firms, " *International Journal of Hospitality Management* 16, no. 4 (1997): 362–374. Murrmann and Murrmann have compiled data on grievance arbitration cases in the hospitality industry from 1985 to 1995. This study provides both an overview of grievance procedures in hospitality as well as interesting cases useful in training managers and supervisors. This article also provides a very good listing of won-loss outcomes by grievance type. For example, the number of "breach of contract" grievances is outlined as well as the outcomes of each.

8. Joan M. Clay and Elvis C. Stephens, "Protected Employee Concerted Activity: Hospitality Industry Implications," *Cornell Hotel and Restaurant Administration Quarterly* 35 (October 1994): 12–15.

9. Zane Reeves, "Use of Employee-Based Grievance Systems," *Review of Public Personnel Administration* 15 (Summer 1995): 73–80.

10. "GAO Survey: Business Leans Toward Use of Dispute Resolution," *Dispute Resolution Journal* 150 (October–December 1995): 22.

Key Terms

arbitration—A process used to settle a labor dispute between a union and management through the use of a third party (known as an arbitrator), whose decision is binding if both the employer and union have previously agreed to be bound by it.

attitudinal structuring—Negotiation strategy in which one or both sides attempt to establish an impression of friendliness, trust, respect, and cooperation in order to manipulate or influence the other.

bargaining in good faith—A practice mandated by the Wagner Act of 1935 whereby management and unions must attempt to reach agreement on disputed issues through negotiation.

binding arbitration—Arbitration process that occurs when the union and management cannot resolve a grievance through negotiations.

boulwarism—Illegal negotiation strategy derived from a tactic developed by Lemuel Boulware, Vice President of Public and Employee Relations at General Electric during the 1960s; calls for management to make a "final offer" early in the negotiations and to refuse to discuss issues any further.

boycott—Situation that occurs when union members refuse to buy products or services offered by a company in which the employees are on strike.

collective bargaining—The negotiation process between unions and management during which contracts are developed.

compensatory damages—In employment litigation, an amount of money awarded to a plaintiff (the employee) that relates directly to the loss of income on the job.

distributive bargaining—Bargaining that occurs when the union and management conflict over major issues. Under such conditions, each side presents a proposal in which one side loses and the other wins.

economic strike—Strike over mandatory issues such as wages or working conditions.

Federal Mediation and Conciliation Service—The federal government source for locating mediators, arbitrators, and mediator-arbitrators.

final offer arbitration—Arbitration process in which the arbitrator must choose either management's proposal or the union's proposal. Decisions made during this process are final.

illegal bargaining issues—Issues prohibited by law from collective bargaining negotiations. Includes closed-shop agreements, any issues that violate EEOC laws, and featherbedding.

impasse—Point at which neither the union nor management will give up on any point or issue and at which agreement is yet to be reached.

integrative bargaining—Bargaining that occurs when the union and management are not necessarily in conflict over an issue, or when both sides have something to gain from bargaining.

intraorganizational bargaining—Negotiation strategy in which both sides must "sell" the agreements reached during negotiation to their own constituents.

jurisdictional strike—Illegal strike based on the issue of which union will represent employees.

just cause clause—Clause in collective bargaining contract that outlines specific guidelines for employee discipline or termination; unions typically want just cause clauses in their contracts.

management rights clause—Clause in collective bargaining contract that gives management the right to control products and services the company makes or delivers, and the right to determine the method and use of employee discipline.

mandatory bargaining issues—Issues discussed during the collective bargaining process that relate directly to the employment relationship. The Wagner and Taft-Hartley Acts stipulate that both union and management must bargain in good faith over these issues.

mediation—A process used to resolve a stalemate in negotiations between union and management in which a third party (known as a mediator) assists by helping the parties to arrive at a voluntary compromise.

past practice—The manner in which work has been done in the past.

progressive discipline—Discipline process in which employees are given increasingly stiffer penalties for infractions; usually progresses from an oral warning, to a written warning, to a suspension, and finally to discharge.

punitive damages—In employment litigation, an amount of money awarded to a plaintiff (the employee) that punishes the other party (the employer) for its actions and conduct.

secondary strike—Illegal strike in which employees go on strike because their employer does business with another employer whose employees are on strike.

sitdown strike—Strike that occurs when union members stop working but remain on the premises.

unfair labor practice—Labor practices specifically prohibited by federal and state laws, particularly those laws regarding either collective bargaining or application of company regulations.

unfair labor practice strike—Strike based on management's refusal to bargain collectively or other unfair labor practices.

voluntary bargaining issues—Issues discussed during the collective bargaining process *only* when both sides want to; discussion is not mandated by law. Issues include pension and benefits rights, supervisory compensation and discipline, and company prices or products.

wildcat strike—Strike not recognized by union leadership. In most wildcat strikes, one group of employees strikes over issues that relate only to their work unit. Employers can replace workers in wildcat strikes and can sue the union for damages.

zero sum issue—Proposal or issue in which one side loses and the other side wins by the same amount.

Review Questions

1. What do managers need to consider when deciding who should be a part of their collective bargaining negotiation team?

2. How do mandatory bargaining issues, voluntary bargaining issues, and illegal bargaining issues differ?

3. What are six non-economic issues typically important to unions during collective bargaining?

4. When can an impasse be declared?

5. What are the differences between management rights clauses and just cause clauses?

6. What are the differences between distributive bargaining and integrative bargaining?

7. Which types of strikes provide the best legal protection for employees? Which types provide the least?

8. What are the differences between arbitration and final offer arbitration? How do these differences affect the outcome of arbitration decisions in most cases?

9. What are the three most common grounds for grievances? Why?

10. What are some of the concerns of non-union properties in establishing grievance procedures?

Internet Sites

For more information, visit the following Internet sites. Remember that Internet addresses can change without notice. If the site is no longer there, you can use a search engine to look for additional sites.

American Arbitration Association
www.adr.org/

Cornell University Law School
www.law.cornell.edu/

Bureau of Labor Statistics
www.bls.gov/

Mini Case Study

Housekeeping employees in your hotel have filed a grievance against you. They say that your hotel failed to abide by the conditions outlined in your collective bargaining agreement with their union. According to the employees, the housekeeping supervisor has under-scheduled personnel in her department so that she and her assistant can make up the rooms themselves—thereby saving the department money. Employees filed a "performance of bargaining unit work" grievance asserting that the manager was taking away their work and attempting to eliminate their jobs.

Discussion Questions

1. Do the employees in this work unit have a legitimate grievance?

2. How could this grievance have been avoided?

3. What position should management assume when presenting its side in this case?

Part IV

Safety, Discipline, and Ethics

Chapter 12 Outline

Occupational Safety and Health Act of 1970
 OSHA Coverage and Scope
 Enforcement of OSHA Standards
 Employee Rights Under OSHA
 Hospitality and OSHA
 Measuring Health and Safety
Employee Stress and Emotional Health
 Sources of Stress
 Stress Scores of Hotel Managers
 Consequences of Stress
 Stress Reduction
Employee Assistance Programs
 Setting Up EAPs
 Costs Saved by EAPs
Other Issues in Safety and Health
 Acquired Immune Deficiency
  Syndrome
 Depression Among Employees
 Wellness Programs
 Smoking in the Workplace
 Work Life/Home Life Issues

Competencies

1. Summarize the history, scope, and goal of the Occupational Safety and Health Act, and describe the enforcement of OSHA standards and requirements. (pp. 391–395)

2. Outline employee rights under OSHA and how these rights apply to the hospitality industry. (pp. 395–399)

3. Identify sources and consequences of stress and list guidelines for reducing stress. (pp. 399–404)

4. Describe the components and benefits of an employee assistance program. (pp. 404–407)

5. Outline the implications of current health issues such as AIDS, depression, wellness programs, workplace smoking, and work life/home life issues. (pp. 407–415)

Health, Safety, and EAPs

This chapter was co-authored by Christine Faja, M.S. candidate, University of Nevada, Las Vegas (UNLV); Kenny Allen, Jr., M.S. candidate, UNLV; and Maxime Lawrence, M.S. candidate, UNLV.

THE NATIONAL SAFETY COUNCIL REPORTS THAT work-related deaths and injuries cost the U.S. economy over $40 billion annually. Employers have a legal responsibility to make every effort possible to limit the number of injuries and deaths in the workplace. In 1998, 5.9 million workers were injured on the job, meaning that 6.7 out of every 100 employees suffered a work-related injury or illness.[1] The most prevalent injuries stem from lifting, pushing, pulling, and holding (annual cost $9.8 billion) and from falls ($8 billion).[2]

Employers have a duty to furnish a safe workplace, free from recognized hazards that can cause serious physical harm. To do so, employers must invest considerable amounts of time and money to promote health and safety in the workplace and to prevent accidents. Employers who shirk this responsibility will eventually face the sanctions and fines of the **Occupational Safety and Health Administration (OSHA)**. Unfortunately, many managers wait until accidents happen or OSHA levies fines against their establishment before addressing these issues. Proactive managers find they can prevent many accidents if they implement programs to recognize and respond to employee health and safety needs. Although these programs cost money, the returns generally outweigh the costs.

This chapter begins by outlining the duties and operation of OSHA in enforcing workplace safety and health standards. The chapter then introduces approaches managers can use to reduce or prevent workplace injuries and to promote good employee health.

Occupational Safety and Health Act of 1970

One of the most controversial pieces of federal legislation enacted since World War II is the **Occupational Safety and Health Act of 1970**. The purpose of this act was to centralize the regulation of work force safety and to expand workplace safety coverage to all workers in the United States.

The act was passed after years of intense lobbying by employee groups, the National Safety Council, and unions. These groups contended that, while many workers in the United States worked in safe environments, many others did not. The Occupational Safety and Health Act was designed to remedy that situation by creating federal legislation that legitimized and standardized workplace safety rules and regulations.

The Occupational Safety and Health Act created three new government agencies: the Occupational Safety and Health Administration, the **Occupational Safety and Health Review Commission (OSHRC)**, and the **National Institute of Occupational Safety and Health (NIOSH)**.

OSHA is a branch of the U.S. Department of Labor. This agency is responsible for formulating and enforcing regulations for on-the-job safety and for issuing citations and penalties. Of the three agencies created by the Occupational Safety and Health Act, OSHA is the most powerful.

The Occupational Safety and Health Review Commission is an appeal board composed of three members appointed by the president of the United States. The main purpose of this body is to adjudicate disputes between OSHA and organizations cited by OSHA.

The National Institute of Occupational Safety and Health is housed in the U.S. Department of Health and Human Services. This agency is responsible for conducting research that evaluates workplace health and safety. Typically, NIOSH develops the regulations and enforcement procedures carried out by OSHA.

OSHA Coverage and Scope

OSHA's first task was to develop safety standards and regulations. Initially, OSHA tried to establish a policy for developing "the no-risk workplace." Under this policy, the agency developed guidelines for making all workplaces free of any risk of injury.

In the late 1970s, the U.S. Supreme Court made a series of judgments against OSHA that forced a major change in policy. These judgments stated that the "no-risk" policy was too strict and too difficult for employers to follow. As a result, OSHA replaced its "no-risk" policy with the "sufficiently risk-free workplace" policy. This policy emphasizes the protection of workers from reasonable and foreseeable health and safety hazards. In enforcing the "sufficiently risk-free workplace" policy, OSHA strives to eliminate known and suspected safety and health hazards from the workplace.

Managers engaged in any form of commerce are subject to OSHA standards. Three different standards are enforceable by OSHA: (1) interim OSHA standards, (2) **permanent OSHA standards**, and (3) **emergency OSHA standards**. Interim standards were set by the secretary of labor to cover the two-year period immediately following the establishment of OSHA. Permanent standards, based on NIOSH research or suggestions by employers, unions, or industry, establish permanent guidelines that businesses must follow. Emergency standards are issued by the secretary of labor when problems in need of immediate correction arise. Most of the standards that the hospitality industry must follow fall into the permanent standards category.

Enforcement of OSHA Standards

OSHA inspectors have the authority to inspect most businesses in the United States. These **compliance officers** inspect workplaces and issue citations for violations of standards. By law, compliance officers must arrive at a workplace unannounced, present their credentials, and hold an opening conference with management. The U.S. Supreme Court has ruled that employers can require OSHA inspectors to obtain a search warrant before conducting any inspection.

Generally, compliance officers begin an inspection by determining if a business has OSHA-required posters displayed in conspicuous places. (Exhibit 1 shows a sample OSHA poster.) These posters explain various aspects of the Occupational Safety and Health Act, and requirements for job safety and health protection.

Once compliance officers confirm poster placement, they have the right to observe and interview employees, inspect for hazards, examine health and safety records, check for first-aid and medical devices, and examine emergency procedures. At the end of this inspection, compliance officers meet a second time with management to discuss their findings, issue citations, suggest improvements, and establish timetables for remedies. If citations are issued, employers have 15 days to appeal to OSHRC. If no appeal is filed within 15 days, citations are final. Penalties of up to $100,000 per willful or repeated violation can be issued by OSHA inspectors. The minimum penalty is $5,000 for each willful violation. In most instances, penalties range from $100 to $400.

Through its Voluntary Protection Programs, OSHA works with employers to find and fix occupational hazards. Nearly 400,000 small businesses have received free OSHA consultations, leading to the correction of 3 million hazards. In the first 30 years of its history, OSHA trained more than 2.1 million people in workplace safety.[3]

Violations. Compliance officers can issue citations for violations in eight categories:

1. Imminent danger

2. Willful or repeated violations

3. Serious danger

4. Non-serious danger

5. Failure to correct a violation

6. Willful violation that causes the death of an employee

7. Posting requirements

8. De minimis (or minimal) violations

Imminent danger violations generally result in a restraining order issued by court action. This order requires a business to cease and desist the work condition or practice that caused the violation.

Record-Keeping Requirements. According to OSHA regulations, each workplace must maintain a file on each employee who logs occupational injuries or illnesses. Employers with no more than 10 employees at any time during the previous year need not comply except to report fatalities or multiple hospitalizations. Properties must document work-related events that result in death, regular medical treatment, loss of work, restricted work activity, or any injury or illness that requires

Exhibit 1   OSHA Job Safety and Health Protection Poster

You Have a Right to a Safe and Healthful Workplace.

IT'S THE LAW!

- You have the right to notify your employer or OSHA about workplace hazards. You may ask OSHA to keep your name confidential.
- You have the right to request an OSHA inspection if you believe that there are unsafe and unhealthful conditions in your workplace. You or your representative may participate in the inspection.
- You can file a complaint with OSHA within 30 days of discrimination by your employer for making safety and health complaints or for exercising your rights under the *OSH Act.*
- You have a right to see OSHA citations issued to your employer. Your employer must post the citations at or near the place of the alleged violation.
- Your employer must correct workplace hazards by the date indicated on the citation and must certify that these hazards have been reduced or eliminated.
- You have the right to copies of your medical records or records of your exposure to toxic and harmful substances or conditions.
- Your employer must post this notice in your workplace.

The *Occupational Safety and Health Act of 1970 (OSH Act)*, P.L. 91-596, assures safe and healthful working conditions for working men and women throughout the Nation. The Occupational Safety and Health Administration, in the U.S. Department of Labor, has the primary responsibility for administering the *OSH Act.* The rights listed here may vary depending on the particular circumstances. To file a complaint, report an emergency, or seek OSHA advice, assistance, or products, call 1-800-321-OSHA or your nearest OSHA office: • Atlanta (404) 562-2300 • Boston (617) 565-9860 • Chicago (312) 353-2220 • Dallas (214) 767-4731 • Denver (303) 844-1600 • Kansas City (816) 426-5861 • New York (212) 337-2378 • Philadelphia 215) 861-4900 • San Francisco (415) 975-4310 • Seattle (206) 553-5930. Teletypewriter (TTY) number is 1-877-889-5627. To file a complaint online or obtain more information on OSHA federal and state programs, visit OSHA's website at www.osha.gov. If your workplace is in a state operating under an OSHA-approved plan, your employer must post the required state equivalent of this poster.

1-800-321-OSHA
www.osha.gov

U.S. Department of Labor   •   Occupational Safety and Health Administration   •   OSHA 3165 more than minor first-aid. Exhibit 2 shows a form designed for this purpose. Record keeping has been made easier in recent years by software programs designed for this purpose. OSHA also provides Internet access to standards and directives at http://www.osha.gov.

All injuries and illnesses must be reported to OSHA within 48 hours of occurrence. Because of these regulations, some employers report as many injuries as possible as "minor first-aid." The hospitality industry was exempted from most record-keeping responsibility in 1983. Since then, the industry has been required to maintain files or submit direct, immediate reports to OSHA only when injuries result in a death or in the hospitalization of five or more employees.[4]

Employee Rights Under OSHA

Under OSHA regulations, employees cannot be punished for refusing to work in an unsafe environment or for reporting violations to OSHA. In addition, employees have the right to know if hazardous or toxic materials are being used in the workplace and to receive proper training in handling such materials when they are present.

The OSHA Hazard Communication Standard requires employers throughout the United States to tell their employees about hazardous materials they may be required to handle on the job. The standard is commonly referred to as **HazComm** or OSHA's right-to-know legislation. HazComm stipulates that material safety data sheets (MSDSs) must be collected for each chemical and filed where employees can read them at any time. Recent action concerning such right-to-know laws and regulations should be followed on a state-by-state basis because standards may vary (see Exhibit 3).

Material safety data sheets are forms that provide information on chemicals or cleaners used at a property. The MSDS form lists the hazardous ingredients, health hazard data, and spill or leak procedures to follow for the product. The MSDS form also lists any special precautions or protective gear required when using the product. These sheets can be obtained from the chemical supplier directly or from a local purveyor.

OSHA stipulates that MSDS forms must be shown to employees who use or are exposed to potentially hazardous products. OSHA also requires employers to follow steps to comply with the standard. OSHA now conducts a review of Haz-Comm compliance with every inspection of a business.

OSHA recommends the establishment of a company-sponsored safety and health program. This program should:

- Have top management leadership
- Clearly establish responsibility for safety
- Identify and immediately correct causes of accidents
- Have a strong training component
- Use accident records to identify problem areas
- Have emergency medical and first-aid materials on the premises and train employees to use them

Exhibit 2   OSHA Log and Summary

Log and Summary of Occupational Injuries and illnesses					
NOTE:	This form is required by Public Law 91-596 and must be kept			RECORDABLE CASES: You are required to record information about every	
	in the establishment for 5 years. Failure to maintain and post			occupational death; every nonfatal occupational illness; and those nonfatal	
	can result in issuance of citations and assessment of penalties.			occupational injuries which involve one or more of the following: loss of	
	(See posting requirements on the other side of form)			conciousness, restriction of work or motion, transfer to another job, or	
				medical treatment (other than first aid)	
				(See definitions on the other side of form)	
Case or File Number	Date of Injury or Onset of Illness	Employee's Name	Occupation	Department	Description of Injury or Illness
Enter a nonduplicating number which will facilitate comparisons with supplementary records.	Enter Mo/Day	Enter first name or initial, middle initial, last name	Enter regular job title, not activity employee was performing when injury occurred or at onset of illness. In the absence of a formal title, enter a brief description of the employee's duties.	Enter department in which the employee is regularly employed or a description of normal workplace to which employee is assigned, even though temporarily working in another department at the time of injury or illness.	Enter a brief description of the injury or illness and indicate the part or part affected. Typical entries for this column might be: Amputation of 1st joint right foref of lower back; Contact dermatitis on both hands; Electrocution - body.
(A)	(B)	(C)	(D)	(E)	(F) PREVIOUS PAGE TOTALS
				TOTALS (Instructions on other side of form)	
OSHA No. 200					

Source: U.S. Department of Labor, Occupational Safety and Health Administration, Washington, D.C.

- Encourage awareness of workplace safety and health issues
- Outline safety and health responsibilities

OSHA also recommends that safety and health programs be developed and administered by a committee of both managers and employees.

Hospitality and OSHA

Approximately 500,000 injuries occur annually in the hospitality industry, a relatively low accident rate overall. Unfortunately, almost 50 percent of these injuries result in 35 or more lost days of work.[5] Kitchen areas can present big safety problems for hospitality operations. For instance, grease build-up in fryers and kitchen exhaust systems can cause fires. Wet floors and spills can contribute to slips and falls. Most other injuries incurred by hospitality employees result from electric partment of Labor

For Calendar Year _____   Page: ____ of ____

Form Approved
O.M.B. No. 1218-0176
See OMB Disclosure
Statement on reverse.

ame

ddress

come of Injury

Type, Extent of, and Outcome of Illness

Nonfatal Injuries						Type of Illness								Fatalities	Nonfatal Illnesses				
Injuries with Lost Workdays					Injuries Without Lost Workdays	CHECK Only One Column for Each Illness (See other side of form for terminations or permanent transfers)								Illness Related	Illnesses with Lost Workdays				Illnesses without Lost Workdays
Enter a Check if injury involves DAYS away from work or restricted work activity or both.	Enter a Check if injury involves DAYS away from work.	Enter number of DAYS away from work	Enter number of DAYS of restricted work activity	Enter a Check if no entry was made in column 1 or 2 but the injury is recordable as defined above.	Occupational Skin Disorder or Disease	Dust Disease of the lungs	Respiratory Conditions due to toxic agents	Poisoning (systemic effects of toxic materials)	Disorders due to physical agents	Disorders associated with repeated trauma	All other occupational illnesses	Enter DATE of death, mm/dd/yy	Enter a CHECK if illness involves DAYS away from work, or DAYS of restricted work activity or both.	Enter a CHECK if illness involves DAYS away from work.	Enter number of DAYS away from work.	Enter number of DAYS of restricted work activity	Enter a CHECK if no entry was made in columns 8 or 9
(2)	(3)	(4)	(5)	(6)	(a)	(b)	(c)	(d)	(e)	(f)	(g) (7)	(8)	(9)	(10)	(11)	(12)	(13)

n of Annual Summary Totals by: _____   Title: _____   Date: _____

POST ONLY THIS PORTION OF THE LAST PAGE NO LATER THAN FEBRUARY 1

shocks or from falls on stairways without protective railings. Hospitality managers should keep a watchful eye on safety within construction sites, laundry areas, and maintenance operations.

Managers can reduce the likelihood of accidents by focusing on three elements: signage, training, and preventive maintenance of equipment. Posting signs near areas where serious accidents can occur can remind employees to be careful. For instance, signs near fryers remind employees of the potential hazards of burns or grease fires and can outline proper equipment use. Training is an effective way to communicate proper use of equipment and property safety standards. Well-structured training is usually effective in minimizing the number and frequency of accidents. A regular program of preventive maintenance—especially for problem-prone areas—can reduce safety risks in the hospitality workplace.

Repetitive Strain Injuries. Repetitive strain injuries (RSI), sometimes known as repetitive stress injuries, command more attention all the time. Employees incur such injuries by repeating the same procedure over and over. Carpal tunnel

Exhibit 3   Michigan Right To Know Law Poster

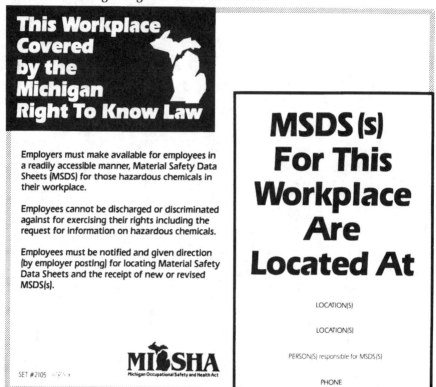

Source: Michigan Department of Labor, Occupational Safety and Health Administration, Lansing, Michigan.

syndrome is a good example of this type of injury. Spending the majority of a work day typing can damage ligaments in the wrist. Video display terminals (VDTs) can also contribute to new forms of injury. Some VDT operators report fatigue, boredom, psychological distress, and eye strain. In addition, keyboard design has been cited as a contributing factor in musculoskeletal problems.[6]

Managers must complete and submit appropriate OSHA accident reports when such injuries occur. Managers can reduce the frequency of some repetitive stress injuries by purchasing desks designed specifically for keyboards and computers, wrist rests, or ergonomic keyboards; by replacing VDT screens with low-glare models; or by adding glare-reducing screens to existing terminals. Such modifications may help decrease carpal tunnel syndrome and VDT trauma incidences in some hospitality work areas where employees spend many hours each day working on computers.

The workstations in quick-service, on-site, and institutional kitchens also place workers at risk for RSI, because workers must perform repetitious food preparation tasks (such as chopping) over long periods of time.[7] OSHA recommends redesign of tools, equipment, workstations, and kitchens to guard against worker injury. Other strategies—such as rotating workers, increasing the variety of tasks done by one worker, and making sure workers take regular rest breaks—have proven effective in promoting safety.[8]

Measuring Health and Safety

OSHA is primarily concerned with creating safe and healthy work environments. Managers can measure their overall safety and health records by using a simple formula. The results of this formula project the number of injuries expected for every 100 employees who work 40 hours for 50 weeks:

$$\frac{N}{TH} \qquad \times \qquad 200,000$$

N	=	number of injuries and illness or lost workdays
TH	=	total hours worked by all employees during calendar year
200,000	=	100 full-time employees $\times$ 40 hour week $\times$ 50 weeks

While there is no "acceptable" level of injuries, this formula does provide information that allows an employer to track the occurrence of injuries over time. In the past, OSHA considered the maintenance of such figures as sound evidence of an employer's effort to maintain a safe and healthy work environment.

Employee Stress and Emotional Health

A 1997 study by the Families and Work Institute of American workers found that 25 percent feel or have felt nervous or stressed too often, and that 13 percent have or have had difficulty coping with the demands of everyday life. Other researchers stated that 40 percent of workers found their jobs extremely stressful, and 25 percent said that their job was the number-one source of stress in their lives. The researchers found that 26 percent of employees felt overwhelmed "often to very often" in their jobs during the preceding month. Of employees who are overworked, 20 percent make a lot more mistakes than those who are not overworked, and 39 percent feel very angry toward their employer.[9]

Also, overworked employees are more likely to have poorer health and neglect caring for their health.[10] Job stress is more strongly associated with health complaints than with financial or family problems. Stress has been linked to a variety of physical ailments from headaches to depression to symptoms that mimic a heart attack.[11]

Employers should pay close attention to workplace stressors because the median absence from work for cases of occupational stress is 23 days, while the median absence for non-stress injuries is one-fourth of that amount.[12] Researchers further noted that more women (40 percent) than men (26 percent) experience high levels of stress. On average, hotel and restaurant managers experience much higher levels of stress than do managers in other fields.[13] Some conclude that high management turnover in the hospitality industry can be traced directly to job-related stress.

Sources of Stress

Some stress on the job is good. Just the right amount of stress can contribute to good job performance and corresponding satisfaction much like, when a guitar is tuned, just the right amount of string tension can contribute to proper tone and corresponding harmonies. However, too much stress can cause guitar strings to stretch or break.

Some people are more prone to stress than others. "Type A" people are typically impatient, hard-driving, competitive individuals who work under strict self-induced time constraints. "Type A" people tend to have higher levels of stress than "Type B" people who characteristically lead unhurried lives. Not all stress relates to personality type, however. Many stress experts identify four different sources of stress, or **stressors**:

- Extra-organizational sources: personal problems with family, marriage, finances, children, and so on

- Individual sources: too much work, failure to manage time effectively, role overload, ambiguity, or conflict

- Group sources: lack of teamwork or demands by team members to over-perform for long periods of time

- Organizational sources: rules and regulations, pressure to produce profits, authoritative management styles, abuse of power, and so on

Stress in the hospitality industry is related to labor shortages, high staff turnover, long and inconvenient hours, and long periods of high-pressure conditions.[14] This stress manifests itself in many ways. Hotel managers, for instance, experience much higher levels of **burnout** than managers in other lines of business.

The incidence of burnout may be higher in service industries because jobs involve a high degree of interaction with customers.[15] Symptoms of burnout are emotional exhaustion, a tendency to depersonalize and become unresponsive to other people, and a low sense of personal achievement. Burnout also manifests itself in turnover, absenteeism, and decreased productivity. The turnover rate among employees is twice as high in service fields as in non-service fields (25–30 percent versus 8–15 percent). The hospitality middle-manager turnover rate is significantly higher than in other service areas. Seventy-six percent of employees said that the most damaging effect of burnout was increased absenteeism, and 70 percent of employees worried about decreased productivity.[16]

Stress is commonly experienced by other hospitality employees as well. For instance, food preparation and service workers are twice as likely to be heavy drinkers as are members of the general public.[17] Ninety-seven percent of surveyed hospitality professionals believe that alcohol and drug abuse is a problem for the industry, with more than half of respondents reporting that the combined effects have reached "worrying" levels. Of almost 1,000 hospitality professionals, 40 percent had seen colleagues take illegal drugs while at work, and 59 percent had seen colleagues drinking to excess on duty. The most common reasons given by people who took drugs at their workplace were "to stay awake during shift" (48 percent) and "to help cope with stress" (also 48 percent).[18]

The Social Readjustment Rating Scale presented in Exhibit 4 identifies common sources of stress. The scale also indicates the rank of each source in terms of its effect on an individual. This scale is based on the highest stressor: death of a spouse. Mean values relate to the extent to which other events approximate that level of stress. Other common conditions that cause stress are loneliness (research has found that social isolation is as dangerous as smoking), high blood pressure, obesity, or high cholesterol. A survey conducted in early 2005 found that 40 percent of workers cited workload as their main cause of stress, 34 percent cited people issues, and 21 percent cited balancing work and life.[19] The presence of any companion, even a pet, can help reduce stress.

Stress Scores of Hotel Managers

In a 1998 study of stress in hotel managers, this author and two colleagues tabulated a score for each individual survey returned. The average score for the 197 participants in the study was 241.5, a score clearly in the danger zone. The percentages of participants scoring in eight different ranges are presented in Exhibit 5. There were no substantially significant differences in the stress levels experienced by GMs based on differences in property size or service levels of their hotels.

Many participating managers reported items that appear on the low end of the 1995 SRRS scales, i.e., items that cause fairly low levels of stress. Exhibit 6 presents items most often mentioned as stressors by hotel managers in this study.

Some of the items on this list—for instance, outstanding personal achievements, vacations, and marriage—would seem to be positive events in the lives of these managers. However, handling the circumstances before and after these events also requires a substantial amount of energy and preparation on the part of the manager. Even a vacation, perhaps the most positive event on the SRRS list, is stressful because it is necessary to plan and make arrangements for others to cover the manager's responsibilities during the absence. While holidays would normally be considered positive for individuals taking this test, this might not be the case for hotel managers, many of whom are much busier during the holiday season.

Consequences of Stress

Too much stress is bad for employees and organizations alike. For individuals, too much stress can lead to alcohol, drug, or tobacco abuse and violent or depressed behavior. In addition to psychological problems, high levels of stress can cause physical problems such as backaches, headaches, irritable bowel syndrome, high blood pressure, and coronary disease. For organizations, stress can lead to high turnover, low productivity, and numerous workers' compensation claims. Approximately 11 to 15 percent of all workers' compensation claims are related to stress.

Stress Reduction

Stress reduction programs have two goals: to reduce individual-induced stress and to reduce organizational-induced stress. Individuals learn to control stress through exercise and diet and by modifying or eliminating their consumption of alcohol, tobacco, or drugs. Stress reduction programs may also include financial and family

Exhibit 4   Standardized Social Readjustment Rating Scores (SRRS)

Rank	Life Event	Mean Value
1.	Death of spouse	119
2.	Divorce	98
3.	Death of a close family member	92
4.	Marital separation	79
5.	Fired at work	79
6.	Personal injury or illness	77
7.	Jail term	75
8.	Death of a close friend	70
9.	Pregnancy	66
10.	Business adjustment	62
11.	Foreclosure on mortgage or loan	61
12.	Gain of a new family member	57
13.	Marital reconciliation	57
14.	Change in health of family member	56
15.	Change in financial state	56
16.	Retirement	54
17.	Change to a different line of work	51
18.	Change in number of arguments with spouse	51
19.	Marriage	51
20.	Spouse begins or ends work	46
21.	Sexual difficulties	45
22.	Mortgage loan	44
23.	Son or daughter leaving home	44
24.	Change in responsibilities at work	43
25.	Change in living conditions	42
26.	Change in residence	41
27.	Trouble with in-laws	38
28.	Begin or end school	37
29.	Outstanding personal achievement	36
30.	Change in work hours or conditions	35
31.	Change in schools	30
32.	Holidays	29
33.	Trouble with boss	29
34.	Change in recreation	29
35.	Low mortgage loan	28
36.	Change in personal habits	27
37.	Change in social activities	27
38.	Change in eating habits	27
39.	Change in sleeping habits	26
40.	Change in the number of family get-togethers	26
41.	Vacation	25
42.	Change in church activities	22
43.	Minor violation of the law	22
	Grand mean for all events	49

Source: M. A. Miller and R. H. Rahe, "Life Changes Scaling for the 1990s," *Journal of Psychosomatic Research* 43, no. 3 (1998): 279–292.

Exhibit 5   A Study of Stress in Hotel Managers

Percentage of Hotel Managers in Each Scoring Range	
Scores	Percentage of Respondents
0	12.9
1–100	12.9
101–150	9.7
151–199	16.1
200–300	12.9
301–400	9.7
401–500	16.1
>500	9.7
	100.0

Source: Robert H. Woods, Misty Johanson, and Michael P. Sciarini, "Stress Factors in the Lives of Hospitality Managers," *Praxis: The Journal of Applied Hospitality Management* 1 (1998): 1–8.

Exhibit 6   Most Frequently Reported Stressors

Percentage of Hotel Managers Reporting Each Stress Factor	
Item	Percentage Reporting
Holidays	56.7
Outstanding personal achievement	39.6
Change in responsibilities at work	39.6
Marriage	32.3
Change in work hours or conditions	30.2
Revision of personal habits	28.2
Change in number of arguments with spouse	24.5
Change in financial state	20.7

Source: Robert H. Woods, Misty Johanson, and Michael P. Sciarini, "Stress Factors in the Lives of Hospitality Managers," *Praxis: The Journal of Applied Hospitality Management* 1 (1998): 1–8.

counseling programs. A simple stress reduction plan might recommend the following guidelines for day-to-day living at home and on the job:

- Rate tasks by importance; address the most important task first.
- Delegate authority whenever possible.
- Set and follow realistic deadlines and schedules.
- Plan ahead to avoid surprises.
- Take frequent "breathers."
- Avoid procrastination.

- Eat sensibly; avoid alcohol, tobacco, and drugs; and exercise at least 20 minutes three times per week.

- Stroke a pet; this can lower stress and blood pressure.

- Get enough sleep. Getting enough sleep is an important step in reducing stress and mistakes at work. According to a survey conducted among 200 senior executives:

  - 45 percent stated that their decision-making ability is seriously hampered by a lack of sleep.

  - 18 percent admitted that lack of sleep caused them to make a decision resulting in serious repercussions for the business.[20]

Reducing the causes of organizational stress includes redesigning jobs to eliminate unnecessary or particularly stressful aspects, rescheduling workflow to eliminate bottlenecks or backups, clarifying roles, and establishing job enrichment programs. Among other programs that reduce organizationally induced stress are retreats, flexible work schedules, job sharing, and employee assistance programs.

Employee Assistance Programs

Estimates are that employees who abuse alcohol and drugs cost U.S. employers astronomical amounts of money. For instance, the U.S. Chamber of Commerce states that drug abuse costs the U.S. economy over $140 billion annually. Research shows that substance abuse can cost a hospitality operation $7,500 per abusing employee annually. These losses are sustained through inefficiency and lost productivity, theft, absenteeism, turnover, reduced employee morale, on-the-job injury, and skyrocketing health care costs. Eighty percent of alcohol abusers in the United States are employed or are dependents of an employee. Because of problems with alcohol:

- U.S. workers miss 33 million workdays a year.

- Absenteeism costs $4 billion due to lost productivity and other losses.

- $36 billion have been spent on health care to treat alcohol-related problems and illnesses.[21]

Information collected by employee assistance programs (EAPs) shows that the 10 to 20 percent of employees with personal problems will account for 80 to 85 percent of an organization's personnel problems. About 30 percent of all absenteeism stems from personal problems.

Some studies gather separate data for alcohol abuse. For instance, the overall cost of alcohol abuse to U.S. employers is about $134 billion annually.[22] In addition, alcohol is responsible for:

- 12,121 cases of alcohol liver disease[23]

- 39 percent of traffic fatalities[24]

The National Council on Alcohol and Drug Dependence has determined that 40 percent of industrial casualties and 47 percent of industrial injuries are alcohol-related. While some of the costs associated with stress and mental or emotional health problems are drug-related, some are not. As illustrated in Exhibit 4, many factors can cause substantial amounts of stress.

EAPs can help employees cope with personal problems like drug and alcohol abuse. Implementation of such programs can help decrease some of the costs associated with alcohol, drug, and personal problems. EAPs have become increasingly popular over the last few years: 74 percent of companies provided them in 2005, up from 68 percent in 2001.[25] Setting up an EAP does not have to be expensive. EAP costs are usually less than one-half of one percent of a company's health care budget. In fact, the costs of EAPs have not gone up in the last 10 to 15 years.[26]

EAPs are as varied as U.S. businesses. In some cases, programs help employees with specific problems like alcohol or drug abuse. In other cases, EAPs include such services as family counseling, financial counseling, and educational or career counseling. There is no single type of EAP; instead, programs vary according to:

- the variety of services offered

- the expertise and training of employee assistance personnel

- the location of the services offered

Most EAPs in the United States offer alcohol and drug abuse counseling, pre-retirement counseling, and stress reduction counseling. About half offer career counseling. Other services offered in employee assistance programs include marital counseling, financial counseling, legal counseling, child care counseling, elder care counseling, and family counseling. According to a 2001 report published by the Institute of Management and Administration, an additional 30 million employees will be covered by EAPs over the next five years.

Setting Up EAPs

Setting up an EAP is a four-stage process. The first stage involves the identification of workplace problems. The second stage is devoted to program development. The third stage is implementation, and the fourth stage is evaluation.

Most EAPs include programs that focus on preventing or reducing drug and alcohol abuse. Many people assume that such programs are typical of EAPs in the hospitality industry since its traditional work force is in the age group most likely to abuse drugs and alcohol. However, employers should assess their individual work environments to determine what programs their employees need most. Assessment—usually conducted by third parties to ensure anonymity—may include observations, interviews, and personality testing.

Once the needs for an EAP have been determined, managers can concentrate on program development. Many EAPs use both internal and external services and programs. Employees generally have an easier time participating in in-house programs conducted on company premises. In-house programs reduce anonymity, however, and a company can be held liable for an employer's negligent or malicious acts during such a program.

Exhibit 7   Referring an Employee to an Employee Assistance Program

When Referring an Employee to an EAP:	
Don't say:	**Do say:**
You seem to have a drinking problem.	You have been late to work three times in two weeks, your performance is slipping, and I've smelled alcohol on your breath.
You are all stressed out. I think you'd better get help.	We have received six complaints from coworkers about you yelling at them. This cannot continue.
The EAP will provide the help you need.	The EAP can help you address your performance.
We would like you to get therapy for your problems.	We would like you to try the EAP for assistance with these concerns.

Source: Jane Easter Bahls, "Handle With Care," *HR Magazine* 44 (1999) 3: 60–65.

Hiring and training personnel for in-house programs may cost more than using external services, which offer advantages over internal programs such as increased anonymity and, sometimes, more professional expertise. When implementing EAPs, the most critical elements are management support, ensurance of employee anonymity or confidentiality, and thorough communication about the services and how employees can access them.

Businesses evaluate an EAP by examining the program's utility. To determine the costs and benefits of an EAP, hospitality managers should first multiply the business's total annual wage cost by .17 (or 17 percent, the national average for "troubled" employees); the resulting number should then be multiplied by 25 percent. The final figure represents the potential loss a company lacking an EAP will incur. EAPs typically reduce this loss by 50 percent. After a program is put in place, an evaluation can examine productivity increases; reductions in health care, insurance, and turnover costs; and the number of employees who use the EAP.

A word of advice for managers on recommending employees for EAP programs: be careful. There have been several instances when businesses have implied to employees that they believe that they need assistance, thereby suggesting that the employee is disabled and covered by ADA. If the employee refuses and the business eventually terminates the employment, the employee can sue under ADA provisions because the "company knew." This happened to Lucky Stores, a chain of supermarkets in California, and the business lost the case. One way to reduce the likelihood that this will happen is in the manager's approach to addressing the employee's problems. For example, the way you say things to an employee can set you up for later ADA troubles. Consider the examples in Exhibit 7.

Costs Saved by EAPs

While EAPs cost money to establish and operate, there is clearly a link between the cost of implementation and reductions in employer expenses. Companies consistently report that they receive at least a 3:1 return for every dollar they invest in an EAP.[27]

One reason EAPs are so successful is that drug and alcohol abuse problems are addressed more successfully within the workplace than outside the workplace. One researcher noted in 1991 that the employee substance abuse recovery rate is 70 to 80 percent when programs are initiated at work.[28] The principal reason for this recovery rate appears to be that employees believed they would lose their jobs if they failed to enroll in company-sponsored EAPs.

While EAPs are used widely by larger employers, they are not used widely by smaller businesses. More than likely, these businesses fear that such programs will be too costly or that their size precludes the need for an EAP. Also, these employers probably figure that the anonymity or confidentiality necessary for an EAP to work would be difficult or even impossible to ensure in a smaller setting. [29]

While some companies have not established EAPs for their employees, others are forging ahead to include broader issues in their EAPs. One trend is to combine EAPs with other health care programs to realize even further reductions in employer costs. Another trend involves the early detection, identification, and referral of employees with problems. Employers are also attempting to increase confidentiality to encourage reluctant employees to use the services. Finally, many businesses are moving EAPs off-site in order to access more professional services.

The market for outsourcing human resource management services is hot and will get hotter. The outsourced HR functions industry grew at an annual rate of 21.9 percent between 2001 and 2005, from a $21.7 billion industry to a $58.5 billion industry in the United States.[30] One source estimates that global expenditures for HR outsourcing will be close to $14 billion in 2009.[31] While many human resources functions are being outsourced, EAPs often lead the pack.[32]

Other Issues in Safety and Health

So far, much of our discussion regarding health issues has been linked to substance abuse and stress. However, these are not the only health-related issues managers and employees face in the hospitality industry. This section addresses several other important health concerns that exist in today's business environment.

Acquired Immune Deficiency Syndrome

While no evidence exists that **Acquired Immune Deficiency Syndrome (AIDS)** can be transmitted through food preparation, hospitality managers have long worried that guests would associate AIDS with food service operations. Many managers have worried about diners boycotting restaurants that employ people with AIDS. In fact, before the Americans with Disabilities Act (ADA), food service and hotel operators lobbied heavily for the Chandler Amendment. This amendment to the ADA would have allowed hospitality managers to assign employees with communicable diseases to non-food handling positions.

If an individual has a communicable disease that is on a list prepared by the Secretary of Health and Human Services, and if that disease can be passed on by handling food, the food service operation can remove that person from the job. The only exception applies when the risk presented by the disease can be eliminated by providing reasonable accommodation.

AIDS is a retrovirus that attacks the body's immune system; the virus weakens the immune system so that the body is unable to fight infection. The scientific name for the virus is human immunodeficiency virus, or HIV. People who test positive for HIV are often described as HIV-positive. Being HIV-positive is not the same as having AIDS. People infected with the virus do not have AIDS until they develop the symptoms. Many people remain HIV-infected but apparently healthy and symptom-free for years.

The national Centers for Disease Control and Prevention (CDC) announced in 1991 that AIDS was the number-one overall killer of Americans 25 to 44 years old. By 1999, new HIV infections in the United States had stabilized at about 40,000 per year. Improved drug therapy helped to reduce AIDS deaths by 68 percent between 1995 and 1997.[33] CDC figures show that women accounted for 27 percent of the estimated 38,730 diagnoses of HIV/AIDS in 2004.[34] The cost of the AIDS epidemic is enormous. By 1995, the CDC estimated that there were two to three AIDS/HIV-positive employees for every 250 employees overall and that 90 percent of HIV-infected Americans were in the workplace. First Union National Bank, with 34,000 employees, estimated that it has 300 to 350 employees with HIV, each of whom will accrue an average of $120,000 in medical bills. That totals $30 to $40 million in medical costs over the next few years, and First Union National is just one example of the prevailing workplace trend.[35] Hospitality companies can use this same scale (two cases per every 300 employees) to determine the number of HIV-positive employees they are likely to have.

For hospitality managers, the biggest problem regarding AIDS is fear of the disease itself. AIDS is transmitted through direct contact with the blood, blood products, or sexual fluid of an infected person, not through casual contact. Unprotected sex and the sharing of hypodermic needles are still recognized as the principal means of transmitting the virus. Many people fail to understand that AIDS does not spread like many other contagious diseases.

Depression Among Employees

It is important that EAPs be prepared to address depression and its affects on the employee. Depression is now the most common health problem around the globe. It affects one in five people during some point in their lifetime. Although depression affects all genders and ages, it is most common in those 24 to 44 years of age, and twice as common in women than in men. Untreated depression can persist for years. Depression can have a huge negative effect on the workplace, for it is estimated that over six million workdays are lost annually due to the illness. In addition, depression can cost many, many working days of reduced productivity per year, since those who are depressed work at a diminished capacity. One employee in 40 is likely suffering from untreated depression.[36]

Wellness Programs

Healthy living has become an obsession to many people in the United States. Many American companies have responded to this trend by establishing **wellness programs** designed to help employees live healthier lives. The theory behind wellness programs is that healthier employees are more likely to be productive, satisfied, and reliable. In that sense, wellness programs are injury prevention strategies.

The American Management Association revealed that 52 percent of all medium-sized companies (1,000 to 10,000 employees) and 57 percent of all large companies (more than 10,000 employees) have established wellness programs for their employees.[37]

Most wellness programs have three components:

- *Health screening and assessment.* Most wellness programs screen and assess employees before enrolling them, primarily to determine health and exercise needs. At a minimum, this process includes physical exams and tests to determine cholesterol, blood sugar, stress, and blood pressure levels.

- *Physical fitness programs.* A component of wellness programs may be classes or facilities for aerobics, jogging, swimming, and weight training or exercise equipment such as bicycles, rowing machines, or treadmills.

- *Education and training.* Many wellness programs offer clinics on smoking cessation, cholesterol reduction, stress reduction, and diet management.

The success of wellness programs in improving employee performance is still up for debate. There is substantial evidence that wellness programs can reduce health care costs for the employer. Consider the results of a wellness program started by Coors Brewing Company in 1980. This program featured a jogging track, weight program, diet training, smoking cessation, and many of the other components we listed earlier. By 1989, Coors reported that their program had resulted in a return of $6.15 for every $1 invested. This money originated from reductions in health care costs, absenteeism, turnover, and workers' compensation claims. Between 1988 and 1989, the national average for health care costs rose 18.6 percent, while the cost for health care at Coors rose only 5.9 percent.[38] Coors claimed that the wellness program also contributed to increases in employee morale, job satisfaction, and general well-being during the same period. Not all companies are as prepared to start wellness programs as Coors was. In fact, many do not know where to start. Some low-cost or free resources for health promotion programs are provided in Exhibit 8.[39]

Smoking in the Workplace

Workplace smoking is a very hot issue. While smokers contend that they have a constitutional right to smoke, nonsmokers contend that passive smoke (smoke from other people's cigarettes) is unhealthy. Education about and emphasis on the hazards of smoking have helped to greatly reduce the number of Americans who smoke.

In most states, hospitality companies have addressed the issue of smoking from a guest perspective. Many states and municipalities now have laws for segregating smokers from nonsmokers in dining rooms and guestrooms.

Wellness advocates contend that smoking reduction in the workplace is very important to maintaining employee health and productivity. Smokers have higher absenteeism rates (40 percent for men and 25 percent for women), more dips in

Exhibit 8   Low-Cost or Free Resources for Health Promotion Programs

The Wellness Councils of America, a nonprofit group based in Omaha, Nebraska, sells memberships for $250 a year. Services include wellness consulting, access to local chapter meetings, and *Healthy, Wealthy, and Wise*, a book that explains how to set up a program. Nonmembers can purchase the book for $95. Call (402) 572-3590.

Wellness in the Workplace: How to Plan, Implement and Evaluate a Wellness Program is available for $9.95 through Crisp Publications in Los Altos, California. Call (800) 442-7477.

The American Institute for Preventive Medicine, in Farmington Hills, Michigan, sells low-cost health promotion publications. One is the *HealthyLife Self-Care Guide*, designed to teach employees how to treat common illnesses and determine when they truly need medical help. Cost: $4.45 a copy, with quantity discounts for 10 or more copies. Call (800) 345-2476.

Occupational Health Strategies Inc., a Madbury, New Hampshire, consulting firm, offers a ready-made wellness program called "Healthy Achievers." For $495 a year, the firm provides a wellness-program manual and then a kit on a new health topic every two months. Call (603) 743-3838.

Healthier People Network Inc., an Atlanta-based nonprofit group, sells a $195 software program that allows a company to conduct health appraisals for employees to gauge their individual health risks, based on their answers to a lifestlye question-naire. The fee also includes a prevention-oriented health newsletter. Call (404) 636-3127.

The National Wellness Institute offers referrals to wellness consultants and to vendors who offer books and audio tapes for corporate wellness programs. In addi-tion, the institute holds a conference every July geared toward companies that want to establish or improve their own wellness programs. Contact the Institute at 1045 Clark St., Suite 210, Stevens Point, Wisconsin 54481. Call (800) 243-8694.

The American Cancer Society is one of several national health organizations that offer health-promotion information to employers, particularly through local chapters. The organization provides pamphlets, videos, and guest workshop speakers at no charge. Contact your local chapter or call (800) 227-2345 for more information.

The American Heart Association offers "Heart at Work," a program that includes ready-made kits of information for wellness workshops on seven topics. Prices range from $200 to $600, depending on the number of kits ordered and the charges levied by local Association chapters. Call (800) 242-9821.

Many health maintenance organizations (HMOs) and other managed care provid-ers offer member employers health promotion services.

productivity (from smoking breaks), and higher medical costs. Overall, Americans who smoke miss up to 10 percent of their workdays.[40] A smoking employee costs the employer at least $1,000 more per year in total direct and indirect healthcare costs.[41]

By 1993, 56 percent of U.S. companies had smoke-free policies.[42] About half the states have enacted legislation to prohibit discrimination against smokers out-side the workplace. These statutes are different from statutes in most states that allow (or require) employers to regulate smoking in the workplace. While hospitality companies everywhere can regulate workplace smoking or prohibit it altogether, they cannot discharge, refuse to hire, or otherwise discriminate against people who smoke outside of work in states that prohibit such discrimination.

The IRS now considers the cost of kicking the smoking habit a deductible medical expense. Because taxpayers can deduct only medical expenses greater than 7.5 percent of their annual salaries, however, this ruling may have little direct impact except in cases where employees include this option in their Section 125 flexible spending account.[43]

Work Life/Home Life Issues

In 1991, *Personnel Journal* bestowed its Optima Award in the Quality of Life category to Marriott Corporation. This award recognized the efforts of Marriott's Department of Work and Family Life to improve the quality of work life among the company's employees. Marriott established this department in 1989 as part of a three-year strategic plan to increase the personal and work satisfaction of its employees.[44]

Marriott is not alone in recognizing the link between the quality of work life and the quality of personal life. More and more American companies see that more and more of their employees regard quality of life as a very important issue. Research suggests that helping families balance **work-family issues** is one of the most pressing challenges companies face today.[45]

Two-Income Families. The increase in quality of work life programs is due to the growing number of two-income and dual-career families in the United States. The Department of Labor predicts that nearly 81 percent of future marriages in the United States will involve dual careers.[46] While dual-career families sometimes enjoy an increase in disposable income, they can also experience unique problems. Many working men and women in their 40s are caught between caring for young children and caring for elderly parents.[47] This "sandwich generation" represents the largest percentage of employed persons in the United States. Not all of these people know how to cope with the problems they face. Some researchers cite inability to deal with personal problems as one cause for the increased number of alcohol, drug, and work-stress problems.

Not everything is rosy for two-career families. Recent research indicates that dual careers may be costing families money. Several studies indicate that well-educated men with working wives are paid and promoted less than men with stay-at-home wives, possibly because they can't clock as much face time (Exhibit 9). In a 1995 survey at Eli Lilly and Company, just 36 percent of workers said it was possible to get ahead and still devote sufficient time to their families—and Lilly has a reputation as one of the most family-friendly companies. Consider the results of a 1997 survey of 236 male managers who earned MBAs from two large northeastern universities between 1975 and 1980. All were married with children. On average, the 84 men married to women who did not work outside the home earned 32 percent more than the 152 men married to women who worked either part-time or full-time. The study was undertaken by Joy Schneer of Rider University in New Jersey, and Frieda Reitman of Pace University.

As incomes began to stagnate in the early 1970s, it has taken a second earner to keep the standard of living of even the most affluent households from falling behind. Now, in 84 percent of married couples, both the husband and wife work.

Exhibit 9   Two-Income Families Face Unique Problems

Average 1993 Income of Men Whose Wives Were:	
Working Outside the Home	Not Working Outside the Home
$95,067	$125,120
Up 48% from 1987	Up 59% from 1987
Percentage of Men Who Received Promotions Whose Wives Were:	
Working Outside the Home	Not Working Outside the Home
28%	38%

Source: Betsy Morris, "Is Your Family Wrecking Your Career (and Vice Versa), *Fortune Magazine* (March 17, 1997): 17–20.

The demands of this new economy wreak havoc on family routines that are the bulwark of childhood. The family dinner has disappeared in many homes as parents work long past the dinner hour. Bedtime slippage follows to give Mom and Dad time—which may or may not be "quality time"—with the kids. The long, unpredictable hours lead to kaleidoscopic child care arrangements. Many households have not one but several babysitters or daycare providers; parents need a flow chart to keep it all straight.

Today's working people provide corporate America with an army of workers, an unprecedented number of them unencumbered. Young people are delaying marriage and children. One-third of women and one-half of men ages 25 to 29 have never married—an all-time high. The percentage of childless women rose from ten percent of 40- to 45-year-olds in 1976 to 17.5 percent in 1994, another all-time high. Some of this childlessness is due to infertility, but a lot is out of choice. Birthrates, which have rebounded slightly to about two per woman after falling to a low of 1.8 a decade or so ago, are buoyed largely by immigrant groups.[48] In the past, employees expected little help from their employers in balancing family and work issues. Today, many employees do expect their employers to help them balance work and family problems.[49] Companies that respond to this expectation are rewarded with lower turnover and absenteeism, increased productivity, and an edge in recruiting. In 2000, 80 percent of Americans listed a family-friendly work schedule as a top priority (Radcliffe Public Policy Center, 2000). In the spring of 2001, the U.S. Department of Labor launched a Twenty-First Century Workforce Initiative to study quality of life issues.[50]

Child and Elderly Care. Child and elderly care are two of the greatest challenges employees encounter while attempting to balance work and family life. For previous generations, it was customary—when economically feasible—for men to work outside the home and for women to stay at home to care for children and elderly parents and manage the household. As a result of socio-economic changes in the United States, both parents are now in the work force.

Parents lose an average of eight working days per year due to child care problems and spend an average of eight hours a year—mostly while at work—arranging for child care.[51] In five out of six two-income families, the work hours of parents do not overlap.[52] Many businesses have responded to the changing schedules of families. Twenty-four-hour grocery stores, all-night laundries, and fast-food restaurants are now common. However, few child-care facilities stay open 24 hours a day, seven days a week; some don't even stay open past 6:00 P.M. on weekdays.

Hospitality businesses are at particular risk for work-family problems because of the industry's high percentage of young employees. Many are starting new families and have a critical need for child care. Hospitality operations that offer child care can reap substantial benefits, not only by attracting quality employees, but by retaining them.

In establishing such programs, properties might consider offering such services as:[53]

- Alternate work patterns or schedules

- Dependent care spending accounts that allot employees designated funds to spend on child care

- Discounts on company-arranged child care

- Subsidized child care

- Company-sponsored child care programs operated by third parties for the benefit of employees

- Child care information and referral services

- Sick-child leave programs

- Onsite child care

Some employees face similar challenges in caring for aging parents. In addition to managing their own lives and families, these employees also manage the care of their elderly parents. Such responsibilities place further demands on employees to take time off work to attend to medical appointments, errands, and other necessities.

A 1997 MetLife study of 1,500 employers found that U.S. businesses lost between $11.4 billion and $29 billion annually in productivity due to elder caregiving. The study identified a large contingent of people who spend from eight to ten hours weekly providing elder care for their parents. The study labeled these people as "caregivers with a glass ceiling" because the time away from work was hurting their careers.

The segment of the population that is 65 or older will have grown from 34.6 million in 1999 to 70 million in 2010, a 137 percent increase. Companies are responding to these needs in a variety of ways, including:

- Flexible work arrangements for workers with elder care issues

- Resource and referral programs

- Long-term care insurance

- Expanded family and medical leave (12 percent of employers in the United States exceed the mandated minimum)

- Flexible spending and dependent care medical accounts

- Adult day care

- Seminars, fairs, and support groups to educate employees.

One example in the hospitality industry is Marriott, which says that about 15 percent of its workforce faces elder care issues. After installing services for these people, Marriott reported that it was able to retain 600 employees whom it would have lost in 1999 alone if it had not had such services.[54] The impact of caring for elders is substantial. According to the National Center for Women and Aging, a worker who cares for an elder will sacrifice, on average, $659,000 in lost wages over his or her lifetime. Approximately 22 million households have at least one person caring for a friend or relative.[55] In 2005, 30–40 percent of Americans were involved in taking care of aging parents.[56]

The biggest work-family stressors that employees with children and elderly parents at home face are: 1) number of hours worked, 2) lack of control over decisions to work overtime, 3) inflexibility of work schedules, 4) irregular starting times for work, and 5) psychologically demanding work. These problems are common to both working men and women. Hospitality employees are at particular risk for such problems given the irregular hours and long shifts of many hotel and restaurant jobs, many of which are held by women. To date, few hospitality operations have developed plans to reduce the effects of work-family conflicts, even though a projected 75 to 90 percent of doctor visits are due to stress-related problems created either at work or at home. The cost of these problems is enormous.[57]

Critical Incidents in the Workplace. A critical incident is any condition that elicits powerful emotional responses and is stressful enough to affect a person's ability to do the job. This includes death, calamity, violence, and illness. The organizational consequences of such incidences can be disastrous; companies should prepare in advance to reduce their risks and to respond when necessary.

In 1992, workplace violence cost $4.2 billion nationally. Critical incidents are estimated to have cost $23.8 billion in the same year (or $250,000 per incident). Organizational effects include:

1. Changes in employee work performance—impaired judgment, absenteeism, memory problems, and inability to make decisions.

2. Changes in relationships between employees—people react differently.

3. Changes in employee perceptions of management—if management doesn't respond "appropriately," it can be considered cold and uncaring.

4. Changes in management-employee relationships—commitment, communication, motivation, and trust are key.

Proper preparation for dealing with critical incidents includes forming a crisis management team to step in immediately, identifying outside assistance resources, conducting an audit to identify vulnerabilities, and developing policies and procedures.

If an incident occurs, the crisis management team should convene immediately to address the incident. It is also important to keep communication lines open with employees and necessary outside sources while working through a problem.

Organizations that fail to manage critical incidents do so because they fail to plan in advance, take responsibility, or provide the time or resources to help employees heal. Unfortunately, too many hospitality companies have experienced the need for critical incident planning in recent years. The worst case scenarios—mass killings in a Luby's Cafeteria and at a McDonald's—are well known. However, less sensational incidents can have serious impact as well; the sudden death or illness of an employee can generate the need for crisis management.

The Ergosmart Workplace. Ergonomics is the applied science of equipment design intended to maximize productivity by reducing operator fatigue and discomfort. It has become part of a manager's responsibility to monitor workplace ergonomics. Failure to implement good ergonomics policies can cost thousands of dollars. According to the U.S. Bureau of Labor Statistics, repetitive strain injuries—many of which can be avoided by thorough attention to ergonomics—are becoming a major cause of workers' compensation claims. Work habits, task design, equipment, individual risks, and other factors can lead to musculoskeletal disorders such as back pain, the most common cause of workers' compensation. Back pain results in 90 million lost work days per year, many of which can be saved simply by buying the right chair or altering equipment. Other factors can lead to headaches, tension, fatigue, and other problems. The Bureau of Labor Statistics and OSHA report that each year, 1.8 million workers suffer from repetitive motion or overexertion injuries. One-third of workplace injuries are caused by musculoskeletal injuries such as carpal tunnel syndrome and back strain. Exhibit 10 provides guidelines for improving computer station ergonomics. Taking such steps can reduce the risk of injuries, workers' compensation claims, and lawsuits.

Endnotes

1. Mary Ann Fitzpatrick and Phyllis King, "Disability Management Pays Off," *Professional Safety* 46 (January 2001): 39–41.

2. *U.S. News and World Report*, 26 March 2001, 10.

3. "Meeting the Mandate: Saving Lives, Preventing Injury, Preserving Health," USDL 00-376, 22 December 2000.

4. Karen Eich Drummond, *Human Resource Management for the Hospitality Industry* (New York: Van Nostrand Reinhold, 1990), 156.

5. Drummond, 156.

6. Naomi Swanson, et al. "The Impact of Keyboard Design on Comfort and Productivity," *Applied Ergonomics* 28 (February 1997): 9–10.

Exhibit 10   Work Station Ergonomics

- The keyboard and monitor should be directly in front of the person to avoid twisting the body.
- The height of the table or chair should allow wrists to be positioned at the same level as the elbow.
- The monitor and typing material should be at or just below eye level.
- The monitor should be a distance of 18 inches to 30 inches from the eyes. Prescription glasses must be for this distance.
- The keyboard should be at a level where wrists are straight, in neutral position, rather than bent forward or flexed for long periods of time.
- The wrists should be able to rest lightly on a pad for support.
- The head and neck should be upright, not tilting forward or to the side.
- The chair should provide lower- and middle-back support.
- The feet should be flat on the floor, or on a footrest, so the knees are parallel at a 90-degree to 110-degree angle. There should be 3 to 6 inches of leg room between one's lap and the keyboard.

7. Foster Frable Jr., "Crystal Ball Shows 2001 Business Anything But Usual With New Regulations, Equipment" 35 (January 15, 2001): 26, 49.

8. www.osha-slc.gov/Web site of the Occupational Safety and Health Administration

9. National Women's Health Resource Center, "Stress Overview," *Contemporary Women's Issues,* 25 May 2005.

10. Ellen Galinsky, James T. Bond, Stacy S. Kim, Lois Nackon, Erin Brownfield, and Kelly Sakai, "Overwork in America: When the Way We Work Becomes Too Much: Executive Summary," Families and Work Institute (2005).

11. National Women's Health Resource Center, http://www.healthywomen.org/.

12. Joyce Crane, "Firms Take Lead on Stress Management for Workers," *Boston Business Journal* 19, no. 41 (1998): 34–35.

13. Mort Sarabakhsh, David Carson, and Elaine Lindgren, "The Personal Cost of Hospitality Management," *Cornell Hotel and Restaurant Administration Quarterly* 30 (May 1989): 72.

14. Ian Buick and Mahesh Thomas, "Why Do Middle Managers in Hotels Burn Out?" *International Journal of Contemporary Hospitality Management* 13, no. 6 (2001): 304–309.

15. Buick and Thomas.

16. Buick and Thomas.

17. Joan M. Lang, "Foodservice Industry: Career Burnout," *Restaurant Business* 90, no. 4 (1991): 131–148.

18. Dan Bignold, "Hospitality Sector Reaches Drink and Drug Crisis Point," *Caterer & Hotelkeeper* 192, no. 4294 (2003).

19. Leah Carlson, "EAP Use Increasingly Centers Around Stress, Family Issues," *Employee Benefit News*, 1 September 2005, 2–4.

20. Robert D. Oxeman, Tami L. Knotts, and Jeff Koch, "Working While the World Sleeps: A Consideration of Sleep and Shift Work Design," *Employee Responsibilities and Rights Journal* 14, no.4 (2002): 145.

21. Roberto Ceniceros, "Most Health Plans Poor at Addressing Alcohol Problems, Researcher Claims," *Business Insurance* 39, no. 33 (2005): 4–6.

22. David Anderson and Eric Goplerud, "Alcohol Problems: Finding Solutions to Save Lives and Money," *Benefits and Compensation Digest* 42, no. 10 (2005): 34.

23. http://www.cdc.gov/nchs/fastats/alcohol.hm, Web site of the Centers for Disease Control and Prevention.

24. Brian Haynes, "DUI Fatalities Falling," *Las Vegas Review-Journal*, 26 September 2005, 1B.

25. Carlson.

26. Tom Anderson, "Employers Should Promote EAPs to Maximize ROI," *Employee Benefit News*, 1 June 2005.

27. "SAP Services: A Natural Extension of EAPs," *Journal of Employee Assistance* (July 2005).

28. Steven A. La Shier, "Safety Professionals Take the Lead: Substance Abuse in the Workplace," *Professional Safety* 36, no. 6 (1991): 50.

29. Ajay K. Saisi, Richard F. Bertramini, and Michael Koller, "Employer Awareness, Attitudes and Referral Practices Regarding Behavioral Problems in the Workplace: Implications for EAPs," *Journal of Professional Services Marketing* 6, no. 8 (1991): 177–192.

30. H. Borg, The Pause Scholarship Foundation, Retrieved November 2, 2005. http://www.mah.se/upload/Omvärlden/Cerrio/Outsourcing%20of%20HR,%20Hakan%20Borg,%20May$202004.pdf.

31. Douglas P. Shuit, "Sea Change," *Workforce Management* 84, no. 6 (2005).

32. Bill Leonard, "HR Update," *HR Magazine* 44, no. 13 (1999): 27–31.

33. "Deadly Self-Deception," *American Medical News*, 14 October 1999, 17.

34. "HIV/AIDS Surveillance Report, 2004," Atlanta: U.S. Department of Health and Human Services, Centers for Disease Control and Prevention (2005).

35. Nancy L. Breuer, "Emerging Trends for Managing AIDS in the Workplace," *Personnel Journal* 74 (June 1995): 125–131.

36. "A Call for Help," *Human Resources*, 4 October 2005.

37. Daniel Stokols, "Integration of Medical Care and Worksite Health Promotion," *JAMA* 27 (12 April 1995): 1136–1143.

38. William K. Coors, "Wellness Comes of Age," *Chief Executive* 63 (1991): 37.

39. Laura M. Litvam, "Preventive Medicine," *Nation's Business* 83 (September 1995): 32–35.

40. William L. Weis, "Can You Afford to Hire Smokers?" *Personnel Administration* 26 no. 5 (1989): 71–78.

41. "Benefits of a Smoke-Free Workplace," Action on Smoking and Health (2000).

42. Jennifer Laabs, "Companies Kick the Smoking Habit," *Personnel Journal* 73 (January 1994): 38–43.

43. Bill Leonard, "HR Update," *HR Magazine* 44, no. 13 (1999): 27–31.

44. Charlene Mayer Solomon, "Marriott's Family Matters," *Personnel Journal* 70 (October 1991): 40–42.

45. William H. Wagel and Hermine Zagat Levine, "HR '90: Challenges and Opportunities," *Personnel* 67, no. 6 (1990): 18–42.

46. Calvin Reynolds and Rita Bennett, "The Career Couple Challenge," *Personnel* 70, no. 30 (1991): 47.

47. Paula Eubanks, "Hospitals Face the Challenges of 'Sandwich Generation' Employees," *Hospitals* 65, no. 7 (1991): 60.

48. Betsy Morris, "Is Your Family Wrecking Your Career? And Vice Versa," *Fortune* 17 March 1997, 70–75.

49. Chris Lae, "Balancing Work and Family," *Training* 28, no. 9 (1991): 25.

50. http://www.dol.gov. Web site of the U.S. Department of Labor.

51. Carol Ann Rudolph, "Child Care and the Work Place," *Bottomline* 7, no. 9 (1990): 20.

52. Jennifer McEnroe, "Split-Shift Parenting," *American Demographics* 13, no. 3 (1991): 53.

53. Lisa R. Coke, "Child Care and Business," *Business and Economic Review* 35, no. 2 (1989): 4–9.

54. Susan J. Wells, "The Elder Care Cap," *HR Magazine* 45, no. 5 (2000): 38–43.

55. Russell V. Gerbman, "Elder Care Takes America by Storm," *HR Magazine* 45, no. 5 (2000): 50–56.

56. Lesley D. Riley and Christopher Bowen, "The Sandwich Generation: Challenges and Strategies of Multigenerational Families," *The Family Journal* 13, no. 1 (2005): 52–58.

57. "American Workers Are Stressed Out," *The Vocational Education Journal* 71 (April 1996): 14.

🔑 Key Terms

AIDS—Acquired Immune Deficiency Syndrome; incurable retrovirus.

burnout—Emotional or physical exhaustion due to stress; often results in employee turnover.

compliance officers—OSHA inspectors.

emergency OSHA standards—Standards issued by the U.S. secretary of labor to correct health and safety problems in the workplace that require immediate attention.

employee assistance program (EAP)—Employer-sponsored counseling program designed to help employees deal with personal problems related to drug or alcohol abuse, stress, family tension, finances, career goals, or other situations that affect their work. EAPs generally involve internal or external counseling services.

ergonomics—Ergonomics is the applied science of equipment design intended to maximize productivity by reducing operator fatigue and discomfort.

HazComm Standard—Hazard Communication Standard; OSHA's regulation requiring employers to inform employees about possible hazards related to chemicals they use on the job.

National Institute for Occupational Safety and Health (NIOSH)—A federal agency whose primary purpose is to carry out research and recommend occupational safety and health standards.

Occupational Safety and Health Administration (OSHA)—An agency within the U.S. Department of Labor created to establish occupational safety and health standards, set up regulations, conduct inspections, issue citations, and propose penalties for noncompliance.

Occupational Safety and Health Review Commission (OSHRC)—Independent federal agency that holds hearings on employer appeals of citations and penalties issued by OSHA.

Occupational Safety and Health Act of 1970—Federal legislation that provides for safe and healthful working conditions for all workers by establishing standards, requiring regular inspections and recordkeeping, and creating policing agencies, including the Occupational Safety and Health Administration.

permanant OSHA standards—Standards issued by OSHA that provide employers with permanent guidelines for workplace safety and health.

repetitive strain injuries (RSI)—Injuries to the body that result from a repeated procedure that stresses a particular part of the body. Carpal tunnel syndrome is considered a repetitive strain injury. Also known as repetitive stress injuries.

stressor—Item or condition that causes stress.

wellness program—Diet, exercise, stress reduction, and health prevention program designed to create a healthier and more satisfied work force.

work-family issues—Issues employees face that are related to balancing the pressures and demands of work and family life.

Review Questions

1. What typically happens when an OSHA compliance officer arrives for an inspection?

2. What rights are provided to employees under OSHA regulations?

3. What are some of the emerging issues that OSHA must deal with in the next few years?

4. What are the seven elements identified by OSHA for good company-sponsored safety and health programs?

5. What are the four causes of employee stress?

6. What are the principal methods of stress reduction?

7. What are some of the principal reasons for instituting an employee assistance program?

8. Why does AIDS present a particular problem for the hospitality industry?

9. What are the primary components in an employee wellness program?

10. What are some of the problems associated with dual-career families?

Internet Sites

For more information, visit the following Internet sites. Remember that Internet addresses can change without notice. If the site is no longer there, you can use a search engine to look for additional sites.

Alcohol Recovery Organizations
www.druginfonet.com/alcohol.htm

American Heart Association
americanheart.org

American Cancer Society
www.cancer.org

Back Pain and Help Groups
www.druginfonet.com:80/backpain.htm

Centers for Disease Control and Prevention
www.cdc.gov/

Center for Substance Abuse Prevention
www.samhsa.gov/

Drug InfoNet
www.druginfonet.com:

Employee Assistance Program Directory
www.eap-sap.com/

Health Resources Publishing
www.healthrespubs.com/

Mind Tools
www.mindtools.com/

National Cancer Institute
www.cancer.gov/

National Clearinghouse for Alcohol and Drug Information
www.health.org/

National Institute of Mental Health on stress management
www.thebody.com/nimh/stress.html

National Institute of Mental Health
www.nimh.nih.gov/

OSHA homepage
www.osha.gov/

U.S. Food and Drug
www.fda.gov/

Mini Case Study

Mary Jones was recently appointed to the new position of director of employee assistance programs at Mega Hotels. Over the objections of her boss, the director of human resources, Mary quickly instituted an alcohol and drug abuse awareness program in each of the hotel's properties. Her boss opposed the program on the basis that Mega Hotels knew little about the kinds of problems its employees faced.

Mary established in-house programs at each property in the chain and hired specialists to implement and supervise the programs. The annual salaries of the five specialists averaged $24,000.

Three months later, the president of Mega Hotels asked for a status report on the employee assistance program. At that time, Mary could report only a five percent employee participation rate. The president was disappointed with this rate and threatened to cancel the program. The president asked Mary to evaluate the progress of the program and to make recommendations for its long-term success.

Discussion Questions

1. What recommendations would you make to Mary about her task?
2. How might she evaluate the effectiveness of the program to date?
3. How could Mary have ensured greater participation in the program from the start?

Competencies

1. Describe the hospitality industry's turnover problem, demonstrate how to calculate turnover rates, and identify the costs of turnover. (pp. 423–430)

2. List causes of turnover, summarize several methods for reducing turnover, and discuss the impact of diversity on turnover. (pp. 430–439)

3. Explain the proper use of discipline in a hospitality organization and describe approaches to employee discipline. (pp. 439–443)

4. Describe possible appeals processes in an employee discipline program. (pp. 443–444)

5. Describe the appropriate use of discharge in an employee discipline program and identify several important concerns associated with using discharge. (pp. 444–449)

6. Outline an effective exit interview system. (pp. 449–451)

13

Turnover, Discipline, and Exits

MOST EMPLOYEES want to work. They want to keep their jobs. Most employees also want to be recognized by their peers and managers for the work they do. Why, then, is turnover such a problem in the hospitality industry? And why, even when unemployment rates are alarmingly high, does the hospitality industry usually still face labor shortages?

This chapter examines the hospitality turnover problem. In that context, it describes the importance of retention programs, the judicious use of discipline, and such organizational exit concerns as discharging employees and exit interviews.

The Turnover Problem

Each time a position is vacated, either voluntarily or involuntarily, a new employee must be hired and trained. This replacement cycle is known as turnover. As a result of current and impending labor shortages, employee turnover is now commanding the attention it deserves. Twenty or 30 years ago, hospitality managers seldom worried about where their employees would come from. At that time, turnover averaged about 60 percent annually for most hospitality companies, and triple-digit turnover was not uncommon. Even so, the supply of available workers always exceeded the demand.

Although turnover was too high even then, management always found reasons to justify it—seasonal work, young employees moving on to other careers, competition from new operations—all of which were valid then and are valid now. But the situation has changed today; turnover remains high, but the supply of available workers has diminished. As a result, the hospitality industry now finds itself critically short of employees. Even though this did not happen overnight, we still ask ourselves, "What happened?"

Two things happened. First, the baby boomers, many of whom were our former hourly employees, grew up. They are now our guests, and their children (the "baby echo") are just beginning to enter the labor market. Second, we failed to address the "temporary employee issue" created by the view held by many hospitality employees that they were just passing through on their way to "real" jobs.

Today the hospitality industry is still fighting high turnover rates. Recent turnover rates per segment in the U.S. restaurant industry, for example, were 129 percent for quick-service restaurants, 119 percent for fast casual/family dining, 101 percent for casual dining, and 83 percent for high-volume, casual dining/fine dining.[1] The rates for managers were 42 percent for quick-service restaurants, 30 percent for fast casual/family dining, 26 percent for casual dining, and 27 percent for high-volume casual dining/fine dining. Unfortunately, therefore, turnover rates remain extremely high for this segment of hospitality, even after years of efforts to curtail the rate.

Some companies have come up with better ways to maintain low turnover rates than others, of course. At the People Report Conference in 2005, the following companies were recognized for their leadership in reducing turnover in their organizations: Donatos Pizza in Columbus, Ohio, for quick service; Pizza Properties, an El Paso, Texas–based franchisee of Peter Piper Pizza, for fast casual/family dining; Los Angeles–based California Pizza Kitchen for full-service casual; and Capital Grille, the steakhouse chain owned by Atlanta-based Rare Hospitality Inc., for high-volume, casual dining/fine dining. People Report also presented T.G.I. Friday's with its Catalyst Award for the company with the most improved hourly and management turnover; after a concerted three-year effort, the casual-dining chain has lowered its turnover to 21 percent for managers and less than 90 percent for hourly workers.

At Donatos (a pizza chain), a 250 percent employee turnover rate was cut in half after a year, and further reduced to 118 percent by the end of 2005. The principal focus in this program was simple: help managers and employees achieve a healthy work/life balance that would improve their performance on the job and at home.[2]

Hospitality is not the only industry interested in stemming the turnover tide. However, the situation is not as grim in other industries. The average annual turnover rate in all industries in the United States is about 13 percent.[3]

Still, these other industries write, talk about, and actively engage in turnover reduction activities as well.

Determining Turnover Rates

The rate of turnover can be calculated for any time period or any group of workers. Unfortunately, not all hospitality organizations use the same methods for calculating turnover. Some include seasonal and part-time employees in their turnover statistics while others do not. One method of calculating turnover rates is to divide the number of terminations for a time period by the average number of employees for the same period. The easiest way to determine the average number of employees is to add the number of employees at the beginning of the period to the number of employees at the end of the period and divide by two. To express the rate as a percentage, multiply the result by 100. The formula is presented below. The example uses the turnover rate for a mid-size restaurant staffed with 25 servers (average); terminations for the year totaled 75:

$$\text{Annual turnover rate} \ = \ \frac{\text{Number of terminations}}{\text{Average number of employees}} \ \times \ 100$$

$$= \ \frac{75}{25} \ \times \ 100$$

$$= \ 300\%$$

Companies use this method simply to determine their total annual (or monthly) turnover rates. This method includes both desirable and undesirable turnover. (Desirable turnover is the loss of undesirable employees; undesirable turnover is the loss of desirable employees.)

A second method adjusts the turnover rate by the loss of undesirable employees (desired turnover). This method first subtracts the desirable terminations (undesirable employees), so that the resulting rate represents only the desirable employees lost (unwanted turnover) during the year or month. To see how it works, we can use the preceding example of 75 terminations for a staff of 25 servers, with the following additional information: 10 of the 75 terminations were desirable terminations—that is, undesirable employees:

$$\text{Unwanted turnover rate} = \frac{\text{Number of terminations} - \text{desired terminations}}{\text{Average number of employees}} \times 100$$

$$= \frac{75 - 10}{25} \times 100$$

$$= 260\%$$

Many managers prefer the second method because they can justify turnover associated with discharges of undesirable employees. In some cases, however, this method provides managers with an opportunity to disguise (or discount the significance of) high turnover rates. These managers might say, "We simply lost employees we didn't want." By including desirable turnover, the first formula may seem to overstate the degree to which turnover is a problem. Nonetheless, its adherents see it as a more accurate figure, in part because there are costs associated even with desired turnover.

The 1998 American Hotel & Lodging Educational Foundation (AH&LEF) survey on turnover, the largest study of its kind ever conducted, found that employee turnover in the lodging industry was about 50.4 percent annually overall.[4] Turnover varies by region, by segment, and by company, but the lodging industry turnover rate is about five times the average of all industries in the United States. Hospitality turnover remains high, but it is not because the problem has been ignored. In fact, a search of relevant databases produced approximately 1,250 citations relating to employee and managerial turnover. While much of this research has led to an increased understanding of many facets of the turnover problem, we have yet to resolve the issue. Turnover continues to be one of the most vexing and disturbing problems lodging managers face.

Much is already known about turnover. For instance, we know that turnover is costly. One study projects that the cost of replacing an employee, whether manager, supervisor, or line-level, can be as high as 100 percent of the annual pay for that employee.[5] Turnover has a significant negative impact on those employees who remain behind after friends and associates leave, and we know that there is a significant positive relationship between high turnover and both low customer retention and investor disinterest. We have also learned from research that there is a positive relationship between organizational stability and turnover, and that high turnover rates therefore create unwanted instability in organizations. Other research has shown us that there is a positive relationship between high turnover and organizational inefficiency.[6] We also know that unwanted turnover can contribute to an organization's inability to build an effective team of employees.

The research literature has also provided us with some valuable information on factors that cause turnover. For instance, we know that there is a positive relationship between turnover reduction and employee training,[7] that individual and group incentives reduce turnover, that salaries paid primarily in commissions and/or bonus compensation programs often lead to higher turnover,[8] that encouraging employees to take part in making decisions (even those with negative impacts) reduces employee turnover,[9] that there is a relationship between organizational size and turnover rates,[10] that self-directed work teams sometimes reduce turnover,[11] and that organizations with high levels of effective communication systems have lower levels of dysfunctional turnover.[12]

Unfortunately, all that we have learned so far has not lead to curing the turnover problem in the lodging industry. Whether because practitioners have not yet accepted that they need to reduce turnover—or whether scholars have not yet discovered and adequately presented the reasons lodging has high turnover and effective methods to reduce it—research continues to indicate that the lodging industry is still in the dark about many issues relating to turnover. While the hospitality industry is not the only one interested in stemming the turnover tide, the situation has not been nearly so grim in other industries. For instance, in the electronics industry, well known for its high turnover, the rate of turnover is about 27 percent. Even in nursing, an occupation known for very high turnover, the rate is "only" 40 percent per year—high, but still less than the hospitality industry's yearly average of 50.4 percent. In the retail grocery industry the turnover rate averages about 35 percent annually. The yearly average for the public sector ranges from five to ten percent. As mentioned previously, the average for turnover in all industries in the United States is about 13 percent annually.[13]

Major Findings of the AH&LEF Study on Turnover

For many years, the general impression was that turnover in the hospitality industry was as high as 100 to 300 percent. This would mean that hospitality employees keep their jobs, on the average, no more than about 12 months, and perhaps no more than three months, while government statistics show the tenure of employees in other industries is about three and a half years. Some analysts believe flawed prior research led to hospitality turnover estimates that were much higher than the figures in the AH&LEF study.

Data for the AH&LEF study was collected from a total of 4,869 lodging properties in the United States. However, because of the method of participation, some data is based on sample sizes ranging from 2,150 properties to 2,719 properties. In all cases, we believe that this is the largest sample ever drawn from the American lodging industry for a study of any kind. The study participants from the four main lodging segments—Luxury, First Class, Mid-Market, and Economy—are representative of the total number of properties in these classes in the United States. This study resulted in several significant findings:

- Perhaps the most important finding is that turnover is simply not as high in the lodging industry as it was previously believed to be. As just noted, prior research led to estimates of hospitality employee turnover as high as 100 to 300 percent annually. The AH&LEF project revealed that turnover nationally among hospitality employees was 50.4 percent in 1997. While still higher than in other industries, and still too high, this turnover is, nevertheless, much lower than anticipated.

- Managerial turnover is also much lower than anticipated. Previous estimates of managerial turnover in the lodging generally have run from 50 to 100 percent. The AH&LEF study revealed that national annual turnover of managers in 1995, 1996, and 1997 was 20 percent, 23 percent, and 15 percent, respectively.

- Supervisory turnover in the lodging industry in 1995 was 19 percent, in 1996 was 22 percent, and in 1997 was 13.5 percent. While previous studies have not collected data on supervisory turnover levels, it was generally assumed that turnover among this group was above that of managers and below that of line-level employees (therefore between 50 to 200 percent, roughly).

- It was assumed that very few lodging properties kept information on turnover that occurs within the first 30 days of hire (research has shown this to be the highest turnover period). The study confirmed this assumption: 92 percent of the properties that participated in the study reported that they do not collect information on their 30-day turnover rates. On the other hand, the eight percent that do collect such data reported that the rate was much lower than anticipated, 24.7 percent. The fact that these properties value and collect such information likely means that they also take steps to reduce turnover during this period. Therefore, we cannot say that turnover in all properties averages 24.7 percent for the first 30 days.

- We also learned that very few properties (5.1 percent) calculate separate turnover rates for part-time and full-time employees. This is significant, because it means that the 50.4 percent turnover rate for 1997 includes both part-time and full-time turnover. Since part-time turnover is both higher and more costly than full-time employee turnover, this indicates that the cost of turnover may even be lower than this study can report.

- More than two-thirds (68.3 percent) of the participating properties maintain separate turnover records on a departmental basis. Many of these properties also calculate turnover on a positional basis. As a result, we have a pretty clear picture of which departments and positions have the highest turnover rates. On the other hand, 31.7 percent of participating properties do not maintain departmental or positional turnover rates, suggesting that not all hotel companies or properties take turnover seriously (or they would collect this information).

- We also learned that different companies and properties calculate turnover differently. While we were able to determine the method that is most popularly used (by 40 percent of the participating properties), this means that 60 percent of the properties use another method: 31.8 percent of participants reported using a second method, and 11.6 percent reported a third method; the remaining 16.6 percent reported various methods. These findings indicate the need for a standardized method of reporting and calculating turnover in the lodging industry.

The results of the landmark AH&LEF study on turnover have more recently been confirmed by other researchers as still accurate. A study of employee retention programs in 2004, for example, confirmed turnover rates of approximately the same percentages as those reported in the AH&LEF study.[14]

The Costs of Turnover

Turnover costs range from $3,000–$10,000 per hourly employee, and can be even higher; as mentioned previously, in some cases the cost could be as high as 100 percent of the employee's annual wage. According to the National Restaurant Association, turnover costs for restaurants average about $5,000 per employee. Turnover costs for managers can average $50,000 or more. Many companies equate the cost of losing one trained manager with the amount of that manager's annual salary; it typically takes about a year for a new manager to become fully productive.

Turnover costs can be classified as tangible or intangible. Tangible costs are incurred directly when replacing employees and range from uniforms to advertisements. Intangible but in many cases significant costs (such as lost productivity) do not relate directly to out-of-pocket expenses.

Separation costs are incurred directly with the loss of a current employee. These costs may include separation or severance pay and the costs associated with conducting exit interviews, maintaining files, removing names from the payroll, terminating benefits, and paying unemployment taxes.

Replacement costs are those associated with recruiting new employees: advertising, pre-employment screening, interviews, testing, staff meetings to discuss applicants, travel expenses for applicants, moving expenses for some applicants, medical exams, and other costs.

Training costs are those associated with orienting new employees, preparing and printing new employee information, creating or purchasing training materials, and conducting training. Lower productivity (on the part of those who are conducting the training as well as those who are being trained) is an intangible cost of training.

Trained employees produce more than new employees who are still learning the job. In restaurants, for instance, trained employees serve more tables and sell more items than do trainees. The result of training is higher productivity. The time it takes for a new employee to reach a satisfactory level of productivity varies. Studies show that it takes about three months for a new employee to reach the level of productivity of a trained employee.[15] Exhibit 1 shows how these costs affected six restaurant companies that participated in a study on turnover.

Other Costs and Effects. High turnover also has other costs and effects (see Exhibit 2). Most analysts regard high turnover rates as indicators of management problems. While this perception hurts some hospitality companies more than others, it

Exhibit 1   Turnover Costs in Six Restaurant Companies

Chain number	Number employed	Number turning over	Turnover percentage	Cost (millions)
Hourly Personnel				
1	1,500	2,250	150%	$ 5.6
2	9,000	9,900	110%	24.7
3	7,500	9,375	125%	23.4
4	900	720	80%	1.8
5	1,300	975	75%	2.4
6	1,650	825	50%	2.0
Managers				
1	100	65	65%	$ 0.65
2	750	375	50%	12.0
3	700	420	60%	4.2
4	75	30	40%	0.3
5	80	40	50%	0.4
6	140	42	30%	0.42

Source: Robert H. Woods and James F. Macaulay, "Rx for Turnover: Retention Programs that Work," *Cornell Hotel and Restaurant Administration Quarterly* 30 (May 1989): 81.

Exhibit 2   Effects of High Turnover

1. Monetary costs
2. Potential for poor service
3. No uniformity of service
4. Low perceptions of managerial effectiveness
5. Revolving door syndrome
6. Lower sales
7. Inability to expand
8. Loss in quality of staff
9. Wages kept down
10. Wasted management time

no doubt also pushes down stock prices industry-wide. Managers should be concerned about curing the turnover problem because of its impact on their own careers. Unwanted turnover curtails company expansion because it eats away at profits. When expansion is curtailed, opportunities for managers diminish. Consequently, those managers who allow the employee turnover problem to persist jeopardize their own chances for advancement and promotion.

Another potential cost is the greater likelihood for unionization in hospitality operations with high turnover. Research on hospitality organizations has shown that employees who are members of unions are significantly less likely to leave their jobs than non-union members. This should indicate to managers that union-ization (sold to employees on the basis of job retention issues) is a greater potential cost factor for hospitality companies with high turnover rates.[16]

Causes of Turnover

Most researchers agree that turnover is more related to internal causes (conditions within a company) than to external causes (the economy, new competition, and so on). Overall, researchers have found three main causes of turnover: (1) low compensation, (2) faulty or inadequate hiring practices, and (3) poor management that weakens morale. Industries or companies with high turnover rates usually exhibit one or more of these conditions.[17]

Other researchers believe that the key to solving turnover problems lies in curing the problem of unmet employee expectations. Employees join an organization with expectations about what the work and the organization will be like. If these expectations are not met, employees often leave. This is the reason realistic job previews are so important.[18]

More than 2,500 studies of turnover have been conducted to date, but not all of the causes of turnover identified pertain to hospitality. Studies of other businesses point to unfavorable work shifts (such as night shifts and irregular hours) as a principal cause of turnover. In contrast, some hospitality employees identify irregular hours as an attractive feature of their employment. While external influences such as unemployment and new job opportunities seem to have little effect on turnover rates in other industries, the reverse seems to be true for hospitality. As most managers know, new hospitality competitors often attract employees from existing operations.

Both managers and employees cite the quality of supervision as the number one cause of turnover in the hospitality industry. More employees leave because they are unhappy with the quality of supervision than for any other reason. Ineffective communication is the second most often cited cause of turnover. Some communication problems are associated with the quality of supervision; ineffective communication among supervisors and employees is often cited as a major cause of turnover. However, communication among employees is also a major turnover factor.

Exhibit 3 lists the top 15 causes of turnover in hotel and restaurant companies. Some suggest that this list should be updated to include drug abuse. The case is strong for including drug abuse as a major cause of hospitality turnover. Methamphetamines, to name just one drug, is causing significant problems in the hospitality and other industries. The United States is currently in what some experts have called a "meth madness" phase because the number of people using methamphetamines is so great. Easy to make and to use, "meth" has made its way into the lives of millions of Americans and is affecting virtually every aspect of their being, including their work lives, of course. Some business leaders have pointed to this epidemic as a major cause of employee turnover, absenteeism, and other problems.[19]

At least 10 of the 15 causes cited in Exhibit 3 are within a unit-level manager's power to correct. The ninth cause on the list—commercialized expectations—may

Exhibit 3   Major Causes of Hospitality Turnover

1. Quality of supervision
2. Ineffective communication
3. Working conditions
4. Quality of co-workers
5. Inappropriate "fit" with company culture
6. Low pay and few benefits
7. Lack of clear definition of responsibilities
8. No direction on what to do
9. Commercialized expectations
10. No career ladder
11. Changes in leadership
12. Limited career opportunities
13. Change in philosophy or practices
14. Lack of clear direction on a company-wide basis
15. Job transferability

Source: Adapted from Robert H. Woods and James F. Macaulay, "R for Turnover: Retention Programs that Work," *Cornell Hotel and Restaurant Administration Quarterly* 30 (May 1989): 87.

be more difficult, but should be possible to control. "Commercialized expectations" refers to the effect of advertising on the performance of service personnel. Briefly, the term implies that guests expect real employees to act the way employees are usually portrayed in advertisements—always smiling, always serving, always at their best. To meet these expectations, hospitality employees must try to display these advertised characteristics. This "acting out" is called "emotional labor." Over time, this type of labor can take a significant emotional toll on employees, because they are often called upon to act in a manner that is inconsistent with how they really feel in a given moment. Behaviorists would call this cognitive dissonance.[20]

Most researchers have found that turnover is a gradual thing. Employees decide to leave over a period of time and because of accumulated reasons. However, this is not always the case, of course. Recent research points to the importance of what are called "shocks" as causes of turnover. Shocks are events, either within or outside the organization, that cause employees to immediately determine to leave an organization. The hurricanes that ravaged the Gulf Coast of the United States in 2005 are examples of such shocks, but so, too, are management decisions to dramatically change how things are done in an operation. For example, a turnover in top managers accompanied by massive changes in workplace rules can lead to immediate employee turnover. One study on the impact of shocks on employee turnover prescribed a series of potential remedies that organizations can take before, during, or after a shock to reduce turnover, including paying attention to past rules, honoring the organization's culture, anticipating the impact of changes on employees, and creating contingency plans for external shocks.[21]

Exhibit 4   Short-Term Remedies for Turnover

1. Surface the organization's culture.
2. Find out why employees leave.
3. Find out why employees stay.
4. Ask employees what they want.
5. Give employees a voice.
6. Make managers aware of their biases.
7. Develop recruiting programs that meet the company's needs.
8. Develop orientation programs that reflect the organization's culture.
9. Take interviewing seriously.
10. Take managing turnover seriously.

Source: Adapted from Robert H. Woods and James F. Macaulay, "Ŗ for Turnover: Retention Programs that Work," *Cornell Hotel and Restaurant Administration Quarterly* 30 (May 1989): 80.

Recent studies have also indicated that such issues as sexual harassment contribute to higher turnover.[22] Even employee health has been identified as a cause of turnover. For example, one study on nutrition recently reported that employees with healthier diets are less likely to leave their jobs. Companies that encourage their employees to eat healthier might reduce unwanted turnover.[23]

Retention Programs: Turnover Remedies

Despite the attention turnover commands, many hospitality companies have no specific plans for addressing it. There are, however, some companies that have developed programs specifically designed to minimize turnover. Most companies that successfully minimize unwanted turnover begin by referring to the problem in positive terms. For this reason, programs designed to reduce turnover are called employee **retention programs.**

Turnover cannot be eliminated completely. In fact, few operators would want such an outcome. New hires can bring in new ideas and fresh energy, so some turnover is desirable. But turnover can be like a disease; if left unattended, it gets worse. The most effective turnover cures are custom-tailored to a particular company. However, general short- and long-term remedies are often helpful.[24]

Short-Term Remedies. Many retention programs can yield immediate results. In some cases, applying the following short-term remedies may be the only action needed. These remedies are listed in Exhibit 4.

Surface the organization's culture. "Culture surfacing" refers to the process of bringing deeply held but often unspoken or unrecognized cultural values, beliefs, and assumptions to the surface, so that what is considered important in an organization's culture can be identified. The best way to do this is to enlist the assistance of a qualified cultural assessor or consultant.[25]

All organizations have a "personality" or a unique character that reflects the values, beliefs, and assumptions that are important in the organization. In one organization, for instance, a key value may be, "Managers should work alongside their employees." In such operations, managers typically roll up their sleeves to wash dishes, check guests in, or do whatever else it takes to get the job done. In other companies, a key value might be, "Managers should merely supervise employees' work." These companies respect managers who can delegate authority effectively and get the job done without having to do it themselves. It would be disastrous for an organization to implement a retention program based on hands-off supervision when the organization favors managers who work alongside employees. This is why the first step in initiating an effective retention program is to better understand the company's culture, so that programs designed to address turnover problems can be culture-specific.

Businesses that have surfaced their cultures and created culture-specific retention programs have found that their programs are much more effective as a result. One such business is Restaurants Unlimited, a Seattle-based chain restaurant company and parent company of Cinnabon, which was able to reduce unwanted turnover to almost zero.

Find out why employees leave. Most hospitality companies do not know why their employees leave. Too few companies correctly collect or use turnover data to identify and cure organizational problems. Exit interviews should be conducted for two reasons: (1) to learn why employees leave, and (2) to learn what can be changed to ensure that more employees do not leave. Managers should develop a profile of employees who leave and document the reasons. This information can be useful during the selection process for new employees. (Exit interviews are discussed in greater detail at the end of the chapter.)

Find out why employees stay. Employees stay for specific reasons. Finding out why they stay is even more important than finding out why they leave, because an employee's reasons for staying can be used to influence other employees to stay. **Attitude surveys** are the simplest and perhaps most effective method of identifying why employees stay. These surveys identify how employees feel about their work and about their work environments. These surveys present a problem, however. Employee responses to attitude surveys may not be totally honest, because some may fear management retaliation for negative feedback. This problem can be overcome by using third-party consultants to collect and analyze the data, since they usually are perceived as more likely to protect employee anonymity.

Ask employees what they want. Marriott Hot-Shoppes used an employee-opinion survey to ask both managers and employees what they wanted from their jobs. Marriott then used information from these surveys to reduce company turnover to less than half the industry averages for both managers and employees.

While opinion surveys are used extensively in many industries, they are not used widely in the hospitality industry. Apparently, many hospitality managers fear that such surveys create unrealistic expectations for employees. Such an attitude may be an indication of management's unwillingness to take employee turnover problems seriously.

Give employees a voice. Employees can voice opinions through grievance procedures, suggestion systems, formal and informal employee-management meetings, counseling services, ombudsmen, attitude surveys, employee-controlled newsletters, hotlines, and many other methods. The more a manager can learn regarding employee feelings about work-related issues, the better.

Make managers aware of their biases. Managers seldom know what employees really want. Typically, managers think the number one concern of employees is money. This is generally not true, although there are exceptions. Employees without enough money to adequately house their families or feed and clothe themselves and their children certainly will put money at the top of their lists. However, once these basic needs are met, employee desires change. A highly standardized test that determines job attribute preferences indicates that managers and employees want almost the same things: recognition for a job well done, a chance to develop skills and abilities, and participation in decision-making about issues that affect them.[26] Making managers aware of what employees want can help them develop retention programs that work.

Develop recruiting programs that meet the company's needs. Many employers are guilty of hiring "warm bodies" to fill immediate job needs. It's hard to fault these labor-poor companies, because they have such pressing needs. These employers know that such employees will not last, but feel they have little choice in the matter; it's either a warm body or no employee. To cure this "warm body" syndrome, managers can develop profiles of the characteristics successful employees should possess and hold out for such job candidates whenever possible. Companies can also develop more creative recruiting methods in order to attract more job candidates.

Develop orientation programs that reflect the organization's culture. Orientation programs should teach the culture of the company. Instead, many companies simply tell new recruits to "follow Jim or Mary Sue around." In many cases, neither Jim nor Mary Sue really knows what it is that management wants new employees to learn. As a result, companies create more turnover by perpetuating bad habits that do not fit in with their culture.

Take interviewing seriously. There is a maxim in the computer industry that cautions, "Garbage in, garbage out." The same goes for interviewing. If poor applicants are hired in the first place, a manager can expect turnover to be high.

Interviewing potential employees is serious business. How well interviews are conducted can determine the amount of turnover a property will have in a given year. Too many managers take this process casually, or even turn it over to less experienced supervisors or employees to conduct; no bigger mistake can be made. Interviews represent the opportunity to determine if an applicant fits the character of the organization and possesses the skills for the job. Many companies reduce their turnover simply by teaching managers to be better interviewers.

Take managing turnover seriously. This directive encompasses all the others. Too often, managers simply do not take turnover seriously enough. Many feel that turnover is not a real problem, or that it is the result of a poor work ethic, or that it is just a fact of life and nothing can be done about it. Managers must realize that turnover is a problem and that something can be done about it. Also, managers must realize that they themselves are often the cause of unwanted turnover.

Exhibit 5   Long-Term Remedies for Turnover

1. Develop socialization programs.
2. Develop training programs in additional languages.
3. Establish career paths.
4. Implement partner/profit-sharing programs.
5. Implement incentive programs.
6. Provide child care and family counseling.
7. Identify alternative sources for employee recruitment.
8. Reconsider pay scales.

Source: Adapted from Robert H. Woods and James F. Macaulay, "℞ for Turnover: Retention Programs that Work," *Cornell Hotel and Restaurant Administration Quarterly* 30 (May 1989): 82.

Long-Term Remedies. As noted, short-term remedies focus on collecting and using information to address immediate concerns. Long-term remedies focus on making organizational changes to create a company in which employees want to work. These remedies take time and often cost money. The cost is determined by the degree of current turnover in a company and by the need for change. The following long-term remedies are listed in Exhibit 5.

Develop socialization programs. Socialization is the ongoing process people experience when they start a new job, join a new club, begin a marriage, or start anything new. As people become accustomed to their surroundings, they learn the rules and how to get things done. Some companies neglect to establish formal socialization programs and leave employees to fend for themselves. This rarely gets employees off to a good start.

Training programs emphasize task completion or development of desired behaviors. Socialization programs, on the other hand, concentrate on teaching employees how to interpret the company's culture and rules (both written and unwritten) so that they can perform their jobs effectively. A study on the socialization programs of Silicon Valley electronics companies showed that employees who received company-sponsored socialization training adapted much more quickly to the values and beliefs of their companies. Hospitality companies should take note, especially since most turnover in the hospitality industry occurs within the first 30 to 60 days of work. A recent study of the impact of socialization on turnover clearly shows a link between effective socialization programs and reduced turnover.[27]

Develop training programs in additional languages. A large number of hourly employees in the United States speak Spanish as their first language. In the hospitality industry, there are many other languages represented in the work force as well. Despite this reality, few hospitality companies offer training in foreign languages. Instead, most hospitality employers rely on bilingual employees to explain company rules, policies, and work responsibilities. This is an abdication of management's responsibility.

Establish career paths. Too many employees see hospitality jobs as only temporary employment on the way to their "real" jobs. This attitude has been fostered by the lack of career ladders for hospitality employees. Some hospitality companies have overcome this problem. For instance, T.G.I. Friday's developed several supervisory levels within its restaurants. By doing so, the company established more rungs on the career ladder for employees interested in moving up. Several companies have developed "hire from within" programs that seek to fill management positions with people from their employee ranks first.

Implement partner/profit-sharing programs. Au Bon Pain, Harman Management Company, Golden Corral, Cheesecake Factory, and Chick-Fil-A are restaurant companies that have used profit-sharing programs effectively to reduce turnover. At Harman Management and Chick-Fil-A, managers can own up to 40 percent of their operations. At Harman, this program has reduced management turnover to below the national average for all industries.

Implement incentive programs. Several hospitality companies have used incentive programs to reduce turnover. South Seas Plantation in Florida, for example, has a program that effectively encourages employees to stay with the company. This program is stair-stepped in the sense that the longer employees stay, the more incentives they are offered. Many companies have developed scholarship programs for employees and their relatives, and have used these programs as incentives to reduce turnover. Other hospitality companies have developed programs in which employees earn points that translate to year-end bonuses.

There are two keys to developing successful incentive programs. First, employees need to be in on the ground floor of program development so that meaningful incentives are chosen. Second, timeframes should not be so unreasonable that few employees ever have a chance of collecting on bonuses, scholarship programs, or other incentives. Employee groups involved in developing incentive programs should help managers determine what timeframes are reasonable.

Provide child care and family counseling. Many U.S. companies offer child care and family counseling. The hospitality industry, however, has been slow to jump on this bandwagon, even though a high percentage of its employees are women with children or women of child-bearing age. Mechanisms that help employees deal with arranging and paying for child care can be valuable features in retention programs. Family counseling and other employee assistance programs are also effective in retaining employees. Unfortunately, the hospitality industry lags behind other industries in these categories as well.

Identify alternative sources for employee recruitment. Historically, the hospitality industry has employed young employees, the age group with the highest turnover levels. Attracting older managers and employees to hospitality companies is not as easy as hanging out a "now hiring senior citizens" sign. Any employee group has specific requirements; seniors are no different. Hospitality companies often must make long-term commitments to providing the type of medical and dental benefits, leave programs, and shortened work shifts that are attractive to senior citizens.

Other non-traditional employee groups include minorities, immigrants, and people with disabilities—all viable recruiting sources. In each case, the rule is the same: identify the needs of the group and offer programs that are specifically attractive to that group.

However, managers must remember that while it is a perfectly legal and laudable goal to seek to hire persons in protected age, race, and national origin groups, there are very strict laws against discriminating against or preferring individuals on the basis of their age, race, or national origins. True "affirmative action programs" must be very carefully crafted and implemented to avoid ruinous litigation later over alleged or perceived illegal discrimination or preference.

Reconsider pay scales. Pay scales in hospitality have been inching upward for the last few years, but the industry's overall rate of pay is still far below the national average. While money alone cannot stop turnover, the lack of it does provide a good reason for employees to consider leaving. For example, on the average, gas station attendants make more than hourly restaurant and hotel employees. Many hospitality businesses could correct this problem by raising pay to more competitive levels. Employers must simply ask themselves whether they would rather pay their employees more money to ensure a longer stay with the company or spend the money on replacing employees who leave. Paying employees more is an investment; turnover costs cannot be recouped.

Keys to Successful Retention Programs. Regardless of the turnover remedies managers choose, three key elements are required for success:

1. Executive-level support
2. Managerial follow-through on program implementation, maintenance, and support
3. Expenditures of time and money

Failure to recognize and provide any one of these key elements can doom retention programs. The place to start when planning a retention program is to compute current turnover costs and then determine the costs and benefits of retention efforts.

A study by the Hay Group of more than 500,000 employees in 300 companies found 50 retention factors.[28] Of these, pay was the least important. Research published in Training and Development, based on 2,000 respondents, confirmed this and cited ten factors that lead to retention:

1. Career growth, learning, and development
2. Exciting and challenging work
3. Meaningful work (making a difference and a contribution)
4. Great people to work with
5. Being part of a team
6. Having a good boss
7. Recognition of work well done
8. Autonomy—a sense of control over one's work
9. Flexible work hours
10. Fair pay and benefits

Applebee's Recipe for Retention Success

With nearly 1,700 restaurants in 49 states and 16 countries, Applebee's is the world's largest casual dining restaurant chain. Recognizing the importance of the turnover issue, it has developed a successful recipe for manager and employee retention. At Applebee's, top management divides all staff members, including unit managers, into three groups: the top 20 percent, middle 60 percent, and lower 20 percent. In its retention program, called "Mix Management," Applebee's top executives assume that turnover will be high among the bottom 20 percent of the chain's employees (managers, supervisors, and line-level employees). The company does not reward managers for keeping overall turnover in their restaurants low; instead, they are rewarded for keeping turnover low among the top 20 percent of the staff. The company does not even set retention standards for the lower 20 percent of performers and assumes that turnover will be high in this group.

The program seems to work. In 2003, the company retained 96 percent of restaurant general managers in the top two groups (that is, the top 20 percent and middle 60 percent of performers). At more junior levels, Applebee's held on to 90 percent of lower-level managers and 80 percent of the hourly employees in the desired categories. The system is based on a working assumption that the loss of a top-20-percent hourly employee costs the company $2,500; the loss of a middle-60-percent employee costs $1,000; and the loss of a bottom-20-percent employee actually lets the company make $500.

Applebee's retention program produces a positive feedback loop. With retention efforts focused on the top 80 percent of employees, many in the bottom 20 percent group will leave and be replaced by a group of new hires. Since some of these new hires may turn out to be top performers, employees who were on the bottom rung of the middle 60 percent group might suddenly find themselves in the lower 20 percent bracket unless they improve their performance. In this way, each bracket should become more competitive as time goes on.

Applebee's uses a software program, APPLEPM, to monitor the success of its employees. (The "PM" in the name stands for "People Management.") Using this system has helped the company reduce the cost of the Mix Management program to about $3 to $7 per employee annually.

Source: Adapted from Aaron Dalton, "Applebee's Turnover Recipe," *Workforce Management*, June 30, 2005.

This report also listed seven steps that managers should take in developing a retention program that works:

1. Collect and analyze all turnover and exit interview information.

2. Conduct a survey to learn company beliefs and attitudes about retention (i.e., what would work).

3. Organize and conduct a "future pull" session. Leap ahead one year and imagine what you are celebrating regarding retention. Set goals this way. For example, one "future pull" might be: "Retained 95 percent of our management team."

4. Gather input and insight from focus groups and interviews of managers and employees.

5. Compile and distribute data. Be sure to use the data you have gathered to plan.

6. Tag a retention champion. You need someone in charge of retention who is empowered to act.

7. Appoint a task force to support the champion.

The Impact of Diversity on Turnover

It is vitally important for managers who are serious about reducing employee turnover to recognize cultural and other differences among today's diverse work force. As hospitality and other industries become more diverse (either purposefully or unintentionally), it may be necessary for managers to review company policies and attitudes in order to retain certain groups of workers. For instance, the growing wave of Latino immigrants is having a profound effect on the U.S. hospitality industry and U.S. society as a whole. The national average of Latino employment in hotels alone will be nearly 30 percent by 2012, up from about 23 percent in 2002. Managing Latino workers effectively requires understanding their culture (this, of course, is also true for other employee groups). Among the differences in managing Latino workers: (1) Latinos identify people by class and role and expect them to act accordingly; (2) Latino workers' notion of time and punctuality is based on nature; and (3) Latinos highly value courtesy during training. The payoff for managers who pay attention to these cultural differences can be great: higher productivity, better service, fewer guest complaints, lower labor costs, and greater profitability.[29]

Similar differences can be noted among other ethnic and cultural groups. A study conducted in the United Kingdom, for instance, noted that turnover was reduced in one hotel company from nearly 100 percent to a low of about 5 percent simply through the institution of policies that created English language training and a buddy system wherein a "buddy" helped to advise workers from other cultures about why the company had policies on different issues.[30]

How can managers successfully address diversity issues? This raises the question of whether one set of rules for everyone is the most effective way to manage a diverse work force, which includes worker groups that understand time, class, communication, and other issues very differently from group to group. In many Asian cultures, for example, employees typically do not question the authority of their supervisors directly, and they may often refuse to state their personal opinions about issues related to work. However, this does not mean that Asian workers do not hold opinions about work issues; they are simply less likely to voice their opinions than employees from other backgrounds. The first challenge for managers is to establish open communication with everyone in their diverse work force. Failure to do so can certainly result in unwanted turnover.

The Use of Discipline

Discipline is an indispensable management tool, but it is also one of the most difficult for managers to use. Too many managers use discipline inconsistently and

Exhibit 6   Sample Set of House Rules

Strict enforcement of these policies will help protect our employees and ensure that our hotel runs in an efficient manner. Listed below are some of the violations which may result in immediate suspension or termination, at the option of the hotel.

- Being discourteous, rude, insubordinate, or using abusive language to a guest or fellow employee.
- Fighting, stealing, unauthorized possession of hotel property, or gambling on hotel premises.
- Unauthorized use of alcohol, possession, use, or appearance of being under the influence of alcohol, narcotics, intoxicants, or other substances prohibited by law, or the abuse of medication whether obtained legally or illegally, while on hotel premises.
- Possession of lethal weapons or other items prohibited by law while on hotel premises.
- Indecent, immoral, or disorderly conduct in the hotel, including willful destruction of property and failure to follow safety procedures.
- Falsification of work or time records, reports, or guest checks.
- Being in an unauthorized area of the hotel while working or in a non-public area of the building after hours without prior permission from your department head.
- Socializing with guests on hotel premises.
- Removing anything from the hotel without permission.
- Sleeping while on duty.

Source: David Wheelhouse, *Managing Human Resources in the Hospitality Industry* (Lansing, Mich.: Educational Institute of the American Hotel & Lodging Association, 1989), 353.

unfairly. Some regard discipline strictly as punishment for past behavior rather than as a means of ensuring proper conduct in the future. In fact, some managers are unaware that discipline can be used to encourage desired behaviors.

Laying the Groundwork

To lay the groundwork effectively for a discipline system that promotes positive behaviors, managers must establish rules of conduct for the workplace and then communicate how those rules should be followed. Employee manuals, training sessions, job descriptions, performance standards, and posted notices are some ways rules can be communicated. Exhibit 6 presents an example of posted conduct rules. The following list of major causes of disciplinary problems shows that the importance of clearly communicating rules and workplace expectations cannot be over-emphasized:[31]

- The employee did not know *what* to do
- The employee did not know *how* to do what he or she was supposed to do
- Unrealistic expectations were set

- The employee and the job were a poor match to begin with
- The employee was not motivated to do a good job

Reread the list; what it identifies is a lack of communication on the part of management.

Understanding the purpose of discipline should be a prerequisite for every manager with disciplinary responsibilities. It is imperative that managers:

- Establish reasonable rules
- Make sure employees know the rules
- Enforce the rules fairly, without discrimination
- Document each employee action or behavior that results in discipline

Approaches to Administering Discipline

There are at least three basic approaches to discipline. In practice, these approaches may overlap; some managers may use elements of any or all of the three. Two of the three—the **hot stove approach** and **progressive discipline**—are traditional approaches; they emphasize the administration of discipline after an employee fails to follow organizational norms and standards. The traditional approaches are reactive in nature, since the behavior precedes disciplinary action. The third approach, normally referred to as **preventive discipline,** is proactive, in that it attempts to establish a means of directing employee behavior.

The Hot Stove Approach. With the hot stove approach, if employees touch a hot stove, they get burned; that is, if they break a rule, they are subjected to disciplinary action. This approach has several foundations:

- *Immediacy:* Corrective action must be taken immediately after an infraction occurs. This links discipline with undesirable performance.

- *Warning:* Managers must provide clear ground rules for behaviors and adequately warn employees that "hot stoves will burn."

- *Consistency:* Corrective action must be consistent; i.e., a hot stove will burn everyone to the same degree.

- *Impersonality:* Discipline must be linked with the behavior, not the person.

- *Appropriateness:* The degree of discipline must equal the extent of the infraction.

This system seems to make sense because it appears to be fair to all employees, and because it correctly establishes which rules result in which disciplinary measures. However, this system has problems. Oddly, the fact that the hot stove does not discriminate is the biggest problem. All employees receive the same punishment for similar infractions; there is no allowance for different situations or individual differences. A new hire who does not fully understand all the rules will be "burned" as badly as the employee who has been with the company for years and has a clear grasp of the rules and what they mean.

Progressive Discipline. Like the hot stove approach, progressive discipline relies on a clear and complete definition of behaviors that will be penalized and the type of disciplinary action that will be meted out for each infraction. A progressive discipline program might dictate that an employee who is tardy for work once will receive an oral warning, an employee who is tardy twice will receive a written warning, and an employee who is tardy three times will be suspended. This step-by-step punitive approach to discipline is very popular. Most progressive discipline programs include four steps:

- *Oral warning:* An informal warning with no documentation

- *Written warning*: A formal warning in which a copy of the documentation is placed in the employee's file

- *Suspension:* Time off, usually without pay

- *Discharge:* Termination of employment

Managers appear to like the hot stove and progressive discipline approaches because of the orderliness they give an operation. Both clearly establish ground rules and emphasize consistent and non-discriminatory treatment of rule-breakers. Any discrimination under either of these systems more or less ensures that grievances, discrimination charges, and lawsuits will be filed. As managers know, it is a lot easier to describe these systems on paper than it is to carry them out. In addition, even under the best circumstances, these types of discipline result in short-term solutions. Both traditional approaches focus on the symptoms rather than on the causes of poor performance. Rule-breaking is a symptom, not a cause.

Preventive (Positive) Discipline. Proponents of preventive or positive discipline point out that the difference between this approach and traditional approaches is that the focus is on the cause rather than on the symptoms of dysfunctional behavior. Communication between supervisor and employee takes place on a "horizontal" level, between adults, with the emphasis on problem-solving rather than on punishment. The underlying assumption is that each employee should have the time and opportunity to correct workplace problems once they are brought to his or her attention.[32]

Positive discipline places disciplinary emphasis on recognizing and reinforcing good performance rather than punishing bad performance. Critical stages in this type of disciplinary system include:

- Oral reminders

- Written reminders

- Paid decision-making leave

- Discharge

At each stage of this process (except discharge), the emphasis is on encouraging good behavior. Oral reminders emphasize what should be done, not what was done wrong. Critics of this type of system contend that paid decision-making leave is counter-productive, because it provides employees with an incentive to perform or behave poorly in order to get a day off with pay. However, research indicates that employees view a day off, even with pay, as a severe punishment, and their behavior often improves as a result of this form of discipline. Some companies call the paid decision-making leave "Decision Day" because the objective is for employees to use the time to decide whether they want to correct the problem and become a productive worker. Some managers require an employee to reflect on the problem that led to the day off and then write an essay outlining a solution to the problem.[33] Some of the largest and most successful companies in the United States use the positive discipline approach.

The principal difference between traditional disciplinary approaches and positive discipline lies in their reactive or proactive natures. Those managers who believe that today's employee is more likely to respond to positive encouragement than to negative punishment are more likely to choose the positive discipline approach over traditional approaches. Many managers have found that positive discipline also encourages a team approach to problem-solving, whereas traditional methods often foster adversarial conditions. Another advantage of positive discipline is that it places a great deal of the burden for improvement upon the individual. Therefore, it improves accountability within the organization and also sometimes helps prevent lawsuits. The non-adversarial positive discipline model encourages managers to address performance problems early, when it is easier to bring about a correction in behavior. For many organizations, the benefit of early correction is the most significant advantage of all.[34]

Appeals Mechanisms

Any effective discipline program has an appeals system for employees. Appeals mechanisms serve two major functions. A systematized appeals process that is widely understood by employees allows each party to present its side of an issue, giving employees a voice in how an issue is settled. In fact, in some cases that are litigated, the mere existence of appeals mechanisms provides evidence of managerial efforts to ensure due process for employees. There are four basic types of appeals processes:

- Hierarchical

- Open-door

- Peer review

- Ombudsman

Hierarchical Appeals Process. The **hierarchical appeals process** is based on an organization's chain of command. In this system, employees who believe that they have been disciplined unfairly appeal first to their immediate supervisor. If unsatisfied with the results at this level, employees appeal at the next level of supervision in the organization. If still unsatisfied, employees can appeal at each succeeding management level until all levels of appeal are exhausted. Appeals generally are made in writing.

Open-Door Appeals Process. Unlike the hierarchical system, an **open-door appeals process** allows employees to appeal to any manager in the organization, regardless of his or her position. While this program works in many cases, it fails in others because managers are reluctant to overrule fellow managers in other departments. Because of this, appeals are often referred back to the immediate supervisor. Another disadvantage of this system is that treatment is sometimes inconsistent—that is, one manager may work diligently to ensure that the appeals process is fair and that employees have a chance for their voice to be heard, while others may take this responsibility lightly.

Peer Review Appeals Process. The **peer review appeals process** typically requires that committees of employees and managers hear appeals and issue final rulings. Employees usually are elected to such committees, while managers are appointed. An advantage of this system is that it allows employees to participate directly in the appeals process. As a result, employees often believe that their appeals were conducted fairly, regardless of the outcomes. When adopting this type of procedure with unionized employees, managers should make sure the process doesn't violate the terms of collective bargaining agreements.

Ombudsman Appeals Process. The **ombudsman appeals process** is widely used in government and in colleges and universities, but is not widely accepted in industry. This system involves the use of an ombudsman who investigates complaints or a mediator who listens to both sides of a case and attempts to mediate an acceptable solution. Ombudsmen have no authority to issue judgments in the event that the two sides cannot agree.

Discharge: A Last Resort

The same managers who use discipline strictly as punishment often view discharge as the ultimate punishment. Most human resources experts are critical of such a view. They question who is punished the most, the employee who must find a new job, or the manager who must replace a discharged employee? For that matter, who is really at fault when a discharge is required, the employee being discharged, or the manager who failed to train, motivate, or otherwise help that employee to perform successfully? In Japan, managers who discharge employees are viewed as failures themselves because they were unable to turn the employees into productive staff members. Many companies in the United States are adopting the same view, largely because it is becoming more difficult and costly to replace lost employees.

Discharging an employee should be a last resort for managers. It should be approached with great caution and extreme seriousness. If a discharge is not properly handled, the employer can end up in court.

Wrongful Discharge

In a survey of 450 human resource executives from varied industries, three out of five reported that their companies were being sued for wrongful discharge. As many as 40 percent of these suits may be legitimate.[35] Wrongful termination lawsuits account for 13 percent of all lawsuits in the United States, second only to shareholder suits.

Before managers exercise the final option to discharge an employee, they should ask themselves the questions below. If they answer "yes" to each of these questions, proceeding with a discharge may be the right thing to do. If they answer "no," the situation described in the question should be corrected before proceeding with a discharge. While the factors in the following questions may not all be critical to a successful legal defense, they all should be considered in the day-to-day management of people:

- Did the employee know what was expected?

- Were the rules clearly and fairly communicated to the employee?

- Did management explain why the rules were important?

- Were the rules that were broken reasonable and important to the organization?

- Is the evidence precipitating the discharge substantial and reliable?

- Is the discipline equal to the seriousness of the offense?

- Was the performance appraisal process fair and complete?

- Did management make a sincere effort to identify poor performers and to correct their behaviors or actions?

- Is punishment for breaking this rule applied consistently to all employees?

Wrongful discharge suits can have a serious impact on an organization. Employees can sue employers for back pay, front pay, and punitive damages in wrongful discharge cases. Both the number of lawsuits and the size of awards have been going up. The number of lawsuits apparently relates directly to passage of the Civil Rights Act of 1991, which includes a codicil that allows employment discontinuation cases to be heard before a jury. The law also capped liability awards at $300,000, which is significantly lower than the average award for wrongful discharge suits that were won prior to passage of the law. Previously, companies could build a case for termination after the fact, i.e., after they were sued. However, in 1995, the U.S. Supreme Court ruled that "after-acquired evidence," or information found out after dismissal, is not usable in court as a defense against wrongful discharge.[36]

Managers who attempt to manipulate employees to quit by transferring or demoting them should be aware that such actions can provide the bases for wrongful discharge suits. A transfer can be viewed as wrongful discharge if it is used as a method of avoiding a termination or layoff; a demotion can be viewed as wrongful discharge if it involves no record of employee wrongdoing. Courts typically view demotions and transfers as wrongful discharge if the new job involves significantly different pay, benefits, responsibilities, travel, and so on, than did the old job. In instances of voluntary resignations, employers are liable if management makes working conditions so bad that employees resign. In such cases, deliberate intent is the key issue in court. To win such cases, employers typically have to prove they could not foresee that resignation would result.

Many companies have gone to great lengths to establish sophisticated systems involving complete documentation and progressive discipline to avoid wrongful discharge suits; many, however, forget to ensure that managers don't actually discharge wrongfully. The easiest wrongful discharge case for an employee to win is one in which the rules are enforced unfairly. Unfortunately, this is the single area in which managers also make the most mistakes. Managers must enforce the same rules and penalties fairly at all times if companies wish to avoid or win wrongful discharge cases. To illustrate how difficult this situation can be, consider the following example:

> Employee A is a steady performer who is well-liked by guests, managers, and fellow employees. However, employee A has a habit of tardiness. Employee B is a poor performer who is not well-liked by either guests, managers, or fellow employees. This employee also has a habit of tardiness. A manager who "solves" his or her problem with employee B by discharging employee B but not employee A is opening the door for a wrongful discharge suit.

As we noted in the section on discipline, managers must understand the purposes of discipline and discharge; they must also know the importance of establishing reasonable rules, communicating the rules, fairly enforcing the rules, and maintaining complete files on each employee action or behavior that results in either discipline or discharge. In addition, one of the best defenses in court is consultation with an independent third party (peer group, outsider, management group) prior to dismissal. This step serves to solidify the decision to terminate, if necessary, and it is more defensible in court.[37]

In addition, many legal and human resources consultants believe the best protection against wrongful discharge litigation is a proactive program in which the employer:

- Effectively communicates the property's employment practices

- Aggressively manages employee performance

- Thoroughly investigates any problem that has the potential to develop into a discharge situation

- Periodically conducts a public policy audit to clarify the property's responsibilities to employees and customers

- Adopts a strict organizational code of ethics

- Adopts procedures for in-house whistleblowing

- Purchases employment practices liability insurance

- Seeks legislative reforms to change unfavorable trends in wrongful discharge litigation[38]

Employment at Will

Under the doctrine of **employment at will,** management can terminate an employee at any time for any reason. Likewise, employees can terminate a relationship with an employer at any time for any reason. Throughout U.S. history, this doctrine has been the predominant rule guiding employer-employee relations. Recently, the country has moved decidedly away from this doctrine toward the philosophy that there is an implied contract between an employer and an employee. At-will employment is dying gradually. Starting with the National Labor Relations Act in the 1930s, to the Civil Rights Act of 1991 and the Family and Medical Leave Act of 1993, employers have faced more and more legal obstacles to at-will employment practices. Continuing court case results have hurt at-will employment. The fact is, whether or not you operate in one of the 45 states that have at-will laws, an employee's right to a jury trial regarding employment issues changes everything. In short, jury members tend to hold that an employee cannot be terminated without "sufficient cause," and are likely to find for the plaintiff if they do not see sufficient cause. While it is still advisable to include an at-will statement for employees to sign during the orientation process, it may not provide an employer protection from an employee who claims wrongful discharge. To be protected, companies must document everything. A detailed employment history can avert a lawsuit and it is always important to document the precise reasons for termination. Although most companies still have them, most courts have adopted reasons to limit the legality of at-will employment documents.

Conflict regarding employment condition—employment at will and contractual employment—has provided a great deal of controversy in recent years. Managers want to claim the right to employ whom they want, when they want. Until recently, this right was generally upheld by the courts. Now the employment climate favors employees. As a result, many employee relations experts assert that managers no longer have the right to enforce employment-at-will arrangements with their employees.

Some experts contend that management can retain the employment-at-will right simply by notifying their employees that this is company policy. These experts suggest that employers can require employees to sign a waiver-of-rights clause included in an employee handbook before employment. Many companies follow this advice and implement such clauses. However, the legal situation is not this clear-cut. For instance, in the 1983 U.S. Supreme Court case *Pine River State Bank v. Matille,* the court ruled that the existence of an employee handbook constituted evidence of an **implied employment contract** between employee and employer. At least 30 state courts have also ruled that the existence and use of employee manuals imply a contract between employer and employee. These rulings were made primarily on the basis of language in the employee manuals that described benefits, grounds for discipline or probation, or equal employment opportunity (EEO) or affirmative action policies, all considered evidence of implied employment contracts. Other elements in employee manuals that may imply a contractual relationship between employers and employees include any language suggesting that an employee can work for a company as long as the employee does a good job, and quoting salaries on an annualized basis.

Human resources consultants continue to recommend that companies publish an at-will policy at the beginning of the employee manual and have each employee sign off on an at-will disclaimer. However, the bottom line for managers is that employment at will is very difficult to sustain at this point. Laws are different in different states; what may be considered evidence of employment at will in one state may be considered evidence of a contract in another. In addition, American society has become so litigious that even cases that employers can clearly win may well end up in court and cost thousands of dollars to resolve.

Some experts believe that managers should give up their rights to employment at will. They contend that employment at will often leads to reduced levels of risk-taking, innovation, or creativity on the part of employees who simply do what they have to do to survive in an organization. Others see employment at will as a prerequisite to ensuring loyalty and productivity.

Public Policy

Employees cannot be fired for exercising their rights as provided by law. In other words, employees cannot be fired for filing workers' compensation claims, serving on juries, refusing to commit perjury, or, in many states, for **whistleblowing**—that is, informing on other employees or managers or turning them in to authorities for illegal acts. Each of these provisions falls under a category known as public policy. These rights have been reaffirmed in more than 40 states as exceptions to either employment at will or employer-employee contract arrangements.

Employers are obligated to follow other employment guidelines provided in federal and state laws. For instance, Section 510 of the Employee Retirement Income Security Act (enacted in 1974) prohibits discharge to avoid paying benefits to employees. The burden of proof is on the employer in this case; employers are obliged to prove they are not discharging employees to avoid paying benefits.

Discharge Interviews

Discharge is the maximum penalty an employer can levy on an employee. As we have noted repeatedly, this step should be taken only as a last resort. Discharge interviews are usually the last step in progressive discipline. The purpose of a **discharge interview** is to: (1) relate the history that has led to the interview, (2) explain why the manager must take such severe disciplinary action, and (3) complete the discharge. There are lots of risks associated with discharging an employee, but managers who follow the rules of discharge should find the task less difficult than they might assume. This does not mean that discharging an employee is an easy or pleasant task, nor should it be.

Managers should observe the following guidelines during discharge interviews:

- Use the meeting to find out what went wrong during employment.

- Read all of the supporting evidence for the discharge and make sure it is available during the interview. Documentation should include records of all disciplinary action against the employee, and past conditions and terms of the disciplinary action.

- Explain specific reasons for the discharge. Managers cannot get by with simply telling an employee, "It didn't work out."

- Respect the dignity of the employee during the interview. The fact that the employee did not work out in this case does not mean that he or she will not find other suitable employment and excel.

- Avoid anger or personal confrontation with the employee.

- Tell the employee that reasons for the discharge should remain confidential at all times.

- As a general rule, have a witness present during the interview. The witness may be needed later to substantiate issues discussed during the interview.

- Most states require that discharged employees be paid in full at the time of discharge. This and other required paperwork should be completed well in advance of the interview.

- Make the employee aware of the appeals process available within the company.

- Suggest other avenues for employment, if appropriate. Also advise the employee that, if contacted for a reference, management will be honest regarding the fact that the employee was discharged.

Most discharge interviews are emotionally charged and can result in unwanted confrontations. By following these guidelines, however, it is more likely that managers will be able to complete them without extreme difficulty.

Exit Interviews

Exit interviews are interviews conducted with employees who leave an organization for any reason, not just because they've been discharged. Employees who leave voluntarily usually do so for good reasons. Managers should be extremely concerned about learning why employees leave. The purpose of exit interviews is to collect information on why employees leave and learn what can be changed to ensure that more employees are not lost. These interviews have been described as an absolutely essential tool for collecting useful information about performance. From an employee's perspective, the exit interview provides an opportunity to vent some frustrations and to achieve closure about leaving a job.

Few hospitality companies use exit interviews to learn why their employees are leaving or what the organization can change for the better. Many hospitality managers use exit interviews only to find out if a departing employee is likely to sue the company. While this is another reason to conduct exit interviews, it is far less important than finding out why good employees leave. As we noted in the section on turnover, losing an employee is very expensive for employers. If information collected during exit interviews enables managers to prevent a single unwanted turnover, the entire process is worth the cost.

Information is not easy to collect from departing employees. Most employers have immediate supervisors conduct exit interviews, but this is the least effective method. Employees often leave because of their supervisor and, as a result, are not likely to be open and honest in an interview with them. In addition, employees often have friends among their co-workers whose jobs they do not want to jeopardize. Many departing employees fear that if they tell the truth during an exit interview, they will not receive a favorable recommendation. Research also shows that many employees don't think that what they say in exit interviews will be taken seriously by the company, because their managers seem to view the process so irreverently.

Exit interviews are most effective when conducted by a third party. A study at Marriott Foodservice, for instance, revealed that departing employees did not give their supervisors the same reasons for leaving as they gave third-party interviewers.

Typically, employees tell their employers that they are leaving because they have found a better job, one that either pays more or provides them with a better opportunity for advancement. This is usually not the case. Most employees leave because they do not like their boss, their work, or their co-workers, not because they are going to make more money or have a better opportunity for advancement.

Guidelines for Conducting Exit Interviews

Exit interviews should be conducted by someone other than the employee's immediate supervisor. The best choice is a third-party external source—a consultant who simply collects the information—or a computer system. Consultants can be hired at relatively inexpensive rates. The cost of losing a single employee through unwanted turnover is much higher than a consultant's fee.

Persons conducting exit interviews should try to learn as much as possible from an employee who is leaving. First, put the employee at ease by ensuring confidentiality. Explain that the information will be used solely for improvements within the company, not for retribution against the departing employee or friends remaining on the job. Ask open-ended questions as much as possible to ensure that the employee has an opportunity to talk about what really caused the turnover. The degree to which questions can be open-ended is determined by the extent to which the employer intends to statistically correlate the information. Conduct the meeting in absolute privacy, with no interruptions, and pay full attention to the departing employee. The following guidelines are helpful:

- Conduct interviews in the final week of employment, but not on the last day, if at all possible. Departing employees are too busy with other issues to give exit interviews their full attention on their final day.

- Make every effort to ensure either anonymity (using computers) or confidentiality.

- Probe for the real reasons employees are leaving. Few employees who are comfortable in their jobs will leave on their own. However, the reasons for leaving are sometimes difficult to learn.

- Schedule a follow-up interview one to three months after the employee leaves. Employees often relate much different (and more accurate) reasons for leaving after they are secure in their new jobs. Having a third party conduct the follow-up works extremely well. Follow-up interviews also represent a good opportunity for employers to find out if departed employees are interested in returning to work.

- Close the interview with guarantees of confidentiality and warm thanks. Remember that departing employees are people whom you may want to hire again someday.

As noted earlier, information obtained in exit interviews should be analyzed and used to help correct conditions that cause employees to leave. Interviews should be conducted with all departing employees, whether the company terminates the relationship or the employee does. Useful information can be gained from all employees.

What You Should Say in an Exit Interview

InfoWorld magazine published an article entitled "Don't Just Leave and Tell: How to Get the Most out of Your Exit Interview." In this article the authors suggested that a departing employee should tell the absolute truth, the real reasons he or she is leaving, even if it burns bridges. An example might be telling the interviewer that you think your manager is bad at his or her job. Several readers took exception to this article and offered different views. These were published in a second article in *InfoWorld*. In this follow-up, some readers offered contrary advice, saying that it is never good to burn your bridges and that instead of telling the truth about things that might hurt you later (in another job interview), that you tell only what the company needs to hear. Other readers agreed with the first article, saying, "Why would you ever want to work for this company again anyway (if they were that bad)?" A third reader offered the view that "exit interview information is for big boys and girls. If the company really wants the information and really intends to use it to better the workplace, you should tell them the truth."

While we cannot suggest that employees leaving their employer should lie about why they are leaving, we do caution employers to realize that not everything they hear in an exit interview may be the truth. Some people simply do not want to burn their bridges. Creating an environment in which you want the truth, regardless of whether it is good or bad, is the best cure for this problem.

Endnotes

1. Dina Berta, "HR Execs at People Report Confab Predict Worsening Labor Shortage," *Nation's Restaurant News*, November 14, 2005: 4–6.

2. Dina Berta, "Donatos Cuts Turnover with Training to Engage Workers," *Nation's Restaurant News*, December 5, 2005: 8–10.

3. Michele Kacmar, Martha C. Andrews, David L. Van Rooy, R. Chris Steilberg, and Stephen Cerrone, "Sure Everyone Can Be Replaced, But at What Cost? Turnover as a Predictor of Unit-Level Performance," *Academy of Management Journal* 49, no. 1 (2006): 133–144.

4. Much of the research that the following discussion is based on is found in Robert H. Woods, Michael P. Sciarini, and William Heck, "Turnover and Diversity Management in the U.S. Lodging Industry," American Hotel & Lodging Educational Foundation, 1998.

5. Dennis Reynolds, Edward A. Merritt, and Andrew Gladstein, "Retention Tactics for Seasonal Employees: An Exploratory Study of U.S. Based Restaurants," *Journal of Hospitality & Tourism Research* 28, no. 2 (2004): 230–241.

6. J. A. Alexander, J. R. Bloom, J. R., and B. A. Nuchols, "Nursing Turnover and Hospital Efficiency: An Organization-Level Analysis," *Industrial Relations* 4, no. 33 (1994): 505–520.

7. George S. Benson, "Employee Development, Commitment, and Intention to Turnover: A Test of 'Employability' Policies in Action," *Human Resource Management Journal* 16 (April 2006): 173.

8. Douglas Wahl and Gangaram Singh, "Using Continuation Pay to Combat Turnover: An Evaluation," *Compensation and Benefits Review* 38, no. 2 (2006): 20–34.

9. N. Magner, R. Welker, and G. Johnson, "The Interactive Effects of Participation and Outcome Favorability on Turnover Intentions and Evaluations of Supervisors," *Journal of Occupational and Organizational Psychology* 69 (1996): 135–143.

10. William Even and David MacPherson, "Employer Size and Labor Turnover: The Role of Pensions" *Industrial and Labor Relations Review* 49 (July 1996): 707–728; and Stephen J. Hiemstra, "Employment Policies and Practices in the Lodging Industry," *International Journal of Hospitality Management.* Special Issue: Strategic Management in the Hospitality Industry, Oxford, England: Pergamon Press, 9, no. 3 (1988): 207–221.

11. Catherine M. Gustafson, "Employee Turnover: A Study of Private Clubs in the USA," *International Journal of Contemporary Hospitality Management* 14, no. 3 (2002): 106–113.

12. John R. Johnson, M. J. Bernhagen, and Mike Allen, "The Role of Communication in Managing Reductions in Work Force," *Journal of Applied Communication Research* 24, no. 3 (1996): 139–164.

13. Kacmar et al.

14. Reynolds et al.

15. Robert H. Woods and James F. Macaulay, "Rx for Turnover: Retention Programs that Work," *Cornell Hotel and Restaurant Administration Quarterly* 30 (May 1989): 81.

16. Steven E. Abraham, Barry A. Friedman, and Randall K. Thomas, "The Impact of Union Membership on Intent to Leave," *Employee Responsibilities and Rights Journal* 17, no. 4 (2005): 201–210.

17. Wim van Breukelen, René van der Vlist, and Herman Steensma, "Voluntary Employee Turnover: Combining Variables from the Traditional Turnover Literature with the Theory of Planned Behavior," *Journal of Organizational Behavior* 25, no. 7: 893–914.

18. Cecil A. L. Pearson, "Turnover Process in Organization," *Human Relations* 48 (April 1995): 405–421.

19. Susan Ladika, "Meth Madness," *HR Magazine* 50, no. 12 (2005): 40–46.

20. For more information on commercialized expectations and emotional labor, see Arlie Russell Hochschild, *The Managed Heart: Commercialization of Human Feeling* (Berkeley, Calif.: University of California Press, 1983).

21. Brooks C. Holtom, Terrence R. Mitchell, Thomas W. Lee, and Edward J. Inderrieden, "Shocks as Causes of Turnover: What They Are and How Organizations Can Manage Them," *Human Resources Management* 44, no. 3 (2005): 333–348.

22. Carra S. Sims, Fritz Drasgow, and Louise F. Fitzgerald, "The Effects of Sexual Harassment on Turnover in the Military: Time-Dependent Modeling," *Journal of Applied Psychology* 90, no. 6 (2005): 1–13.

23. "Wellbeing—Nutrition: A Feeding Frenzy for Healthy Productivity," *Employee Benefits*, December 7, 2005: S20.

24. Substantial portions of the following two sections are adapted from Woods and Macaulay, 83–89.

25. For a complete explanation of how to surface an organization's culture see Robert H. Woods, "More Alike Than Different: The Culture of the Restaurant Industry," *Cornell Hotel and Restaurant Administration Quarterly* 30 (August 1989): 82–98; Woods, "Ten Rules for Culture Consultants," *The Consultant* 23, no. 3 (1990): 52–53; Woods, "Deep Meaning: Understanding Your Restaurant's Culture," *Restaurant Personnel Management* 4, no. 2 (1990): 4–7; and Woods, "Surfacing Organizational Culture: The Northeast Restaurants Case," *International Journal of Hospitality Management* 10, no. 4 (1991): 339–357.

26. For a complete review of job attribute tests see Robert W. Eder and N. Roth Tucker, "Sensitizing Management Students to Their Misconceptions of Line Worker Job-Attribute Preferences," *Organizational Behavior Teaching Review* 12, no. 8 (1987): 93–100. Organizations that include employees in strategic planning sessions enjoy dramatically reduced turnover rates, simply as a result of employees feeling more involved in the organization's management process. See Lillian T. Eby, Tammy D. Allen, and Andi Brinley, "A Cross-Level Investigation of the Relationship Between Career Management Practices and Career-Related Attitudes," *Group & Organization Management* 30, no.6 (2005): 565–587.

27. David G. Allen, "Do Organizational Socialization Tactics Influence Newcomer Embeddedness and Turnover?" *Journal of Management* 32, no. 2 (2006): 237–256.

28. Beverly Kaye and Sharon Jordan-Evans, "Retention Tag: You're It," *Training and Development* 54, no. 4 (2000): 29–34.

29. Woodruff Imberman and Mariah DeForest, "Take Care of Your Latino Workers," *Lodging Hospitality* 60, no. 14 (2004): 54–56.

30. Nic Paton, "A Turnaround in Turnover," *Personnel Today*, November 15, 2005: 27–29.

31. Kate Drummond, *Human Resource Management for the Hospitality Industry* (New York: Van Nostrand Reinhold, 1990): 261–262.

32. Cynthia J. Guffey and Marilyn M. Helms, "Effective Employee Discipline," *Public Personnel Management* (Spring 2001): 111–127.

33. Brenda Baik Sunoo, "Positive Discipline—Sending the Right or Wrong Message," *Personnel Journal* 75 (August 1996): 109–111.

34. Guffey and Helms.

35. Shari Caudron, "Angry Employees Bite Back in Court," *Personnel Journal* 75 (December 1996): 32–38. More recent research of lawsuits filed in the United States shows that the number of wrongful discharge lawsuits has not abated at all. See David H. Autor, John J. Donohue, and Stewart J. Schwab, "The Costs of Wrongful-Discharge Laws," November 18, 2002, *MIT Department of Economics. Working Paper No. 02-41;* and *Stanford Law & Econmics Olin Working Paper No. 243;* and *Stanford Law School, Public Law Research Paper No. 49.*

36. Wayne E. Barlow, "The After-Acquired Evidence Defense: Where Do We Stand Now?" *Personnel Journal* 74 (June 1995): 152–156.

37. Ralph H. Baxter, Jr., "Protecting Against Exposure," *National Law Review* 16 (February 1994): 1.

38.   Susan Gardner, Glenn M. Gomes, and James F. Morgan, "Wrongful Termination and the Expanding Public Policy Exception: Implications and Advice," *S.A.M. Advanced Management Journal* (Winter 2000): 38, 44.

Key Terms

attitude survey—A needs assessment method designed to determine when behavioral training is required; also a questionnaire or other information-gathering tool designed to determine how employees feel about work issues.

discharge interview—A meeting between an employee and employer in which the purpose is to terminate the employee's employment.

employment at will—Employment policy stipulating that employers can discharge employees at any time for any reason.

exit interview—Meeting conducted between an employer and an employee leaving the organization that attempts to identify specific training needs or other work-related problems.

hierarchical appeals process—A process that employees who feel they have been treated unfairly can use to take their concerns to succeeding levels of the chain of command.

hot stove approach—An approach to discipline based on immediate punishment for each offense.

implied employment contract—An agreement that is inferred from information in employee and training manuals and other documents suggesting that employees have the right to work for their employer as long as they do a good job.

open-door appeals process—A process used by employees who feel they have been treated unfairly to take their concerns to any manager.

peer review appeals process—A process used by employees who feel they have been treated unfairly to take their concerns to boards made up of other employees and managers.

preventive discipline—A type of discipline emphasizing recognition of good behavior instead of bad behavior.

progressive discipline—Discipline process in which employees are given increasingly stiffer penalties for infractions; usually progresses from an oral warning, to a written warning, to a suspension, and finally to discharge.

replacement costs—Turnover costs associated with replacing lost employees (recruiting, advertising, uniforms, manuals, interviewing, and other related costs).

retention program—Program designed to reduce turnover.

separation costs—Turnover costs associated with exit interviews, separation pay, closure of employee benefits files, and unemployment taxes.

training costs—Turnover costs associated with preparing new employees to be productive (orientation, training instruction, training materials, and so forth).

turnover—The rate at which employees leave a company or work unit.

turnover costs—Tangible or intangible costs incurred by a hospitality operation to replace an employee.

whistleblowing—The act of informing authorities of illegal or unethical actions taken by one's employer.

wrongful discharge—Charge brought against an employer for terminating employees without due process or without substantial efforts to first call an employee's attention to improper work habits and to help the employee change; terminating an employee's employment without sufficient reason.

 Review Questions

1. Why should employee discharge be viewed as a last-resort disciplinary step?
2. What are three organizational causes of discipline problems?
3. What are three individual causes of discipline problems?
4. How does the "hot stove approach" compare with progressive discipline?
5. How does positive discipline differ from progressive discipline?
6. What processes should a manager go through before discharging an employee?
7. Under what circumstances might an employee file a wrongful discharge lawsuit that would be difficult for managers to defend?
8. What are some circumstances that may lead employees to believe that they have an implied employment contract for lifetime work?
9. How does the concept of employment at will compare with implied employment contracts?
10. What is an effective exit interview system?

 Internet Sites

For more information, visit the following Internet sites. Remember that Internet addresses can change without notice. If the site is no longer there, you can use a search engine to look for additional sites.

For additional information, search "wrongful discharge" using any Web search engine. Many sites are home pages for attorneys offering services related to employment issues.

Sample employee discipline policy
www.db.erau.edu/appm/policy/
8-3-5.html

U.S. Census Bureau
www.census.gov

U.S. Consumer Information Center   Workforce Management
www.pueblo.gsa.gov   www.workforce.com

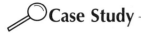

Case Study

Can One Month Destroy Seven Years? Lucy at Risk in an At-Will State.

Henry is the maintenance manager at an older hotel that has been renovated in recent years. He is a newcomer to the property and just reached his six-month anniversary. Lucy is his administrative assistant. She supports him and the entire three-shift operation by entering and updating work orders on a computerized maintenance management system. She has been with the property for seven years and has performed well through a few organizational changes.

The department workload has been particularly heavy since the new wing opened in September. Around the beginning of October, Henry noticed that Lucy sometimes arrived back late from lunch breaks. It is now late October. Last week, Lucy started to fall behind in her paperwork. On Tuesday and Wednesday she arrived late and took long lunches. She called in sick on Friday and again this past Monday.

On Tuesday Henry checked in with Lucy when she arrived for work and asked if she was feeling better. She did not look at him, but mumbled, "As well as could be expected." Two maintenance personnel, Jeff and Jim, entered the office and began finishing up their paperwork. Henry told Lucy about an all-employee meeting first thing Wednesday morning and said it was important that she be there, both as a valuable maintenance-team member and as an employee of the property as a whole. She sighed that she would be there. But Wednesday morning she didn't show up for the meeting; she didn't even call in. Jeff and Jim commented on her absence to Henry, "Either something's really wrong, or she's really fed up with you." Henry agreed and said, "If she is messing around with me, she's not going to get away with it." He began mulling over in his mind the option of firing her. In the at-will state in which their property was located, he could fire for no reason at all.

Right after lunch on Wednesday, Henry looked over the week's time sheets and noticed that Lucy had listed 8 hours of work for each day she had been gone, Friday and Monday, plus 5 overtime hours. She had attached a note to her time sheet that read: "Henry, I took some work home Thursday night to try and catch up. I hope that's all right."

Lucy showed up around 2 P.M. on Wednesday. Henry confronted her and said her attendance pattern and some other behaviors were unacceptable. He said he wanted to schedule a counseling session with her first thing Thursday morning. Lucy, visibly upset, quickly agreed. She worked haltingly for the rest of Wednesday.

Thursday morning there was no sign of Lucy. Fifteen minutes after she was supposed to have met with Henry, one of the supervisors under Henry brought him a message from her saying she felt too stressed about the meeting and too overwhelmed with her workload to come. Henry called her at home right away to find out what exactly was going on. Lucy repeated much of what she had said in the phone message: she was exhausted; she was overwhelmed by the workload and stressed about meeting with him. She added that she wasn't even sure if she wanted to work at the hotel anymore. Henry listened but said a face-to-face talk would be important for an in-depth discussion of the issues. He asked Lucy if she would be willing to meet with him first thing the next morning—Friday. She agreed.

Now it's Friday. Lucy arrives and is seated in Henry's office with the door closed. Henry begins, "Lucy, I'm glad you came this morning. I've been worried about you. You've been taking longer lunches than you should be sometimes, and you haven't changed that pattern, even when I've talked with you about it. And now, in the last couple weeks, you've been late or missing or sick a lot. Yesterday you violated our policy that says you should call your direct supervisor when you're not coming in. I saw the note you attached to last week's time sheet; you know you're not supposed to take overtime without my advance permission. Can you tell me what the problem is?"

Lucy reacts quickly. "There's been so much to do lately, and no one has helped me a bit! Did you ever stop to think about how that new wing would affect my job? This place has been like a war zone—work orders everywhere, a computer that's a piece of junk, the phone ringing off the hook, and people standing in line to tell me what a lousy job I'm doing. Every morning it's been all I could do to get up and face the day. Now I'm just not sure I want to put up with it anymore."

"Whoa, now, slow down," says Henry. "Let's start at the beginning." He asks about the workload, especially since the new wing's opening, and Lucy shares how abandoned she felt when the department hired several new maintenance workers, but gave no extra support on the administrative end. The computer has been down every few weeks for as much as three days at a time. When it is up and running, it's much slower than it should be at accessing and saving information. And Lucy is uncomfortable with the amount of attention—sometimes unwelcome attention—focused on her, the sole woman in the department. Henry listens carefully, noting and apologizing for those things for which he is most clearly at fault. He acknowledges those feelings and perceptions he can understand, even when he thinks she's wrong.

"Well," says Henry, "let's talk now about how things should work for someone in your position. How did it work before I got here?" Lucy brightens a little as she reminisces about how she was able to meet the various challenges of her work in the earlier years. She mentions how housekeeping now fails to get work orders in to her in time to affect the room status update for the front desk by 2 P.M. She also lists the names of several newer maintenance workers who are particularly rude when she gets behind. Henry pulls out the job description for her position, and they together discuss some ideas based on that.

Henry responds to Lucy's concerns about the rude workers, the workload, and the unacceptably late housekeeping work orders by saying he can do something about those issues. He says he'll talk to his own boss about the possibility of getting a part-time assistant to work with her. "However," he says, "there are some parts of your job description that are nonnegotiable. You were wrong to take those overtime hours without asking me. The rule about calling your direct supervisor when you'll be gone is still a rule—it's not fair to me, and it's not fair to make the other supervisor play middleman for you. I cannot, we as a department cannot afford to have an administrative assistant with irregular attendance. All our maintenance workers are counting on you and me to organize their work and keep them focused and busy. Beyond that, the front desk, housekeeping, sales—lots of departments are affected when we're backed up. Ultimately, the property loses guests." Lucy shifts in her seat. "I think you have given the property a lot in past years, and you are still valuable to us now. But you can't go on dealing with the problems here by not showing up. If you hide your head in the sand one more time, your job will not be here for you when you come out. Do I make myself clear?" Lucy nods, stone-faced.

Lucy leaves the office. Henry heads straight for the human resources office to talk with Brad, the HR director, about his meeting. He tells Brad, "I don't know what to do with Lucy. We don't have any employment problems written up in her file, but now all this has happened." Henry recounts the events of the last month or so, including the meeting he just had. "I really doubt she's going to come through. She seems near the point of no return in her own mind. I'm uneasy with keeping someone like that. Any effort she makes to change will be just a show until she knows she's off 'probation.' Then she'll go right back to the way she is now. But what do you think we should do with her?"

Discussion Questions

1. Should Henry have handled his meeting with Lucy any differently? How so?

2. If you were Brad, the human resources director, what advice would you give Henry?

3. Is Lucy guilty of willful disregard for her employer? gross misconduct? At what point did she cross the line?

Case number: 35613CA

The following industry experts helped generate and develop this case: Philip J. Bresson, Director of Human Resources, Renaissance New York Hotel, New York, New York; and Jerry Fay, Human Resources Director, ARAMARK Corporation, Atlanta, Georgia.

Chapter 14 Outline

Competencies

1. Describe philosophical perspectives on the social responsibility of business. (pp. 461–464)

2. Explain typical responses of businesses to the call for social responsibility, and outline the pros and cons associated with social responsibility. (pp. 464–468)

3. Describe examples of how hospitality companies are socially responsible, and discuss how they might conduct a social responsibility audit. (pp. 468–473)

4. Summarize ethical issues in business, including how businesses can assess ethical behavior, recent ethical issues in American business, and ethical issues in human resources management. (pp. 473–478)

14

Social Responsibility and Ethics

This chapter was co-authored by Cecil R. Torres, Jr., M.Ed., HRTD, Ph.D. candidate, University of Nevada, Las Vegas.

BY DEFINITION, social responsibility is the obligation of an organization's management to make decisions and take actions that enhance the welfare and interests of society as a whole. Social responsibility is not corporate charity; it is not enough for organizations to simply parcel out charitable contributions. Managers today must be responsive to a broad spectrum of societal groups. Managers must realize that their businesses are an important part of society, and society plays an integral role in the success of their businesses. As managers look to the future, more and more of them see being socially responsible as playing a key role in helping them sustain long-term organizational success.

Ethics has always been important in business. Unfortunately, its importance has been highlighted in recent years by notable ethical lapses on the part of top executives in companies like Enron, WorldCom, and Adelphia. These and other examples of spectacular ethical implosions by U.S. companies have led some Americans to believe that all companies engage in unethical practices. This is unfortunate, because most American businesses have a social conscience and follow the rules.

In this chapter, we will take a look at differing philosophical perspectives on just how socially responsible businesses should be. We will examine the pros and cons of social responsibility from a business perspective, and describe how the hospitality industry tries to be socially responsible. We will conclude the chapter with a look at ethical issues in business; specifically, how ethical behavior can be measured in organizations, recent ethical issues in American business, and ethical dilemmas managers face when dealing with human resources issues.

Philosophical Perspectives on the Social Responsibility of Business

In the early twentieth century, the prevailing view among business leaders was that business had a responsibility only to those who had a direct interest in its success. This view was exemplified by the powerful robber barons of the era—Rockefeller, Vanderbilt, Carnegie—and others who controlled much of the business activity in the United States. "Social responsibility" in this era was often addressed through charity. The great robber barons gave millions of dollars to their charitable pursuits, but they felt no pangs of guilt when they paid their employees slave wages or broke strikes by force. Politically and economically, this period was characterized by the belief that government had no role in business, and business had no role in government. This was known as laissez-faire economics. Philosophically, this period was characterized by Herbert Spencer's social Darwinism theory, which asserted that the fittest people in society would survive and rise to the top.

The stock market crash of 1929 and the worldwide Great Depression that soon followed brought an end to the laissez-faire policies of the early twentieth century. In response to the great human suffering and massive economic problems of the 1930s, the U.S. government began to play a larger and larger role in regulating business activities. The many federal programs begun under Franklin D. Roosevelt's New Deal typify the era. Philosophically, this period was dominated by Keynesian economic theory, which advocated active federal intervention in many business enterprises. The government assumed more responsibility for providing for the health and economic welfare of U.S. citizens.

In the mid-1960s, the relationship between business and society shifted again. This time, businesses were encouraged to get directly involved in the broader society's attempt to cure society's ills. Since the sixties, Americans have come to expect more and more of business leaders. In the latter part of the twentieth century, it began to be widely accepted that businesses had an important role in promoting and preserving the overall health of society and had a responsibility to help address society's problems. As we begin the twenty-first century, more businesses are accepting the fact that to be optimally successful, they must be seen as good citizens by their customers and others in society.

However, not all of today's business leaders agree that corporations have a responsibility to society at large. Their opinions appear to be split among three different philosophies.

Traditional Philosophy

As noted earlier, during the early part of the twentieth century it was believed that the overriding goal of business was the maximization of profits. This philosophy is still held by many business leaders. Some of the characteristics of this belief are:

- The saying, "What's good for business is good for society"
- The desire for government to maintain a hands-off role in business
- A "buyer beware" attitude in business transactions
- Managers being accountable only to their superiors

Stakeholder Philosophy

A second widely held view—the **stakeholder philosophy**—contends that managers are responsible not only to their superiors and their shareholders but also to certain groups of **stakeholders**. Generally, stakeholders are those groups and individuals—both within and outside an organization—who have a stake in a

Exhibit 1   Typical Stakeholders of a Hotel Company

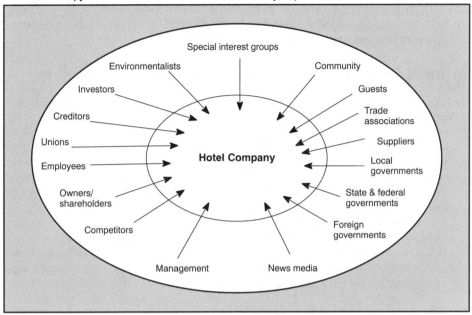

company's performance. For example, the stakeholders of a large international hotel chain range from guests and employees to environmentalists and foreign governments. Exhibit 1 shows typical stakeholders of a hotel.

The stakeholder philosophy reflects "enlightened self-interest." Managers who hold this view recognize that responding to their stakeholders is ultimately good for business. An example is the approach that Johnson & Johnson took following the Tylenol scare of 1982, in which seven people in the Chicago area died from taking Tylenol capsules laced with cyanide. Johnson & Johnson immediately responded by pulling Tylenol off store shelves to protect its customers. This show of good faith helped Johnson & Johnson retain the trust of its consumers. This philosophy was also typified more recently by Starbucks Coffee which, when faced with the triple-homicide of three of its workers at a Starbucks store in Washington, D.C., took the unusual action of chartering a plane and flying the company's president to Washington overnight, offering a reward for the capture of the murderers, and turning the profits of the store over to the families of the slain employees in perpetuity.

Affirmative Philosophy

The third major philosophical approach to social responsibility is the **affirmative philosophy**. This approach is typified by companies that anticipate changes in stakeholder needs and voluntarily curtail activities that may be seen as damaging to society as a whole. Companies that curtailed business interests in South Africa in the mid-1980s in protest of that country's apartheid political system exemplified the affirmative philosophy. This approach can be seen in many different companies today, through such activities as donating leftover food to homeless shelters, providing housing for victims of natural and other disasters, and offering educational opportunities to employees and their families.

Business Responses to the Call for Social Responsibility

From these three philosophical bases, businesses today generally take one of four approaches to society's demands to behave in a socially responsible way:

- *Obstructive response.* When businesses engage in an **obstructive response,** they may deny responsibility for an activity that has negatively affected society in some way; claim that the evidence condemning the company's products, services, or actions is misleading or distorted, and/or place obstacles in the path of investigations. One of the most famous cases of a company engaging in this type of behavior is that of Union Carbide. On December 3, 1984, a holding tank in a Union Carbide pesticide plant in Bhopal, India, malfunctioned and released tons of methyl isocyanate gas into the atmosphere. Thousands of people were killed within hours, and several thousand more were permanently disabled. Union Carbide took the obstructive approach of forcing the government of India to prove the company liable, which eventually happened when the Supreme Court of India ruled as such. To this day the company is resisting efforts to clean up the site.[1]

- *Defensive response.* When businesses take a **defensive response,** they admit to some errors or omissions, but only do what is legally required to correct the situation. This approach is typified by companies that do not curtail questionable or controversial activities until legal action is taken. This approach is typified by Exxon's response to the events surrounding the *Exxon Valdez* oil spill in Alaska, the worst environmental disaster to occur at sea in history. Not only was the company slow to respond initially, it is still appealing the punative damages award in this case, some 17 years later.[2]

- *Accommodating response.* Businesses that react to situations with an **accommodating response** accept their responsibility to society at large and try to meet all of the legal, economic, and ethical responsibilities of a situation. The reaction just mentioned of Starbucks after the tragic shooting of its Washington, D.C., employees typifies this type of response.

- *Proactive response.* Businesses characterized by **proactive responses** take action to be social responsible before an incident occurs or before pressure from government agencies or special interest groups force them to take action. DuPont took a proactive approach when it voluntarily instituted a program to repurchase used Freon and chlorofluorocarbons (chemicals that it had manufactured) to help reduce the impact of such waste on the environment.

Exhibit 2 presents examples of proactive, socially responsible programs that businesses can engage in.

Exhibit 2   Sample Proactive Social Responsibility Programs

- Youth programs (community youth centers, youth mentoring programs, after-school programs)
- Recycling, waste reduction, and conservation programs
- Responsible purchasing (product safety, environmental concerns)
- Code of conduct for suppliers
- Support for local charities
- Progressive labor policies (diversity programs, competitive wages and benefits, safety programs, health/fitness programs for workers, and so on)
- Support for programs (at the local, national, and/or international level) to end hunger
- House-the-homeless programs (e.g., Habitat for Humanity)
- Disaster relief
- Anti-drug campaigns

The Pros of Social Responsibility

Within many of today's corporations, there is still an ongoing debate between starting or supporting programs that benefit society or simply pursuing traditional financial goals. However, there are numerous "real-world" examples showing that a policy of social responsibility can enhance a corporation's financial success. Corporations that take social responsibility seriously find it is far more than just a public relations gesture. Businesses that are socially responsible can benefit in the following ways:

- *Reduced operating costs.* Businesses can save money by putting recycling and energy conservation programs into practice. The Coalition for Environmentally Responsible Economies (CERES) provides a nonprofit network for businesses, advocacy groups, and trade unions to plan for environmental responsibility and follow a ten-point code of conduct. Preventing waste is a top priority, and hotels that are part of this network look for ways to cut down on discarded paper, plastic, and food products. By switching to a "lean and green" program to recycle waste, reduce daily washing of linens, and convert to energy-efficient utility sources, lodging properties can not only save money, they can make money by attracting a new, environmentally conscious clientele. For example, in the first three months of its eco-friendly program, the Boston-based Saunders Hotel Group lowered its operating expenses and brought in $1 million in new business. The Rocky Mountain Institute calculated that "green" buildings can increase worker productivity by as much as 16 percent. An air filtration system developed by EcoSmart Healthy Properties can help hotels slash their electric bills by 30 percent. The Fairmont Palliser in Calgary, Alberta, reuses the water that cools the compressors in ice machines and freezer units, reducing water consumption by one-third.[3]

- *Enhanced image and reputation.* A study of *Fortune* magazine's annual list of "Most Admired Companies" shows that the emphasis is shifting from top producers to companies with programs promoting social responsibility. Other media lists and business awards that are concerned with corporate reputation (e.g., *Business Ethics* magazine's "100 Best Corporate Citizens," American Business Ethics Awards, and the Better Business Bureau Torch Award for Marketplace Ethics) use a range of ethical considerations as criteria in determining the companies' rankings. Increasingly, consumers are paying attention to these reports. When there is a choice, many consumers prefer a company with a social conscience.

- *Greater customer loyalty.* A 2005 study on consumer behavior reported that many consumers base their purchase decision in part on whether the company they are purchasing from is ethical and socially responsible. A study conducted by *Forbes* magazine confirmed this result, finding that fully 47 percent of the American public makes decisions on where to purchase products based on their understanding of whether or not the companies they are buying from are socially responsible.[4]

- *Increased ability to attract and retain employees.* Often employees are attracted by the corporate culture of companies that are socially responsible. One survey of employees revealed that for 42 percent of the respondents, a company's ethical integrity directly influenced their decision to work for the company. Companies with low employee turnover save on recruitment, training, and other employee costs. At Starbucks, employee turnover is less than a third of the turnover average for the retail food industry. This is attributed to Starbuck's socially responsible practices, which includes a full benefits package for part-time employees.[5]

- *Greater access to capital.* In 2005, Social Investment Forum reported that $2.29 trillion (up from $2.16 trillion in 2003) was invested in companies which engaged in socially responsible actions. Many people like to feel good about where their investment dollars are going.

- *Potential avoidance of fines.* A business that has developed strong social programs and ethics initiatives may greatly reduce the chance that it will have to pay large fines resulting from wrongful, fraudulent, discriminatory, or illegal activities. With the revision of the U.S. Federal Sentencing Guidelines, companies demonstrating "good corporate citizenship" can substantially reduce potential penalties when misconduct does occur. In this and other ways, local and national government bodies are starting to reward companies that are proactive in addressing social issues and are trying to be good corporate citizens.

Another benefit to businesses that are proactive when it comes to social issues is that such a philosophy puts them in agreement with an increasing number of their shareholders. Companies that have their heads in the sand when it comes to social responsibility sometimes find themselves under attack from within. More and more companies today are being subjected to what are known as "shareholder activism" campaigns. The following campaigns show some of the societal issues that are on the minds of shareholders:

- McDonald's agreed to add sexual orientation to its non-discrimination statement, thanks to a campaign led by Trillium Asset Management Corporation. (Trillium Asset Management advertises itself as "the largest independent investment management firm dedicated solely to socially responsible investing."[6])

- General Electric finally promoted a woman into a top operating management position, in part because of a behind-the-scenes dialogue with Aquinas Funds, a mutual funds company in Dallas, Texas, which is also dedicated to socially responsible investing.

- Universal Health Services of Pennsylvania, the country's third largest hospital management company, agreed to formally request that its suppliers phase out polyvinyl chloride (PVC) in medical products, following a resolution filed by Citizens Advisers, Inc., of Portsmouth, New Hampshire.

- Hewlett-Packard agreed to review global environmental standards for suppliers, and T. Rowe Price agreed to take steps toward disclosing Equal Employment Opportunity data, thanks to shareholder resolutions (later withdrawn after the companies complied) by Walden/U.S. Trust Company of Boston.

- Paychex announced it had hired a search firm to seek out women and minorities for its board of directors, following the threat of a shareholder resolution by the Calvert Group of Bethesda, Maryland.

The Cons of Social Responsibility

Business leaders who do not believe it is their responsibility to be proactive social leaders often use one or more of the following six arguments against businesses engaging in proactive social responsibility programs:

1. The benefits of responsible social action are difficult to measure in terms of the bottom line.

2. The cost of social responsibility can be high, and businesses can rarely increase their prices to cover it.

3. The time that managers spend on social issues is time taken away from efforts to keep their businesses afloat and profitable in a highly competitive business environment.

4. There are too many different issues espoused by too many special interest groups for business leaders to respond to all of them.

5. Unlike political leaders, business leaders are not directly accountable to the people. Therefore, they should feel no need to engage in socially progressive activities just because the public wants or expects them to.

6. Business already has enough power. Allowing the business world to engage in actions designed to directly impact society would give it too much power.

Despite these six reasons, corporate social responsibility is the watchword for most progressive companies in the early twenty-first century. According to the Millennium Poll on Corporate Responsibility, "two in three citizens want companies to go beyond their historical role of making profits, paying taxes, employing people, and obeying all laws; they want companies to contribute to broader societal goals."[7] Many companies are responding to this desire. Most Fortune 500 companies, for example, incorporate social responsibility programs into their operations. While the effect on consumer behavior of businesses trying to be socially responsible is not completely understood, marketplace polls and academic studies show that consumers generally have more confidence in companies that are socially responsible and follow a set of ethical guidelines.[8]

Social Responsibility and the Hospitality Industry

The hospitality industry often gets a bad rap for its perceived approach to social responsibility. For instance, the public is much more likely to know that the hospitality industry is one of the largest consumers of polystyrene containers (those plastic "to go" boxes) than it is to know that the hospitality industry has been a leader in programs to feed the homeless. One reason for this is that bad news gets more attention than good news. The fact is, many hospitality companies are engaged in proactive social responsibility programs today and have been for many years. The following are just a few examples of the programs and initiatives hospitality companies engage in regularly:

- Share Our Strength (SOS) is a nationwide consortium of restaurants, suppliers, and others that raises money for hunger relief and sponsors many other programs to help the hungry in America. SOS stages an annual benefit meal and supports National Hunger Awareness Day to raise public awareness about the problem of hunger in the United States and throughout the world.

- Many hospitality companies donate "leftovers" (unused, wholesome food) to charitable organizations. Legislation that helped free up the hospitality industry (and other industries, such as the retail grocery industry) to donate more food was the Bill Emerson Good Samaritan Food Donation Act. This act limits liability for companies that donate food products for the benefit of the community.

- In 2006, Hilton announced that it has made it even easier for members of its highly popular guest reward program, Hilton HHonors, to convert their HHonors points and contribute to a variety of charitable organizations. Through Hilton's newly created Hilton Family Giving Back Program, Hilton guests who wish to contribute their HHonors points to worthy causes can contribute to such organizations as the American Red Cross, the City of Hope Cancer Center, and the National Coalition for the Homeless.

- At Kimpton Hotel & Restaurant Group, the San Francisco–based boutique hotel company, 65 percent of its hotel and restaurant employees nationwide volunteered their time and expertise to make a positive social and environmental difference on a local level during Kimpton Cares Month. They donated blood, raised money for humane societies, planted trees, collected food for the hungry, and participated in many other charitable activities. The Kimpton Cares program, of which Kimpton Cares Month is only a part, runs throughout the year and is affiliated with such national charity organizations as the Trust for Public Land and Dress for Success (a nonprofit organization committed to helping disadvantaged women thrive in the workplace).

- In 2003, Darden Restaurants, the largest casual dining restaurant company in the world, established an endowed chair in Diversity and Business Ethics to study ways that hospitality companies can be more socially responsible.

- Sol Meliá, a Spanish hotel and resort chain with approximately 350 hotels and resorts in 30 countries, is supporting UNICEF (the United Nations Children's Fund) through a new "Sol Meliá Solidarity Fund." For every hotel reservation made through solmelia.com, the company will donate 1 euro to UNICEF.

- Many hospitality companies have become very active in the movement to "green America" through reuse and recycling programs and the proper handling and elimination of waste and environmental pollutants. Overall, the hospitality industry is much more active in environmental causes than many other industries, for practical as well as ethical reasons. It is in a hotel company's economic interest, for example, when it builds a resort in a beautiful, remote setting to take measures to make sure the setting stays beautiful; otherwise, guests will not patronize the resort if the natural beauty surrounding the resort is spoiled. "Green" Hotels Association offers a listing of hotels that save water, save energy, and reduce solid waste—while saving money. The association's Web site lists reuse and recycling ideas and gives examples of what other hotels are doing in the area of protecting the environment.

Conducting a Social Responsibility Audit

Hospitality companies interested in assessing how socially responsible they are can conduct a social responsibility audit. Most audits compare a company's socially responsible performance to five factors:

1. Established expectations for each department or organizational unit in terms of responses to consumer affairs, employee relations, environmental concerns, and so forth.

2. Established priorities of what each unit will try to accomplish, and when.

3. Established objectives, including an outline of how the company will reach each objective.

4. Commitment of department or unit resources, including analysis of costs and benefits associated with resource allocations.

5. Objective evaluation on an established, periodic basis to determine the extent to which each objective has been achieved.

Social audits are tools that companies use to identify or define their social and environmental impacts, measure and evaluate the impacts, communicate their performance internally and externally, and make continual improvement in such areas as community and customer relations, employment practices, human rights issues, environmental responsibility, and ethical behavior. Companies conduct social audits of their operations for a number of reasons: to be more strategic about their corporate social responsibility (CSR); to quantify the non-financial aspects of their community involvement and other CSR-related activities; to identify potential liabilities; and in response to stakeholder requests for increased disclosure. To date, European companies have taken the lead in creating the most comprehensive social audits, though there are leadership examples in many countries outside Europe as well, including Peru, South Africa, and the United States.

There are a variety of standards that hospitality and other companies are using to measure and disclose their social performance. These include industry benchmarking tools and frameworks, mandatory and non-mandatory legislation in some countries, and voluntary codes developed by nongovernmental organizations and private-sector consultancies. What follows are just a few examples of sources for social accounting standards:

- *Quality Scoring Framework.* The New Economics Foundation and the Institute of Social and Ethical Accountability created the Quality Scoring Framework, based on principles for social and ethical accounting, auditing, and reporting. The system—which assesses the quality of a company's audit, not its corporate social responsibility performance—is based on eight key principles, each of which involves seven questions, which are scored on a scale of 0 to 4. The scoring process for each of the 56 questions yields an aggregate score for each principle, which can be plotted to provide a visual representation of a company's social-accounting process and how well it meets both company and stakeholder needs.

- *Sunshine Standards for Corporate Reporting to Stakeholders.* Proposed by the Washington, D.C.–based Stakeholder Alliance—an association of individuals and organizations from environmental, consumer, and religious organizations—the "Sunshine Standards" describe "the information that corporations should routinely provide in an annual Corporate Report to Stakeholders." The standards cover a wide spectrum of information, from "customer information needs" (related to actions against the corporation, product contents, and other issues) and "employee information needs" (job security, health and safety risks, equal opportunity employment data, employee grievances) to "community information needs" (company ownership, financial data, environmental impact, taxes paid, job creation data, investments, charitable contributions) and "society's information needs" (trade with hostile nations, major government contracts, fines levied against the company, and so on).

- *Ethical Accounting Statement.* This statement was developed by two professors at the Copenhagen Business School, with the first actual statement produced at Sbn Bank, a major Danish financial institution. Since then, roughly 50 private and public enterprises in Denmark have embraced "ethical accounting" as a means of introducing and maintaining values-based management and organizational ethics. The Ethical Accounting Statement (see Exhibit 3) provides measures of how well an organization lives up to the shared values it has committed itself to follow.

Exhibit 3 Minimum Requirements for an Ethical Accounting Statement

- It is based on the shared values that the stakeholders have defined in a conversation process.
- It uses questionnaires based on concrete expressions of the shared values.
- It is developed at regular intervals by representatives of the stakeholders.
- It is published even if the results are unpleasant for one or more stakeholders.
- It is designed so that it is impossible to identify individual respondents.
- It gives no stakeholder a monopoly on interpreting the results. Interpretation takes place in an ongoing dialog between the stakeholders.
- It is not a strategic tool that a single stakeholder can use to further his or her goals. The mutual balance between stakeholders protects against bias and facilitates the dynamic attunement of values and positions.
- It provides the starting point for new dialogs aimed at proposing concrete actions in areas where the organization should improve its support of a shared value—and for the development of the next Ethical Accounting Statement.

Source: DiversityInc.com (www.diversityinc.com), a webzine specializing in the study of diversity and how it affects companies' relationships with their key stakeholders: employees, suppliers, customers, investors, and others.

Steps in Conducting Social Responsibility Audits. The approaches of hospitality companies to social auditing and accounting are as varied as their approaches to corporate social responsibility. There are few templates to follow in establishing the goals, metrics, scope, and standards of social accounting, just as there are few standards to follow in most other aspects of the social auditing process, such as what standards of performance should be used, how frequently to evaluate the results of a social audit, whether and how to report the results to internal and external audiences, and what actions companies should take in response to audit results.

A company need not begin with an exhaustive, company-wide audit; most companies find it useful to begin with smaller, more informal and focused audits that may be more appropriate to their immediate needs. The following are some strategies to consider:

- *Determine the audit's scope and process.* The scope may be as narrow as a single program, department, or facility, or as comprehensive as imaginable, including all aspects of all parts of a company's worldwide operations. Evaluations can involve surveys, interviews, dialogs, focus groups, and data analysis.
- *Define and engage stakeholders.* It is important to determine at the onset the stakeholder groups that will be part of the audit—both as potential participants (providing input to the company) and as "customers" (people who will receive copies of the completed audit). Some companies' primary stakeholder group is internal—their employees—while other companies select from any or all of a variety of external stakeholders: suppliers, customers, investors, community groups, regulators, nongovernmental organizations, academic organizations, and the news media.

- *Identify benchmarks.* Before information is collected, it is necessary to determine how the audit will be evaluated—that is, the measures of success that will be used. To do this, it may be helpful to conduct research on what other companies are doing in the area of corporate social responsibility. Such benchmarking can help identify "best practices" or establish a baseline of minimum requirements.

- *Review documents.* A thorough audit will include a review of all relevant reports, both internal reports as well as external ones sent to governmental agencies and others. This review will help establish the internal and external expectations of the company and may also include baselines of compliance. The review also will provide indications of where the company has, or hasn't, met its commitments, including the commitments established by its mission statements and other policy documents.

- *Review management systems.* It is important to gain a complete understanding of the management policies and practices that exist within the company for the specific areas covered by the audit. A comprehensive audit will review all of these systems and assess their strengths and weaknesses.

- *Summarize the findings.* The audit should reach some conclusions about what was learned. In some cases, this may involve weighing the findings against the measures of success identified earlier, both quantitatively and qualitatively. In other cases, it may involve more descriptive, impressionistic assessments of the findings. In any event, an audit should include the costs and benefits of the company's corporate social responsibility programs, the company strengths and weaknesses in policy statements and management systems, feedback from stakeholders, and a list of issues worth exploring in future audits.

- *Verify results.* More and more companies are having their social responsibility audits verified by credible, independent third parties, such as an accounting firm, management consultancy firm, or nongovernmental organization with knowledge and expertise in the area of social audits. In many such cases, the third-party organization is also involved with the design and implementation of the audit. In addition to having a third-party verification, it may be helpful to have the report reviewed by a few key stakeholders before it is officially released, to ensure that the report is comprehensive and balanced.

- *Share the findings.* Not all social responsibility audits are intended for public consumption; some companies prefer to limit their use to internal audiences. However, many companies release their audits widely, sending them to a diverse spectrum of stakeholders—those involved with the audits as well as those who aren't. Potential audiences include shareholders, regulators, community organizations, environmental organizations, labor unions, and the news media. Some companies also make them available on the Internet.

- *Create mission statements.* Based on the results of the audit, it may be appropriate to create one or more new mission statements for company departments or other areas, or create a single, overarching mission statement or ethical policy for the entire company.

- *Repeat the process.* Social responsibility audits are most useful when they are conducted on a regular basis, enabling companies and stakeholders to track progress over a period of time.

Ethical Issues in Business

Progressive managers promote corporate social responsibility at both the organizational and individual levels, recognizing that the two efforts are interdependent. No company can enjoy an atmosphere where corporate social responsibility thrives unless there is a commitment to the importance of ethical behavior at the individual level.[9] Although people develop their strongest beliefs about ethics early in life, these beliefs grow and change with experience. One of the most powerful influences on a person's worldview and behavior is the workplace. Therefore, managers who emphasize the importance of ethical behavior can positively impact the way their employees conduct business.

Although the importance of ethics in business has been recognized since the first businesses were created, in the past few decades the topic of business ethics has enjoyed a wave of renewed interest. Many organizations have been created over the years to help business managers create workplace cultures that encourage ethical behavior. For example, the Ethics Resource Center was founded in 1922 in Washington, D.C., to help individuals and companies improve their ethical practices. The Center publishes research and provides benchmarks to improve organizational ethics; its newsletter, *Ethics Today,* is published monthly in e-mail format and is sent free to registered subscribers. The International Business Ethics Institute was founded in 1994 to promote business ethics and corporate responsibility; it sponsors a Roundtable Discussion Series, publishes *International Business Ethics Review,* and helps companies establish effective international ethics programs. The Society for Business Ethics, founded in 1980, is an international organization of scholars engaged in the academic study of business ethics. The society conducts research and publishes *Business Ethics Quarterly.* An increasing number of colleges and universities are offering business ethics classes as part of their business curriculums.

Although the unethical conduct of companies often receives the most attention, many organizations in recent years have created codes of ethics (see Exhibit 4) and are taking other steps to improve their records on ethics. For example, by 2006 nearly 65 percent of U.S. companies had developed ethics training programs for their managers.[10] For such programs to work, they need:

- Top management support

- Open discussion of realistic ethical scenarios that employees and managers are likely to face

- A mechanism for allowing and encouraging managers and employees to report ethical violations

- An organizational culture that rewards ethical conduct

Exhibit 4   Sample Code of Ethics

CODE OF ETHICS
HOSPITALITY SERVICE AND TOURISM INDUSTRY

1. We acknowledge ethics and morality as inseparable elements of doing business and will test every decision against the highest standards of honesty, legality, fairness, impunity, and conscience.

2. We will conduct ourselves personally and collectively at all times such as to bring credit to the service and tourism industry at large.

3. We will concentrate our time, energy, and resources on the improvement of our own product and services and we will not denigrate our competition in the pursuit of our own success.

4. We will treat all guests equally regardless of race, religion, nationality, creed or sex.

5. We will deliver all standards of service and product with total consistency to every guest.

6. We will provide a totally safe and sanitary environment at all times for every guest and employee.

7. We will strive constantly, in words, actions and deeds, to develop and maintain the highest level of trust, honesty and understanding among guests, clients, employees, employers and the public at large.

8. We will provide every employee at every level all of the knowledge, training, equipment and motivation required to perform his or her tasks according to our published standards.

9. We will guarantee that every employee at every level will have the same opportunity to perform, advance, and will be evaluated against the same standard as all employees engaged in the same or similar tasks.

10. We will actively and consciously work to protect and preserve our natural environment and natural resources in all that we do.

11. We will seek a fair and honest profit, no more, no less.

Source: Stephen S.J. Hall, ed., *Ethics in Hospitality Management: A Book of Readings* (Lansing, Mich.: Educational Institute of the American Hotel & Lodging Association, 1992): 23.

The key element in ethics programs is support from the top. Managers and employees are likely to reflect the views and actions of their superiors, because the business's reward systems are usually established and managed by top executives. One could argue that employees who exhibit unethical behavior often simply reflect the behavior of their superiors. Exhibit 5 shows how this process can occur by depicting two different types of communication systems in organizations. As Exhibit 5 shows, creating an environment that fosters open communication, positive confrontations, and truthfulness results in normative behavior that

Exhibit 5 Communication Outcomes

ORGANIZATIONAL VALUE: HONESTY

Action by Managers

Limited Communication	Open Communication
• Instills fear	• Instills confidence
• Discourages differing views	• Encourages differing views
• Avoids confrontations	• Supports positive confrontation
• Suppresses bad news	• Rewards truthfulness
Belief: Encourages agreement, not questions	Belief: Welcomes disagreement, questions
Norm: Defensive, deceptive	Norm: Truthful, candid communication

---

Source: Adapted from Roy Serpa, "Creating a Candid Corporate Culture," *Journal of Business Ethics* 4 (1985): 425–430.

stresses honesty, truthfulness, and candid communication (an ethical environment). Environments that limit communication, discourage differing viewpoints, and reward only good news result in defensive, deceptive communication (an environment that is likelier to encourage unethical behavior).

The challenge for managers is to create cultures in which truthful, candid communication is the norm. This challenge is especially incumbent on top managers and other leaders within a business, because employees follow their lead when making decisions.

Assessing Ethical Behavior in Organizations

Three philosophical approaches have been used over the years to assess whether an organizational or individual action is ethical: the utilitarian approach, the moral rights approach, and the social justice approach:

* The **utilitarian approach** assumes that actions that present the greatest net good for society as a whole are ethical.

* The **moral rights approach** assumes that conduct that does not interfere with another's rights and does not coerce another party is moral and ethical.

* The **social justice approach** assumes that cultural differences cause different societies to establish varying ethical standards. Hence, what might be considered ethical in one culture could be considered unethical in another.

Other methods of assessing ethical behavior in organizations have been offered in recent years. Most of them fall into three categories, normally referred to as: (1) the three-stage approach, (2) the critical questions approach, and (3) the balance sheet approach.

The **three-stage approach** consists of:

Steps to Implementing a Company Ethics Program

Companies interested in developing or enhancing their ethics programs may want to consider some or all of the following steps:

- Earn the commitment of the CEO and senior management.
- Develop or affirm company values/mission/vision statement that refers to ethics.
- Develop an ethics or corporate responsibility committee of the Board of Directors.
- Articulate some type of standards of business practices; this can be global in scope.
- Develop ethical decision-making processes.
- Integrate an emphasis on ethics into regular business plans, policies, meetings and everyday activities.
- Develop an ethics communication strategy.
- Implement an ethics training program.
- Seek buy-in from employees.
- Hire an ethics officer or establish appropriate ethics management systems to foster ethical conduct and to respond to allegations of misconduct.
- Create a system that rewards ethical behavior and penalizes unethical behavior.
- Develop annual evaluation systems to gauge the company's progress.

Source: Adapted from Business for Social Responsibility (BSR), a membership organization for companies seeking to sustain commercial success in ways that demonstrate respect for ethical values, people, communities, and the environment. The BSR Web site can be found at www.bsr.org.

- Developing an understanding of general ethical principles
- Developing ethical principles to apply to real business situations as they arise
- Identifying cases that provide good examples of the applied principles

The second method, the **critical questions approach,** consists of asking company executives to answer broad questions about ethical conduct in their company, such as:

- Who are the authorities? What are the rules and precedents?
- What are the existing agreements?
- Is there a conflict with existing principles?

This second approach has also resulted in the development of questions that address specific issues, such as, "What is our attitude toward employee theft, the work ethic, blame-shifting, etc.?"

With the **balance sheet approach** to assessing ethical behavior, managers, whenever they must make an important decision, draw a line down the middle of a sheet of paper and list the ethical pros of the decision on one side of the line, the ethical cons on the other. While the balance sheet approach might provide managers with a good starting point, many decisions may not lend themselves to this simplistic approach.

Recent Ethical Issues in American Business

In recent years, American businesses large and small have been caught engaging in unethical and illegal business practices. The impact on the managers and employees of many of these companies has been dramatic. In the Enron bankruptcy, for example, company executives were sentenced to prison, and employees who had been encouraged by the company to invest in Enron stock lost nearly $1.2 billion in stock value; for many, their Enron stock represented their entire retirement savings.[11] Other prominent companies also have been caught behaving unethically, including WorldCom, Global Crossing, Adelphia, Arthur Andersen, Tyco International, Cendant, and others.

In response to widespread abuse of accounting and other business practices among U.S. companies, Congress passed the Sarbanes-Oxley Act in 2002.

The Sarbanes-Oxley Act. The Sarbanes-Oxley Act is designed to curb unethical business practices by increasing reporting requirements and requiring companies and their executives to follow much more stringent ethical guidelines. The act requires American companies to make several changes in how they conduct business. Foremost among them is the requirement for publicly owned companies to submit an annual assessment of the effectiveness of their internal financial auditing controls to the Securities and Exchange Commission (SEC). The act also requires external auditors to report on the effectiveness of internal control systems put in place by company managers. All publicly owned U.S. companies and their subsidiaries, and all foreign-owned companies trading stock in the United States, are required to submit these reports. In addition, this act established the Public Company Accounting Oversight Board (PCAOB), which operates under the supervision of the SEC to monitor submissions to the SEC.

Under the Sarbanes-Oxley Act, chief executive officers and chief financial officers must certify in writing that their companies' annual and quarterly SEC reports do not contain any false statements or omissions, and that company financial statements are a fair representation of the financial condition of the company. Certification of the procedures for preparing and disclosing this information are also required. A corporate officer who accidentally or unknowingly fails to follow these reporting guidelines can receive up to $1 million in fines and ten years in prison. Those guilty of purposeful unethical behavior in regard to the reporting guidelines can receive up to $5 million in fines and 20 years in prison.

One of the most noticeable developments in the corporate world since passage of the Sarbanes-Oxley Act is the privatization of public companies. Since Sarbanes-Oxley applies only to publicly traded companies, some companies have gone private to avoid the act's regulations. On the surface, this certainly appears to be an unethical reaction to a law designed to protect Americans and American investors from corporate fraud. The likely result of this move to privatization will be that laws will be passed to cover nonpublic companies, too.

Whistleblowers. A whistleblower is a current or former manager or employee of an organization who reports unethical behavior on the part of the organization to people or entities that have the power to take corrective action. Generally the unethical behavior is a violation of a law, rule, or regulation, or is otherwise a direct threat to the public interest. Perhaps the best known U.S. whistleblower is Jeffrey Wigand, who revealed that some top executives of the big U.S. tobacco companies not only knew that cigarettes were addictive, they also directed their companies to add carcinogenic ingredients to the tobacco in cigarettes to boost their addictive effect. His story was popularized in the movie *The Insider.*

Whistleblowers in the business world are protected by federal and state "whistleblower laws" that allow them to report misconduct without fear of retaliation from their companies. Whistleblowers have played prominent roles in uncovering unethical behavior in companies such as Enron, WorldCom, and others. When passed, this law was assumed to apply to both private business and governmental agencies. However, in May of 2006 the U.S. Supreme Court ruled that the approximately 20 million U.S. public employees (employees who hold government positions, from city to federal governments) are not protected under current whistleblower laws. This was immediately seen as a blow to efforts to identify unethical and illegal business practices in the United States.[12] Whether this ruling becomes a major setback in the campaign to ensure ethical business practices is yet to be determined.

Ethical Issues in Human Resources Management

Much of human resources management is based on making choices about employees and employment issues. How these choices are made is often subject to ethical considerations. For example, human resources managers are often faced with supervisors who want to hire a certain individual for a specific position. The supervisors announce an open position in their departments, then want to hire a specific individual for that position without further search. This presents a problem for human resources managers, who know that, legally and ethically, they should allow other applicants to pursue the position.

Other human resources issues that challenge a manager's ethical conduct on a regular basis include:

- *Hiring.* When job applicants ask about promotion opportunities, do you describe their prospects for promotion in realistic terms, or portray a "best case scenario" because you need them to take the job?

- *Orientation.* Do you tell new employees how things really are in the organization, or how you wish they were? Do you paint a rosier picture of the organization than is warranted?

- *Discharging employees.* Do you make a deal with an unwanted employee to leave quietly, or use "just cause" to dismiss the employee and risk a wrongful discharge suit?

How managers deal with these and other human resources issues will depend in part on the ethical standards established within their organizations.

Endnotes

1. http://en.wikipedia.org/wiki/Bhopal_Disaster.

2. http://en.wikipedia.org/wiki/Exxon_Valdez_oil_spill.

3. Sara J. Welch, "The Color of Money," Successful Meetings 50 (March 2001):49–55. For updates on eco-friendly hotels, please see "Green" Hotels Association at www.greenhotels.com and Green Seal at www.greenseal.org.

4. Lois A. Mohr and Deborah J. Webb, "The Effects of Corporate Social Responsibility and Price on Consumer Responses," Journal of Consumer Affairs 39 (2005): 121; and www.forbes.com.

5. N. Craig Smith, "Corporate Social Responsibility: Whether or How?" California Management Review 45 (2005): 4, 59.

6. www.trilliuminvest.com.

7. www.mori.com/polls/1999/millpoll.shtml.

8. Sankar Sen and C. B. Bhattacharya, "Does Doing Good Always Lead to Doing Better? Consumer Reactions to Corporate Social Responsibility," JMR, Journal of Marketing Research, 38 (May 2001): 225–243.

9. Harvey S. James, Jr., "Reinforcing Ethical Decision-Making Through Organizational Structure," Journal of Business Ethics 28 (November 2000): 43–58.

10. E. McQueeney, "Making Ethics Come Alive," Business Communication Quarterly 69(2) (2006): 158–171.

11. Roberta Romano, "The Sarbanes-Oxley Act and the Making of Quack Corporate Governance," Yale Law Journal, 114 (2005): 3.

12. Gina Holland, "High Court Limits Whistleblower Lawsuits," May 30, 2006, Forbes online at ww.forbes.com/technology/feeds/ap/2006/05/30/ap2780736.html.

 # Key Terms

accommodating response—A response to social problems caused by a business that is characterized by the business accepting responsibility and following legal, economic, and ethical guidelines to remedy the problems.

affirmative philosophy—A philosophy that assumes that business has a responsibility to serve society.

balance sheet approach—An approach to ethical decision-making that consists of listing the ethical pros and cons of a decision on a sheet of paper.

critical questions approach—A method of assessing ethical standards in a business, based on the process of asking critical questions about ethical conduct.

defensive response—A response to social problems caused by a business that is characterized by the business admitting some errors but doing only what is legally required to correct the situation.

moral rights approach—An approach to ethics that assumes that actions are moral and ethical if they do not interfere with another's rights and do not coerce another party.

obstructive response—A response to social problems caused by a business that is characterized by the business denying responsibility, hiding evidence, and stonewalling investigations.

proactive response—A response to social problems caused by a business that is characterized by the business voluntarily doing everything it can to resolve the problems, or to head off potential problems before they develop.

profit maximization management—A philosophical view of the role of business that contends that the only responsibility a business has is to maximize its profits for the benefit of its owners/shareholders.

quality-of-life management—A philosophy that contends that business has a responsibility to help make society better.

social Darwinism—The application of Darwinism to the study of human society; specifically, a theory in sociology that social order is the result of natural selection.

social justice approach—An approach to ethics that assumes that cultural differences cause different societies to establish varying ethical standards.

social responsibility—The obligation an organization's management has to make decisions and to take actions that will enhance the welfare and interests of society as a whole.

stakeholder philosophy—A business philosophy emphasizing that managers should be responsible to societal groups that have a stake in the company's performance.

stakeholders—Groups that have either direct or indirect interests in the welfare and activities of an organization or business. Examples of the stakeholders for a typical hotel company include owners, stockholders, employees, unions (if applicable), customers, suppliers, creditors, trade associations, government agencies (at the local, state, and federal levels), media outlets, competitors, and special interest groups.

three-stage approach—A method of assessing the ethical actions of a business based on developing an understanding of general ethical principles, developing ethical principles to apply to real business situations, and identifying cases that provide good examples of the applied principles.

utilitarian approach—An approach to ethics that assumes actions representing the greatest net good for society as a whole are most ethical.

  Review Questions ————————————————————————————————————

1. What are the differences between the traditional, stakeholder, and affirmative philosophies of the social responsibility of business?

2. What are four typical responses of businesses to the call for social responsibility, and how do they differ from each other?

3. What are the pros and cons for businesses of social responsibility programs?

4. In what ways are hospitality companies addressing social responsibility issues?

5. What are some steps in conducting a social responsibility audit?

6. What are four key factors for the successful implementation of a business's ethics training program?

7. What are three approaches to assessing whether a business decision or behavior is ethical?

8. How has the Sarbanes-Oxley Act affected U.S. business ethics?

9. What is a whistleblower?

10. What are some ethical issues in human resources management?

 Internet Sites —————————————————————————

For more information, visit the following Internet sites. Remember that Internet addresses can change without notice. If the site is no longer there, you can use a search engine to look for additional sites.

Business Ethics Online
www.business-ethics.com

Business for Social Responsibility
www.bsr.org

CERES
www.ceres.org

CorpWatch
www.corpwatch.org

CSRwire
www.csrwire.com

Ethics Resource Center
www.ethics.org

"Green" Hotels Association
www.greenhotels.com

Green Seal
www.greenseal.org

International Association for Business and Society
www.iabs.net

International Business Ethics Institute
www.business-ethics.org

JeffreyWigand.com
www.jeffreywigand.com

Kimpton Hotel & Restaurant Group
www.kimptonhotels.com

List of Business Ethics Organizations
www.societyforbusinessethics.org/organizations.htm

Share Our Strength
www.strength.org

Social Investment Forum
www.socialinvest.org

Society for Business Ethics
www.societyforbusinessethics.org

UNICEF
www.unicef.org

United States Office of Government Ethics
www.usoge.gov

Mini Case Studies

Mini Case 1

The U.S.-based Megahotel Company has been very successful in establishing operations throughout the country. In recent years, Megahotels has also successfully established hotels in most major European business capitals. The company has decided to establish itself as a worldwide entity. This decision is based primarily on top management's belief that to effectively compete on an international scale, the company must provide its services to business travelers around the globe. In this way, U.S. or European travelers can stay in the company's hotels anywhere they travel. Top management sees this expansion as critical in preventing business travelers from using the competition. As the vice president of marketing recently noted, "We cannot risk forcing our guests to use competing hotels too often. After a few stays, these guests might decide to switch hotels permanently, simply because they can stay with the same property everywhere they travel."

To reach its new goal, Megahotels is now negotiating with the government of a developing country to place a property in the business district in that country's capital. A foreign-based hotel company is negotiating for the same location.

After several weeks of fruitless negotiations in which Megahotels seemed to get further and further from its goal while the competitor seemed to get closer to signing a contract, a mid-level government official visited the offices of Megahotels' director of international operations. The official's conversation was brief:

"The government of my country is considering signing a contract with Megahotels to allow building your hotel. However, your competition now has the inside track on that site. I believe that within days your competitor will have a signed deal. The reason for this is that your competitor has provided our government with certain 'gifts' which will enable cabinet ministers and others to realize personal profit. In addition, your competitor has promised to provide complimentary hotel rooms for our cabinet ministers in your country. If you could meet those gifts, I am certain the government will decide to give you the permission you seek."

After this meeting, the director of international operations called the key management team together and relayed what had just taken place. The problem seemed obvious-either pay a bribe to the government or lose the contract.

Discussion Questions

1. What makes you think that this may be a very realistic scenario?
2. Is it ethical to provide what the local government representative asked for?
3. Is it unethical to provide rooms for the government officials?
4. What action would you take and how would you justify this action?

Mini Case 2

As an assistant manager in a restaurant company with an eye on his future, Bob wants to do as much as possible to ensure his career progression. He works longer hours, spends more time focusing on customer service and loyalty and has learned how to train employees more effectively. Recently, however, Bob has become disturbed by some actions of his superiors which, to him, do not seem to be ethical. For instance, at the end of last month Bob was asked by the GM to inflate the inventory in order to show a better bottom-line performance for the last month. The GM explained that, while this is technically unethical, the last month was unusual in the sense that the restaurant had an accident in which the cooler malfunctioned overnight and many food products spoiled. To further explain this, the GM noted that, from his perspective, inventories are meant to capture long-range use of resources, not once-only events.

Discussion Question

1. Should Bob inflate the inventory as requested by his GM? If not, what should he do?

Mini Case 3

Really Big Hotels company has grown quickly in the last few years. Today, they operate 30 hotels along the Arizona–Southern California corridor. Because of competition for employees with other industries, the company has instituted a policy (in accordance with federal regulations) of taking employment documents at face value. If an applicant has a social security number, for instance, the company now has a policy of accepting it regardless of whether the manager believes that the number belongs to the applicant. The result is that the company has begun hiring many illegal aliens to work in its hotels. Problems have arisen from this. For example, recently the company received a letter from a woman in Seattle, Washington, who claims that the social security number used by one of the company's employees is really hers, that the employee or others stole the number to allow for employment.

Discussion Question

1. What action should the company take?

Mini Case 4

XYZ Restaurants Corp. has recently completed its annual external audit of financial records. The outside auditing firm employed to conduct this audit has presented the results to the company president and asked for her approval and signature on the document. However, the president is unsure of the results and unwilling to attest to the results of the audit. In last month's corporate board meeting, members openly demanded the resignation of the president on the grounds that she is holding up company progress through her actions. The board has also determined that, in its opinion, her signature is not needed on these documents.

Discussion Question

1. How should be president respond?

Index